INSTRUCTOR'S RESOURCES

to accompany

Robin S. Rosenberg and Stephen M. Kosslyn

ABNORMAL PSYCHOLOGY

Meera Rastogi

University of Cincinnati, Clermont College

WORTH PUBLISHERS

Instructor's Resources
by Meera Rastogi
to accompany
Rosenberg and Kosslyn: *Abnormal Psychology*

© 2011 by Worth Publishers

Printed in the United States of America

ISBN 10: 1-4292-3472-5
ISBN 13: 978-1-4292-3472-6

First printing 2010

Worth Publishers
41 Madison Avenue
New York, NY 10010
www.worthpublishers.com

Contents

Preface

These **Instructor's Resources** are designed for use with Robin S. Rosenberg and Stephen M. Kosslyn's *Abnormal Psychology* and were written with both experienced and novice instructors in mind. The suggestions in these pages are meant to assist in developing unique, original, and dynamic lesson plans that best present the material in the text and spark creative ways of teaching and learning. The activities, media recommendations, lecture enhancements, additional readings, and much more are included to expand on the topics presented in the text and offer a chance to go beyond in teaching *Abnormal Psychology*.

Each chapter of the Instructor's Resources begins with a brief outline of the textbook chapter that quickly highlights chapter headings, concepts, learning objectives, textbook tools and correlates these with classroom activities, lecture enhancements, and media recommendations. Following the brief chapter outline, each Instructor's Resource chapter contains:

- Detailed Outline—material covered in the text chapter is organized and summarized for classroom lectures.

- Learning Objectives—highlight the main concepts and skills that students should take away from the chapter.

- Key Terms—all key terms from the text chapter are listed and defined.

- Textbook Tools—important figures and tables pulled from the text so that the instructor can easily refer students to these tools.

- Lecture Enhancements—outside materials that can help to enhance your lectures. They highlight current issues or themes in the field and topics that pique students' interest. The objective, length, summary, key lecture topics, as well as additional resources and questions for students are included for each enhancement.

- Learning Activities—activities that can be completed by students in class, usually in small groups. The objective, time to complete, additional resources (such as Web sites), and questions for students are included for each activity.

- Media Recommendations—relevant films, film clips, and Web sites that can be used during lecture to further learning and discussion. The objective, length of the film or clip, summary, as well as additional resources (such as Web sites), and questions for students are included for each media recommendation.

- Student Handouts—further help students to consolidate and integrate the text material.

- Each chapter concludes with a list of Additional Resources, which includes journal articles, books, and films that can further your students' knowledge.

Note that you can access these materials on the Instructor's Resource CD-ROM or on the Book Companion Site at www.worthpublishers.com/rkabpsych1e/.

Video Tool Kit for
Abnormal Psychology by Rosenberg and Kosslyn

All videos can be found at www.worthvideotoolkit.com.
The video clips noted with an * indicate that they are also found on our Instructor's DVD.

The History of Abnormal Psychology

CHAPTER OUTLINE

CHAPTER HEADINGS	INSTRUCTION IDEAS AND TEXTBOOK CORRELATIONS
THE THREE CRITERIA FOR DETERMINING PSYCHOLOGICAL DISORDERS	**Learning Objectives:** 1.1, 1.2 **Learning Concepts:** distress, impairment in daily life, psychosis (hallucinations and delusions), risk of harm **Learning Activity 1.1:** Does This Person Have a Mental Illness? **Textbook Tool:** Figure 1.1 **Worth Tool Kit for Abnormal Psychology:** *Grey Gardens*: Exploring the Definition of Psychological Disorders
Context and Culture	**Learning Objective:** 1.3 **Learning Concepts:** culture, culture-bound symptoms (*koro*, genital-shrinking fears, possession trance) **Lecture Enhancement 1.1:** Cultural Influences on Defining Mental Illness **Lecture Enhancement 1.2:** Is Mental Illness a Myth? **Textbook Tools:** Table 1.1; Case 1.1
VIEWS OF PSYCHOLOGICAL DISORDERS BEFORE SCIENCE	**Learning Objectives:** 1.4, 1.5 **Learning Concepts:** ancient views of psychopathology (supernatural forces; exorcism; Chinese *Qi;* Greeks—imbalance of four humors; medical model; Romans—balance of emotions; The Middle Ages—possession; and the Renaissance—demonic possession and witches), asylums, novel humane treatments, moral treatment, neurasthenia **Learning Activity 1.2:** What Are Your Views on the Causes of Mental Illness? **Lecture Enhancement 1.3:** Salem Witch Trials and Ergot Poisoning **Media Recommendation 1.1:** *Grey Gardens* **Lecture Enhancement 1.4:** Ethics of Filming the Beales **Textbook Tool:** Table 1.2
THE TRANSITION TO SCIENTIFIC ACCOUNTS OF PSYCHOLOGICAL DISORDERS	**Learning Objectives:** 1.6, 1.7, 1.8 **Learning Concepts:** hypnosis, psychoanalytic theory, psychosexual stages, neurosis, psychosis, defense mechanisms, psychodynamic theory, the humanist response **Learning Activity 1.3:** Comparing Your Ideal and Real Selves

	Media Recommendation 1.2: Freud's Early Years **Textbook Tools:** Figure 1.2; Table 1.3
SCIENTIFIC ACCOUNTS OF PSYCHOLOGICAL DISORDERS	**Learning Objective:** 1.9 **Learning Concepts:** behaviorism, cognitive contribution
Social Forces	**Learning Objectives:** 1.10, 1.11 **Learning Concepts:** attachment style, social support
Biological Explanations	**Learning Objective:** 1.12 **Learning Concept:** medical model **Lecture Enhancement 1.5:** Explore the Genes to Cognition Online Web Site
The Modern Synthesis of Explanations of Psychopathology	**Learning Objective:** 1.13 **Learning Concepts:** diathesis-stress model, biopsychosocial approach, three types of factors underlying psychological disorders, neuropsychosocial approach, feedback loops **Lecture Enhancement 1.6:** Explore the Treatment of the Mentally Ill Today **Media Recommendation 1.3:** Normal or Abnormal? **Textbook Tools:** Figures 1.3, 1.4

LEARNING OBJECTIVES

After reading this chapter, students should be able to:

1.1 Describe the three criteria for defining psychological disorders.

1.2 Discuss the different types of impairments people may experience.

1.3 Describe how culture and context shape three criteria for defining psychological disorders.

1.4 Articulate how mental illness was viewed throughout history, noting particular shifts in views based on religion and science.

1.5 Identify major figures of the moral movement, noting the particular changes in treatment and the resulting consequences.

1.6 Identify the major contributions of psychoanalytic and psychodynamic theory, such as the three levels of consciousness, three structures of the mind, psychosexual stages of development, and the role of defense mechanisms.

1.7 Compare the core assumptions of psychoanalytic theory to humanistic theory.

1.8 Explain Rogers's explanation of psychological distress.

1.9 Identify the core beliefs of the behaviorism and cognitive movements.

1.10 Describe the four types of parent-child attachment.

1.11 Describe the role of social support in the development of mental illness.

1.12 Describe the connection between biological factors and mental illness.

1.13 Describe the modern explanations of psychopathology: diathesis–stress, biopsychosocial, neuropsychosocial, and feedback loops.

KEY TERMS

Abnormal psychology: The subfield of psychology that addresses the causes and progression of psychological disorders; also referred to as psychopathology.

Psychological disorder: A pattern of thoughts, feelings, or behaviors that causes significant personal *distress,* significant *impairment* in daily life, and/or significant risk of harm, any of which is unusual for the context and culture in which it arises.

Psychosis: An impaired ability to perceive reality to the extent that normal functioning is not possible. The two types of psychotic symptoms are hallucinations and delusions.

Hallucinations: Sensations that are so vivid that the perceived objects or events seem real, although they are not. Hallucinations can occur in any of the five senses.

Delusions: Persistent false beliefs that are held despite evidence that the beliefs are incorrect or exaggerate reality.

Culture: The shared norms and values of a society that are explicitly and implicitly conveyed to its members by example and through the use of reward and punishment.

Asylums: Institutions to house and care for people who are afflicted with mental illness.

Moral treatment: The treatment of the mentally ill that provided an environment in which people with mental illness were treated with kindness and respect and functioned as part of a community.

Psychoanalytic theory: The theory that thoughts, feelings, and behaviors are a result of conscious and unconscious forces continually interacting in the mind.

Id: According to Freud, the seat of sexual and aggressive drives, as well as of the desire for immediate gratification of physical and psychological needs.

Superego: According to Freud, the seat of the conscience, which works to impose morality.

Ego: According to Freud, the psychic structure that is charged with mediating between the id's demands for immediate gratification and the superego's high standards of morality, as well as the constraints of external reality.

Psychosexual stages: According to Freud, the sequence of five distinct stages of development (oral, anal, phallic, latency, and genital) through which children proceed from infancy to adulthood; each stage has a key task that must be completed successfully for healthy psychological development.

Neurosis: According to psychoanalytic theory, a pattern of thoughts, feelings, or behaviors that expresses an unresolved conflict between the ego and the id or between the ego and the superego.

Defense mechanisms: Unconscious processes that work to transform psychological conflict so as to prevent unacceptable thoughts and feelings from reaching consciousness.

Mental processes: The internal operations that underlie cognitive and emotional functions (such as perception, memory, and guilt feelings) and most human behavior.

Mental contents: The specific material that is stored in the mind and operated on by mental processes.

Behaviorism: The approach to psychology that focuses on understanding directly observable behaviors in order to understand mental illness and other psychological phenomena.

Diathesis–stress model: The model that proposes that a psychological disorder is triggered when a person with a predisposition—a diathesis—for the particular disorder experiences an environmental event that causes significant stress.

Biopsychosocial approach: The view that a psychological disorder arises from the combined influences of three types of factors—biological, psychological, and social.

Neuropsychosocial approach: The view that a psychological disorder arises from the combined influences of neurological, psychological, and social factors—which affect and are affected by one another through feedback loops.

CHAPTER GUIDE

Chapter Introduction

The Beales.   Edith ("Big Edie") and Edith ("Little Edie") Beale lived together for 29 years in a 28-room mansion known as the Grey Gardens in an affluent town in New York. They lived in squalor and grew more eccentric as time passed. Did Big or Little Edie have a psychological disorder? The subfield of psychology that addresses the causes and progression of psychological disorders is called *abnormal psychology.*

I.   THE THREE CRITERIA FOR DETERMINING PSYCHOLOGICAL DISORDERS

LEARNING ACTIVITY 1.1: Does This Person Have a Mental Illness?

Objective: This exercise will help students identify the differences between normal and abnormal behavior.

Time: 15 Minutes

Directions: Label three parts of the room as:
1. Person HAS a mental illness.
2. Person MAY HAVE a mental illness.
3. Person DOES NOT HAVE a mental illness.

Read the three scenarios below, and have students stand in the part of the room that reflects their opinion about whether the individual has, may have, or does not have a mental illness.

Case 1:
Marcus can get through most days feeling okay, however he rarely feels happy. Some days he feels so sad it is difficult to get out of bed, but he is able to force himself to get up. He used to enjoy going for walks, but he no longer feels motivated or sees the purpose in getting exercise; so he spends most of his time in bed or watching television.

Case 2:
Laney thinks she has been infected with a virus that creates robotic cells that are eating away at her organs. Laney refuses to go to her physician because she is afraid of getting more infections that will accelerate this process.

Case 3:
Angela dislikes being around groups of people, so she spends most of her time at home. She has spent time in large groups during college, but she tends to get nervous when she is in large groups. She makes excuses when her friends invite her to parties, but likes to have people over for dinner.

Summary: This exercise will help students see the criteria clinicians use to determine what is abnormal behavior. Students will see that there is sometimes a fine line between what is normal versus abnormal but the three criteria described in this chapter will help you to determine the difference. Their discussion and reflections on different perspectives will serve to guide them in a thought-provoking way toward understanding the general criteria for determining whether a person has a psychological disorder and will help transition them into the next section.

Questions to Students and Discussion: Where do you draw the line when distinguishing between symptoms that suggest a disorder and characteristics of someone's personality? Was this activity difficult? Why? How do we decide what is a disorder?

- A *psychological disorder* is a pattern of thoughts, feelings, or behaviors that causes (1) significant personal *distress,* (2) significant *impairment* in daily life, and/or (3) significant *risk of harm,* any of which is unusual for the context and culture in which it arises.
- To merit the diagnosis of a psychological disorder, at least one of the following three elements for determining whether someone has a psychological disorder must have a substantial effect on that person's life. [See *Figure 1.1.*]

A. Distress

- **Distress** is anguish or suffering that all of us experience at different times in our lives.
- To be considered abnormal, the distress is often out of proportion to a situation or context.

B. Impairment in Daily Life

- **Impairment in daily life** is a significant reduction of an individual's ability to function in some area of life.
- A person considered to have a psychological disorder must be impaired to a greater *degree* than most people in a similar situation.

1. Types of Impairment

A *psychosis* is an impaired ability to perceive reality so that normal functioning is not possible (e.g., schizophrenia).

a. Two Forms of Psychotic Symptoms:

- *Hallucinations* are sensations so vivid that the perceived objects or events seem real, yet are not (e.g., hearing voices and seeing images or stimuli).
- *Delusions* are persistent false beliefs held despite evidence that the beliefs are incorrect or exaggerate reality (see the following examples).

(1) Types of delusions:

- Paranoid or persecutory (e.g., people—the FBI, aliens, neighbors—are after the individual)
- Delusional jealousy (e.g., the individual's intimate partner is dating or interested in another person)
- Delusions of grandeur (e.g., the individual is more powerful, knowledgeable, or influential than Jesus and/or the individual is a different person, such as the president)
- Somatic delusions (e.g., part or all of the individual's body is defective or functioning abnormally)

C. Risk of Harm

- The element of **risk of harm** refers to symptoms of a disorder that may lead to life or property damage.
- The risky behavior is a symptom of a psychological disorder.
- The behavior must be outside the normal range and can be accidental or intentional. The individual's thoughts or actions may lead him or her to put other people's lives at risk.

D. Context and Culture [see *Table 1.1*]

- The three elements used for determining whether someone has a psychological disorder—level of distress, impairment, and risk of harm—must be considered within the context and culture in which they arise.

- Behavior that seems inappropriate may make sense from another individual's point of view depending on his or her cultural perspective.
- *Culture* is defined as the shared norms and values of a society.
- Each society defines mental health, mental illness, and even distress for itself.

1. **Culture-Bound Symptoms [generally observed only in certain countries]**

   - *Koro* is an intense fear that an individual's penis—or nipples and vulva—will retract into the body and cause death. It is found in Southeast Asia. [See *Case 1.1.*]
   - **Genital-shrinking fears** have been reported in India and in West African countries.
   - **Possession trance** occurs when spirits purportedly take over an individual's body (often a woman's) and cause it to participate in a ritual.

LECTURE ENHANCEMENT 1.1: Cultural Influences on Defining Mental Illness

Objective: To examine how culture has influenced what we define as mental illness.

Time: 10 Minutes

The text notes that "in 1851, Dr. Samuel Cartwright of Louisiana wrote an essay in which he declared that slaves' running away was evidence of a serious mental disorder, which he called 'drapetomania.'" Also, the text notes that "homosexuality was officially considered a psychological disorder in the United States until 1973, when it was removed from the *Diagnostic and Statistical Manual of Mental Disorders,* the manual used by mental health clinicians to classify psychological disorders."

Summary: This lecture enhancement will help students learn how culture shapes the way mental illness is defined. The instructor may choose to highlight other examples of such cases (e.g., the diagnosis of homosexuality as a mental illness, hysteria).

Questions to Students and Discussion: Who defines mental illness? Who decides what is a mental illness? How do those who are privileged (by class, race, gender, etc.) influence the definition of psychological disorders? How can we use these two examples as a warning?

LECTURE ENHANCEMENT 1.2: Is Mental Illness a Myth?

Objective: To explore how diagnosing mental illness helps or hinders people.

Time: 5–10 Minutes

Watch Online: Szasz, http://www.youtube.com/watch?v=Qj7GmeSAxXo (YouTube search term "Szasz").

The text notes that "Thomas Szasz (1960) argued that because all people engage in 'us-versus-them' thinking, it is easy for a society to stigmatize people who are noticeably different. That is, culturally undesirable behaviors, emotional difficulties, and coping problems may be inaccurately called mental illness. In fact, Szasz proposed that mental illness is actually a myth."

Summary: In this video, Szaz argues that behavior alone (typical or atypical) should not be labeled as a disease because of the stigma that these labels carry. This video highlights an opposite view of mental illness than we see in psychology and psychiatry.

Questions to Students and Discussion: Do diagnoses stigmatize people? Do we label behaviors as disorders because we dislike the behaviors or because they are symptoms of an illness? In what ways does diagnosing people help or hinder them?

II. VIEWS OF PSYCHOLOGICAL DISORDERS BEFORE SCIENCE

LEARNING ACTIVITY 1.2: What Are Your Views on the Causes of Mental Illness?

Objective: This activity serves a pretest assessment of students' current understanding of the etiology of mental illness.

Time: 15–20 Minutes

Directions: Ask students to free write on the following questions:
1. What do you think causes mental illness?
2. How has your thinking changed over time?
3. How do others explain the reasons for mental illness?
4. What questions do you have about the causes of mental illness?

Summary: Students will assess their current knowledge and thoughts about the causes of mental illness. The instructor can use student responses to find themes in answers and connect these to the explanations of mental illness in this chapter.

Questions to Students and Discussion: Can you group your answers into categories? If so, what are these categories? Is there an emphasis on some explanation(s) rather than on others? Why? Were any of your classmates' thoughts surprising?

A. Ancient Views of Psychopathology

Two Possible Causes of Mental Illness.   Earliest accounts of abnormal thoughts, feelings, and behaviors focused on supernatural forces and bodily imbalance.

1. **Supernatural Forces**

    The belief was that ***supernatural forces,*** spirits or demons possessing bodies as punishment for transgressions, caused psychological disorders.

    - An ***exorcism,*** a ritual or ceremony intended to force the demon(s) to leave the body, was performed. This was the best choice of treatment at that time.
    - Exorcisms were common in ancient Egypt and Mesopotamia.

2. **Chinese *Qi***

    Another ancient belief, still common today, was that bodily and spirit imbalances in the life force, called the ***Chinese Qi*** [pronounced as "chee"], caused disorders.

    - The *Qi* flows through 12 channels of the body to the organs.
    - Restoration and balance occur through acupuncture and herbal medicines.

3. **Ancient Greeks and Romans**

    Mental illness was believed to be a body illness due to **imbalance of four humors,** or bodily fluids: (1) black bile, (2) blood, (3) yellow bile, and (4) phlegm. [See *Table 1.2.*]

    - Examples: Mania, or excessive energy, is caused by too much blood and yellow bile. Melancholy, or anguish, is caused by too much black bile.
    - Treatment included (1) changes in diet, (2) medicine, and (3) surgery (bloodletting).
    - Hippocrates (Greek, 460–377 B.C.E.) rejected a supernatural explanation. Instead, he viewed mental illness a result of brain abnormalities. The view that all illnesses have

a basis in biological disturbances is called the ***medical model,*** named after Hippocrates. Galen (Roman, 131–201 C.E.) believed in the ***balance of emotions***—that psychological disorders could result from imbalances in humors which then produced emotional problems.

B. Forces of Evil in the Middle Ages and the Renaissance

1. The Middle Ages

- From 500–1400 C.E., people believed mental illness was caused by battles between good and evil for the **possession** of an individual's soul.
- Prophets and visionaries were believed to be possessed by the devil or inspired by the will of God.
- Men and women with mental illness were possessed by demons or were being punished for their sins.
- Treatment included exorcism, torture to use pain to drive out the evil, starvation, and other bodily punishment.
- However, as early as the 10th century, Islamic institutions were caring humanely for those with mental illness.

2. The Renaissance

- From the 15th through 17th centuries, mental illness continued to be viewed a result of **demonic possession.**
- **Witches** possessed by or in league with the devil were scapegoats for the community's personal and societal problems (e.g., sickness, drought, and crop failures). These "witches" were often burned alive, a practice that spread throughout Europe and the American colonies.
- Treatments for mental illness focused on eliminating the demonic forces, in one way or another.

LECTURE ENHANCEMENT 1.3: Salem Witch Trials and Ergot Poisoning

Objective: To learn more about the practice of witch hunts in American colonies and our early explanations of the cause of mental illness.

Video Clip and Discussion: 30 Minutes

Full Program and Discussion: 60 Minutes

Watch Online: PBS' *Secrets of the Dead: The Witches Curse,* http://www.pbs.org/wnet/secrets/previous_seasons/lessons/lp_salem_videos.html

Scientists now believe that the women who exhibited signs that suggested they were witches actually suffered from ergot poisoning, a fungus that produces hallucinations and delusions. This PBS program explores a scientific explanation of the odd behavior of the Salem witches.

Summary: This program does an excellent job of highlighting cultural explanations for mental illness during the witch hunts. Students will learn about ergot poisoning and the power of labels.

Questions to Students and Discussion: Reflect on the evidence provided by the scientist. Do you think ergot poisoning is caused the symptoms exhibited by the witches? What evidence can you provide to support your opinion?

C. Rationality and Reason in the 18th and 19th Centuries

- Descartes proposed that mind and body are distinct—bodily illness arises from bodily abnormalities, whereas mental illness arises from mental abnormalities.
- John Locke, 17th-century British philosopher, believed insanity is caused by irrational thinking—it could be treated by helping people regain their rational and logical thought process.

1. Asylums

The Renaissance, the age of enlightenment, witnessed the founding of *asylums,* or institutions to house and care for the mentally ill.

- Asylums were founded by religious orders.
- The first one opened in Valencia, Spain, in 1409.
- Asylums regressed from places of refuge for patients to overcrowded, restrictive facilities housing delinquents and street dwellers.
- Most famous from this era was the Hospital of St. Mary of Bethlehem in London (eventually referred to as "Bedlam," which became a word meaning "confusion and uproar").

a. Hospital of St. Mary of Bethlehem (Bedlam):

- In 1547, that institution shifted from being a general hospital to an asylum used to incarcerate the mad, particularly those who were poor.
- Residents were chained to the walls or floor or put in cages and displayed to a paying public much like animals in a zoo.

MEDIA RECOMMENDATION 1.1: *Grey Gardens*

Objective: To observe and learn more about the Beale women.

Time: 100 Minutes

Film and Discussion: 130 Minutes

Discussion Only: 30 Minutes

Watch Online: *Grey Gardens* (1975 and 2009 versions)
Grey Gardens' fan site: http://www.greygardens.com/
Remake of *Grey Gardens:* http://www.hbo.com/films/greygardens/
This film portrays the Beale women in their dilapidated home, Grey Gardens.

Summary: Students will find it surprising that these affluent women live in such a chaotic environment. Students will be able to apply the criteria of distress, impairment, and culture and context to identify the Beales' abnormal behavior.

Questions to Students and Discussion: Do the Beale women meet the criteria for abnormality? Why or why not? How ethical was it to film these women? What could have helped these women?

LECTURE ENHANCEMENT 1.4: Ethics of Filming the Beales

Objective: To watch footage of *Grey Gardens* and discover the ethical issues surrounding both filming and talking about people with mental illnesses.

Time: 5–10 Minutes

Watch Online: The original trailer for *Grey Gardens,* http://www.youtube.com/watch?v=mum WYU5aHBU (YouTube search term "Grey Gardens")

Explore Online: The official *Grey Gardens* website, http://www.greygardens.com/

See the textbook for a descriptive analysis of the Beales. Highlight criteria in the text that might help the students examine if the Beales were just an eccentric pair or meet the criteria for defining mental illness.

Summary: As students watch the original trailer of the Beales, students can describe the types of behaviors that might be considered abnormal. Students will also see the amazing footage of the Beales' life and determine the ethics surrounding such a film.

Questions to Students and Discussion: Do you think *Grey Gardens* exploits the Beales? Does the film play into stereotypes about people with psychological disorders? Are the Beales able to provide informed consent? How does the treatment of the Beales compare to the treatment that people with mental illnesses have received in the past? Is YouTube, or films like this one, the new "zoo" where we as viewers pay to watch those who lack full control over their circumstances?

2. **Novel Humane Treatments [early attempts to treat mental illness using humane methods]**

   a. **Franz Mesmer:**

   - Mesmer (1734–1815) used mesmerism to treat hysterias by unblocking animal magnetism—an electromagnetic fluid that flowed in the body through fine channels.

   - To unblock the electromagnetic flow, he passed his own magnetic hands over the patient's body in what he called "magnetic passes."

   - A scientific commission, headed by Benjamin Franklin, discredited the theory of electromagnetism and the treatment.

   b. **Phillipe Pinel:**

   - The French physician (1745–1826) transformed asylum life at the Salpêtrière and Bicêtre Hospitals in Paris by removing patients' chains and stopping "treatments" involving bleeding, starvation, and physical punishment.

   - He identified partial insanity—that some patients were mostly rational and could be treated through psychological means, such as reasoning.

   - This treatment was one of the first mental treatments for mental disorders.

   c. **Francis Willis:**

   - Willis treated King George III in 1788 by creating blisters on his skin to draw out the "evil humors" and restraining him in an effort to bring him to his senses.

   - Willis also tried to talk people out of their delusions, another mental treatment for mental disorders.

   - His timely treatment of the king was hailed as a cure for insanity.

3. **Moral Treatment**

   a. **Quakers:**

   - Quakers in York, England, developed a ***moral treatment*** for the mentally ill that provided a community atmosphere of kindness and respect.

   - After a year, over 90% of the residents recovered, at least temporarily.

   b. **Dr. Benjamin Rush:**

   - In the United States, Dr. Rush (1745–1813), while at the Pennsylvania Hospital in Philadelphia, moved the mentally ill from filthy basement cells to rooms above ground level, gave them mattresses and meals, and treated them with respect.

c. Dorothea Dix:

- A schoolteacher and lifelong humanitarian, Dix (1802–1887) worked tirelessly to ensure that the mentally ill were housed separately from criminals and treated humanely, in both public and private asylums.

d. Public Asylums:

- Moral treatment became popular, and asylums' populations increased tenfold as people with epilepsy and other neurological disorders, ordinarily jailed, flocked to the asylums.
- As a result, public mental institutions became overcrowded and underfunded.
- Personnel resorted to using sedation and other methods of management to control the patient population.

4. Neurasthenia

Neurasthenia is an example of a medical problem that can bring on mental illness.

a. Description:

Neurasthenia is nerve weakness accompanied by the symptoms of low mood and mental and physical fatigue. In the United States, the pace of life increased with the advent of the telegraph and the railroad and thus more and more men and women were diagnosed with neurasthenia.

b. Treatment:

Treatment, administered by a physician, included rest, sedatives, and induced vomiting or bleeding.

III. THE TRANSITION TO SCIENTIFIC ACCOUNTS OF PSYCHOLOGICAL DISORDERS

A. Freud and the Importance of Unconscious Forces

- Sigmund Freud (1856–1939), the Viennese neurologist, helped to make the study of psychological disorders a science.
- He developed new methods for diagnosis and treatment (many still in use today).
- He proposed a rich and intricate theory, which still influences many clinicians today.

B. The Beginnings of Freud's Contributions

For 4 months, Freud studied with French neurologist Jean-Martin Charcot, professor at Salpêtrière Hospital in Paris. Charcot:

- proposed that (1) people with hysteria have susceptible nerves, and (2) symptoms could be cured by **hypnosis.**
- would suggest to his hypnotized patients that their symptoms would go away, and they often did.

Free Association. Freud developed free association as an improvement over hypnosis.

- During free association, patients are encouraged to say whatever thoughts occur to them.
- Part of Freud's free association involved talking, or the "talking cure," which he thought would reduce unconscious conflicts, thereby providing relief from hysteria and other mental disorders.

MEDIA RECOMMENDATION 1.2: Freud's Early Years

Objective: The purpose of this film is to show students Freud's early life and experiences and how these experiences shaped his theories and work.

Time: 120 Minutes

Watch Online: *Young Dr. Freud* (2002), http://www.pbs.org/youngdrfreud/ (A preview of the film is available at this link.) This is a two-part series examining the early life and career of Sigmund Freud.

Summary: After watching this film, students will have a better understanding of psychoanalytic theory and Freud's personal and professional experiences.

Questions to Students and Discussion: How did Freud's own struggles influence his theories? Describe the progression of his theory.

1. **Psychoanalytic Theory**

   Freud developed ***psychoanalytic theory*** (Greek *psyche,* meaning "mind").

   - The theory proposes that thoughts, feelings, and behaviors are a result of conscious and unconscious forces continually interacting in the mind.
   - According to the theory, the mind functions across three levels of consciousness.

   a. **Freud's Three Levels of Consciousness:**
      - The *conscious* consists of thoughts and feelings that are a part of normal awareness.
      - The *preconscious* consists of thoughts and feelings that a person does not perceive, which might enter conscious awareness in the future.
      - The *unconscious* includes thoughts and feelings that cannot be perceived or called into awareness, which have power to influence a person.
      - Abnormal behavior results from banishing our unacceptable sexual and aggressive impulses to our unconscious.
      - In the unconscious, they inevitably gain strength and find release through our feelings, thoughts, or actions.

   b. **Three Psychological Structures of the Mind Distinguished by Freud [see *Figure 1.2*]:**
      - ***Id:*** The seat of physical, sexual, and aggressive drives demanding immediate gratification of needs without regard to consequences. Called the *pleasure principle.*
      - ***Superego:*** The seat of individual conscience, working to impose morality by inducing feelings of guilt to constrain urges.
      - ***Ego:*** Mediates among the id's demands, the superego's sense of morality, and the constraints of external reality. Normal egos handle this process well; weak egos will not mediate well, and anxiety and other symptoms result.

2. **Psychosexual Stages**

   Freud discovered that children *must* pass through *each of* five distinct developmental stages (the oral, anal, phallic, latency, and genital stages) from infancy to adulthood.

These five *psychosexual stages* require a person to complete a key task for healthy psychological development.

- Four stages involve *erogenous zones* (the mouth, genitals, and anus), which demand satisfaction.
- Some children do not satisfy the needs of a stage until adulthood, and some never do, developing a *fixation*—a tendency for thoughts, feelings, and behaviors to relate to the stage that wasn't satisfied.

3. Mental Illness, According to Freud

Freud proposed two general categories of mental illness: neuroses and psychoses.

- *Neurosis:* A pattern of thoughts, feelings, or behaviors that expresses an unresolved conflict between the ego and the id or between the ego and the superego. An anxiety neurosis, extreme "free-floating fear," latches onto different objects or possibilities (e.g., every coincidence is an evil omen).
- **Psychosis:** A break from reality causing conflict between the ego's view of reality and reality itself. According to the psychoanalytic view, schizophrenia involves a psychosis.

4. Defense Mechanisms [see *Table 1.3*]

Defense mechanisms are unconscious. The ego transforms conflicts in a way that prevents unacceptable thoughts and feelings from reaching consciousness.

- Successful defense mechanisms can decrease anxiety.
- Anna Freud extended this work.
- Conflicts and threats can possibly cause a psychological disorder when a particular defense mechanism is relied on too heavily.

5. Psychoanalytic Theory Beyond Freud

Freud's theory is now called **psychodynamic theory** and has attracted many adherents. It has been renamed, developed, and modified.

a. Modifications to Psychoanalytic Theory:
- Normal versus abnormal development of the self
- Additional sources of motivation, such as feelings of inferiority, and their influence
- The development and work of the ego
- The possibility that our species has certain inborn and unconscious archetypes (an *archetype* is an abstract, ideal characterization of a person, object, or concept) that channel some aspects of motivation
- Research by Karen Horney et al. on the connection between moment-to-moment interactions between child and parent and psychological disorders

6. Evaluating Freud's Contributions

Psychodynamic theory faces two challenges:

- Its guiding principles and corresponding treatments rest primarily on subjective interpretations of what patients say and do.
- The theory is not generally amenable to scientific testing.

C. The Humanist Response

1. Reaction to Freud's Notions

The **humanist response** was developed as a reaction to Freud's two notions:

- Mental processes are governed by the same cause-and-effect relations that govern all machines and are driven by sexual and aggressive impulses.
- Humans don't really have free will because our behavior is in response to unconscious processes.

2. Humanistic Psychology

This area of psychology focuses on free will, innate goodness, creativity, and the self. Mental health clinicians with this outlook, such as Carl Rogers (1902–1987), are often called *humanists.*

3. Carl Rogers

Rogers, in 1942, proposed that symptoms of distress and mental illness arise when a potential route to personal growth is blocked [e.g., a person lacks a coherent, unified sense of self or there is a mismatch, or *incongruence,* between the ideal self (the qualities a person wants to have) and the real self (the qualities the person actually has)].

- Rogers developed *client-centered therapy* to help people reduce the incongruence and create solutions to their problems by releasing their "real selves."
- In accordance with this approach of self-empowerment, Rogers referred to people as "clients," indicating that they were not sick and powerless "patients," that they had control over their own lives, and that they were interested in self-improvement through engagement with mental health services.

LEARNING ACTIVITY 1.3: Comparing Your Ideal and Real Selves

Objective: Apply Rogers's theory to your own life to help solidify the concepts.

Time: 15 Minutes

Directions: Ask students to:
1. List five characteristics of who they would like to be.
2. List five characteristics that they possess currently.

Summary: As students see how Rogers's theory can be applied to their own lives, the instructor can link student responses to the development of psychological disorders (e.g., depression).

Questions to Students and Discussion: How congruent, or similar, do you think these two lists are? How might big or little differences between the lists reflect a person's level of distress or overall feelings about himself or herself?

D. Lasting Contributions of Psychodynamic and Humanist Approaches

1. Mental Processes

Psychodynamic theory rested on the fundamental insight of mental processes, which proved crucial for development of later theories and treatments. *Mental processes* are internal operations underlying cognitive and emotional functions (e.g., perception, memory, and guilt feelings) and most human behavior.

2. Mental Contents

The theory's focus on *mental contents*—the specific memories, knowledge, goals, and other material that are stored and processed in the mind—has led to much fruitful research.

3. Mental Processes and Contents Are Hidden

The notion that some mental processes and mental contents are hidden away from consciousness has proven invaluable to understanding psychopathology.

IV. SCIENTIFIC ACCOUNTS OF PSYCHOLOGICAL DISORDERS

A. Behaviorism

1. Founders

Behaviorism was spearheaded by American psychologists Edward Lee Thorndike (1874–1949), John B. Watson (1878–1958), Clark L. Hull (1884–1952), and, most famously, B. F. Skinner (1904–1990).

2. Objectives

It focuses on understanding directly observable behaviors rather than unobservable mental processes and contents. Behaviorists proposed scientifically testable mechanisms that may explain how maladaptive behavior arises.

3. Ivan Pavlov

A Russian physiologist, Pavlov (1849–1936), accidentally discovered an association between reflexive behavior and its antecedents, associations created by processes sometimes referred to as *Pavlovian conditioning.* He studied and observed the following in dogs:

- Dogs increased their salivation both *while* they were eating and *right before* they were fed (which he did not predict).
- Dogs began salivating when they heard the feeder's approaching footsteps.
- The feeder's footsteps (a neutral stimulus) became associated with the stimulus of food in the mouth.
- The dogs then salivated when hearing the footsteps—the dogs' past association between the feeder's footsteps and subsequent food led to a behavior change.
- Researchers have found that reflexive fear-related behaviors (such as a startle response) can be conditioned in the same fashion.

4. An Important Insight

An important insight of behaviorism is that a person's behavior, including maladaptive behavior, can result from learning—from a previous association with an object, situation, or event.

5. Lasting Impact

The behaviorists' emphasis on controlled, objective observation and on the importance of the situation, however, had a deep and lasting impact on the field of psychopathology.

B. The Cognitive Contribution

Cognitive psychology is an area of psychology from the late 1950s and early 1960s that studies direct connections between observable events and mental processes. This area of psychology uses the analogy of information processing by a computer.

- Researchers developed new, behaviorally based methods to track the course of hidden mental processes. These mental processes began to be demystified.

- The **cognitive contribution** to understanding psychological disorders is its focus on specific changes in mental processes.

- Psychiatrist Aaron Beck (b. 1921) and psychologist Albert Ellis (1913–2007) each focused on the content of people's thoughts: how irrational and inaccurate thinking can contribute to psychological disorders. Treatment involves shifting, or *restructuring*, people's faulty beliefs and irrational thoughts.

- Cognitive theories do not fully explain why an individual's mental processes and contents are biased in a *particular* way.

C. Social Forces

Various researchers and theorists in the last half of the 20th century recognized the connection between social forces and mental illness. Many social forces (the loss of a relationship, abuse, trauma, neglect, poverty, discrimination) produce high levels of stress.

1. Quality of Parent-Child Relationships: Attachment Styles

a. John Bowlby and Mary Ainsworth:

- Each examined *attachment style*–the particular way a person relates to intimate others.

- Researchers have delineated four types of attachment styles.

(1) Bowlby's four attachment styles:

- **Secure attachment.** These children became upset when their mother left, but quickly calmed down upon her return.

- **Resistant/anxious attachment.** These children became angry when their mother left and remained angry upon her return, sometimes even hitting her

- **Avoidant attachment.** These children had no change in their emotions based on their mother's presence or absence.

- **Disorganized attachment.** These children exhibited a combination of resistant and avoidant styles and also appeared confused or fearful with their mother.

- Children who did not have a secure attachment style (those with a resistant/anxious, avoidant, or disorganized style) were more likely to develop symptoms of psychological disorders.

- Attachment styles can be different in different cultures.

2. Social Support

- **Social support** can buffer the effects of negative life events.

- The absence of protective relationships increases the risk for developing a psychological disorder in the face of a significant stressor.

- Social forces do not fully account for how and why psychological disorders arise.

D. Biological Explanations

- Biological researchers discovered that the final stage of syphilis damages the brain and leads to abrupt changes in mental processes, including psychotic symptoms.

- The discovery of a causal link between syphilis and general paresis heralded a resurgence of the medical model, the view that psychological disorders have underlying biological causes.

- According to the **medical model,** once biological causes are identified, appropriate medical treatments can be developed, such as medications.
- Scientists have examined genes, neurotransmitters, and abnormalities in brain structure and function associated with mental illness.
- Psychological disorders cannot be explained simply on the bases of biological factors. The context of people's lives must be considered.

LECTURE ENHANCEMENT 1.5: Explore the Genes to Cognition Online Web Site

Objective: Students will learn about mental health neuroscience findings.

Time: 30 Minutes

Explore Online: The Genes to Cognition Online Web site, http://www.g2conline.org/

Introduce the students to this Web site that focuses on cognitive disorders, cognitive processes, and research approaches, and explore together the modern neuroscience explanations of psychological disorders.

Summary: As students explore this amazing Web site, they will understand the complex interaction of the neuropsychosocial feedback loops that explain psychological disorders.

Questions to Students and Discussion: Select one disorder and identify three causes or explanations of the disorder. Bring your findings into class. Which disorders did you and the other students choose? Were you surprised by the findings? What do you want to know more about?

E. The Modern Synthesis of Explanations of Psychopathology

Researchers have increasingly recognized that no single theory or factor can explain a psychological disorder. The following two psychopathological approaches integrate multiple factors.

1. **The Diathesis–Stress Model [see *Figure 1.3*]**

   - *The diathesis–stress model* claims that a psychological disorder is triggered when a person with a predisposition—a *diathesis*—for the particular disorder experiences significant stress.
   - The same stress would not affect a person who did not have the predisposition; a person who did have a diathesis for a psychological disorder would be fine if he or she could avoid high-stress situations. Essentially, both factors are required to trigger a disorder.
   - The diathesis may be a biological factor, such as a genetic vulnerability, or it may be a psychological factor, such as a cognitive vulnerability (e.g., when irrational or inaccurate negative thoughts about oneself contribute to depression).
   - The stress is often a social factor. It can be acute (e.g., being the victim of a crime) or less intense but chronic (e.g., recurring spousal abuse, poverty, or overwork).

MEDIA RECOMMENDATION 1.3: Normal or Abnormal?

Objective: Students will learn about how the pharmaceutical industry, our culture, and social contexts contribute to the development of depression.

Time: 71 Minutes

Watch Clip Online: *We Don't Live Under Normal Conditions: A Film About Depression and Suicide* (2000), http://www.aperiofilms.com/wdlunc.html (clips of the film are available)

This film challenges our notions of psychological disorders by arguing that depression may be a natural feeling in the context in which we live. The film juxtaposes the personal lives of people affected by depression with the pharmaceutical industry's desire for profit.

Summary: After watching the film, students will understand the complex causes of psychological disorders. Students will view multiple arguments about how the pharmaceutical industry, our culture, and social contexts contribute to the development of depression.

Questions to Students and Discussion: Which case was the most powerful? Why? What do you think about the various facts highlighted in the film? Do you agree that the pharmaceutical industry plays a role in what is considered normal or abnormal? If so, what are the costs to society? To the individual?

2. **The Biopsychosocial and Neuropsychosocial Approaches**

a. **Three Types of Factors:**

- The **three types of factors underlying psychological disorders** are: (1) biological—genetics, the structure and function of the brain, and the function of other bodily systems; (2) psychological—behaviors; and (3) social—social interactions and the environment in which they occur.

- The biopsychosocial approach identifies these three factors and documents the ways these factors contribute to a disorder. There are two problems with the traditional biopsychosocial approach: (1) The approach does not specifically focus on the brain, the organ that is responsible for cognition and affect; and (2) sometimes the biopsychosocial approach is used to identify the set of factors that caused a disorder but considers the factors in isolation, thus missing the big picture.

b. **The Neuropsychosocial Approach: Refining the Biopsychosocial Approach:**

The **neuropsychosocial approach** has two defining features: (1) the way it characterizes the factors, and (2) the way it characterizes their interactions.

(1) **Emphasis on the brain:**

- The biopsychosocial approach was revised to incorporate recent discoveries about the brain and how psychological and social factors affect brain function.

- The approach underscores the role of the brain—brain structures and functions—in contributing to psychological disorders.

(2) **Emphasis on feedback loops:**

- Neurological, psychological, and social factors are usually involved simultaneously and are constantly interacting through **feedback loops:** Each factor is affected by the others and also feeds back to affect the other factors. [See *Figure 1.4.*]

- Interactions among neurological, psychological, and social factors are common.

LECTURE ENHANCEMENT 1.6: Explore the Treatment of the Mentally Ill Today

Objective: Discuss the current treatment of people with severe mental illness.

Time: 30 Minutes

Explore Online:

Examine the National Alliance for the Mentally Ill *Grading the States 2009* report, http://www.nami.org/gtsTemplate09.cfm?Section=Grading_the_States_2009

Listen and look at Michael Nye's Fine Line Exhibit of voices, images, and stories of people with mental illness, http://www.michaelnye.org/fineline/

AND

Either listen to NPR's *All Things Considered* audiofile on "Settlements in Mental Health Cases Face Scrutiny" (in Georgia), http://www.npr.org/templates/story/story.php?storyId=102503173

This audio clip highlights the poor treatment of people in state institutions.

OR

Examine the United States Department of Justice Civil Rights of Institutionalized Persons Act, http://www.usdoj.gov/crt/split/cripa.php

Summary: After reviewing these sites, students will gain an understanding of the current state of the treatment of those with mental illness. The instructor can highlight similarities and differences to the historical explanations of mental illness covered in this chapter.

Questions to Students and Discussion: How is the treatment of people with mental illness different or similar to the various historical treatments covered in this chapter? What improvements do you think are needed?

ADDITIONAL MEDIA RECOMMENDATIONS

Hovde, E., Meyer, M., Maysles, A., Maysles, D., & Froemick, S. (Directors). (1975). *Grey Gardens* [Film]. United States: Portrait Films.

This film captures the lives of the eccentric Beale family, relatives of Jacqueline Kennedy.

Collins, R. (Director). (2000). *We don't live under normal conditions: A film about depression and suicide* [Film]. United States: Fanlight Productions.

This film takes a critical look at depression through the eyes of diverse people in the United States. The film integrates interesting facts about the pharmaceutical companies, the history of diagnosis and mental illness, and how homophobia and racism contribute to the development of mental illness. Clips from the film can be found here: http://www.aperiofilms.com/About theFilm.html

Barraclough, J. (Producer), & Lewis, M. (Director). (2008). *Secrets of the dead: Witches curse* [Television series episode]. Arlington, VA: PBS.

This PBS program examines the possible role of ergot poisoning in the Salem witch trials of 1692. It is an excellent source for discussion of the tensions between religious and scientific explanations of mental illness. Clips of the program can be seen here: http://www.pbs.org/wnet/secrets/previous_seasons/case_salem/about.html

Navasky, M., & O'Connor, K. (Producers and Directors). (2005). *The new asylums* [Television series episode]. Boston, MA: WGBH Educational Foundation.

Many people who are mentally ill are now being housed in prisons. This Frontline episode explores why this is happening. Watch the program online: http://www.pbs.org/wgbh/pages/frontline/shows/asylums/view/

Goodman, B., & Maggio, J. (Producers and Directors). (2008). *The lobotomist* [Television series episode]. Boston, MA: WGBH Educational Foundation.

Dr. Walter Freeman performed hundreds of lobotomies on people to "cure" them of their mental illness. However, there is no scientific evidence that the lobotomy is an effective treatment. Watch the program online: http://www.pbs.org/wgbh/amex/lobotomist/program/

Wiseman, F. (Director). (1967). *Titicut follies* [Film]. United States: Grove Press.

This is a documentary, originally banned, about a prison for the criminally insane. Recommended with caution.

WEB SITES

Time Lines

History of Abnormal Psychology: This Web site provides a time line of the beliefs and treatment of mental illness from prehistoric times (10,000 B.C.E.–3,000 B.C.E.) to the mental hygiene movement (1940s). See: http://www3.niu.edu/acad/psych/Millis/History/2002/mainsheet.htm

Timeline Treatments for Mental Illness: See: http://www.pbs.org/wgbh/amex/nash/timeline/index.html

Photos of Institutions and Early Treatments

Photos of Psychiatric Institutions Around the World: See: http://www.newsweek.com/id/159114

Forms of Early Psychiatric Treatment: See: http://web.mac.com/paul.stermer/Psychological_Links_of_Interest/Treatments.html

Treatment of People with Mental Illness Today

National Alliance on Mental Illness: Examines the treatment of people with mental illness today. See: http://www.nami.org/Content/NavigationMenu/Inform_Yourself/About_Mental_Illness/About_Mental_Illness.htm

Modern Neuroscience

Genes to Cognition Online Web Site: Explores modern neuroscience explanations of many psychological disorders. See: http://www.g2conline.org/

Podcast

"The Anatomy of a Lobotomist" (2007, 60 minutes, Shrink Rap Radio). See: http://www.podcastdirectory.com/podshows/1279834

Understanding Psychological Disorders: The Neuropsychosocial Approach

CHAPTER 2

CHAPTER OUTLINE

CHAPTER HEADINGS	INSTRUCTION IDEAS AND TEXTBOOK CORRELATIONS
Chapter Introduction	**Learning Objective:** 2.1 **Learning Concepts:** etiology, neuropsychosocial factors **Learning Activity 2.1:** Exploring the Causes of Disorders
NEUROLOGICAL FACTORS IN PSYCHOLOGICAL DISORDERS	
Brain Structure and Brain Function	**Learning Objectives:** 2.2, 2.3, 2.4, 2.5, 2.6, 2.7 **Learning Concepts:** nervous system, central nervous system (CNS), peripheral nervous system, occipital lobe, parietal lobe, temporal lobe, frontal lobe, limbic system, three main types of neurons, structure, function, synapse, neurotransmitters, dopamine, serotonin, acetylcholine, adrenaline, noradrenaline, glutamate, gamma-amino butyric acid (GABA), endogenous cannabinoids, abnormal communications among neurons, the HPA axis, cortisol **Learning Activity 2.2:** Personal Application of the Nervous System **Learning Activity 2.3:** Simon Says **Media Recommendation 2.1:** Memorizing Brain Parts and Functions **Media Recommendation 2.2:** Psychobiology of Conflict **Media Recommendation 2.3:** Neuroscience Exploration **Media Recommendation 2.4:** Neurotransmitters **Learning Activity 2.4:** Act Out a Neuron **Textbook Tools:** Figures 2.1, 2.2, 2.3, 2.4, 2.5, 2.6
The Genetics of Psychopathology	**Learning Objective:** 2.8 **Learning Concepts:** genes, genotypes, phenotypes, behavioral genetics, twin and adoption studies
FEEDBACK LOOPS IN ACTION: The Genes and the Environment	**Learning Concepts:** feedback loops: the genes and the environment **Lecture Enhancement 2.1:** Exploring Complex Inheritance

PSYCHOLOGICAL FACTORS IN PSYCHOLOGICAL DISORDERS	
Behavior and Learning	**Learning Objectives:** 2.9, 2.10, 2.11 **Learning Concepts:** classical conditioning, operant conditioning, observational learning **Media Recommendation 2.5:** Little Albert Footage **Lecture Enhancement 2.2:** The Truth Behind Little Albert **Learning Activity 2.5:** Phobias and Classical Conditioning **Media Recommendation 2.6:** *Supernanny* and Operant Conditioning **Learning Activity 2.6:** Operant Conditioning and Personal Examples **Media Recommendation 2.7:** Bobo Doll Experiment Footage **Textbook Tools:** Figure 2.7; Table 2.1
Mental Processes and Mental Contents	**Learning Objective:** 2.12 **Learning Concepts:** mental processes and mental contents **Media Recommendation 2.8:** Gloria and Cognitive Therapy **Textbook Tools:** Figures 2.8, 2.9, 2.10; Table 2.2
Emotion	**Learning Objectives:** 2.13, 2.14, 2.15 **Learning Concepts:** emotion, mood, temperament **Textbook Tools:** Figures 2.9, 2.10
SOCIAL FACTORS IN PSYCHOLOGICAL DISORDERS	
Family Matters	**Learning Objectives:** 2.16 **Learning Concepts:** family interaction style, child maltreatment, parental psychological disorders
Community Support	**Learning Concepts:** community support, social support
Social Stressors	**Learning Objectives:** 2.17 **Learning Concepts:** socioeconomic status (SES), discrimination, bullying **Media Recommendation 2.9:** Poverty, Race, and Health **Learning Activity 2.7:** APA's Office of Socioeconomic Status **Textbook Tool:** Case 2.1 **Worth Video Tool Kit for Abnormal Psychology:** Florida Anti-Bullying Bill: Acommunity Response, Cruel Intentions: A Social Experiment
Culture	**Learning Objectives:** 2.18 **Learning Concepts:** culture, acculturation
FEEDBACK LOOPS IN ACTION: LEARNED HELPLESSNESS	**Learning Activity 2.8:** Finding the Best Treatments **Learning Activity 2.9:** Mock Clients Using Theater Students

LEARNING OBJECTIVES

After reading this chapter, students should be able to:

2.1 Define etiology.

2.2 Describe the parts of the nervous system and the role of the nervous system in psychological disorders.

2.3 Identify the location and describe the major functions of the four lobes of the brain.

2.4 Describe the key structures of the limbic system and their roles in psychological disorders.

2.5 Define and locate the main structures of the neuron.

2.6 Describe the role of neurotransmitters in psychological disorders.

2.7 Explain how hormones can affect our ability to cope.

2.8 Identify the role of genetics in psychological disorders.

2.9 Explain how classical conditioning can cause certain psychological disorders.

2.10 Apply operant conditioning to the development of psychological disorders.

2.11 Describe how observational learning might play a role in psychological disorders.

2.12 Explain how mental processes and contents contribute to the development of psychological disorders.

2.13 Identify how emotion plays a role in psychological disorders.

2.14 Describe the four major temperaments and their connection to psychological disorders.

2.15 Define expressed emotion.

2.16 Describe the ways that child maltreatment places individuals at a higher risk for developing psychological disorders.

2.17 Identify social stressors that place individuals at risk for developing psychological disorders.

2.18 Articulate how culture and acculturation influence mental health.

KEY TERMS

Etiology: The factors that lead a person to develop a psychological disorder.

Cerebral cortex: The outer layer of cells on the surface of the brain.

Neurons: Brain cells that process information related to physical, mental, and emotional functioning.

Brain circuits: Sets of connected neurons that work together to accomplish a basic process.

Brain systems: Sets of brain circuits that work together to accomplish a complex function.

Action potential: The wave of chemical activity that moves from the cell body down the axon when a neuron fires.

Synapse: The place where the tip of the axon of one neuron sends signals to another neuron.

Neurotransmitters: Chemicals that are released at the terminal buttons and cross the synaptic cleft.

Neuromodulators: Chemicals that modulate (alter) the way neurotransmitters affect the receiving neuron. Some chemicals that act as neurotransmitters can also act as neuromodulators in certain circumstances, and vice versa.

Receptors: Specialized sites on dendrites and cell bodies that respond only to specific molecules.

Reuptake: The process of moving leftover neurotransmitter molecules in the synapse back into the sending neuron.

Hormones: Neurotransmitter substances that are released directly into the bloodstream and often function primarily as neuromodulators.

Mendelian inheritance: The transmission of traits by separate elements (genes).

Genes: Segments of DNA that control the production of particular proteins and other substances.

Genotype: The sum of an organism's genes.

Phenotype: The sum of an organism's observable traits.

Complex inheritance: The transmission of traits that are expressed along a continuum by the interaction of sets of genes.

Behavioral genetics: The field that investigates the degree to which the variability of characteristics in a population arises from genetic versus environmental factors.

Heritability: An estimate of how much of the variation in a characteristic within a population (in a specific environment) can be attributed to genetics.

Monozygotic twins: Twins who have basically the same genetic makeup (although it may differ in how often specific genes are repeated) because they began life as a single fertilized egg (zygote), which then divided into two embryos; also referred to as *identical twins.*

Dizygotic twins: Twins who developed from two fertilized eggs and so have the same overlap in genes (50%) as do siblings not conceived at the same time; also referred to as *fraternal twins.*

Classical conditioning: A type of learning that occurs when two stimuli are paired so that a neutral stimulus becomes associated with another stimulus that elicits a reflexive behavior; also referred to as *Pavlovian conditioning.*

Unconditioned stimulus (UCS): A stimulus that reflexively elicits a behavior.

Unconditioned response (UCR): A behavior that is reflexively elicited by a stimulus.

Conditioned stimulus (CS): A neutral stimulus that, when paired with an unconditioned stimulus, comes to elicit the reflexive behavior.

Conditioned response (CR): A response that comes to be elicited by the previously neutral stimulus that has become a conditioned stimulus.

Conditioned emotional responses: Emotions and emotion-related behaviors that are classically conditioned.

Stimulus generalization: The process whereby responses come to be elicited by stimuli that are similar to the conditioned stimulus.

Operant conditioning: A type of learning in which the likelihood that a behavior will be repeated depends on the consequences associated with the behavior.

Reinforcement: The process by which the consequence of a behavior *increases* the likelihood of the behavior's recurrence.

Positive reinforcement: The type of reinforcement that occurs when a desired reinforcer is received after a behavior, which makes the behavior likely to occur again in the future.

Negative reinforcement: The type of reinforcement that occurs when an aversive or uncomfortable stimulus is *removed* after a behavior, which makes that behavior more likely to be produced again in the future.

Punishment: The process by which an event or object that is the consequence of a behavior *decreases* the likelihood that the behavior will occur again.

Positive punishment: The type of punishment that takes place when a behavior is followed by an undesirable consequence, which makes the behavior less likely to recur.

Negative punishment: The type of punishment that takes place when a behavior is followed by the removal of a pleasant or desired event or circumstance, which decreases the probability of that behavior's recurrence.

Learned helplessness: The state of "giving up" that arises when an animal is in an aversive situation where it seems that no action can be effective.

Observational learning: The process of learning through watching what happens to others; also referred to as *modeling.*

Cognitive distortions: Dysfunctional, maladaptive thoughts that are not accurate reflections of reality and contribute to psychological disorders; also called *cognitive vulnerabilities.*

Emotion: A short-lived experience evoked by a stimulus that produces a mental response, a typical behavior, and a positive or negative subjective feeling.

Affect: An emotion that is associated with a particular idea or behavior, similar to an attitude.

Inappropriate affect: An expression of emotion that is not appropriate to what a person is saying or not appropriate to the situation.

Flat affect: A lack of, or considerably diminished, emotional expression, such as occurs when someone speaks robotically and shows little facial expression.

Mood: A persistent emotion that is not attached to a stimulus; it exists in the background and influences mental processes, mental contents, and behavior.

Temperament: The various aspects of personality that reflect a person's typical emotional state and emotional reactivity (including the speed and strength of reactions to stimuli).

High expressed emotion: A family interaction style characterized by hostility, unnecessary criticism, or emotional overinvolvement.

Social support: The comfort and assistance that an individual receives through interactions with others.

Social causation: The hypothesis that the daily stressors of urban life, especially as experienced by people in a lower socioeconomic level, trigger mental illness in those who are vulnerable.

Social selection: The hypothesis that those who are mentally ill "drift" to a lower socioeconomic level because of their impairments; also referred to as *social drift.*

CHAPTER GUIDE

Chapter Introduction

The factors that may lead a person to develop a psychological disorder, its *etiology,* include:

- **Neurological factors,** which are abnormalities in brain structures, neuron or neurotransmitter function, and genes
- **Psychological factors,** which include feelings, beliefs, thoughts, and goals

- **Social factors** such as finances, family relationships, and society and culture
- The interactions among these factors and the effects they have on each other via feedback loops—the neuropsychosocial approach

LEARNING ACTIVITY 2.1: Exploring the Causes of Disorders

Objective: To introduce students to the multiple explanations of psychological disorders.

Time: 10 Minutes

Directions:
1. Have students meet in small groups and come up with three causes of the Beales' behavior.
2. After students have discussed their ideas in groups, write all the ideas on the board.
3. Using the content of the textbook as a guide, organize these ideas according to which category they fall under: neurological, genetic, environmental, learning, cognitive distortions, emotional dysfunction, temperament, family, and culture.

Summary: Students will enjoy hearing about the number of explanations and different perspectives on the etiology of psychological disorders. Currently, the neuropsychological perspective dominates the media and thus students should explain mental illness due to structural or neurochemical causes.

Questions to Students and Discussion: What explanations were most common? What explanations were most rare? What do you think are the top one or two reasons why the students in your classroom lean toward the explanations that they do?

I. NEUROLOGICAL FACTORS IN PSYCHOLOGICAL DISORDERS

Genes interact with the environment and sometimes contribute to psychopathology.

A. Brain Structure and Brain Function

1. A Quick Tour of the Nervous System

a. The Central Nervous System and the Peripheral Nervous System:

- The *central nervous system (CNS)* has two parts: the brain and spinal cord. It is the seat of memory, consciousness, perception, and voluntary action.
- The *peripheral nervous system (PNS)* has two parts: the sensory-somatic nervous system and the autonomic nervous system. [See *Figure 2.1.*]

b. The Autonomic Nervous System:

- The sensory-somatic nervous system is part of the PNS that connects the brain to the outside world via senses (inputs) and muscles (outputs).
- The *autonomic nervous system (ANS)* is the part of the PNS that plays a major role in our response to stress. It controls involuntary functions (heart, digestive tract, blood vessels) and has two components: the sympathetic nervous system and the parasympathetic nervous system.
  - **i.   Sympathetic nervous system (SNS):** This system acts in emergencies. It speeds up a person's heart and dilates the pupils, and it slows down digestion (fight-or-flight, or stress, response). [*Figure 2.1.*] The *hypothalamic-pituitary-adrenal axis (HPA axis)* produces cortisol, which readies the muscles for physical exertion. [*Figure 2.1.*] The cortisol level often remains high when under chronic stress. The HPA axis and cortisol are involved in depression and

stress-related psychological disorders, such as posttraumatic stress disorder (PTSD).

  ii. **Parasympathetic nervous system (PNS):** This system calms a person down after a crisis: The PNS slows the heart, contracts the pupils, and increases digestion. Failure of the PNS to counteract the effects of the SNS has been associated with various psychological problems.

LEARNING ACTIVITY 2.2: Personal Application of the Nervous System

Objective: To have students apply their knowledge about the nervous system to their own experience.

Time: 5 Minutes

Directions:
  1. Ask students to think of a stressful situation.
  2. Then have them identify how their nervous system responded to the situation, referring to the terms found in this section, "Brain Structure and Brain Function."
  3. Also, have the students describe and discuss how they were able to calm themselves down.

Summary: This exercise highlights how the sympathetic nervous system activates in emergencies while the parasympathetic nervous system helps to calm the system down. Students will become more aware of how their bodies react to stressful situations and thus connect the material to their own lives.

Questions to Students and Discussion: Do you know someone who has an overactive parasympathetic nervous system? What symptoms does he/she show? How do you think this person can reduce this activity?

c. **The Four Brain Lobes:**

One part of the central nervous system, the brain, has four major lobes—all four lobes are found on each side (called a *hemisphere,* or *half-sphere*) of the brain (the right side and the left side). [See *Figure 2.2.*] Starting with the back of the brain:

- The **occipital lobe** is located in the back of the brain and is dedicated to vision.
- The **parietal lobe** is located at the top of the back of the brain, processes spatial information (location of objects), and plays a role in self-awareness.
- The **temporal lobe** is located under the temple. It stores visual memories, processes auditory information, decodes the meaning of speech, and contributes to conscious experience. When functioning abnormally, it produces intense emotions and auditory hallucinations.
- The **frontal lobe** is located behind the forehead and plays a role in feeling emotions, using emotional responses in decision making, and general thinking and problem solving. It is involved in programming actions and controlling body movements and is the seat of executive functioning, which plans for the future and problem-solves. Schizophrenia is associated with this lobe when abnormalities both in this lobe and in executive functioning are present.

LEARNING ACTIVITY 2.3: Simon Says

Objective: To have students locate the four lobes.

Time: 5 Minutes

Directions: Have students touch the different lobes on their head using the Simon Says game rules. Go through the exercise with the students once and then have one of the students in the class lead the game.

Summary: Students will learn where the lobes are located and the physical movement should help to solidify this information.

Questions to Students and Discussion: What lobes were most difficult to remember? What techniques can you use to aid in your memory of the four lobes?

MEDIA RECOMMENDATION 2.1: Memorize Brain Parts and Functions

Objective: To memorize the brain parts and functions.

Time: 19 Minutes

Media and Discussion: 25 Minutes

Discussion Only: 5 Minutes

Watch Online: Psych Files, Episode 72: *Memorizing the Parts of the Brain,* http://www.thepsych-files.com/2008/09/22/episode-72-video-memorize-the-parts-of-the-brain/

This brief podcast shows numerous mnemonic devices to help students learn how to remember the different brain structures and functions. A written summary of each technique is provided.

Summary: Students will learn various mnemonic devices to help them remember the names and functions brain structures. Students will enjoy seeing these memory techniques as well as learning the names and definitions.

Questions to Students and Discussion: Now that you've heard the podcast, how many structures and functions can you recall? What structures do you still find challenging to remember? Can you or anyone in your class create a better or easier mnemonic device?

d. The Cortex and Beneath the Cortex:
- The *cerebral cortex* is the outer layer of cells on the brain surface.
- It contains the majority of the brain's *neurons* (the cells that process information related to our physical, mental, and emotional functioning).
- Most brain functions described earlier are carried out primarily in the cortex of the corresponding lobes.
- Important functions are carried out in *subcortical areas*—areas beneath the cortex—such as the limbic system, thalamus, nucleus accumbens, basal ganglia, and cerebellum. [See *Figure 2.3.*]
    - i. **Limbic system:** This system plays a role in emotions. Three of the more important components are the: (1) hypothalamus—which governs bodily functions associated with eating, drinking, and temperature and also plays a role in emotions and pleasure; (2) amygdala—which is central to producing and per-

ceiving strong emotions, especially fear; and (3) hippocampus—which stores new information in memory.

    ii. Thalamus: The functioning of this subcortical area of the brain is critical for sleep and attention. Abnormalities are associated with schizophrenia.

    iii. Nucleus accumbens: This subcortical area registers reward and learning from experience. It is involved in addiction.

    iv. Basal ganglia: This area is involved in automatic responses. Abnormalities are associated with repetitive thoughts or behavior, such as obsessive-compulsive disorder.

    v. Cerebellum: The cerebellum helps manage physical coordination, attention, and automatic motions.

MEDIA RECOMMENDATION 2.2: Psychobiology of Conflict

Objective: To apply a psychobiological understanding of couples' relationships and conflicts.

Time: 60 Minutes

Media and Discussion: 90 Minutes

Discussion Only: 30 Minutes

Listen Online: *A Psychobiological Approach to Couples Therapy,* with Dr. Stan Tatkin, Podcast #179, http://www.shrinkrapradio.com/?s=NEUROBIOLOGY&searchsubmit=Find

This podcast explores psychobiological explanations of couples' conflicts by examining how our brain and nervous system respond to conflict. There is a transcript available of this podcast through the Shrink Rap Radio Web site.

Summary: Students will learn how our hardwired biological system sets us up to face certain challenges in relationships. Students will also be able to relate concepts from this chapter and podcast to their personal relationships.

Questions to Students and Discussion: Why do we have such a difficult time being calm in arguments? Do you agree with Tatkin's view of relationships? Why or why not?

MEDIA RECOMMENDATION 2.3: Neuroscience Exploration

Objective: To explore neuroscience through interactive and hands-on activities.

Time: 5–30 Minutes

Medium and Discussion: 45 Minutes

Discussion Only: 15 Minutes

Explore Online:
(1)   Neuroscience for Kids, http://faculty.washington.edu/chudler/experi.html
(2)   Neuroimaging Primer and Images, http://www.med.harvard.edu/AANLIB/home.html

Neuroscience for Kids provides interactive and other activities for studying the brain and neurons. Even though the activities are intended for children in grades 1 through 5, college students will enjoy many of these sites. In particular, students will enjoy making a three-dimensional model of the neuron and coloring and labeling the neuroscience pictures.

Neuroimaging Primer and Images compares images of the normal brain with various diseased-brain images. The Web site includes Harvard lecture notes, 3D imaging, and diseased-brain "tours."

Summary: Both of these Web sites are useful for exploring the structures of the brain. Students can explore these sites to learn more about neuroimaging.

Questions to Students and Discussion: Which activities did you enjoy? Why? Which activities did you not enjoy? Why? Can you think of another creative way to learn information from this chapter?

2. Neurons

- All brain activity depends on neurons. Malfunctions at the neuronal level often contribute to psychological disorders. Most neurons interact with others. They either (1) activate, or turn on, other neurons, or (2) inhibit, or turn off, other neurons.
- The **three main types of neurons** are:
  i.   **Sensory neurons:** Receive input from sense organs (eyes, ears, etc.)
  ii. **Motor neurons:** Carry output that stimulates muscles and glands
  iii. **Interneurons:** Lie between other neurons and make up most of the brain's neurons
- *Brain circuits* are sets of connected neurons that work together to accomplish a basic process (such as recoiling from a hot stove after touching it).
  i.   Sets are organized into **brain systems,** which can encompass large portions of one or more lobes.
  ii. Psychopathology may arise if brain circuits are not working properly.
  iii. Psychopathology may also arise when neurons fail to communicate, which leads brain circuits to produce incorrect outputs.

a. The Cell Body [the Structure and Function of the Neuron]:

- The **structure** of the neuron: The neuron consists of three parts: (1) a receiving end, (2) a sending end, and (3) a *cell body* (the middle part). [See *Figure 2.4.*]
- The *nucleus* of the neuron regulates all neuron functions.
- The *cell membrane* is the outer covering.
- The **function** of the neuron: When the neuron is stimulated enough, (1) very small holes, or *channels,* in the membrane open; (2) the balance of chemicals changes; and (3) the neuron then fires, thus sending information to other neurons.
- Each neuron registers the sum total of both the stimulating and the inhibiting inputs. The neuron then balances the inputs and only fires if the stimulating inputs substantially outweigh the inhibiting ones.

b. The Axon:

- The *axon* is the part of the neuron that sends signals when a neuron fires.
- It is a long, threadlike structure, covered with a fatty, insulating layer called a *myelin sheath.*
- A single axon branches out extensively, sending signals to many neurons at the same time.
- When a neuron fires, a wave of chemicals (**action potential**) moves from the cell body to the end of the axon. Chemicals are then released and stored in the *terminal buttons.*
- If a neuron does not fire when it should, the brain circuit of which it is a part will not function correctly and psychopathology may result.

c. The Dendrites:

- *Dendrites* stimulate neurons to fire; they receive signals from other neurons.
- They are highly branched to simultaneously receive many signals.
- Signals received from other neurons move along the dendrites of the receiving neurons to their cell bodies.
- Sometimes neurons receive inputs directly on their cell bodies. The inputs are produced not only by other neurons but also by *glial cells.*
  - **i.** Glial (meaning "glue" in Greek) cells care, support, and feed neurons.
  - **ii.** The brain contains about 10 times as many glial cells as neurons.
  - **iii.** These cells stimulate neurons and modulate input from other neurons.
- Some psychopathology is caused by loss of dendrites and/or glial cells, possibly brought on by pre- or postnatal stress).

3. Chemical Signals

- The way neurons communicate is crucial to understanding psychopathology.
- Psychological disorders involve faulty signaling among neurons; medications alter/fix the production and processing of signals.
- To understand these signaling problems, we need to understand chemical signaling: (1) what happens at the synapse, (2) what neurotransmitters and neuromodulators do, (3) the nature of chemical receptors, and (4) what can go wrong with chemical communication between neurons.

a. The Synapse:

- When a neuron fires and chemicals are released at the terminal button, the chemicals usually contact another neuron at a **synapse,** the place where the axon tip of one neuron nestles against the dendrite of another neuron and sends signals.
- Most of the time the two neurons are not physically connected, but instead the chemicals (or neurotransmitters) carry the signal across a gap, the *synaptic cleft.* [See *Figure 2.5.*]
- Problems at the synapse can result in psychopathology.

b. Neurotransmitters and Neuromodulators:

- *Neurotransmitters* are the chemicals that are released from the axon tip (at the terminal button).
- *Neuromodulators* are chemicals that affect the function of neurotransmitters, sometimes by altering events at the synapse (i.e., by slowing down the removal of molecules of the neurotransmitters from the synaptic cleft).
- Because some chemicals can act as neurotransmitters sometimes and as neuromodulators other times, the term *neurotransmitter substances* is now used to include both neurotransmitters and neuromodulators.
- The following neurotransmitter substances play roles in psychological disorders depending in part on their nature and on the neural transmission process.

(1) Dopamine:

- Involved in reward, motivation, and the executive functions of the frontal lobe, including body movements.
- Too little dopamine is linked to attention-deficit/hyperactivity disorder and depression; too much dopamine is linked to aggression and schizophrenia.

(2) **Serotonin:**

- Involved in mood, sleep, and motivation.
- Largely an inhibitory neurotransmitter.
- Too little serotonin is linked to depression and obsessive-compulsive disorder; too much may reduce motivation.

(3) **Acetylcholine:**

- Plays an important role in the hippocampus, where it helps to process new information in memory.
- Also found in the ANS and is involved in the fight-or-flight (or panic) response.
- Too little acetylcholine is linked to delusions; too much can contribute to spasms, tremors, and convulsions.

(4) **Adrenaline (or Epinephrine):**

- Plays a role in attention and the body's fight-or-flight response.
- Too little adrenaline contributes to depression; too much can lead to over-arousal and feelings of apprehension or dread.

(5) **Noradrenaline (or Norepinephrine):**

- Plays a role in attention and the fight-or-flight response.
- Too little contributes to distractibility, fatigue, and depression; too much is implicated in schizophrenia and anxiety disorders.

(6) **Glutamate:**

- Involved in registering pain and forming new memories. This is a fast-acting excitatory neurotransmitter.
- Too little glutamate is associated with other disorders, notably schizophrenia; too much is linked to various disorders, including substance abuse.

(7) **Gamma-amino butyric acid (GABA):**

- A common inhibitory substance.
- Too little GABA is associated with anxiety and (possibly) panic disorder; too much appears to undermine motivation.

(8) **Endogenous cannabinoids:**

- Involved in emotion, attention, memory, appetite, and the control of movements.
- Too little is associated with chronic pain; an excess is associated with eating disorders, memory impairment, attention difficulties, and possibly schizophrenia.

MEDIA RECOMMENDATION 2.4: Neurotransmitters

Objective: To compare and contrast the different neurotransmitters.

Time: 20 Minutes

Explore Online: Search google.com, using the search term "neurotransmitters and drugs chart," or see here: http://ocw.mit.edu/ans7870/SP/SP.236/S09/lecturenotes/drugchart.htm

This Web site summarizes different types of drugs and neurotransmitters. The chart also explains the function of each neurotransmitter.

Summary: Students will appreciate the structure of this chart as it quickly summarizes the different neurotransmitters and their functions. Students might try developing their own chart using information from the lecture and textbook.

Questions to Students and Discussion: Which neurotransmitter(s) plays a role in happiness? Which neurotransmitter(s) affects memory? Which neurotransmitter(s) plays a role in anxiety?

c. Chemical Receptors:

- *Receptors* of neurons receive chemical messages and respond only to specific molecules because the receptors work like a lock and key. [*Figure 2.5.*]
- They are located on the dendrites or cell body.
- Neurotransmitters *bind* to receptors (instead of locking or unlocking them) and excite or inhibit them.
- A small number of neurotransmitters often bind to many different types of receptors.
- The effect of a firing neuron depends on how its neurotransmitters bind to receptors on the receiving neuron—i.e., the same chemical can have different effects on a neuron depending on which kind of receptor it binds to.

LEARNING ACTIVITY 2.4: Act Out a Neuron

Objective: To show students visually how a neuron works.

Time: 20 Minutes

Directions: Use this exercise in front of the class, and then have students replicate the exercise in small groups.
1. Ask for at least 5 volunteers.
2. Have 2 people play the dendrites (1 from the firing neuron and 1 postsynaptic) and have 2 people play the axon.
3. Have 1 person play the terminal button and give this student balls of paper as the neurotransmitters.
4. Have the dendrite receive the message and send (wiggle) it down through the axon.
5. Show students how the chemical or neurotransmitter is used to communicate to the next neuron but is not passed throughout the neuron.

Summary: This exercise helps students to visualize neural communication.

Questions to Students and Discussion: Now that you have done this activity, are you still confused about any part of the process? What questions do you have about neural transmission? How does psychopathology develop in the neural transmission process?

d. Abnormal Communications Among Neurons:

There are three ways in which communications can be disrupted among neurons at the synaptic cleft:

- Neurons might have too many or too few dendrites or receptors.
- Sending neurons might produce too much or too little of a neurotransmitter substance.

- Events following a neuron firing might go awry. *Example:* After a neuron fires and sends neurotransmitter chemicals to another neuron, not all of these molecules bind to receptors. When molecules linger in the synaptic cleft and need to be removed, special chemical processes operate to **reuptake** these neurotransmitters, moving them back into the sending neuron. If reuptake does not operate properly, sometimes a psychological disorder can result.

4. Hormones and the Endocrine System

- Hormones are neurotransmitter substances released into the bloodstream, often functioning as neuromodulators and having a widespread effect by activating or modulating neuron activity. [See *Figure 2.6.*]

- Traumatic events can disrupt this often helpful mechanism and contribute to psychological disorders.

- Hormones are produced by glands in the endocrine system.

- Hormones affect the **HPA axis** by releasing **cortisol** (produced by the adrenal gland) to cope with emergencies (cortisol breaks down fats and proteins and converts them to sugar for more energy).

- Abnormal amounts of cortisol (produced in the adrenal glands above the kidneys) have been linked to anxiety and depression.

- Some substances, such as adrenaline, function as neurotransmitters in the brain and also as **hormones** in the body. Thus, researchers must consider not only amounts of a transmitter substance but also the nature of the neurons that have receptors for that substance and the circuits in which they participate.

B. The Genetics of Psychopathology

Genes affect physical traits, the brain (and, through the brain, thinking, feeling, and behavior), and our vulnerability to particular psychological disorders.

- Gregor Mendel (1866), an Augustinian monk, formulated the idea of **Mendelian inheritance,** or the transmission of traits by genes. The two most important aspects are (1) each parent transmits a distinct "element" to its offspring that specifies each trait, and (2) one element may dominate the other "recessive" element in the expression or nonexpression of the trait in the offspring. The offspring will show the effect of the recessive element only if it receives two copies of the recessive element, one from each parent.

- Watson and Crick (mid-20th century) identified as **genes** those segments of DNA that control the production of particular proteins. [*Figure 2.6.*]

- For many traits, gene variants (alleles) determine how those traits are expressed.

- The sum of an organism's genes is called its **genotype,** but the observable traits are called the **phenotype.**

- For most traits, genes work together to cause particular traits; such traits are expressed along a continuum, and the joint action of these genes produces **complex inheritance.**

- Almost all psychological disorders that have a genetic component, such as schizophrenia and depression, arise in part through complex inheritance.

1. Behavioral Genetics

Behavioral genetics examines genetic versus environmental factors in the expression of genes. Genes and environment interact through feedback loops; thus the phenotype is described as the product of genes in a specific environment—the same genes can have different effects in different environments.

a. Heritability:

- *Heritability* is an estimate of how much of a variation in a characteristic within a population (in a specific environment) can be attributed to genetics.

- Many variables can affect the estimate of the heritability of a given psychological disorder.

- Environmental effects of heritability are difficult to assess. One particular difficulty is the wide variance in how situations and events are perceived and understood, such as how children of different ages perceive divorce.

b. Twin and Adoption Studies:

- Identical twins (or *monozygotic twins*) have basically the same genetic makeup because they begin life as a single fertilized egg (or *zygote*) that then divides to become two embryos.

- Fraternal twins (or *dizygotic twins*) begin life as different fertilized eggs and are like any other nonidentical siblings in terms of their genetic similarity: They have about 50% overlap in the genes that vary among humans.

- Researchers who compare the characteristics of monozygotic twins and dizygotic twins try to control the environment as much as possible and then attempt to draw conclusions about the contribution of genes in that environment.

- Researchers take twins who were separated at birth and raised in different homes, and then compare them to twins who were raised in the same home. Researchers also study unrelated children who were adopted and raised together, then compare them to unrelated children who were reared in different homes. In both cases, it is not easy to disentangle the effects of **genes and the environment.**

- The *reciprocal gene–environment model* is the name for the relationship in which genetic differences also influence the environment.

- Researchers now assess whether individuals have specific alleles of different genes to attempt to find associations between the presence or absence of those alleles and psychological disorders. The research has proved difficult because many genes contribute to most disorders and they interact in complex ways.

C. FEEDBACK LOOPS IN ACTION: The Genes and the Environment

1. The Environment Affects the Genes

A person's genes are regulated by the environment. Some genes are activated as a result of experience or interactions with the environment. That is, genes do not determine behavior, but rather predispose one to be influenced by the environment. Having specific genes can make a person at risk for a particular psychological disorder, but other factors can influence the expression of the genes.

2. The Genes Affect the Environment

- **Passive interaction** is the process where the parents' genes affect the child's environment—and the child receives these influences. (*Example:* A parent is shy and thus limits the social interaction or outlets of the child.)

- **Evocative interaction** (or **reactive interaction**) is the process where a person's inherited traits encourage other people to behave in particular ways—hence the person's social environment is affected by his or her genes. (*Example:* People respond to and behave toward a tall person in unique ways.)

- **Active interaction** is the process where each of our genes influences the environments we actively seek out or avoid. (*Example:* A person's sensitivity to stimulation causes him to prefer staying home at night.)

LECTURE ENHANCEMENT 2.1: Exploring Complex Inheritance

Objective: To explore the interaction of the multiple factors contributing to psychological disorders.

Time: 1 Hour

Media and Discussion: 90 Minutes

Discussion Only: 30 Minutes

Explore Online: Genes to Cognition Web site, http://www.g2conline.org/#

This Web site explores modern neuroscience explanations of many psychological disorders.

Have students pick a disorder and watch several of the video explanations to explore the multiple factors that contribute to the disorder. Next, have students articulate key factors that play a role in the development of a disorder by describing the roles of (1) genes, (2) biochemicals, (3) cells, (4) brain anatomy, (5) cognition, and (6) environment.

Summary: Genes and environment influence one another and affect the expression of inheritance. Students will learn about the complex nature and causes of psychological disorders. Students will enjoy the different videos and Web resources on each disorder.

Questions to Students and Discussion: What did you learn about the complex inheritance of the disorder you picked?

II. PSYCHOLOGICAL FACTORS IN PSYCHOLOGICAL DISORDERS

Previous learning, mental processes and contents, and emotions can play roles in psychological disorders.

A. Behavior and Learning

Many behaviors related to psychological disorders can be learned. Therefore, some psychological disorders are a consequence of one of three types of learning: **classical conditioning, operant conditioning,** and **observational learning.**

1. Classical Conditioning

Classical conditioning (or Pavlovian conditioning) is a type of learning that occurs when two stimuli are paired so that a neutral stimulus becomes associated with another stimulus (which then elicits a reflexive behavior/response). By experiencing these pairings, the person then responds to the neutral stimulus alone.

- *Unconditioned stimulus (UCS)* is the stimulus that reflexively elicits a behavior. It requires no prior conditioning to elicit a response.
- *Unconditioned response (UCR)* is the natural or reflexive behavior elicited from the unconditioned stimulus. (*Example:* A loud noise [UCS] reflexively elicits a startle response [UCR].)

- *Conditioned stimulus (CS)* is the neutral stimulus that is conditioned—after pairing—to elicit the reflexive behavior. (*Example:* The white rat was the CS in Little Albert's case.) Its ability to elicit a response is conditional on being paired with a UCS.

- *Conditioned response (CR)* is the elicited response to the UCS (the previously neutral stimulus) after the pairings. (*Example:* In Little Albert's case, it was the startle response to the rat alone.) [See *Figure 2.7.*]

- *Conditioned emotional responses* are emotions and emotion-related behaviors that are developed through classical conditioning. People who are more emotionally reactive, or *neurotic,* are more likely to develop these responses.

- *Stimulus generalization* occurs when stimuli similar to the CS elicit the reflexive behavior. (*Example:* Little Albert developed a fear of other white furry things.)

- Classical conditioning helps explain phobias, mechanisms of substance abuse and dependence, and specific types of sexual disorders.

MEDIA RECOMMENDATION 2.5: Little Albert Footage

Objective: To learn about classical conditioning by watching real footage of the Little Albert experiment.

Time: 3 Minutes

Media and Discussion: 15 Minutes

Discussion Only: 10 Minutes

Explore Online: Search YouTube for footage from the Little Albert experiment, using the suggested search terms "Little Albert" and "Watson."

Watch Online: http://www.youtube.com/watch?v=y1URoX4QaMc&feature=related

This original footage shows the Little Albert experiment.

Summary: Students will learn about classical conditioning through the footage of the Little Albert study. The experiment is slightly disturbing and may raise ethical questions.

Questions to Students and Discussion: Identify the unconditioned and conditioned stimuli and responses. Does this experiment raise any ethical issues?

LECTURE ENHANCEMENT 2.2: The Truth Behind Little Albert

Objective: To learn about the facts of the Little Albert study.

Time: 20 Minutes

Media and Discussion: 40 Minutes

Discussion Only: 20 Minutes

Listen Online: Psych Files, Episode 47: *The Little Albert Study: What You Know Is Mostly Wrong,* http://www.thepsychfiles.com/2008/02/19/episode-47-the-little-albert-study-what-you-know-ismostly-wrong/

This podcast challenges what we know about the Little Albert case and argues that the details about the case have been exaggerated. The podcast author uses a variety of sources to support his arguments.

Suggested Key Lecture Points:
I.   Introduction
      A. What we know of the Little Albert story is not all true.
      B. Many times details are passed down incorrectly and this lecture enhancement seeks to straighten out some of the incorrect aspects of this case study.
II.   Incorrect Information About the Little Albert Study
      A. Little Albert was conditioned to fear a white rat, *not* a white rabbit, as most assume or have been taught.
      B. This fear is thought to have generalized to all white furry things but his fear was not as strong as Watson had suggested or implied.
      C. Albert was conditioned to fear the Santa Claus mask; this was *not* a generalized fear.
III. Correct Information About the Little Albert Study
      A. His name was Albert and he was nine months old.
      B. He was conditioned to fear a white rat.
      C. Watson did try to condition Albert to wooden blocks, a dog, coat, white cotton, a white glove, and a Santa Claus mask.
      D. Watson appears to have misrepresented some of the findings from this case.

Summary: After learning about the real facts of this case study, students will be amazed with the inaccuracies that have been reported regarding this case. These inaccuracies will raise questions about the study and emphasize the importance of replications of studies.

Questions to Students and Discussion: What scientific principles are lacking in the Little Albert case? How might we replicate the Little Albert study today? What ethical considerations are needed? How did the embellishments heighten public interest in the study? What cautions should we use when learning about the findings of research studies?

Additional Resources: Harris, B. (1979). Whatever happened to Little Albert? *American Psychologist, 34*(2), 151–160.

LEARNING ACTIVITY 2.5: Phobias and Classical Conditioning

Objective: To apply classical conditioning principles to the understanding of phobias.

Time: 30 Minutes

Directions: Have students pick a phobia and apply the principles of classical conditioning to the phobia in writing or as part of a class discussion. Read the following to the students to help guide them:

"What might serve as the neutral object? This is usually the feared object. What might this neutral object be paired with? This is usually a stimulus that causes a natural response."

Note to Instructor: Please be sensitive to students in the class who might have a phobia and/or be taking medication for a phobia.

Summary: Pairings of natural and neutral stimuli can easily explain the development of phobias. Students will apply their understanding of classical conditioning to the development of a phobia. Students will most likely enjoy applying information from theory to real life.

Questions to Students and Discussion: How might you use the same principles of classical conditioning to countercondition a phobia?

2. Operant Conditioning

- *Operant conditioning* is a type of learning that depends on the consequences associated with a behavior. It usually involves voluntary behaviors, whereas classical conditioning usually involves reflexive behaviors.

- A behavior is more likely to be repeated when followed by a positive consequence and is less likely to be repeated when followed by a negative consequence.

- It contributes to various psychological disorders, such as depression, anxiety disorders, substance abuse disorders, eating disorders, and self-regulation problems.

- It relies on two types of consequences: reinforcement and punishment.

a. Reinforcement:

Reinforcement is the process by which the consequence of a behavior increases the likelihood of a behavior's recurrence. The consequence is called the *reinforcer.* There are two types of reinforcements: positive reinforcement and negative reinforcement.

- *Positive reinforcement* occurs when the receipt of a desired reinforcer makes the behavior likely to reoccur. *Example:* A drug may lead to a pleasant state (the reinforcer), thus making the person more likely to take the drug again.

- *Negative reinforcement* occurs when the removal of an aversive or uncomfortable stimulus makes a behavior more likely to reoccur. *Example:* A man has a phobia of dirt, so he constantly washes his hands. The act of washing his hands is negatively reinforced by the consequence of removing his discomfort about the dirt, which makes him more likely to wash his hands again the next time they get a bit dirty.

b. Punishment:

Punishment is a process that decreases the likelihood that a behavior will occur again due to the consequence of that behavior. The consequence of the behavior can be an event or an object. There are two types of punishment: positive punishment and negative punishment.

- *Positive punishment* takes place when a behavior is followed by an undesirable consequence which makes the behavior less likely to recur. *Example:* Every time a young boy sings along with the radio, his older sister makes fun of him (an undesirable consequence): In the future, he won't sing as often when she's around.

- *Negative punishment* occurs when a behavior is followed by the removal of a pleasant or desired event or circumstance which decreases the probability of that behavior's recurrence. *Example:* A teenager stays out too late with friends causing her parents to take away her access to television (or something else she likes) for a week. [See *Table 2.1.*]

- *Learned helplessness* is a state of giving up that occurs when an individual is in an aversive situation where it seems that no action can be effective. It is considered to be a model for certain types of depression. *Example:* Sometimes people who are emotionally abused give up trying to change the situation and become depressed and vulnerable to stress-related problems.

MEDIA RECOMMENDATION 2.6: *Supernanny* and Operant Conditioning

Objective: To have students apply their knowledge of operant conditioning to real-world examples.

Time: 5 Minutes

Media and Discussion: 10 Minutes

Discussion Only: 5 Minutes

Watch Online: Selected *Supernanny* clips, http://www.supernanny.com/

Explore Online: Search YouTube.com using the suggested search term "Supernanny."

The *Supernanny* Web site has numerous clips from the show as well as advice columns, blog pages, and a forum for parents.

Summary: From the clips you or your students select, students will observe how reinforcers increase behaviors while punishments decrease behaviors. Both reinforcements and punishments are used by the Supernanny to shape the behavior of children.

Questions to Students and Discussion: Provide examples of how the caregivers inadvertently reinforced behaviors. Describe the changes in reinforcements and punishments that were needed. Do you think you can apply these techniques to your own behavior?

LEARNING ACTIVITY 2.6: Operant Conditioning and Personal Examples

Objective: To provide personal examples of operant conditioning principles using the worksheet provided.

Time: 20–30 Minutes

Directions: Under the heading "Personal Example" in Worksheet 2.1, ask students to write about a time when they either applied a principle of reinforcement listed or their behavior was influenced as the outcome of a reinforcement.

Summary: Students will be able to understand the concepts of operant conditioning using their own personal examples.

Questions to Students and Discussion: Which concepts were difficult to understand? Which were easiest?

3. **FEEDBACK LOOPS IN ACTION: Classical Conditioning and Operant Conditioning Revisited**

   All three factors—psychological, neurological, and social—interact through feedback loops to affect adaptive and maladaptive learning.

4. **Observational Learning**

   Observational learning results from watching what happens to others (social factor); from the observations, a person is guided in her own behavior and expectations (psychological factor).

   - Primarily a psychological factor and includes our mental processes (attention, perception, interpretation, and motivation).

   - Social factors involved include who the model is, his or her status, and the relationship to the observer.

MEDIA RECOMMENDATION 2.7: Bobo Doll Experiment Footage

Objective: To observe the original footage of the Bobo doll experiment and learn about observational learning.

Time: 5 Minutes

Media and Discussion: 10 Minutes

Discussion Only: 5 Minutes

Watch Online: Original footage of the Bobo doll experiment on video.google.com, using search terms "Bandura" and "Bobo doll experiment," or type in http://video.google.com/videoplay?docid=4586465813762682933

This original footage shows the observational learning experiment, the Bobo doll experiment.

Summary: The Bobo doll experiment reveals the power of observational learning. Students will enjoy watching the footage from the Bobo doll study as they will observe how easily "seeing" becomes "doing."

Questions to Students and Discussion: How has observational learning affected your own behavior? How do you think observational learning can influence the development of psychological disorders or symptoms?

B. Mental Processes and Mental Contents

1. Mental Processes

We all have biases in our mental processes. Mental processes involved in attention, perception, and memory may be biased in the following particular ways.

- **Selective attention bias** results in selecting or enhancing certain stimuli and may be related to a disorder. (*Example:* Focusing on dirt or germs)
- **Perception bias** results when registering and identifying specific stimuli. (*Example:* Spiders or particular emotional expressions)
- **Memory bias** involves storing, retaining, and recalling emotional information relevant to a particular disorder. (*Example:* A preoccupation with bodily sensations in those with hypochondriasis)

2. Mental Contents

The mental contents of people's thoughts can play a role in the development of psychological disorders.

- *Cognitive distortions,* also called *cognitive vulnerabilities,* are dysfunctional, maladaptive thoughts. These vulnerabilities can make a person at risk for psychological disorders. (*Example:* A woman believes she is unlovable and that if her boyfriend really knew her, he couldn't love her.)
- Recognizing dysfunctional thoughts and adopting realistic, adaptive thoughts can reduce psychological problems. [See *Table 2.2.*]
- Cultural factors may contribute to what appear to be maladaptive cognitive distortions. (*Example:* Some cultures have a social norm of responding to a compliment with a self-deprecating statement.)
- The interaction of mental processes and distortions affect each other [see *Figure 2.8*] and make people more vulnerable to psychopathology.

MEDIA RECOMMENDATION 2.8: Gloria and Cognitive Therapy

Objective: To observe cognitive therapy facilitated by Albert Ellis.

Time: 9 Minutes

Media and Discussion: 20 Minutes

Discussion Only: 10 Minutes

Watch Online: Search YouTube, using the search terms "Gloria" and "Albert Ellis," http://www.youtube.com/watch?v=sHSnYKkeWgE&feature=related

OR

Purchase: Shostrom, E. L. (Producer). (1965). *Three approaches to psychotherapy.* Orange, CA: Psychological Films.

This film features three approaches of counseling (person-centered, gestalt, and cognitive therapies). Founders of these therapies (Rogers, Perls, and Ellis) use their techniques while working with a patient named Gloria.

Summary: Students will enjoy comparing the different approaches that each therapist uses with Gloria.

Questions to Students and Discussion: Can you identify key terms/concepts Ellis uses in this session? How effective do you think Ellis is in working with Gloria? Would you personally like to have Ellis as a therapist? Why or why not?

C. Emotion

Many psychological disorders include problems that involve *emotions,* short-lived experiences caused by stimuli (physical or mental) that produce mental responses, behaviors, and feelings.

- *Affect* is an emotion associated with a particular idea or behavior. It also describes how emotion is expressed: inappropriate affect and flat affect.
  - i. *Inappropriate affect* is an expression of an individual's emotion that is not appropriate to what he or she is saying or is not appropriate to the situation. (*Example:* A person laughs at a funeral.)
  - ii. *Flat affect* is a lack of, or diminished, emotional expression. (*Example:* A person shows little facial expression.) Some people with schizophrenia display inappropriate affect or flat affect. *Labile* is the term used to describe affect that changes too rapidly and may indicate a psychological disorder.
- A *mood* is a persistent emotion that is not attached to a stimulus, that lurks in the background, and that influences mental processes, mental contents, and behavior.

1. **Emotions and Behavior**

   Emotions and behavior can be closely linked in various ways. [See *Figure 2.9.*]

   - People are more likely to participate in activities and behave in ways that are consistent with their emotions.
   - A change in behavior can lead to a change in emotion. The fact that changing behaviors can alter emotions is the basis of a number of psychological treatments—emotions and behavior dynamically interact.

2. Emotions, Mental Processes, and Mental Contents

Emotions affect behavior, mental processes, and mental contents. [See *Figure 2.10.*] Emotions also contribute to biases in attention, perception, and memory. Mental processes can affect emotions in the following ways:

- The self-serving attributional bias can protect against depression and occurs when people typically attribute positive events—but not negative events—to their own personality trait. This serves to increase or preserve a person's positive view of himself.
- Emotion can affect the attributions we make. *Example:* Walter Scott and colleagues found that, among depressed individuals, those who were irritable and hostile were more likely to blame their negative life events on others.

3. Emotions, Moods, and Psychological Disorders

Many psychological disorders are marked by impaired or inappropriate emotions, emotional experiences, or emotional expression. Examples of inappropriate emotions and some associated disorders include:

- Excesses of mood, such as depression and mania (mood disorders)
- Flat affect (schizophrenia)
- Absence of normal emotional experiences (dissociative disorders)
- Emotions or moods that don't fit the context
- Difficulty regulating emotions, thoughts, and behaviors (personality disorders), which can begin in childhood and last through adulthood and which can lead to:
    i. **Externalizing Problems** (towards others): These problems are characterized by too little control of emotion and related behaviors and by disruptive behavior. Primary effects are on others and/or the environment and are usually observable to others. (*Example:* delinquency)
    ii. **Internalizing Problems** (toward the self): These are characterized by negative internal experiences, such as anxiety, withdrawal, and depression. The primary effect is on the troubled individual rather than on others and is less observable to others. (*Example:* depression)
    iii. **Other Problems:** These problems do not fit into the two previous categories. (*Examples:* eating, learning, and substance-related disorders)
    iv. **Personality Disorders:** These disorders are inflexible and maladaptive stable personality traits characterized by difficulty regulating emotions. (*Examples:* impulsiveness and rapid changes in emotion)

4. Brain Bases of Emotion

Emotion is a psychological but also a neurological response. There are two general types of human emotions, each with its own circuit in the brain.

- **Approach Emotions:** Positive emotions (such as love and happiness) are activated more in the left frontal lobe. Optimism is associated with left frontal lobe activation, and depression is associated with relatively less activity in the left frontal lobe.
- **Withdrawal Emotions:** Negative emotions (such as fear and sadness) are activated more in the right frontal lobe. Approach and withdrawal tendencies are genetically determined or learned—likely a combination of the two. LeDoux has suggested that different brain systems contribute to different emotions. Some brain systems are independent or not easy to control, while others rely on conscious interpretation to stimuli or events.

5. Temperament

Temperament refers to aspects of personality that reflect a person's typical emotional state and reactivity and has the following characteristics:

- Largely innate and influences behavior in infancy and early childhood.
- May contribute to neurological vulnerability for certain disorders, even at an early age.
- In some cases a psychological disorder is simply an extreme form of temperament. *Example:* Social phobia may be an extreme form of shyness.
- Genes contribute about one-half of the variability in temperament.

Cloninger et al. proposed an influential, contemporary theory of temperament characterized by the following four dimensions:

- *Novelty seeking* consists of searching out and reacting positively to novel stimuli. It is associated with being impulsive, avoiding frustration, losing one's temper easily, dopamine activity, and disorders that involve impulsive or aggressive behaviors.
- *Harm avoidance* consists of reacting very negatively to harm and, when possible, avoiding it. It is associated with mood and motivation variations and the actions of serotonin.
- *Reward dependence* involves repeating behaviors that elicit desired outcomes. It is associated with attention and stress response and the actions of norepinephrine.
- *Persistence* is a continued effort toward a goal despite frustration. It is associated with certain genes that lead to low levels of dopamine.

Researchers have found associations between specific genes and these dimensions of temperament. The complexity of inheritance and underlying neurological bases are at work.

III. SOCIAL FACTORS IN PSYCHOLOGICAL DISORDERS

Family, community, and culture are social forces that help to shape who we become.

A. Family Matters

Family-related social factors, such as style of interaction among family members, child maltreatment, and parental psychological disorders, can contribute to or perpetuate psychological disorders.

1. Family Interaction Style and Relapse

Family members sometimes exhibit **high expressed emotion,** such as becoming hostile, voicing unnecessary criticism, or becoming emotionally overinvolved.

- Schizophrenia is likely to recur in U.S. and Chinese families who show high expressed emotion.
- When family members push the schizophrenic family member to change, that stress can make the disorder worse; when family members are educated about the disorder and productive communications, relapse rates generally decline.
- High expressed emotion is not associated with disorder relapse in all cultural or ethnic groups, such as Mexican American and African American families.

2. Child Maltreatment

Children exposed to neglect, verbal abuse, physical abuse, and sexual abuse are associated with higher risks for a variety of psychological disorders. Maltreatment exerts influence indirectly through:

- **An Altered Bodily and Neurological Response to Stress:** This creates higher baseline levels of cortisol in mistreated children and this stress response continues into adulthood.
- **Behaviors Learned Through Maltreatment:** Some children can exhibit learned helplessness and are more likely to be victimized as adults.
- **Biases in Discriminating and Responding to Facial Expressions:** Physically abused children are more likely to perceive photographs of faces as conveying anger.
- **Difficulties in Attachment:** Children are less likely to develop a secure type of attachment.
- **Increased Social Isolation:** Physically abused children report feeling more socially isolated.

However, not all abused children develop psychological disorders.

3. Parental Psychological Disorders

- The third family-related factor, having a parent (or parents) with a disorder, may contribute to a child's vulnerability to develop a psychological disorder.
- Not only genetics but also the disordered parent's displayed attitude may affect the amount and type of vulnerability.
- Types of vulnerabilities fall under the categories of learning, mental processes, cognitive distortions, emotional regulation, or social interactions.

B. Community Support

Social support—the comfort and assistance that an individual receives through interactions with others—can buffer stress experienced throughout life. Conversely, lack of it can cause vulnerabilities to developing a disorder.

C. Social Stressors

Poverty and discrimination are social factors associated with psychological disorders.

1. Socioeconomic Status

Socioeconomic status (SES) is defined in terms of education, income, and occupational level in a socioeconomic group. People from low SES backgrounds have a higher rate of psychological disorders. Theories of how SES contributes to the development of psychological disorders follow:

- *Social Causation:* Socioeconomic disadvantages and stress cause psychological disorders. [See *Case 2.1.*]
- *Social Selection* (or *Social Drift*): People who are vulnerable to psychological disorders, and who then develop a disorder, "drift" to a lower SES. One study showed that if SES conditions improve, symptoms of disorders improve.

2. Discrimination

There is an increased risk of distress and psychological disorders associated with **discrimination.**

- Women and other members of ethnic, racial, or sexual minority groups may experience discrimination in any aspect of life, which can lead to chronically higher levels of stress; this increases risk.
- African Americans and Hispanics are no more likely to experience psychological disorders than are Whites, possibly because they receive protective buffering from social support, such as ethnic identity, spirituality, and religion.

MEDIA RECOMMENDATION 2.9: Poverty, Race, and Health

Objective: To learn about the ways poverty, race, and gender affect one's health.

Time: 45 Minutes to 4 Hours

Media and Discussion: 45 Minutes +

Discussion Only: 15 Minutes

Watch Online: All or parts of Adelman, L. (Producer). (2008). *Unnatural causes: Is inequality making us sick?* San Francisco, CA: Newsreel, http://www.unnaturalcauses.org/

This seven-part documentary series will help students learn how poverty and race interact to affect health.

Summary: Students will be amazed at how poverty, race, and gender influence our physical and mental health.

Questions to Students and Discussion: How does racism play a role in health outcomes? How does being poor affect one's health?

LEARNING ACTIVITY 2.7: APA's Office of Socioeconomic Status

Objective: To read about APA's interest in how poverty affects mental health.

Time: 20 Minutes

Directions:
1. Have students explore the Web site of the American Psychological Association's new Office of Socioeconomic Status to learn about concerns about poverty and mental health, http://www.apa.org/pi/ses/
2. Have students read the office's latest newsletter or task force report to find out the role of SES on psychological well-being.
3. Instructors can examine the teaching resources on the inclusion of SES in psychology courses.
4. Lead students in a discussion of their findings.

Summary: Poverty and social class are often overlooked in the psychological literature. However, SES is an extremely important factor that affects health and well-being. Students will read about the many ways poverty affects mental health.

Questions to Students and Discussion: Are you surprised by the powerful impact of poverty? How can clinicians and researchers be more inclusive and aware of the role of poverty on health?

3. **Bullying**

When a child experiences this untoward behavior that may be unrelated to the victim's membership in an ethnic, racial, or other group that is being bullied, it can contribute to psychological problems in childhood and adulthood, especially internalizing problems.

4. **War**

War often inflicts extreme and prolonged stress on soldiers and civilian victims. The effects are partly determined by proximity to fighting and duration of combat.

D. Culture

Every **culture** promotes an ideal of healthy functioning, which can differ from culture to culture.

- Some cultures are *collectivist,* placing a high value on getting along with others.
- Some cultures are *individualist,* valuing independence and autonomy.
- Individuals with personality traits different from those valued by their culture may eventually feel isolated and develop poor self-esteem and possibly psychological disorders.

1. **Culture Can Suppress or Facilitate Behaviors**

According to the *problem suppression-facilitation model,* values, social norms, accepted child-rearing practices, and other cultural factors can minimize or amplify the child's natural behavioral tendencies.

2. **Acculturation**

This adaptation of the values and behaviors when living in a new culture is often stressful.

- Children who move to a new culture, with parents, in their formative years and who retain the values and views of the original culture are often forced to choose between the values and views of these two competing cultures. This makes these children prone to developing psychological disorders.
- Other acculturation-influencing factors include the starkness of differences between cultures, reasons for leaving a culture (such as traumatic causes including war and famine), changes in SES after moving, and discrimination encountered in the new culture.
- Some groups of individuals who immigrate to the United States tend to have lower rates of psychological disorders than their American-born counterparts of similar age.
- Not all immigrant groups fare equally. *Example:* Puerto Rican immigrants do not fair as well as Mexican immigrants.

IV. FEEDBACK LOOPS IN ACTION: LEARNED HELPLESSNESS

- Rats that receive uncontrollable shocks undergo different brain changes than do rats that receive controllable shocks.
- In the presence of a second rat, learned helplessness is less severe than when rats are shocked alone.
- In humans, similar mechanisms may contribute to depression, with associated behaviors that resemble learned helplessness. Social factors such as abuse, discrimination, and poverty can lead to changes in beliefs as well as changes in the brain that are associated with depression.

LEARNING ACTIVITY 2.8: Finding the Best Treatments

Objective: To have students apply the information they have learned to particular treatment cases.

Time: 20–30 Minutes

Directions:
1. After reviewing this chapter, click on the link from the following source: Suler, J. (n.d.). *Which treatment is best? The people and their problems.* Retrieved on April 30, 2009, from http://www-usr.rider.edu/~suler/whichtx.html.
2. Follow the directions at the top of the Web page on how to use the handouts on the Web site page.

Note to Instructor: Be aware that the suggested answers to the handouts appear at the bottom of the page; you'll want to exclude these when printing student copies.

Summary: This activity examines which treatments might be best for specific problems. Students will enjoy applying their knowledge of treatments to specific problems. Students will notice more than one approach might be needed or possible.

Questions to Students and Discussion: How difficult was this exercise for you? Did you want to choose more than one treatment for each case? Why or why not? Did you tend to choose one type of treatment more often? If so, why do you think you have this tendency?

LEARNING ACTIVITY 2.9: Mock Clients Using Theater Students

Objective: To role-play different types of therapy with mock clients.

Time: 15–30 Minutes

Directions:

Collaborate with your school's theater department.
1. Invite students from an acting class to attend your class and play different clients, while you demonstrate the different forms of treatment.
2. Provide student actors with cases from the textbook and have your class guess the treatments/ perspectives you emphasize—that is, after each client session, have your students determine which treatment technique was used.

Summary: Students will enjoy seeing these therapies acted out versus passively hearing or reading about them.

Questions to Students and Discussion: There are many different treatments available, as you read in this chapter. Which techniques worked? Which did not work? What other techniques might have been helpful?

ADDITIONAL RESOURCES

Journal Articles

Afifi, T. O., Brownridge, D. A., Cox, B. J., & Sareen, J. (2006). Physical punishment, childhood abuse and psychiatric disorders. *Child Abuse & Neglect, 30,* 1093–1103.

Alegría, M., Canino, G., Shrout, P. E., Woo, M., Duan, N., Vila, D., Torres, M., Chen, C., & Meng, X. (2008). Prevalence of mental illness in immigrant and non-immigrant U.S. Latino groups. *American Journal of Psychiatry, 165,* 359–369.

Baer, J. C., & Martinez, C. D. (2006). Child maltreatment and insecure attachment: A meta-analysis. *Journal of Reproductive and Infant Psychology, 24,* 187–197.

Bandura, A., Ross, D., & Ross, S. A. (1961). Transmission of aggression through imitation of aggressive models. *Journal of Abnormal and Social Psychology, 63,* 575–582.

Bhugra, D., & Ayonrinde, O. (2001). Racism, racial life events and mental ill health. *Advances in Psychiatric Treatment, 7,* 343–349.

Breslau, J., Kendler, K. S., Su, M., Aguilar-Gaxiola, S., & Kessler, R. C. (2005). Lifetime risk and persistence of psychiatric disorders across ethnic groups in the United States. *Psychological Medicine 35,* 317–327.

Costello, E. J., Compton, S. N., Keeler, G., & Angold, A. (2003). Relationships between poverty and psychopathology: A natural experiment. *JAMA: Journal of the American Medical Association, 290,* 2023–2029.

Finzi-Dottan, R., & Karu, T. (2006). From emotional abuse in childhood to psychopathology in adulthood: A path mediated by immature defense mechanisms and self-esteem. *Journal of Nervous and Mental Disease, 194,* 616–621.

Kalivas, P. W., & Volkow, N. D. (2005). The neural basis of addiction: A pathology of motivation and choice. *American Journal of Psychiatry, 162,* 1403–1413.

Books

Faraone, S. V., Tsuang, M. T., & Tsuang, D. W. (2001). *Genetics of mental disorders: What practitioners and students need to know.* New York: Guilford.
    This is a basic text on genetics and pathology.

Lambert, K., & Kinsley, C. H. (2005). *Clinical neuroscience.* New York: Worth Publishers.
    Examines the neurobiological aspects of mental disorders.

Plomin, R., DeFries, J. C., McCLearn, G. E., & McGuffin, P. (2008). *Behavioral genetics.* New York: Worth Publishers.
    Learn about the intersection among psychology and genetics.

Pogrebin, A. (2009). *One and the same: My life as an identical twin and what I've learned about everyone's struggle to be singular.* New York: Doubleday.
    Explore what it is like to be a twin while also trying to develop a "singular" identity.

Thompson, R. F. (1993). *The brain, a neuroscience primer* (2nd ed.). New York: W. H. Freeman.
    This book is a basic text on neuroscience.

WEB SITES

Modern Neuroscience

Genes to Cognition Online Web Site: Study a three-dimensional brain and explore modern neuropsychosocial factors affecting various psychological disorders. See: http://www.g2conline.org/

Mental Health Reports

Surgeon General's Report: United States Public Health Service. (2001). *Mental health: Culture, race, and ethnicity. A supplement to mental health: A report of the Surgeon General.* See: http://www.surgeongeneral.gov/library/mentalhealth/cre/

WORKSHEET 2.1
APPLYING OPERANT CONDITIONING

Type of Reinforcement	What Occurs	Result	Personal Example
Positive reinforcement	Appealing consequence follows a behavior.	Increases behavior	
Negative reinforcement	Undesired stimulus is removed following a behavior.	Increases behavior	
Positive punishment	Undesired stimulus follows a behavior.	Decreases behavior	
Negative punishment	Pleasant stimulus is removed after behavior.	Decreases behavior	

Clinical Diagnosis and Assessment

CHAPTER

3

CHAPTER OUTLINE

CHAPTER HEADINGS	INSTRUCTION IDEAS AND TEXTBOOK CORRELATIONS
DIAGNOSING PSYCHOLOGICAL DISORDERS	**Learning Objective:** 3.1 **Learning Activity 3.1:** Who Is Emil Kraepelin?
Why Diagnose?	**Learning Objective:** 3.1 **Learning Concepts:** diagnosis **Textbook Tool:** Case 3.1
A Cautionary Note About Diagnosis	**Learning Concepts:** bias, stigmatizing labels **Learning Objective:** 3.1 **Learning Activity 3.2:** Stigma Busting **Learning Activity 3.3:** Advocacy in the Abnormal Psychology Classroom **Lecture Enhancement 3.1:** Overview of the Stigma of Mental Illness
Reliability and Validity in Classification Systems	**Learning Objective:** 3.2 **Learning Concepts:** reliable, valid
The Diagnostic and Statistical Manual of Mental Disorders (DSM)	**Learning Objectives:** 3.3, 3.4 **Learning Concepts:** the evolution of DSM, multiaxial system, criticisms of the DSM-IV-TR **Lecture Enhancement 3.2:** The DSM-V **Learning Activity 3.4:** Multiaxial Diagnosis of Someone You Know or a Celebrity **Textbook Tools:** Figure 3.1; Tables 3.1, 3.2, 3.3, 3.4
The People Who Diagnose Psychological Disorders	**Learning Objective:** 3.5 **Learning Concepts:** clinical psychologists, counseling psychologists, clinical psychiatrists, mental health professionals with master's degrees **Learning Activity 3.5:** Comparison of the Professions
ASSESSING PSYCHOLOGICAL DISORDERS	**Learning Concepts:** clinical assessment, neurological and biological factors, psychological factors, social factors **Worth Video Tool Kit for Abnormal Psychology:** Making an Assessment

Assessing Neurological and Other Biological Factors	**Learning Objective:** 3.6 **Learning Concepts:** assessing brain structure and function, assessing neurotransmitter activity, neuropsychological assessment **Lecture Enhancement 3.3:** Neuroimaging Techniques **Learning Activity 3.6:** Case Examples from the Bender Gestalt Test **Textbook Tool:** Figure 3.2
Assessing Psychological Factors	**Learning Objectives:** 3.7, 3.8 **Learning Concepts:** clinical interview, tests of psychological functioning **Media Recommendation 3.1:** Watch a Clinical Interview **Lecture Enhancement 3.4:** Testing Controversies **Learning Activity 3.7:** Case Examples of the MMPI-2 **Textbook Tools:** Figure 3.3; Tables 3.5, 3.6
Assessing Social Factors	**Learning Objective:** 3.9 **Learning Concept:** family functioning **Learning Activity 3.8:** A Family Genogram **Learning Activity 3.9:** Mental Health Treatments in the Developing World **Textbook Tool:** Figure 3.4
Assessment as an Interactive Process	
DIAGNOSING AND ASSESSING ROSE MARY AND REX WALLS	

LEARNING OBJECTIVES

After reading this chapter, students should be able to:

3.1 Identify arguments in support of, and against, clinical diagnosing and the classification system.

3.2 Define the terms *reliability* and *validity* as they pertain to the Diagnostic and Statistical Manual of Mental Disorders.

3.3 Accurately describe the evolution of the DSM.

3.4 Name the five axes of the DSM-IV-TR.

3.5 Distinguish the differences in training among various mental health professionals.

3.6 State the different ways professionals examine the brain's structures, function, and neurotransmitter and hormone levels.

3.7 Describe how psychologists assess psychological factors through the clinical interview, observation, and the self-report.

3.8 Differentiate between malingering and factitious disorder.

3.9 Describe the importance of including family, community, and cultural factors in clinical assessment.

KEY TERMS

Diagnosis: The identification of the nature of a disorder.

Clinical assessment: The process of obtaining relevant information and making a judgment based on the information.

Diagnostic bias: A systematic error in diagnosis.

Reliable: Yielding consistent results; a key characteristic of a measure (such as a classification system or assessment tool).

Valid: Having a high degree of accuracy; a key characteristic of a measure (such as a classification system or assessment tool).

Prognosis: The likely course and outcome of a disorder.

Prevalence: The number of people who have a disorder in a given period of time.

Comorbidity: The presence of more than one disorder at a time in a given patient.

Clinical psychologist: A mental health professional who has a doctoral degree that requires several years of related coursework and several years of treating patients while receiving supervision from experienced clinicians.

Counseling psychologist: A mental health professional who has either a Ph.D. from a program that focuses on counseling or an Ed.D. from a school of education.

Psychiatrist: A mental health professional who is also an M.D. and has completed a residency that focuses on psychiatric disorders.

Psychiatric nurse: A mental health professional who has an M.S.N. degree, plus a C.S. certificate in psychiatric nursing.

Social worker: A mental health professional who has an M.S.W. and is trained to provide psychotherapy to help individuals and families.

Computerized axial tomography (CT): A neuroimaging technique that uses X-rays to build a three-dimensional image (CT or CAT scan) of the brain.

Magnetic resonance imaging (MRI): A neuroimaging technique that creates especially sharp images of the brain by measuring the magnetic properties of atoms in the brain; MRI allows more precise diagnoses when brain abnormalities are subtle.

Positron emission tomography (PET): A neuroimaging technique that measures blood flow (or energy consumption) in the brain and requires introducing a very small amount of a radioactive substance into the bloodstream.

Functional magnetic resonance imaging (fMRI): A neuroimaging technique that uses MRI to obtain images of brain functioning, which reveal the extent to which different brain areas are activated during particular tasks.

Magnetic resonance spectroscopy (MRS): A neuroimaging technique that uses magnetic resonance to assess levels of neurotransmitter substances in the brain.

Neuropsychological testing: The employment of assessment techniques that use behavioral responses to test items to draw inferences about brain functioning.

Clinical interview: A meeting between clinician and patient during which the clinician asks questions related to the patient's symptoms and functioning.

Malingering: Intentional false reporting of symptoms or exaggeration of existing symptoms, either for material gain or to avoid unwanted events.

Factitious disorder: A psychological disorder marked by the false reporting or inducing of medical or psychological symptoms in order to assume a "sick" role and receive attention.

Projective test: A tool for personality assessment in which the patient is presented with ambiguous stimuli (such as inkblots or stick figures) and is asked to make sense of and explain them.

CHAPTER GUIDE

Chapter Introduction

A *diagnosis* is the identification of the nature of a disorder. It is made by assigning an individual's symptoms to a specific classification. Once a diagnosis is known, previously documented symptoms of the classification will lend insight into more than what was initially apparent. For example, a diagnosis could indicate:

- The disorder's possible causes
- Its course over time
- Its possible treatments
- Why the disorder was developed
- Whether the symptoms might shift in frequency or intensity over time
- Which specific treatments might be more effective and which might be less effective

The *clinical assessment* is the process of obtaining relevant information and making a judgment about mental illness based on the information. The assessment is used to:

- Gather relevant information to make an informed diagnosis
- Gather information about specific ways the individual is impaired and the degree of impairment
- Determine areas of functioning that are not impaired

I.   DIAGNOSING PSYCHOLOGICAL DISORDERS

The first modern, diagnostic *classification system* for mental illness was developed by Emil Kraepelin (1856–1926), a German psychiatrist.

Kraepelin's Classification System.

- Identified symptoms and course (its progression over time) of psychological disorders
- Utilized systematic observations of patients—led to outlining the hallmarks of schizophrenia today
- Helped form today's diagnostic system

LEARNING ACTIVITY 3.1: Who Is Emil Kraepelin?

Objective: To provide students with biographical information about Kraepelin and the evolution of the classification system of mental disorders.

Time: 30 Minutes

Directions: Have the students work in small groups to locate various resources (books, articles, Web sites, etc.) to answer the following questions about Kraepelin:

1. Where was Kraepelin born?
2. What is he most famous for? What disorders did he study long-term?
3. Why did he develop a classification system?
4. Which famous psychologist did he study under?
5. If you could go back in time, what questions would you like to ask Kraepelin?

Summary: Students will be impressed to learn about Kraepelin's advanced understanding of how symptoms can present themselves on a continuum and the neurological and biological factors that influence disorders.

Questions to Students and Discussion: What are the highlights of the path Kraepelin followed in developing the classification system and studying psychological disorders? Did his collaborations with Wilhelm Wundt influence his structured approach to studying disorders? If so, in what ways?

A. Why Diagnose?

Classification systems of mental disorders categorize and label psychological disorders, making it possible to advance in learning from one case to the next and to decide how best to help or treat each person with unusual symptoms or combinations of symptoms. Diagnosing patients using classification systems of mental disorders benefits the patient and clinician in the following ways:

- Provides a shorthand (labels) of words and phrases and a measuring stick for symptoms
- Allows the grouping of certain abnormal thoughts, feelings, and behaviors into unique constellations of symptoms
- Conveys information about the etiology (cause) of the disorder, its course, and indications for its treatment
- Enables researchers to study the causes, the course, and the effects of treatments for disorders
- Can indicate that the individual is in need of attention (including treatment), support, or benefits (*Examples:* special services at school, special accommodations or services from insurance or the government at home or work, considerations affecting outcomes of court proceedings)
- Can provide great relief to the patient in no longer feeling alone in having particular problems; patient can learn more about disorders and treatments once known [see *Case 3.1*]

B. A Cautionary Note About Diagnosis

Clinicians and researchers can work toward avoiding bias and stigma by examining the possibilities in detail.

1. Diagnostic Bias

Diagnostic bias is a systematic error in diagnosis. Potential bias demands the need to keep in mind the following cautions:

- Certain people (due to race, sexual orientation, age, etc.) may receive a particular diagnosis disproportionately.
- Lack of familiarity with the cultural background of clients may lead to misdiagnoses or misinterpretations.
- Culture can influence symptoms experienced—the unique constellations of symptoms of cultural groups not found in the North American classification system will

sometimes explain underdiagnosis of those groups. Also, language differences between patients and clinicians can make accurate assessments difficult.

2. **Diagnosis as a Stigmatizing Label**

    Patients, once diagnosed with a disorder, may receive **stigmatizing labels** because of it. A diagnosis can have any or all of the following deleterious effects:

    - Influences how we view and treat the person
    - Can lead some patients to blame themselves and try to hide their problems
    - Can create shame and prevent some from obtaining needed treatments

LEARNING ACTIVITY 3.2: Stigma Busting

Objective: To help students understand the social justice issue of mental health stigma.

Time: 1 Hour

Directions: Assign students to eight small groups where they will examine various aspects of the stigma of mental illness.

Group 1: Read about stigma through the National Alliance on Mental Illness (NAMI), http://www.nami.org and summarize the key points.
Group 2: Interview a consumer(s) of mental health therapies about their experiences with stigma.
Group 3: Interview students outside of the class about their first impressions/thoughts on people with psychological disorders.
Group 4: Read and describe the work of a national group called "Active Minds," found at http://www.activeminds.org/.
Group 5: Through TV or Internet, examine how certain TV shows portray those with mental illness (*Mental, Law and Order,* and others).
Group 6: Discuss how mental illness is perceived in your family. Do people in your family talk about their mental health? Why or why not?
Group 7: Read and describe the National Mental Health Awareness Campaign, http://www.nostigma.org/.
Group 8: Examine NAMI's StigmaBusters Group and Archives, http://www.nami.org/template.cfm?section=fight_stigma.

The National Alliance on Mental Illness (NAMI) is "dedicated to improving the lives of individuals and families affected by mental illness." The Web site contains a plethora of information, from articles and videos to information on medications and recent legislative action.

Active Minds "supports chapters of student-run mental health awareness, education, and advocacy groups on campuses that seek to increase awareness of mental health issues and encourage students to seek help as soon as it is needed."

The National Mental Health Awareness Campaign is a "nationwide nonpartisan public education campaign that was launched as part of the 1999 White House Conference on Mental Health. It is dedicated to battling stigma, shame, and myths surrounding mental disorders."

Note to Instructor: Groups 2, 3, and 6 will require work outside of the school setting and may need additional time.

Summary: Mental health stigma is very powerful and often goes unnoticed. Students should see that stigmas can have powerful consequences, such as preventing someone from seeking treatment. Emphasize to them that it is important to be aware of, and reduce, stigma when possible.

Questions to Students and Discussion: What did you learn about stigma? Are certain disorders or treatments more stigmatized than others? How might stigma affect the individual's feelings about or likelihood to seek treatment? What are ways we can challenge the stigma?

LEARNING ACTIVITY 3.3: Advocacy in the Abnormal Psychology Classroom

Objective: As a follow up to Learning Activity 3.2, students will learn about ways to advocate for people with mental illnesses.

Time: 2 Hours

Directions: Have students choose one of the following:
1. Write a letter to a television company about the representation of the mentally ill in a specific television program or in an episode of a television program.
2. Develop an Active Minds chapter at your institution, http://www.activeminds.org/.
3. Cosponsor a Mental Health Awareness Day with your institution's counseling center, http://www.nostigma.org/.
4. Develop a brochure or flyer to bring about awareness of ways we stigmatize people with psychological disorders, http://www.nami.org.

Summary: Students will enjoy these types of service-learning or advocacy activities because they allow students to apply and synthesize in-class knowledge to real-world settings.

Questions to Students and Discussion: How did you feel about your route of advocacy? Do you feel like it may help? What else might you do, or what might your class do as a group?

LECTURE ENHANCEMENT 3.1: Overview of the Stigma of Mental Illness

Objective: To provide students with information about stigma and up-to-date research on the topic.

Time: 38 Minutes

Media and Discussion: 58 Minutes

Discussion Only: 20 Minutes

Read Online: Dingfelder, S. F. (2009). Stigma: Alive and well. *Monitor on Psychology, 40*(6), 56–60, http://www.apa.org/monitor/2009/06/stigma.html

Dingfelder's online article reveals new research suggesting that people might be making real progress in being less fearful of those with mental illness.

Watch and Listen Online: Nye, M. (2006). *Fine Line: Mental health/mental illness, a documentary of voices, stories, and portraits,* http://www.michaelnye.org/fineline/videoreviews.html

Listen to the audio files of/look at photographs of consumers, http://www.michaelnye.org/fineline/photoaudio.html

In addition to the Fine Line documentary, the Michael Nye Web site includes detailed information about the contents of the documentary, history, Nye's biography, and audio clips.

Lecture Points: New research by Pescosolido, published in the *Journal of Health and Social Behavior* (Vol. 41, No. 2), finds that 68% of Americans do not want someone with a mental illness marrying into their family and 58% do not want people with mental illnesses in their workplaces. Additionally, U.S. newspaper articles are more likely to mention violence or criminality when discussing the topic of mental illness. These stereotypes are likely to be internalized by individuals with disorders, which can prevent individuals from seeking needed treatments.

Summary: Stigma toward mental illness is highly prevalent in our culture, yet it is often overlooked. This lecture enhancement will further solidify students' understanding of stigmas and the powerful consequences they can cause, such as preventing someone from seeking treatment. Thus it is important to be aware of and reduce stigma when possible.

Questions to Students and Discussion: What are ways that you or people you know stereotype individuals with mental illness? What effect might this have on those individuals' willingness to seek treatment?

C. Reliability and Validity in Classification Systems

Classification systems that produce consistent results over time are ***reliable.*** Classification systems or measures (such as criteria) that are accurate are considered ***valid.***

Potential Problems Concerning Reliability in Diagnosis.

- The criteria for disorders are unclear and rely on the clinician's judgment.
- Significant overlap among disorders makes it difficult to distinguish among them.

Importance of Reliability and Validity of Classification Systems.

- Classification systems must be accurate because they are used to study etiology, prognosis (the likely course and outcome of a disorder), and effectiveness of treatments for disorders.
- In order to use these systems for research, the prevalence of each disorder (the number of people having the disorder in a given period of time) must be large enough for researchers to find people with the disorder.

Potential Problems Concerning Validity in Diagnosis.

- The criteria are too restrictive, and thus the prevalence is very low, leaving very little to discover about the disorder's course or treatment.
- The criteria are too broad and the disorder is very common, and thus the criteria may reflect a set of different (but possibly related) problems or even include aspects of normal psychological functioning.

D. The Diagnostic and Statistical Manual of Mental Disorders (DSM)

- Currently in its fourth edition and published by the American Psychiatric Association
- Describes the characteristics of many psychological disorders
- Identifies *criteria* (kinds, number, and duration of symptoms) for diagnosing each disorder
- Uses a *categorical* classification system—someone either has or does not have a disorder (versus on a continuum)
- Now substantially overlaps with the International Classification of Diseases (ICD), 10th edition, allowing research using one system to be applied to the other system

1. **The Evolution of DSM**

   - The original version was published in 1952 and had a strong psychodynamic approach in its classifications.

   - The second edition was published in 1968 and contained only minor changes.

   - The first two editions contained reliability and validity problems partially due to heavy reliance on the psychodynamic approach, causing the clinician to draw inferences and make judgments.

   - The third edition (DSM-III), published in 1980, set out to improve reliability and validity. DSM-III was unique in that it:
     i. Did not rest on the psychodynamic, or any other, theory of psychopathology
     ii. Focused on overt behaviors and symptoms rather than inferences
     iii. Listed and further developed explicit criteria based on research for each disorder
     iv. Included a system to record diagnoses and additional relevant information that could affect diagnosis, prognosis, and treatment

   - DSM-III (and DSM-III-R) also had problems, such as:
     i. Some DSM-III criteria were not clear and contained inconsistencies.
     ii. The DSM-III-R (*R* for "Revised") was published in 1987, had greater reliability, but still contained validity problems (criteria at times were too restrictive).

2. **The Multiaxial System of DSM-IV-TR**

   - The weaknesses of DSM-III-R led to DSM-IV (1994), which specified new disorders and revised some disorders' criteria.

   - A revised and expanded DSM-IV-TR (2000; *TR* stands for "Text Revision") includes, for each disorder, more current information and new information on prevalence, course, gender and cultural issues, and ***comorbidity***—the presence of more than one disorder at a time in a given patient.

   - DSM-IV-TR defines 17 major categories of psychological problems [see *Table 3.1*] and nearly 300 mental disorders (almost triple the number in DSM-III).

   - For the fifth edition, additional disorders, such as "Internet addiction" and "night eating syndrome," may be included.

   - The **multiaxial system** of DSM-IV-TR includes five *axes* used to diagnose a patient, plan treatment, aid in prognosis, or for research. [See *Table 3.2.*]

The Multiaxial System	Example
Axis I: Diagnosed disorder	Social phobia and bulimia nervosa
Axis II: Personality disorders and mental retardation	*Personality disorders* such as antisocial personality disorder
Axis III: General medical conditions	Visual problems and hip fracture
Axis IV: *Psychosocial* and environmental problems	Discrimination and marital conflict
Axis V: Global Assessment of Functioning (numerical estimate between 1 and 100 indicating the patient's overall functioning within the past year)	GAF = 83 [see *Table 3.3*]

LECTURE ENHANCEMENT 3.2: The DSM-V

Objective: To explore various issues facing the new edition of the DSM, scheduled to be released in 2012.

Time: 1 Hour 20 Minutes

Read Online: DSM-V: The Future Manual, the American Psychiatric Association, http://www.psych.org/MainMenu/Research/DSMIV/DSMV.aspx

The article details the history of the making of this newest DSM version up to the current time.

Lecture Points:
I. DSM-V
    A. Planning for the manual began in 1999, and research is currently underway.
    B. Work groups and members were announced in May 2008 and include the following topics:
        1. ADHD
        2. Anxiety
        3. Child-Adolescence
        4. Eating
        5. Mood
        6. Neurocognitive
        7. Neurodevelopmental
        8. Personality
        9. Psychosis
        10. Sexual-GID
        11. Sleep-Wake
        12. Somatic Distress
        13. Substance-Related
II. Work Groups
    A. "Each work group meets regularly, in person and on conference calls."
    B. Each group reviews the strengths and weaknesses of the DSM-IV-TR.
    C. Research questions and hypotheses are developed.
    D. These areas are then investigated using current literature and data.
    E. Research plans will be developed to be "tested in *DSM-V* field trials involving direct data collection."

Note to Instructor: For current work group summaries and findings, please consult: http://www.psych.org/MainMenu/Research/DSMIV/DSMV/DSMRevisionActivities.aspx

Summary: Students will be impressed with the amount of money, research, and time that has been committed to revising the current DSM. For example, the director of the DSM-V was chosen in the year 2000!

Questions to Students and Discussion: What newer disorders or behaviors do you think should be included in the DSM-V? What other information should be included?

LEARNING ACTIVITY 3.4: Multiaxial Diagnosis of Someone You Know or Celebrity

Objective: To learn how to apply the five axes to a real-life person.

Time: 45 Minutes

Explore Online: Skim through various disorders to make your diagnosis, http://allpsych.com/disorders/dsm.html. This Web site contains a current list of DSM-IV-TR disorders and diagnostic codes.

Directions: Diagnose someone you know or a celebrity using the five axes. If you choose someone you know, make sure not to use the person's real name so that you do not disclose personal and confidential information without that person's consent.

Note to Instructor: Caution students about diagnosing others or themselves when they have very little knowledge and training in psychology.

Summary: By creating a multiaxial diagnosis, students will better understand the multiaxial system. This exercise will teach students that each "client" will be assessed in five different ways according to the axes.

Questions to Students and Discussion: How difficult was it to make the diagnosis? What was most difficult? What was least difficult? What questions do you have about diagnosing?

3. **Criticisms of DSM-IV-TR**

    This edition's classification system has been criticized on a number of grounds. (You will find examples expounding on the clinical and diagnostic repercussions of these oversights in the textbook chapter.)

    a. **Determining Clinical Significance:**

    This determination of symptoms is subjective, and professionals' judgments vary.

    b. **Disorders as Categories, Not Continua:**

    Disorders are not classified on continuums so that number of symptoms would indicate severity of the disorder. [See *Figure 3.1.*]

    c. **Heterogeneous Groups Have the Same Disorder:**

    Groups of people diagnosed with the same disorder do not always share the same list of symptoms; thus sometimes an individual with a diagnosed disorder will need to be treated differently than other individuals with that same diagnosis. [See *Table 3.4.*]

    d. **Symptoms Are Weighted Equally:**

    The problem with this is that each symptom may not be equally important.

    e. **Duration Criteria Are Arbitrary:**

    Some duration criteria are not supported by research. Furthermore, applying a duration criteria to an individual means that someone's diagnostic status can change literally overnight.

    f. **Some Sets of Criteria Are Too Restrictive:**

    Criteria for some disorders are so restrictive that most of the patients with appropriate symptoms don't meet all the criteria to be diagnosed. They are then diagnosed as having *psychotic disorder NOS* (not otherwise specified).

    g. **Psychological Disorders Are Created to Ensure Payment:**

    More patients are being diagnosed with DSM disorders, some of which are not valid, since DSM disorders are more likely to receive insurance reimbursement.

    h. **Medical Illnesses Are Made into Psychological Disorders:**

    The DSM is beginning to include medical disorders, some of which are clearly not *psychological* disorders, partly to help ensure that psychological treatments for these medical disorders are paid for by insurance companies. However, another reason for the push to include these medical disorders is because clinicians have found that some medical disorders can be treated successfully using certain psychological treatments, such as treatment to relieve symptoms of irritable bowel syndrome. These reasons do not justify the inclusion of these disorders in the DSM.

i. Social Factors Are Deemphasized:

Maybe because, in general, the DSM-IV-TR does not address the causes of disorders, it also doesn't explicitly acknowledge the social factors that often contribute to disorders (but, see also Axis IV in the textbook).

j. Comorbidity Is Common:

About half of the people who have one psychological disorder have at least one additional disorder; thus, DSM-IV-TR disorders may be more like symptom clusters whose validity can be questioned.

k. Overlooks Commonalities Across Diagnostic Categories:

It is difficult for researchers to identify, across the DSM's 17 categories, the commonalities between disorders. This difficulty arises when disorders are frequently comorbid (such as depression and anxiety) or when various disorders have common symptoms.

E. The People Who Diagnose Psychological Disorders

Individuals who work in the mental health field have varying academic degrees, preparation, training, and perspectives on mental illness. The following table provides an easy comparison of these professions and resources for students wanting additional information. The categories include:

Title	Degree	Description	Additional Information
1. Clinical Psychologists and Counseling Psychologists*			
Clinical psychologists	Ph.D. (doctor of philosophy) or a Psy.D. (doctor of psychology)	Provide *psychotherapy,* helping patients cope with difficulties. The doctorate includes several years of coursework (on mental processes, learning theory, psychological testing, assessment, treatments, and ethics) and years of treating patients while receiving supervision.	Society of Clinical Psychology http://www.apa.org/divisions/div12/aboutcp.html
Counseling psychologists	Ph.D. or an Ed.D. (doctor of education)	Provide psychotherapy. More training in vocational testing, career guidance, multicultural issues, and psychotherapy. Tend to work with healthier people.	Division of Counseling Psychology http://div17.org/
Also: Clinical neuropsychologists	Ph.D.	Examine the effects of brain damage and neurological diseases (such as Alzheimer's disease) on thoughts, feelings, and behaviors.	Division of Clinical Neuropsychology www.div40.org/

Title	Degree	Description	Additional Information
2. Psychiatrists, Psychiatric Nurses, and General Practitioners*			
Psychiatrists	M.D. (doctor of medicine) plus a residency focusing on psychiatric disorders	Qualified to prescribe medications. Usually have not been taught how to interpret psychological tests nor conduct research in psychopathology.	American Psychiatric Association http://www.psych.org/
Psychiatric nurses	M.S.N. (master of science in nursing), plus a C.S. (clinical specialization) certificate in psychiatric nursing; may also be certified as a psychiatric nurse practitioner (N.P.)	Work in a hospital, clinic, or private practice providing psycho-therapy; work closely with doctors to administer and monitor patient medications; sometimes prescribe medications.	American Psychiatric Nurses Association http://www.apna.org/
General practitioners (G.P. or family doctors)	M.D. (doctor of medicine)	May diagnose and prescribe medication for some psychological disorders and/or refer patients to see a mental health professional.	American Medical Association http://www.ama-assn.org/
3. Mental Health Professionals with Master's Degrees*			
Social workers	M.S.W. (masters of social work)	Sometimes trained to provide psychotherapy; connect individuals and families to appropriate community social services.	National Association of Social Workers www.socialworkers.org/
Marriage and family therapists (counselors)	M.F.T. (masters in family therapy)	Trained to provide psychotherapy to couples and families; sometimes hold doctorates.	American Association of Marriage and Family Therapy http://www.aamft.org/
	or M.A.	Trained in some area of counseling or clinical psychology, but schooling requires fewer classes and less research and clinical training than M.F.T.s. Some counselors may have training in *pastoral counseling,* or faith-based counseling.	American Counseling Association http://www.counseling.org/

*These are headings found in the textbook.

Note: Terms in the left column that are boldfaced and italicized are key terms.

LEARNING ACTIVITY 3.5: Comparison of the Professions

Objective: To have students spend ample time comparing and contrasting professions of interest.

Time: 30 Minutes

Directions: All of the many different professions in the mental health field have different degrees, training, and coursework. The table on the preceding pages summarizes the similarities and differences, which will make it easier for students to compare the various careers. Have students identify two professions listed in the table that interest them, and have them compare and contrast the two.

Share the following resources for finding information on salary, job outlook, and more, using the Occupational Outlook Handbook, http://www.bls.gov/OCO/

Summary: Students will be surprised by the number of possible careers there are in the mental health field. Students will gain insight and information about a career they may wish to pursue.

Questions to Students and Discussion: Which career is more appealing to you? Why? In what ways can you get involved in the profession now? What surprised you?

II. ASSESSING PSYCHOLOGICAL DISORDERS

Types of Information Included in a Clinical Assessment. The types of information included in a **clinical assessment** are influenced by several factors related to the assessment:

- The **reason for the assessment** determines the questions that are to be asked and answered by the assessment. *Possible reasons* for making an assessment include:
  i.   To obtain additional information for a diagnosis
  ii. To monitor the course of the symptoms
  iii. To determine what treatment might be most beneficial
  iv. To monitor the progress of treatment
- The **type of clinician** making the assessment determines the types of information obtained.
- The **setting** in which the clinician works determines how much information is gathered (assessments made as part of research tend to be more comprehensive).
- **Financial issues** related to the assessment determine what specific methods of obtaining information will—and will not—be paid for.

Assessment Reliability, Validity, and Cultural Considerations. There are several factors to keep in mind when making a clinical assessment.

- **Reliability:** Clinicians or researchers should obtain the same information and use the same methods when assessing the same patient. Assessments can be reliable but not valid.
- **Validity:** The instrument of assessment should assess the problem or aspect of functioning that is intended to assessed. Assessments can be valid but not reliable.
- **The patient's cultural background** may influence assessment tools used, interpretation, and comparison data used and its validity.

Three Main Categories of Factors in Assessment. A complete clinical assessment can include information from any or all of the following categories:

- **Neurological and other biological factors** (the structure and functioning of brain and body)

- **Psychological factors** (behavior, emotion and mood, mental processes and contents, and past and current ability to function)
- **Social factors** (social context of the patient's problems, living environment and community, family history and family functioning, relationship history, financial resources, and social support)

A. Assessing Neurological and Other Biological Factors

Clinicians **assessing neurological** (and other biological) **structure and function** determine if abnormal behaviors, feelings, or thoughts are affected by a medical problem, such as a brain tumor or abnormal hormone levels. Also, researchers are now looking for neurological and biological factors that may be related to particular disorders.

1. **Assessing Abnormal Brain Structures with X-rays, CT Scans, and MRIs**

   Neuroimaging techniques for providing images of the brain include the following:

   - **X-rays** are one-dimensional pictures.
   - *Computerized axial tomography (CT)* (*tomography* is a Greek word meaning "section") creates a CT scan, or CAT scan, by building an image of a person's brain, slice by slice.
   - *Magnetic resonance imaging (MRI)* makes clear and more precise images of the brain. MRIs work in the following way:
     i.   A large magnet is turned on and causes atoms to align with its magnetic field.
     ii. Another magnetic field from a different angle is activated and turns some of the atoms away from their first alignment.
     iii. When the second field is turned off, the atoms reorient with the first field and create a recorded signal.
     iv. This signal is translated into an image that shows where the atoms were located and indicates damaged tissue and abnormal parts of the brain.

2. **Assessing Brain Function with PET Scans and fMRI [see *Figure 3.2*]**

   - *Positron emission tomography (PET)* measures blood flow in the brain and requires an injection of a small amount of radioactive substance into the bloodstream. Next, while the patient performs a task, active brain regions take up more of the radioactive substance, which is measured and sent to a computer that creates a three-dimensional brain image of activity. Brighter colors indicate higher radiation (greater activity). Drawbacks of using PET scanning include:
     i.   Radioactive substances must be injected.
     ii. The person must perform the same task for at least 40 seconds.
     iii. A single test can cost $2,000.
   - *Functional magnetic resonance imaging (fMRI)* is currently the most widely used method for measuring human brain function. Neuroimaging with fMRI typically relies on three facts:
     i.   Iron affects the way hydrogen atoms in water molecules respond to the magnetic fields used in fMRI.
     ii. The presence of oxygen diminishes this effect of iron.
     iii. Hemoglobin has iron atoms in its structure, and the effects of the iron are different when the hemoglobin carries oxygen than when it has been stripped of its oxygen (because the oxygen was used for cell metabolism).
   - The fMRI scan measures the oxygenated hemoglobin that accumulates in the activated region. Brain regions that are not activated draw less blood, and the oxygen

carried by the blood gets used up. The difference in oxygen levels due to brain activity is reflected in the fMRI images. The advantages and disadvantages of fMRI over PET are as follows:

i. The advantages of fMRI are not having to use radiation and the ability to construct images in just a few seconds.

ii. Disadvantages include: a participant must lie in a narrow, noisy machine, and metal objects containing iron (magnetic objects) cannot be brought into the machine.

3. **Neurotransmitter and Hormone Levels**

Researchers use the following methods of **assessing neurotransmitter activity:**

- *Magnetic resonance spectroscopy (MRS)* (researchers are just beginning to develop this method) relies on magnetic resonance to assess levels of neurotransmitters. *Example:* The MRS scans of brains of 8-year-old children exposed to cocaine in the womb showed high levels of creatine in the frontal lobes, which may indicate the brain's attempt to repair damaged tissue.

- Measurements of chemical by-products of neurotransmitters in blood, urine, or cerebrospinal fluid (the fluid that surrounds the brain and spinal cord) give a sense of the role of neurotransmitters in psychological disorders. *Example:* In the cerebrospinal fluid of patients with major depression or post-traumatic stress disorder (PTSD), researchers found higher levels of a by-product of *substance P* (a neurotransmitter that helps register pain). More substance P was present when patients viewed aversive videos.

- PET techniques that use *ligands,* radioactive molecules that mimic neurotransmitters, can reveal where receptors for given neurotransmitters are located as well as dysfunctional receptor systems. *Example:* A *ligand* that mimics serotonin injected in the blood of healthy volunteers showed that people with higher levels of anxiety showed less binding of this ligand.

- Assessing the levels of specific hormones may determine their possible contribution to mental illness. *Example:* Symptoms of depression are sometimes caused by low levels of the hormone thyroxin; therefore thyroid supplements can be prescribed as part of treatment.

LECTURE ENHANCEMENT 3.3: Neuroimaging Techniques

Objective: To show students additional neuroimaging information and images.

Time: 30 Minutes

Media and Discussion: 45 Minutes

Discussion Only: 15 Minutes

Explore Online: MRI/PET images from The Whole Brain Atlas, http://www.med.harvard.edu/AANLIB/home.html

The Whole Brain Atlas Web site includes a neuroimaging primer based on Harvard Medical School lecture notes and compares images of the normal brain with various diseased-brain images. The Web site also includes 3-D imaging and more.

Video clips comparing various imaging techniques, Genes to Cognition Web site, http://www.g2conline.org. (To find these clips, click on "neuroimaging" under the Research Approaches heading. Then, click on any of the items of interest at the top of the site.)

Use the Genes to Cognition Web site to study a 3-D brain and explore modern neuropsychosocial factors affecting various psychological disorders.

Neuroscience for Kids, http://faculty.washington.edu/chudler/image.html

Neuroscience for Kids offers simple descriptions of numerous imaging techniques.

Note to Instructor: These Web sites will help students visualize the concepts and teaching points in the suggested lecture.

Lecture Points:
I.   Methods of Studying Brain
    A. The following methods assess the structure of the brain:
        1. Electrical stimulation of the brain (ESB) uses an electrical current to directly stimulate the brain.
        2. Computerized axial tomography (CAT or CT scan) works by taking a series of X-rays to reveal brain abnormalities.
    B. The following methods assess brain activity:
        1. Electroencephalogram (EEG) records electrical activity by attaching electrodes to the scalp to record brain waves. It is used in sleep and relaxation research.
        2. Positron emission tomography (PET scan) measures brain activity after giving a patient an injection of radioactive glucose.
    C. The following method assesses both structure and activity:
        1. Magnetic Resonance Imaging (MRI) uses magnetic fields to study the activity structures of the brain.
    D. See text for additional methods of studying the brain

Summary: There are many different techniques used to study the brain. This lecture enhancement provides a quick overview of the different methods and a number of Web resources and videos to supplement these notes and the text. Students will be amazed with how far technology has come and the type of opportunities that exist for future research.

Questions to Students and Discussion: What did you find interesting about the technique you studied? Why? Which method(s) might be most useful for what type of problem(s)?

   4. Neuropsychological Assessment

   Neuropsychological testing uses behavioral responses to test items to draw conclusions about brain functioning. A **neuropsychological assessment** is advantageous because it:

   • Distinguishes the effects of brain damage from psychological problems (*Example:* disrupted speech can be caused by either of these)

   • Determines whether the brain damage is contributing to psychological problems (*Example:* frontal lobe damage can disrupt the ability to inhibit aggressive behavior)

   • Gives a broad picture of the brain's functioning, which can more readily suggest parts of the brain that are damaged (unlike functional neuroimaging, which identifies brain areas activated during a given task)

   • Is less expensive and easier to administer than neuroimaging and can be given in any quiet place

   Neuropsychological tests assess complex abilities (such as judgment or planning) or specific abilities (*Example:* recognizing faces measured by the Facial Recognition Test). Examples of neurological assessments include the following:

- During one version of the **Facial Recognition Test,** a patient is shown a photo of a "target" face then a set of six photos of faces from which the patient must pick out the target. In another version, there are three target photos to be recognized and the six photos differ in lighting and orientation.
- **Bender Visual-Motor Gestalt Test-II** (2nd edition) assesses the integration of visual and motor functioning. Patients are shown a series of simple to complex drawings and must reproduce them.
- **Luria-Nebraska Neuropsychological Battery** consists of 14 tests that measure different abilities.
- **Halstead-Reitan Neuropsychological Battery** consists of 10 tests that measure different abilities.

LEARNING ACTIVITY 3.6: Case Examples from the Bender Gestalt Test

Objective: To show students how brain injury and substance abuse can affect the patient's performance on this assessment.

Time: 30 Minutes

Directions: Have students read portions of Lacks, P. (1999). *Bender Gestalt screening for brain dysfunction.* New York: Wiley. Students should compare the Bender Gestalt case results from individuals with different disorders.

Note to Instructor: Please consider getting permission to photocopy examples from the book or bring the book to class so students can see the images.

This book has numerous case examples of Bender Gestalt results. Students are amazed to see how brain dysfunction impacts what appears to be the easy task of drawing simple shapes.

Summary: Students will find it very interesting to compare Bender Gestalt results from individuals with different disorders.

Questions to Students and Discussion: Are you surprised to see how relatively easy it is for images to become so distorted? What does this tell you about brain function and brain damage?

B. Assessing Psychological Factors

Mental health researchers and clinicians employ interviews and tests of cognitive and personality functioning to ascertain specifics about psychological functioning depending on the purpose of the assessment. Types of psychological assessment follow.

1. Clinical Interview

The *clinical interview* is a meeting between clinician and patient during which the clinician asks questions related to the patient's symptoms and functioning. This interview provides two types of information: (1) the content of the answers to the interview questions and (2) the manner in which the person answers them. Questions may focus on symptoms, general functioning, degree and type of impairment, and the patient's relevant history.

There are three types of clinical interviews (see the table on the following page):

- The **unstructured interview** allows the clinician to ask whatever questions he or she deems appropriate, depending on the patient's responses.
    i.   **Advantage:** It allows the clinician to pursue topics and issues specific to the patient.
    ii. **Disadvantages:** Different clinicians may arrive at different diagnoses due to one's choice of interview topics, and the interviewer may neglect to gather information about context and culture.
- During the **structured interview,** the clinician uses a fixed set of questions to guide the interview.
    i.   **Advantage:** It yields more consistent and reliable diagnoses because each clinician asks the same questions.
    ii. **Disadvantage:** Diagnoses may be less valid because the questions asked may not be relevant to the patient's particular symptoms, issues, or concerns.
- The *semistructured interview* incorporates specific questions to guide the interview, but the clinician has flexibility in asking additional relevant questions.

TYPES OF CLINICAL INTERVIEWS

Interview Type	Description	Advantages	Disadvantages
Unstructured	Clinician creates questions deemed appropriate, depending on the patient's responses	Pursues topics and issues specific to the patient

Gives freedom to choose questions, which helps guarantee relevance to patient's presenting problem | May lead to different diagnoses by different clinicians who each gather different information

May forget to gather information about contextual and cultural factors

May be time-consuming

May not be as reliable and valid as assessment techniques that use tests |
| Structured | Clinician asks only a fixed set of questions | Yields more consistent and reliable diagnoses because the same questions are asked by each clinician | Diagnosis may be less valid if questions do not cover patient's symptoms, issues, or concerns

May be time-consuming

May not be as reliable and valid as assessment techniques that use tests |
| Semistructured | Clinician asks a fixed set of questions and creates relevant follow-up question

(*Examples:* a mental status exam and the *Structured Clinical Interview for the DSM-IV, Axes I and II*) | Gives freedom to choose follow-up questions, which helps guarantee that the questions are relevant to the patient's presenting problem | May be time consuming

May not be as reliable and valid as assessment techniques that use tests |

MEDIA RECOMMENDATION 3.1: Watch a Clinical Interview

Objective: To observe a clinical interview to learn about the information gathered.

Time: 10 Minutes (Video 1); 2 Minutes (Video 2)

Media and Discussion: 25 Minutes (Video 1); 10 Minutes (Video 2)

Discussion Only: 8 to 15 Minutes

Watch Online: Search YouTube using the search term "intake interview" or http://www.youtube.com/watch?v=YA-T_UhRITY

This video shows a clip of an anonymous intake interview during which the clinician covers a wide range of topics in order to collect background information on the client.

Search YouTube using the search terms "clinical interview" and "clinical interviewing" or http://www.youtube.com/watch?v=CrqNa9a9PZY

Although this video shows a clip of a medical interview, it provides students with an example of the type of historical data that is gathered through an initial interview.

Summary: Students will enjoy watching real-life intake interviews and will be impressed by the amount of information the professionals obtain in a short period of time.

Questions to Students and Discussion: What are the major areas covered by the clinician? What did the clinician not cover? What surprised you? Why?

a. Observation:

All types of interviews provide an opportunity for making observations and inferences about different aspects of a patient, such as the following:

(1) **Appearance:** Cleanliness, appropriate dress, or other, sometimes subtle, aspects of a person's appearance should be noted. (*Example:* A person with bulimia nervosa may have puffed checks.)

(2) **Behavior:** Body language, facial expressions, movements, and speech can provide insights into the following aspects of psychological functioning:

    (a) **Emotions:** *Examples:* upbeat, "low," intense, uncontrollable, inappropriate to the situation

    (b) **Movement:** *Examples:* restlessness, lack of movement

    (c) **Speech:** *Examples:* very fast speech suggesting anxiety, mania, or certain kinds of substance abuse; very slow speech suggesting depression or other kinds of substance abuse

    (d) **Mental processes:** *Examples:* talking to someone not in the room, obvious memory problems, lack of concentration or focus

(3) **More on behavior:** Behaviors that seem unusual should be interpreted with an understanding of the patient's cultural background. *Example:* Japanese people often express less emotion in their faces; therefore, not only might a show of little emotion be in the normal range, but a small angry outburst could indicate a larger problem.

b. Patient's Self-Report:

The clinician will ask the patient for a verbal self-report of his or her *history*—past factors or events that may illuminate the current difficulties. The patient's self-report helps the clinician put the patient's current difficulties in context and determine whether the patient's psychological functioning is maladaptive or adaptive given the environmental circumstances.

The following are some of the problems, or drawbacks, of the patient's self-report, some of which involve deception or bias:

(1) *Malingering:* Patients intentionally report having symptoms that they don't actually have or exaggerate symptoms they do have for material gain or in order to avoid unwanted events.

(2) *Factitious disorder:* Patients intentionally pretend to have symptoms or even induce symptoms so that they can assume "sick" roles and receive attention.

(3) **Memory bias:** Patients may report what they remember, but emotions can bias the frequency, intensity, or duration of the those memories.

(4) **Reporting bias:** Patients may report inaccuracies or distortions because of a desire to appear a particular way.

(5) **Psychological impairment:** Patients who are sufficiently impaired may confuse their internal world with reality and thus report inaccuracies.

(6) **Immaturity of children as patients:** Children may lack adequate insight and/or the verbal ability to be reliable reporters of their mental health status.

c. Semistructured Interviews:

The clinician who wants to tailor his interview to cover specific ground will perform a semistructured interview, which combines a list of standard questions with follow-up questions formulated by the clinician. Information on the two formats of the semistructured interview follows.

- The *mental status exam* is not used to obtain information that corresponds to the categories in DSM-IV-TR, but is used broadly to create a portrait of the individual's general psychological functioning. The exam elicits information from the patient about:
  i. The reported problem and its history
  ii. Functioning in different areas of life
  iii. Ability to reason and perform simple math
  iv. Problems in memory and judgment
- The questions in the *Structured Clinical Interview for DSM-IV, Axes I and II* (SCID-I and SCID-II) correspond to DSM-IV-TR criteria lists. This format is generally used as part of research to help diagnose patients according to the DSM-IV-TR. [See *Table 3.5.*]
  i. The SCID provides modules corresponding to different disorder categories.
  ii. Each module starts with a question about symptoms in an effort to match symptoms with categories of disorders.
  iii. If the patient does not have those symptoms, the remainder of that module is skipped.
  iv. If the patient does have those symptoms, the clinician asks the patient the remaining questions in the module.
  v. In general, no interpretation is needed.

2. Tests of Psychological Functioning

Many different **tests of psychological functioning** are available. Some assess a wide range of abilities and areas (cognitive and personality assessments) and others assess a narrow range (short-term memory and specific symptoms).

a. Cognitive Assessment:

- Cognitive functioning is typically assessed using intelligence tests.
- *The Wechsler Adult Intelligence Scale,* 4th edition (WAIS-IV, revised in 2008) and the *Wechsler Intelligence Scale for Children,* 4th edition (WISC-IV, revised in 2003) are the most commonly used intelligence assessments.
- Choice of scale depends on the patient's age.
- These scales determine the *intelligence quotient (IQ):* Average intelligence is set at 100 and normal intelligence ranges from 85 to 115. IQs of 70 to 85 are in the *borderline* range, and 70 and below signify mental impairment/delay.
- Both scales include subtests that assess four types of abilities:
  i. **Verbal comprehension:** verbal understanding
  ii. **Perceptual reasoning:** nonverbal reasoning
  iii. **Working memory:** concentration, recall, and mental manipulation of information
  iv. **Processing speed:** attention and utilization of information
- Current versions of intelligence tests minimize cultural influences, in part by:
  i. Excluding items requiring cultural knowledge specific to one group
  ii. Including specific norms for different ethnic groups
- Neuropsychological testing can also be used for cognitive assessments.
  i. A typical neuropsychological battery assesses basic cognitive functions (perception, memory, and language comprehension).
  ii. Other cognitive tests focus purely on cognitive functions without addressing which parts of the brain contribute to the functions.

LECTURE ENHANCEMENT 3.4: Testing Controversies

Objective: To examine the various perspectives on testing.

Time: 60 Minutes

Media and Discussion: 90 Minutes

Discussion Only: 30 Minutes

Explore Online:

Tulenko, J. (2002). *Frontline: Testing Our Schools.* WGBH Educational Foundation. http://www.pbs.org/wgbh/pages/frontline/shows/schools/

Testing Our Schools focuses on the controversies related to standardized testing. The *Frontline* links include "No Child Left Behind," "The Challenge of Standards," and "Testing. Teaching. Learning?" Click on the pictures to explore parent guides, video excerpts, transcriptions from the broadcasts, and more.

Lecture Points:
I. No Child Left Behind Was Passed in 2001
   A. Thus all children in grades 3-8 will take an annual test in reading and math.
   B. The test is based on "Standards of Learning," which are determined state by state.
II. Rationale for Testing
   A. So all students have the same expectations.

    B. To increase standards for all students.
    C. To hold schools accountable.
III. Problems with Standardized Tests
    A. Many teachers focus the class on the test.
    B. Correlations with grades are moderate or zero. Test performance is more likely to predict early but not later college grades. The correlation depends on time of grades and narrowness of scores.
    C. Poor academic environments are not addressed.
IV. What Should We Do?
    A. Should we emphasize student experience, achievement, interests, and attitudes?
    B. Can we measure skills needed for college (for example, curiosity, creativity, etc.)?

Summary: Many students in your class will have participated in state graduation exams and will appreciate the controversies that surround testing. Students will enjoy discussing alternatives to this form of "high stakes" testing.

Questions to Students and Discussion: Do graduation tests measure only a limited type of intelligence? What are the benefits and consequences of this form of cognitive test? What other methods might we use?

b. Personality Assessment

Various psychological tests assess different aspects of personality functioning. Two such tests are inventories and projective tests.

(1) Inventories:

These are questionnaires with items pertaining to many different problems and aspects of personality. When test questions are included, they are sorted into *scales,* with each scale assessing a certain facet of personality. The most commonly used inventory is the *Minnesota Multiphasic Personality Inventory,* 2nd edition (MMPI-2):

- Developed in the 1930s to identify people with mental illness and revised in 1989 to include a wider range of racial, ethnic, and other group norms
- Consists of 567 true and false questions that ask about behavior, emotions, mental processes and contents, and other areas
- Takes 60 to 90 minutes to complete
- Available in three formats: paper and pencil, a CD recording, and a computer version
- Has been translated into many languages and used in many countries
- Includes validity and clinical scales:
    i. *Validity scales* assess whether the individual's responses are likely to be valid or if the respondent is trying to appear psychologically healthier or more impaired than he or she actually is. The validity scales are labeled "Cannot Say," "Lie," "Infrequency," and "Correction."
    ii. *Clinical scales* assess symptoms of various disorders and problems. The clinical scales are labeled "Hypochondriasis," "Depression," "Hysteria," "Psychopathic Deviate," "Masculinity-Femininity," "Paranoia," "Psychasthenia," "Schizophrenia," "Hypomania," and "Social Introversion." [See *Table 3.6* and *Figure 3.3.*]

LEARNING ACTIVITY 3.7: Case Examples of the MMPI-2

Objective: To apply students' knowledge of the MMPI-2 scales to case examples.

Time: 30 Minutes

Directions: View more than 20 different MMPI-2 sample reports at http://psychcorp.pearsonassessments.com/pai/ca/research/publications/samplerpts/reslist.htm
 1. Scroll down the page until you see the reports labeled MMPI-2.
 2. Pick two sample reports and find the page with the MMPI-2 Validity Scales and Clinical Scales.
 3. Refer to *Table 3.6* and *Figure 3.3* in your textbook, and identify which items are low and which items are high. (For the Validity and Clinical Scales, these would be scores below 50 or above 65.)
 4. What conclusions can you make about the person from viewing these scales?

The MMPI-2 assesses a wide range of areas of a client's personality. The MMPI-2 report contains a visual profile of the patient's score. Additionally, the report includes items of concern and findings.

Summary: Students will find the actual examples of the MMPI-2 profiles very interesting. They will learn more about the specific scales by applying the textbook information about the MMPI-2 to the case examples.

Questions to Students and Discussion: What might the presenting problems of these clients be? Are the tests valid? Why or why not? What are potential areas you might explore with this client? What are the limits of this type of test?

 (2) **Projective tests:**

 Projective tests produce information about facets of a patient's personality that are less likely to emerge in a self-report, such as systematic biases in mental processes.

 • During a projective test, such as the well-known *Rorschach test,* a patient is presented with an ambiguous stimulus (*Examples:* an inkblot or a group of stick figures) and asked to explain the stimulus.

 • The *Rorschach test* was developed by Herman Rorschach (1884–1922) and includes 10 inkblots, one on each of 10 cards. This test and projective tests in general have been criticized for two related reasons:
 i. It does not appear to be valid (i.e., assess what it says it is measuring).
 ii. It is not necessarily reliable (results can be inconsistent from one day to the next).

 • The Exner scoring system is a systematic and comprehensive scoring system for the Rorschach test developed by John Exner (1974).
 i. The system has been shown to be reasonably reliable, and it also assesses psychosis reasonably well.
 ii. It is not as effective in assessing psychological disorders in general.
 iii. The norms of the system might lead to misdiagnosing people as having a disorder they do not have.

 • Another projective test, the *Thematic Apperception Test (TAT),* uses detailed black-and-white drawings that often include people. The test was developed by Christiana Morgan and Henry Murray (1935).

    i. The test is used to discern motivations, thoughts, and feelings without asking the patient directly.

    ii. The patient is asked to explain the drawings by answering: What is happening in the picture? What has just happened? What will happen next? What might the people in the picture be thinking and feeling?

    iii. Responses may reflect unconscious beliefs, desires, fears, or issues.

    iv. Although responses on the TAT may be interpreted freely by the clinician or according to a scoring system, only 3% of clinicians using TAT rely on a scoring system.

    v. Furthermore, responses to the drawings can be ambiguous, and clinicians may be unable to judge between usual and wishful feelings, thoughts, and behaviors without having to ask the patient directly.

C. Assessing Social Factors

Symptoms arise in a context, and part of a thorough clinical assessment is collecting information about social factors such as family functioning, community, and culture.

1. Family Functioning

- Various aspects of **family functioning** can affect a person's mental health; thus clinicians may interview all or some family members or ask patients about how the family functions.

- The *Family Environment Scale* is a tool that assesses family functioning. Family members' answers create a profile of the family environment (family organization, control and conflict issues, family values, and emotional expressiveness).

LEARNING ACTIVITY 3.8: A Family Genogram

Objective: To assess family dynamics and functioning by creating a map of family relationships, patterns, and mental illness.

Time: 1 Hour

Directions: Get permission to photocopy some examples of family genograms from Gerson, McGoldrick, and Petry's (2008) *Genograms: Assessment and Intervention.* Hand out several different genograms to students and ask them to identify the family patterns of mental illness.

Summary: Students will be surprised at the patterns of mental illness in the person's families. This exercise will solidify the genetic factor of mental illness.

Questions to Students and Discussion: What did you find out about the family you chose? What was surprising? What relational patterns or mental illnesses does your genogram show?

2. Community

Learning about the patient's **community** informs the clinician about normal functioning in that environment ("community" may include where the patient not only lives but also where he or she spends a lot of time, such as school or the workplace).

Clinicians also assess the patient's capacity to manage daily life in his or her job or community, the patient's ability to communicate needs and interact with others according to norms, and whether the patient would benefit from social skills training.

3. Culture

Culture influences the amount and type of symptoms people will report to a mental health clinician, which thereby affects the diagnosis. Cultural differences may underlie, at least in part, the dramatic differences in the apparent rates of serious mental illness reported across countries. [See *Figure 3.4*—For this WHO study, a mental illness was considered *serious* if the individual was unable to carry out his or her normal activities for at least 30 days in the past year.]

LEARNING ACTIVITY 3.9: Mental Health Treatments in the Developing World

Objective: To discuss the lack of access to mental health treatments in some countries.

Time: 25 Minutes

Media and Discussion: 35 Minutes

Discussion Only: 10 Minutes

Read Online: Clay, R. C. (2009). Bridging the treatment gap. *Monitor on Psychology, 40*(6), 30–31; http://www.apa.org/monitor/2009/06/treatment.aspx

This article describes the lack of mental health services in other countries.

Watch Online: The Mental Health Gap Video, http://video.who.int/streaming/mental_health.wmv

This video explores the lack treatments for people with mental illness in different countries.

Directions: Have the class analyze and discuss the statistics, such as possible reasons for certain countries' lower scores and any barriers that might prevent seeing better mental health statistics in those countries in the future.

Summary: Students will be surprised about mental health services and treatments available to patients in other countries as compared to the United States.

Questions to Students and Discussion: How can we better spread effective treatments in other countries? What are the pros and cons of doing this? How can we be culturally sensitive in addressing barriers and stigma in other countries?

D. Assessment as an Interactive Process

Mental health researchers and clinicians learn about patients from assessing psychological and social factors, and sometimes neurological and other biological factors. Information about each type of factor should not be considered in isolation, but rather should influence how the clinician understands the other types of information. Furthermore, the patient's culture must be taken into account as part of the assessment.

III. DIAGNOSING AND ASSESSING ROSE MARY AND REX WALLS

Psychological, social, and neurological forms of assessment are applied to the case of Rose Mary and Rex Walls. No direct clinical assessment can be made; the ability to make a diagnosis is therefore limited because the information has been obtained through their daughter's recollection and not through Rose Mary and Rex Walls directly.

ADDITIONAL READINGS

Journal Articles

Abreu, J. M. (1999). Conscious and nonconscious African American stereotypes: Impact on first impression and diagnostic ratings by therapists. *Journal of Consulting and Clinical Psychology, 67,* 387–393.

Clay, R. C. (2009). Bridging the treatment gap. *Monitor on Psychology, 40*(6), 30–31.

Corrigan, P. W., & Watson, A. C. (2001). Paradox of self-stigma and mental illness. *Clinical Psychological Science Practice, 9,* 35–53.

Dingfelder, S. F. (2009). The military's war on stigma. *Monitor on Psychology, 40*(6), 53–56.

Dingfelder, S. F. (2009). Stigma: Alive and well. *Monitor on Psychology, 40*(6), 56–60.

Wahl, O. F. (1999). Mental health consumers' experience of stigma. *Schizophrenia Bulletin, 25,* 467–478.

WHO World Mental Health Survey Consortium. (2004). Prevalence, severity, and unmet need for treatment of mental disorders in the World Health Organization World Mental Health Surveys. *JAMA: Journal of the American Medical Association, 291,* 2581–2590.

Clinical Diagnosis and Assessment Books and Memoirs

Baden, A. L., & Wong, G. (2008). Assessment issues for working with diverse populations of elderly: Multiculturally sensitive perspectives. In L. A. Suzuki & J. G. Ponterotto (Eds.), *Handbook of multicultural assessment: Clinical, psychological, and educational applications* (pp. 594–623). San Francisco: Jossey-Bass.

This chapter covers assessment issues with the elderly.

Corrigan, P. W. (2005). *On the stigma of mental illness.* Washington, DC: APA.

Read more about the ways we can challenge the stigma of mental illness.

Groth-Marnat, G. (2003). *Handbook of psychological assessment.* New York: John Wiley and Sons.

This is an excellent book that describes the various psychological assessments and interpretations.

U.S. Department of Health and Human Services. (1999). *Mental health: A report of the Surgeon General.* Rockville, MD: Author. Retrieved January 15, 2007, from http://mentalhealth.samhsa.gov/cre/ch2.asp.

Learn about the rates of mental illness among various ethnic groups in this succinct report.

Walls, J. (2005). *The glass castle.* New York: Scribner's.

This book tells the story of Walls' experience growing up with two emotionally and financially unstable parents.

WEB SITES

American Academy of Family Physicians Genogram Template: Students can use this genogram template to analyze their own family history, a celebrity, or consumer of mental health services. See: http://www.aafp.org/fpm/2001/0300/fpm20010300p49-rt1.pdf

Assessment Psychology Online: Provides a wealth of resources, including sample assessments and information about widely used assessments. See: http://www.assessmentpsychology.com

Psychological Testing: A Guide to Psychology and Its Practice: This Web site provides an overview of different types of psychological tests, reasons for using assessments, and rights of consumers. See: http://www.guidetopsychology.com/testing.htm

Foundations of Treatment

CHAPTER 4

CHAPTER OUTLINE

CHAPTER HEADINGS	INSTRUCTION IDEAS AND TEXTBOOK CORRELATIONS
Chapter Introduction	**Textbook Tool:** Table 4.1
TREATMENTS THAT TARGET NEUROLOGICAL FACTORS	
Medications to Change Brain Functioning (Psychopharmacology)	**Learning Objectives:** 4.1, 4.2 **Learning Concepts:** goals and methods of medication, schizophrenia, depression, anxiety disorders **Textbook Tool:** Figure 4.1
Changing Brain Function Through Brain Stimulation	**Learning Objectives:** 4.3, 4.4 **Learning Concepts:** electroconvulsive therapy, transcranial magnetic stimulation **Media Recommendation 4.1:** TMS in Action
Biofeedback	**Learning Objective:** 4.5 **Media Recommendation 4.2:** The Portable Stress Eraser **Worth Video Tool Kit for Abnormal Psychology:** Kitty Dukakis: An Advocate for ECT
Changing Brain Structure Through Neurosurgery	**Learning Objective:** 4.6 **Media Recommendation 4.3:** *The Lobotomist*
Targeting Neurological Factors in Younger and Older Populations	**Learning Objective:** 4.7 **Media Recommendation 4.4:** *Medicating Kids* and *The Medicated Child*
TREATMENTS THAT TARGET PSYCHOLOGICAL FACTORS	**Learning Objective:** 4.8
Psychodynamic Therapy: Core Assumptions	**Learning Objectives:** 4.9, 4.10 **Learning Concepts:** goals of psychoanalysis and psychodynamic therapy, methods of psychodynamic therapy

	Learning Activity 4.1: Identify Your Id, Ego, and Superego **Media Recommendation 4.5:** *The Language of Dreams* and *Dream Interview Method* **Learning Activity 4.2:** Examine Your Own Transference **Media Recommendation 4.6:** Transference in Relationships **Textbook Tools:** Table 4.2; Case 4.1
Client-Centered Therapy	**Learning Objectives:** 4.11, 4.12 **Learning Concepts:** goals and methods of client-centered therapy **Media Recommendation 4.7:** Carl Rogers and Gloria **Learning Activity 4.3:** Client-Centered Therapy Role-Play
Cognitive-Behavior Therapy	**Learning Objectives:** 4.13, 4.14, 4.15, 4.16, 4.17 **Learning Concepts:** goals and methods of behavior therapy, role of classical conditioning, role of operant conditioning, additional methods **Media Recommendation 4.8:** Virtual Reality Therapy **Media Recommendation 4.9:** Systematic Desensitization **Learning Activity 4.4:** Identify Your Triggers **Learning Activity 4.5:** Analyze *Supernanny* **Learning Activity 4.6:** Develop a Behavioral Goal **Learning Activity 4.7:** Examining Your ABCs **Learning Activity 4.8:** Acting Out Your Cognitive Distortions **Learning Activity 4.9:** Personal Cognitive Distortions **Textbook Tools:** Figures 4.2, 4.3, 4.4; Tables 4.3, 4.4
Incorporating Technology Into Treatment	**Learning Objective:** 4.18 **Learning Concepts:** technology for between-session work, cybertherapy **Worth Video Tool Kit for Abnormal Psychology:** Train Your Brain: Dr. Robert Reiner Teaches Patients to Deal with Their Phobias Using Virtual Reality to Overcome a Fear
Targeting Psychological Factors in Younger and Older Populations	**Learning Objective:** 4.19 **Media Recommendation 4.10:** Play Therapy
TREATMENTS THAT TARGET SOCIAL FACTORS	**Learning Objective:** 4.20
Interpersonal Therapy (IPT)	**Learning Objectives:** 4.21, 4.22 **Learning Concepts:** goals and methods **Textbook Tool:** Table 4.5
Family and Systems Therapy	**Learning Objectives:** 4.23, 4.24 **Learning Concepts:** goals and methods **Textbook Tools:** Figure 4.5; Case 4.2
Group Therapy	**Learning Objective:** 4.25 **Worth Video Tool Kit for Abnormal Psychology:** Family Therapy with a Divorced Family, The Angry Couple: Couples Therapy
Community-Based Treatment	**Learning Objectives:** 4.26 **Learning Concepts:** inpatient treatment, partial hospitalization, residential treatment, self-help, prevention programs **Learning Activity 4.10:** Attend a Group or Community Workshop

Targeting Social Factors in Younger and Older Populations	**Learning Objective:** 4.27
Treating a Multicultural Population	**Learning Objective:** 4.28 **Learning Concepts:** how ethnicity can influence treatment, using mental health services, bridging a cultural gap between patient and clinician **Media Recommendation 4.11:** Hold Your Breath **Lecture Enhancement 4.1:** Ethnicity and Mental Health Care **Tools:** Figures 4.6, 4.7; Case 4.3
Finances and Managed Care	**Learning Objective:** 4.29
CREATING A TREATMENT PLAN	
Choosing a Specific Treatment	**Learning Objective:** 4.30
Choosing One or More Treatments	

LEARNING OBJECTIVES

After reading this chapter, students should be able to:

4.1 Describe the types of medications that change brain functioning.

4.2 Identify the types of medications used to treat schizophrenia, depression, and anxiety disorders.

4.3 Summarize the practice of electroconvulsive therapy.

4.4 Describe the new practice of transcranial magnetic stimulation.

4.5 Describe the process of biofeedback.

4.6 Articulate the best time to use neurosurgery.

4.7 Clarify the adjustments needed when treating neurological factors in older and younger populations.

4.8 Identify the major types of treatments that target psychological factors.

4.9 Compare and contrast psychoanalysis and psychodynamic therapy.

4.10 Name and describe the specific methods used in psychodynamic therapy.

4.11 Describe the major goals of client-centered therapy.

4.12 Name and describe the specific methods used in client-centered therapy.

4.13 Summarize the major goals of behavior therapy.

4.14 Compare and contrast the methods used in behavior therapy.

4.15 Describe the major goals of cognitive therapy.

4.16 Compare and contrast the methods used in cognitive therapy.

4.17 Describe the main components of dialectical behavior therapy.

4.18 Discuss the various ways technology can be incorporated into treatment.

4.19 Describe adjustments to treatments that target psychological factors needed for older and younger populations.

4.20 Compare and contrast treatments that target social factors.

4.21 Describe the major goals and techniques used in interpersonal therapy.

4.22 Name and define the four themes of relationship problems in interpersonal therapy.

4.23 Compare and contrast family and systems therapy.

4.24 Describe the major goals and techniques used in systems therapy.

4.25 Describe how group therapy can be used as a treatment.

4.26 Name and describe the various forms of community-based treatments.

4.27 Identify ways to modify treatments that target social factors in younger and older populations.

4.28 Describe ways that ethnicity can influence treatment.

4.29 Describe ways that managed care affects treatment possibilities.

4.30 Identify how clinicians select a specific treatment.

KEY TERMS

Treatment (for psychological disorders): The use of a procedure or substance to reduce or eliminate psychological problems or symptoms of psychological disorders and/or improve quality of life.

Biomedical treatments: Treatments that are designed to reduce target symptoms and/or improve quality of life by changing brain functioning, hormonal activity, or another aspect of bodily functioning.

Psychopharmacology: The use of medication to reduce or eradicate symptoms of psychological disorders; also the study of such treatment.

Agonists: Medications that mimic the effects of a neurotransmitter or neuromodulator and activate a particular type of receptor.

Antagonists: Medications that bind to a receptor site on a dendrite (or cell body) and prevent the neurotransmitter in the synapse from binding to that receptor or cause less of it to bind.

Reuptake inhibitors: Medications that partially block the process by which a neurotransmitter is reabsorbed into the terminal button, thus increasing the amount of the neurotransmitter in the synaptic cleft.

Antipsychotic medications: Medications that reduce certain psychotic symptoms; also called *neuroleptic medications.*

Benzodiazepines: Medications commonly known as tranquilizers.

Electroconvulsive therapy (ECT): A procedure that causes a controlled brain seizure in order to reduce or eliminate the symptoms of certain psychological disorders.

Transcranial magnetic stimulation (TMS): A procedure that sends sequences of short, strong magnetic pulses into the cerebral cortex via a coil placed on the scalp; TMS sometimes is used in an effort to reduce or eliminate the symptoms of certain psychological disorders.

Biofeedback: A technique by which a person is trained to bring normally or unconscious bodily activity, such as heart rate or muscle tension, under voluntary control.

Psychoanalysis: The intensive psychotherapy based on Freud's view that psychopathology arises from unconscious conflict.

Psychodynamic therapy: A form of psychotherapy based on psychoanalysis but that involves less frequent sessions, less emphasis on aggressive and sexual drives, and more attention to present experiences.

Therapeutic alliance: The positive relationship between the therapist and the patient.

Free association: The psychodynamic technique in which patients report aloud their train of thought, uncensored.

Interpretation: The psychodynamic technique in which the therapist infers the unconscious meaning or motivation behind a patient's words and behaviors and shares these inferences with the patient.

Dream analysis: The psychodynamic technique in which the therapist interprets the content of a patient's dreams.

Transference: The psychodynamic process by which patients interact with the therapist in the same manner that they did with their parents or other important figures in their lives.

Client-centered therapy: A humanistic therapy developed by Carl Rogers that is intended to promote personal growth so a client can reach his or her full potential.

Cognitive-behavior therapy (CBT): The form of treatment that combines methods from cognitive and behavior therapies.

Behavior therapy: The form of treatment that rests on the ideas that (1) maladaptive behaviors, cognitions, and emotions stem from previous learning; and (2) new learning can allow patients to develop more adaptive behaviors, cognitions, and emotions.

Cognitive therapy: The form of treatment that rests on the ideas that (1) mental contents influence feelings and behavior, and (2) correcting irrational thoughts and incorrect beliefs will therefore lead to a better mood and more adaptive behavior.

Habituation: The process by which repeated exposure reduces the emotional response to a stimulus that elicits fear, anxiety, or arousal.

Exposure: The behavioral technique that involves repeated contact with a feared or arousing stimulus in a controlled setting.

Systematic desensitization: The behavioral technique that involves learning to relax in the presence of a feared stimulus.

Exposure with response prevention: The behavioral technique in which a patient is carefully prevented from engaging in his or her usual maladaptive response after being exposed to a stimulus.

Stimulus control: The behavioral technique for changing the frequency of a maladaptive conditioned response by controlling the frequency or intensity of exposure to the stimulus that elicits the response.

Behavior modification: The use of operant conditioning principles to change maladaptive behavior.

Shaping: The procedure of reinforcing small and then progressively larger components of changed behavior until the desired complex behavior is exhibited.

Extinction: The process of eliminating a behavior by not reinforcing it.

Secondary reinforcers: Objects and events that do not directly satisfy a biological need but are desirable nonetheless.

Token economy: A treatment program that uses secondary reinforcers to change behavior.

Rational-emotive behavior therapy (REBT): The form of treatment in which a patient's irrational thoughts are transformed into rational ones, which in turn leads to more positive emotions and adaptive behaviors.

Psychoeducation: The process of educating patients about research findings and therapy procedures relevant to their situation.

Dialectical behavior therapy (DBT): The form of treatment that includes elements of CBT as well as an emphasis on validating the patient's experience, a Zen Buddhist approach, and a dialectics component.

Cybertherapy: Internet-based therapy.

Interpersonal therapy (IPT): The form of treatment that is intended to improve the patient's skills in relationships so that they become more satisfying.

Family therapy: The form of treatment that involves either the family as a whole or some portion of it.

Systems therapy: The form of treatment that is designed to change the communication or behavior patterns of one or more family members in the context of the family as a whole; also known as *family systems therapy.*

Validate: A systems therapy technique by which the therapist demonstrates an understanding of each family member's feelings and desires.

Reframe: A systems therapy technique by which the therapist offers new ways to conceive of, or frame, the family's or identified patient's problem.

Paradoxical intention: A systems therapy technique by which the therapist suggests that the problem behavior be allowed to continue or even increase in intensity or frequency.

Group therapy: The form of treatment in which several patients with similar needs meet together with one or two therapists.

Outpatient treatment: Treatment that does not involve an overnight stay in a hospital.

Inpatient treatment: Treatment that occurs while a patient is in a psychiatric hospital or in a psychiatric unit of a general hospital.

Partial hospitalization: Treatment that is provided at a hospital or other facility, but the patient does not sleep there; such treatment is less intensive than inpatient treatment but more intensive than outpatient visits.

Residential treatment: Treatment in which patients stay in a staffed facility where they sleep, eat breakfast and dinner, and perhaps take part in evening groups.

Bibliotherapy: Using self-help materials as part of therapy.

Prevention programs: Programs that are designed to prevent, or inhibit the development or progression of, psychological problems or disorders.

Managed care: A type of health insurance plan that restricts access to specialized medical care by limiting benefits or reimbursement.

Chapter Guide

CHAPTER INTRODUCTION

Treatment (for psychological disorders) is defined as the use of a procedure or substance to reduce or eliminate specific symptoms and/or to improve the general quality of life.

- Some treatments are provided for guidance; no abnormalities are involved.
- Symptoms focused on in treatment are called *target symptoms.*
- General quality of life encompasses psychological, social, and material well-being.
- Specific quality-of-life issues include relationships, self-care, and integration into society.
- All treatments can be categorized according to the type of factor they target: neurological, psychological, or social. [See *Table 4.1.*]
- Feedback loops are created, whereby treatment of certain factors can affect other factors.

I. TREATMENTS THAT TARGET NEUROLOGICAL FACTORS

Biomedical treatments reduce target symptoms by changing (1) brain functioning, (2) hormonal activity, or (3) another aspect of bodily functioning regulated by the brain. The goal of these treatments is to change neurological functioning. The following are methods used:

A. Medications to Change Brain Functioning (Psychopharmacology)

Psychopharmacology is the use or study of using medication to reduce or eradicate symptoms of psychological disorders. The treatment is administered via (1) pills, (2) skin patches, or (3) injection.

1. Goals of Medication

Medication can affect neurological and/or psychological factors by increasing or decreasing specific types of brain activity.

2. Methods of Medication

Medication can alter neural activity in several ways. [See *Figure 4.1.*]

- An *agonist* mimics the effects of a neurotransmitter or neuromodulator, thus activating a receptor or receptors.
- An *antagonist* binds to a receptor site on the dendrite. The binding of the neurotransmitter to the receptor is then lessened or reduced.
- A medication can cause additional neurotransmitters from the terminal button to be released into the synapse.
- A medication can increase/decrease the level or activity of other substances that activate/inactivate a neurotransmitter.
- A *reuptake inhibitor* partially blocks *reuptake* (neurotransmitter molecules left in the synapse, which are reabsorbed into the terminal button to be recycled later), thus increasing neurotransmitters in the synaptic cleft.

Note: The table on the following page summarizes the methods of medication just described.

Type of Medication	How It Works	Examples
Agonists	Mimic the neurotransmitter or a neuromodulator and activate the receptor	L-dopa
Antagonists	Bind to a receptor site and prevent the neurotransmitter from binding to the receptor or cause less of it to bind	Antipsychotic medications
Reuptake inhibitors	Block reuptake of neurotransmitter, thus increasing the amount of neurotransmitter in the synaptic cleft	Prozac, Zoloft, Celexa

3. **Medications for Specific Disorders**

The following table summarizes the type of medications used to treat specific psychological disorders.

Disorder	Treatment Medication
Schizophrenia	• *Antipsychotic medications* (or *neuroleptic medications*) • Reduce certain psychotic symptoms but do not cure the disorder
Depression	• *Selective serotonin reuptake inhibitors (SSRIs), serotonin norepinephrine reuptake inhibitors (SNRIs), tricyclic antidepressants (TCAs), or monoamine oxidase inhibitors (MAOIs)*
Anxiety Disorders	• *SSRIs, SNRIs,* or *antidepressants* such as *tricyclics*—can be effective for long-term treatment. • *Benzodiazepines* (or *tranquilizers*)—effective for short-term treatment.

B. Changing Brain Function Through Brain Stimulation

Two other biomedical techniques that can change patients' brain functioning more directly than medications are electroconvulsive therapy and transcranial magnetic stimulation. These methods are used only when other types of treatment have been unsuccessful.

1. **Electroconvulsive Therapy (ECT)**

Electroconvulsive Therapy (ECT) induces brain seizures to reduce/eliminate symptoms of psychological disorders. After a patient receives a muscle relaxant and anesthesia, an electric current is passed through his or her head via electrodes on the scalp. Typical ECT entails 6–12 sessions over several weeks.

2. **Transcranial Magnetic Stimulation (TMS)**

Transcranial Magnetic Stimulation (TMS) sends sequences of short, strong magnetic pulses into the cerebral cortex via a coil placed on the scalp. Each pulse lasts only 100–200 microseconds.

MEDIA RECOMMENDATION 4.1: TMS in Action

Objective: To provide an overview of transcranial magnetic stimulation treatment as applied to a real-life case and to illustrate how transcranial magnetic stimulation can affect the brain's language center.

Time: 2 Minutes (Video 1); 4 Minutes (Video 2)

Media and Discussion: 10 Minutes

Discussion Only: 5 Minutes

Watch Online: View a short video clip describing how repetitive transcranial magnetic stimulation can help treat depression. Search YouTube using the search terms "Transcranial Magnetic Stimulation" or http://www.youtube.com/watch?v=stJFwxVH2_s

Further explore TMS by viewing this clip showing a news reporter whose speech production is interrupted using transcranial magnetic stimulation. Search YouTube using the search terms "Transcranial Magnetic Stimulation Lets You Deactivate Selected Parts of Your Brain" or http://www.youtube.com/watch?v=XJtNPqCj-iA

Students will become aware of how transcranial magnetic stimulation affects the brain and, in turn, behavior.

Summary: These video clips show how TMS affects the brain and how it can be used for psychological treatments and physical illnesses. Students will be amazed with this new form of treatment and will also understand how transcranial magnetic stimulation affects the brain.

Questions to Students and Discussion: What are your concerns about this form of treatment? Are you concerned that this treatment has not been approved by the FDA? How might this treatment revolutionize mental-health care?

C. Biofeedback

Biofeedback is a technique by which an individual is trained to bring involuntary or unconscious bodily activity (heart rate or muscle tension) under voluntary control. Electrical leads placed on the body measure biological activity (pulse rate or muscle tension level), and the patient learns to keep the targeted biological activity within the desired range.

MEDIA RECOMMENDATION 4.2: The Portable Stress Eraser

Objective: To show students a fairly new personal and portable biofeedback device.

Time: 3 Minutes (Web); 8 Minutes (Video clip)

Media and Discussion: 16 Minutes

Discussion Only: 5 Minutes

Explore Online: Learn about the StressEraser, a new portable biofeedback device, at http://stresseraser.com/

View a short clip illustrating how biofeedback can be used to reduce stress. Search YouTube using the search terms "the stress eraser" or http://www.youtube.com/watch?v=0oSfKN-Cl2U

Summary: Students will learn about how the StressEraser (a biofeedback tool) can help to reduce anxiety by focusing on one's bodily reactions and breathing.

Questions to Students and Discussion: Do you think this treatment should be covered by insurance? Why might some companies not reimburse patients for this type of treatment? Would you find this type of treatment helpful? Why?

D. Changing Brain Structure Through Neurosurgery

Neurosurgery or brain surgery is used only rarely when all other treatments have failed. During neurosurgery, specific brain structures or connections with other parts of the brain are destroyed or severed, which changes brain functioning and reduces the intensity or frequency of maladaptive behaviors.

MEDIA RECOMMENDATION 4.3: *The Lobotomist*

Objective: To learn about the controversial history of neurosurgery.

Film: 60 Minutes

Film and Discussion: 90 Minutes

Discussion Only: 30 Minutes

Watch Online: View the film at http://www.pbs.org/wgbh/amex/lobotomist/

The PBS Web site also has patients' stories, detailed time lines of the treatment of the mentally ill, an online forum, and additional links.

Dr. Walter Freeman performed numerous lobotomies without full knowledge of how this surgery was affecting patients.

Summary: This film does an excellent job of showing how critical thinking is essential for safe practices. The film reveals how unexamined beliefs and practices can be harmful.

Questions to Students and Discussion: What prevented Walter Freeman from having better insight into the consequences of the lobotomies he was performing? What ethical rules did he violate? How can we prevent this type of treatment from occurring in the future?

E. Targeting Neurological Factors in Younger and Older Populations

Patients at two ends of the developmental continuum—children (including adolescents) and older adults—may respond somewhat differently than do young and middle-aged adults; thus biomedical treatments may be modified in the following ways.

1. **Targeting Neurological Factors in Younger Patients**

   - Dosage and frequency of medications are prescribed off-label (because most medications have not been tested on younger patients), and so may need to be adjusted as well as monitored for adverse side effects more frequently in younger populations.

   - ECT has rarely been used to treat children and adolescents, and thus such therapy lacks clear guidelines for use with younger patients.

   - Interest in using brain stimulation techniques to treat children and adolescents is increasing because of the side effects of various antidepressant medications in young patients.

MEDIA RECOMMENDATION 4.4: *Medicating Kids* and *The Medicated Child*

Objective: To explore the controversies involving putting children on medication

Films: 60 Minutes Each

Film and Discussion: 90 Minutes Each

Discussion Only: 30 Minutes

Watch Online: Gaviria, M., and Smith, M. (2001). *Frontline: Medicating Kids*. WGBH Educational Foundation. http://www.pbs.org/wgbh/pages/frontline/shows/medicating/

Smith, M. (2008). *Frontline: The Medicated Child*. WGBH Educational Foundation. http://www.pbs.org/wgbh/pages/frontline/medicatedchild/

Medicating Kids focuses on ADHD diagnosis and treatment controversies. *The Medicated Child* examines the side effects of using medication to treat psychiatric illnesses in children. The PBS Web site also includes interviews, updates, and resources for parents and teachers.

Summary: These films will help your students understand the benefits and drawbacks of treating childhood forms of mental illness with medication.

Questions to Students and Discussion: What do you think are the pros and cons of medicating kids? What are the alternatives to medication?

2. Targeting Neurological Factors in Older Patients

- Older adults are typically more sensitive to medications and may need lower dosages.
- Many older adults take medications to treat physical problems and these medications can adversely affect their mood, cognitive functioning, or behavior; these side effects and symptoms may cause older adults to be misdiagnosed.
- Electroconvulsive therapy is particularly effective with older depressed patients.

II. TREATMENTS THAT TARGET PSYCHOLOGICAL FACTORS

A variety of psychological treatments differ in the factors they target, goals, and methods. Psychological treatments include psychodynamic therapy, client-centered therapy, and cognitive-behavior therapy (CBT).

A. Psychodynamic Therapy: Core Assumptions

- *Psychic determinism* is the belief that all behavior has underlying psychological causes.
- According to Freud, there are three psychic structures of the mind: the id (pleasure principle), the ego (reality principle and mediator), and the superego (moral principle).
- Problems arise from conflicts among the id, superego, and ego.
- Treatment focuses on talk therapy, in which clients talk about their problems and the therapist interprets unconscious causes.

LEARNING ACTIVITY 4.1: Identify Your Id, Ego, and Superego

Objective: To apply the concepts of the three structures of the mind.

Time: 20–30 Minutes

Directions: Have students provide examples of their own internal dialogue with their id, ego, and superego.

Summary: The students' examples will clarify the mental processes associated with each of these concepts.

Questions to Students and Discussion: What part of your personality tends to be most dominant? How does your ego negotiate conflicts between the superego and the id? What psychological problems might you be at risk for due to the dominance of one structure?

1. **The Goals of Psychoanalysis and Psychodynamic Therapy**

   - The ultimate goal is to help patients handle impulses and urges more adaptively by understanding one's past and how those events influence one's unconscious urges and current difficulties.

   - Gaining *insight* or awareness of the unconscious urges improves one's ability to handle one's impulses, which leads to more productive choices.

   - In *psychoanalysis,* intensive psychotherapy based on Freud's view that psychopathology arises from unconscious conflict, patients meet with their *psychoanalyst* four or five times per week, and the average patient participates in 835 sessions over at least 4 years.   .

   - The most common treatment based on psychodynamic theory is *psychodynamic therapy,* which typically has fewer sessions, less emphasis on aggressive and sexual drives, and more attention on present experiences.

   - Both psychoanalysis and psychodynamic therapy aim to help patients understand that their unconscious motivations influence their behaviors in specific ways and to help them make better choices

2. **Methods of Psychodynamic Therapy**

   Psychodynamic therapies use a variety of methods. [See *Table 4.2.*]

   a. **Therapeutic Alliance:**

   Therapeutic alliance refers to the positive relationship between therapist and patient, providing the trust and goodwill to undertake the therapeutic work.

   b. **Free Association:**

   Free association is the technique in which patients report aloud their train of thought uncensored.

   c. **Interpretation:**

   Interpretation is the technique in which the therapist infers the unconscious meaning or motivation behind a patient's words and behaviors, sharing his insights with the patient.

   d. **Dream Analysis:**

   Dream analysis is the technique in which the therapist interprets the content of a patient's dreams.

   e. **Resistance:**

   This technique in which the therapist uses the patient's conscious or unconscious attempts to hinder treatment to increase awareness or insight. [See *Case 4.1.*]

   f. **Transference:**

   Transference is the technique in which the therapist uses the patient/therapist interaction in the same manner as the patient did with parents or other important figures in his or her life as a way to encourage the patient to better understand his or her transferred feelings and how these feelings influence his or her behavior.

	Psychoanalysis	Psychodynamic Therapy
Frequency	Four or five times a week	Usually not more than twice a week
Duration	Years, or indefinitely	A few years or less
Seating arrangements	Patient lies on a couch; the analyst sits behind the patient, off to the side, out of the patient's view.	Patient and therapist both sit on chairs, facing each other.
Emphasis	More emphasis on sexual and aggressive urges and childhood experiences	Less emphasis on sexual and aggressive urges; more emphasis on current—rather than past—experiences

MEDIA RECOMMENDATION 4.4: *The Language of Dreams* and *Dream Interview Method*

Objective: To learn about current dream analysis methods through two podcasts featuring interviews with Robert Hoss, former president of the International Association for the Study of Dreams, and Gayle Delaney, founder of the International Association for the Study of Dreams.

Media: 60 Minutes Each

Media and Discussion: 90 Minutes Each

Discussion Only: 30 Minutes

Listen Online: Hoss, R. (May 15, 2007). *The Language of Dreams.* Shrink Rap Radio podcast number 90.

Delaney, G. (July 28, 2007). *Dream Interview Method.* Shrink Rap Radio podcast number 103.

http://www.shrinkrapradio.com/?s=dream+interview+method&searchsubmit=Find

Summary: After listening to these programs, students will be able to identify how dreams can be used to reveal unconscious conflicts experienced by the client.

Questions to Students and Discussion: After listening to these programs, do you think Freud's belief in latent content of dreams is true? Why or why not?

LEARNING ACTIVITY 4.2: Examine Your Own Transference

Objective: To understand how our past relationships affect our current relationships.

Time: 30–40 Minutes

Directions: Think about a recent conflict or strong reaction you had to an interpersonal event. For example, remember the last time you got really angry or sad. Write what happened and how you were feeling. Now write about a time in your early childhood when you felt the same way.

Summary: Psychoanalytic theory looks for connections between our early relationships with our caregivers and current triggers.

Questions to Students and Discussion: Were you able to find a connection between the current and past events?

MEDIA RECOMMENDATION 4.6: Transference in Relationships

Objective: Through an interview with couples therapist Harville Hendrix, students will explore how transference can affect couples and how Imago Therapy is used to heal early childhood wounds.

Time: 3 Minutes

Media and Discussion: 20 Minutes

Discussion Only: 15 Minutes

Watch Online: Search YouTube using the search terms "Harville Hendrix couples therapy" or http://www.youtube.com/watch?v=ABedIDJh94I&feature=related

Summary: Students will enjoy seeing a modern adaptation of psychoanalytic principles. Students will gain insight into ways one's childhood affects present-day relationships.

Questions to Students and Discussion: How do you think transference is expressed in the therapeutic setting? How can a therapist use transference to help with healing?

B. Client-Centered Therapy

Carl Rogers developed *client-centered therapy,* a humanistic therapy intended to promote personal growth so that a client can reach his or her full potential.

1. The Goal of Client-Centered Therapy

- To decrease the incongruence between the ideal and real selves by modifying the ideal self or realizing that the real self is closer to the ideal self than previously thought
- To develop an integrated sense of self
- To enhance the ability for clients to reach their full potential

2. Methods of Client-Centered Therapy

The two basic tenets of client-centered therapy are that the therapist should express:

a. Genuine Empathy:

The therapist accurately reflects the key parts or essential components or feelings of what the client said.

b. Unconditional Positive Regard:

The therapist expresses positive feelings and worth for the client, regardless of what the client expresses.

MEDIA RECOMMENDATION 4.7: Carl Rogers and Gloria

Objective: To observe client-centered therapy.

Time: 45 Minutes

Media and Discussion: 65 Minutes

Discussion Only: 20 Minutes

Watch Online: Search YouTube, using the following terms "Carl Rogers" and "Gloria."
Part 1: http://www.youtube.com/watch?v=ZBkUqcqRChg
Part 2: http://www.youtube.com/watch?v=m30jsZx_Ngs&feature=related
Part 3: http://www.youtube.com/watch?v=RX_Y3zUPzEo&feature=related
Part 4: http://www.youtube.com/watch?v=zHxl5NtcDow&feature=related
Part 5: http://www.youtube.com/watch?v=L19nXMvbS8E&feature=related

In this five-part film, famed psychologist Carl Rogers meets with Gloria and, using client-centered therapy, explores her concerns.

Summary: As students watch Rogers interact with Gloria they can identify client-centered techniques. Students will also be able to see the effect these techniques have on Gloria.

Questions to Students and Discussion: Name and describe the specific client-centered methods used in this film. Would you like to see Rogers as your personal therapist? Why or why not?

LEARNING ACTIVITY 4.3: Client-Centered Therapy Role-Play

Objective: To have students role-play as the client and the therapist during a client-centered therapy session.

Time: 20 Minutes

Directions: Have students break up into pairs. Assign one student to be the "therapist" and one student to be the "client." Give students 5–10 minutes each to play the therapist and client. When playing the client, the student should describe a current upsetting or a difficult situation. The therapist should use client-centered techniques of empathy and unconditional positive regard.

Summary: Students will gain insight into how client-centered techniques are used in the therapy setting.

Questions to Students and Discussion: How did it feel to be the client? How did it feel to be the therapist? What did you enjoy or dislike about using these techniques?

C. Cognitive-Behavior Therapy

Cognitive and behavioral therapies were originally two separate forms of therapy. But because their approaches are complementary, they are frequently combined into what is called *cognitive-behavior therapy (CBT)*.

- According to *behavior therapy,* maladaptive behaviors, cognitions, and emotions stem from previous learning.
- New learning can allow patients to develop more adaptive behaviors, cognitions, and emotions.

1. The Goals of Behavior Therapy

- Founded by Joseph Wolpe (1915–1997), behavior therapy is based on well-researched principles of learning.
- It stresses changing behavior rather than identifying unconscious motivations or root causes of problems.

2. Methods of Behavior Therapy

- Focus on the *ABC*s of an unwanted behavior pattern: the *antecedents* of the behavior (the stimuli that trigger the behavior), the *behavior* itself, and the *consequences* of the behavior (which may reinforce the behavior).
- *Homework* refers to tasks that the patient completes between therapy sessions.

a. The Role of Classical Conditioning in Behavior Therapy:

Conditioning adaptive and new emotional responses using classical conditioning principles.

(1) Treating anxiety and avoidance:

(a) This method involves repeated contact with the (feared or arousing) stimulus in a controlled setting, creating a hierarchy of feared events (from least to most feared), and an ***exposure*** process by having contact with the least-feared item on the hierarchy. The anxiety symptoms diminish within 20–30 minutes or less. [See *Table 4.3.*]

Patients in therapy can experience exposure in three ways:
- *imaginal exposure,* forming mental images of the stimulus
- *virtual reality exposure,* exposure to a computer-generated (often very realistic) representation of the stimulus
- *in vivo exposure,* which is exposure to the actual stimulus

MEDIA RECOMMENDATION 4.8: Virtual Reality Therapy

Objective: To observe virtual reality therapy.

Time: 5 Minutes (Video 1); 5 Minutes (Video 2); 48 Minutes (Audio Clip)

Media and Discussion: 90 Minutes

Discussion Only: 10–20 Minutes

Explore Online: View a clip of a woman facing her fear of subways using virtual reality therapy. Search YouTube using the search terms "virtual reality therapy" or http://www.youtube.com/watch?v=CQgKEp_NhHk

Learn how virtual images and "smells" from the Iraq War are used to treat PTSD. Search YouTube using the search terms "Not a Game: Inside Virtual Iraq" or http://www.youtube.com/watch?v=R6kl2BuhKmM&NR=1

Listen to the creator of a video game used to treat PTSD in U.S. soldiers who served in the Iraq War. Rizzo, A. (August 28, 2006). *Virtual Reality and Psychology.* Shrink Rap Radio podcast number 48.

http://www.shrinkrapradio.com/2006/08/24/48-virtual-reality-and-psychology/

Summary: Students will learn about how technology can aid in treatment through the use of virtual reality therapy.

Questions to Students and Discussion: What are the pros and cons of each of the three treatments?

(b) Systematic desensitization relies on the fact that a person cannot be relaxed and anxious at the same time, but this form of treatment is not as efficient or effective as exposure therapy. In ***systematic desensitization,*** the patient learns to become physically relaxed through *progressive muscle relaxation,* constructs a hierarchy of experiences related to the feared stimulus (ordering them from least to most feared), practices becoming relaxed, and continues to remain relaxed while imagining increasingly feared experiences.

(2) **Treating compulsive behaviors:**

The patient is carefully prevented from engaging in the usual maladaptive response after being exposed to the stimulus.

MEDIA RECOMMENDATION 4.9: Systematic Desensitization

Objectives: To provide an additional description of systematic desensitization and an example of progressive muscle relaxation.

Time: 2 Minutes (Video clip); 1–8 Minutes (Audio clips)

Media and Discussion: 10–20 Minutes

Discussion Only: 5–10 Minutes

Explore Online: View a discussion on the use of systematic desensitization for a snake phobia. Search YouTube using the search terms "systematic desensitization" or http://www.youtube.com/watch?v=LcojyGx8q9U

Listen to audio clips teaching the skills of deep breathing and muscle relaxation, posted by the University of Wisconsin-Madison's University Health Center, http://forms.uhs.wisc.edu/relaxation.php

Summary: Students will enjoy hearing about the major principles behind systematic desensitization. Also, after playing out one or two of the audio clips in class, students will be amazed to observe how relaxed they feel. Students will then appreciate the effect of relaxation techniques.

Questions to Students and Discussion: Why do you think these techniques are helpful? Do you think they would help you? What might be difficult about using these techniques?

(3) **Treating habitual maladaptive behaviors:**

This method seeks to limit the patient's contact with the stimulus (called ***stimulus control***) and involves controlling the frequency or intensity of exposure to the stimulus that elicits the response.

LEARNING ACTIVITY 4.4: Identify Your Triggers

Objective: To apply the concept of stimulus control to oneself.

Time: 10–15 Minutes

Directions: Think of a behavior you are trying to control. What are your triggers that cause this behavior? Are there ways to avoid or control those triggers? Describe ways you can control them.

Summary: This exercise highlights the triggers in your environment that might cause an undesired behavior.

Questions to Students and Discussion: If you learn to identify and limit these triggers, do you think your target behavior will decrease? Why?

b. The Role of Operant Conditioning in Behavior Therapy:

Operant conditioning is used to modify maladaptive behaviors using reinforcement and punishment (also called *behavior modification*).

(1)   Making use of reinforcement and punishment:

Reinforcement and punishment set appropriate consequences that follow maladaptive or desired behaviors.

(2)   Making use of extinction:

Extinction is the process of not reinforcing a behavior with the end goal of eliminating the behavior.

(3)   Keeping track of the ABCs through self-monitoring

Self-monitoring tools (a daily log of activities, feelings, and thoughts [see *Figure 4.2*] help a patient become aware of *triggers,* or antecedents to problematic behavior.

LEARNING ACTIVITY 4.5: Analyze *Supernanny*

Objective: To identify the basic terms and concepts of operant and classical conditioning in real-life situations.

Time: 30–40 Minutes

Directions: Watch a segment of the TV series *Supernanny* at http://abc.go.com/primetime/supernanny/index?pn=index. Identify the reinforcers and punishments. Also identify the ways that Nanny Jo uses classical conditioning (*Example:* the naughty chair).

Summary: Nanny Jo clearly uses learning principles to identify what reinforces the children's bad behavior. She then uses these techniques to shape and change the parents' and children's behavior.

Questions to Students and Discussion: What works or doesn't work? Why?

LEARNING ACTIVITY 4.6: Develop a Behavioral Goal

Objective: To apply behavioral therapy methods in order to change a targeted behavior.

Time: 30 Minutes

Directions: Identify a behavior you would like to change. List primary and secondary reinforcers that you can use to help you achieve your goal. Describe a way to create a token economy for your goal.

Summary: Students will gain skills at applying behavioral theories and concepts to real life. In particular, they will identify reinforcements and punishments that they can apply to a specific behavior.

Questions to Students and Discussion: Which reinforcers are most effective? Less effective?

3. **The Goals of Cognitive Therapy**

To modify patient's automatic but irrational or incorrect beliefs (a process called *cognitive restructuring*).

4. **Methods of Cognitive Therapy**

Developed by Albert Ellis and Aaron Beck, who both placed importance on identifying and challenging irrational thoughts and on assigning patients homework.

a. Ellis's Rational Emotive Behavior Therapy (REBT):

- In *rational emotive behavior therapy (REBT)* the patient's irrational thoughts are transformed into rational ones, and this process leads to positive emotions and adaptive behaviors.

- The REBT therapist systematically examines the A, B, and Cs and then uses the D, E, and Fs to intervene:

(1) The interventional steps of REBT:

An *activating* event triggers the patient's *belief*, which leads to a highly charged emotional *consequence.* The therapist helps the patient *dispute* any irrational beliefs by highlighting their destructive or illogical quality, which leads to a new *effect,* idea, or pattern of emotion, or behavior. Finally, the patient can strengthen the effect through *further action.* [See *Figure 4.3.*]

LEARNING ACTIVITY 4.7: Examining Your ABCs

Objective: To apply Ellis's theory to oneself.

Time: 30 Minutes

Directions: Identify a current upsetting situation. Identify the (A) *activating event,* your (B) *belief* about the event, and (C) the emotional *consequence* of your belief. Now play Dr. Ellis, and (D) *dispute* that belief. What is the new (E) *emotion* or *effect,* and what is a (F) *further* action you can take to strengthen it?

Summary: This exercise shows how Dr. Ellis applies REBT to a client's issue.

Questions to Students and Discussion: Did you find this helpful? Why or why not?

---

b. Beck's Cognitive Restructuring:

Beck examined faulty automatic thoughts that pop into awareness without effort.

- Beck had patients test these thoughts, which they discovered were faulty, and that discovery led to more rational and realistic thoughts.

- Beck identified common cognitive distortions that lead to negative automatic thoughts. [See *Figure 4.4* and *Table 4.4.*]

LEARNING ACTIVITY 4.8: Acting Out Your Cognitive Distortions

Objective: Have students think of personal examples of cognitive distortions and then act them out.

Time: 30 Minutes

Directions: Break up into groups of three to four students. Select a cognitive distortion and act it out. Have the class guess which distortion you are enacting.

Summary: We all commit cognitive distortions, and this exercise shows common examples of distorted thinking.

Questions to Students and Discussion: Which distortions are most common for you? How do you think you can stop yourself from incorporating these distortions?

LEARNING ACTIVITY 4.9: Personal Cognitive Distortions

Objective: To apply the cognitive distortions to one's own life.

Time: 20 Minutes

Directions: The table on *Worksheet 4.1* lists some cognitive distortions. Describe a personal example for each distortion.

Summary: We all have cognitive distortions and this exercise shows common examples of distorted thinking.

Questions to Students and Discussion: Which distortions are your most common ones? How do you think you can stop yourself from making and then holding on to them?

5. **Methods of Cognitive-Behavior Therapy**

   Psychoeducation is an additional cognitive therapy technique that educates patients about research findings and therapies relevant to the situation or issue.

6. **Dialectical Behavior Therapy (DBT)—CBT Plus More**

   a. **What Is DBT?**

   - *Dialectical behavior therapy (DBT)* is a relatively new type of therapy developed specifically for treating people with *borderline personality disorder* (an Axis II disorder) that includes elements of CBT as well as an emphasis on validating the patient's experience, a Zen Buddhist approach, and a dialectics component.

   - *Dialectical* refers to tolerating and integrating contradictory feelings, beliefs, and desires.

   - DBT utilizes particular tools and methods to change specific thoughts, feelings, and behaviors.

   - DBT involves individual and group therapy and uses a strong collaborative patient-therapist bond.

   - DBT adds three other components:

   (1) **Emphasis on validating the patient's experience:**

       Recognition of how past experiences and personal strengths and weaknesses influence one's perception of a current issue

   (2) **Mindfulness:**

       Nonjudgmental awareness of one's life or situation

   (3) **Dialectics component:**

       Acknowledgement and acceptance of one's opposing feelings, beliefs, and desires

D. Incorporating Technology into Treatment

- Technology allows for more efficient and effective treatments and between-session work.

- Using computer software or Web sites to facilitate cognitive restructuring, for educational information, or for online blank forms.

- Using computer software to provide virtual reality exposure treatment.

1. **Using Technology for Between-Session Work**

   Significant between-session work using technology includes **self-monitoring** via use of PDAs, smartphones, or programmable computer software.

   a. **Reminders of Self-Monitoring:**
      - To assess one's thoughts, mood, and symptom level
      - To perform certain mental tasks (such as coming up with a rational response to an automatic thought)
      - To perform certain physical behaviors (such as a relaxation technique).

2. **Cybertherapy**

   Cybertherapy is Internet-based therapy, or therapy at a distance.

   a. **Cybertherapeutic Possibilities:**
      - *E-therapy,* or e-mail exchanges between patient and therapist
      - E-mail exchanges between patient and therapist in addition to face-to-face meetings
      - Real-time, online chats between patient and therapist
      - Real-time, face-to-face video chats (using Webcams) between patient and therapist

   b. **Cybertherapeutic Concerns:**
      - *Imposters* who are neither professionally trained nor licensed
      - *Privacy,* since confidentiality and privacy cannot be guaranteed
      - *Incomplete communication,* because e-mail communication lacks important non-verbal cues
      - Little research comparing cybertherapy to in-person therapy (either in general or for specific disorders)

E. Targeting Psychological Factors in Younger and Older Populations

Treatments may need to be modified for these two populations.

1. **Targeting Psychological Factors in Younger Patients**
   - Match the cognitive and emotional level of the younger patient.
   - Employ parental assistance as needed with homework assignments.
   - Utilize *play therapy* for younger children, who may not be able to discuss their problems in detail or may have poor insight into their problems.

MEDIA RECOMMENDATION 4.10: Play Therapy

Objective: To expand on the description of play therapy.

Time: 5 Minutes

Media and Discussion: 10 Minutes

Discussion Only: 5 Minutes

Explore Online: Search YouTube, using the search terms "Anne Murphy Play Therapy" or http://www.youtube.com/watch?v=rl9e9A8IG2I

Summary: This video clip will teach your students about play therapy. Students will enjoy watching play therapy and learning about why this form of therapy is helpful in treating children.

Questions to Students and Discussion: Do you think play therapy can help children express themselves? What are the dangers and strengths of this type of therapy?

2. Targeting Psychological Factors in Older Patients

Treatments may need to be modified in cases of significant cognitive slowing or impairment or memory problems.

III. TREATMENTS THAT TARGET SOCIAL FACTORS

Treatments that target social factors aim to reduce symptoms and/or improve quality of life by improving one's relationships and sense of community. Treatments that target social factors include interpersonal, family, and group therapy and community-based treatment. These treatments must be modified and adapted according to the specific populations receiving treatment.

A. Interpersonal Therapy (IPT)

Interpersonal therapy (IPT) focuses on the patient's relationships and is loosely based on psychodynamic theory.

1. The Goal of Interpersonal Therapy

Improving the patient's skills in relationships, so relationships become more satisfying; as relationships improve, so do the patient's thoughts and feelings, and the symptoms of psychological disorders lessen.

2. Interpersonal Therapy's Four Themes of Relationship Problems

a. Unresolved Grief:

The therapeutic goal is to help with mourning.

b. Role Transition:

Therapeutic goals are to help with expectations, needed social support, and skills.

c. Role Dispute:

Therapeutic goals are to identify the dispute and develop new ways of interacting.

d. Interpersonal Deficits:

Therapeutic goals are to increase interpersonal skills through the patient-therapist relationship and transfer these skills to new relationships. [See *Table 4.5.*]

3. Methods Used in Interpersonal Therapy

- The therapist links aspects of the patient's current relationships with one of the four kinds of problems in relationships.
- Next, the therapist, in cooperation with the patient, sets about enhancing problematic aspects of relationships by doing the following:
  - i.   Teaching the patient to consider the consequences of his/her actions in a relationship
  - ii. Having the patient role-play his/her interactions with significant others
  - iii. Heightening the patient's awareness of feelings that he/she has ignored or pushed aside

    iv. Helping the patient to improve his or her communication skills

    v. Encouraging the patient to tell others how he or she feels in an appropriate manner.

- IPT is a short-term therapy, usually lasting 16 sessions.

- Treatment manuals guide the goals, techniques, and topics for each session to ensure proper implementation of the treatment.

B. Family and Systems Therapy

Family therapy and systems therapy seek to change maladaptive family interactions and increase family support for one another.

1. Family Therapy

Family therapy is a form of treatment that involves either the family as a whole or some portion of it.

- The family (versus an individual) is the focus of the treatment.

- The therapeutic process can occur, using any theoretical approach.

2. Systems Therapy: A Different Way of Thinking About the Family

Systems therapy is designed to change the communication or behavior patterns of one or more family members.

- The focus is on communication and power within the family.

- The family is referred to as the *patient* and the individual member with a psychological disorder as the *identified patient.*

- The identified patient's symptoms are viewed as a result of that individual's intentional or unintentional attempts to maintain or change a pattern within the family or to convey a message to family members.

a. The Goals of Systems Therapy:

To identify and then change maladaptive patterns of interaction and communication among family members.

b. Methods of Systems Therapy:

- Interview family members about the history of the family.

- Establish who is close and distant and how feelings, issues, and conflicts tend to be handled within the family. [See *Figure 4.5.*]

- Examine roles of parents and identify an underinvolved parent (*Example:* a parent who doesn't interact much with his or her child), an overinvolved parent (*Example:* a parent who spends inordinate amounts of time with the child, perhaps finishing his or her sentences), or a conflicted parental relationship.

- A systems therapist might implement ***paradoxical intention***—by suggesting that the problem behavior be allowed to continue, or even increase in intensity or frequency. [See *Case 4.2.*]

C. Group Therapy

- In ***group therapy,*** several patients with similar needs meet together with one or two therapists for a single session, sessions that continue over years, or within some specified time limit (such as 12 weeks).

- Group therapy can be rooted in any of a variety of theoretical orientations, such as psychodynamic or cognitive-behavioral.

D. Community-Based Treatment

Community-based treatment occurs in the patient's community, neighborhood, town, or city. Most people seeking mental health care receive *outpatient treatment*—treatment that does not involve an overnight stay in a hospital and may occur in a therapist's private office, in a community mental health center or mental health clinic, in an outpatient unit of a hospital, or, for those seeking pastoral counseling, within their church, synagogue, or mosque.

1. Inpatient Treatment

Inpatient treatment is the term for treatment that occurs while a patient is in a psychiatric hospital or psychiatric unit of a general hospital; it is the most intensive level of treatment and is provided mainly in either of the following situations:

- Individuals are believed to be at risk of harming themselves or another person (or have already done so).
- Individuals cannot adequately take care of themselves.

2. Partial Hospitalization

- For *partial hospitalization,* a hospital or other facility provides this treatment, but the patient does not sleep there.
- This type of treatment is appropriate for people who are not actively dangerous to themselves or others.
- Partial hospitalization lasts from 2–12 hours daily.
- Examples include *day treatment programs* and *evening programs.*

3. Residential Treatment

- During *residential treatment,* patients stay in a staffed facility where patients sleep, eat breakfast and dinner, and take part in evening group therapy.
- During the day, patients go elsewhere, such as to a partial hospitalization program, school, or work.
- Residential treatment is for people who do not need the intensity of inpatient care, but need supervised care during the evening and night.

4. Self-Help

- Self-help groups act as a supplement to individual therapy or in place of therapy.
- The focus of self-help groups is on a particular problem or disorder.
- The leader is not clinically trained, although a mental health professional may advise the group.
- Attending a self-help group can diminish feelings of shame and isolation, as well as provide support and valuable information.

LEARNING ACTIVITY 4.10: Attend a Group or Community Workshop

Objective: To provide students with an opportunity to learn about community-based mental health and group therapy.

Time: 60–80 Minutes

Directions: Attend a local self-help group (*Examples:* Alcoholics Anonymous, Depression and Bipolar Support Alliance Group, etc.).

Summary: Students often have stereotypes about who attends community groups. Many students think that group members will be "crazy" or disheveled. Attending a group will teach students that people with mental illnesses look and act like they or people they know do.

Questions to Students and Discussion: What did you find most interesting about this experience? Do you think community supported treatments are helpful? What are some problems with this form of treatment? Would you recommend your group to a friend?

a. Self-Help Books and Materials:

(1) Bibliotherapy:

Bibliotherapy refers to the therapist advising patients to read relevant books to understand causes and treatments for their disorder.

(2) The Internet:

Provides educational materials, chat rooms that serve as support groups, and interactive self-help treatments

(3) Interactive self-help computerized programs:

Involves automatically adapting to the user's responses; they are more complex than a self-help book or video, but they are unlikely to surpass live therapy in terms of patient satisfaction and quality of treatment

5. Prevention Programs

- Prevent or inhibit the development of psychological problems or disorders
- Target any or all neuropsychosocial factors, but the creation of such programs relies crucially on social factors
- Offer ways of dealing with a number of issues, including early intervention for people who have been identified as having an elevated risk of a particular psychological disorder, such as
  i. those with a family history of a particular disorder
  ii. those who have experienced a traumatic event
  iii. children whose parents have divorced

E. Targeting Social Factors in Younger and Older Populations

Treatments for children and older adults that target social factors may need to be modified in the following ways.

1. Targeting Social Factors in Younger Patients

- Family therapy is used for children with psychological disorders and may focus on parental guidance, instructing parents how to interact more adaptively with their children.
- Group therapy for children and adolescents helps develop social skills with peers.
- Parental groups may help parents to improve parenting skills and decrease their isolation.
- Consultation with schools and teachers may help specific child-teacher or child-peer interactions.

2. Targeting Social Factors in Older Patients

- Treatment may involve family therapy to help the patient and family members plan long-term care.
- Sessions may include members of an elder's health care team.

F. Treating a Multicultural Population

In 2025, approximately 40% of adults and almost half of all children in the United States will be from a racial or ethnic minority group. One social factor that may affect treatment is the demographic characteristics of the patient. [See *Figure 4.6.*]

1. How Ethnicity Can Influence Treatment

- The patient's ethnic background, race, or sexual orientation can influence the type of treatment used or modifications to the treatment.

- Differences between the patient and therapist can lead to misunderstandings about treatment goals, methods, and expectations.

MEDIA RECOMMENDATION 4.11: Hold Your Breath

Objective: To explore the role of ethnicity in treatment.

Time: 58 Minutes

Media and Discussion: 90 Minutes

Discussion Only: 30 Minutes

Watch Online: A clip of Grainger-Monson, M. (2005). *Hold your breath.* Fanlight Productions. Program in Bioethics and Film. Stanford Center for Biomedical Ethics. http://medethicsfilms.stanford.edu/holdyourbreath/trailer.html

Purchase: http://fanlight.com/catalog/films/456_hyb.php

This film portrays Kochi, an Afghan immigrant, who develops terminal cancer. Trouble ensues from the conflicts with Kochi's religious beliefs and cultural miscommunication between the physician and Kochi's family.

Summary: Students will be amazed at how easily cultural miscommunication can occur. Students can identify possible causes of the miscommunication and can discuss how to avoid these in their own professional work.

Questions to Students and Discussion: What are the cultural miscommunications that occurred? How could they have been prevented? What are possible miscommunications that could occur in the clinical setting?

LECTURE ENHANCEMENT 4.1: Ethnicity and Mental Health Care

Objective: To explore possible forms of discrimination in the mental health system and in treatment.

Time: 30–40 Minutes

Explore Online: U.S. Department of Health and Human Services. (2001). *Mental health: Culture, race, and ethnicity. A supplement to mental health: A report of the Surgeon General.* Rockville, MD: U.S. Department of Health and Human Services, Substance Abuse and Mental Health Services Administration, Center for Mental Health Services. Retrieved October 12, 2008, from http://www.surgeongeneral.gov/library/mentalhealth/cre/sma-01-3613.pdf

Explore: Sue, D. W., Capodilupo, C. M., Torino, G. C., Bucceri, J. M., Holder, A. M., Nadal, K. L., & Esquilin, M. (2007). Racial microaggressions in everyday life: Implications for clinical practice. *American Psychologist, 62*(4), 271–286.

Summary: Both documents discuss the mental health system's treatment of ethnic minorities. The first report examines the differences in treatment and mental health care utilization by ethnicity. The second article explores unintentional forms of racism by white counselors toward their minority clients.

Questions to Students and Discussion: What do you think needs to be improved in the mental health system's treatment of minorities? How could changes be accomplished?

2. Using Mental Health Services

Minorities generally do not use mental health services as often as do Whites. Several reasons for the underutilization of services among minority groups include:

- Lesser likelihood of their having health insurance coverage, which reduces their ability to pay for treatment.

- Existence of mental health treatment barriers such as geographic limits and limited English proficiency [see *Figure 4.7*]

- Mistrust based on past experiences, when minority groups felt disrespected or judged unfairly

- Awareness of past abuses by mental health institutions and professionals, including fear of being "experimented on"

- Possibility of mental health care carrying a stigma in some communities

- The tendency to sometimes seek alternative services—for example, from a minister or traditional healer who is a member of their community—before turning to standard mental health services

- The more frequent seeking of treatment from their primary care physician

3. Bridging a Cultural Gap Between Patient and Clinician

Cultural competence, or tailoring treatment to the needs of a specific cultural group or its members, leads to higher use and benefit of treatments and includes:

- Awareness of the biases and assumptions the clinician has about mental health, mental illness, and treatment

- Understanding of the different biases and assumptions held by people from other ethnic groups

- Collaborative development of treatment goals that respect the patient's background

a. Cultural Competence and Medication:

- Awareness that people from ethnic groups may respond to medication differently than people who do not belong to these groups

- Client's preference for counseling over medication

- The possibility that different ethnic groups may metabolize drugs differently

b. Culturally Specific Treatment:

- When appropriate, clinicians who speak the patient's language act as translators

- Specific outreach programs to community members about mental health treatment that fits in with the particular ethnic group's view of mental health and mental illness

c. Cultural Sensitivity in Treatment:

- Avoiding the assumption that a patient's different ethnic or racial background or sexual orientation will lead to misunderstandings
- Therapist sensitivity to *possible* differences
- Therapist inquiring about ways that the patient's culture, sexual orientation, or difference in background from the therapist's own may influence symptoms or treatment [see *Case 4.3*]

G. Finances and Managed Care

Managed care is a plan that restricts access to specialized medical care by limiting benefits or reimbursement, thus minimizing expenses without restricting necessary services by:

- Restricting the number of inpatient days
- Restricting the mental health facilities to those who have previously negotiated an agreed on rate
- Paying for partial hospitalization rather than inpatient care
- Restricting the number of days a patient can remain in partial hospitalization
- Limiting the number of outpatient sessions or services covered

To minimize the adverse effects of these restrictions, in 2008, the U.S. Congress passed the Wellstone-Domenici Mental Health Parity Act; the Act mandates that most insurance plans provide comparable levels of treatment benefits for mental and physical health.

IV. CREATING A TREATMENT PLAN

We've considered many different types of treatment, but which particular course of treatment should someone choose?

A. Choosing a Specific Treatment

How would a clinician decide what type of treatment to offer? The choice of treatment depends on the following:

- The clinician's training
- The types of treatment the patient is willing to try
- The types of treatment most appropriate for a particular problem

B. Choosing One or More Treatments

A given patient may receive more than one form of treatment depending on:

- The nature of the problem
- The patient's preferences
- Whether a single treatment sufficiently alleviates symptoms or improves quality of life
- Constraints arising from health insurance coverage or finances
- Treatments that directly target different factors, including neurological, psychological, or social factors

ADDITIONAL READINGS

Barber, C. (2008, February). The medicated Americans: Antidepressant prescriptions on the rise. *Scientific American.* Retrieved October 11, 2008, from http://www.sciam.com/article.cfm?id= the-medicated-americans

Beck, A. T. (2005). The current state of cognitive therapy: A 40-year retrospective. *Archives of General Psychiatry, 62,* 953–959.

Bernal, G., & Scharrón-Del-Río, M. R. (2001). Are empirically supported treatments valid for ethnic minorities? Toward an alternative approach for treatment research. *Cultural Diversity and Ethnic Minority Psychology, 7,* 328–342.

Beutler, L. E. (2002). The dodo bird is extinct. *Clinical Psychology: Science and Practice, 9,* 30–34.

Carter, E. M., & McGoldrick, M. (2004). *The expanded family life cycle: Individual, family, and social perspectives.* Needham Heights, MA: Allyn & Bacon.

Falicov, C. J. (1998). *Latino families in therapy: A guide to multicultural practice.* New York: Guilford Press.

Helms, J. E., & Cook, D. A. (1999). *Using race and culture in counseling and psychotherapy: Theory and process.* Needham Heights, MA: Allyn & Bacon.

Lin, K. M., & Cheung, F. (1999). Mental health issues for Asian Americans. *Psychiatric Services, 50,* 774–780.

Lin, K. M., Cheung, F., Smith, M., & Poland, R. E. (1997). The use of psychotropic medications in working with Asian patients. In E. Lee (Ed.), *Working with Asian Americans: A guide for clinicians* (pp. 388–399). New York: Guilford Press.

Linehan, M. M. (1993). *Cognitive-behavioral treatment of borderline personality disorder.* New York: Guilford Press.

Minuchin, S. (1974). *Families and family therapy.* Cambridge, MA: Harvard University Press.

Ng, C. H. (1997). The stigma of mental illness in Asian cultures. *Australian and New Zealand Journal of Psychiatry, 31,* 382–390.

Ready, D. J., Pollack, S., Rothbaum, B. O., & Alarcon, R. D. (2006). Virtual reality exposure for veterans with posttraumatic stress disorder. *Journal of Aggression, Maltreatment & Trauma, 12,* 199–220.

U.S. Department of Health and Human Services. (2001). *Mental health: Culture, race, and ethnicity. A supplement to mental health: A report of the Surgeon General.* Rockville, MD: U.S. Department of Health and Human Services, Substance Abuse and Mental Health Services Administration, Center for Mental Health Services. Retrieved October 12, 2008, from http://www.surgeongeneral.gov/library/mentalhealth/cre/sma-01-3613.pdf

Wampold, B. E. (2001). *The great psychotherapy debate: Models, methods, and findings.* Mahwah, NJ: Erlbaum.

ADDITIONAL MEDIA RECOMMENDATIONS

Berlinger, J., & Sinofsky, B. (Directors). (2004). *Some kind of monster.* [Film]. United States: Radical Media.
    This film takes viewers inside the intimate and personal group therapy sessions with the band Metallica.

Forman, M. (Director). (1976). *One flew over the cuckoo's nest.* [Film]. United States: Fantasy Films.

This film is set inside a psychiatric hospital and shows the results of a lobotomy.

Levinson, S., Leight, W., Wahlberg, M., Garcia, R., Barclay, P., & Levi, H. (Producers). (2008). *In treatment.* [Television series]. Home Box Office Incorporated.

This cable television series follows the practice of a psychoanalyst, capturing sessions with his patients.

LeVine, D. J., & Levine, D. (Writers). (2009) *Mental.* [Television series]. Atlanta, GA: Fox Broadcasting.

This series follows a psychiatrist working as the director of mental services as a Los Angeles hospital and shows intense, often controversial, treatments for serious forms of mental illness.]

Oz, F. (Director). (1991). *What about Bob?* [Film]. United States: Touchstone Pictures.

The film illustrates one therapist's struggle with establishing boundaries with his client, Bob.

Ramis, H. (Director). (1999). *Analyze this.* [Film]. United States: Village Roadshow Pictures.

This film takes a look at an atypical approach to therapy.

Shostrom, E. (Producer and Director). (1986). *Three approaches to psychotherapy.* [Film]. Orange, CA: Psychological Films.

This three-part film demonstrates the client-centered therapy approaches of Carl Rogers, Frederick Perls, and Albert Ellis.

WORKSHEET 4.1
FIVE COMMON COGNITIVE DISTORTIONS

Cognitive Distortion	Definition	Personal Example
Dichotomous thinking or black-and-white thinking	Extremes of an idea	
Mental filtering	Focusing on the negative qualities and overlooking positive qualities	
Mind reading	Assuming what other people are thinking about you	
Catastrophic exaggeration	Assuming the worst possible circumstance will happen and that you can't handle it	
Control beliefs	Believing that unless you maintain control things will spin totally out of control	

Researching Abnormality

CHAPTER OUTLINE

CHAPTER HEADINGS	INSTRUCTION IDEAS AND TEXTBOOK CORRELATIONS
Chapter Introduction	**Learning Activity 5.1:** Thinking Like a Psychopathology Researcher
USING THE SCIENTIFIC METHOD FOR UNDERSTANDING ABNORMALITY	
The Scientific Method	**Learning Objectives:** 5.1, 5.2 **Learning Concepts:** identify a question, collect initial data, develop a hypothesis, collect data to test the hypothesis, develop a theory, test the theory **Textbook Tool:** Figure 5.1
Types of Scientific Research	**Learning Objective:** 5.3, 5.4, 5.5, 5.6, 5.7, 5.8 **Learning Concepts:** conduct research with experiments, quasi-experimental design, independent and dependent variables, control groups and conditions, unintentional bias, internal and external validity, correlation does not imply causation, measuring a correlation, statistical significance, using correlational methods, uses and limits of case studies **Learning Activity 5.2:** Identifying the Independent and Dependent Variables **Learning Activity 5.3:** Does Correlation Mean Causation? **Media Recommendation 5.1:** The *Up* Series **Lecture Enhancement 5.1:** Feral Children **Learning Activity 5.4:** Design Your Own Experiment **Learning Activity 5.5:** Comparison of Research Methods **Textbook Tool:** Figures 5.2, 5.3; Table 5.1; Case 5.1
Ethical Guidelines for Research	**Learning Objective:** 5.9 **Learning Activity 5.6:** Informed Consent Forms **Textbook Tool:** Table 5.2
RESEARCH CHALLENGES IN UNDERSTANDING ABNORMALITY	

Challenges in Researching Neurological Factors	**Learning Objective:** 5.10
Challenges in Researching Psychological Factors	**Learning Objective:** 5.11 **Learning Concepts:** biases in mental processes that affect assessment, research challenges with clinical interviews, research challenges with questionnaires
Challenges in Researching Social Factors	**Learning Objective:** 5.12 **Learning Concepts:** investigator-influenced biases, experimenter expectancy effects, reducing experimenter expectancy effects with a double-blind design, reactivity **Media Recommendation 5.2:** Facilitated Communication **Textbook Tools:** Figures 5.4, 5.5 **Worth Video Tool Kit for Abnormal Psychology:** Scientific Method: How Double Blind Clinical Trials Are Done
RESEARCHING TREATMENT	
Researching Treatments That Target Neurological Factors	**Learning Objectives:** 5.13, 5.14 **Learning Concepts:** drug effect or placebo effect, dropouts
Researching Treatments That Target Psychological Factors	**Learning Objectives:** 5.15, 5.16, 5.17, 5.18, 5.19, 5.21 **Learning Concepts:** common factors, specific factors, controlling possible confounding variables with analogue studies, [therapy versus no treatment], [determining the most effective treatment], [best therapy for treating a specific disorder], randomized clinical trials, importance of follow-up assessment, exclusion criteria, manual-based treatment, allegiance effect, empirically supported treatment/evidence based practice, criticisms of RCTs, ethical research on experimental treatments, therapy dose-response relationship **Lecture Enhancement 5.2:** Common Factors **Media Recommendation 5.3:** What Really Works in Therapy? **Lecture Enhancement 5.3:** Is Therapy Helpful? **Textbook Tools:** Figures 5.6, 5.7; Tables 5.3, 5.4 **Worth Video Tool Kit for Abnormal Psychology:** The Controversy of Antidepressants for Children
Researching Treatment That Targets Social Factors	**Learning Objective:** 5.21 **Learning Concepts:** matching patient and therapist by gender and ethnicity, culturally sanctioned placebo effects
FEEDBACK LOOPS IN ACTION: The Placebo Effect	

LEARNING OBJECTIVES

After reading this chapter, students should be able to:

5.1 Identify the stages of the scientific method.

5.2 Apply the stages of the scientific method to psychopathology research.

5.3 Compare and contrast the different types of scientific research.

5.4 Identify independent and dependent variables.

5.5 Describe the importance of the control group and random assignment.

5.6 Compare and contrast internal and external validity.

5.7 Describe the main components of the quasi-experimental design.

5.8 Identify the strengths and weaknesses of correlational, case, single-participant studies, and meta-analyses.

5.9 List the information to be included when obtaining informed consent.

5.10 Identify key challenges when researching neurological factors.

5.11 Identify key challenges when researching psychological factors.

5.12 Identify key challenges when researching social factors.

5.13 Describe the importance of the placebo in neurological studies.

5.14 Identify the problems that result due to participant dropouts.

5.15 Name and describe the common factors.

5.16 Describe the challenges researchers face when wanting to study specific factors.

5.17 Provide empirical support for the effectiveness of treatment.

5.18 Explain the dodo bird verdict.

5.19 Describe the components of randomized clinical trials.

5.20 Identify the strengths and weaknesses of randomized clinical trials.

5.21 Describe the results of the therapy-dose response relationship, gender and ethnicity matching, and culturally sanctioned placebo effects.

KEY TERMS

Scientific method: The process of gathering and interpreting facts that can lead to the formulation of a new theory or the validation of an existing theory.

Data: Numerical measurements or systematic observations of phenomena.

Replication: The process of repeating a study using the same data collection methods under identical or nearly identical conditions to obtain data that should have the same characteristics as the original study.

Hypothesis: A preliminary idea that is proposed to explain a set of data.

Theory: A principle (or set of principles) that explains a set of data.

Predictions: Hypotheses that should be confirmed if a theory is correct.

Experiments: Research studies in which investigators intentionally manipulate one variable at a time, and measure the consequences of such manipulation on one or more other variables.

Independent variable: A variable that a researcher manipulates.

Dependent variable: A variable that may change as a result of manipulating the independent variable.

Confounding variables: Factors that might inadvertently affect the variables of interest in an experiment; also called *confounds*.

Control group: A group of participants in an experiment for which the independent variable is not manipulated, but which is otherwise treated identically to the experimental group.

Bias: Any inadvertent influence on factors that can affect data in systematic ways.

Random assignment: Assigning participants to each group in a study using a procedure that relies on chance.

Population: The complete set of possible participants.

Sample: The small portion of a population that is examined in a study.

Sampling bias: The distortion in data that can occur when the participants in an experiment have not been drawn randomly from the relevant population under investigation.

Internal validity: A characteristic of a study that measures what it purports to measure because it has controlled for confounds.

External validity: A characteristic of a study whose results generalize from the sample to the population from which it was drawn and from the conditions used in the study to similar conditions outside the study.

Correlation: The relationship between the measurements made of two variables in which a change in the value of one variable is associated with a change in the value of the other variable.

Correlation coefficient: A number that quantifies the strength of the correlation between two variables; the correlation coefficient is most typically symbolized by r.

Statistically significant: The condition where the probability of obtaining the value of a statistical test is greater than what would be expected by chance alone.

Epidemiology: The type of correlational research that investigates the rate of occurrence, the possible causes and risk factors, and the course of diseases or disorders.

Longitudinal studies (in studies of psychopathology): Research studies that are designed to determine whether a given variable is a risk factor by using data collected from the same participants at various points in time.

Case study (in studies of psychopathology): A research method that focuses in detail on one individual and the factors that underlie that person's psychological disorder or disorders.

Single-participant experiments: Experiments with only a single participant.

Meta-analysis: A research method that statistically combines the results of a number of studies that address the same general question.

Response bias: The tendency to respond in a particular way, regardless of what is being asked by the question.

Social desirability: A bias toward answering questions in a way that respondents think makes them "look good" (i.e., that they think is socially desirable), even if the responses are not true.

Experimenter expectancy effect: The experimenter's intentionally or unintentionally treating participants in ways that encourage particular types of responses.

Double-blind design: A research design in which neither the participant nor the researcher knows the group to which specific participants have been assigned or the predicted results of the study.

Reactivity: A behavior change that occurs when one becomes aware of being observed.

Placebo effect: A positive effect of a medically inert substance or procedure.

Attrition: The reduction in the number of participants during a research study.

Common factors: Helpful aspects of therapy that are shared by virtually all types of psychotherapy.

Specific factors: The characteristics of a particular treatment or technique that lead it to have unique benefits, above and beyond those conferred by common factors.

Analogue study: Research in which treatment is provided in a way that is analogous to the way it is usually provided, but that is conducted under controlled conditions in a laboratory setting, thereby minimizing confounds.

Randomized clinical trial (RCT): A research design that has at least two groups—a treatment group and a control group (usually a placebo control)—to which participants are randomly assigned.

Allegiance effect: A pattern in which studies conducted by investigators who prefer a particular theoretical orientation tend to obtain data that support that particular orientation.

Dose-response relationship: The association between more treatment (a higher dose) and greater improvement (a better response).

CHAPTER GUIDE

Chapter Introduction

This chapter explores various methods used to study psychopathology, examines problems with these studies, and explains ways researchers attempt to address these challenges.

LEARNING ACTIVITY 5.1: Thinking Like a Psychopathology Researcher

Objective: The purpose of this activity is to increase students' excitement about the topic of research by having them identify questions and possible methods to research the identified questions.

Time: 20 Minutes

Directions:
1. Have students meet in small groups and develop a psychopathology-related question they would like to answer. For example, students might want to know whether therapy or medication is more effective for treating depression.
2. Ask students what methods they might use to answer this question. For example, will they use surveys, clinicians' observations, interviews?
3. Have students write their question and methods on the board.
4. After students have posted their responses, highlight similarities and differences among the methods to study the same problem.
5. Highlight student examples in your review of the steps of the scientific method.

Summary: This exercise will get students thinking about the ways to study psychopathology, the challenges that face researchers in choosing the best design, and how to enhance critical-thinking skills.

Questions to Students and Discussion: What kinds of psychopathology-related questions would a survey best answer? What kinds of questions would a clinical observation best answer? What kinds of questions would an interview best answer?

I. USING THE SCIENTIFIC METHOD FOR UNDERSTANDING ABNORMALITY

The *scientific method* is the process of gathering and interpreting facts that can lead to the formulation of a new theory or the validation of an existing theory.

A. The Scientific Method Includes the Following Steps [see *Figure 5.1*]:

1. Collect Initial Observations

- Sometimes the researcher's initial observations lead directly to the next steps, but they may also lead the researcher to describe the phenomenon more carefully and systematically by collecting data.

- Collecting *data* (numerical measurements or methodical observations of phenomena) helps in developing scientific facts. *Example:* questionnaires answered by people who have recently gone through a breakup or depression after receiving medication and counseling.

- In most scientific fields, properly collected data can be **replicated,** or similar findings arrived at, under identical or nearly identical conditions.

- Researchers collect data about *variables*—measurable characteristics of the object or event of interest, such as measurements of brain activity, hormone or symptom levels, behavior, and observed family interactions.

- Variables include categorical and continuum types.
  i. **Categorical variables** are records of nonnumerical information.
  ii. **Continuum variables** are numbers on a scale or range.

2. Identify a Question

The process of explaining a set of observations begins by asking a specific question, which identifies an area where properly conducted research can point toward an answer.

3. Develop a Hypothesis

A *hypothesis* is a preliminary idea that is proposed to explain a set of data or relationship among the variables in the question you've asked.

4. Collect Data to Test the Hypothesis

Researchers systematically collect data to test the hypothesis; this might include recruiting participants to complete questionnaires, brain scans, measurements, etc.

5. Develop a Theory

A *theory* is a principle (or set of principles) that explains a set of data and provides an answer to the question identified by the researcher.

6. Test the Theory

Researchers collect and examine additional data that might lead to *predictions*— hypotheses that should be confirmed if a theory is correct.

B. Types of Scientific Research

There are many ways to study specific questions, and each have strengths and weaknesses; the various research methods include experiments and quasi-experimental designs, correlational studies, case studies, single participant experiments, and meta-analyses.

1. Conducting Research with Experiments

Experiments are research studies in which investigators intentionally manipulate one variable at a time and measure the consequences of such manipulation on one or more other variables; they are the ideal method for conducting research.

a. Independent Variables and Dependent Variables:

Two kinds of variables: those that are manipulated and those that are measured. *Independent variables* are the variables that a researcher manipulates or changes. *Dependent variables* are variables that are measured in terms of the changes that occur as a result of manipulation of the independent variable.

LEARNING ACTIVITY 5.2: Identifying the Independent and Dependent Variables

Objective: To have students practice identifying independent and dependent variables.

Time: 30 Minutes

Directions: Have students write in large letters on one side of a piece of paper "IV" (for independent variables) and on the other side "DV" (for dependent variables). For each of the following research conditions, ask students to show you the IV or DV side of the piece of paper. In large lecture rooms, you can have students use clickers or turn to the right (for independent variables) or left (for dependent variables).

1. The research question: "Does the drug Viagra increase male sexual drive?" In a study, one group of men receives Viagra while another group of men receives a placebo.
2. The research question: "Is virtual reality therapy helpful in treating flying phobias?" In a study, half of the participants learn to relax while watching various images related to flying on a plane while the other half of participants watch a nature film.
3. The research question: "Is the thought-stopping technique (in which clients are told to yell 'Stop' when they have obsessive thinking) helpful in reducing obsessive-compulsive symptoms?"

Summary: This activity offers students a chance to practice identifying independent and dependent variables in psychopathology research. It also provides a way to make a quick assessment of students' understanding of these concepts

Questions to Students and Discussion: (1): "Is Viagra the IV or the DV?" (It's the IV.) "Is the level of sexual desire the IV or the DV?" (It's the DV.); (2): "Is the virtual-reality treatment the IV or the DV?" (It's the IV.) "Is the level of anxiety the IV or the DV?" (It's the DV.); (3): "Is the thought-stopping technique the IV or DV?" (It's the IV.) "Is the number of obsessive-compulsive symptoms the IV or DV?" (It's the DV.)

- Limitations of experimental research:
    i. Researchers cannot cause certain variables (such as creating a loss in a person's life or causing depression in clients); thus, researchers are limited in what they can study.
    ii. All research is vulnerable to ***confounding variables*** (or *confounds*), factors that might inadvertently affect the variables of interest in the experiment. To minimize the possibility of confounds, the researcher should try to examine every reasonable hypothesis that might explain the effect.

b. **Control Groups and Conditions:**

   Control groups and conditions limit the effect of confounds in an experiment. The experimental group (or groups) and the ***control group*** are treated identically throughout the experiment, but the control group does not receive the manipulation. Control groups should have similar characteristics as the experimental group and each group should be treated similarly.

c. **Bias:**

   - ***Bias*** occurs when the researcher consciously or inadvertently treats the experimental and control groups differently (*Example:* smiling more in the presence of one group than another).
   - To control against bias, researchers use ***random assignment,*** in which each participant has the same chance of being assigned to the control or experimental group.

- The *population* is the complete set of possible participants (*Example:* all rats or all people, or in certain cases all people of a certain age, gender, or race). The *sample* is the small portion of the population examined in the study.
- *Sampling bias* occurs when the participants are not drawn randomly from the relevant population, which prevents the research from being generalized or applied to the wider population.

d. Internal and External Validity:

Informs the consumer about the quality of the research.

- *Internal validity* is high if it controls for confounding variables, thus increasing the likelihood that the independent variable is responsible for variations in the dependent variable.
- *External validity* is high when the results generalize from the sample (the particular participants) to the general population. If a study does not have internal validity, it cannot have external validity; however, internal validity does not guarantee external validity.

2. Quasi-Experimental Design

- **Quasi-experimental designs** rely on groups that already exist because in many cases, random assignment is not ethical, desirable, or possible.
- Participants are sorted into groups according to specific criteria, yet researchers still try to control for possible confounding variables.

3. Correlational Research

- **Correlational research** is utilized when independent variables can't or shouldn't be manipulated.
- Researchers thus can study the relationship among variables by looking at the *correlation,* or the relationship between two variables when a change in the value of one variable is associated with a change in the value of the other variable.

a. Characteristics of Correlations:

- The stronger the correlation, the more closely related the variables are.
- There are no independent and dependent variables in correlational research because no manipulation is taking place; instead, naturally occurring variations among measurements of different variables are compared.
- **Correlation Does Not Imply Causation.** A correlation measures a relationship but does not demonstrate that one variable *causes* the other.
- Correlations do not control for possible confounding variables.

LEARNING ACTIVITY 5.3: Does Correlation Mean Causation?

Objective: Students often have difficulty understanding that correlation does not mean causation. In order to drive this idea home, use the following correlations to explore possible third factors that influence the two variables.

Time: 20 Minutes

Directions: Post the following correlations on the board and ask students to come up with an explanation for the results. Next, have them think of a third variable that is likely to affect/cause both variables.

1. Couples that cohabitate are more likely to get divorced.
2. If a community has more churches, it is likely to have more bars.
3. The higher number of televisions per person in a country is related to longer life expectancy.
4. The more household appliances a couple has the more frequently the couple has sex.
5. The more people pray for someone in the hospital the faster the patient heals.
6. The higher the amount of ice cream consumed the more drownings in a community.

Sources for the correlations:
1–3: Ferguson, T. J. Utah State University. *Correlation does not imply causation.*
http://www.mrbakerrocks.info/Correlation%20Does%20Not%20Imply%20Causation.doc
4–6: Unknown.

Summary: These examples highlight why correlation does not mean causation. Students should see that there are a number of variables that can explain the correlations.
1. Third variable: couples may be more liberal and thus more open to divorce.
2. Third variable: larger communities have more bars and churches.
3. Third variable: wealthier communities can afford more televisions and tend to have higher life expectancies.
4. Third variable: wealthier couples have more appliances and possibly less stress.
5. Third variable: social support can be linked to more prayer and better health.
6. Third variable: ice cream consumption increases in the summer, a season when there are more people in the water.

Questions to Students and Discussion: Does correlation imply causation? Why or why not?

b. Measuring a Correlation:

- A *correlation coefficient* is a number that indicates the strength between any two variables (most typically symbolized by r).

- A positive number between 0 and $+1$ signifies that the variables change in the same direction; both variables either increase or decrease in the same general pattern.

- A negative number from 0 to -1 indicates that the variables change in opposite directions in the same general pattern; one goes up while the other goes down.

- When plotting two variables on a graph, putting one variable on each axis, you can see whether or not the variables change together. The closer the data points are to a straight line, the stronger the correlation. [See *Figure 5.2.*]

c. Statistical Significance:

- *Statistical significance* means that the correlation is not due to chance and is more meaningful when the research uses a larger sample.

- **Probability** or p indicates the likelihood that the correlation is due to chance. The p value is found in the appendices of most statistics textbooks.

- $p < .01$ means that the probability that the correlation is due to chance is less than 1 in 100.

- $p < .05$ means the probability that the correlation is due to chance is less than 5 in 100; this is usually considered the cutoff for statistical significance.

d. Using Correlational Methods:

- Most psychopathology research is correlational.

- *Epidemiology* is a type of correlational research that investigates the rate of occurrence, the possible causes and risk factors (*Examples:* the age of onset of a disorder, the number of people in the family who have had symptoms of the disorder, and socioeconomic status), and the course or severity of diseases or disorders in relation to other variables.

- *Longitudinal studies* collect data from the same participants over time. For example, some longitudinal studies track a group of children or adults over time and observe whether a disorder develops.

MEDIA RECOMMENDATION 5.1: The *Up* Series

Objective: To show students a visual image of a longitudinal study. The films can be shown in class or assigned for students to watch on their own.

Time: YouTube clip of *49 Up:* 2 Minutes, 54 Seconds
Seven Up: 39 Minutes
7 Plus Seven: 52 Minutes
21: 100 Minutes
28 Up: 136 Minutes
35 Up: 123 Minutes
42: Forty Two Up: 139 Minutes
49 Up: 134 Minutes

Watch Online:
Clips of the film can be seen on YouTube (use search terms "Up Series") or
http://www.youtube.com/watch?v=_rQ1V7m0Kfs

Description: In 1964, *Seven Up* featured 14 English children from diverse socioeconomic backgrounds. Every seven years, director Michael Apted met with as many members of the original group as possible in order to find out about their lives, decisions, and development. This documentary series shows a longitudinal study that examines the same participants repeatedly over time.

Questions to Students and Summary: For how many years were the participants tracked so far? What is this type of study called? What can't researchers determine from this type of study?

4. **Case Studies**

   Case studies focus on one individual and multiple factors that may underlie that person's psychological disorder or disorders and can alert clinicians to possible factors that may exacerbate symptoms of a particular disorder. [See *Case 5.1.*]

LECTURE ENHANCEMENT 5.1: Feral Children

Objective: The case study of Genie helps students understand the strengths and weaknesses of the case approach. Specifically, students will learn about when case studies are particularly useful, as well as ethical issues that may arise in clinical case studies.

Time: 1 Hour, 15 Minutes

Media and Discussion: 2 Hours

Discussion Only: 45 Minutes

Explore Online:
Nova: *Secrets of the Wild Child.* Transcripts and teacher's guide available at:
http://www.pbs.org/wgbh/nova/transcripts/2112gchild.html

The BBC version of *Secrets of the Wild Child* can be found on YouTube (using the search terms "Genie Wild Child") or http://www.youtube.com/watch?v=ICUZN462qMw

Winfrey, O. (2009). The little girl found living like an animal.
Photos, summary, and guide to working with traumatized children can be found at:
http://www.oprah.com/dated/oprahshow/oprahshow-20081016-feral-child

Lecture Points:
1. Genie was a 13-year-old girl who was raised in isolation in her Los Angeles home, tied to a potty chair, and never taught to speak.
2. Genie was a case study in which psychologists could test their theories of nature versus nurture. Psychologists were particularly interested in finding out whether Genie had passed the "critical" period of learning language. Since psychologists cannot ethically cause severe neglect, Genie's "case" allowed them to study neglect, language development, and attachment in ways they are unable to otherwise.
3. Genie was able to learn some basics of language, attachment, and social interaction. However, her knowledge remained limited. It was unclear whether Genie was mentally retarded from birth or whether her difficulties were due to severe isolation and abuse.
4. The psychologists struggled with custody issues, overworking Genie, long-term care, and dual roles of the therapist and the scientist.
5. For current research on the same topic, see child psychiatrist Dr. Bruce Perry's discussion—featured in the Oprah clip—of the effects of extreme neglect on brain development. The episode shows brain scans of normal children and those of neglected children.

Summary: This enhancement highlights the strengths and weaknesses of the case approach. The case approach allows psychologists to examine clients who have life experiences that cannot be ethically created in an experiment. However, many ethical issues can arise through case studies, as seen in Genie's case.

Questions to Students and Discussion: Who was Genie? Why is Genie so interesting to psychologists? What did they find out? What ethical issues were raised by this case study?

    a. Uses and Limits of Case Studies:
    Case studies are used:

- to demonstrate aspects of diagnoses, etiology, or treatment(s);
- to provide support for (or evidence against) a hypothesis or theory; and
- to train other mental health professionals, who are given case studies in order to propose diagnoses and appropriate treatments.

    A limitation of case studies is:

- It is impossible to *generalize* from a single case because findings from a case study cannot necessarily be extended to other similar cases, as there are many confounding factors.

5. Single-Participant Experiments

Single-participant experiments are experiments with only a single participant. Watson and Rayner conducted a single-participant experiment with Little Albert. Single-participant experiments may rely on the *ABAB design.*

- A is the baseline condition (before treatment), B is the behavior during the treatment (*Example:* behavior modification, or any other type of treatment).
- The data on the target behavior in the baseline phase (A) are compared to the data on that behavior in the next phase (B).
- The second A phase is the measured behavior when the treatment is withdrawn and the second B is when the treatment is presented again.

LEARNING ACTIVITY 5.4: Design Your Own Single-Subject Experiment

Objective: Students will create their own single-subject design.

Time: 20 Minutes

Directions:
1. Identify a behavior you would like to change, for example, to stop smoking.
2. Identify a type of treatment for this behavior, for example, chewing gum instead of smoking.
3. Hypothetically graph the ABAB phases using *Figure 5.3* as a guide.
   - Identify the baseline and treatment phases.
   - Label the *x* (targeted behavior) and *y* (time) axes.
   - Hypothetically chart the data.

Summary: This exercise helps students see how a researcher might use a single-subject experiment to study a treatment.

Questions to Students and Discussion: What did you like about this type of design? What are the design's limitations or drawbacks?

a. Uses and Limitations of Single-Participant Experiments:

Single-participant experiments are used:

- to help clinicians determine which interventions may be effective for a patient's behavior with the same problem and in similar circumstances.

Limitations of single-participant experiments are:

- results of one study cannot be generalized to others because the results are specific to that individual.
- confounding variables limit the generalizability.

6. Meta-Analysis

Meta-analysis is a research method that statistically combines the results of a number of studies, thus increasing the size of the overall data set which determines whether certain variables are related. But meta-analysis has some drawbacks:

- Many studies fail to find significant effects and, therefore, are never published (called the *file drawer problem*).
- Meta-analyses should be followed up with new studies that directly test their conclusions. [See *Table 5.1.*]

LEARNING ACTIVITY 5.5: Comparison of Research Methods

Objective: To provide students with a quick comparison and summary of the research methods.

Time: 30 Minutes

Directions: Ask students to form small groups and complete the table provided in *Worksheet 5.1.*
1. Ask: "In your own words, provide a brief description of the research method."
2. Ask: "Identify each method's benefits and limitations."
3. Ask: "Provide a psychopathology-related example for each type of research."

Summary: *Worksheet 5.1* asks students to summarize the different types of psychopathology research and provide an example for each.

Questions to Students and Discussion: Which method appeals to you most? Why? Which method appeals to you least? Why? Share your examples with a neighboring group.

C. Ethical Guidelines for Research

How do researchers decide which research studies are ethical and which are not?
The ethical code for psychologists states that the following are needed for ethical studies:

- *Informed consent* occurs when the participant understands what is involved in the study and he or she agrees to participate. The participant must be able to withdraw from the study at any time. [*Specific information that is included on informed consent forms can be found in Table 5.2.*]

- *Debriefing* occurs when investigators ask participants about their positive and negative experiences in the study in order to determine if the study needs to be adjusted to minimize harmful aspects and to clear up any misconceptions that the participant may have about the study.

- *Approval* occurs when the Institutional Review Board (IRB), which is composed of scientists, clinicians, and community members, examines the study's risks and benefits, and grants/denies approval of the study.

LEARNING ACTIVITY 5.6: Informed Consent Forms

Objective: Students will examine informed consent forms used in real studies.

Time: 10 Minutes

Directions:
1. Bring a consent form to class and, using the form along with the textbook, ask students the questions shown here.
2. Search for consent forms on google.com (use search terms "psychology consent forms") or download one from one of the following Web sites:
   http://www.muhlenberg.edu/depts/psychology/docs/informedconsent.doc
   http://www.socialpsychology.org/consentform.htm

Description: The consent forms reveal the APA ethical principles that are used in real studies.

Questions to Students and Discussion: Using information from your textbook, what information is missing from the form? What key pieces of information are included? Does anything surprise you about the form? Is there anything you personally feel should be included? Are there differences between Web-based survey consent forms and in-person survey consent forms?

II. RESEARCH CHALLENGES IN UNDERSTANDING ABNORMALITY

Major challenges to research on the nature and causes of abnormality from the neuropsychosocial, psychological, and social approaches are the following:

A. Challenges in Researching Neurological Factors

With the exception of genetics, the techniques that assess neurological factors identify abnormalities in brain structure or function, either directly with neuroimaging or indirectly with neuropsychological testing or by measuring the level of stress hormones in the bloodstream. Such abnormalities are associated (correlated) with specific disorders or symptoms. Thus, the results cannot confirm whether:

- the abnormality existed before the disorder's symptoms
- the symptoms arose because of the abnormality
- a third factor affected the symptoms and the abnormality

Researchers still do not yet have a complete understanding of the function of the brain's structures.

B. Challenges in Researching Psychological Factors

Scientists who study psychological factors examine specific mental contents, behaviors, emotions, or biases in mental processes; this type of research has the following challenges:

1. **Biases in Mental Processes That Affect Assessment**

   - Assessing psychological factors via self-report or report by others can yield inaccurate information because of biases in what people perceive, remember, and report.
   - Individual biases influence recall and reporting.

2. **Research Challenges with Clinical Interviews**

   - Patients' responses may be affected by being asked questions by an interviewer in person. [See *Figure 5.4.*]
   - Family members or friends may have their own biases that will affect the information a clinician is seeking about a patient.

3. **Research Challenges with Questionnaires**

   - Both limiting choices in response to an item to "yes" or "no" and offering an undefined range of answers can lead to biased results.
   - *Response bias* refers to a tendency to respond in a particular way, regardless of what is being asked by the questions. The tendency to agree or *acquiesce* can be reduced by wording half the items negatively.
   - *Social desirability* refers to answering questions in a way that the respondents think make them "look good" (that is, in a way that they think is socially desirable) even if the answer is not true.
   - Some individuals have a tendency to rate most items as an "Average" response especially if they think their responses are too high or too low. [See *Figure 5.5.*]

C. Challenges in Researching Social Factors

For research on psychopathology, a key part of the context is defined by other people.

- Social factors include the ways that the presence or behavior of the investigator and the beliefs and assumptions of a particular culture can influence the responses of participants.

1. **Investigator-Influenced Biases**

   The social interaction between investigator and participant can influence the data in the following ways:

   a. Experimenter Expectancy Effects:

   Experimenter expectancy effect refers to the experimenter's intentionally or unintentionally treating participants in ways that encourage particular types of responses and thus may influence the results of the data and lower the validity of the study.

   b. Reducing Experimenter Expectancy Effects with a Double-Blind Design:

   Double-blind studies refer to studies in which neither participants nor researchers know if participants are assigned to the experimental or control group.

MEDIA RECOMMENDATION 5.2: Facilitated Communication

Objective: This video will show students how easy it is for researchers and clinicians to influence studies and clients to behave in ways they desire.

Time: 60 Minutes

Film and Discussion: 90 Minutes

Discussion Only: 30 Minutes

Directions:
Have students watch the program listed below on their own or in class. (You may choose to only show a clip of the film.)

Explore Online:
Palfreman, J. (1993). *Frontline: Prisoners of silence.* WGBH Educational Foundation.
Transcript of the program: http://www.pbs.org/wgbh/pages/frontline/programs/transcripts/1202.html

Search Google Videos (using search terms "frontline prisoners of silence") or
http://video.google.com/videoplay?docid=3439467496200920717&ei=ydONSrXmAajaqwKqqair
Dw&q=frontline+facilitated+communication&hl=en

Description: The film shows how one's own biases can prevent one from thinking critically about a treatment. This examination of facilitated communication reveals how easy it is for researchers and clinicians to subtly influence the behavior of clients.

Questions to Students and Discussion: What is facilitated communication? In what ways did the clinicians influence their clients? Describe the study used to examine facilitated communication. What methods did the researcher use to control the study? Why do you think people still believe in facilitated communication despite the evidence? What warnings might this film have for you when you become a professional?

   c. Reactivity:

   Reactivity is a behavior change that occurs when one becomes aware of being observed; because of this, the researcher is not collecting authentic data.

2. **Effects of Community Standards on Individual Behavior**

   Different communities have different standards on what is appropriate behavior; thus the participants may be influenced by their community's standards.

3. Cultural Differences in Evaluating Symptoms

Some disorders are culture-specific or may have different words or concepts for describing certain symptoms. These differences can pose challenges to researchers.

III. RESEARCH TREATMENT

Which treatment is most effective for which disorder? Does treatment even work? Treatment research is challenging but important for finding the most effective forms of prevention and treatment.

A. Researching Treatments That Target Neurological Factors

1. Drug Effect or Placebo Effect?

One way to find out if a neurological treatment is helpful is to randomly assign some participants to receive the medication while the other participants receive a *placebo,* which is an inert substance or a procedure that itself has no direct medical value; often, it is simply a sugar pill. The *placebo effect,* or the positive effect of such a substance, can be strengthened or weakened by the outward qualities of the placebo and how it is administered.

- A higher dose of pills has a greater effect.
- Capsules have a better effect than pills.
- Injections have a stronger effect than capsules.
- The dispensing person who is empathic and friendly produces a larger effect than a nonempathic person.
- Placebos perceived to be more expensive are more effective than those thought to be less expensive.

2. Dropouts

Attrition is the reduction in the number of research participants during a study. If researchers have uneven attrition in the experimental and control groups, it is difficult to draw conclusions.

B. Researching Treatments That Target Psychological Factors

Table 5.3 shows the number of variables that researchers can study when targeting psychological factors. Variables include therapy, patient, therapist, and patient-therapist interactions.

1. Common Factors

Common factors are helpful aspects of therapy that are shared by virtually all types of psychotherapy and may cause relief for the client, which makes it difficult to study the effectiveness of specific techniques.
   Common factors can include:

- place to share problems
- explanation or validation of the problems
- encouragement for risk taking
- hope
- a positive relationship

LECTURE ENHANCEMENT 5.2: Common Factors

Objective: This enhancement will provide students with more detailed information about the common factors.

Time: 20 Minutes

Introduction
What helps people change? Be specific.

Common Factors
Hubble, Duncan, and Miller (1999) discuss Lambert's work on the common factors. They provide an excellent pie chart depicting the common factors. They note that Lambert's work found that client characteristics, the therapeutic alliance/relationship, placebo effect/hope, and specific technique/procedure accounted for changes in therapy. Each of these factors accounted for a different amount of change. Client characteristics account for 40%, the therapeutic relationship accounts for 30%, hope/placebo effect accounts for 15%, and specific technique/procedure accounts for 15%. Thus, the authors argue that the relationship is an important element in creating change.

Source: Asay, T. P., & Lambert , M. J. (1999). The empirical case for the common factors in therapy: Quantitative findings. In M. A. Hubble, B. L. Duncan, and S. D. Miller (Eds.), *The heart and soul of change: What works in therapy* (pp. 33–56). Washington, DC: American Psychological Association.

Summary: This enhancement provides additional details about the common factors research.

Questions to Students and Discussion: Do you agree or disagree with the authors? Would you add any other factors to the ones you have learned about?

MEDIA RECOMMENDATION 5.3: What Really Works in Therapy?

Objective: Students will enjoy this interesting podcast with researcher and author Scott Miller (author of *The heart and soul of change: What works in therapy*).

Time: 60 Minutes

Media and Discussion: 1 Hour, 20 Minutes

Discussion Only: 20 Minutes

Explore Online:
Van Nuys, D. (December 14, 2006). What really works in therapy with Scott Miller, Ph.D. Shrink Rap Radio podcast number 66.
http://www.shrinkrapradio.com/2006/12/14/66-what-really-works-in-therapy/

Transcript is available at http://www.shrinkrapradio.com/66.pdf

Description: This podcast shows some of the problems in treatment and what can be done to improve the therapeutic process.

Questions to Students and Discussion: What are some of the problems Miller identifies in the diagnostic system? What is the percent of people who are better off having treatment than those untreated? How does Miller suggest clinicians can improve treatment? On what basis does Miller criticize RCTs? What was particularly shocking for you in this podcast?

2. **Specific Factors**

Specific factors are the unique benefits of the particular treatment or technique under investigation that cannot be accounted for by the common factors.

3. **Controlling Possible Confounding Variables with Analogue Studies**

There are many possible confounding variables that may influence results. [See *Table 5.3*.]

- An *analogue study* is a type of treatment research that is conducted under controlled conditions in a laboratory setting, thereby minimizing confounds. Thus, the therapy is provided in a similar way to traditional therapy while controlling as many variables as possible.

4. **Is Therapy Better Than No Treatment?**

Researchers use a number of ways to address this question:

- W*ait-list control group* and the treatment group will have pre- and post-assessments. The pretest allows researchers to establish a *baseline symptom level*.
- Placebo control groups, where participants meet with the "placebo therapist" who does not use active treatment techniques, allow researchers to measure effects above and beyond meeting with someone and having someone who listens to their concerns.

Researchers have conducted such studies for half a century and have concluded:

- Therapy really does make a difference.
- Treatment shows a larger effect, when compared to a wait-list control group, than the placebo group because of the effects of common factors. [See *Figure 5.6*.]

LECTURE ENHANCEMENT 5.3: Is Therapy Helpful?

Objective: To explore additional information on whether therapy helps or hurts.

Time: 30 Minutes

Lecture Points:

The first well-known study on therapy was conducted by Eysenck (1952). He summarized 24 outcome studies and found that 72% of individuals receiving no therapy group showed improvement, 66% receiving combination therapy showed improvement, and 44% receiving psychoanalysis showed improvement. Eysenck concluded that "no therapy is as good as some therapy" because his research showed treatment was not effective.

A second study by Smith, Glass, and Miller (1980) utilized the meta-analysis technique and found an effect of .85, which means that the "average client is better off than 80% of those with no treatment." They concluded that these results are equal to or better than medical and educational treatments, and therefore, that therapy does work.

Lambert and Bergin's (1994) study found that no type of therapy works best; instead, the common factors are more important and make the difference for client change.

In 1995, *Consumer Reports* collected 4000 responses and found that most participants were satisfied with all mental health professionals *except* marriage counselors. Those who saw a therapist for 6 months compared to those who saw a doctor tended to feel better and those who were in therapy longer reported more improvement.

What are the problems with these studies?

1. Are the control and treatment groups equivalent?
2. Are the groups receiving other services (medical, group, informal support)?
3. Efficacy studies versus effectiveness studies

    a. Efficacy studies or clinical trials: control extraneous variables; while high in internal validity, do not represent the real world; are best at assessing actual treatment; are carefully scripted; involve random assignment

    b. Effectiveness studies: are correlational/quasi-experimental; are best at assessing general effect

4. Placebo effect

Sources:

Consumer Reports. (1995). Mental health: Does therapy help? *Consumer Reports, 60*(11), 734–739.

Eysenck, H. J. (1952). The effects of psychotherapy: An evaluation. *Journal of Consulting Psychology, 16,* 319–324.

Lambert, M. J., & Bergin, A. E. (1994). The effectiveness of psychotherapy. In A. E. Bergin and S. L. Garfield (Eds.), *Handbook of psychotherapy and behavior change,* 4th edition (pp. 143–189). Oxford: John Wiley & Sons.

Smith, M. L., Glass, G. V., & Miller, T. L. (1980). *The benefits of psychotherapy.* Baltimore: Johns Hopkins University Press.

Summary: Several major studies have been conducted on the effectiveness of therapy. Although early studies did not show promising results, more recent studies have concluded that therapy is effective and that 80% of those treated are better off than those not treated.

Questions to Students and Discussion: Why is it difficult to assess whether therapy helps people? What kinds of studies are best at assessing the effectiveness of therapy?

5. Is One Type of Therapy Generally More Effective Than Another?

The *dodo bird verdict* of psychotherapy found that no specific therapy was superior to another. The dodo bird is from *Alice's Adventures in Wonderland;* Dodo says: "*Everybody* has won, and all must have prizes."

6. Is One Type of Therapy Better for Treating a Specific Disorder?

This research sought to address whether any particular type of therapy was more effective than others in treating a specific disorder and was studied using randomized clinical trials.

a. Randomized Clinical Trials:

A *randomized clinical trial (RCT)* has participants randomly assigned to at least two conditions (the treatment or control group) and takes place at multiple locations.

Example: The National Institute of Mental Health (NIMH) compared four treatments over 16 weeks—interpersonal therapy (IPT), cognitive behavioral therapy (CBT), *imipramine* with supportive sessions with a psychiatrist, and a placebo medication together with supportive sessions with a psychiatrist. Various dependent variables were measured. The 18-month follow-up revealed:

- The CBT group had a larger sustained effect and fewer relapses.

- In the most severely depressed patients, IPT and imipramine were more effective than CBT.

- The "collaborative bond" between therapist and patient had a stronger influence on treatment outcome than did the type of treatment.

b. The Importance of Follow-up Assessment:

Follow-up assement helps to examine the long-term benefits for patients (or their relapses). Researchers can identify relapse risk factors and make adjustments to treatment.

c. Exclusion Criteria:

Researchers ideally seek participants who have one disorder but most people have more than one disorder in real life (thus reducing external validity).

d. Manual-Based Treatment:

RCTs prefer to use manual-based treatment, typically lasting 6 to 16 sessions, to ensure similar treatment among participants.

- More than 108 different treatment manuals for adults have been created.
- Research can then isolate and manipulate a specific variable in treatment and measure its effects.

e. Allegiance Effect:

Allegiance effects are studies conducted by investigators who prefer a particular theoretical orientation and who tend to obtain data that support that particular orientation.

f. Empirically Supported Treatments/Evidence-Based Practice:

Empirically supported/empirically validated treatments are well-designed and well-conducted studies that are effective for a particular disorder.

g. Criticisms of RCTs:

- *Exclusion criteria* limits the generalizability of a study's results.
- *Homogenous samples;* since most RCT participants are White and middle-class.
- *Overly rigid manual-based treatments* have less favorable results.
- *Relative effectiveness* because manual-based versus non-manual-based treatments have similar results.
- *Therapy quality* may inadvertently affect the results.
- *Common factors versus specific techniques* may be a less important issue than patient variables, therapist variables, and patient-therapist interaction variables. [See *Table 5.3.*]
- *Length of treatment* in RCTs tends to be brief and focus on only one problem.
- *Problems with DSM diagnostic groups* since people with the same disorder can have different symptoms.
- *The most important dependent variables* are difficult to identify since it is unclear what is most important in helping clients feel better.
- *Applying the results to individual patients* may not apply since the data is aggregated.

Some of the criticisms of RCTs can be summed up by noting the difference between a treatment's *efficacy* and *effectiveness.*

- Efficacy is assessed within the carefully controlled confines of RCTs in a research clinic.
- Effectiveness is assessed in nonresearch settings, the place where most clinicians treat patients, without excluding them because of multiple diagnoses.

7. Ethical Research on Experimental Treatments

Research must be approved by an IRB and new/experimental treatments must follow additional guidelines such as:

- Discuss the experimental nature of the treatment.
- Clarify what services the control group will or will not receive.

- Inform participants about how they will be assigned to the treatments.
- Provide treatment alternatives if person withdraws.
- Explain any compensation/costs of participating. [See *Table 5.4.*]

8. **The Therapy Dose-Response Relationship**

   The *dose-response relationship* is the correlation between the number of sessions and the client's response to treatment.

   - More sessions result in better outcomes.
   - For certain disorders, the early stages of treatment have the best response. [See *Figure 5.7.*]
   - We do not know if an increased number of sessions *causes* the increased response or if a third factor causes an increase in sessions and response.

C. Researching Treatment That Targets Social Factors

Treatment research may also examine social factors and social context.

1. **Matching Patient and Therapist by Gender and Ethnicity**

   Matching patient and therapist by ethnicity, gender, and age does not have beneficial effects.

   - Flaherty and Adams (1998) found that clients are more likely to drop out of therapy when the therapist is male.
   - If a client strongly prefers a therapist with a similar ethnic or racial background, the therapy may have better outcomes.
   - Research on this topic is difficult because of confounding variables, desire for similar values, ethnicity, acculturation level, and broad versus specific ethnic matching issues.

2. **Culturally Sanctioned Placebo Effects**

   Across different cultures and time, communities have sought the help of healers to successively treat psychopathology. Advertising medication to consumers may also cause the placebo effect.

D. FEEDBACK LOOPS IN ACTION: The Placebo Effect

Social factors or cultural norms influence what consumers see as appropriate treatment. These norms influence the patient's expectations (a psychological factor) about the effectiveness of the treatment.

ADDITIONAL READING

Asay, T. P., & Lambert, M. J. (1999). The empirical case for the common factors in therapy: Quantitative findings. In M. A. Hubble, B. L. Duncan, and S. D. Miller (Eds.), *The heart and soul of change: What works in therapy* (pp. 33–56). Washington, DC: American Psychological Association.

Lambert, M. J., & Bergin, A. E. (1994). The effectiveness of psychotherapy. In A. E. Bergin and S. L. Garfield (Eds.), *Handbook of psychotherapy and behavior change* (4th ed., pp. 143–189). Oxford, England: John Wiley & Sons.

Wampold, B. E. (2001). Practical interpretations of outcome research in psychotherapy through the examination of effect sizes. *Clinician's Research Digest, Supp. 24,* n.p.

Wampold, B. E., & Bhati, K. S. (2004). Attending to the omissions: A historical examination of evidence-based practice movements. *Professional Psychology: Research and Practice, 35,* 530–570.

WEB SITES

American Psychological Association (2002): Ethical principles of psychologists and code of conduct. See: http://www.apa.org/ethics/code2002.pdf

NARSAD: The world's leading charity dedicated to mental health research. See: http://www.narsad.org

National Institute of Mental Health: One of the largest organizations that conducts mental health research. They provide free e-mail updates and an enormous amount of information on psychopathology research. See: http://www.nimh.nih.gov/index.shtml

Society for Research in Psychopathology: This organization is focused on connecting people who conduct research on psychopathology. See: http://www.psychopathology.org/

WORKSHEET 5.1
RESEARCH METHODS IN PSYCHOPATHOLOGY

Complete the following table to provide a summary of the different research methods.

Research Method	Brief Description	Benefits	Limitations	Example
Experiments				
Quasi-experimental design				
Correlational research				
Case studies				
Single-participant experiments				
Meta-analysis				

CHAPTER

6

Mood Disorders and Suicide

CHAPTER OUTLINE

CHAPTER HEADINGS	INSTRUCTION IDEAS AND TEXTBOOK CORRELATIONS
Chapter Introduction	**Media Recommendation 6.1:** Kay Redfield Jamison **Textbook Tools:** Table 6.1
DEPRESSIVE DISORDERS	
The Building Block of Depressive Disorders: Major Depressive Episode	**Learning Objective:** 6.1 **Learning Concepts:** affect, behavioral and physical symptoms, cognitive symptoms, stages of MDE **Textbook Tools:** Table 6.2; Case 6.1
Major Depressive Disorder	**Learning Objectives:** 6.2, 6.3, 6.4, 6.5 **Learning Concepts:** specifiers, depression in children and adolescents **Media Recommendation 6.2:** Postpartum Depression **Lecture Enhancement 6.1:** Premenstrual Dysphoric Disorder **Media Recommendation 6.3:** Light Therapy for Depression **Media Recommendation 6.4:** Teen Depression **Media Recommendation 6.5:** *The Killer at Thurston High* **Textbook Tools:** Table 6.3; Case 6.2 **Worth Video Tool Kit for Abnormal Psychology:** Overview of Depression
Dysthymic Disorder	**Learning Objective:** 6.6 **Textbook Tools:** Tables 6.4, 6.5; Case 6.3
Understanding Depressive Disorders	**Learning Objectives:** 6.7, 6.8, 6.9 **Learning Concepts:** neurological factors, brain systems, neural communication, stress-related hormones, genetics, psychological factors, attentional biases, dysfunctional thoughts, rumination, attributional style, learned helplessness, social factors, stressful life events, social exclusion, social interactions, culture, gender differences **Learning Activity 6.1:** Applying the Negative Triad of Depression **Learning Activity 6.2:** Applying the Depressive Attributional Style **Learning Activity 6.3:** Stressful Life Events Scale **Learning Activity 6.4:** Insiders and Outsiders

	Lecture Enhancement 6.2: Men and Depression **Textbook Tools:** Figures 6.1, 6.2; Table 6.6; Worksheet 6.1 **Worth Video Tool Kit for Abnormal Psychology:** Irritability and Depression
Treating Depressive Disorders	**Learning Objectives:** 6.7, 6.8, 6.9 **Learning Concepts:** targeting neurological factors, medication, brain stimulation, targeting psychological factors, behavioral methods, cognitive methods, cognitive behavioral therapy compared to medication, targeting social factors, interpersonal therapy, family systems **Media Recommendation 6.6:** Rob McGruder and the ECT Odyssey **Media Recommendation 6.7:** TMS for Depression **Textbook Tools:** Figure 6.3
BIPOLAR DISORDERS	
The Building Blocks for Bipolar Disorders	**Learning Objective:** 6.10 **Learning Concepts:** manic episode, mixed episode, hypomanic episode **Textbook Tools:** Table 6.7; Case 6.4
The Two Types of Bipolar Disorder	**Learning Objective:** 6.11 **Learning Concepts:** bipolar I versus bipolar II disorder, bipolar disorder and creativity? **Learning Activity 6.5:** The Sylvia Plath Effect **Textbook Tools:** Tables 6.8a, 6.8b, 6.9
Cyclothymic Disorder	**Learning Objective:** 6.12 **Textbook Tools:** Figure 6.4; Table 6.10; Case 6.5
Understanding Bipolar Disorders	**Learning Objectives:** 6.13, 6.14, 6.15 **Learning Concepts:** neurological factors, brain systems, neural communication, genetics, psychological factors, social factors **Textbook Tools:** Figure 6.5
Treating Bipolar Disorders	**Learning Objectives:** 6.13, 6.14, 6.15 **Learning Concept:** targeting neurological factors, targeting psychological factors, targeting social factors **Textbook Tools:** Figures 6.6, 6.7 **Worth Video Tool Kit for Abnormal Psychology:** Age and Onset of Bipolar Disorder, Bipolar Disorder and Its Symptoms, Diagnosis: Bipolar Disorder
SUICIDE	
Suicidal Thoughts and Suicide Risks	**Learning Objective:** 6.16 **Learning Concepts:** thinking about, planning, and attempting suicide, risk and protective factors for suicide **Textbook Tools:** Tables 6.11, 6.12
Understanding Suicide	**Learning Objective:** 6.17 **Learning Concepts:** neurological factors, brain system and neural communication, genetics, psychological factors, social factors **Textbook Tools:** Figure 6.8; Tables 6.13, 6.14

Preventing Suicide	**Learning Objectives:** 6.18, 6.19 **Learning Concepts:** targeting neurological factors, targeting psychological factors, targeting social factors **Media Recommendation 6.8:** Exploring Suicide Prevention Programs **Textbook Tools:** Figures 6.9, 6.10; Table 6.15 **Worth Video Tool Kit for Abnormal Psychology:** Suicide: A Guide for Prevention

LEARNING OBJECTIVES

After reading this chapter, students should be able to:

6.1 Describe the building blocks of the depressive disorders.

6.2 Identify affect, behavior, and cognition typical of depressive disorders.

6.3 Describe the two stages of MDEs.

6.4 Describe the symptoms of an MDE.

6.5 Name and describe several specifiers of depression.

6.6 Explain the difference between MDE and Dysthymia.

6.7 Identify neurological causes and treatments of depression.

6.8 Identify psychological causes and treatments of depression.

6.9 Identify social causes and treatments of depression.

6.10 Describe the building blocks of the bipolar disorders.

6.11 Articulate the differences between bipolar I and bipolar II disorder.

6.12 Explain the differences between cyclothymia and the bipolar disorders.

6.13 Identify neurological causes and treatments of the bipolar disorders.

6.14 Identify psychological causes and treatments of the bipolar disorders.

6.15 Identify social causes and treatments of the bipolar disorders.

6.16 Describe gender and cultural differences in suicide rates.

6.17 Describe the neurological, psychological, and social factors that contribute to suicide.

6.18 Identify the neurological, psychological, and social approaches to suicide prevention.

6.19 Identify how the neurological, psychological, and social factors might have influenced each other.

KEY TERMS

Mood disorders: Psychological disorders characterized by prolonged and marked disturbances in mood that affect how people feel, what they believe and expect, how they think and talk, and how they interact with others.

Major depressive episode (MDE): A mood episode characterized by severe depression that lasts for at least 2 weeks.

Anhedonia: A difficulty or inability to experience pleasure; a state in which activities and intellectual pursuits that were once enjoyable no longer are, or at least are not nearly as enjoyable as they had been.

Vegetative signs (of depression): Psychomotor symptoms coupled with changes in appetite, weight, and sleep.

Psychomotor agitation: An inability to sit still, evidenced by pacing, hand-wringing, or rubbing or pulling the skin, clothes, or other objects.

Psychomotor retardation: A slowing of motor functions indicated by slowed bodily movements and speech (in particular, longer pauses in answering) and lower volume, variety, or amount of speech.

Hypersomnia: Sleeping more hours each day than normal.

Prodromes: Early symptoms of a disorder.

Premorbid: Referring to the period of time prior to a patient's illness.

Major depressive disorder (MDD): The mood disorder marked by five or more symptoms of depression lasting more than 2 weeks.

Age cohort: A group of people born in a particular range of years.

Seasonal affective disorder (SAD): Recurrent depression that follows a seasonal pattern.

Phototherapy: Treatment for depression that uses full-spectrum lights; also called *light-box therapy.*

Dysthymic disorder: A depressive disorder that involves fewer of the symptoms of a major depressive episode, but the symptoms persist for a longer period.

Double depression: Having both major depressive disorder and dysthymic disorder.

Selective serotonin reuptake inhibitors (SSRIs): Medications that slow the reuptake of serotonin from the synapses.

Tricyclic antidepressants (TCAs): Older antidepressants named after the three rings of atoms in their molecular structure.

Monoamine oxidase inhibitors (MAOIs): Antidepressant medications that increase the amount of the enzyme monoamine oxidase in the brain.

Bipolar disorders: Mood disorders in which a person's mood is often persistently and abnormally upbeat or shifts inappropriately from upbeat to markedly down.

Manic episode: A period of at least 1 week characterized by abnormal and persistent euphoria or expansive mood or irritability.

Expansive mood: A mood that involves unceasing, indiscriminate enthusiasm for interpersonal, sexual, or occupational interactions.

Flight of ideas: Thoughts that race faster than they can be said.

Rapid cycling (of moods): Having four or more episodes that meet the criteria for any type of mood episode within 1 year.

Cyclothymia: Mood disorder characterized by chronic, fluctuating mood disturbances with numerous periods of hypomanic symptoms and numerous periods of depressive symptoms that do not meet the criteria for an MDE.

Mood stabilizer: A category of medication that minimizes mood swings.

Lithium: The oldest mood stabilizer; it is administered as a salt.

Suicidal ideation: Thoughts of suicide.

CHAPTER GUIDE

Chapter Introduction

This chapter reviews ***mood disorders:*** mood disturbances that affect how people feel, what they believe and expect, how they think and talk, and how they interact with others.

- Eight percent of Americans experience at least one mood disorder per year.

- Mood disorders are among the leading causes of disability worldwide.
- Kay Redfield Jamison is a psychologist who studies mood disorders and wrote *An Unquiet Mind* (1995), in which she recounts her own experiences with bipolar disorder.

MEDIA RECOMMENDATION 6.1: Kay Redfield Jamison

Objective: To provide students with additional information about Jamison and her experiences with a bipolar disorder.

Time: 30 Minutes

Film and Discussion: 45 Minutes

Discussion Only: 15 Minutes

Explore Online: Personal Reflections on Manic-Depressive Illness (Search YouTube using search terms "Kay Redfield Jamison" or http://www.youtube.com/watch?v=CxRLap9xLag&feature= related)

Description: This video features Kay Redfield Jamison as she highlights key features of her illness and treatment.

Summary: This video will help students learn about Jamison's experience with a bipolar disorder. Students will also gain insight into treatment issues for bipolar disorders.

Questions to Students and Discussion: What key words does Jamison use to describe her manic versus depressive symptoms? What struggles did she face as she started treatment? Why is she so vocal about her experiences? What was most surprising to you about what she describes?

Two categories of mood disorders:

- Depressive disorders (categorized by a low mood)
- Bipolar disorders (categorized by periods of an up or manic mood and times when the person's mood is low)

The four types of mood disorder episodes aid in diagnosis:
[See *Table 6.1.*]

- A *major depressive episode* has depressive symptoms.
- A *manic episode* has euphoric or irritable moods. The euphoric mood is extremely positive and may not necessarily be appropriate to the situation.
- A *hypomanic episode* has less severe euphoria or irritability.
- *Mixed episode* has symptoms of major depressive and manic episodes.

I. DEPRESSIVE DISORDERS

What does it mean to say that someone is depressed?

A. The Building Block of Depressive Disorders: Major Depressive Episode

All of the depressive disorders include some form of a major depressive disorder.

- A ***major depressive episode (MDE)*** is characterized by severe depression that lasts for at least 2 weeks.
- An MDE includes affective (mood), behavior, and cognitive symptoms (known as the ABCs). [See *Table 6.2.*]

1. **Affect, the Mood Symptoms of Depression**

   Affect or mood symptoms of depression include:

   - *Anhedonia* is a state in which activities and intellectual pursuits that were once enjoyable no longer are, or at least are not nearly as enjoyable as they had been.
   - Anhedonia can lead to social withdrawal and unexplained sadness or crying.

2. **Behavioral and Physical Symptoms of Depression**

   Vegetative signs of depression include psychomotor agitation or psychomotor retardation, along with changes in appetite, weight, and sleep.

   - *Psychomotor agitation* is an inability to sit still, evidenced by pacing, hand wringing, or rubbing or pulling the skin, clothes, or other objects.
   - *Psychomotor retardation* is a slowing of motor functions indicated by slowed bodily movements and speech (in particular, longer pauses in answering) and lower volume, variety, or amount of speech.
   - Sleep changes include insomnia, which is difficulty sleeping; *hypersomnia,* which is sleeping more hours each day than normal; and sleep irregularities during *rapid eye movement (REM)* sleep, the sleep period that helps to process emotional memories.
   - Other changes include feeling less energetic, tired, or fatigued.

3. **Cognitive Symptoms of Depression**

   Depressed clients tend to have the following thoughts or cognitive symptoms:

   - Feeling worthless or guilt-ridden
   - Evaluating oneself negatively, not based on reality
   - Ruminating (repetitive thoughts) over failings
   - Misinterpreting statements by others as indicators of one's worthlessness
   - Feeling responsible for negative events
   - Blaming oneself for the depression and the inability to function
   - Difficulty thinking, remembering, concentrating, and making decisions [see *Case 6.1 and Table 6.2*]

B. Major Depressive Disorder

If a client meets the criteria for a major depressive episode, he/she is diagnosed as having **major depressive disorder (MDD).**

- A *major depressive disorder* is defined as an individual having five or more symptoms of depression lasting more than 2 weeks.
- A single *episode* is when an individual has an MDD one time.
- A *recurrent depression* is more common and is when a person has more than one episode.
- Increasingly frequent episodes, episode clusters, or isolated episodes followed by periods without symptoms are common. [See *Table 6.3*.]
- Depression and anxiety commonly occur together and may have a common, previously unknown, cause.

1. **Specifiers**

   Specifiers are specific sets of symptoms that occur together or in particular patterns that aid in treatment and prognosis.

Examples of specifiers include:

a. *Melancholic features:*

Including anhedonia, mood fluctuations (which may be worse in the morning), and appetite loss

b. *Atypical depression:*

Characterized by improved mood when experiencing positive events and at least two of the following: hypersomnia, weight gain, heavy feelings in arms or legs, sensitivity to rejection, and lack of response to medication

c. *Catatonic features:*

Affecting motor symptoms, causing clients to hold odd postures for long periods of time or experience restlessness

d. *Psychotic feature:*

Occur rarely, and include hallucinations (of the five senses) or delusions (beliefs not based on reality)

e. *Chronic depression:*

The continuations of an MDE for 2 years

f. *Postpartum onset:*

Occurring within 4 weeks of giving birth (this time range varies); women who experienced recurrent depression before giving birth are at most risk [see *Case 6.2*]

MEDIA RECOMMENDATION 6.2: Postpartum Depression

Objective: To inform students about the firsthand experience of women with postpartum depression.

Time: 22 Minutes

Film and Discussion: 30–40 Minutes

Discussion Only: 10–20 Minutes

Explore Online: *Family Secrets—Beyond Baby Blues.* Search Joost.com using the search terms "postpartum depression" or http://www.joost.com/272ij5h/t/Family-Secrets-Beyond-Baby-Blues #id=272ij5h

Description: The video explores the challenges of family members as they struggling to cope with one mother's postpartum depression.

Summary: Students will learn about one family's firsthand experience of postpartum depression. Students will be able to see symptoms and possible treatments for this type of depression.

Questions to Students and Discussion: What did you find surprising about this video? What expectations of yours were confirmed? Identify some of the key symptoms of depression.

LECTURE ENHANCEMENT 6.1: Premenstrual Dysphoric Disorder

Objective: To examine the MDE specifier of premenstrual dysphoric disorder (PMDD) and identify possible treatments.

Time: 30–60 Minutes

Description: Students will watch a short video and listen to a lecture on the symptoms and treatments for PMDD.

Watch Online: *The Biology of PMDD.* Search YouTube using the search terms "premenstrual dysphoric disorder" or http://www.youtube.com/watch?v=nj3qIMO6Glk&feature=related

Summary: Students will learn about rates of occurrence, criteria for diagnosing PMDD, risk factors, and treatment (described below in more detail).

Rates: Currently 5% of U.S. women qualify for diagnosis of PMDD; 20% of women have significant symptoms.

Criteria for Diagnosis: (1) Five or more of the MDE symptoms over 1 year, (2) symptoms occur during the last week of luteal phase (when progesterone and estrogen are withdrawn leading to dysregulation of the HPA system) and end at the beginning of menses, and (3) symptoms are significant enough to interfere with occupation and/or relationships.

Risk factors: (1) family history of premenstrual syndrome, and (2) personal history of MDE and/or postpartum depression.

Treatments: (1) Medications that can reduce the hormonal fluctuations such as certain birth control pills, (2) antidepressants or antianxiety medications that reduce the chemical fluctuations, (3) vitamins for vitamin deficiency: B6, calcium, magnesium, and (4) diet and exercise.

Additional Suggestions: Family members may also benefit from tips on how to cope with a loved one suffering from PMDD, such as how to offer empathy. Also, discussing symptoms and possible treatments for PMDD is advisable (though not during the luteal phase).

Reference:
Pearlstein, T., & Steiner, M. (2008). Premenstrual dysphoric disorder: Burden of illness and treatment update. *Journal of Psychiatry & Neuroscience, 33*(4), 291–301.

Questions to Students and Discussion: What are the symptoms of PMDD? Can you identify the risk factors for PMDD? What are some treatments?

    g. *Seasonal affective disorder (SAD):*

        Recurrent depression that follows a seasonal pattern; can occur in winter or summer

        (1) Winter depression symptoms:

- Recurrent depressive episodes
- Hypersomnia
- Increased appetite
- Weight gain
- Irritability
- Symptoms beginning in autumn and continue through the winter
- Symptoms alleviated or less severe in summer
- 4–6% of the general population affected
- Average age of onset is 23 years
- Four times more common in women than in men
      i. *Treatment:* **phototherapy** (*light-box therapy*) using full-spectrum lights

        (2) Summer depression symptoms:

- Beginning in late spring
- Poor appetite and weight loss
- Less sleep
- Psychomotor changes
      i. *Treatment:* antidepressant medication

MEDIA RECOMMENDATION 6.3: Light Therapy for Depression

Objective: To educate students about seasonal affective disorder and treatment using light boxes.

Time: 7 Minutes (Part 1), 8 Minutes (Part 2)

Media and Discussion: 30 Minutes

Discussion Only: 20 Minutes

Watch Online: Two-part video on light therapy for depression. Search YouTube using search terms "SAD and light therapy" or http://www.youtube.com/watch?v=BKSIgu0_QBM&feature=related and http://www.youtube.com/watch?v=IwneIN8icfQ&feature=related

Description: The video shows Professor Raymond Lam, of the University of British Columbia, talking about symptoms and treatment of seasonal affective disorder.

Summary: Students will learn additional information about seasonal affective disorder and light therapy for this type of MDE.

Questions to Students and Discussion: Describe the typical path of seasonal affective disorder.

What was surprising in this video? Why do people resist being treated for SAD? Who is most at risk for SAD? How are light boxes different than typical lights? How does light therapy work?

2. **Depression in Children and Adolescents**

   - 1–3% of elementary-school children and 5–8% of teenagers are depressed per 6-month period.
   - Childhood or adolescent depression does not predict depression in adulthood unless first episode is during the teenage years.
   - Teens with depression have a higher likelihood of dropping out of school or having an unplanned pregnancy.

MEDIA RECOMMENDATION 6.4: Teen Depression

Objective: To educate students about adolescent depression symptoms and warning signs.

Time: 3 Minutes (Video 1), 27 Minutes (Video 2)

Video and Discussion: 60 Minutes

Discussion Only: 30 Minutes

Watch Online:
Learn about teen depression by watching *Real Life Teens—Teen Depression*. Search YouTube using the search terms "teen depression" or http://www.youtube.com/watch?v=pAvm4BJwhso&feature=related

Explore adolescents' experiences with depression further by watching *Keeping Kids Healthy: Clinical Depression in Children*. Search http://video.google.com using the search terms "adolescent depression" or http://video.google.com/videoplay?docid=-1559115186254879470&ei=8FatSom ZJYqhlAf6oZyjAw&q=adolescent+depression&hl=en&client=firefox-a#

Summary: These videos highlight the experience of depression for teens. Students will gain additional information about how depression expresses itself in teens.

Questions to Students and Discussion:
In *Real Life Teens—Teen Depression,* describe the symptoms of depression the teens experience. What are warning signs of teen depression? What are ways adolescents cope with depression?

In *Keeping Kids Healthy: Clinical Depression in Children,* what signs of depression did the adolescents show? What ways did they try to cope? What are ways to prevent depression in teens? How were the teens' experiences similar or different? What treatments were recommended?

MEDIA RECOMMENDATION 6.5: *The Killer at Thurston High*

Objective: To identify symptoms and warning signs of depression in Kip Kinkel's diary entries and to also gain awareness of the extreme consequences of untreated depression when accompanied by social factors.

Time: 60 Minutes

Film and Discussion: 90 Minutes

Discussion Only: 30 Minutes

Description: This program explores the neurological, psychological, and social factors that led to Kip Kinkle's killing his parents and two classmates.

Source: *The Killer at Thurston High* (May 2004). PBS.
http://www.pbs.org/wgbh/pages/frontline/shows/kinkel/

Explore Online: Excerpts from Kinkel's diary:
http://www.pbs.org/wgbh/pages/frontline/shows/kinkel/kip/writings.html

Summary: Students can identify symptoms and warning signs in Kinkel, and understand how neurological, psychological, and social factors interact to produce depression in teens.

Questions to Students and Discussion: Identify the (a) neurological, (b) psychological, and (c) social factors that led to Kinkel's depression. What might have prevented this tragedy? What surprised you in the film or in Kinkel's diary?

C. Dysthymic Disorder

- *Dysthymic disorder* has fewer symptoms than MDD, but the symptoms last for at least 2 years and are not alleviated for longer than 2 months at any time. [See *Table 6.4.*]
- *Double depression* is when a person with dysthymic disorder develops an MDE.
  i. Patients with double depression are likely to have more than one MDE and may require longer treatment. [See *Case 6.3 and Table 6.5.*]

D. Understanding Depressive Disorders

Neurological, psychological, and social factors help to explain the etiology of depressive disorders.

1. Neurological Factors

Brain systems, neural communication, stress-related hormones, and genetics are the neurological factors that contribute to depressive disorders.

a. Brain Systems:

- Depressed people have lower activity in a part of the frontal lobe that communicates with the amygdala (our primal emotion center) and emotion centers in the brain.
- Those with depression are unable to regulate emotions normally and experience a lack of motivation.
- Overactivity in the limbic system (specifically the basal ganglia) is related to severe depression.

b. Neural Communication:

- Depression can result from problems with neurotransmitter release, amount of neurotransmitters remaining in the synapse, and receptor interactions.
- The *catecholamine hypothesis* is one explanation of this dysfunction.
  - **i.** The hypothesis is that depression is caused by low levels of norepinephrine (NE).
  - **ii.** Fewer norepinephrine by-products were found in the urine and cerebrospinal fluid of depressed individuals.
  - **iii.** Autopsies show denser norepinephrine receptors in depressed brains. Thus, researchers believe the brain compensates for low NE by increasing the number of NE receptors.

c. Stress-Related Hormones:

- The *stress–diathesis model* of depression focuses on the HPA axis (hypothalamic-pituitary-adrenal axis).
- The HPA axis triggers the release of the stress hormone cortisol. An increased level of cortisol is linked to increased sensitivity and affects serotonin function. [See *Figure 6.1*.]
- Cortisol is believed to decrease the size of the hippocampus (a structure in the brain that helps form new memories) since it is smaller in depressed people.
- "Stressed" rats (due to early separation from their mothers) had higher HPA axis activity, levels of corticotropin-releasing factor (CRF), and density of CRF receptors.
- Antidepressant medication reduces HPA axis activity in stressed rats.
- Oddly, the HPA axis activity increases in typical depression and decreases in atypical depression.

d. Genetics:

- Monozygotic twins share their genes but dizygotic twins share only half of their genes.
- Genes influence how a person responds to stressful events but the environment determines *how* the genes are expressed.

2. Psychological Factors

Psychological factors include attentional biases, dysfunctional thoughts, rumination, attribution style, and learned helplessness.

a. Attentional Biases:

People who are depressed are more likely to focus on negative expressions, words, scenes, and depressive stimuli.

b. Dysfunctional Thoughts:

Beck's (1967) *negative triad of depression* describes how depressed individuals have negative views about (1) the world, (2) the self, and (3) the future.

LEARNING ACTIVITY 6.1: Applying the Negative Triad of Depression

Objective: To apply the concepts of the negative triad of depression to a real-life situation.

Time: 10 Minutes

Directions: Assign students to small groups and have them come up with 2–3 examples of times when they, or someone they know, have had negative views about the world, themselves, and the future.

OR

Ask students to listen to audio tapes or videos of people with depression and have them identify the negative triad.

Summary: Students will learn how to identify negative types of thinking among people who are depressed. Students will learn to differentiate the ways in which depression causes negative views of the world, the self, and the future.

Questions to Students and Discussion: Have you ever experienced the negative triad of depression? If so, what was it like? If not, what prevents you from thinking this way?

c. Rumination:

Stress-reactive rumination has been linked to depression and is characterized by repetitive thoughts about negative stressful life events, such as:

- How the stressful event was all my fault
- What the occurrence of the stressor means about me
- How things like this always happen to me

d. Attributional Style:

- Attributions are explanations of events; there are two types (internal and external).
- People who have an *internal attributional style* blame themselves for negative events; this style is linked to depression.
- Those with an *external attributional style* blame negative events on the environment; this style is not linked to depression.
- People with *depressive attributional style* are likely to show:
  i. More *internal* versus *external* attributions
  ii. *Stable* (enduring causes) versus *unstable* (local, transient causes) explanations
  iii. *Global* (general, overall causes) versus *specific* (particular, precise causes) explanations. [See *Table 6.6.*]

LEARNING ACTIVITY 6.2: Applying the Depressive Attributional Style

Objective: Students will learn about the depressive attributional style among people with depression.

Time: 20 Minutes

Directions: Have students work alone or in small groups and have them apply either an internal, stable, or global explanation to a recent event. Have students then select another attributional style to apply to the same event in order to compare and contrast the two. [Use *Worksheet 6.1* for this exercise.]

Summary: Students will see how certain attributional styles are linked to depression.

Questions to Students and Discussion: Identify a recent event you experienced. Now apply internal, stable, and global explanations to this event. Next, apply external, unstable, and specific attributions to the same example. Compare the two attributions. Why do you think the first type is linked to depression?

e. Learned Helplessness:

Learned helplessness is not based on dysfunctional attributions; it arises when a person gives up trying to change or escape a negative situation.

3. Social Factors

Social factors that are linked to depression are stressful life events, social exclusion, social interactions, culture, and gender differences.

a. Stressful Life Events:

Seventy percent of MDE episodes occur after a significant life stressor.

LEARNING ACTIVITY 6.3: Stressful Life Events Scale

Objective: Students will identify their level of stress and risk factors for depression.

Time: 20 Minutes

Directions: Have students complete the Life Events Stress Test, available at http://www.stresstips.com/lifeevents.htm. Discuss the results.

Summary: This activity has students identify the life stressors currently affecting them and connect this with their risk for developing depression.

Questions to Students and Discussion: How many stressors are you currently facing? Which stressors are more powerful than other stressors? For those of you experiencing a high number of stressors, how do you feel? How at risk are you to developing depression?

b. Social Exclusion:

Ethnic minorities, LGBTQ persons, and people from low SES groups may experience prejudice, alienation, or violence. (*Example:* homosexuals who experience community alienation or violence, which may be linked to higher levels of depression.)

LEARNING ACTIVITY 6.4: Insiders and Outsiders

Objective: To have students experience what it is like to be an "outsider" or an "insider."

Time: 45 Minutes

Directions: Make labels for students to wear with the following words: "Hug Me," "Shake My Hand," "Smile at Me," "Ignore Me." Also include some labels that are blank, with no words on them. (Try to have the same number of each label.) The labels should then be placed on the upper chest, high enough so it can be seen by other students, but not by the student who is wearing it.

1. Tell students to get up from their chairs and interact with each other for 5 minutes.

2. During the 5-minute interaction, you will see groups form. Those with "Hug Me," "Smile at Me," and "Shake My Hand" will tend to have a good time and group together. Those with "Ignore Me" and the Blank labels will tend to form their own group and dislike the exercise.

Summary: By doing this exercise, students are able to see how being in a certain group has benefits and drawbacks. The students who are isolated or become "outsiders" are at a higher risk for depression.

Questions to Students and Discussion: How did you feel while doing this exercise? In our society, what groups have "Shake My Hand," "Smile At Me," or "Hug Me" labels? In our society, what groups have blank or "Ignore Me" labels? How can being an "outsider" be linked to depression?

c. Social Interactions:

- Spending time with someone who is depressed or anxious can lead to depression.
- Another factor associated with depression is the way people typically interact with others; these patterns begin in infancy and are partly based on the consistency and quality of the caregiver's interactions with the child. When children are distressed, they display one of the following three patterns:
  - i. *Secure attachment,* or using the caregiver for comfort and support, leading to positive adult relationships
  - ii. *Avoidant attachment,* or actively avoiding the caregiver, leading to distant adult relationships
  - iii. *Anxious-ambivalent attachment,* or alternating between wanting support and withdrawing from the caregiver, leading to anxious adult relationships
- Adults with avoidant and anxious-ambivalent attachment are more vulnerable to depression.

d. Culture:

- Some cultures express mental illness somatically by complaining about bodily aches.
- Cultures vary on which symptoms they take seriously.
- A culture can also influence and change the people in it.

e. Gender Differences:

Why are women three times as likely as men to be diagnosed with depression?

- Women are more likely to have a ruminative response to stress.
- Socialization leads women to have higher rates of body dissatisfaction, which can lead to negative thinking.
- Women are more likely to report symptoms of depression than men.
- Family members are more likely to recognize depression in females than males.

LECTURE ENHANCEMENT 6.2: Men and Depression

Objective: To educate students about how depression manifests itself differently in men.

Time: 60 Minutes

Summary: Students will learn the following key points from your lecture:
1. Depression rates in men peak at ages 35–45.
2. Men who are more traditional experience higher levels of distress but are less likely to seek help.
3. Men are less likely to seek help for their problems in general.

Socialization of men:

What does it mean to be a man? How does a man decide he needs help?

1. Why don't men seek help?
   a. They are socialized to not seek help.
   b. This is especially true for more traditional men.
   c. There is a stigma against men seeking help.
2. This socialization creates "masked depression" in which people, in this instance men, are unable to see the signs of depression.
   a. Men cope with depression with alcohol abuse, delinquency, reckless behavior, and anger.
   b. Studies show men are affected by grief more and diagnosed more with alcohol problems.
   c. Men may have alexithymia (literally, "lack of word") or the inability to articulate emotions.

Pollack has proposed a "major depressive disorder–male type." Criteria for a major depressive disorder male type include:

1. Withdrawal
2. Workaholism and burnout
3. Denial of pain (physical or psychological?)
4. Demands for autonomy
5. Avoiding help
6. Increase or decrease in sex
7. Increase in angry outbursts
8. Substance abuse
9. Denial of sadness
10. Harsh self criticism
11. Depleted mood or impulsivity
12. Trouble concentrating, maintaining weight, or sleeping

Prevention Program:

National Institute of Mental Health, Men and Depression

http://www.nimh.nih.gov/health/topics/depression/men-and-depression//index.shtml

References:

Cochran, S. V. (2005). Masked depression: New developments and critical concepts for diagnosis and treatment. Paper presented for the Annual APA Convention 2005.

Cochran, S. V., & Rabinowitz, F. E. (1999). *Men and depression.* San Diego: Academic Press.

Pollack, W. (1998). Mourning melancholy and masculinity: Recognizing and treating depression in men. In W. Pollack and R. Levant (Eds.), *A new psychotherapy for men* (pp. 147–166). New York: Wiley.

Winerman, L. (2005, June). Helping men . . . to help themselves [Electronic version]. *APA Monitor on Psychology, 36*(6), 57.

Questions to Students and Discussion: Why do men seek help for depression less frequently than do women? Identify the criteria that indicate someone may be a major depressive–male type.

4. FEEDBACK LOOPS IN ACTION: Depressive Disorders

- Genetic vulnerability, stress, environment, and certain styles of thinking interact and produce depression.
- Coyne's interactional theory of depression states that someone who is vulnerable to depression may unintentionally alienate supportive people, which then confirms the person's negative view of self and his or her prospects for the future. [See *Figure 6.2.*]

E. Treating Depressive Disorders

Treatments target neurological, psychological, and social factors.

1. Targeting Neurological Factors

Medication and brain stimulation are the two neurological treatments for depression.

a. Medication:

Medications that treat depression include:

- *Selective serotonin reuptake inhibitors (SSRIs),* medications that slow the reuptake of serotonin from the synapses.
  - **i.** Examples of SSRIs are *fluoxetine* (Prozac), *paroxetine* (Paxil), and *sertraline* (Zoloft).
  - **ii.** *SSRIs* work by slowing the reuptake of serotonin from the synapses.
  - **iii.** The major benefit of SSRIs is that they have fewer side effects than other types of medication.
  - **iv.** Drawbacks include decreased sexual interest, the *Prozac poop-out* (which refers to patients getting less benefit from the dose over time) and greater risk for suicidal thoughts or attempts in children and adolescents.

- *Tricyclic antidepressants (TCAs),* older antidepressants named after the three rings of atoms in their molecular structure.
  - **i.** *Amitriptyline* (Elavil) is one example of a TCS.
  - **ii.** Benefits are that they are as effective as Prozac and do not decrease sexual interest as SSRIs do.
  - **iii.** Drawbacks include side effects such as low blood pressure, blurred vision, dry mouth, and constipation.

- *Monoamine oxidase inhibitors (MAOIs),* antidepressant medications that increase the amount of the enzyme monoamine oxidase in the brain.
  - **i.** *Phenelzine* (Nardil) is one example of an MAOI.
  - **ii.** Benefits include effectiveness in treating atypical depression.
  - **iii.** Drawbacks include food limitations (wine, cheese, and other foods containing a substance called tyramine).
  - **iv.** MAOIs are now available as a skin patch.

(1) Other medications

- **Newer medications: Serotonin/norepinephrine reuptake inhibitors (SNRIs):**
  Medications that affect serotonin and norepinephrine.
  - **i.** Examples include *venlafaxine* (Effexor) and *duloxetine* (Cymbalta).

- **Newer medications: Noradrenergic and specific serotonergic antidepressants (NaSSAs):**
  Medications that affect noradrenaline (norepinephrine) and serotonin.
  - **i.** *Mirtazapine* (Remeron) is one example of an NaSSA.

(2) Nonprescription treatments

- **St. John's wort (Hypericum perforatum)**
  - **i.** Helps those with mild to moderate depression and sometimes even those with severe depression.
  - **ii.** Benefits include fewer side effects.
  - **iii.** Drawbacks include dry mouth or dizziness.

- **S-adenosyl-ʟ-methionine (SAMe)**
  i. **SAMe or ademetionine** is as effective as imiprimine.
  ii. Benefits include quickly reducing depression in about a week.

b. **Brain Stimulation:**
- Electroconvulsive therapy (ECT) and transcranial magnetic stimulation (TMS) both treat depression through brain stimulation.
  i. ECT is used only when symptoms are severe, other medications cannot be used due to side effects or other medical reasons, the patient has psychotic depression that does not respond to medication, or medication or psychotherapy has not helped to reduce symptoms.
  ii. Drawbacks include memory loss for events prior to the procedure and lack of information about how ECT works.
  iii. Treatment is administered for 6–12 sessions and occurs two to three times a week over several weeks and in conjunction with medication to prevent relapses.

MEDIA RECOMMENDATION 6.6: Rob McGruder's ECT Odyssey

Objective: Students will learn about the benefits and drawbacks of ECT.

Time: 22 Minutes

Media and Discussion: 40 Minutes

Discussion Only: 18 Minutes

Listen Online: Hear from Rob McGruder as he seeks relief from bipolar disorder through ECT: http://www.npr.org/templates/story/story.php?storyId=1135970

Summary: The NPR audio segment explores a real-life experience of ECT. Students learn about the benefits and drawbacks of this treatment.

Questions to Students and Discussion: What surprised you in listening to Rob's story? What symptoms of MDE is Rob showing? What are some of the side effects of ECT, according to Rob? What stigma is associated with ECT treatments?

- In TMS, high-intensity magnetic pulses are sent through the brain.
  i. Benefits include ease of administration, fewer side effects than ECT, and FDA approval if other treatments fail.
  ii. Drawbacks include ill-defined treatment guidelines, including critical features such as where to position the coils and how often to administer the treatment.

MEDIA RECOMMENDATION 6.7: TMS for Depression

Objective: Students will learn about and hear TMS.

Time: 22 Minutes

Media and Discussion: 30 Minutes

Discussion Only: 8 Minutes

Listen Online: This NPR audio clip describes TMS: http://www.npr.org/templates/player/media Player.html?action=1&t=1&islist=false&id=1135970&m=135970.

Summary: Georgia decided to try TMS to treat her depression. The audio clip takes the listener through the treatment process.

Questions to Students and Discussion: How does TMS work? What does undergoing TMS feel like? What questions do you have about TMS?

2. **Targeting Psychological Factors**

   Psychological treatments include behavioral and cognitive methods.

   a. **Behavioral Methods:**
   - *Behavioral activation* refers to specific techniques to change depressive behaviors.
   - Examples include self-monitoring, scheduling daily pleasurable activities, decreasing avoidant behaviors, and problem solving.
   - Behavioral activation works better than cognitive techniques for both moderate and severe depression.

   b. **Cognitive Methods:**
   - The focus is on reducing or changing distorted thoughts.
   - Patients are asked to collect data and assess the accuracy of their beliefs, which in turn reduces the symptoms of depression.
   - However, only about 35% maintain improvement 18 months later.

   c. **Cognitive-Behavior Therapy Compared to Medication:**
   - CBT is as effective as medication.
   - CBT works better than medication when side effects can lead to noncompliance or when patients decide to stop taking the medication.
   - Medication and CBT in combination are more effective than medication alone.

3. **Targeting Social Factors**

   Interpersonal and family systems therapy treat social factors.

   a. **Interpersonal Therapy:**
   - Interpersonal therapy for depression focuses on four aspects of the patient's relationships.
   - The four aspects of relationships include:
     i. Improving social and communication skills
     ii. Resolving significant relationship conflicts
     iii. Examining grief
     iv. Addressing transitions in interpersonal roles
   - IPT has resulted in a decrease in depressive symptoms, has been used in treating postpartum depression in women at high risk, and can be used alone or in combination with CBT.

   b. **Family Systems Therapy:**
   - Family systems therapy addresses family dysfunctional interaction patterns or family conflicts.
   - This form of therapy is used to help resolve intergenerational conflict in immigrant families.

4. **FEEDBACK LOOPS IN TREATMENT: Depressive Disorders**

- Neurological, psychological, and social treatments all share the goal of reducing depressive symptoms.
- One treatment will affect the others. [See *Figure 6.3.*]

II. BIPOLAR DISORDERS

The second category of mood disorders is ***bipolar disorders,*** in which a person's mood is often persistently and abnormally upbeat or shifts inappropriately from upbeat to markedly down.

A. Building Blocks for Bipolar Disorders

There are four types of mood episodes for bipolar disorders—the major depressive episode, the *manic episode,* the *mixed episode,* and the *hypomanic episode.*

1. **Manic Episode**

   The ***manic episode*** is a discrete period of at least 1 week characterized by abnormally euphoric feelings, intense irritability, or an *expansive mood.*

   - During an ***expansive mood,*** the person exhibits unceasing, indiscriminate enthusiasm for interpersonal, sexual, or occupational interactions. [See *Table 6.7.*]
   - Symptoms may include:
     i. Increase in focused goal-directed activity
     ii. Grandiosity
     iii. Rapid or loud speech
     iv. *Flight of ideas* or thoughts that race faster than they can be said [see *Case 6.4*]
     v. Increased distractibility
     vi. Reckless pursuit of pleasurable activities
     vii. Lack of awareness of consequences
     viii. Sharpened senses

2. **Mixed Episode**

   - A *mixed episode* involves symptoms of both manic *and* major depressive episodes.
   - A mixed episode may last weeks or months, and all of the symptoms may disappear or evolve into an MDE or manic episode.
   - These episodes are more common in young people and those over 60 years old, and they are more common among males than females.
   - Symptoms may include:
     i. Agitation
     ii. Insomnia
     iii. Appetite dysregulation
     iv. Psychotic features
     v. Suicidal thinking

3. **Hypomanic Episode**

   - A *hypomanic episode* is a distinct period of persistent and pervasive elated, irritable, or euphoric mood, which is less distressing and debilitating than mania.
   - These episodes do not include psychotic symptoms or flight of ideas.
   - Symptoms of a hypomanic episode must last for a minimum of 4 days, compared to 1 week for a manic episode.

- Symptoms include:
  - **i.** Uncritical self-confidence but not grandiosity
  - **ii.** Increased efficiency and creativity
  - **iii.** Loud and rapid speech that can be interrupted

B. The Two Types of Bipolar Disorder

There are two types of bipolar disorder: bipolar I disorder and bipolar II disorder.

1. Bipolar I Versus Bipolar II Disorder

- Both disorders have manic symptoms at varying levels.

- Bipolar I is more severe and has mixed or manic episodes and possibly an MDE.

- Bipolar II is less severe and alternates between hypomania and MDE. [See *Tables 6.8a, 6.8b,* and *6.9.*]

- *Rapid cycling* is defined as having four or more episodes that meet the criteria for any type of mood episode within 1 year; it can occur in both bipolar I and bipolar II, but is more common with bipolar II disorder and occurs more often in women. Rapid cycling is unique to the bipolar disorders.

- People of different races and ethnicities are equally likely to be afflicted with bipolar disorders.

2. Bipolar Disorder and Creativity?

Are people with bipolar disorder more creative?

- Studies have suggested a link but have numerous methodological problems because many studies lack random selection or suffer from overreliance on biographical accounts and rater biases.

LEARNING ACTIVITY 6.5: The Sylvia Plath Effect

Objective: To have students learn about the connection between mental illness and creativity.

Time: 30 Minutes

Read Online: This article in the *APA Monitor* explores the link between creativity and mental illness: http://www.apa.org/monitor/nov03/plath.html

Summary: Students will read about arguments on each side of this issue. One interesting research result: "[I]n a more recent retrospective study of 1,629 writers, Kaufman found that poets—and in particular female poets—were more likely than fiction writers, nonfiction writers and playwrights to have signs of mental illness, such as suicide attempts or psychiatric hospitalizations" (Bailey 2003).

Source: Bailey, D. S. (Nov. 2003). The "Sylvia Plath" effect. *Monitor, 34*(10), 42.

Questions to Students and Discussion: Do you think creativity and mental illness are connected? How do you support your argument? Do you find creative writing or writing about yourself to be emotionally beneficial or harmful? What questions do you have about this topic?

C. Cyclothymic Disorder

- *Cyclothymia* is a more chronic but less intense version of bipolar II disorder characterized by chronic, fluctuating mood disturbances with numerous periods of hypomanic symptoms and numerous periods of depressive symptoms (but which do not meet MDE criteria).

- The disorder has a lifetime prevalence of 0.4–1.0%.
- Men and women are equally affected.
- Symptoms are expressed in early adolescence or young adulthood.
- 15–50% of people with cyclothymia develop some type of bipolar disorder. [See *Table 6.10, Case 6.5,* and *Figure 6.4.*]

D. Understanding Bipolar Disorders

Neurological, psychological, and social factors interact to produce bipolar disorder.

1. **Neurological Factors**

   Brain functioning and genetics are neurological factors associated with bipolar disorders.

   a. Brain Systems:
   - The amygdala is enlarged and overactive in people with a bipolar disorder.
   - These differences may lead to stronger emotional reactions.

   b. Neural Communication:
   - Three neurotransmitters are involved in bipolar disorder—serotonin, norepinephrine, and glutamate.
   - Serotonin and norepinephrine play a role in bipolar disorders.
   - Lithium (a mood stabilizer) lowers norepinephrine levels and reduces bipolar symptoms.
   - During manic episodes, the left frontal lobes produce too much glutamate (an excitatory neurotransmitter).

   c. Genetics:
   Research suggests genes influence who will develop bipolar disorder:

   - A person is at a 4–24% risk of developing the disorder if there is a first-degree relative who has bipolar disorder.
   - Monozygotic twins have a 40–70% chance of developing the disorder if one twin develops a bipolar disorder.
   - Dizygotic twins have a 5% chance of developing the disorder if one twin develops bipolar disorder.
   - Depressive and bipolar disorders may share the same genetic vulnerability.
     i. If a dizygotic twin has a bipolar disorder, the other twin has an 80% chance of developing a mood disorder.

2. **Psychological Factors: Thoughts and Attributions**
   - The cognitive distortions, negative thinking, and internal attribution style that affect people with depression also affect people with a bipolar disorder during MDEs.
   - Residual effects of manic episodes can cause continued cognitive deficits (attentional difficulties, learning, memory, executive functioning, and problem solving).

3. **Social Factors: Social and Environmental Stressors**
   - Significant social stressors occur prior to experiencing the first episode.
   - Family-related stress can contribute to relapse.
   - Stress can worsen the course of symptoms.

4. **FEEDBACK LOOPS IN ACTION: Bipolar Disorders**
   - Neurological, psychological, and social factors interact to produce the bipolar disorders. [See *Figure 6.5.*]

E. Treating Bipolar Disorders

Treatments target neurological, psychological, and social factors.

1. **Targeting Neurological Factors: Medication**

   a. Mood Stabilizers:

   Mood stabilizers are medications that minimize mood swings.

   - *Lithium* is the oldest mood stabilizer.
     - **i.** Lithium is a type of salt.
     - **ii.** It affects several neurotransmitters.
     - **iii.** Side effects can include coordination problems, vomiting, muscular weakness, blurred vision, and ringing in the ears; regular blood tests are recommended.
     - **iv.** Lithium only works for half of patients who take it.
   - Other mood stabilizers can be effective.
     - **i.** These medications help those with recurring manic episodes.
     - **ii.** Included are antiepileptic medications (or *anticonvulsants*) such as *divalproex* (Depakote), *carbamazepine* (Tegretol), *lamotrigine* (Lamictal), and *gabapentin* (Neurontin).

   b. Problems with Medication:

   - Blunting of emotions and other positive aspects of mania can occur.
   - Antidepressant medication alone can trigger mania.

2. **Targeting Psychological Factors: Thoughts, Moods, and Relapse Prevention**
   - Teaching clients about patterns of thought and behavior that minimize the risk of relapse
   - Medication compliance
   - CBT that focuses on medication compliance, sleeping strategies, and early recognition of symptoms has been helpful.

3. **Targeting Social Factors: Interacting with Others**
   - Treatments focus on establishing consistent social patterns (sleep, eating, etc.) and better social interactions (reducing conflict, etc.).
   - See *Figure 6.6* for an example of a Daily Log of Social Rhythms.
   - Family treatments focus on reducing criticism and negative family interactions.
   - Group therapy and self-help groups can decrease isolation and shame.

4. **FEEDBACK LOOPS IN TREATMENT: Bipolar Disorder**

   Successful treatments target multiple factors such as neurological, psychological, and social aspects of the bipolar disorder. [See *Figure 6.7.*]

III. SUICIDE

A. Suicidal Thoughts and Suicide Risks

- Suicide is ranked 11th among causes of death in the United States and Canada.
- Approximately 32,000 people die by suicide each year in the United States. [See *Table 6.11.*]

1. **Thinking About, Planning, and Attempting Suicide**

    a. **Suicidal ideation:**

    Suicidal ideation is when people may have thoughts of death or thoughts about committing suicide.

    - Behaviors indicative of suicidal ideation include:
        i. Giving away possessions
        ii. Saying goodbye to friends or family
        iii. Talking about death or suicide generally or about specific plans to commit suicide
        iv. Making threats of suicide
        v. Rehearsing a plan for suicide
    - Some suggest a sixth axis be added to a diagnosis for an evaluation of a patient's suicidal risk.
    - *Parasuicidal behavior* is behavior associated with suicide but is not a suicide attempt. (*Example:* self injury)

2. **Risk and Protective Factors for Suicide**

    - People who have a psychological disorder are at a higher risk for attempting suicide.
    - People with a major depressive disorder (50%), personality disorders (40%), and substance-related disorders (up to 50%) are more likely to commit suicide.
    - Substance use (inhibits one's ability to reason), history of attempts, and being gay or lesbian plays a role in suicide. [See *Table 6.12.*]

B. Understanding Suicide

The interactions among neurological, psychological, and social factors can help us to understand suicide.

1. **Neurological Factors**

    a. **Brain Systems and Neural Communication:**
    - People who commit suicide have fewer neurons in the part of the brain that produces serotonin, produce less serotonin, and have fewer serotonin receptors in their brains.
    - Low levels of serotonin is associated with impulsivity, which may increase the likelihood of committing suicide.

    b. **Genetics:**
    - Researchers have not yet identified a gene associated with suicide but have found a genetic link with depression.
    - Future research may focus on examining genes related to serotonin.

2. **Psychological Factors: Hopelessness and Impulsivity**

    Poor coping and problem-solving skills, and, especially, hopelessness are psychological factors linked to suicide.

3. **Social Factors: Alienation and Cultural Stress**

    - Social and cultural factors affect suicide rates. [See *Table 6.13.*]
    - Durkheim (1897/1951) believed individualistic communities place people at higher risk for suicide. This theory may, in part, account for the increasing worldwide sui-

cide rate among young men. [See *Table 6.14.*] Men commit suicide five times more than women, but this rate differs according to the country.

- Socially related protective factors and method of suicide may explain these gender differences.

4. **FEEDBACK LOOPS IN ACTION: Suicide**

Neurological, psychological, and social factors contribute to suicide. [See *Figure 6.8.*]

C. Preventing Suicide

- Prevention measures include management of crises, suicide hotlines, long-term interventions, and treatment of related disorders.
- Research on suicide prevention has examined neurological, psychological, and social factors.

1. **Targeting Neurological Factors: Medication**

- Medications and ECT (as a last resort) are neurological interventions that can target those with suicidal thoughts.
- Khan and colleagues (2000) used RCTs and found similar rates of attempted and completed suicides when comparing those taking newer antidepressants versus placebos. However, those with serious suicidal intent are often excluded from RCTs.

2. **Targeting Psychological Factors: Reducing Feelings of Hopelessness**

- If someone is suicidal, the first goal is safety.
- Once the person is safe, psychological interventions are used to examine triggers and problem-solving and coping skills.
- Clinicians also assess and treat depression and substance abuse and may use CBT.

3. **Targeting Social Factors: Social Programs, Social Awareness**

- Programs that target social factors seek to prevent suicide long-term by reducing child abuse, improving access to mental health care, decreasing substance abuse, and increasing employment.
- Suicidal prevention and awareness is also helpful. [See *Table 6.15.*]

MEDIA RECOMMENDATION 6.8: Exploring Suicide Prevention Programs

Objective: To learn about various prevention programs and resources.

Time: 30 Minutes

Media and Discussion: 60 Minutes

Discussion Only: 30 Minutes

Explore Online:
Center for Disease Control Suicide Prevention Resources, Activities, and Audiofiles:
http://www.cdc.gov/ViolencePrevention/suicide/index.html

National Institute of Mental Health Facts, Resources, Research, and Funding:
http://www.nimh.nih.gov/health/topics/suicide-prevention/index.shtml

National Strategy for Suicide Prevention Facts, Resources, Events: http://mentalhealth.samhsa.gov/suicideprevention/2000.asp

Summary: Through this media exploration, students can identify specific activities and resources for suicide prevention.

Questions to Students and Discussion: Name three prevention strategies. Describe three resources that are available to the public. In exploring the online data, what aspect of suicide prevention most surprised you?

4. FEEDBACK LOOPS IN PREVENTION: Suicide

- The Air Force instituted a comprehensive suicide prevention program to reduce the number of suicides.
- The suicide rate fell by 33%. [See *Figure 6.9.*]
- The homicide and family violence rates also decreased.
- *Figure 6.10* shows the feedback loops of prevention.

ADDITIONAL READINGS

Abramson, L. Y., Alloy, L. B., Hogan, M. E., Whitehouse, W. G., Donovan, P., Rose, D. T., Panzarella, C., & Raniere, D. (1999). Cognitive vulnerability to depression: Theory and evidence. *Journal of Cognitive Psychotherapy, 13,* 5–20.

Abramson, L. Y., Metalsky, G. I., & Alloy, L. B. (1989). Hopelessness depression: A theory-based subtype of depression. *Psychological Review, 96,* 358–372.

Abramson, L. Y., Seligman, M. E., & Teasdale, J. D. (1978). Learned helplessness in humans: Critique and reformulation. *Journal of Abnormal Psychology, 87,* 49–74.

Antonuccio, D. O., Danton, W. G., & DeNelsky, G. Y. (1995). Psychotherapy versus medication for depression: Challenging the conventional wisdom with data. *Professional Psychology: Research & Practice, 26,* 574–585.

Goodwin, F. K., & Jamison, K. R. (1990). *Manic-depressive illness.* New York: Oxford University Press.

Jamison, K. R. (1989). Mood disorders and patterns of creativity in British writers and artists. *Psychiatry, 52,* 125–134.

Jamison, K. R. (1993). *Touched with fire: Manic-depressive illness and the artistic temperament.* New York: Free Press.

Marano, H. E. (2003). Bedfellows: Insomnia and depression. *Psychology Today,* July/August, n.p. Retrieved May 4, 2007, from http://psychologytoday.com/articles/pto-20030715-000001.html.

Nolen-Hoeksema, S. (2000). The role of rumination in depressive disorders and mixed anxiety/depressive symptoms. *Journal of Abnormal Psychology, 109,* 504–511.

Nolen-Hoeksema, S. (2001). Gender differences in depression. *Current Directions in Psychological Science, 10,* 173–176.

Parker, G., Gladstone, G., & Chee, K. T. (2001). Depression in the planet's largest ethnic group: The Chinese. *American Journal of Psychiatry, 158,* 857–864.

Mood Disorder Memoirs and Novels

Behrman, A. (2003). *Electroboy: A memoir of mania.* New York: Random House.
Take a trip with Behrman and experience the thrill and downside of mania.

Berger, D., & Berger, L. (1992). *We heard the angels of madness: A family guide to coping with manic depression.* New York: Harper Collins.

  Written from the perspective of a mother and sister dealing with a family member suffering from bipolar depression.

Birmingham, A. (2006). *The crazy inside: A poetic journey through manic depression.* Lulu.com.

  Birmingham chronicles her battle with bipolar depression through this collection of poems and photographs.

Burak, C. S., & Remington, M. G. (1994). *The cradle will fall.* New York: Donald I. Fine.

  Remington's tale (cowritten with the psychiatrist who treated her) about her experiences with a postpartum depression, which leads to her kill her child and injure herself.

Jamison, K. R. (1995). *An unquiet mind: A memoir of moods and madness.* New York: Vintage Books.

  An exploration of Jamison's experience with bipolar disorder.

Manning, M. (1995). *Undercurrents: A life beneath the surface.* San Francisco: Harper Collins.

  A psychologist writes about her experience with depression and ECT.

Plath, S. (1971). *The bell jar.* New York: Bantam Books.

  Plath's infamous, semi-autobiographical novel, published one month before the author's suicide, tells the story of a college student's descent into depression, resulting in her hospitalization.

Wertzel, E. (1994). *Prozac nation: A memoir.* New York: Houghton Mifflin.

  Wertzel describes her high school and college struggles with depression and/or bipolar disorder.

ADDITIONAL MEDIA RECOMMENDATIONS

Berman, S. S., & Pulcini, B. (Directors). (2003). *American splendor* [Film]. USA: Good Machine.

  This film features the true story of Harvey Pekar, a Cleveland cartoonist, who suffers from MDEs.

Daldry, S. (Director). (2003). *The hours* [Film]. USA: Paramount Pictures.

  An exploration of depression and suicide in the lives of three women.

David, J. (Director). (1987). *Four lives: A portrait of manic depression* [Film]. USA: Jonathon David Films.

  A powerful, educational film that features diverse expressions of bipolar disorder.

Jeffs, C. (Director). (2003). *Sylvia* [Film]. UK: BBC Films.

  A biography of the American writer Sylvia Plath, who struggled with debilitating depression and ultimately committed suicide.

Steel, E. (Director). (2007). *The bridge* [Film]. USA: Easy There Tiger Productions.

  This controversial documentary shows successful and attempted suicides at the Golden Gate Bridge. Web site: http://www.thebridge-themovie.com/new/index.html

WEB SITES

Bipolar World: A Web site for mental health consumers. See: http://www.bipolarworld.net/

Child and Adolescent Bipolar Foundation: This site offers a plethora of resources and a space to chat. See: http://www.bpkids.org/site/PageServer

Depression and Bipolar Support Alliance: Resources, training, and information about support groups. See: http://www.dbsalliance.org/site/PageServer?pagename=home

Lifeline Gallery: Stories of Hope and Recovery: Listen to real people talk about their experiences with suicide. See: http://www.lifeline-gallery.org/

Madison Institute of Medicine: This is the most comprehensive source for information on bipolar disorder treatments. See: http://www.miminc.org/aboutmimmain.asp

Mental Help Network: This site offers solid information on various disorders. See: http://www.mentalhelp.net/

NIMH Video on Depression: This four-minute video covers signs and symptoms of depression. See: http://www.nimh.nih.gov/health/topics/depression/index.shtml

PsychEducation: Information on a number of mental illnesses presented and updated by Dr. Jim Phelps. See: http://www.psycheducation.org/

WORKSHEET 6.1

	Internal (personal)		External (environmental)	
	Stable	Unstable	Stable	Unstable
Global				
Specific				

Anxiety Disorders

CHAPTER OUTLINE

CHAPTER HEADINGS	INSTRUCTION IDEAS AND TEXTBOOK CORRELATIONS
COMMON FEATURES OF ANXIETY DISORDERS	
What Is Anxiety?	**Learning Objectives:** 7.1, 7.2 **Learning Concepts:** What is anxiety? **Learning Activity 7.1:** Rate My Anxiety
The Fight-or-Flight Response Gone Awry	**Learning Objective:** 7.3 **Learning Concepts:** fight-or-flight response gone awry **Media Recommendation 7.1:** The Stress Response **Textbook Tools:** Figure 7.1 **Worth Video Tool Kit for Abnormal Psychology:** Anxiety Disorders: Identify the Disorder
Comorbidity of Anxiety Disorders	**Learning Concepts:** comorbidity of anxiety disorders **Media Recommendation 7.2:** Overview of Anxiety Disorders **Textbook Tools:** Figure 7.2
GENERALIZED ANXIETY DISORDER	
What Is Generalized Anxiety Disorder?	**Learning Objective:** 7.5 **Learning Concepts:** What is generalized anxiety disorder? **Media Recommendation 7.3:** The Experience of GAD **Textbook Tools:** Tables 7.1, 7.2; Case 7.1
Understanding Generalized Anxiety Disorder	**Learning Objectives:** 7.6, 7.7, 7.8 **Learning Concepts:** understanding and treating generalized anxiety disorder, neurological (brain systems, neural communication, genetics), psychological, and social factors (stressors) **Textbook Tool:** Figure 7.3
Treating Generalized Anxiety Disorder	**Learning Objectives:** 7.9, 7.10 **Learning Concepts:** targeting neurological factors: medication, psychological factors (behavioral and cognitive), social factors **Learning Activity 7.2:** Muscle Relaxation **Textbook Tools:** Figures 7.4, 7.5

PANIC DISORDER (WITH AND WITHOUT AGORAPHOBIA)	**Learning Concepts:** panic attack
The Panic Attack—A Key Ingredient of Panic Disorder	**Learning Objective:** 7.11 **Textbook Tools:** Table 7.3
What Is Panic Disorder?	**Learning Concepts:** What is panic disorder? **Media Recommendation 7.4:** Panic Disorder **Textbook Tools:** Table 7.6; Case 7.2
What Is Agoraphobia?	**Learning Concepts:** What is agoraphobia? **Textbook Tools:** Table 7.6; Case 7.3
Understanding Panic Disorder and Agoraphobia	**Learning Objectives:** 7.12, 7.13 **Learning Concepts:** understanding panic disorder and agoraphobia, neurological (brain systems, neural communication, genetics), psychological (learning and cognitive), and social factors **Textbook Tool:** Figure 7.6; Case 7.2
Treating Panic Disorder and Agoraphobia	**Learning Objectives:** 7.14, 7.15 **Learning Concepts:** treating panic disorder and agoraphobia, targeting neurological (medication), psychological (behavioral and cognitive methods), and social factors (group and couples therapy) **Textbook Tools:** Figure 7.7; Table 7.7
SOCIAL PHOBIA (SOCIAL ANXIETY DISORDER)	**Worth Video Tool Kit for Abnormal Psychology:** Cognitive Therapy for Panic Disorder, Cognitive Therapy for Agoraphobia: A Success Story
What Is Social Phobia?	**Learning Objective:** 7.16 **Learning Concepts:** What is social phobia? **Textbook Tools:** Tables 7.8, 7.9; Case 7.4
Understanding Social Phobia	**Learning Objectives:** 7.17, 7.18 **Learning Concepts:** understanding social phobia, neurological (brain systems, neural communication, genetics), psychological (cognitive and classical and operant conditioning), and social factors (parent-child interactions and culture) **Textbook Tool:** Figure 7.8; Case 7.4
Treating Social Phobia	**Learning Objectives:** 7.19, 7.20 **Learning Concepts:** treating social phobia, neurological (medication), psychological (exposure and cognitive restructuring) and social factors (group interactions) **Textbook Tools:** Figures 7.9, 7.10
SPECIFIC PHOBIAS	**Learning Concepts:** understanding and treating specific phobias **Textbook Tools:** Tables 7.10, 7.11; Case 7.5
What Is Specific Phobia?	**Learning Objective:** 7.21 **Learning Concepts:** What is specific phobia?
Specifics About Specific Phobias	**Learning Activity 7.3:** Do You Have a Phobia?

Understanding Specific Phobias	**Learning Objectives:** 7.22, 7.23 **Learning Concepts:** understanding specific phobias, neurological (brain systems, neural communication, genetics), psychological (faulty estimations and conditioning), and social factors (modeling) **Textbook Tool:** Figures 7.11, 7.12
Treating Specific Phobias	**Learning Objectives:** 7.24, 7.25 **Learning Concepts:** treating specific phobias, targeting neurological (medication), psychological (behavioral and cognitive), and social factors **Media Recommendation 7.5:** Virtual Reality Therapy **Textbook Tools:** Figure 7.13; Table 7.12
OBSESSIVE-COMPULSIVE DISORDER	**Worth Video Tool Kit for Abnormal Psychology:** Real People Cope with Real Fears: Alter Egos in Virtual World
What Is Obsessive-Compulsive Disorder?	**Learning Objective:** 7.26 **Learning Concepts:** What is obsessive-compulsive disorder? **Media Recommendation 7.6:** Living with OCD **Textbook Tools:** Tables 7.13, 7.14, 7.15; Case 7.6
Understanding Obsessive-Compulsive Disorder	**Learning Objectives:** 7.27, 7.28 **Learning Concepts:** understanding obsessive-compulsive disorder, neurological (brain systems, neural communication, genetics), psychological (behavioral and cognitive), and social factors (stress, culture), and feedback loops **Media Recommendation 7.7:** Religion and OCD **Textbook Tool:** Figures 7.14, 7.15
Treating Obsessive-Compulsive Disorder	**Learning Objectives:** 7.29, 7.30 **Learning Concepts:** treating obsessive-compulsive disorder, targeting neurological (medication), psychological (behavioral and cognitive), and social factors (family therapy) **Lecture Enhancement 7.1:** Hoarding **Textbook Tool:** Figure 7.16
POSTTRAUMATIC STRESS DISORDER	**Learning Objectives:** 7.31
Stress Versus Traumatic Stress	**Learning Objectives:** 7.32 **Learning Concepts:** stress versus traumatic stress **Textbook Tool:** Table 7.16
What Is Posttraumatic Stress Disorder?	**Learning Concepts:** What is posttraumatic stress disorder? **Lecture Enhancement 7.2:** Race-Based Traumatic Stress Injury **Textbook Tools:** Tables 7.17, 7.18; Case 7.7
Criticisms of the DSM-IV-TR Criteria for Posttraumatic Stress Disorder	**Learning Concepts:** criticisms of the DSM-IV-TR criteria
Understanding Posttraumatic Stress Disorder	**Learning Objectives:** 7.33, 7.34 **Learning Concepts:** understanding posttraumatic stress disorder, neurological (brain systems, neural communication, genetics),

	psychological (history of trauma, comorbidity, and conditioning), and social factors (socioeconomic stress, social support, culture) **Lecture Enhancement 7.3:** Stages of Sexual Assault Survival **Textbook Tool:** Figure 7.17
Treating Posttraumatic Stress Disorder	**Learning Objectives:** 7.35, 7.36 **Learning Concepts:** treating posttraumatic stress disorder, targeting neurological (medication), psychological (behavioral and cognitive) and social factors (safety, group exposure, family education) and feedback loops **Textbook Tool:** Figure 7.18
HOWARD HUGHES AND ANXIETY DISORDERS	

LEARNING OBJECTIVES

After completing this chapter, students will be able to:

7.1 Describe the common features of anxiety disorders.

7.2 Define anxiety.

7.3 Describe the flight-or-fight response and its relation to anxiety disorders.

7.4 Explain the components of the tripartite model of anxiety and depression.

7.5 Describe the DSM-IV-TR criteria of generalized anxiety disorder.

7.6 Describe the neurological explanations of generalized anxiety disorder.

7.7 Identify psychological and social causes of generalized anxiety disorder.

7.8 Describe the interactions among neuropsychosocial factors for generalized anxiety disorder.

7.9 Identify neurological, psychological, and social treatments for generalized anxiety disorder.

7.10 Describe the interactions among neurological, psychological, and social treatments for generalized anxiety disorder.

7.11 Describe the DSM-IV-TR criteria of panic disorder (with and without agoraphobia).

7.12 Identify the neurological, psychological, and social causes of panic disorder (with and without agoraphobia).

7.13 Describe the interactions among neuropsychosocial causes of panic disorder (with and without agoraphobia).

7.14 Identify the neurological, psychological, and social treatments for panic disorder (with and without agoraphobia).

7.15 Describe the interactions among neuropsychosocial treatments for panic disorder (with and without agoraphobia).

7.16 List the DSM-IV-TR criteria for social phobia.

7.17 Describe the neurological, psychological, and social causes of social phobia.

7.18 Explain how the neuropsychosocial causes for social phobia interact.

7.19 Articulate the neurological, psychological, and social treatments for social phobia.

7.20 Explain how the neuropsychosocial treatments for social phobia interact.

7.21 List the DSM-IV-TR criteria and four types of specific phobia.

7.22 Describe the neurological, psychological, and social causes of specific phobia.

7.23 Explain how the neuropsychosocial causes for specific phobia interact.

7.24 Articulate the neurological, psychological, and social treatments for specific phobia.

7.25 Explain how the neuropsychosocial treatments for specific phobia interact.

7.26 List the DSM-IV-TR criteria for obsessive compulsive disorder.

7.27 Describe the neurological, psychological, and social causes for obsessive-compulsive disorder.

7.28 Explain how the neuropsychosocial causes for obsessive-compulsive disorder interact.

7.29 Articulate the neurological, psychological, and social treatments for obsessive-compulsive disorder.

7.30 Explain how the neuropsychosocial treatments for obsessive-compulsive disorder interact.

7.31 List the DSM-IV-TR criteria for posttraumatic stress disorder.

7.32 Describe the differences between stress and traumatic stress.

7.33 Describe the neurological, psychological, and social causes of posttraumatic stress disorder.

7.34 Explain how the neuropsychosocial causes for posttraumatic stress disorder interact.

7.35 Articulate the neurological, psychological, and social treatments for posttraumatic stress disorder.

7.36 Explain how the neuropsychosocial treatments for posttraumatic stress disorder interact.

KEY TERMS

Anxiety: A sense of agitation or nervousness, which is often focused on an upcoming possible danger.

Anxious apprehension: Anxiety that arises in response to a high level of fear of a particular stimulus.

Anxiety disorder: A category of psychological disorders in which the primary symptoms involve extreme anxiety, intense arousal, and/or extreme attempts to avoid stimuli that lead to fear and anxiety.

Fight-or-flight response: The automatic neurological and bodily response to a perceived threat; also called the *stress response.*

Panic: An extreme sense (or fear) of imminent doom, together with an extreme stress response.

Phobia: An exaggerated fear of an object or a situation, together with an extreme avoidance of the object or situation.

Generalized anxiety disorder (GAD): The anxiety disorder characterized by uncontrollable worry and anxiety that do not have a specific focus.

Hypervigilance: A heightened search for threats.

Panic attack: A specific period of intense dread, fear, or a sense of imminent doom, accompanied by physical symptoms of a pounding heart, shortness of breath, shakiness, and sweating.

Panic disorder: The anxiety disorder characterized by frequent, unexpected panic attacks, along with fear of further attacks and possible restrictions of behavior in order to prevent such attacks.

Agoraphobia: The persistent avoidance of situations that a person fears will trigger another panic attack.

Concordance rate: The probability that both twins will have a characteristic or disorder, given that one of them has it.

In vivo exposure: The behavioral therapy method that consists of direct exposure to a feared or avoided situation or stimulus.

Interoceptive exposure: The behavioral therapy method in which patients intentionally elicit the bodily sensations associated with panic so they can habituate to those sensations and not respond with fear.

Social phobia: The anxiety disorder characterized by intense fear of public humiliation or embarrassment, together with the avoidance of social situations likely to cause this fear; also called *social anxiety disorder.*

Specific phobia: The anxiety disorder characterized by intense anxiety or fear related to a specific situation or object.

Obsessions: Thoughts, images, or impulses that persist or recur, are intrusive—and therefore difficult to ignore—and are inappropriate to the situation.

Compulsions: Repetitive behaviors or mental acts that a person feels driven to carry out and that usually correspond thematically to an obsession.

Obsessive-compulsive disorder (OCD): The anxiety disorder characterized by one or more obsessions, which may occur together with compulsions.

Posttraumatic stress disorder (PTSD): The anxiety disorder that arises a month or more after a traumatic event and that involves a persistent reexperiencing of the event, avoiding stimuli related to the event, and symptoms of anxiety and hyperarousal that persist for at least a month.

Acute stress disorder: The anxiety disorder that arises within a month after a traumatic event and that involves reexperiencing the event, avoiding stimuli related to the event, and symptoms of anxiety, hyperarousal, and dissociation that last for less than a month.

CHAPTER GUIDE

Chapter Introduction

Anxiety disorders involve significant fear, agitation, and nervousness. They can impair functioning in any or all spheres of life and anxiety symptoms can take many different forms.

This chapter includes six types of DSM-IV-TR anxiety disorders: generalized anxiety, panic disorder, social phobia, specific phobia, obsessive-compulsive disorder, and posttraumatic stress disorder.

I.   COMMON FEATURES OF ANXIETY DISORDERS

This section describes anxiety, its connection to the fight-or-flight response, and comorbidity with depression.

A. What Is Anxiety?

- *Anxiety* refers to a sense of agitation or nervousness, which is often focused on an upcoming potential danger.

- Anxiety can be adaptive because it prepares us for crises but extreme anxiety can lead to problems.

- *Anxious apprehension* is extreme anxiety in response to a high level of fear of a particular stimulus.

- *An **anxiety disorder*** involves extreme anxiety, intense arousal, and extreme attempts to avoid stimuli that lead to fear and anxiety.

LEARNING ACTIVITY 7.1: Rate My Anxiety

Objective: Students will be able to see the continuum of anxiety among their peers.

Time: 30 Minutes

Directions:
1. Post the following signs around the room: A lot, Sometimes, Rarely, Never.
2. Ask students to rate the degree to which they experience one or more of the following symptoms, by standing by the corresponding sign.
3. Ask students to complete "I have experienced _____."
   - Sweating
   - Trembling or shaking
   - Feeling dizzy, light-headed
   - Fear of losing control
   - Chills or hot flashes
   - Anxiety about being in a crowd
   - Anxiety about traveling
   - Fear of receiving an injection
   - Fear of snakes
   - A tendency to worry about things
   - Having to check the stove more than one time before leaving

Summary: Highlight the range and diversity of experiences in the class. Explain that anxiety disorders cover a range of symptoms on a continuum. Underscore that some anxiety is adaptive but can also be maladaptive. *Example:* Anxiety can motivate a student to study for an exam (adaptive), but if the anxiety interferes with the student's ability to concentrate or perform well on the exam then the anxiety is maladaptive and causes distress.

Questions to Students and Discussion: Do you think your anxiety helps you? Harms you? Why?

B. The Fight-or-Flight Response Gone Awry

- The **fight-or-flight response** (or *stress response*) occurs when an individual perceives a threat.
  - **i.** The brain and body respond by preparing either to fight (exert physical energy) or to take flight (run away). [See *Figure 7.1.*]
- An overactive stress response can lead to misinterpretations of physical responses or:
  - **i.** *Panic* or extreme sense (or fear) of imminent doom
  - **ii.** *Phobia* (derived from the Greek word for fear, *phobos*), an exaggerated fear of an object or a situation, together with an extreme avoidance of the object or situation
- Fifteen percent of Americans will have some type of anxiety disorder in their lifetime; this has almost doubled from 1990 to 2003 for unclear reasons.
- Women are twice as likely as men to be diagnosed with one of the anxiety disorders. This difference is possibly due to biological differences during pregnancy or puberty, or cultural factors.

MEDIA RECOMMENDATION 7.1: The Stress Response

Objective: To show students a visual of the stress response's effect on the brain and body.

Time: 3 Minutes

Video and Discussion: 20 Minutes

Discussion Only: 17 Minutes

Watch Online: Video on the science of the stress response. Search YouTube using the search term "stress response" or http://www.youtube.com/watch?v=RyP8L3qTW9Q

Description: This short video shows how stress affects the body and mind.

Summary: Students will see how stress affects the brain and body and how it can be adaptive or maladaptive. A minimal amount of stress can help energize and motivate us (*Example:* responding to a crisis), but at high levels it can debilitate us (*Example:* becoming paralyzed from responding or concentrating).

Questions to Students and Discussion: How is the stress response adaptive? Describe the stress response in the brain and body. How are anxiety and stress related? How does modern life affect our stress levels?

C. Comorbidity of Anxiety Disorders

- Symptoms of anxiety are seen in many other disorders, so clinicians must note the primary presenting problem or by-product symptoms.
- Over 50% of people with anxiety disorders are depressed; thus anxiety and depression commonly occur together.
- Some professionals have proposed the three-part model of anxiety and depression, which explains the difference between the two disorders and how they overlap.
    i. *High level of negative emotions* is what is shared by both anxiety and depression.
    ii. *Low level of positive emotions* is a symptom of depression, but generally not a symptom of anxiety disorders.
    iii. *Physiological hyperarousal* (overarousal) is found in anxiety disorders, but not in depression. [See *Figure 7.2.*]

MEDIA RECOMMENDATION 7.2: Overview of Anxiety Disorders

Objective: To provide students with a quick overview of anxiety disorders.

Time: 7 Minutes

Video and Discussion: 20 Minutes

Discussion Only: 13 Minutes

Watch Online: Search YouTube using the search terms "anxiety overview" or http://www.youtube.com/watch?v=_Cr7IomSy8s

Description: This video provides an overview of the neuropsychosocial factors in anxiety disorders.

Summary: Students will learn the major anxiety disorders, bodily responses, and consequences of anxiety disorders.

Questions to Students and Discussion: How does anxiety affect the body? What are the different anxiety disorders? What are the consequences of having an anxiety disorder?

What questions do you have about anxiety disorders?

II. GENERALIZED ANXIETY DISORDER

A. What Is Generalized Anxiety Disorder?

- *Generalized anxiety disorder (GAD)* is characterized by uncontrollable worry and anxiety that does not have a specific focus. [See *Table 7.1.*]
- The worry and anxiety primarily focus on family, finances, work, and illness.
- People with GAD worry when things go well; thoughts intrude into their awareness, and they cannot stop worrying.
- Symptoms are present for at least half the days during a 6-month period. [See *Table 7.1* and *Case 7.1.*]
- People with GAD feel restless and have difficulty concentrating and sleeping. [See *Table 7.2.*]

1. GAD and Depression

- Both disorders have high comorbidity.
- People with both disorders are likely to have had their symptoms arise at a younger age, to have more severe symptoms of each disorder, and to function less well than those who have only one of the two disorders.
- Among people over 50 years old—the age group in which GAD is most common—depression often arises after GAD.

MEDIA RECOMMENDATION 7.3: The Experience of GAD

Objective: To understand the neuropsychosocial factors of GAD.

Time: 3 Minutes

Video and Discussion: 20 Minutes

Discussion Only: 17 Minutes

Watch Online: Dr. Erdelyi, a professor of psychology at Brooklyn College, discusses the neuropsychosocial factors of GAD. Search YouTube using the search terms "what is generalized anxiety disorder?" or http://www.youtube.com/watch?v=dRmBJhtys9g

Description: This brief clip provides an overview of generalized anxiety disorder and includes visuals of the neuron.

Summary: Students will understand and be able to visualize the neuropsychosocial factors in GAD.

Questions to Students and Discussion: What are the symptoms of GAD? What are the neurological, psychological, and social factors in GAD? What questions do you have about GAD?

B. Understanding Generalized Anxiety Disorder

Neurological, psychological, and social factors and the feedback loops among them help us understand GAD.

1. Neurological Factors

Brain systems, neural communication and genetics are the neurological factors that play a role in the development of GAD.

a. Brain Systems:

- Patients with GAD have more gray and white matter in the superior temporal gyrus, an area used in hearing and language comprehension.
- The superior temporal gyrus is larger in the right hemisphere than the left, and the size difference is more extreme in people with severe anxiety.
- The right hemisphere may be involved in a coping activity since the frontal lobes have many connections to the limbic system and the autonomic nervous system.

b. Neural Communication:

People with GAD may have dysfunctional GABA, serotonin, and norepinephrine activity, which affect reward responses, motivation, and attention.

c. Genetics:

Heritability for GAD is equal for men and women and is estimated at as low as 15–20% and as high as 40%.

2. Psychological Factors: Hypervigilance and the Illusion of Control

People with GAD have the following psychological characteristics:

- People with GAD experience *hypervigilance,* a heightened search for possible threats, by scrutinizing their surroundings.
- Their worries and thoughts feel as if they are out of control.
- Worrying prevents anxiety from becoming panic and is a negative reinforcer.

3. Social Factors: Stressors

- Stressful life events can trigger symptoms of GAD in someone who is neurologically vulnerable to developing it.
- People with GAD view themselves as having serious problems in relationships.

4. FEEDBACK LOOPS IN ACTION: Understanding Generalized Anxiety Disorder

GAD may be caused by neurological, physiological, or genetic factors and affect psychological perceptions of social events. [See *Figure 7.3.*]

C. Treating Generalized Anxiety Disorder

Treatment for GAD can target neurological, psychological, or social factors.

1. Targeting Neurological Factors: Medication

- *Buspirone* (Buspar), an antianxiety medication, reduces the symptoms of GAD by decreasing serotonin release, which causes changes in the amygdala.
- Decreasing serotonin levels reduces the responsiveness of key parts of the amygdala and dampens learned fear.
- Those with GAD and depression need a serotonin/norepinephrine reuptake inhibitor (such as paroxetine [Paxil] and *escitalopram* [Lexapro]).

- Symptoms return when the medication is stopped, so behavioral and cognitive therapies in combination with medication are strongly recommended.

2. **Targeting Psychological Factors**

The goals of psychological treatments include increasing a patient's sense of control over thoughts and worries, increasing the ability to accurately appraise potential threats, and decreasing muscle tension.

a. Behavioral Methods:

There are three main behavioral methods to treat GAD that focus on breathing as well as muscle tension and behaviors associated with worry.

- *Breathing retraining*—patients learn to increase awareness and control of breathing by taking deep, relaxing breaths.
- *Muscle relaxation training*—patients identify tense muscles and then relax them through standard relaxation techniques or *biofeedback.*
- *Exposure*—patients prolong exposure to their worries for about 30 minutes and then list rational responses to the worst outcomes they imagined. [See *Figure 7.4.*]

LEARNING ACTIVITY 7.2: Muscle Relaxation

Objective: To have students experience muscle relaxation.

Time: 3 Minutes

Audio and Discussion: 20 Minutes

Discussion Only: 17 Minutes

Listen Online: University of Wisconsin-Madison's Counseling Center's Relaxation Exercises MP3: http://forms.uhs.wisc.edu/relaxation.php

Description: This is an audio clip of a muscle relaxation exercise.

Directions:
1. Turn the lights off or low.
2. Have students close their eyes.
3. Play the audio clip.
4. Slowly put the lights on and have students open their eyes.

Summary: Students will experience deep relaxation from this exercise and will understand how such exercises help to treat GAD and other anxiety disorders.

Questions to Students and Discussion: How did you feel after this exercise? Why were you instructed to tense and release muscles rather than to simply relax? What are the pros and cons of such a treatment?

b. Cognitive Methods:

Cognitive methods include the following:

- *Psychoeducation* teaches about GAD symptoms and available treatment.
- *Meditation* teaches how to "let go" of thoughts and reduce the time spent thinking about worries.
- *Self-monitoring* helps patients become aware of cues that lead to anxiety and worry.

- *Problem solving* teaches patients to identify the specific problem and ways to use cognitive restructuring.
    - *Cognitive restructuring* helps patients to identify and to shift automatic, irrational thoughts related to worries. [See *Figure 7.4.*]

3. **Targeting Social Factors**

    Few treatments for GAD specifically target social factors but, instead, seek to change thoughts, behaviors, and feelings.

4. **FEEDBACK LOOPS IN TREATMENT: Generalized Anxiety Disorder**

    Behavioral and cognitive methods can increase awareness and lead to neurological changes, which can affect social factors. [See *Figure 7.5.*]

III. PANIC DISORDER (WITH AND WITHOUT AGORAPHOBIA)

A *panic attack* is a specific period of intense dread, fear, or a sense of imminent doom, accompanied by physical symptoms of a pounding heart, shortness of breath, shakiness, and sweating.

A. The Panic Attack—A Key Ingredient of Panic Disorder [see *Table 7.3*]

- Symptoms generally begin quickly, peak after a few minutes, and disappear within an hour.
- Some attacks are cued and are associated with certain objects, situations, or sensations.
- Attacks can occur at any time, even while sleeping.
- At some point in their lives, 30% of adults are affected.
- Symptoms may interfere with daily life and may cause people to avoid certain situations and environments.

B. What Is Panic Disorder?

- *Panic disorder* is marked by frequent, unexpected panic attacks, along with fear of further attacks and possible restrictions of behavior in order to prevent such attacks.
- The frequency, unpredictability, and individual response determine if a person has a panic attack or a disorder. [See *Tables 7.4, 7.5* and *Case 7.2.*]
- The symptoms are similar across cultures, but may include themes of magic or witchcraft depending on the culture.

MEDIA RECOMMENDATION 7.4: Panic Disorder

Objective: To show students the experience of panic disorders and an overview of basic facts.

Time: 3 Minutes

Video and Discussion: 15 Minutes

Discussion Only: 12 Minutes

Watch Online: Search Videojug.com using the search terms "panic disorder" or http://www.videojug.com/interview/panic-disorder.

Description: This video provides an overview of different aspects of panic disorder and students will hear from an expert about the key symptoms and risk factors of panic disorder.

Summary: Students will enjoy hearing from an expert who actually treats clients with panic disorder. Students may be surprised at how panic attacks can cause a vicious cycle where clients are "panicked" about having a panic attack.

Questions to Students and Discussion: Describe panic disorder. What are the risk factors of panic disorder? What are the consequences of having panic disorder? What are the common treatments for panic disorder?

C. What Is Agoraphobia?

- *Agoraphobia* (which literally means "fear of the marketplace") refers to the persistent avoidance of situations that a person fears are likely to trigger a panic attack.

- Most people have agoraphobia with panic attacks; though agoraphobia can occur on its own, it is not common. [See *Table 7.6.*]

- Diagnosis will be *panic disorder with agoraphobia* (if the patient also has panic disorder) or *agoraphobia without history of panic disorder* (if the patient had never had panic disorder).

- Between one third and one half of those with panic disorder also have agoraphobia.

- Extreme agoraphobia prevents one from functioning normally. [See *Case 7.3.*]

D. Understanding Panic Disorder and Agoraphobia

Neurological, psychological, and social factors can help us to understand panic disorder and agoraphobia.

1. Neurological Factors

Brain systems, neural communication, and genetics contribute to panic disorder and agoraphobia.

a. Brain Systems:

- Hyperventilation and medically safe substances, such as sodium lactate (a salt produced in sweat) and caffeine, can trigger panic attacks in people who have panic disorder.

- People who experience panic attacks have a low threshold for detecting decreased oxygen in the blood.

- People with panic disorder cannot hold their breath as long as control participants can.

- When shown panic-inducing stimuli, people with panic disorder have more activity in the right frontal lobe.

- Withdrawal or escape emotions are easily induced in people with panic disorder. [See *Figure 7.6.*]

b. Neural Communication:

- Too much norepinephrine is found in people who have anxiety disorders.

- The locus coeruleus (located in the brain stem and which plays a key role in the alarm system) produces norepinephrine, and may be overly sensitive in people with panic disorder, producing too much norepinephrine.

- However, people with panic attacks do not have high levels of stress-related hormones (*Example:* cortisol), so panic is different than the stress response.

- Serotonin may also play a role in panic disorder and affects the locus coeruleus in complex ways.

c. Genetics:

- First-degree biological relatives of people with panic disorder are up to eight times more likely to develop the disorder than are control participants.
- This rate increases to 20 times more likely if the relative developed panic disorder before 20 years of age.
- *Concordance rate* is the probability that both twins will have a characteristic or disorder given that one of them has it; this rate is 24% for identical (monozygotic) twins, compared to 11% fraternal (dizygotic) twins.

2. Psychological Factors

Behavioral and cognitive perspectives help to explain panic disorder and agoraphobia.

a. Learning: An Alarm Going Off:

- A first panic attack may arise in response to a stressful or dangerous event and may condition a person to be sensitive to *false alarms* or the symptoms associated with panic attacks.
- *Interoceptive cues* are cues received from the interior of the body, which may trigger fear, panic, or a *fear of fear* (when arousal causes fear that one might have a panic attack). [See *Case 7.2.*]

b. Cognitive Explanations: Catastrophic Thinking and Anxiety Sensitivity:

- *Catastrophic thinking* is the *misinterpretion* of bodily signals that some individuals with panic disorder make.
- Catastrophic thinking is connected to *anxiety sensitivity,* in which a person believes bodily sensations indicate upcoming harmful consequences.
- Nocturnal panic attacks occur at the beginning of sleep when one transitions into deep sleep but do not occur during rapid eye movement (REM) sleep.

3. Social Factors: Stressors, "Safe" People, and a Sign of the Times

- People with panic disorder have had a higher than average number of such stressful events during childhood and adolescence, and for 80% of people with panic disorder, it appeared after a stressful life event.
- The presence of a safe or close person can help to reduce symptoms, yet the person with panic disorder may not learn to address with his or her symptoms.
- Levels of anxiety seem to be increasing in the United States and might be due to environmental stressors.

4. FEEDBACK LOOPS IN ACTION: Understanding Panic Disorder

Neurological, psychological, and social factors help explain panic disorder and agoraphobia. [See *Figure 7.6.*]

E. Treating Panic Disorder and Agoraphobia

The following are various types of treatments commonly used for panic disorder.

1. Targeting Neurological Factors: Medication

- Benzodiazepines (such as *alprazolam* [Xanax] and *clonazepam* [Klonapin]) are short-term treatments that reduce symptoms within 36 hours. Side effects include drowsiness, slowed reaction times, withdrawal or tolerance to the medications.

- Antidepressants (such as an SNRI, an SSRI, or a TCA [tricyclic antidepressant]) may be a better long-term treatment, but they can take up to 10 days to have an effect.

2. Targeting Psychological Factors

- Cognitive-behavioral therapy (CBT) is the most enduring treatment and can be implemented in a self-help format.
- Behavioral methods focus on accurate assessments of bodily signals of arousal, and cognitive methods focus on the challenging misappraisal of bodily sensations and mistaken inferences.

a. Behavioral Methods: Relaxation Training, Breathing Retraining, and Exposure:

- Breathing retraining (taking long deep breaths) stops the progression from arousal to panic attack and increases one's sense of control.
- Exposure methods encourage clients to resume activities they started avoiding due to the panic symptoms.
- *In vivo exposure* is direct exposure to the feared or avoided situation or stimulus. *Imaginal exposure* is exposure to mental images of the fear-inducing stimuli, progressing from least- to most-anxiety-inducing situations. Sixty to seventy percent improve even up to 6–15 months later.
- *Interoceptive exposure* refers to the behavioral therapy method in which the client intentionally elicits the panic symptoms. Symptoms tend to decrease within 30 minutes. This treatment shows clients that symptoms will alleviate without the anticipated consequences of a heart attack or death. [See *Table 7.7.*]

b. Cognitive Methods: Psychoeducation and Cognitive Restructuring:

Psychoeducation describes the biology of panic and explains how catastrophic thinking and anxiety sensitivity can lead panic attacks to develop into panic disorder.

3. Targeting Social Factors: Group and Couples Therapy

- Therapy groups allow clients a space in which to share their experiences and decrease their sense of isolation.
- Couples therapy can help decrease reliance on the safe person.
- Family members and friends can be solicited to provide additional support.

4. FEEDBACK LOOPS IN TREATMENT: Panic Disorder

- Medication can affect neurological functioning, which results in changes in thoughts, feelings and behaviors.
- CBT leads to enduring treatments. [See *Figure 7.8.*]

IV. SOCIAL PHOBIA (SOCIAL ANXIETY DISORDER)

A. What Is Social Phobia?

- *Social phobia,* also called *social anxiety disorder,* is an intense fear of public humiliation or embarrassment, together with the avoidance of social situations likely to cause this fear. [*See Table 7.8.*]
- Social phobia may be *specific* to performances or *generalized* to most social situations. [See *Case 7.4.*]

- Symptoms of Social Phobia include:
  i. People with social phobia show extreme sensitivity to criticism, to rejection, and to not living up to others' expectations.
  ii. Fear or dread of evaluation and scrutiny are shown.
  iii. Panic attacks rarely occur when one is alone. [See *Tables 7.8, 7.9.*]

B. Understanding Social Phobia

Neurological, psychological, and social factors can help us to understand social phobia.

1. Neurological Factors

Brain systems, neural communication, and genetics all play a role in social phobia.

a. Brain Systems and Neural Communication:

- The amygdala is more strongly activated when people with social phobia are afraid.
- People who have social phobia have dysfunctional hippocampus and cortical areas.
- The right hemisphere appears to also play a part in this disorder.
- Dopamine activity, basal ganglia activity, and serotonin activity are decreased in people with social phobia.

b. Genetics:

- The heritability of social phobia is about 37% on average (with a range of 12–60% in various studies).
- This genetic component may also predispose a person to develop autism or have fragile X syndrome; social factors and environment determine which one of these disorders is expressed.

2. Psychological Factors

Cognitive biases and distortions, classical conditioning, and operant conditioning are all psychological factors related social phobia.

a. Cognitive Biases and Distortions:

- People with social phobia have particular biases in attention and memory.
- Lundh and Ost (1996) found that after viewing a series of faces, people with social phobia recognized the faces they judged as being critical, whereas people without social phobia were more likely to recognize faces they judged as accepting.
- People with social phobia seem to be vigilantly looking for social threats and criticism.
- People with social phobia are more likely to judge their performance negatively and ruminate on their performance.

b. Classical Conditioning:

People with social phobia pair social situations (conditioned stimulus) with negative experiences (unconditioned stimulus).

c. Operant Conditioning:

Avoiding social situations decreases the likelihood of unpleasant experiences, thus reinforcing the avoiding behavior.

3. Social Factors

Interactions with family members and the influence of culture are social factors in social phobia.

a. Parent-Child Interactions:

Extreme overprotection by parents is associated with childhood anxiety.

b. Culture:

- Culture influences concerns about social interactions and highlights expected behaviors.

- *Taijin kyofusho* is the Japanese fear of body odor or blushing that might be offensive to the Japanese, whereas North Americans and Europeans might be afraid of certain verbal or behavioral actions.

4. **FEEDBACK LOOPS IN ACTION: Understanding Social Phobia**

Genetics can lead to neurological vulnerabilities that may affect one's thinking and be exacerbated by certain social situations. [See *Figure 7.8.*]

C. Treating Social Phobia

Neurological, psychological, and social factors are targeted to treat social phobias.

1. **Targeting Neurological Factors: Medication**

- *Propranolol* (a beta-blocker also known as Inderal) is the medication used for isolated performances. Beta-blockers bind epinephrine and norepinephrine receptors and decrease their sensitivity.

- SSRIs, such as *paroxetine* (Paxil) or *sertraline* (Zoloft); SNRIs, such as *venlafaxine* (Effexor) and *nefazodone* (Serzone); and NaSSAs, such as *mirtazapine* (Remeron), can also help treat social phobia.

- These medications decrease the activation of the amygdala and the locus coeruleus.

2. **Targeting Psychological Factors: Exposure and Cognitive Restructuring**

- CBT effectively reduces activity in certain brain areas.

- Furmark et al. (2002) assigned participants to one of three groups: SSRI *citalopram*, CBT, and waiting list. After 9 weeks, patients in the two treatment groups had improved to the same degree but the wait list group had not improved. [See *Figure 7.9.*]

3. **Targeting Social Factors: Group Interactions**

- In group cognitive behavioral therapy, members try out new skills to help them reduce arousal, a treatment that is as effective as medication.

- Self-help organizations exist for people who are afraid of public speaking. (*Example:* www.toastmasters.org)

4. **FEEDBACK LOOPS IN TREATMENT: Social Phobia**

CBT affects neurological and psychological factors, which influence social factors. [See *Figure 7.10.*]

V. SPECIFIC PHOBIAS

A. What Is Specific Phobia?

- A *specific phobia* as an intense anxiety or fear related to a specific situation or object. [See *Table 7.10* and *Case 7.5.*]

- There are five types of specific phobia.

1. **Animal Type**

   - *Animal type* specific phobia involves an extreme fear or avoidance of any variety of animal (most common fears include snakes and spiders).
   - Symptoms emerge in childhood.

2. **Natural Environment Type**

   - *Natural environment* specific phobia focuses on heights, water, or storms. [See *Case 7.5.*]
   - Symptoms emerge during childhood.

3. **Blood-Injection-Injury Type**

   - *Blood-injection-injury* specific phobia produces a strong response to seeing blood, having injections, sustaining bodily injuries, or watching surgery.
   - The phobia runs in families and emerges in early childhood.
   - A typical and unique response in the blood-injection-injury phobia is an increased arousal, followed by a rapid decrease in heart rate and blood pressure, which may cause fainting.

4. **Situational Type**

   - *Situational type* specific phobia involves a fear of a particular situation (*Example:* being in an airplane, elevator, or a enclosed space or driving a car).
   - Onset is generally later—in the mid-20s.
   - Usually symptoms are accompanied by unexpected panic attacks.
   - Situational phobia has a gender ratio, age of onset, and family history similar to that of panic disorder with agoraphobia.

5. **Other Type**

   Other type specific phobia does not fall into the previous four categories. (*Examples*: fear of falling down when not near a wall, fear of costumed characters, fear of choking or of vomiting, fear of contracting an illness)

B. Specifics About Specific Phobias

- People with one specific phobia are likely to have another; so specific phobia may be specific or generalized.
- Phobias have an evolutionary advantage of protection.

LEARNING ACTIVITY 7.3: Do You Have a Phobia?

Objective: To have students explore the diverse range of phobias outside of class.

Time: 10–20 Minutes

Explore Online: http://www.phobialist.com/

Description: This Web site provides a lengthy list of phobias. Students will have fun exploring the various types of phobias.

Summary: Students will see the wide variety of phobias—some probably known to them and others that may surprise them.

Questions to Students and Discussion: What are the names for the phobias you have? Which phobia was most surprising to you? Why? What questions do you have about phobias?

C. Understanding Specific Phobias

Neurological and psychological factors appear to weigh more heavily than social factors.

1. Neurological Factors

Brain systems and genes seem to play a role in the development of specific phobia.

a. Brain Systems:

- The amygdala of people with specific phobia is more strongly activated to fear stimuli than to controls.
- The *somatosensory cortex* (registers sensations on the body) is activated when feared stimuli are shown, and participants reported tactile sensations and visual imagery during the study.

b. Neural Communication:

- Too little GABA activity (an inhibitory neurotransmitter) may influence the experience of specific phobia.
- Lower levels of acetylcholine are associated with higher levels of anxiety, are linked to serotonin activity, and may play a role in anxiety.

c. Genetics:

- Genes predispose one to certain specific phobias.
- Men and women have an equal chance of animal phobia but have different chances of developing agoraphobia, situational phobia, and blood-injection-injury phobia. [See *Figure 7.11.*]

2. Psychological Factors

Three primary psychological factors contribute to specific phobia.

a. Faulty Estimations:

People with a specific phobia overestimate the idea that something bad will happen to them.

b. Conditioning: Classical and Operant:

- Recent research does not support the idea that classical conditioning plays a role in the development of specific phobias.
- Avoidance of the feared object can be negatively reinforced because as one avoids the anxiety provoking stimulus, he/she reduces the anxiety.

3. Social Factors: Modeling

Seeing a person exhibit a fear is enough to cause the fear to develop in the observer.

4. FEEDBACK LOOPS IN ACTION: Understanding Specific Phobias

Neurological vulnerabilities, genetics, faulty cognitions, and negative reinforcement can help us understand specific phobias. [See *Figure 7.12.*]

D. Treating Specific Phobias

Neurological or psychological factors are usually the primary target of treatments.

1. Targeting Neurological Factors: Medication

- Medication is usually unnecessary because CBT treatment is highly effective in treating a specific phobia.

- *D-cycloserine* is thought to treat the neural basis of fear extinction.

2. **Targeting Psychological Factors**

- CBT has up to 90% lasting improvement rates even after only one session.

a. **Behavioral Method: Exposure:**

- *Graded exposure* is a first-line treatment in which the patient and the therapist progress through a hierarchy of anxiety-producing stimuli or events as fast as the patient can tolerate. (*Example:* exposure treatment for social anxiety)
- Virtual reality exposure works as well for certain phobias.

MEDIA RECOMMENDATION 7.5: Virtual Reality Therapy

Objective: To show students virtual reality therapy for phobias.

Time: 5 Minutes

Media and Discussion: 20 Minutes

Discussion Only: 15 Minutes

Watch Online: Search YouTube using search terms "virtual reality therapy" or http://www.youtube.com/watch?v=CQgKEp_NhHk

Description: This demonstration shows how virtual reality therapy can be used to treat a panic disorder with agoraphobia.

Summary: Students can see how virtual reality therapy helps clients to experience the physical sensations in a safe environment while clients gain relaxation skills.

Questions to Students and Discussion: What are the pros and cons of virtual reality therapy? How does virtual reality therapy work? Which phobias do you think virtual reality therapy would be most effective in treating? Why or why not?

- *Applied tension* works by having the patient tense bodily muscles, increasing blood pressure—thus preventing fainting—and then exposing the patient to the feared stimulus. It is the treatment of choice for the blood-injection-injury type of specific phobia.

b. **Cognitive Methods:**

- Clients identify and challenge irrational thoughts.
- Group CBT may be appropriate for some specific phobias but does not address social factors. [See *Table 7.12.*]

3. **Targeting Social Factors: A Limited Role for Observational Learning**

Observational learning is not an effective tool for treating specific phobia.

4. **FEEDBACK LOOPS IN TREATMENT: Specific Phobias**

CBT causes neurological changes and shows greater improvement than medication alone. [See *Figure 7.13.*]

VI. OBSESSIVE-COMPULSIVE DISORDER

A. What Is Obsessive-Compulsive Disorder?

- *Obsessions* are thoughts, images, or impulses that persist or recur, are intrusive—and therefore difficult to ignore—and are inappropriate to the situation.
- *Compulsions* are repetitive behaviors (*Example:* avoiding stepping on sidewalk cracks) or a mental act (*Example:* silently counting to 10) that a person feels driven to carry out; a compulsion usually corresponds thematically to an obsession.
- *Obsessive-compulsive disorder (OCD)* is characterized by one or more obsessions, which may occur together with compulsions. [See *Tables 7.13, 7.14, 7.15* and *Case 7.6.*]

MEDIA RECOMMENDATION 7.6: Living with OCD

Objective: Students will be shown real-life cases of severe obsessive-compulsive disorder and learn to identify symptoms.

Time: 15 Minutes (Preview Time: 3 Minutes)

Film and Discussion: 30 Minutes

Discussion Only: 15 Minutes

Watch Online: *Obsessive-Compulsive Disorder.* Films for the Humanities and Sciences. Preview clip online: http://ffh.films.com/id/8897/Obsessive-Compulsive_Disorder.htm

Description: This short film shows two severe cases of OCD: a man who thinks he killed someone and a young woman who performs daily rituals.

Summary: This video highlights several cases of severe OCD. Students will learn about what it is like to live with OCD and about the range of symptoms in this disorder.

Questions to Students and Discussion: Name the individuals and their symptoms of OCD. What symptoms surprised you the most? Why? What would life be like with these symptoms?

B. Understanding Obsessive-Compulsive Disorder

OCD can be understood by considering neuropsychosocial factors and their interactions with psychological and social factors.

1. Neurological Factors

a. Brain Systems:

- The basal ganglia set up a loop of repetitive activity. [See *Figure 7.14.*]
- This neural loop is thought to play a key role in obsessive thoughts.
- Dysfunctional connections among the frontal lobes, the thalamus, and the basal ganglia may also play a role in OCD.
- Larger amounts of gray matter in the frontal lobes and smaller amounts in the posterior portions of the brain may explain the increase of activity in the frontal regions, but such brain abnormalities have not been found in all studies.
- Abnormal birth, epilepsy, head trauma, infection of the brain or the membranes, or childhood streptococcal infection may lead to OCD symptoms.

   b. Neural Communication: Serotonin:
   - Too little serotonin activity can lead to OCD symptoms.
   - However, OCD can arise for different reasons.

   c. Genetics:
   - Twin studies have shown that if one monozygotic (identical) twin has OCD, the other is very likely (65%) to have it, but the rate is lower (only 15%) for dizygotic (fraternal) twins.
   - OCD is more common among relatives of OCD patients (10.3% of whom also have OCD) than among relatives of control participants (of whom only 2% also have OCD).

2. **Psychological Factors**

   Psychological factors focus on operant conditioning.

   a. Behavioral Explanations: Operant Conditioning and Compulsions:

   Compulsive behavior provides short-term relief from anxiety that is produced by an obsession and is thus reinforcing (through operant conditioning the behavior is negatively reinforced). [See *Figure 7.15.*]

   b. Cognitive Explanations: Obsessional Thinking:
   - People with OCD tend to have unacceptable thoughts leading to uncomfortable feelings.
   - People with OCD tend to pay more attention and remember threatening stimuli.

3. **Social Factors**

   Stress and culture are the social factors that can influence the particular content of symptoms.

   a. Socioeconomic Stress:

   Onset of OCD often follows a stressor, and the severity of the symptoms is often proportional to the severity of the stressor.

   b. Culture:

   Culture and religion can influence the content of obsessions or compulsions.

MEDIA RECOMMENDATION 7.7: Religion and OCD

Objective: To see how religion can influence the types of obsessions and compulsions one experiences.

Time: 1 Hour

Media and Discussion: 1 Hour and 15 Minutes

Discussion Only: 15 Minutes

Watch Online: On the Web site of the *Dr. Phil* show, search using the terms "OCD nightmares" or http://drphil.com/shows/show/490/

Description: Students will learn how religion influences the types of obsessions and compulsions experienced by 18-year-old Liz.

Summary: This video highlights a severe case of OCD where symptoms have been influenced by the client's religious beliefs. For example, Liz hangs crosses all over walls and performs Hail Mary's throughout the day to relieve her obsessive thinking.

Questions to Students and Discussion: What symptoms does Liz have? How do her religious beliefs affect her obsessions and compulsions? What do you think life is like for Liz? What types of treatment might be helpful for Liz?

4. **FEEDBACK LOOPS IN ACTION: Understanding Obsessive-Compulsive Disorder**

Increased activity in the neural loop can cause OCD, which can be reinforced through behavior and influenced by culture. [See *Figure 7.15.*]

C. Treating Obsessive-Compulsive Disorder

1. **Targeting Neurological Factors: Medication**

- An SSRI is the first form of medication used in treating OCD (*paroxetine* [Paxil], *sertraline* [Zoloft], *fluoxetine* [Prozac], *fluvoxamine* [Luvox], or *citalopram* [Celexa]).
- TCAs can also be used in high doses (*clomipramine* [Anafranil]), though those with an early onset are less responsive.
- Those with *severe* OCD may receive transcranial magnetic stimulation (TMS) or neurosurgery.
   i. TMS is a series of very fast pulses of a very strong magnetic field sent to part of the brain, disrupting neural activity.
   ii. Neurosurgery is a last resort and aims at disrupting the circuit that underlies the symptoms of OCD.

2. **Targeting Psychological Factors**

Behavioral and cognitive methods are effective at treating OCD.

   a. **Behavioral Methods: Exposure:**

   Exposure with response prevention is the typical treatment in which clients are exposed to a feared situation or stimulus and are prevented from engaging in the compulsion.

   b. **Cognitive Methods: Cognitive Restructuring:**

   Cognitive methods help clients to reduce irrational thoughts and obsessions and increase accurate assessment of these thoughts.

3. **Targeting Social Factors: Family Therapy**

Family therapy educates the family about treatments and goals and increases normal functioning.

4. **FEEDBACK LOOPS IN TREATMENT: Obsessive-Compulsive Disorder**

Neurological, psychological, and social treatments all target symptoms of OCD and interact with one another. [See *Figure 7.16.*]

LECTURE ENHANCEMENT 7.1: Hoarding

Objective: Students will learn about a possible subtype of OCD called "hoarding."

Time: 30–45 Minutes

Film: Montag, K. (2004). *Packrat.* Fanlight Productions. http://www.fanlight.com/catalog/films/410_prat.php

Watch Online: Search YouTube using the search term "hoarding" or http://www.youtube.com/watch?v=YVtRIZmTdPU

Key Lecture Points:
1. Definition of hoarding: "Collecting and being unable to discard excessive quantities of goods and objects that are of limited or no value."
   - Must impact living space
   - Must create distress
2. Characteristics of hoarders
   - Usually ego-syntonic—they do not see their behavior as abnormal
   - Poor outcomes when treated with medication
   - Driven by obsessive doubting
   - May be caused by problems with impulse control (trichotillomania [pulling out one's hair], skin picking, gambling)
   - Psychoanalysis—stuck in anal stage
   - Fifty percent of patients show no other OCD symptoms
3. Deficits
   - Information processing problems: decision making, organization, and memory
   - Problems with emotional attachment to possessions: sentimental, past events, comfort, safety
   - Assumption about nature and importance of possessions: control over and responsible for possessions, remember things
   - Behavioral avoidance: avoidance of decision making, potential mistakes, emotional upset
4. Onset
   - Childhood and adolescence
   - Twenty to thirty percent of people with OCD also express hoarding problems
   - Sixty percent are compulsive buyers
   - Fifty percent are trying to acquire free things
5. Treatment
   - Antidepressants—higher dose and longer treatment needed
   - Prevent incoming clutter
   - Create method for discarding
   - Create methods for organization
   - Schedule cleanup
   - Relapse prevention

References:

Feusner, J., & Saxena, S. (2005). Compulsive hoarding. *Current Psychiatry, 4*(3), 13–26.

Grisham, J. R., & Barlow, D. H. (2005). Compulsive hoarding: Current research and theory. *Journal of Psychopathology and Behavioral Assessment, 27*(1), 45–52.

Grisham, J. R., Brown, T. A., Liverant, G. I., & Campbell-Sills, L. (2004). The distinctiveness of compulsive hoarding from obsessive-compulsive disorder. *Journal of Anxiety Disorders, 19,* 767–779.

Summary: Students see what hoarding is, what its characteristics are, when it typically begins during the life cycle, and the treatments for it.

Questions to Students and Discussion: What is hoarding? How is it related to OCD? What are some symptoms? What are the various types of treatments?

VII. POSTTRAUMATIC STRESS DISORDER

   - A *stress disorder* has three types of persistent symptoms:
     i. The individual *reexperiences the traumatic experience* through flashbacks or reliving.
     ii. There is *avoidance* of anything related to the trauma, or the individual experiences a sense of *numbness*.

   iii. *The individual has increased arousal and anxiety,* which leads to sleep difficulties and hypervigilence.

- *Acute stress disorder* is a type of stress disorder in which a person experiences dissociation, combined with the symptoms just listed, emerging within 4 weeks of a traumatic event and lasting less than 1 month.

- **Posttraumatic stress disorder (PTSD)** is a type of stress disorder that is diagnosed if the symptoms listed last more than 1 month.

A. Stress Versus Traumatic Stress

A traumatic event is when the experience involved:

- The threat of death, the threat of experiencing of serious injury, or a threat to the physical integrity of self or others [and]

- The response involved intense fear, helplessness, or horror. Note: In children, this may be expressed instead by disorganized or agitated behavior.

   1. *Factors that affect the development of a stress disorder*

     a. The kind of trauma:

     Violence is more likely to lead to a stress disorder than are natural disasters.

     b. The severity of the traumatic event, its duration, and its proximity:

     Being in close proximity to a traumatic event and the occurrence of multiple traumatic events lead to a more severe stress disorder.

   2. *Assumptions that are challenged by a traumatic event*

- *The belief that the world is fair and just and people get what they deserve* can be challenged by traumatic events.

- *The belief that it is possible to trust others and be safe* can be challenged by traumatic events.

- *The belief that it is possible to be effective in the world* challenges people's belief that they can effectively protect themselves.

- *The sense that life has purpose and meaning* can be challenged by traumatic events.

B. What Is Posttraumatic Stress Disorder?

- *Posttraumatic stress disorder (PTSD)* is diagnosed when people who have experienced a trauma
   i. Persistently reexperience the traumatic event
   ii. Avoid stimuli related to the event
   iii. Have symptoms of anxiety and hyperarousal; these symptoms must persist for at least a month [See *Tables 7.17* and *7.18,* and *Case 7.7.*]

- **Acute stress disorder** also involves reexperiencing the traumatic event, avoiding stimuli related to the event, and exhibiting symptoms of anxiety and hyperarousal and symptoms of dissociation within 4 weeks of the trauma.

- Symptoms of dissociation include:
   i. Feeling emotionally detached or numb
   ii. Feeling less aware of the environment ("being in a daze")
   iii. *Derealization,* in which the external world seems strange, unreal, or feels as if one is seeing the world through a pane of glass

    iv. *Depersonalization,* in which the perception or experience of oneself is altered and one feels like an observer, seeing oneself from the outside

    v. *Dissociative amnesia,* or loss of memory of important elements of the traumatic event

LECTURE ENHANCEMENT 7.2: Race-Based Traumatic Stress Injury

Objective: To explore the possibility of racism causing a stress disorder.

Time: 30 Minutes

Description: Students will read and discuss Bryant-Davis, T. (2007). Healing requires recognition: The case for race-based traumatic stress. *The Counseling Psychologist, 31*(1), 135–143.

Key Lecture Points
1. Definition of Race-Based Trauma:
   - An emotional injury that is motivated by hate or fear of a person or group of people as a result of their race
   - A racially motivated stressor that overwhelms a person's capacity to cope
   - A racially motivated, interpersonal severe stressor that causes bodily harm or threatens one's life integrity
   - A severe interpersonal or institutional stressor motivated by racism that causes fear, helplessness or horror
2. Race-Based Trauma versus Typical Traumas Associated with PTSD
   - Nonphysical stressors can be traumatic
   - Psychological component of race-based trauma is emphasized
   - Consequences due to race are included (*Example:* neglect)

References:
Bryant-Davis, T. (2007). Healing requires recognition: The case for race-based traumatic stress. *The Counseling Psychologist, 35*(1), 135–143.

Carter, R. T. (2007). Racism and psychological and emotional injury: Recognizing and assessing race-based traumatic stress. *Counseling Psychologist, 35*(1), 13–105.

Summary: Students will be able to identify race-based trauma and see how it differs from typical traumas associated with PTSD.

Questions to Students and Discussion: Do you agree that race-based incidents can cause traumatic stress? Why or why not? How is race-based trauma different and/or similar to typical traumatic events? What are the psychological effects and consequences of race-based trauma? As a future professional, what is important for you to know about race-based trauma?

C. Criticisms of the DSM-IV-TR Criteria for Posttraumatic Stress Disorder

The diagnosis of PTSD is somewhat controversial for the following reasons:

- Distress after a traumatic event is not pathological.
- Symptoms of PTSD are similar to anxiety and depression.
- Original criteria only included extreme events, but current criterion includes less traumatic events.
- "Secondhand victimization" is included.

- The status of "victim" is now sought for legal, financial, or psychological reasons.
- PTSD is the only diagnosis for which people can sue for compensation and thus may lead to overdiagnosis.

D. Understanding Posttraumatic Stress Disorder

Neurological, psychological, and social factors can help us to understand PTSD.

1. Neurological Factors

Neurological factors that contribute to PTSD arise from interactions between the frontal lobe and the amygdala, serotonin, and genetics.

a. Brain Systems:

- Research shows that people with PTSD respond more strongly and have a higher heart rate in response to trauma-related stimuli.
- MRI studies show that people with PTSD have a smaller hippocampus, which may make individuals susceptible to trauma-induced memory deficits.
- The limbic system and visual perception areas are highly activated in people with PTSD.
- People with PTSD have highly activated amygdala when viewing fearful faces and deactivation in the Broca's area when viewing trauma-related stimuli.

b. Neural Communication:

- People with PTSD have lower levels of cortisol.
- The locus coeruleus (a small structure in the brainstem) produces norepinephrine, a neurotransmitter that may be involved in PTSD and when high levels are injected into people with PTSD, anxiety, panic, and traumatic memories are triggered.

c. Genetics:

A genetic predisposition to develop PTSD does exist but plays a smaller role than the environment in predicting PTSD.

2. Psychological Factors: History of Trauma, Comorbidity, and Conditioning

- A history of depression or other psychological disorders will affect the development of PTSD.
- The beliefs that one is unable to control stressors and that the world is a dangerous place make a person vulnerable to PTSD.
- People with lower IQs have more severe symptoms, but this finding is based only on correlational research and may be caused by another factor or factors.
- Classical and operant conditioning help explain avoidance behaviors.

LECTURE ENHANCEMENT 7.3: Stages of Sexual Assault Survival

Objective: To learn about the stages of sexual assault post-trauma.

Time: 20–30 Minutes

Watch Online: Search YouTube using the search terms "How men can help a sexual assault survival" or http://www.youtube.com/watch?v=j0g14GUARh0

Search YouTube using the search terms "rape and sexual assault's aftermath" or http://www.youtube.com/watch?v=OutNrRch2OY

Key Lecture Points:
1. What Is Rape?
   Forcible sexual intercourse with a person who does not give consent
2. How Common Is Rape?
   One out of 10 women reported having experienced a rape or attempted rape in her lifetime.
3. Effects of Sexual Assault:
   - PTSD rates are higher for rape than any other crime.
   - Ninety percent of survivors have symptoms in the first month.
   - Fifty percent have symptoms in 3 months.
4. Stages of Sexual Assault Survival:
   - Stage 1: Anticipatory Stage
     i. The potential victim senses danger and threat.
     ii. Dissociation may occur—"spacing out," being in a cloud.
   - Stage 2: Impact Stage
     Within 2 weeks of the assault the victim experiences:
     i. Helplessness
     ii. Numbness, shock
     iii. Blaming oneself for resisting and nonresisting
     iv. Vivid recollections of the assault—reliving assault
     v. Fears
     vi. Controlled reactions: repressing
     vii. Worsening of physical and/or mental illness
   - Stage 3: Reconstitution Stage
     i. Attempting to resume life
     ii. Experiencing lingering strong emotions
     iii. Possible development of maladaptive coping mechanisms (*Examples:* six times more likely to use prescription drugs, three times more likely to use marijuana, six times more likely to use cocaine, twenty-six times more likely to develop a serious drug problem, thirteen times more likely to abuse alcohol)
   - Stage 4: Resolution
     i. Less intense emotions
     ii. Feelings of anger

References:

Matsakis, A. (2003). *The rape recovery handbook.* Oakland, CA: New Harbinger.

Santrock, J. W. (2008). *Adolescence* (12th ed.). Boston: McGraw Hill.

Summary: Students will see the four stages of sexual assault, post-trauma, and the behaviors and feelings accompanying each stage.

Questions to Students and Discussion: Identify in sequence the four stages of sexual assault, post-trauma. What are the characteristic responses for each stage?

3. Social Factors

Social factors determine whether PTSD develops.

a. Socioeconomic Stress:

SES affects one's ability to cope and may place one in more vulnerable, traumatic situations.

b. Social Support:

People who receive support from others immediately after a trauma have a lower risk of developing PTSD.

c. **Cultural Expression of Symptoms:**

Cultural patterns influence coping skills and style.

4. **FEEDBACK LOOPS IN ACTION: Understanding Posttraumatic Stress Disorder**

Neurological, psychological, and social differences among individuals lead to their different responses to traumatic events and make some people more vulnerable to developing PTSD after a trauma. [See *Figure 7.17.*]

E. Treating Posttraumatic Stress Disorder

1. **Targeting Neurological Factors: Medication**

- SSRIs (*sertraline* [Zoloft] and *paroxetine* [Paxil]) are the first-line medications for treating the symptoms of PTSD and should be taken for at least 9 months.

- *Propranolol* (a beta-blocker, also called Inderal) may decrease future symptoms of PTSD if taken soon after a traumatic event. This treatment is still in the experimental stages.

- Transcranial magnetic stimulation may reduce PTSD symptoms, but this treatment is also in the preliminary stages.

2. **Targeting Psychological Factors**

a. **Behavioral Methods: Exposure, Relaxation, and Breathing Retraining:**

Imagining exposure or in vivo exposure helps to habituate and reduce the trauma symptoms.

b. **Cognitive Methods: Psychoeducation and Cognitive Restructuring:**

- Educating patients about PTSD helps to make symptoms more understandable and less frightening.

- Reevaluating the meaning and misattributions of the event also helps clients.

- CBT can help prevent acute stress disorder from evolving into PTSD.

3. **Targeting Social Factors: Safety, Support, and Family Education**

- Family or couples therapy teaches about PTSD symptoms and suggests ways to offer support.

- Interpersonal therapy may help those who are not interested in CBT.

4. **FEEDBACK LOOPS IN TREATMENT: Posttraumatic Stress Disorder**

Individuals with PTSD brought on by a traffic accident received 12 weeks of group CBT. Participants reported fewer neurological and psychological symptoms. [See *Figure 7.18.*]

VIII. HOWARD HUGHES AND ANXIETY DISORDERS

Howard Hughes clearly suffered from OCD and experienced a number of physical and environmental stressors that exacerbated his symptoms.

ADDITIONAL READINGS

Antony, M. M., Craske, M. G., & Barlow, D. H. (1995). *Mastery of your specific phobia.* New York: Graywind Publications.

Antony, M. M., & Swinson, R. P. (2000). *The shyness and social anxiety workbook.* Oakland, CA: New Harbinger Publications.

Anxiety Disorders Association of America. Retrieved September 23, 2002, from http://www.adaa.org/GettingHelp/Articles/ShirlyB.asp

Barlett, D. L., & Steele, J. B. (1979). *Howard Hughes: His life and madness.* New York: Norton.

Baxter, L. R. (1992). Neuroimaging studies of obsessive compulsive disorder. *Psychiatric Clinics of North America, 15,* 871–884.

Brown, P. H., & Broeske, P. H. (1996). *Howard Hughes: The untold story.* Cambridge, MA: Da Capo Press.

Campbell, E., & Ruane, J. (1999). *The Earl Campbell story.* Toronto: ECW Press.

Colas, E. (1998). *Just checking: Scenes from the life of an obsessive-compulsive.* New York: Pocket Books.

Dolan, A. (2006, April 3). The obsessive disorder that haunts my life. *Daily Mail.* Retrieved on February 25, 2009 from http://www.dailymail.co.uk/pages/live/articles/showbiz/showbiznews.html?in_article_id=381802&in_page_id=1773

Fowler, R. D. (1986). Howard Hughes: A psychological autopsy. *Psychology Today, 20,* 22–33.

Herman, J. (1992). *Trauma and recovery.* New York: Basic Books.

Kaplan, A. (2007). Hoarding: Studies characterize phenotype, demonstrate treatment. *Psychiatric Times, 24*(6). Retrieved on February 25, 2009, from http://www.psychiatrictimes.com/showArticle.jhtml?articleId=199202770

The Hughes legacy: Scramble for the billions. (1976, April 19). *Time Magazine.* Retrieved June 28, 2007, from http://www.time.com/time/magazine/article/0,9171,914059,00.html

Anxiety Disorders Memoirs and Novels

Bell, J. (2007). *Rewind, replay, repeat: A memoir of obsessive-compulsive disorder.* Center City, MN: Hazeldon.

A radio newscaster describes his experiences with OCD.

Colas, E. (1998). *Just checking: Scenes from the life of an obsessive-compulsive.* New York: Pocket Books.

This is a memoir about a young woman with OCD.

Rand, R. (2004). *Dancing away an anxious mind: A memoir about overcoming panic disorder.* Madison, WI: University of Wisconsin Press.

A nationally recognized writer and radio producer recounts how dancing helped her deal with panic disorder.

Raskin, M. (2004). *The anxiety expert: A psychiatrist's story of panic.* Bloomington, IN: Authorhouse.

Raskin experienced a lifetime of panic disorders until she sought therapy and uncovered childhood abuse.

Sanford, M. (2008). *Waking: A memoir of trauma and transcendence.* New York: Rodale Books.

After experiencing an accident that killed his father and sister, Sanford struggles with paralysis as he attempts to get on with his life.

Sebold, S. (2002). *Lucky: A memoir.* New York: Back Bay Books.

Sebold recounts her rape and post-survival, experience with PTSD, and the conviction of her perpetrator.

ADDITIONAL MEDIA RECOMMENDATIONS

Amiel, J. (Director). (1995). *Copycat* [Film]. USA: Regency Enterprises.

A profiler becomes fearful of a serial killer.

Anderson, P. T. (Director). (2002). *Punch-Drunk Love* [Film]. USA: New Line Cinema.

    A man struggles with his anxiety and social phobia as he falls in love.

Brooks, J. (Director). (1997). *As Good As It Gets* [Film]. USA: TriStar Pictures.

    An eccentric man with obsessive-compulsive disorder finds an unlikely female companion who helps him to face his symptoms.

Garcia, E., & Griffin, N. (Writers). (2003). *Matchstick Men* [Film]. USA: Warner Brothers Pictures.

    An obsessive-compulsive con artist seeks therapy so he can continue "working."

Jeunet, J. (Director). (2001). *Amelie* [Film]. France: Claudie Ossard Productions.

    A woman with anxiety falls in love.

Redford, R. (Director). (1981). *Ordinary People* [Film]. USA: Paramont Pictures.

    A boy struggles to cope after a boating accident kills his brother.

Scorsese, M. (Director). (2004). *The Aviator* [Film]. USA: Miramax Studies, Inc.

    A biography of Howard Hughes and his struggles with OCD.

WEB SITES

Anxiety Disorders Association of America: Resources promoting public and professional awareness of anxiety disorders. See: http://www.adaa.org/

Mental Health Network: Includes information and resources about anxiety disorders including a long list of free videos. See: http://www.mentalhelp.net/poc/center_index.php?id=1&cn=1

National Center for Posttraumatic Stress Disorder: Contains information for veterans, the general public, providers and researchers. See: http://www.ptsd.va.gov/

NIMH on Anxiety Disorders: Provides an overview of anxiety disorders and treatments. See: http://www.nimh.nih.gov/health/topics/anxiety-disorders/index.shtml

Obsessive Compulsive Foundation: Provides information about OCD and has a national campaign and spokesperson. See: http://www.ocfoundation.org/

Dissociative and Somatoform Disorders

CHAPTER OUTLINE

CHAPTER HEADINGS	INSTRUCTION IDEAS AND TEXTBOOK CORRELATIONS
Chapter Introduction	**Learning Objective:** 8.1 **Learning Activity 8.1:** Who Is Anna O.?
DISSOCIATIVE DISORDERS	
Dissociative Disorders: An Overview	**Learning Objectives:** 8.2, 8.3 **Learning Concepts:** overview, normal versus abnormal dissociation, cultural variations of pathological dissociation
Dissociative Amnesia	**Learning Objectives:** 8.4, 8.5, 8.6, 8.7 **Learning Concepts:** understanding dissociative amnesia, neurological factors, brain systems, neural communication, psychological factors, disconnected mental processes, dissociation theory, neodissociation theory, social factors, indirect effects **Media Recommendation 8.1:** Case Examples of Dissociative Amnesia **Textbook Tools:** Tables 8.1, 8.2; Case 8.1
Dissociative Fugue	**Learning Objectives:** 8.8, 8.9 **Learning Concepts:** what is dissociative fugue?, understanding dissociative fugue, neurological factors, psychological factors, related to hypnotizability, social factors: combat stress **Media Recommendation 8.2:** The Man with No Past **Textbook Tools:** Tables 8.3, 8.4; Case 8.2
Depersonalization Disorder	**Learning Objectives:** 8.9, 8.10, 8.11, 8.12, 8.13 **Learning Concepts:** what is depersonalization disorder?, understanding depersonalization disorder, neurological factors, brain systems, neural communication, psychological factors: cognitive deficits, social factors: childhood emotional abuse **Media Recommendation 8.3:** Living with Depersonalization Disorder **Textbook Tools:** Figure 8.1; Tables 8.5, 8.6; Case 8.3 **Worth Video Tool Kit for Abnormal Psychology:** Grisi Siknis

Dissociative Identity Disorder	**Learning Objectives:** 8.14, 8.15, 8.16, 8.17, 8.18, 8.19 **Learning Concepts:** what is dissociative identity disorder?, criticisms of the DSM-IV-TR criteria, understanding dissociative identity disorder, neurological factors: alters in the brain, brain systems, neural communication, genetics, psychological factors, social factors: a cultural disorder, two models for the emergence of alters, the posttraumatic model, the sociocognitive model, the debate about dissociative identity disorder **Media Recommendation 8.4:** Interview with Truddi Chase **Media Recommendation 8.5:** Interview with Chris Sizemore **Media Recommendation 8.6:** Hypnosis, Dissociation, and Trauma **Textbook Tools:** Tables 8.7, 8.8; Case 8.4
Treating Dissociative Disorders	**Learning Objectives:** 8.20, 8.21, 8.22 **Learning Concepts:** targeting neurological factors: medication, targeting psychological and social factors: coping and integration **Textbook Tools:** Figure 8.2 **Worth Video Tool Kit for Abnormal Psychology:** Dissociative Identity Disorder
SOMATOFORM DISORDERS	
Somatoform Disorders: An Overview	**Learning Concepts:** somatoform disorders: an overview **Textbook Tools:** Table 8.9
Somatization Disorder	**Learning Objectives:** 8.23, 8.24, 8.25 **Learning Concepts:** what is somatization disorder?, criticisms of the DSM-IV-TR criteria, understanding somatization disorder, neurological factors: genetics, psychological factors: misinterpretation of bodily signals, social factors, social stress, social learning, cultural influences on symptoms **Textbook Tools:** Figure 8.3; Tables 8.10, 8.11; Case 8.5 **Worth Video Tool Kit for Abnormal Psychology:** Undiagnosed Medical Disorder
Conversion Disorder	**Learning Objectives:** 8.26, 8.27, 8.28 **Learning Concepts:** what is conversion disorder?, criticisms of the DSM-IV-TR criteria, understanding conversion disorder, neurological factors, brain systems, genetics, psychological factors: self-hypnosis, social factors: stress response **Textbook Tools:** Figures 8.4, 8.5; Tables 8.12, 8.13; Case 8.6
Hypochondriasis	**Learning Objectives:** 8.29, 8.30, 8.31 **Learning Concepts:** what is hypochondriasis?, hypochondriasis and anxiety disorders: shared features, understanding hypochondriasis, neurological factors, brain systems, neural communication, genetics, psychological factors: catastrophic thinking about the body, social factors: stress response **Textbook Tools:** Tables 8.14, 8.15; Case 8.7
Body Dysmorphic Disorder	**Learning Objectives:** 8.32, 8.33, 8.34 **Learning Concepts:** what is body dysmorphic disorder?, diagnosing body dysmorphic disorder versus other disorders, understanding body

	dysmorphic disorder, neurological factors, psychological factors: focus on imperfections, social factors: cultural emphasis on certain body features **Lecture Enhancement 8.1:** Males and Body Image **Media Recommendation 8.7:** *Whole* **Textbook Tools:** Tables 8.16, 8.17; Case 8.8 **Worth Video Tool Kit for Abnormal Psychology:** Impact of Body Dysmorphic Disorder, Facing Themselves, Body Dysmorphic Disorder Alters Individual Self-Perception, Treatment for Body Dysmorphic Disorder
Is Somatoform Disorder a Useful Concept?	**Learning Objective:** 8.35
Treating Somatoform Disorders	**Learning Objective:** 8.36 **Learning Concepts:** targeting neurological factors, targeting psychological factors: cognitive-behavior therapy, targeting social factors: support and family education **Textbook Tools:** Figure 8.6; Tables 8.18, 8.19
FOLLOW-UP ON ANNA O.	

LEARNING OBJECTIVES

After reading this chapter, students will be able to:

8.1 Describe the overarching characteristics of dissociative disorders.

8.2 Distinguish between normal and abnormal forms of dissociation.

8.3 Name and describe cultural forms of dissociation.

8.4 Identify the symptoms of dissociative amnesia.

8.5 Describe the neurological factors that play a role in dissociative amnesia.

8.6 Explain the differences between the dissociation and neodissociation theories.

8.7 Specify the social factors that play a role in dissociative amnesia.

8.8 Identify the symptoms of dissociative fugue.

8.9 Describe the neurological, psychological, and social factors that play a role in dissociative fugue.

8.10 Identify the symptoms of depersonalization disorder.

8.11 Identify the role of brain systems and neural communication in depersonalization disorder.

8.12 Describe the psychological and social factors that affect depersonalization disorder.

8.13 Identify how the neurological, psychological, and social factors interact in depersonalization disorder.

8.14 Identify the symptoms of dissociative identity disorder.

8.15 Explain the criticisms of the dissociative identity disorder diagnosis.

8.16 Describe the neurological factors that affect dissociative identity disorder.

8.17 Identify the psychological and social causes of dissociative identity disorder.

8.18 Compare and contrast the posttraumatic stress and sociocognitive models.

8.19 Recognize the debates about dissociative identity disorder.

8.20 Identify neurological, psychological, and social treatments for dissociative disorders.

8.21 Describe the interactions among the neurological, psychological, and social treatments for dissociative disorders.

8.22 Describe the overarching characteristics of dissociative disorders.

8.23 Identify the symptoms of somatization disorder.

8.24 Highlight the criticisms of the DSM criteria for somatization disorder.

8.25 Describe the neurological, psychological, and social factors and interactions that influence somatization disorder.

8.26 Identify the symptoms of conversion disorder.

8.27 Highlight the criticisms of the DSM criteria of conversion disorder.

8.28 Describe the neurological, psychological, and social factors and interactions that influence conversion disorder.

8.29 Identify the symptoms of hypochondriasis.

8.30 Compare and contrast hypochondriasis and anxiety disorders.

8.31 Describe the neurological, psychological, and social factors and interactions that influence hypochondriasis.

8.32 Identify the symptoms of body dysmorphic disorder.

8.33 Compare and contrast body dysmorphic disorder with other disorders.

8.34 Describe the neurological, psychological, and social factors and interactions that influence body dysmorphic disorder.

8.35 Explain the weaknesses of the concept of somatoform disorders.

8.36 Describe the neurological, psychological, and social treatments and interactions that influence somatoform disorder.

KEY TERMS

Hysteria: An emotional condition marked by extreme excitability and bodily symptoms for which there is no medical explanation; hysteria is not a DSM-IV-TR disorder.

Dissociative disorders: A category of psychological disorders in which perception, consciousness, memory, or identity are dissociated to the point where the symptoms are pervasive, cause significant distress, and interfere with daily functioning.

Dissociation: The separation of mental processes—such as perception, memory, and self-awareness—that are normally integrated.

Amnesia: Memory loss, which is usually temporary but, in rare cases, may be permanent.

Identity problem: A dissociative symptom in which an individual is not sure who he or she is or may assume a new identity.

Derealization: A dissociative symptom in which the external world is perceived or experienced as strange or unreal.

Depersonalization: A dissociative symptom in which the perception or experience of self—either one's body or one's mental processes—is altered to the point of feeling like an observer, as though seeing oneself from the "outside."

Dissociative disorders: A category of psychological disorders in which perception, consciousness, memory, or identity are dissociated to the point where the symptoms are pervasive, cause significant distress, and interfere with daily functioning.

Dissociative amnesia: A dissociative disorder in which the sufferer has significantly impaired memory for important experiences or personal information that cannot be explained by ordinary forgetfulness.

Dissociative fugue: A dissociative disorder that involves sudden, unplanned travel and difficulty remembering the past, which can lead patients to be confused about who they are and sometimes to take on a new identity.

Depersonalization disorder: A dissociative disorder whose primary symptom is a persistent feeling of being detached from one's mental processes or body, although people who have this disorder may also experience derealization.

Dissociative identity disorder (DID): The dissociative disorder characterized by the presence of two or more distinct *alters* (personality states or identities), each with their own characteristics and history, that take turns controlling the person's behavior.

Somatoform disorders: A category of psychological disorders characterized by complaints about physical well-being that cannot be entirely explained by a medical condition, substance use, or another psychological disorder.

Somatization disorder (SD): A somatoform disorder characterized by multiple physical symptoms that are medically unexplained and impair an individual's ability to function.

Pain disorder: A somatoform disorder that occurs when psychological factors significantly affect the onset, severity, or maintenance of significant pain.

Conversion disorder: A somatoform disorder that involves sensory or motor symptoms that do not correspond to symptoms that arise from known medical conditions.

Hypochondriasis: A somatoform disorder marked by preoccupation with a fear or belief of having a serious disease, but this preoccupation arises because the individual has misinterpreted his or her bodily sensations or symptoms.

Body dysmorphic disorder: A somatoform disorder characterized by excessive preoccupation with a perceived defect or defects in appearance.

CHAPTER GUIDE

Chapter Introduction

- Dr. Joseph Breuer diagnosed Anna O. with *hysteria,* an emotional condition marked by extreme excitability and bodily symptoms for which there is no medical explanation.
- Hysteria is currently not a DSM-IV-TR disorder, but hysteria symptoms are similar to two DSM-IV-TR categories of disorders: dissociative and somatoform disorders, both featured in this chapter.
- *Dissociative disorders* are a category of psychological disorders in which perception, consciousness, memory, or identity are dissociated to the point where the symptoms are pervasive, cause significant distress, and interfere with daily functioning. The chief symptom is *dissociation,* the separation of mental processes that are normally integrated.
- *Somatoform disorders* include persistent bodily symptoms that have no medical cause.

LEARNING ACTIVITY 8.1: Who Is Anna O.?

Objective: To describe the case of Anna O. and show how her case relates to dissociative and somatoform disorders.

Time: 20–30 Minutes

Directions: Ask students to look up two Web sites that contain information about Anna O.'s background, symptoms, and treatments.

This exercise will highlight the key findings about Anna O. and how these findings relate to dissociative and somatoform disorders.

Summary: Students will see the symptoms of dissociative and somatoform disorders.

Questions to Students and Discussion: Describe Anna O.'s background. What symptoms did she experience? What types of treatments were used to help her? What information would you like to know more about if you were treating Anna O.? What information surprised you?

I.   DISSOCIATIVE DISORDERS

A. Dissociative Disorders: An Overview

The symptoms of dissociation:

- May arise suddenly or gradually
- Can be brief or chronic
- Have four types:
    i.   *Amnesia* or memory loss
    ii. *Identity problems* in which a person does not know who he/she is or takes on a new identity
    iii. *Derealization* in which the environment seems strange and unreal
    iv. *Depersonalization* in which the person feels like he/she is an observer of his/her life

1.   Normal Versus Abnormal Dissociation

- Occasional dissociating is normal and part of everyday life.
- Dissociation can also be part of religious or cultural rituals (such as the possession trance).
- To be considered abnormal, symptoms must be pervasive, and cause distress and impairment.
- Only 2% of the U.S. population reports abnormal dissociation.

2.   Cultural Variations in Pathological Dissociation

Dissociative symptoms vary by culture. (*Example:* in Indonesia and Malaysia, people may experience fleeting episodes of profanity, amnesia, and a trancelike state—symptoms known as *latah.*)

3.   Types of Dissociative Disorders

There are four types of dissociative disorders:

- *Dissociative amnesia*
- *Dissociative fugue*
- *Depersonalization disorder*
- *Dissociative identity disorder*

Dissociative disorder not otherwise specified (DDNOS) refers to the diagnosis for people whose symptoms do not meet all the criteria of one of the four types of dissociative disorders, and is a common diagnosis that needs further research.

B. Dissociative Amnesia

1. What Is Dissociative Amnesia?

- *Dissociative amnesia* is a dissociative disorder in which the sufferer has significantly impaired memory for important experiences or information that cannot be explained by ordinary forgetfulness. [See *Table 8.1.*]
- Dissociative amnesia takes several forms:
  - **i.** *Generalized amnesia:* one forgets his/her entire life; a very rare condition.
  - **ii.** *Selective amnesia:* one can remember only some parts of a period of time.
  - **iii.** *Localized amnesia:* memory is lost for a specific period of time and often triggered by a stressful event. [See *Table 8.2; Case 8.1.*]

MEDIA RECOMMENDATION 8.1: Case Examples of Dissociative Amnesia

Objective: To illustrate the lived experience of dissociative amnesia.

Time: 2 Minutes

Video and Discussion: 10 Minutes

Discussion Only: 8 Minutes

Watch Online: Search YouTube using the search terms "dissociative amnesia" and "NBC News" or http://www.youtube.com/watch?v=23Pum-7-pyM

This NBC news clip focuses on localized amnesia due to childhood sexual abuse.

Summary: Students will learn about how memories are recovered and how a therapist can influence them.

Questions to Students and Discussion: What type of dissociative amnesia is featured in this clip? Why did one survivor discredit his memories while another one confirms hers? What controversies surround these types of memories?

---

2. Understanding Dissociative Amnesia

Neuropsychosocial factors can help explain dissociative amnesia.

a. Neurological Factors: Brain Trauma?

The neurological factors that affect dissociative amnesia are not clear.

(1) Brain systems:

Prolonged stress damages the hippocampus (brain structure that stores new information in the memory) and thus does not operate well under new stress.

(2) Neural communication:

The adrenal glands produce the hormone cortisol when one is under stress. Researchers have found that monkeys and humans with excessive cortisol have a smaller hippocampus; however, it is unclear whether this plays a role in dissociative amnesia.

b. Psychological Factors: Disconnected Mental Processes:

The *dissociation* and *neodissociation theories* focus on traumatic experiences as the cause of dissociation.

(1) Dissociation theory:

- Dissociation theory argues that traumatic experiences cause arousal and cognitive dysfunction, which causes memory to be dissociated from other aspects of cognition.
- Arousal disruption theory may be a better name for this theory.
- The theory does not explain the purpose of the dissociation.

(2) Neodissociation theory:

Neodissociation theory argues that memory operates independently and creates an amnestic barrier and cuts off information from awareness.

c. Social Factors: Indirect Effects:

Traumas are common for people with a dissociative disorder, possibly because the anxiety may lead to dissociative symptoms.

C. Dissociative Fugue

Dissociative fugue may manifest in sudden, unplanned travel and difficulty remembering the past. This combination can lead sufferers to be confused about who they are and sometimes to take on a new identity.

1. What Is Dissociative Fugue?

- Episodes can last from a few hours to months.
- The individual functions normally but may have no memories of being in a fugue state. [See *Tables 8.3, 8.4;* and *Case 8.2.*]

MEDIA RECOMMENDATION 8.2: The Man with No Past

Objective: To learn about the lived experience of dissociative fugue.

Time: 23 Minutes (Part I), 24 Minutes (Part II)

Video and Discussion: 41–55 Minutes

Discussion Only: 18 Minutes

Watch Online: Search http://www.veoh.com for *The man with no past.*

This two-part video shows what it's like to suffer from dissociative fugue. Students will learn about 25-year-old David Fitzpatrick, who has no recollection of his past.

Summary: Students will be shocked to learn about David's loss of memory and how he had to rebuild even basic knowledge. For example, in addition to general knowledge, David had to relearn information about his family members. His journey to recover his memory is complicated as he learns about the unlikable person he was before the fugue.

Questions to Students and Discussion: What surprised you about this video? What are David's symptoms and how do they compare with the DSM criteria for dissociative fugue? How was David's family affected by his illness?

a. Cultural Forms of Dissociative Fugue:

- Running syndrome involves a sudden trancelike state in which a person runs until exhausted then falls asleep, and has no memories of the experience afterwards.
- Populations most likely to experience running syndromes include:

    i. *Pibloktoq* (native Arctic people)

    ii. *Grisi siknis* (Miskito of Nicaragua and Honduras)

    iii. *Amok* (Western Pacific cultures)

2. Understanding Dissociative Fugue

Neuropsychological factors can help us understand dissociative fugue.

a. Neurological Factors:

- Research has found that people with dissociative fugue have less activation in the frontal and temporal regions and right hemisphere as compared to controls when recalling aspects of their lives. (The right hemisphere is known to play a role in the retrieval of autobiographical memories.)

- In one study, a patient who lost his memory about his past and also of his native language, German, performed poorly on frontal lobe function assessments. This patient also had lower frontal and parietal lobe activation, which showed he was not pretending to forget his native language.

- High levels of stress-related hormones may affect memory retrieval for those with dissociative fugue.

b. Psychological Factors: Related to Hypnotizability?

Research has found that those with dissociative fugue are more hypnotizable, but it is unclear whether being more hypnotizable makes a person more vulnerable to dissociative fugue, having experienced a fugue state makes a person more hypnotizable, or a third variable may cause both an increase in hypnotizability and dissociative fugue.

c. Social Factors: Combat Stress:

- Significant stressors may cause dissociative fugue.

- Symptoms overlap with trances and other cultural phenomenon.

D. Depersonalization Disorder

People with depersonalization disorder experience a *persistent* feeling of being detached from their thought process or body.

1. What Is Depersonalization Disorder?

- The person feels separate from his/her body but knows he/she is not detached.

- There is a feeling of lack of control over one's behavior, which leads to feelings of being swept away by life events. [See *Tables 8.5 and 8.6.*]

- Meditation and hypnotic trances considered symptoms of depersonalization can also be normal behaviors.

- Symptoms are somewhat similar to those of anxiety, and in fact the comorbid anxiety symptoms are what often lead the person to seek help.

MEDIA RECOMMENDATION 8.3: Living with Depersonalization Disorder

Objective: To learn about the lived experience of depersonalization disorder.

Time: 6 Minutes

Video and Discussion: 15 Minutes

Discussion Only: 9 Minutes

Watch Online: Search YouTube using the search terms "living with depersonalization disorder" or http://www.youtube.com/watch?v=3axCvSr7UmE&feature=related

This short clip features the personal experience of someone who has depersonalization disorder.

Summary: Students will learn about what it is like to live with depersonalization disorder. In particular, the person highlights symptoms of feeling outside of herself and feeling in a "dreamlike" state. She also discusses possible causes of depersonalization such as trauma or drug abuse.

Questions to Students and Discussion: How does this young woman describe depersonalization disorder? What other disorders can one experience in addition to depersonalization disorder? What are possible causes of this disorder?

2. Understanding Depersonalization Disorder

Neurological factors can best explain depersonalization disorder; however, less is known about psychosocial factors.

a. Neurological Factors:

(1) Brain systems:

Individuals with depersonalization disorder have high levels of activity in the frontal lobes (possibly due to the high level of emotional control/suppression) while showing low levels of activation in the emotion areas when remembering emotion words.

(2) Neural communication:

Norepinephrine production (associated with the autonomic nervous system) is dysfunctional in patients with depersonalization disorder and may cause blunted emotional responses.

b. Psychological Factors: Cognitive Deficits:

- Patients have short-term memory loss and impaired spatial reasoning due to attention problems.
- It is unclear whether the attention problems are the cause or the effect of the disorder.

c. Social Factors: Childhood Emotional Abuse:

- Stressful events such as severe and long-lasting emotional abuse can cause depersonalization disorder.
- Stress, mood, fear, and new settings can make the symptoms worse. [See *Case 8.3.*]

d. FEEDBACK LOOPS IN ACTION: Depersonalization Disorder:

One hypothesis is that when stress is suppressed (in the frontal lobes) it can lead to feelings of disconnection. If a person catastrophizes the feeling or event, this can lead to further anxiety, especially if he/she has a family member suffering from a mental illness.

E. Dissociative Identity Disorder

- Formerly known as multiple personality disorder.
- Possibly the most controversial of all DSM-IV-TR disorders.

1. What Is Dissociative Identity Disorder?

- ***Dissociative identity disorder (DID)*** is the presence of two or more distinct *alters* (personality states or identities), each with its own characteristics and history, that take turns controlling the person's behavior.

- Each alter has its own name, mannerisms, speaking style, medical problems, and history.
- Number of alters ranges from 2 to 100 (with most people with DID having 10 or fewer alters). [See *Tables 8.7, 8.8; Case 8.4.*]

MEDIA RECOMMENDATION 8.4: Interview with Truddi Chase

Objective: To learn about the lived experience of dissociative identity disorder.

Time: 7 Minutes

Video and Discussion: 15 Minutes

Discussion Only: 8 Minutes

Watch Online: Search YouTube using the search terms "interview with Truddi Chase" or http://www.youtube.com/watch?v=NDUw-yCRBUM&feature=related

This clip features Truddi Chase, author of *When the Rabbit Howls.*

Summary: Students will see Chase as she talks about the sexual abuse she experienced as a young child and how she developed 92 different alters to deal with the abuse.

Questions to Students and Discussion: What role did abuse play in the development of her alters? What affect did Chase's experiences have on Oprah? Why did Chase title her book *When the Rabbit Howls?*

2. **Criticisms of the DSM-IV-TR Criteria**

   Criticisms of the DID diagnosis include:
   - The diagnosis of DID does not define "personality states" or "identities," which makes it difficult to differentiate between "normal" mood fluctuations versus separate identities.
   - DSM-IV-TR does not indicate how to identify when an alter has "taken control" (Criterion B), so it is left up to the therapist's judgment.
   - DID is difficult to distinguish from malingering since people can easily fake symptoms.
   - There is difficulty in differentiating DID from rapid cycling bipolar disorder because both involve sudden changes in mood and demeanor.

3. **Understanding Dissociative Identity Disorder**

   Although these factors may conflict, neurological, psychological, and social factors can help us understand DID.

   a. **Neurological Factors: Alters in the Brain?**
      - Research has shown that each alter has knowledge about information acquired by other alters.
      - Genes can make individuals sensitive to stress and may contribute to the development of the disorder.

      (1) **Brain systems:**
         - Research has shown that an alter recognizes previously learned material when another alter was dominant.
         - Some memories are unavailable to alters; this may be due to the orbital frontal cortex (which regulates cognitive and emotional processes).

- Early abuse may affect normal brain development and prevent typical development of the self.
- A PET scan study revealed that the brain responded differently to stories of personal trauma depending on the alter that was dominant. This study also found that the area of the brain for autobiographical memories was activated only when the alter knew about the abuse. However, these results may be influenced by self-hypnosis.

(2) Neural communication:

Since DID is associated with early childhood abuse, and stress-related hormones alter brain development and subsequent brain functioning, we can assume these play a role in the development of DID. However, researchers are unclear of the specific links.

(3) Genetics:

Almost half of the variance in abnormal dissociations can be attributed to genes.

b. Psychological Factors:

Patients with DID are highly hypnotizable and can easily dissociate.

c. Social Factors: A Cultural Disorder?

- Prior to 1976, DID was a rare disorder. After the made-for-television movie *Sybil* aired, the number of DID diagnoses increased.
- Other cultures have an extremely low or zero prevalence rate of DID (*Examples:* India and China).

d. FEEDBACK LOOPS IN ACTION: Two Models for the Emergence of Alters:

The posttraumatic and sociocognitive models are two models of dissociative identity disorder, which includes neurological, psychological, and social factors.

(1) The posttraumatic model:

- Because of frequent episodes of abuse and coping through dissociation, the child's dissociated state can develop its own memories, identity, and way of interacting with the world, thus becoming an alter.
- However, many children are abused and do not develop DID, although many of these children do easily dissociate.

(2) The sociocognitive model:

The therapist unintentionally causes the patient to act in ways that are consistent with the symptoms of DID by subtly prompting the client.

4. The Debate About Dissociative Identity Disorder

- Some argue that therapists and the media subtly influence clients' symptoms of DID (sociocognitive model).
- We can neither be sure that all people with DID have been abused nor can we disconfirm the abuse.

MEDIA RECOMMENDATION 8.5: Interview with Chris Sizemore

Objective: To learn about the lived experience of DID through a famous case.

Time: 23 Minutes

Video and Discussion: 40 Minutes

Discussion Only: 17 Minutes

Watch Online: Search YouTube using the search terms "Multiple Personality Disorder on HardTalk" or click http://www.youtube.com/watch?v=kLGluMf-cH8&feature=related

The famous made-for-television movie *Three Faces of Eve* is based on the real-life story of Chris Sizemore, who is featured in these three clips. She addresses her experiences with her alters and her treatment.

Summary: Students will see how alters are experienced by a person with MPD and what the treatment for this disorder is, including the role of the person's family.

Questions to Students and Discussion: Describe Chris's different alters. Which alter does she miss the most and why? What treatment did she receive? What role did her family play in Chris's treatment? What surprised you most about this case?

MEDIA RECOMMENDATION 8.6: Hypnosis, Dissociation, and Trauma

Objective: To learn about the controversies surrounding hypnosis and dissociative disorders.

Time: 60 Minutes

Audio and Discussion: 90 Minutes

Discussion Only: 30 Minutes

Listen Online: Wise Counsel Podcast: An Interview with John Kihlstrom, Ph.D., on hypnosis, dissociation, and trauma (recording date February 2009), http://www.mentalhelp.net/poc/view_index. php?idx=119&d=1&w=9&e=29046

This podcast provides an overview of dissociative disorders and in particular highlights research on dissociative identity disorder and the use of hypnosis. Kihlstrom examines different types of research studies that have looked at DID.

Summary: Students will learn about the dissociative disorders and how hypnosis is used in treating them.

Questions to Students and Discussion: Describe the first few cases of DID mentioned in the podcast. What is Kihlstrom's perspective on the connection between trauma and DID? What is the difference between retrospective and prospective studies? How does hypnosis affect memory?

F. Treating Dissociative Disorders

Most dissociative disorders resolve themselves without treatment; since these disorders are so rare, little is known about the most effective treatments.

1. **Targeting Neurological Factors: Medication**

    People do not receive medication for DID, but they may receive medication for a comorbid disorder or for anxiety or mood symptoms that arise in response to the dissociative symptoms.

2. **Targeting Psychological and Social Factors: Coping and Integration**

    - Psychological treatments focus on helping clients reinterpret symptoms to decrease avoidance, increase stress-management skills, and address the dissociated memories or identities.
    - The post-traumatic model maps each alter's personality, recovers memories of abuse, and integrates the alters.

- The sociocognitive model ignores the alters in order to extinguish any mention of the alters.

- Hypnosis is sometimes used as part of treatment to help the patient learn and integrate the multiple alters but is controversial because of possible therapist suggestion and patient susceptibility.

- Reducing possible traumatic stress is also a helpful treatment.

3. FEEDBACK LOOPS IN TREATMENT: Dissociative Disorders

- Hypnosis involves helping the patient become aware of and integrate the alters.

- Hypnosis does allow patients to remember dissociated information but memories can be susceptible to the therapist's suggestions. [See *Figure 8.2.*]

II. SOMATOFORM DISORDERS

A. Somatoform Disorders: An Overview

- ***Somatoform disorders*** are complaints about physical well-being that cannot be entirely explained by a medical condition, substance use, or another psychological disorder.

- Somatoform disorders are "rule out" diagnoses because clinicians must clarify whether the symptoms do indeed suggest a medical problem. [*See Table 8.9.*]

- Symptoms must cause impairment and distress, and are involuntary.

- Somatoform disorders, in general, are rare, but they are the most common type of psychological disorder diagnosed in medical settings.

- Hippocrates described somatoform symptoms as caused by a wandering uterus (*hysteria*, from the Greek word *hystera*, meaning "uterus"). *Hysteria* was often used to refer to bodily symptoms that lack a medical explanation; in addition, patients with hysteria typically describe their symptoms dramatically.

- Somatoform disorders are different from *factitious disorder*, in which people *intentionally* induce symptoms for attention.

- Somatoform disorders all feature a *bodily preoccupation* and *symptom amplification*.

B. Somatization Disorder

Somatization disorder (SD) is multiple physical symptoms that are medically unexplained and impair an individual's ability to function.

1. What Is Somatization Disorder?

Patients must have four different types of medically unexplained symptoms: pain and gastrointestinal, sexual, and pseudoneurological symptoms. [See *Tables 8.10, 8.11; Case 8.5.*]

a. What Is a Pain Disorder?

- A ***pain disorder*** is different from SD and occurs when psychological factors significantly affect the onset, severity, or maintenance of significant pain.

- Symptoms must cause distress or impairment, and malingering or factitious disorder must be ruled out.

2. Criticism of the DSM-IV-TR Criteria

- Symptoms are equally weighted, despite some symptoms being more serious.

- The number of required symptoms was decided arbitrarily and was not based on research.

- The criteria do not include the client's misperceptions of bodily sensations and symptoms.
- It is possible that the symptoms might be indicative of a different psychological disorder (*Example:* anxiety).

3. **Understanding Somatization Disorder**

   a. **Neurological Factors: Genetics:**
   - A large-scale twin study found that genetic effects may account for as much as half of the variability in SD but the exact role of genetics is unclear, and individual experiences may affect the development of SD.
   - SD is more frequent in the relatives of people with hypochondriasis.

   b. **Psychological Factors: Misinterpretation of Bodily Signals:**
   - The client's preoccupation, amplification, and faulty beliefs about bodily symptoms lead to distress.

   c. **Social Factors:**
      (1) **Social stress:**

      SD often develops after a major stressor such as the death of a loved one.

      (2) **Social learning:**
      - People with SD may have developed this behavior through observational learning because many people with SD have had an ill parent.
      - Attention from friends and family can reinforce the behavior through operant conditioning.

      (3) **Cultural influences on symptoms:**
      - Somatic symptoms may be an acceptable form of expressing helplessness.
      - Culture seems to influence the prevalence of SD as Puerto Ricans are 10 times more likely to develop SD than the general U.S. population.
      - Lower SES groups are more likely to develop SD possibly due to feeling more helpless.

   d. **FEEDBACK LOOPS IN ACTION: Somatization Disorder:**

      Genetic predisposition may cause misinterpretations of bodily symptoms that are then reinforced by family members. [See *Figure 8.3.*]

C. Conversion Disorder

Conversion disorder involves sensory or motor symptoms that do not correspond to those that arise from known medical conditions.

1. **What Is Conversion Disorder?**
   - Symptoms of this disorder are not faked or developed consciously.
   - Symptoms cause distress and impairment.
   - Conversion disorder symptoms are limited to sensory and motor symptoms that appear to be neurological but do not follow neurological pathways. [*See Figure 8.4.*]
   - All possible medical causes must be ruled out to receive a conversion disorder diagnosis. [See *Figure 8.4; Table 8.12.*]

   a. **Three Types of Symptoms in Conversion Disorder:**
      (1) *Motor symptoms* that worsen when receiving attention (*Examples:* tics or jerks, muscle spasms, swallowing problems, staggering, and *pseudoparalysis*)

(2) *Sensory symptoms* that do not follow an actual nerve pathway (*Examples:* blindness, double vision, deafness, auditory hallucinations, and lack of feeling on the skin)

(3) *Seizures or pseudoseizures* that do not have a neurological origin and cannot be treated with seizure medication [see *Table 8.13; Case 8.6*]

2. Criticisms of the DSM-IV-TR Criteria

- Some researchers argue that conversion disorder is just a variant of SD since they both are bodily expressions of psychological distress.

- Other researchers believe that conversion symptoms are more like dissociative symptoms that disrupt sensory or motor functioning.

- Some see conversion disorder as a type of factitious disorder in which the person plays the sick role to get attention and avoid responsibilities.

3. Understanding Conversion Disorder

a. Neurological Factors:

(1) Brain systems:

- Clinicians must rule out the possibility that the client is faking his/her symptoms.

- Neuroimaging has found that activity in the brain is different for those who fake motor symptoms than for those with conversion disorder.

- Researchers compared brain activation in clients reporting sensory deficits in one limb and not the other. The "normal limb" registered pain (in the thalamus, the anterior cingulate cortex, the insula, and part of the frontal lobe). In the deficit limb, these structures were not activated and some areas were deactivated (the primary and secondary areas of the somatosensory cortex and parts of the parietal and frontal lobes). [See *Figure 8.5.*]

- Another neuroimaging study examined patients with conversion disorder who had a loss of sensation and motor control in one hand. A vibration device stimulated both hands but decreased blood flow in the thalamus, and the basal ganglia were found on the side opposite the affected hand. When the symptoms subsided these structures responded normally.

- Conversion disorder may be misdiagnosed and may reflect underlying medical problems.

(2) Genetics:

There may be a genetic link for conversion disorder, but it is difficult to differentiate between the role of family modeling and that of genetics.

b. Psychological Factors: Self-Hypnosis?

- Those with conversion disorder may inadvertently hypnotize themselves so that they are not consciously aware of the sensations in some part of their body or suggest to themselves that they have certain symptoms.

- Support for this argument is that the location of brain activation is similar for hypnosis and paralysis.

c. Social Factors: Stress Response:

The greater the stressor, the more severe are the conversion symptoms.

D. Hypochondriasis

- *Hypochondriasis* is a preoccupation with a fear or belief by people that they have a serious disease, but this preoccupation arises because they have misinterpreted their bodily sensations or symptoms.

- Patients with hypochondriasis strongly believe something is medically wrong despite reassurance from physicians.

1. What Is Hypochondriasis?

- Patients with hypochondriasis have *poor insight* into their condition and are preoccupied with health problems.

- Symptoms must cause distress or impairment for at least 6 months. [See *Tables 8.14, 8.15; Case 8.7.*]

2. Hypochondriasis and Anxiety Disorders: Shared Features

- Hypochondriasis has similarity to anxiety disorders and should, according to some researchers, be renamed *health anxiety disorder.*

- Symptoms of hypochondriasis include high levels of fear and anxiety, perceived danger, avoidance of certain stimuli, and obsessive thoughts about illness.

3. Understanding Hypochondriasis

a. Neurological Factors:

Brain systems, neural communication, and genetics are involved.

(1) Brain systems:

- Brain studies have found amygdala activation in patients with obsessive-compulsive disorder (OCD) when viewing OCD-related words, but not in those with hypochondriasis.

- Brain activation patterns are more similar, but not identical, to those with panic disorder.

(2) Neural communication:

Serotonin dysfunction may cause symptoms of hypochondriasis.

(3) Genetics:

- Genetics account for about a third of the variation in nonmedical bodily disorders.

- Results are mixed about a genetic link between hypochondriasis and OCD.

b. Psychological Factors: Catastrophic Thinking About the Body:

Psychological factors that contribute to hypochondriasis include biased thinking, excessive focus on unpleasant bodily sensations, misinterpretation of sensations as a sign of illness or disease, *catastrophic thinking,* and the remembering of health-related words more than non-health-related words.

c. Social Factors: Stress Response:

- Stressful events can trigger hypochondriasis.

- People with this disorder report experiencing more stressors than those without the disorder.

- Attention from caretakers may reinforce symptoms.

E. Body Dysmorphic Disorder

Body dysmorphic disorder, dysmorphophobia, is diagnosed when someone is excessively preoccupied with a *perceived* defect or defects in appearance; it is excessive because the defect is either imagined or slight.

1. What Is Body Dysmorphic Disorder?

- Physical imperfections cause distress or consume so much energy that daily functioning is impaired. [See *Table 8.16.*]
- Common preoccupations include thinning or excessive hair, acne, wrinkles, scars, complexion (too pale, too dark, too red, and so on), facial asymmetry, or the shape or size of some part of the face or body. The focus of these may change.
- People with BDD think that others are staring at them or talking about a "defect."
- They believe that the perception of the defect is accurate.
- People with BDD compulsively exercise, diet, shop, and pick at their skin, to hide a defect.
- Hours are spent looking in or avoiding the mirror. [See *Case 8.8.*]
- Social situations may be avoided.
- People with BDD may seek out surgery or perform self-surgery. *Example:* scar removal or teeth alterations. [See *Table 8.17.*]

a. Culture and Body Dysmorphic Disorder:

- Symptoms are similar across cultures.
- *Koro,* a condition in Southeast Asia, refers to a person becoming preoccupied with the belief that a body part (penis, labia, nipples, or breasts) is shrinking. The symptoms do not last as long as with body dysmorphic disorder.

2. Diagnosing Body Dysmorphic Disorder Versus Other Disorders

BDD shares similar features to anxiety disorders: anxiety-causing stimuli, avoidance, excessive fear of evaluation, obsessions, and time-consuming compulsions.

3. Understanding Body Dysmorphic Disorder

a. Neurological Factors:

- The frontal-temporal portions of the brain may play a role in body dysmorphic disorder symptoms.
- Dysfunctional serotonin may affect symptoms.
- There may be a genetic link between OCD and BDD.

b. Psychological Factors: Focus on Imperfections:

- Cognitive biases include being distracted by emotional information, hyperfocus on certain body parts and imperfections, and *catastrophic thinking* that imperfections will lead to dreadful consequences.
- People with BDD avoid anxiety-provoking situations (such as looking in the mirror).

c. Social Factors: Cultural Emphasis on Certain Body Features:

The body parts of focus differ across cultures.

LECTURE ENHANCEMENT 8.1: Males and Body Image

Objective: To inform students about muscle dysmorphia in males.

Lecture: 15 Minutes

Video and Lecture: 33 Minutes

Lecture Key Points:
I.   Introduction
    A. What messages do males receive about how they should look?
    B. From whom, what, and where do they receive these messages?
    C. What are some concrete examples of the messages they receive?
II. Who is at risk?
    A. Higher rates associated with male athletes in sports in which weight plays a role (wrestling, running, boxing).
    B. Higher rates of eating disorder have been found among gay men.
III. What is muscle dysmorphia?
    A. It is a reverse type of anorexia where an individual sees himself as smaller than he wants to be.

Optional Resources:
Cambridge Educational. (2002). *Body image for boys.* [Film]. Films for the Humanities and Sciences. http://ffh.films.com/id/4589/Body_Image_for_Boys.htm

Keel, P. (2005). *Eating disorders.* New York: Prentice Hall.

Summary: Students will learn what muscle dysmorphia is, the specific messages that males receive that may lead to muscle dysmorphia, and which males are most at risk.

Questions to Students and Discussion: What is muscle dysmorphia? Is it a gender-related disorder? Why do you think this is so? Who is most at risk for muscle dysmorphia? What messages do people receive that put them at risk?

MEDIA RECOMMENDATION 8.7: *Whole*

Objective: To learn about a form of BDD in which people wish to become amputees.

Time: 55 Minutes

Film and Discussion: 90 Minutes

Discussion Only: 35 Minutes

Watch Online: Gilbert, M. (2003). *Whole: A Documentary* [Film]. Melody Gilbert and FRZN Productions. http://www.whole-documentary.com/

This film highlights the experience of people who want to become amputees despite having no medical problems. Students will learn about a rare form of body dysmorphic disorder in which people wish to have their healthy limbs amputated.

Summary: Students will be surprised to learn about people who wish to become "whole" by amputating fully functioning limbs. For example, many of the people featured in the film believe their limbs should not be part of their bodies and will go to drastic measures to get a limb amputated.

Questions to Students and Discussion: What are your thoughts about this film? Why do you think these people wish to become amputees? Should they be allowed to have this as an elective surgery?

F. Is Somatoform Disorder a Useful Concept?

- Some researchers think that the symptoms of somatoform disorder could be symptoms of other disorders such as mood and anxiety disorders.
- Some cultures reject the division between the mind and body.
- Inter-rater reliability is a problem, as different clinicians often make different diagnoses for the same patient with somatoform symptoms.
- Somatoform disorders may be more accurately viewed as a medical illness.
- Alternatively, somatoform disorders may be unexplained.
- As we learn more about somatoform disorders, they may be moved to another category.
- Medical technology may help to uncover underlying medical problems.

G. Treating Somatoform Disorders

1. **Targeting Neurological Factors**

   - SSRIs or St. John's wort can treat the anxiety-related symptoms of somatoform disorders.
   - Minimal rigorous research has been done on the effectiveness of medication in treating somatoform disorders. [See *Table 8.18.*]

2. **Targeting Psychological Factors: Cognitive-Behavior Therapy**

   - Cognitive-behavioral therapy (CBT) is the treatment of choice.
   - CBT focuses on identifying and changing irrational thoughts. [See *Table 8.19.*]

3. **Targeting Social Factors: Support and Family Education**

   - A therapist may help by understanding the experience of someone with this disorder and how the symptoms affect the client's daily life.
   - Family therapy may be used to modify possible reinforcements for the dysfunctional behaviors.

4. **FEEDBACK LOOPS IN TREATMENT: Somatoform Disorders**

   - One form of treatment will affect the other factors. [See *Figure 8.6.*]

III. FOLLOW-UP ON ANNA O.

- Anna was hospitalized for morphine and chloral hydrate addiction (both prescribed by Breuer).
- Eventually, she became a social worker, orphanage director, and founder of a home for unwed mothers where the women were taught skills to support themselves and their children.

ADDITIONAL READINGS

Journal Articles

Adityanjee, Raju G. S., & Khandelwal, S. K. (1989). Current status of multiple personality disorder in India. *American Journal of Psychiatry, 146,* 1607–1610.

Albertini, R. S., & Phillips, K. A. (1999). Thirty-three cases of body dysmorphic disorder in children and adolescents. *Journal of the American Academy of Child & Adolescent Psychiatry, 38,* 453–459.

Borch-Jacobsen, M. (1997). Sybil: The making of a disease: An interview with Dr. Herbert Spiegel, *The New York Review,* April 27, 1997, p. 60.

Martorano, J. T. (1984). The psychological treatment of Anna O. In M. Rosenbaum & M. Muroff (Eds.), *Anna O.: Fourteen contemporary reinterpretations* (pp. 85–100). New York: Free Press.

Dissociative and Somatoform Disorders Books and Memoirs

Breuer, J., & Freud, S. (1955). *Studies on hysteria* (Vol. 2). (J. Strachey, Trans.). London: Hogarth Press. (Original work published 1895.)
     The book features several cases of "hysteria" as seen from the eyes of Breuer and Freud.

Freeman, L. (1990). *The story of Anna O.* New York: Paragon House.
     This book is discussed throughout this chapter.

Maggard, B. S. (2008). *Fugue: Through a glass darkly.* Create Space.
     The fictional story of a young woman who survives an accident but then cannot remember her past.

Oxnam, R. B. (2005). *A fractured mind: My life with multiple personality disorder.* New York: Hyperion Books.
     Oxnam is a China scholar who finds out he has multiple personality disorder.

Simeon, D. (2008). *Feeling unreal: Depersonalization disorder and the loss of self.* New York: Oxford University Press.
     This comprehensive book highlights personal accounts, research, and treatments for depersonalization disorder.

ADDITIONAL MEDIA RECOMMENDATIONS

Berman, S. R., & Pulcini, R. (Directors). (2003). *American splendor.* [Film]. USA: Good Machine.
     This film shows how hypochondriasis and mood disorders can overlap. The film focuses on a cartoonist who struggles with health issues, relationships, and depression.

Fincher, D. (Director). (1999). *Fight club.* [Film]. USA: Art Linson Productions.
     A young professional struggles with two aspects of his identity.

Gilbert, M. (Director). (2003). *Whole.* [Film]. St. Paul, MN: Melody Gilbert & FRZN Productions.
     This documentary focuses on individuals who want to be amputees despite having no medical problems.

Nolan, C. (Director). (2000). *Memento.* [Film]. USA: Newmarket Films.
     This film features a man who cannot form long-term memories due to hippocampal damage.

Petrie, D. (Director). (1976). *Sybil.* [Film]. USA: Lorimar Productions.
     A made-for-television movie featuring Sally Field as a young teacher who discovers she has dissociative identity disorder.

WEB SITES

Body Dysmorphic Disorder Central: This site offers information on treatment, resources, and additional information. See: http://www.bddcentral.com/

Depersonalization Support Community: This site provides a number of resources (chat rooms, treatments, support, and links) for people with depersonalization disorder. See: http://www.dpselfhelp.com/forum/

Substance Use Disorders

CHAPTER OUTLINE

CHAPTER HEADINGS	INSTRUCTION IDEAS AND TEXTBOOK CORRELATIONS
SUBSTANCE USE, ABUSE, AND DEPENDENCE	
Substance Use Versus Intoxication	**Textbook Tool:** Table 9.1
Substance Abuse and Dependence	**Learning Objectives:** 9.1, 9.2, 9.3, 9.4, 9.5, 9.6, 9.7 **Learning Concepts:** use becomes abuse, common liabilities model, gateway hypothesis, factors associated with progressing from entry drugs to hard drugs, substance abuse as a category or on a continuum?, comorbidity, polysubstance abuse, prevalence and costs, culture and context **Learning Activity 9.1:** Continuum Case Examples **Textbook Tools:** Figures 9.1, 9.2, 9.3, 9.4; Tables 9.2, 9.3, 9.4; Cases 9.1, 9.2
Culture and Context	**Learning Objective:** 9.7 **Learning Concept:** culture and context **Lecture Enhancement 9.1:** Youth Substance Use Rates
STIMULANTS	
What Are Stimulants?	**Learning Objectives:** 9.8, 9.9, 9.10, 9.11, 9.12, 9.13, 9.14 **Learning Concepts:** cocaine and crack, amphetamines, methamphetamine, Ritalin, Methylenedioxymethamphetamine (MDMA), nicotine **Media Recommendation 9.1:** The Meth Epidemic **Media Recommendation 9.2:** Memoirs of Meth Addiction from a Father and a Son **Textbook Tools:** Tables 9.4, 9.5; Cases 9.3, 9.4
Understanding Stimulants	**Learning Objectives:** 9.15, 9.16, 9.17, 9.18 **Learning Concepts:** brain and neural communication I—dopamine and abuse, the dopamine reward system, effects of cocaine and

	methamphetamine on the brain, brain systems and neural communication II—beyond dopamine, psychological factors, observational learning, operant conditioning, classical conditioning, social factors, family relations, peers, norms and perceived norms, sociocultural factors **Media Recommendation 9.3:** Stimulant Use at the Mouse Party **Learning Activity 9.2:** Drugs on Neurons **Learning Activity 9.3:** Comparison of Neighborhoods **Textbook Tools:** Figures 9.5, 9.6, 9.7; Tables 9.6, 9.7, 9.8
DEPRESSANTS	
What Are Depressants?	**Learning Objectives:** 9.19, 9.20, 9.21 **Learning Concepts:** alcohol, blood alcohol concentration, binge drinking, alcohol dependence, sedative-hypnotic drugs, barbiturates, benzodiazepines **Learning Activity 9.4:** What Is Your BAC? **Textbook Tools:** Figure 9.8; Case 9.5
Understanding Depressants	**Learning Objective:** 9.22 **Learning Concepts:** neurological factors, brain systems and neural communication, chronic alcohol drinking and withdrawal, biological by-products of alcoholism, why we get hangovers, genetics of alcoholism, family and twin studies, alcohol and adoption studies, alcoholism and chromosomal markers, psychological factors, social factors, changing cultural norms and alcohol abuse, community norms, diversity and drinking **Media Recommendation 9.4:** Children of Alcohol **Textbook Tools:** Figure 9.9; Tables 9.8, 9.9
OTHER ABUSED SUBSTANCES	
What Are Other Abused Substances?	**Learning Objectives:** 9.23, 9.24, 9.25 **Learning Concepts:** narcotic analgesics, heroin, progression to injection, hallucinogens, LSD, marijuana, dissociative anesthetics, phencyclidine (PCP), ketamine **Media Recommendation 9.5:** Hofmann's Potion **Lecture Enhancement 9.2:** Over-the-Counter Medication Abuses **Textbook Tool:** Case 9.6
Understanding Other Abused Substances	**Learning Objective:** 9.26 **Learning Concepts:** neurological factors, brain systems and neural communication, psychological factors, social factors **Textbook Tools:** Figures 9.10, 9.11; Tables 9.7, 9.8 **Worth Video Tool Kit for Abnormal Psychology:** Chemically-Induced Hallucinations
TREATING SUBSTANCE USE DISORDERS	
Goals of Treatment	**Learning Objective:** 9.27 **Learning Concept:** goals of treatment

Targeting Neurological Factors	**Learning Objective:** 9.28 **Learning Concepts:** detoxification, medications **Media Recommendation 9.6:** Topiramate and Naltrexone **Textbook Tool:** Table 9.10
Targeting Psychological Factors	**Learning Objective:** 9.29 **Learning Concepts:** motivation, stages of change, motivational enhancement therapy, cognitive-behavior therapy, 12-step facilitation, matching treatment to patient **Textbook Tools:** Figure 9.12; Tables 9.11, 9.12
Targeting Social Factors	**Learning Objectives:** 9.30, 9.31 **Learning Concepts:** residential treatment, community-based treatment, family therapy **Learning Activity 9.5:** Attend an AA Meeting **Media Recommendation 9.7:** Flipping the World—Drugs Through a Blue Lens **Textbook Tool:** Figure 9.13

LEARNING OBJECTIVES

After reading this chapter, students will be able to:

9.1 Describe the differences between substance use, abuse, and dependence.

9.2 Define substance use, intoxication, tolerance, and withdrawal.

9.3 Compare and contrast the common liabilities model and gateway hypothesis.

9.4 Identify the factors that contribute to the movement from entry to harder drugs.

9.5 Define the terms "comorbidity" and "polysubstance abuse," and provide examples of each.

9.6 Describe two costs of substance abuse.

9.7 Identify the role of culture in the rates of substance abuse.

9.8 Describe how stimulants affect the body and name six types.

9.9 Describe the effects of crack and cocaine use and abuse.

9.10 Identify the effects of amphetamine use and abuse.

9.11 Name the effects of methamphetamine use and abuse.

9.12 Describe the effects of Ritalin use and abuse.

9.13 Identify the effects of MDMA use and abuse.

9.14 Describe the effects of nicotine use and abuse.

9.15 Explain how stimulants affect the brain and neural communication.

9.16 Describe the psychological factors that influence stimulant abuse and dependence.

9.17 Name the social factors that influence stimulant abuse and dependence.

9.18 Describe how sociocultural factors influence stimulant abuse and dependence.

9.19 Explain how depressants affect the body and name the two major types.

9.20 Describe the effects of alcohol.

9.21 Describe the effects of sedative-hypnotic drugs.

9.22 Explain how neurological, psychological, and social factors influence depressant abuse and dependence.

9.23 Name and describe how narcotic analgesics affect the body.

9.24 Name and describe how hallucinogens affect the body.

9.25 Name and describe how dissociative anesthetics affect the body.

9.26 Describe the neurological, psychological, and social factors that influence other substance abuse and dependence.

9.27 Name the two ultimate goals of treatment.

9.28 Describe the different forms of neurological treatments for substance abuse and dependence.

9.29 Indentify the different forms of psychological treatments for substance abuse and dependence.

9.30 Name the different forms of social treatments for substance abuse and dependence.

9.31 Describe how the neurological, psychological, and social factors influence one another.

KEY TERMS

Psychoactive substance: A chemical that alters mental ability, mood, or behavior.

Substance use disorders: Psychological disorders characterized by abuse of or dependence on psychoactive substances.

Substance intoxication: The reversible dysfunctional effects on thoughts, feelings, and behavior that arise from the use of a psychoactive substance.

Substance abuse: A pattern of use of a psychoactive substance that leads to harm or other adverse effects.

Substance dependence: The persistent and compulsive use of a psychoactive substance, despite its negative effects on work, relationships, and health or its legal consequences.

Tolerance: The physiological response that arises from repeated use of a substance such that more of it is required to obtain the same effect.

Withdrawal: The set of symptoms that arises when a regular user decreases or stops intake of an abused substance.

Common liabilities model: The model that explains how neurological, psychological, and social factors make a person vulnerable to a variety of problematic behaviors, including substance abuse and dependence; also called *problem behavior theory*.

Gateway hypothesis: The proposal that use can become abuse when "entry" drugs serve as a gateway to (or the first stage in a progression to) use of "harder" drugs.

Polysubstance abuse: A behavior pattern of abusing more than one substance.

Dopamine reward system: The system of neurons, primarily in the nucleus accumbens and ventral tegmental area, that relies on dopamine and gives rise to pleasant feelings.

Reward craving: The desire for the gratifying effects of using a substance.

Relief craving: The desire for the temporary emotional relief that can arise from using a substance.

Drug cues: The stimuli associated with drug use that come to elicit conditioned responses through their repeated pairings with use of the drug.

Delirium tremens (DTs): The symptoms of alcohol withdrawal marked by confusion, convulsions, visual hallucinations, and fever.

Detoxification: Medically supervised withdrawal for those with substance dependence; also referred to as *detox*.

Antabuse: A medication for treating alcohol abuse and dependence that induces violent nausea and vomiting when it is mixed with alcohol.

Stages of change: A series of five stages that characterize how ready a person is to change problematic behaviors: precontemplation, contemplation, preparation, action, and maintenance.

Motivational enhancement therapy: A form of treatment specifically designed to boost a patient's motivation to decrease or stop substance use by highlighting discrepancies between stated personal goals related to substance use and current behavior; also referred to as *motivational interviewing.*

CHAPTER GUIDE

I. SUBSTANCE USE, ABUSE, AND DEPENDENCE

A *psychoactive substance* (commonly referred to as a drug) is a chemical that alters mental ability, mood, or behavior. These substances are used for one or more of the following purposes: therapeutic (*Example:* antidepressants), nontherapeutic (*Example:* alcoholic drinks for unwinding), or intoxication (*Example:* drugs used to get "wasted"). Frequent use can lead to abuse or dependence.

- *Substance use disorders* are characterized by abuse of or dependence on psychoactive substances.

- Once dependent, people abuse a substance because of its affect on mood, behavior, and/or cognition or because it prevents withdrawal symptoms.

- Substance use disorders cause impairment of function and of cognition or affect an imbalance of thoughts and motivation and can cause exacerbation of underlying psychological symptoms.

A. Substance Use Versus Intoxication

- *Substance intoxication* is defined as reversible dysfunctional effects on thoughts, feelings, and behavior that arise from the ingestion of a psychoactive substance. [See *Table 9.1.*]

- *Substance use* is a general term for having used a substance—via smoking, swallowing, snorting, injecting, or otherwise absorbing it—that does not indicate the extent or effect of use.

B. Substance Abuse and Dependence

- The term *addiction* refers to the compulsion to seek and use a psychoactive substance. The term is avoided by some clinicians and researchers because of its widespread overuse (*Examples:* addictions to chocolate, work, sex, love, and Internet use), which obscures its meaning.

- As already noted, *intoxication* refers to the direct results of using a substance; *substance abuse,* a pattern of harmful use of a psychoactive substance, focuses more on the indirect effects of repeated use, such as legal problems, unmet obligations, or reckless behavior while using the substance. [See *Table 9.2.*]

- *Substance dependence* is the pattern of persistent and compulsive use of a psychoactive substance, despite its negative effects on work, relationships, and health or its legal consequences. It refers mostly to direct effects of use. [See *Table 9.3.*]

- Neurologically based symptoms of substance dependence are tolerance and withdrawal. [See *Figure 9.1.*]
  i. *Tolerance* occurs when, with repeated use, more of a substance is required to obtain the same effect.
  ii. *Withdrawal* refers to the set of symptoms that arises when a regular user decreases intake of a substance. It occurs because the body continues to compensate for the repeated influx of a drug after the user has stopped taking the drug.

iii. For some substances that lead to tolerance with regular use, the absence of them may not also cause withdrawal symptoms. (*Example:* LSD.) In contrast, marijuana is one drug that can lead to withdrawal symptoms but may not always cause tolerance to be experienced, while PCP causes neither tolerance nor withdrawal.

1. Use Becomes Abuse

Substance abuse can develop in three ways:

- Unintentionally, such as through the environment
- When physician-prescribed medication produces psychoactive side effects
- Intentionally
- When a drug is used for its psychoactive effects (most research targets this path toward abuse)

a. Common Liabilities Model:

The **common liabilities model,** or *problem behavior theory,* explains how neurological, psychological, and social factors make a person vulnerable to problematic behaviors that include substance abuse and dependence.

- A study found that certain problem behaviors (drug and alcohol use, early sexual intercourse, delinquent behaviors) were exhibited by a group of adolescents who later developed substance abuse and that these behaviors may stem from the same underlying factors.
- Impulsivity is an important common liability that leads to substance abuse and other problems.
- There is a high comorbidity between substance use disorders and impulse-control disorders.

b. Gateway Hypothesis:

The **gateway hypothesis,** and related *stage theory,* claims that "entry drugs" (*Examples:* cigarettes and alcohol) serve as a first step into more serious drug use (use of "harder" drugs).

- Research is mixed: some, but not all, youths who used entry drugs progressed to marijuana use, and then some of these youths went on to use even harder drugs. [See *Case 9.1.*]
- Adolescents and young adults do not generally try other illegal drugs without first having used marijuana. [See *Figure 9.2.*]
- The typical progression of drug use is initiation, experimentation, casual use, regular use, abuse, and dependence.

c. Factors Associated with Progressing from Entry Drugs to Hard Drugs:

The two factors associated with the progression from entry drugs to hard drugs are age and quantity:

(1) Age:

The younger individuals are when first using a drug, the more likely they are to abuse drugs later in life—and the less likely they are to decrease or stop abusing them.

(2) Quantity:

The more drugs individuals use at the outset, the more likely they are to continue toward becoming substance dependent.

2. Substance Abuse as a Category or on a Continuum?

- Currently, substance abuse and substance dependence are considered separate diagnoses that are not both to be applied to the same patient.
- Some research suggests that this distinction is artificial and that use, abuse, and dependence should be viewed quantitatively on a continuum, defined by frequency, quantity, and duration of use. [See *Figure 9.3.*]

LEARNING ACTIVITY 9.1: Continuum Case Examples

Objective: To help students understand the differences between use, abuse, and dependence.

Time: 20 Minutes

Directions:
1. Have students generate examples of individuals who have had problems with substance use, abuse, and dependence.
2. Students should find examples of varying levels of abuse; have them examine their personal experience, the media, films, etc., to generate the list.
3. Collect all of the examples.
4. Use their examples to create a continuum (similar to *Figure 9.3*) on the classroom wall or floor.
5. As you read the cases aloud, have students stand on (or near, if you use a wall) that part of the continuum they believe corresponds to the case example.

Summary: Students will notice the subjectivity involved in judging cases according to whether the individual used, abused, or had dependence on a substance. Students should be made aware of hidden factors that might lead them to "misdiagnose" a case example. For example, Mel Gibson was pulled over for driving while intoxicated. Would he meet the criteria of abuse or dependence?

Questions to Students and Discussion: Which cases were most difficult to categorize? Why? Which cases were the easiest? Why? What are the strengths and problems of these categories?

3. Comorbidity

- In 1993, almost half of the people with alcohol abuse or dependence also had another DSM-IV-TR disorder.
- Also in 1993, almost three-fourths of those with drug use or dependence had another DSM disorder.
- The most frequent comorbid disorders are mood disorders (depression), posttraumatic stress disorder (PTSD), schizophrenia, and *attention-deficit/hyperactivity disorder (ADHD).*
- Clinicians may infer that an individual whose substance abuse developed *after* the development of another psychological disorder is self-medicating, that is, using substances to alleviate the disorder's symptoms.

4. Polysubstance Abuse

- *Polysubstance abuse* is a behavior pattern of abusing more than one substance.
- Polysubstances can be dangerous because of possible drug interactions. [*See Case 9.2.*]

5. Prevalence and Costs

In 2007, about 9% of Americans ages 12 and older, that is, 22.3 million individuals, exhibited substance abuse or dependence.

- Men are more likely to be diagnosed with substance abuse or dependence; women are more likely to be diagnosed with abuse or dependence on prescription medications.

- Native Americans have the highest rates of alcohol abuse or dependence, while Asian Americans have the lowest rates.

- Illegal substance abuse or dependence is more likely among African Americans, although this same group is least likely, after Asian Americans, to have alcohol abuse or dependence.

- There is wide variation within ethnic groups, and the prevalence rates of racial and ethnic groups provide only a general overview and only at a particular moment in time.

- Substance abuse and dependence affects not only the individual but also family, friends, coworkers, and colleagues. Examples of effects on all ages may include violence, neglect, chaos and stress, guilt, shame, children taking on adult roles and responsibilities, and other emotional and behavioral problems.

- The total economic cost of substance abuse in the United States was estimated to be $250 billion a year in 2006.

- There is a high correlation of substance abuse and dependence with unemployment. [See *Figure 9.4.*]

C. Culture and Context

- The distinction between use and abuse depends on the cultural context.
- There are four categories of patterns of use:
  i. Abstinence
  ii. Constrained (only for rituals)
  iii. Common activity
  iv. Fiesta (during celebrations)

LECTURE ENHANCEMENT 9.1: Youth Substance Use Rates

Objective: To examine current rates of substance use, abuse, and dependence among U.S. youth.

Time: 30 Minutes

Lecture Points:
I. Introduction
   A. Do you think substance abuse rates have increased or decreased among U.S. youth?
   B. What reasons can you provide to help explain your thoughts?
II. Study Background
   A. The University of Michigan's Institute for Social Research has conducted the *Monitoring the Future (MTF)* survey since 1975.
   B. Currently, the survey studies drug use among 8th, 10th, and 12th graders.
III. 2007–2008 Survey Findings
   A. Positive Results
      1. Illicit drug use declined among 10th graders. This finding does not include marijuana. "Lifetime use decreased from 18.2 to 15.9%, past-year use declined from 13.1 to 11.3 percent, and past-month use decreased from 6.9 to 5.3 percent."

2. Cigarette smoking fell to the lowest rates among 10th graders (but not for 8th and 12th graders).
        3. Amphetamine use among 10th graders declined. Crystal methamphetamine and crack cocaine use declined among 12th graders.
        4. Alcohol use among 10th graders decreased.
    B. Areas Needing Improvement
        1. Decreases in marijuana use have leveled off. "Past-year use was reported by 10.9% of 8th graders, 23.9% of 10th graders, and 32.4% of 12th graders."
        2. "In 2008, 15.4% of 12th graders reported using a **prescription drug** nonmedically within the past year."
        3. Perceptions of harm from using LSD among 12th graders and perceptions of harm from marijuana use among 8th graders have declined.

Summary: Students will be surprised to learn that illicit drug use among youth has declined, yet 8th graders seem to perceive LSD and marijuana use as safer than in previous years. Students may also raise methodological issues regarding survey research as adolescents may not be honest with their responses.

Resource: NIDA InfoFacts: High School and Youth Trends (2008), http://www.nida.nih.gov/info-facts/hsyouthtrends.html

Questions to Students and Discussion: What explanations can you give for the positive results and areas of concern? How might teachers and health officials address the areas of concern? Do you agree or disagree with this study? Why or why not? What concerns might you have about the research design? Do you think adolescents are honest when responding to questions about drug use?

II. STIMULANTS

Stimulants increase activity and arousal in the central nervous system and require repeated use for effect.

A. What Are Stimulants?

   1. **Cocaine and Crack**

   a. Cocaine:
   - Made from the coca plant, it operates as an anesthetic.
   - Initial use produces a heightened sense of well-being.
   - Prolonged use causes paranoia, hallucinations (due to spontaneous firing of sensory neurons), compulsive and repetitive behavior, increase in blood pressure, and loss of appetite. [See *Table 9.4.*]

   b. Crack:
   - Smoked crack acts quicker and stronger than cocaine.
   - Initial positive effects of crack use include heightened sense of well-being, energy, and mental clarity.
   - Aftereffects of crack use include depression and cravings. [See *Case 9.3.*]

   2. **Amphetamines**

   Effects of **amphetamines** are the same as those of cocaine but last longer.

   - Common amphetamines include *benzedrine* (racemic-amphetamine sulfate), *dexedrine* (dextroamphetamine), and *adderall* (a combination of amphetamine salts).

- Amphetamines are usually taken as a pill, snorted or diluted, or injected.
- Legal use includes treatments for ADHD and narcolepsy.
- They may cause irreversible damage to memory and physical coordination.
- Additional side effects are irritability and violent behavior.
- Withdrawal may cause depression, fatigue, irritability, and anxiety. [See *Case 9.4.*]

3. **Methamphetamine**

   Methamphetamines are also called "meth" or "speed."

   - Methamphetamines are related to amphetamines but are stronger, have a longer effect, and can be swallowed, smoked, or injected.
   - They create an intense rush that quickly leads to abuse and dependence.
   - Negative effects of methamphetamine use include irritability, heart problems, hallucinations, paranoia, dopamine and serotonin dysfunction (which causes motor and memory problems and difficulty with emotion regulation), and increased blood pressure (which can lead to a stroke). [See *Table 9.5.*]

MEDIA RECOMMENDATION 9.1: The Meth Epidemic

Objective: To explore the neuropsychosocial factors in meth dependence.

Time: 60 Minutes

Media and Discussion: 90 Minutes

Discussion Only: 30 Minutes

Watch Online: Byker, C., & McMahon, K. (2006), *Frontline: The Meth Epidemic.* WGBH Educational Foundation. http://www.pbs.org/wgbh/pages/frontline/meth/

This *Frontline* episode shows a fascinating analysis of the factors that play a role in methamphetamine addiction.

Summary: Students will better understand the neurological, psychological, and social factors that affect meth use and will see that physical deterioration and personal loss are some of the more significant consequences of meth dependence.

Questions to Students and Discussion: How is meth made? Were you shocked by the physical and psychological effects of meth dependence? What shocked you most and why? What factors have contributed to the rise and fall of meth abuse?

MEDIA RECOMMENDATION 9.2: Memoirs of Meth Addiction from a Father and a Son

Objective: To hear the personal experiences of a father and son affected by meth dependence.

Time: 39 Minutes

Media and Discussion: 60 Minutes

Discussion Only: 21 Minutes

Listen Online: *Fresh Air* (February 26, 2008), *Memoirs of Meth Addiction from a Father and a Son.* http://www.npr.org/templates/story/story.php?storyId=25552288

This *Fresh Air* interview explores the impact of meth dependence from the perspectives of a father and his drug-addicted son.

Summary: Students should gain a better understanding of how meth dependence impacts the individual and the family. They will also gain insight into the personal experience of a real individual with meth dependence.

Questions to Students and Discussion: How did Nic Sheff justify his use of meth? What changes in Nic's behavior did David report? What factors played a role in Nic's developing his addiction?

4. **Ritalin**

   Methylphenidate hydrochloride, or **Ritalin,** is prescribed for ADHD and works similarly to, but slower than, cocaine.

   - People can abuse Ritalin in any of three ways: swallowing pills, inhaling or snorting crushed pills, or injecting a liquid form of the drug.
   - Abuse causes alertness, increased attention, and decreased appetite.
   - Adverse side effects include heart problems and stroke.

5. **MDMA (Ecstasy)**

   Methylenedioxymethamphetamine (MDMA) is more commonly called Ecstasy, "E," or "X" and is taken as a tablet.

   - MDMA causes increased energy, distorted perceptions, empathy, sensitivity to touch, and reduced anxiety.
   - MDMA abuse can cause poor mood and emotional control, anxiety, aggression, sleeping problems, decreased appetite, impaired memory and cognitive functioning, poor concentration, depression, and fatigue.
   - Frequent users may experience withdrawal symptoms.
   - MDMA causes increased blood pressure, heart rate, dehydration, and hypothermia.

6. **Nicotine**

   Tobacco's active ingredient, **nicotine,** is a stimulant.

   - Nicotine can be inhaled, chewed, or smoked.
   - Nicotine causes alertness, dizziness, increased blood pressure, and irritability.
   - Nicotine enters the bloodstream and at the same time carbon monoxide enters the lungs and produces tar.
   - Chronic use can lead to lung cancer, emphysema, and breathing problems.
   - Tobacco abuse and dependence is the number 1 preventable cause of death in the United States.
   - Withdrawal symptoms include insomnia, anxiety, irritability, and decreased concentration.

B. **Understanding Stimulants**

   1. **Brain Systems and Neural Communication I: Dopamine and Abuse**

      Stimulant abuse affects specific neurotransmitters.

a. The Dopamine Reward System:

The *dopamine reward system* is the system of neurons, primarily in the nucleus accumbens and ventral tegmental area, that relies on dopamine and gives rise to pleasant feelings.

- Stimulant drugs affect the dopamine reward system. [See *Figure 9.5.*]
- Researchers have found that rats will press a lever repeatedly and even sacrifice food and drink if they receive stimulation in the dopamine reward system.
- The *dopaminergic hypothesis* of substance abuse argues that drug abuse is a result of the reward system where a person needs more of the substance to feel "normal."
- People may be more susceptible to drug abuse and dependence due to fewer dopamine receptors in the brain and thus need additional stimulation for effects.

MEDIA RECOMMENDATION 9.3: Stimulant Use at the Mouse Party

Objective: To see the effects of different substances on the brain.

Time: 15 Minutes

Media and Discussion: 30 Minutes

Discussion Only: 15 Minutes

Watch Online: *Mouse Party,* http://learn.genetics.utah.edu/content/addiction/drugs/mouse.html

This interactive video illustrates how various substances affect the brain. The step-by-step clips walk students through this complex process.

Directions:
1. Select a mouse that has used your drug of interest.
2. Pick up the mouse and place him in the chair.
3. Watch and listen as the audio and visual clips illustrate and explain how the substance affects the brain.

Summary: Students will enjoy the visual images of how various drugs affect the mice and will be able to describe this process more easily.

Questions to Students and Discussion: Describe the step-by-step process of how each drug affects the brain. What surprised you about this process? Why? What remains unclear?

LEARNING ACTIVITY 9.2: Drugs on Neurons

Objective: To act out the process of how a drug affects the neural communication processes.

Time: 20–30 Minutes

Directions:
1. Ask for 5 volunteers.
2. Have 3 students create a neuron (label the dendrites, cell body, and axon/terminal button).
3. Have 2 students play the role of the substance.
4. Show students *Figures 9.5* and *9.6.*
5. Have students act out normal neuron communication and then have them show how the substance affects this process.

Summary: This activity will solidify students' understanding of how drugs affect the neural communication process.

Questions to Students and Discussion: How does dependence develop due to this process? Explain. What remains unclear? How would this process look different with a different substance?

b. Effects of Cocaine and Methamphetamine on the Brain:

- Cocaine and methamphetamines bind to dopamine transporters and thus allow dopamine to linger in the synapse and cause the postsynaptic neuron to fire. [See *Figure 9.6.*] Long-term methamphetamine use creates transporter dysfunction.

- Chronic methamphetamine use can lead to permanent brain damage. [See *Figure 9.7.*]

2. Brain Systems and Neural Communication II: Beyond Dopamine

- Gamma-aminobutyric acid (GABA), glutamate, and serotonin also play a role in substance dependence.

- The GABAergic system includes the prefrontal cortex, which motivates behavior (in this case drug-seeking behavior).

- The glutamate system affects the cortical and limbic regions by producing the reinforcing effects of abuse and withdrawal symptoms.

- The serotonin system plays a role in eating, drinking water, sexual behavior, and response to pain and produces the desire for cocaine.

- These systems interact with one another.

- MDMA affects the dopamine reward system and the serotonin system. MDMA binds to serotonin transporters and sends a message to the neurons to produce less serotonin.

- However, nicotine affects only acetylcholine receptors (called *nicotinic receptors*), which increase the release of dopamine and inhibit the effects of other neurotransmitters. [See *Table 9.6.*]

3. Psychological Factors: From Learning to Coping

- Types of **psychological factors,** such as **observational learning, operant conditioning,** and **classical conditioning,** play a role in stimulant abuse and dependence.

a. Observational Learning:

Substance abuse or dependence may develop through observation of family, peers, celebrities, or mentors. Research on observational learning is correlational, and thus we cannot assume causation.

b. Operant Conditioning:

Operant conditioning influences stimulant use in four ways.

(1) Positive reinforcement:

If stimulant use is followed by pleasurable experiences, use increases. *Reward craving* occurs where even the thought of stimulant use creates a desire for the gratifying effects.

(2) Negative reinforcement—alleviating a negative state:

Use of the drug may alleviate negative feelings and thus use becomes reinforced. *Relief craving* is the craving for the drug when experiencing negative emotions.

(3)   **Negative reinforcement—alleviating withdrawal symptoms:**

Stimulant use can alleviate withdrawal symptoms and thus use becomes reinforced.

(4)   **Immediate reinforcement:**

Research has shown that people who abuse substances prefer immediate, smaller reinforcements over delayed, larger reinforcements. These same people prefer larger, delayed losses over smaller, immediate losses.

c. **Classical Conditioning:**

Drug cues are stimuli associated with drug use and can activate the dopamine reward system. [See *Table 9.7.*]

4.   **Social Factors**

Negative family interactions and peer relations are associated with higher risk of developing a substance use disorder.

a. **Family Relations:**

A correlational study found that youth who abused substances were less likely to feel close to their family. However, dysfunctional family interactions (*Examples:* abuse, domestic violence, or parental substance abuse) are more likely to be linked with youth substance abuse.

b. **Peers:**

Spending time with peers who also use these substances can lead to socialization into a subculture that accepts drug use.

c. **Norms and Perceived Norms:**

One's perception of norms may lead to increased use.

d. **Sociocultural Factors:**

- Stressors (such as economic hardships or unemployment) may lead to more use.
- Exposure to ads about legal psychoactive substances is more often present in economically disadvantaged areas. [See *Table 9.8.*]

LEARNING ACTIVITY 9.3: Comparison of Neighborhoods

Objective: To compare the number of ads and access to substances in different neighborhoods.

Time: 30–60 Minutes

Directions:
1. Ask students to identify one local middle-class neighborhood and one economically depressed neighborhood.
2. Organize a group trip to each neighborhood and ask students to compare the access to alcohol (liquor stores, delis, etc.) and the number of billboards and ads for legal substances (cigarettes, alcohol) in each neighborhood.

Summary: This exercise will provide students with real-life comparisons of the amount of risk for abuse and dependence people are exposed to in different socioeconomic settings.

Questions to Students and Discussion: What were your conclusions after this trip? On what bases did you form these conclusions? What surprised you? Why? What might be done to address this problem?

III. DEPRESSANTS

A. What Are Depressants?

Depressants include alcohol, opiates, barbiturates, and benzodiazepines. Depressants decrease activity and awareness. Tolerance can develop, and cutting back can produce withdrawal symptoms.

1. **Alcohol**

    - Six percent of Americans ages 12 and up are thought to abuse **alcohol.**
    - Abuse differs by ethnicity, with Native Americans having the highest prevalence of abuse and Blacks having lower abuse rates than Whites.

    a. **Blood Alcohol Concentration:**

      - **Blood alcohol concentration** is affected by
        i.   Number of consumed drinks
        ii.   Time period of consumption
        iii. When the person has last eaten
        iv.   The person's weight
        v.   Gender [See *Figure 9.8.*]
      - The type of glass may influence the amount of alcohol consumed, with people consuming more in shorter, wider glasses than with taller, narrow ones.
      - Women have less total water content in their bodies, which lessens the ability to dilute the alcohol and thus alcohol has a greater effect on women.
      - Genes and tolerance level can explain individual differences.

LEARNING ACTIVITY 9.4: What Is Your BAC?

Objective: To identify your own blood alcohol concentration on a typical night out.

Time: 20 Minutes

Explore Online: The Blood Alcohol Content Calculator at http://www.ou.edu/oupd/bac.htm

This Web site allows students to enter the type and number of drinks, their weight, and time factors. The analysis shows students how impaired they would be using the various reported factors.

Directions:
  1. Ask students to record the number of drinks they consume in a given night.
  2. Direct the students to enter the requested information on the Web site.

Summary: Students will gain insight into the various factors that affect one's blood alcohol concentration. Many students may be surprised how their typical drinking habits place them at a high level of impairment.

Questions to Students and Discussion: Were you surprised by your results? Why or why not? How can you use this information to modify your behavior? How might the BAC Calculator be helpful to others?

---

    b. **Binge Drinking:**

      - **Binge drinking,** or *heavy episodic drinking,* occurs when a person drinks until his or her blood alcohol concentration reaches at least 0.08% in a 2-hour period (which generally translates into four or more drinks for women, five or more for men) and can lead to abuse or dependence.

- Binge drinking among college students depends on age (older students binge-drink less), gender of students (females binge-drink less), and if students attend an all-female or coed school (students at all-female schools binge-drink less).

- Binge drinking increases dangerous behaviors. (*Examples:* driving while under the influence, having unprotected sex, an increase in sexual activity.)

c. Alcohol Dependence:

- **Alcohol dependence** has the following four symptoms:
  i. Craving or strong need; urge to drink
  ii. Loss of control over the amount one drinks
  iii. Physical dependence such as nausea, sweating, shakiness, and anxiety after stopping drinking
  iv. Tolerance, which causes the person to consume more alcohol to achieve the same feelings [See *Case 9.5.*]

- Abuse and dependence may cause memory problems and *blackouts* (periods of time while intoxicated where the person cannot remember what happened).

2. Sedative-Hypnotic Drugs

- These drugs reduce pain and anxiety, relax muscles, lower blood pressure, slow breathing and heart rate, and induce sedation and sleep.

- They can cause similar effects as alcohol: impaired physical coordination and judgment, increased aggression and sexual behavior, lowered inhibitions, increased sense of well-being, memory problems, confusion, poor concentration, fatigue, and respiratory arrest.

- They can be lethal when combined with alcohol.

- There are two types: barbiturates and benzodiazepines.

a. Barbiturates:

- Examples of barbiturates include *amobarbital* (Amytal), *pentobarbital* (Nembutal), and *secobarbital* (Seconal) and are usually prescribed for sleep difficulties.

- Barbiturates are abused by those with and without a prescription.

- Repeated use of barbiturates leads to tolerance.

- Withdrawal symptoms include agitation, restlessness, hallucinations, confusion, and possibly seizures.

- Medical consultation is needed for proper withdrawal.

b. Benzodiazepines:

- Benzodiazepines are prescribed for muscle pain, as a sleep aid, or for short-term anxiety treatment.

- Examples include *lorazepam* (Ativan), *triazolam* (Halcion), *chlordiazepoxide* (Librium), *diazapam* (Valium), and *alprazolam* (Xanax).

- Dependent patients are advised to gradually taper off use and seek medical consultation.

B. Understanding Depressants

1. Neurological Factors

This section will explore the effects of depressants on the GABAergic system, neural bases of alcohol abuse and dependence, and the role of genetics in alcoholism.

a. Brain Systems and Neural Communication:

- The GABAergic system inhibits the anxiety process, and those who experience anxiety are more likely to find depressants reinforcing.
- Alcohol and other depressants not only depress the nervous system but also inhibit other systems, which then causes more casual and impulsive behaviors.

(1) Chronic alcohol drinking and withdrawal:

- Alcohol consumption induces the production of dopamine, and long-term use stimulates the production of *endogenous opioids* or pleasure chemicals.
- When chronic drinkers stop, they no longer produce the *endogenous opioids* and thus may experience unpleasant opioid withdrawal.

(2) Biological by-products of alcoholism:

- Frequent drinkers may become malnourished. (*Example:* Some may develop deficiencies of vitamin B1, which causes brain atrophy.)
- *Korsakoff's syndrome* is a chronic memory problem due to brain atrophy caused from alcohol abuse. [*See Figure 9.9.*]
- *Cirrhosis* of the liver is caused by scar tissue, which impairs liver function. Cirrhosis is due to chronic alcohol use.

(3) Why we get hangovers:

- A hangover occurs the day after intoxication. Symptoms include headache, nausea, dizziness, and disorientation.
- One cause of hangovers is dehydration from our kidneys, which use the body's water to clean out the toxins in the blood.
- The liver uses a two-step process to break down alcohol, first producing acetaldehyde (a toxin) which is then converted into acetate (a harmless substance). Some people cannot convert the acetaldehyde to acetate and thus their bodies retain the toxins that were produced by the liver.
- Some people drink more to reduce withdrawal symptoms of alcohol.
- Withdrawal symptoms, also called **delirium tremens (DTs)**, experienced by heavy drinkers include headaches, weakness, tremors, anxiety, high blood pressure, seizures, increased heart rate and breathing, fever, agitation, irritability, confusion, convulsions, and hallucinations.

b. Genetics of Alcoholism:

(1) Family and twin studies:

- Biological offspring of alcoholics are twice as likely to become alcoholics as those without a family history of alcoholism.
- Twin studies have also shown a genetic link; some report that 54% of the variance is attributed to genetics.

(2) Alcoholism and adoption studies:

- Those who were adopted by nonalcoholics but had alcoholic biological parents were more likely to abuse alcohol as adults.
- There may be two types of alcoholism: Type I and Type II.
- Type I alcoholism is less severe, has later onset, can be modified with the environment, and occurs in both men and women.
- Type II alcoholism has an earlier onset, is less modified by the environment, and occurs only in men.

(3)   **Alcoholism and chromosomal markers:**

Chromosome 11 may serve as the genetic link to alcoholism. This gene may make people more vulnerable or serve as a protective mechanism. (*Example*: Asians have a gene that magnifies the effect of alcohol, which causes increased heart rate and nausea.) [See *Table 9.9.*]

2.   **Psychological Factors**

Observational learning, operant conditioning (including both positive and negative reinforcement), and classical conditioning can contribute to substance abuse or dependence.

3.   **Social Factors**

Dysfunctional family interactions, peer use of depressants, norms about depressant use, economic hardship, and unemployment can contribute to substance abuse or dependence. [See *Table 9.8.*]

MEDIA RECOMMENDATION 9.4: Children of Alcohol

Objective: To learn about parental alcohol abuse and how it affects children.

Time: 18 Minutes

Media and Discussion: 30 Minutes

Discussion Only: 12 Minutes

Watch Online: Cardinal, G. (1984), *Children of Alcohol.* National Film Board of Canada. http://www.nfb.ca/film/children_of_alcohol/

This powerful film features several children who have watched their parents abuse alcohol.

Summary: Students will understand the social consequences for children whose parents abuse alcohol. The text discusses observational learning as a cause of substance abuse and dependence.

Question to Students and Discussion: What were the various consequences the children experienced due to their parents' behavior? Do you think the camp is an effective outlet for these children? Describe specific behaviors these children might be observing that may cause future drug dependence.

---

a. **Changing Cultural Norms and Alcohol Abuse:**

- As social mores and norms for women have changed, alcohol abuse has increased for American women.
- Cultures influence appropriate and inappropriate alcohol use.
- Research has shown that when youth are exposed to more ads for alcohol, it correlates to the assumption by young people that alcohol use is greater than it actually is in reality.

b. **Community Norms, Diversity, and Drinking:**

- White students attending colleges with more diversity had lower rates of binge drinking, possibly due to exposure to a wider range of views regarding alcohol use.
- Asian and Black Americans ages 20 and under are least likely to binge-drink.

IV. OTHER ABUSED SUBSTANCES

This section describes the abuse of narcotic analgesics, hallucinogens, and dissociative anesthetics.

A. What Are Other Abused Substances?

1. Narcotic Analgesics

- Derived from the opium poppy plant or chemically related substances; narcotic analgesics are sometimes referred to as *opiates, opioids,* or *exogenous opioids* (*exogenous* means "arising from an outside source")
- Include methadone, heroin, codeine, morphine, and synthetic derivatives found in pain-relief medications (*oxycodone* [OxyContin], *hydrocodone* [Vicodin], *meperidine hydrochloride* [Demerol], *propoxyphene* [Darvon], and *hydromorphone* [Dilaudid])
- Can be injected, snorted, or taken by mouth
- Produce pleasant, relaxing effects but are highly addictive
- Aftereffects include apathy, unhappiness, impaired judgment, fidgeting, and sluggishness and begin within 8 hours after use
- Withdrawal symptoms include flu-like symptoms such as nausea and vomiting, muscle aches, watery eyes, dilated pupils, sweating, fever, diarrhea, insomnia, depressed mood, irritability, and restlessness

a. Heroin:

- **Heroin** is a very addictive strong opioid. It produces a strong euphoria, but has a letdown that increases cravings.
- Tolerance can cause irritability because of the failure to reach the same high previously felt.

(1) Progression to Injection:

- Typical users start by snorting heroin, then injecting the substance under the skin (called *skin popping*), and finally by injecting the drug into the blood vessels (called *mainlining*).
- Associated medical conditions include pneumonia, liver disease, clogged blood vessels, AIDS, hepatitis, and collapsed veins.

2. Hallucinogens

- Less predictable and influenced by the user's expectations
- Induce sensory or perceptual distortions—hallucinations in any of the senses
- Include LSD, *mescaline, psilocybin,* and *marijuana*

a. LSD:

- **LSD** use alters visual and auditory sensations and perceptions and may cause *synesthesia,* a blending of senses that might lead the user to "see" musical notes or "hear" colors.
- Effects start 30 to 90 minutes after ingestion and last up to 12 hours.
- A bad trip includes feelings of anxiety, fear, dread, losing control, going crazy, or dying.
- Those who have a bad trip alone are at risk of hurting themselves.
- Aftereffects include psychosis and flashbacks (called *hallucinogen perception disorder,* where involuntary sensory distortions occur when taking the drug).

- Recurrent use leads to tolerance.
- Discontinued use does not cause withdrawal symptoms, although some have enduring psychotic symptoms.

MEDIA RECOMMENDATION 9.5: Hofmann's Potion

Objective: To learn about alternative views on LSD use.

Time: 56 Minutes

Media and Discussion: 90 Minutes

Discussion Only: 34 Minutes

Watch Online: Littlefield, C. (2002). *Hofmann's Potion.* National Film Board of Canada. http://www.nfb.ca/film/hofmanns_potion/

This film explores the origins of LSD, times when LSD was used as a treatment, and alternative perspectives on LSD use.

Summary: Students will gain an understanding of multiple perspectives on LSD use.

Questions to Students and Discussion: How was LSD discovered? How does LSD affect our perceptions? What are the various "experts'" perspectives on how LSD affects our perceptions? What were some of the original uses of LSD? Do you agree that Whites should be allowed to use LSD if it is legal to use among Native American populations? Why or why not?

b. Marijuana:

- **Marijuana** is dried leaves and flowers of the hemp plant (*cannabis sativa*).
- Resin from the hemp plant's flowering tops is *hashish.*
- *Tetrahydrocannabinol* (THC) is the active ingredient of marijuana and hashish.
- Its effects are more subtle than other hallucinogens and include perceptual distortions, vivid sensations, feeling that time has slowed down, and cognitive and motor impairment.
- It activates the dopamine reward system; the experience depends on the user's mood and expectations.
- Withdrawal symptoms include irritability, anxiety, depression, decreased appetite, and disturbed sleep.
- Chronic use affects learning, memory, motivation, and increased risk of heart attack—even when not under its direct influence.

3. Dissociative Anesthetics

- Produces a sense of detachment from the user's surroundings—a *dissociation*; *anesthetic* refers to the drugs originally used as anesthetics for surgery
- Act like depressants but also affect glutamate, producing distorted visual and auditory perceptions
- The most commonly used dissociative anesthetics are PCP and ketamine

a. Phencyclidine (PCP):

- **Phencyclidine (PCP)** is also known as "angel dust" or "rocket fuel" and became a popular street drug in the 1960s.

- PCP can be snorted, ingested or smoked.

- Users report feeling powerful and invulnerable, which places them at risk for violence or suicide.

- Medical effects of high use include decreased breathing and heart rate, sweating, coordination problems, and numbness. PCP is dangerous even in small amounts.

- Higher doses may cause hallucinations, delusions, paranoia, disordered thinking, and other schizophrenia-like symptoms. [See *Case 9.6.*]

b. Ketamine:

- **Ketamine** is known as "Special K" or "Vitamin K" and can be injected or snorted.

- It causes anesthesia, hallucinations, and short-acting, less-intense PCP-like effects.

- Abuse can cause temporary memory loss, impaired cognitive abilities, loss of contact with reality, violent behavior, and potentially fatal breathing and heart problems.

LECTURE ENHANCEMENT 9.2: Over-the-Counter Medication Abuses

Objective: To examine the abuse of over-the-counter medications.

Time: 60 Minutes

Lecture Points:
I.   Over-the-Counter Abuses
   A. Cough Medicines
      1. Rate
         a. The number of dextromethrophan overdoses in young people ages 9 to 17 has increased more than 10 times—from 23 cases in 1999 to 375 cases in 2004.
         b. The chemical dextromethrophan, or DXM, is the ingredient found in over 200 products (including Robitussin DM, Nyquil, Vicks Formula 44, and Coricidin HBP Cough & Cold tablets).
         c. Street names among teenagers include Robo, Skittles, Triple C's, Dex, Vitamin D, and Tussin.
      2. Effects
         a. Dissociative hallucinations and out-of-body experiences or a PCP-like high
         b. Affects brain chemistry like morphine (opioid)
         c. Medical complications include coma, negative reactions when mixed with other meds, unconsciousness, seizures, liver destruction, addiction, and tolerance
   B. Inhalants—nail polish remover, gasoline, glue, cleaners, hairspray, spray paint, gases
      1. Rates
         a. 22.9 million Americans have used an inhalant once in their lives. Four percent of 4th graders used it at least once (2003-2004 study); 17.3% of 8th graders; 12.4% of 10th graders; and 11.9% of 12th graders
      2. How It Works
         a. Sniffing, huffing (using a cloth in mouth), sniffing in bag
         b. Absorbed in lungs and distributed through brain and body (similar to alcohol)
         c. Breaks down myelin sheath, which causes difficulty sending messages and muscle problems
         d. Causes problems with hippocampus and results in difficulty learning new things
         e. Stops nerve cell activity in cerebral cortex
         f. Affects the cerebellum and slows movement

3. Effects
   a. Mind altering
   b. Slurred speech, lack of coordination
   c. Long-term consequences include harm to important organs, heart damage, fewer blood cells, and long-term attention problems

Resource: NIDA InfoFacts: Prescription and Over-the-Counter Medications, http://www.drugabuse.gov/Infofacts/PainMed.html

Summary: Students will be surprised to learn about over-the-counter abuse among youth. Students will also benefit from learning about the neurological and psychological consequences of inhalant abuse. For example, students will learn how certain substances deteriorate the myelin sheath and affect specific brain structures, which in turn affects speech and coordination and may lead to interpersonal problems.

Questions to Students and Discussion: What surprises you about this information? How might we use different social factors to prevent such abuses?

B. Understanding Other Abused Substances

1. Neurological Factors

a. Brain Systems and Neural Communication

The other abused substances have different effects on the brain and neural systems.

(1) Narcotic analgesics:
   - Heroin slows down the central nervous system and binds to opioids in the brain, which causes pain reduction and stimulates the dopamine reward system.
   - Longer-term use of heroin reduces the brain's production of endorphins and thus intensifies withdrawal symptoms.

(2) Hallucinogens:
   - Early marijuana use can cause atrophy of natural cannabinoid receptors (particularly in the hippocampus and cerebellum).
   - The hippocampal atrophy may cause memory problems. [See *Figure 9.10.*]

(3) Dissociative anesthetics:
   - These can alter glutamate activity, inducing brain activity, which may cause violent, impulsive behavior.
   - Glutamate also plays a role in memory, pain perception, and environmental responses.
   - High levels of glutamate are toxic and may lead to cell death causing cognitive deficits.

b. Genetics of Other Types of Substance Abuse:
   - A twin study found that genes as well as shared and unique environmental factors all influence substance abuse.
   - Forty-five percent of the variance is due to genes, 20% to environmental factors, and 35% to nonshared environmental factors for marijuana dependence.

2. Psychological Factors
   - Observational, operant, and classical conditioning all influence substance abuse. [See starred items in *Table 9.7.*]

- Classical conditioning explains the finding that environmental factors (like the place where a person uses heroin) can trigger the brain to prepare for the dose of heroin by dampening the effect of the about-to-be-taken drug and may lead to an overdose.

3. **Social Factors [see starred items in *Table 9.8*]**

   Dysfunctional family interactions, peer use, economic hardship, and unemployment are associated with drug abuse and dependence.

4. **FEEDBACK LOOPS IN ACTION: Understanding Substance Use Disorders**

   - Neurological, psychological, and social factors all influence substance abuse and dependence and each other.
   - A study found that children of parents who had alcohol dependence tended to exhibit negative emotions (sadness, anger, aggression), while those with drug-dependent parents had lower self-control and harm avoidance. [See *Figure 9.11.*]

V. TREATING SUBSTANCE USE DISORDERS

A. Goals of Treatment

There are two possible **goals of treatment:** *abstinence* (which has higher relapse rates and may use medications that reduce or block the high) and *harm reduction* (to reduce harm to self and society due to drug abuse and dependence).

B. Targeting Neurological Factors

Detoxification and medications address neurological factors.

1. **Detoxification**

   Detoxification (also referred to as *detox*) is medically supervised withdrawal for those with substance dependence. It can be gradual and may require medical supervision.

2. **Medications**

   Medications can work by reducing or blocking pleasant effects, reducing unpleasant effects such as withdrawal, or helping the user abstain from the drug. Relapse prevention strategies should accompany the use of medication.

   a. Stimulants:
   - *Bupropion* (Zyban) affects dopamine and can reduce cravings for nicotine and methamphetamines.
   - *Nicotine replacement therapy* (*Examples:* skin patches, chewing gum, nasal inhalers or sprays) is a better alternative to smoking and can help one taper off use.

   b. Depressants:
   - *Disulfram* (***Antabuse***) is a drug used to treat alcohol abuse that causes nausea and vomiting when one drinks alcohol, thereby slowly decreasing one's use of alcohol (and possibly cocaine). However, taking Antabuse is voluntary.
   - *Naltrexone* (reVia) is the most widely used treatment for alcohol abuse, post-detoxification; it works by reducing the dopamine reward system activity.
   - *Acamprosate* is more common in Europe and reduces cravings through the NMDA receptors. A combination of naltrexone and acamprosate has been found to be most effective.
   - *Atenolol* (a beta-blocker) helps to reduce seizures and DTs caused by detoxification.

MEDIA RECOMMENDATION 9.6: Topiramate and Naltrexone

Objective: To learn about naltrexone and topiramate.

Time: 2 Minutes

Media and Discussion: 10 Minutes

Discussion Only: 8 Minutes

Watch Online: Search Healthcentral.com with the search terms "new help for alcohol" or http://www.healthcentral.com/video/408/2529.html
This video explores one person's success with topiramate.

Search Healthcentral.com with the search terms "makeover for alcohol" or http://www.healthcentral.com/video/408/2399.html
This video explores one person's success with naltrexone.

Summary: Students will learn about how topiramate and naltrexone target the dopamine reward system to reduce the desire for and effects of alcohol.

Questions to Students and Discussion: How do these medications work? How have they changed the patients' lives? What questions do you have about this method of treatment?

c. Narcotic Analgesics [see *Table 9.10*]:

- *Methadone* is a synthetic opiate that prevents a high from heroin. Drawbacks of methadone treatment include: it is only effective for 24 hours, it might be sold on the black market since it may produce a slight high, it can only be given at a clinic, and it does not block the high from other drugs.

- *LAAM* (levo-alpha-acetyl-methadol) blocks narcotic analgesics up to 72 hours and does not produce a high. Drawbacks of LAAM include heart problems.

- *Buprenorphine* (Subutrex) and *naloxone* (Suboxone) treat narcotic analgesic abuse or dependence. Naltrexone can also treat opiate dependence (often used with buprenorphine) and works best with those individuals who are highly motivated.

- *Clonidine* (a beta-blocker) can help with withdrawal symptoms.

d. Hallucinogens:

- Those who want to stop with LSD abuse can just quit without experiencing withdrawal symptoms.

- Marijuana abuse and dependence are treated by addressing psychological and social factors.

C. Targeting Psychological Factors

There are four psychological factors that are targeted: motivation, expectations, involvement, and decreasing conditioned behaviors.

1. Motivation

Motivation strongly affects success of treatment.

a. Stages of Change:

The *stages of change* identify the readiness of the client to change behaviors associated with substance abuse and dependence. There are five stages a person goes through:

   (1) **Precontemplation:**

     Individual does not admit there is a problem and has no plan to change.

   (2) **Contemplation:**

     Individual identifies the problem but no action is made.

   (3) **Preparation:**

     Individual becomes prepared to change and has made a plan and intention.

   (4) **Action:**

     Individual makes changes in behavior.

   (5) **Maintenance:**

     Individual continues building on changes, tries to prevent relapse, and may need support to prevent relapses.

       These stages are not mutually exclusive and people often regress to an earlier stage.

  b. Motivational Enhancement Therapy:

- *Motivational enhancement therapy* (also referred to as *motivational interviewing*) is specifically designed to boost patients' motivation to decrease or stop substance use by highlighting discrepancies between stated personal goals related to substance use and current behavior.

- Therapists promote behavior change through highlighting discrepancies, increasing motivation, and discussing positive and negative consequences of use, reasons to quit, and how to begin change.

- This form of therapy works best when there is a positive relationship between client and therapist; however, benefits fade over one year.

2. Cognitive-Behavior Therapy

- **Cognitive-behavior therapy (CBT)** focuses on three themes:
  - **i.** understanding
  - **ii.** changing the antecedents and consequences of abuse and dependence
  - **iii.** developing alternative behaviors

- *Abstinence reinforcement* is where one increases positive consequences of abstinence. This is one form of *contingency management,* and it works by reinforcing desired behaviors or when undesired behaviors do not occur.

- Possible reinforcements include monetary vouchers [see *Figure 9.12*], reduction of counseling sessions, more convenient appointment times, or allowing a person a small supply of methadone, thus reducing the number of clinic trips.

- Positive incentives work best, but relapse increases once rewards are discontinued.

- Other CBT methods include increasing healthy coping skills, self-monitoring, cognitive restructuring, problem-solving, and relaxation techniques. [See *Table 9.11*.]

3. Twelve-Step Facilitation (TSF)

- **Twelve-step facilitation (TSF)** is based on the 12 steps or principles that form the basis of *Alcoholics Anonymous (AA).* [See *Table 9.12*.]

- AA views alcohol abuse as a disease that is out of one's control and focuses on motivation. Furthermore, AA groups are leaderless, whereas TSF groups are led by a professional.

- Narcotics Anonymous (NA) and other similar groups use the 12-step format.

4. Matching Treatment to Patient

- A large study compared TSF, CBT, and motivational enhancement and found that all patients improved regardless of type of treatment. No specific patient-treatment matches were found.

- However, polysubstance abusers need a single program that addresses polysubstance abuse, and those with a dual diagnosis fare better when the other disorder is treated as well as the abuse or dependence.

D. Targeting Social Factors

Social factors focus on treating interpersonal and community antecedents and consequences of abuse and dependence.

1. Residential Treatment

- Some people need a therapeutic environment 24 hours a day, seven days a week.

- These types of programs can help people change more quickly.

2. Community-Based Treatment

a. Group Therapy:

Cognitive behavior therapy, role-playing, and social skills training can be used in a group setting where the person can also have peer support.

b. Self-Help Groups:

Self-help groups (also called support groups; examples include Alcoholics Anonymous and Narcotics Anonymous) hold regular meetings, can act as supplemental treatment, and view a belief in a higher power as part of treatment.

- *Sponsors* are sober individuals who serve as mentors and can be contacted when newer members experience cravings or temptations to drink again.

- Nonreligious groups include Secular Organizations for Sobriety, Women for Sobriety, Rational Recovery, and Smart Recovery.

- Research has shown that once-a-week attendance is associated with continued abstinence.

LEARNING ACTIVITY 9.5: Attend an AA Meeting

Objective: To observe a self-help treatment.

Time: 60–90 Minutes

Directions: Visit Alcoholics Anonymous online to find a meeting near you, http://www.aa.org

Please make sure to only attend "open" meetings, as some of the meetings are closed to nonmembers.

Summary: Students will observe firsthand how self-help treatments for alcohol abuse and dependence work.

Questions to Students and Discussion: Describe your thoughts and feelings before attending the meeting. What were you surprised about? How was the meeting conducted?

3. Family Therapy

Outpatient **family therapy** has been shown to help adolescents abstain from substance abuse. Family therapy seeks to address communication, power, and control issues.

4. **FEEDBACK LOOPS IN TREATMENT: Substance Use Disorders**

- Interventions are successful if one:
    - **i.** Completes the treatment and is not using or abusing the substance
    - **ii.** Experiences few harmful consequences from use
    - **iii.** Decreases use of the substance
    - **iv.** Behaves more responsibly
    - **v.** Feels better
    - **vi.** Conforms to societal norms
- Successful treatments use a neuropsychosocial approach. [See *Figure 9.13.*]

MEDIA RECOMMENDATION 9.7: Flipping the World — Drugs Through a Blue Lens

Objective: To learn about drug addiction from people who have recovered.

Time: 30 Minutes

Media and Discussion: 45 Minutes

Discussion Only: 15 Minutes

Watch Online: Simpson, M. (2000). *Flipping the World.* National Film Board of Canada http://www.nfb.ca/film/flipping_the_world_drugs_through_a_blue_lens/

This documentary is an intimate look at the people behind the term "substance youth." Several young people interview and befriend substance abusers with the supervision of police.

Summary: Students will see the dramatic before-and-after experiences of young people who are battling severe addictions.

Questions to Students and Discussion: What were the youths' responses to this experience? Which transformation was most shocking? Why?

ADDITIONAL READINGS

Austin, A. M., Macgowan, M. J., & Wagner, E. F. (2005). Effective family-based interventions for adolescents with substance use problems: A systematic review. *Research on Social Work Practice, 15,* 67–83.

Blair, N. A., Yue, S. K., Singh, R., & Bernhardt, J. M. (2005). Depiction of substance use in reality television: A content analysis of *The Osbournes. British Medical Journal, 331,* 1517–1519.

Daley, D. C., & Salloum, I. (1999). Relapse prevention. In P. J. Ott, R. E. Tarter, and R. T. Ammerman (Eds.), *Sourcebook on substance abuse: Etiology, epidemiology, assessment, and treatment* (pp. 255–263). Needham Heights, MA: Allyn & Bacon.

Hettema, J., Steele, J., & Miller, W. R. (2005). Motivational interviewing. *Annual Review of Clinical Psychology, 1,* 91–111.

Prochaska, J. O., Velicer, W. F., Rossi, J. S., Goldstein, M. G., Marcus, B. H., Rakowski, W., et al. (1994). Stages of change and decisional balance for 12 problem behaviors. *Health Psychology, 13,* 39–46.

Staines, G. L., Magura, S., Foote, J., Deluca, A., & Kosanke, N. (2001). Polysubstance use among alcoholics. *Journal of Addictive Diseases, 20,* 53–69.

Substance Use Disorders Memoirs and Novels

Burroughs, A. (2004). *Dry: A memoir.* New York: Picador.
   Burroughs describes his recovery from alcoholism.

Frey, J. (2005). *A million little pieces.* New York: Anchor.
   Frey describes his experience in rehab for alcoholism and drug addiction.

Knapp, C. (1997). *Drinking: A love story.* New York: Dial Press.
   A successful journalist goes to rehab after a lifetime of drinking.

Salant, J. (2008). *Leaving dirty Jersey: A crystal meth memoir.* New York: Simon Spotlight Entertainment.
   An upper-class teenager skips out on rehab and goes on a crystal meth binge.

Zailckas, K. (2006). *Smashed: Story of a drunken girlhood.* New York: Penguin.
   Describes Zailckas' experience of binge drinking in college.

ADDITIONAL MEDIA RECOMMENDATIONS

Aronofsky, D. (Director). (2000). *Requiem for a dream* [Film]. USA: Artisan Entertainment.
   This film features four individuals who are addicted to various substances from diet pills to heroin. The film does an amazing job of showing the pleasurable effects of the drugs as well as the horrifying consequences.

Bole, D. (Director). (1996). *Trainspotting* [Film]. UK: Channel Four Films.
   Scottish youths suffer the consequences of their addiction to heroin.

Figgis, M. (Director). (1995). *Leaving Las Vegas* [Film]. USA: Initial Productions.
   This film captures the unlikely friendship of a Hollywood screenwriter and a prostitute as the screenwriter commits a slow suicide from alcohol abuse.

Gilliam, T. (Director). (1998). *Fearing and loathing in Las Vegas.* [Film]. USA: Fear and Loathing LLC.
   A journalist and lawyer travel to Las Vegas taking a number of drugs along the way. The film shows the effects of cocaine, LSD, and other substances.

Levine, J. (Director and Writer). (2008). *The wackness.* [Film]. USA: Occupant Films.
   A high school student spends his summer selling marijuana and trading marijuana for therapy with a psychologist.

WEB SITES

Alcohol

Alcoholics Anonymous: Provides meeting sites, videos, resources, and a calendar of events. See: http://www.aa.org/?Media=PlayFlash

Methamphetamines

Faces of Meth: The site features before-and-after photos of meth users over periods ranging from 1 month to 5 years. In this case, a picture really is worth a thousand words. See: http://www.drugfree.org/Portal/DrugIssue/MethResources/faces/index.html

KCI: Anti-Meth Site: Provides personal letters and stories of those touched by methamphetamine abuse and dependence. The site includes shocking photos of the long-term effects of meth use. See: http://www.kci.org/meth_info/meth_letters.htm

Ecstasy

The Neurobiology of Ecstasy: This free PowerPoint presentation shows the short- and long-term neurological effects of ecstasy use. See: http://www.drugabuse.gov/pubs/teaching/teaching4/teaching.html

Addiction and Recovery Information

The Elephant on Main Street: An Interactive Community About Addictions and Recoveries: An online discussion forum and blog that includes resources on screenings, advocacy for families, and recovery meetings. See: http://www.elephantonmain.com/index.html

Faces and Voices of Recovery: Seeks to help those affected by substance abuse and dependence through advocacy. The Recovery Resources include personal stories of recovery and advocacy. See: http://www.facesandvoicesofrecovery.org/

Neurobiological Effects of Drugs

Mouse Party: This interactive site was created by the University of Utah's Genetic Science Learning Center and allows the viewer to see how various drugs affect the brain. See: http://learn.genetics.utah.edu/content/addiction/drugs/mouse.html

The Neurobiology of Drug Addiction: Provides a free PowerPoint presentation that describes the biological aspects of cocaine and heroin addiction. See: http://www.nida.nih.gov/pubs/teaching/Teaching2/Teaching.html

General National Institute on Drug Abuse: Provides up-to-date information on drug use and abuse. Also provides PowerPoint presentations, free publications, and resources for teachers. See: http://www.nida.nih.gov/

Substance Abuse and Mental Health Services Administration: Provides information on treatment, services, free publications, and statistics. See: http://www.samhsa.gov/

Eating Disorders

CHAPTER
10

CHAPTER OUTLINE

CHAPTER HEADINGS	INSTRUCTION IDEAS AND TEXTBOOK CORRELATIONS
Chapter Introduction	**Learning Objective:** 10.1
ANOREXIA NERVOSA	
What Is Anorexia Nervosa?	**Learning Objectives:** 10.2, 10.3 **Learning Concepts:** anorexia nervosa according to DSM-IV-TR, two types of anorexia nervosa: restricting and binge-eating/purging **Media Recommendation 10.1:** Stories of Anorexia **Learning Activity 10.1:** What's Your Body Image? **Textbook Tools:** Figure 10.1; Tables 10.1, 10.2; Case 10.1
Medical, Psychological, and Social Effects of Anorexia Nervosa	**Learning Objectives:** 10.4, 10.5 **Learning Concepts:** anorexia's medical effects, psychological and social effects of starvation **Media Recommendation 10.2:** Medical Effects of Anorexia
Problems with the DSM-IV-TR Definition of Anorexia Nervosa	**Learning Objective:** 10.6 **Learning Concepts:** problems with the diagnostic criteria, problems with the types of anorexia **Lecture Enhancement 10.1:** Models and Weight
BULIMIA NERVOSA	**Learning Objectives:** 10.7, 10.8 **Learning Concepts:** medical effects of bulimia nervosa **Media Recommendation 10.3:** Stories of Bulimia **Textbook Tools:** Tables 10.3, 10.4; Case 10.2, 10.3
Problems with the DSM-IV-TR Diagnostic Criteria	**Learning Objectives:** 10.9, 10.10, 10.11 **Learning Concepts:** problems defining binge eating, problems with the types of bulimia, is bulimia distinct from anorexia? **Learning Activity 10.2:** Compare and Contrast Anorexia and Bulimia
Eating Disorder Not Otherwise Specified	**Learning Objective:** 10.12

UNDERSTANDING EATING DISORDERS	
Neurological Factors: Setting the Stage	**Learning Objective:** 10.13 **Learning Concepts:** brain systems, neural communication: serotonin, genetics
Psychological Factors: Thoughts of and Feelings About Food	**Learning Objective:** 10.14 **Learning Concepts:** thinking about weight, appearance, and food, excessive concern with weight and appearance, abstinence violation effect, operant conditioning: reinforcing disordered eating, personality traits as risk factors, dieting, restrained eating, and disinhibited eating, other psychological disorders as risk factors **Lecture Enhancement 10.2:** Pro MIA and Pro ANA Web sites **Textbook Tools:** Figures 10.2, 10.3, 10.4
Social Factors: The Body in Context	**Learning Objectives:** 10.15, 10.16 **Learning Concepts:** the role of family and peers, the role of culture, eating disorders across cultures, the power of the media, objectification theory **Learning Activity 10.3:** Messages **Learning Activity 10.4:** What Is the Cultural Ideal? **Textbook Tools:** Figures 10.5, 10.6, 10.7; Case 10.4 **Worth Video Tool Kit for Abnormal Psychology:** Eating Disorders Don't Discriminate, Eating Disorders
TREATING EATING DISORDERS	
Targeting Neurological and Biological Factors: Nourishing the Body	**Learning Objective:** 10.17 **Learning Concepts:** a focus on nutrition, medical hospitalization, medication **Media Recommendation 10.4:** What Is Good Nutrition?
Targeting Psychological Factors: Cognitive-Behavior Therapy (CBT)	**Learning Objective:** 10.18 **Learning Concepts:** CBT for anorexia, CBT for bulimia, using CBT manuals to treat eating disorders, efficacy of CBT for treating eating disorders **Textbook Tool:** Table 10.5
Targeting Social Factors	**Learning Objectives:** 10.19, 10.20 **Learning Concepts:** interpersonal therapy, family therapy, psychiatric hospitalization, prevention programs **Learning Activity 10.5:** Create a Prevention Program for Youth **Lecture Enhancement 10.3:** Prevention: What Works **Lecture Enhancement 10.4:** Obesity **Textbook Tool:** Figure 10.8
FOLLOW-UP ON MARYA HORNBACHER	

LEARNING OBJECTIVES

After completing this chapter, students will be able to:

10.1 Define bulimia and anorexia nervosa.

10.2 Identify the DSM-IV-TR criteria for anorexia nervosa.

10.3 Differentiate between the two types of anorexia.

10.4 Name the medical effects of anorexia nervosa.

10.5 Describe the psychological and social effects of starvation.

10.6 Identify the problems with anorexia nervosa diagnostic criteria and the two types.

10.7 Identify the DSM-IV-TR criteria for bulimia nervosa.

10.8 Describe the medical effects of bulimia nervosa.

10.9 Identify the problems in defining binge eating.

10.10 Name several problems with the types of bulimia nervosa.

10.11 Compare and contrast anorexia and bulimia nervosa.

10.12 Describe the eating disorder not otherwise specified (EDNOS) disorder.

10.13 Explain the neurological causes of eating disorders (these include the brain systems, neural communication, and genetics).

10.14 Identify psychological factors in eating disorders (these include the role of thoughts, conditioning, personality traits, modifications to eating, and other factors).

10.15 Describe the role of social factors in eating disorders (these include family and peers, culture, media, and objectification theory).

10.16 Explain how neurological, psychological, and social factors influence one another.

10.17 Name and describe neurological and biological forms of treating eating disorders (such as improved nutrition, hospitalization, and medication).

10.18 Name and describe how cognitive-behavior therapy can treat eating disorders.

10.19 Describe treatments that target social factors (including interpersonal and family therapy, hospitalization, and prevention programs).

10.20 Explain how the neurological, psychological, and social factors influence one another.

KEY TERMS

Eating disorders: A category of psychological disorders characterized by abnormal eating and a preoccupation with body image.

Anorexia nervosa: An eating disorder characterized by being at least 15% below expected body weight along with using various methods to prevent weight gain.

Bulimia nervosa: An eating disorder characterized by binge eating along with vomiting or other behaviors to compensate for the large number of calories ingested.

Amenorrhea: The suppression of menstruation; this condition is diagnosed after three consecutive missed menstrual cycles.

Binge eating: Eating much more food at one time than most people would eat in the same context.

Purging: Attempting to reduce calories that have already been consumed by vomiting or using diuretics, laxatives, or enemas.

Eating disorder not otherwise specified (EDNOS): The diagnosis given when an individual's symptoms of disordered eating cause significant distress or impair functioning but do not meet the full criteria for a diagnosis of anorexia nervosa or bulimia nervosa.

Partial cases: The designation given to cases in which patients have symptoms that meet only some of the necessary criteria, but not enough symptoms to meet all the criteria for the diagnosis of a disorder.

Subthreshold cases: The designation given to cases in which patients have symptoms that fit all the necessary criteria, but at levels lower than required for the diagnosis of a disorder.

Binge-eating disorder: A provisional diagnosis of the variant of an eating disorder characterized by frequent episodes of rapid uncontrolled eating of large quantities of food, even when not hungry, without subsequent purging; according to DSM-IV-TR, patients with binge-eating disorder receive a diagnosis of EDNOS.

Abstinence violation effect: The condition that arises when the violation of a self-imposed rule about food restriction leads to feeling out of control with food, which then leads to overeating.

Restrained eating: Restricting intake of specific foods or overall number of calories.

Objectification theory: The theory that girls learn to consider their bodies as objects and commodities.

Maudsley approach: A family treatment for anorexia nervosa that focuses on supporting parents as they determine how to lead their child to eat appropriately.

CHAPTER GUIDE

Chapter Introduction

Marya Hornbacher, who is reported on throughout this chapter, developed bulimia nervosa at the age of 9. By age 15 she had anorexia nervosa. At age 23, after being hospitalized six times and institutionalized once, along with receiving many hours of therapy, Hornbacher wrote *Wasted: A Memoir of Anorexia and Bulimia.*

Eating disorders are defined as a category of psychological disorders characterized by abnormal eating and a preoccupation with body image. There are two DSM-IV-TR specific types of eating disorders:

- *Anorexia nervosa:* An eating disorder characterized by being at least 15% below expected body weight along with using various methods to prevent weight gain.

- *Bulimia nervosa:* An eating disorder characterized by binge eating along with vomiting or other behaviors to compensate for the large number of calories ingested.

I. ANOREXIA NERVOSA

A. What Is Anorexia Nervosa?

- Also called *anorexia*
- Person maintains a low normal weight and prevents weight gain
- Places people at high risk for death as 10% to 15% of people hospitalized die from the disorder

MEDIA RECOMMENDATION 10.1: Stories of Anorexia

Objective: To hear personal stories of anorexia.

Time: 4 Minutes (Video 1), 87 Minutes (Video 2), 9 Minutes (Video 3)

Media and Discussion: 24–120 Minutes

Discussion Only: 20 Minutes

Watch Online: Search YouTube using the search terms "anorexia real story" or http://www.youtube.com/watch?v=tOouAmEEsnlc

This short clip features a young woman in recovery from anorexia.

Search YouTube using the search terms "E! True Hollywood Story-Karen Carpenter" or http://www.youtube.com/view_play_list?p=FC82D5A428E287CA&search_query=e%21+true+hollywood+story+karen+carpenter

This program (which is presented in eight 10–11 minute segments) features music from The Carpenters and Karen's struggle with anorexia.

Search YouTube using the search terms "Superstar The Karen Carpenter Story" or http://www.youtube.com/watch?v=XrAA6VMIPb0

This interesting film by now-famous director Todd Haynes tells the Karen Carpenter story using Barbie dolls.

Summary: Students will find the personal stories shocking and powerful. These lived experiences help to highlight and bring to life the symptoms discussed in this chapter.

Questions to Students and Discussion: What symptoms did the women express? Why did the women develop eating disorders? What struggles did they face? What were the underlying reasons for developing anorexia?

1. **Anorexia Nervosa According to DSM-IV-TR**

    Four criteria must be met to receive the diagnosis of anorexia nervosa:

    - Refusing to maintain at least 85% of expected weight (based on age and height)
    - Intense fear of gaining weight or becoming fat; self-worth and emotional well-being fluctuate based on weight gain or loss
    - Body image distortions [see *Figure 10.1*]
    - *Amenorrhea* or the suppression of menstruation, a condition diagnosed after three consecutive missed menstrual cycles [see *Tables 10.1, 10.2; Case 10.1*]

LEARNING ACTIVITY 10.1: What's Your Body Image?

Objective: To examine one's own body image.

Time: 10 Minutes

Activity and Discussion: 20 Minutes

Discussion Only: 10 Minutes

Directions:
1. Have students open their textbook to *Figure 10.1,* which shows representations of different body types.
2. Ask the students to cover the items below the continuum. Instructors may want to create a continuum for males and females.
3. Have students identify which figure matches their ideal image, which figure they feel is most attractive to men/women, and where on the continuum they think and feel their body image is.
4. Ask students to then look at the items noted under the continuum and the sidebar description.

Note to Instructor: Body image is a sensitive issue to many people and thus students may not be comfortable sharing the results of this activity with their classmates. Instructors may also want to provide a list of resources and the University or College counseling information for those who need additional support.

Summary: Students will be amazed at how their estimates of themselves and others are unrealistic.

Questions to Students and Discussion: What surprises you about the results? Which categories were most/least accurate? What factors might cause these discrepancies?

2. **Two Types of Anorexia Nervosa: Restricting and Binge-Eating/Purging**

   People with anorexia maintain their low weight in two ways:

   a. **Restricting Type:**

      The typical type of anorexia where the person undereats

   b. **Binge-Eating/Purging:**

      The type where the person binges and purges

      (1) *Binge eating:*

         When a person eats much more food at one time than most people would eat in the same context

      (2) *Purging:*

         An attempt to reduce calories that have already been consumed by vomiting or using diuretics, laxatives, or enemas

B. **Medical, Psychological, and Social Effects of Anorexia Nervosa**

   Serious side effects include the following:

   1. **Anorexia's Medical Effects**

      • The heart muscle becomes thinner because the body searches for energy sources and begins to cannibalize itself.

      • Muscle wasting occurs because the body begins to break down muscle to obtain calories.

      • Additional medical effects include low heart rate and blood pressure, abdominal bloating or discomfort, constipation, loss of bone density (leading to osteoporosis and easily fractured bones), and a slower metabolism (which leads to lower body temperature, difficulty tolerating cold temperatures, and downy hairs forming on the body to provide insulation).

      • Visible medical effects include dry and yellow-orange skin, brittle nails, and hair loss.

      • Less obvious symptoms include irritability, fatigue, headaches, and hyperactivity or restlessness (possibly as a result of starvation and is also observed in starved animals).

      • Methods of purging (vomiting, diuretics, laxatives, and enemas) may all lead to dehydration and then to an *electrolyte imbalance*—salts that are critical for neural transmission and muscle contractions, including that of the heart muscle.

MEDIA RECOMMENDATION 10.2: Medical Effects of Anorexia

Objective: To learn about the effects of anorexia in later adulthood.

Time: 8 Minutes

Media and Discussion: 13 Minutes

Discussion Only: 5 Minutes

Watch Online: "The Ballet World" from MCPhee, L. (2000). *Dying to Be Thin.* WGBH Educational Foundation and Twin Cities Public Television, Inc. http://www.pbs.org/wgbh/nova/thin/program.html

This segment features a former dancer who spent many years battling anorexia. She now has difficulty walking and feels she is "paying for" starving herself in her earlier years. This clip also shows a bone scan revealing the shocking effects anorexia has on bone density.

Summary: Students will be interested in learning about the ways in which anorexia affects functioning in later life.

Questions to Students and Discussion: Describe the physical consequences of anorexia. Were you surprised by how anorexia has lingering effects on the body?

2. **Psychological and Social Effects of Starvation**

    A 1940s study on starvation found that when young men lost 25% of their weight and received half their usual amount of caloric intake for six months, they showed the following symptoms:

    - Increased sensitivity to light, cold, and noise
    - Decreased sleep, sex drive, mood, and loss of humor
    - Increased symptoms of depression, anxiety, talking and dreaming about food, collecting and sharing recipes
    - Hoarding food and random items such as old books and knick-knacks
    - Persisting effects even after returning to their normal caloric intake

C. Problems with the DSM-IV-TR Definition of Anorexia Nervosa

Criticisms of the DSM-IV-TR include problems with the criteria and the two types of anorexia.

1. **Problems with the Diagnostic Criteria**

    Three of the four criteria are considered problematic:

    a. **Refusal to Maintain a Healthy Body Weight (Criterion A):**

    Research has shown this factor does not predict medical status, prognosis, or outcome and the 85% cutoff point does not consider growth during puberty or cultural differences.

    b. **Fear of Becoming Fat or of Gaining Weight (Criterion B):**

    This "fear" is not always present in non-Western cultures (for example, Hong Kong) and the criteria should focus more on controlling eating.

c. Amenorrhea (Criterion D):

Some women with low weight do not experience amenorrhea, and amenorrhea may occur without significant weight loss.

2. Problems with the Types

People often shift from one type to the next. For example, a person who was once a binge-eating/purging type may switch to the restricting type.

LECTURE ENHANCEMENT 10.1: Models and Weight

Objective: To discuss the weight expectations of models.

Time: 20 Minutes

Lecture Points:

In February 2007, five models were "excused" from a show in Madrid for being too thin. The Madrid City Council, which sponsors the fashion week, ordered that every model in the show must have a body mass index (BMI) of at least 18. Following this ruling, Milan's fashion week also tightened its restrictions on underweight models.

Summary: The modeling field has a reputation for being overly focused on thinness. Students will be surprised to learn about this new rule that excuses models for being too thin.

Resource: Wilson, E. (2007, Jan 6). Health guidelines suggested for models. *The New York Times.* http://www.nytimes.com/2007/01/06/business/06thin.html

Question to Students and Discussion: Do you think a BMI of 18 is high enough? Should fashion shows have minimum BMI for models? Why or why not?

II. BULIMIA NERVOSA

A. What Is Bulimia Nervosa?

Bulimia nervosa (also called *bulimia*) is characterized by repeated episodes of binge eating followed by inappropriate efforts to prevent weight gain.

- There are two types of bulimia: purging and nonpurging.
  i. *Purging type* uses vomiting, diuretics, laxatives, or enemas.
  ii. The *nonpurging type* prevents weight gain through fasting or excessive exercise.
- Low weight and amenorrhea characterize anorexia but not bulimia.
- Bulimia occurs at twice the rate as anorexia.
- Both anorexia and bulimia are more common in women than men. [See *Tables 10.3, 10.4; Case 10.2.*]

MEDIA RECOMMENDATION 10.3: Stories of Bulimia

Objective: To learn about people's experiences with bulimia.

Time: 16 Minutes

Media and Discussion: 26 Minutes

Discussion Only: 10 Minutes

Watch: Search www.dailymotion.com using the search terms "intervention bulimia Jesse" or http://www.dailymotion.com/video/x8eew1_interventionbulimiajessie_shortfilms

This video clip shows Jesse's struggle with bulimia and how her illness affects her family.

Summary: Students will learn about the symptoms of bulimia and some of the feelings that underlie this disorder.

Questions to Students and Discussion: What symptoms of bulimia does Jesse have? What seems to underlie her bulimia? How did Jesse's illness affect her family?

B. Medical Effects of Bulimia Nervosa

Serious physical and medical problems include:

- Chronic vomiting may cause swelling of the jaw (due to parotid and salivary glands) and erosion of dental enamel (which may cause cavities and other problems).
- Ipecac may cause heart and lung problems.
- Laxatives may cause intestinal problems, constipation, abdominal bloating and discomfort, fatigue, irregular menstruation, and dehydration, which may lead to an electrolyte imbalance. [See *Case 10.3.*]

C. Problems with the DSM-IV-TR Diagnostic Criteria

Criticisms of the criteria include problems defining binge eating, bulimia types, and the overlap among bulimia and anorexia.

1. Problems Defining Binge Eating

- Binge eating is subjective and the definition varies widely.
- Time periods listed are not based on research.

2. Problems with the Types of Bulimia

- Meaningful differences have not been found between the two types of bulimia.
- Impulsivity (stealing, running away, seeking out danger) predicts course and prognosis but not type.

3. Is Bulimia Distinct from Anorexia?

- Half of people with anorexia develop bulimia; thus some have argued the disorders are phases of one another.
- Binge-eating/purging anorexia shares more overlap with bulimia than the restricting type of anorexia.
- The restricting anorexia type is distinct in the eating approach and coping style (for example, emotion regulation).

LEARNING ACTIVITY 10.2: Compare and Contrast Anorexia and Bulimia

Objective: To learn the similarities and differences between anorexia and bulimia.

Time: 20 Minutes

Directions: Have students complete *Worksheet 10.1* to help them compare and contrast anorexia and bulimia.

Summary: Students will be surprised that the two disorders have a lot of overlap. Students will also be able to see some clear distinctions between the disorders.

Questions to Students and Discussion: What are the similarities between these two disorders? What are some distinct differences?

D. Eating Disorder Not Otherwise Specified

Eating disorder not otherwise specified (EDNOS) is the diagnosis given when an individual's symptoms of disordered eating cause significant distress or impair functioning but do not meet the full criteria for a diagnosis of anorexia nervosa or bulimia nervosa.

- Diagnosed in 4% to 6% of Americans
- People with EDNOS fall into one of three groups:
  i.   *Partial cases* are when the person meets some, but not enough, of the anorexia or bulimia diagnostic criteria. For example, a woman meets all criteria except amenorrhea.
  ii. *Subthreshold cases* are where a person has a lower level of symptoms than the criteria specifies. For example, bingeing only once a week.
  iii. *Binge-eating disorder* is a provisional diagnosis and is where a person has uncontrolled eating of large amounts of food, is overweight, and is distressed by the binge-eating. This disorder occurs in men and women equally and is more common than anorexia and bulimia combined.
- Three changes are needed for an alternative system of categorizing anorexia and bulimia.
  i.   Delete the purging and non-purging types of bulimia.
  ii. Combine the binge-eating/purging bulimia with anorexia to further differentiate these disorders from the restricting type of anorexia, or place these disorders on a continuum.
  iii. The binge-eating/purging types of anorexia and bulimia should be on the same continuum.

III. UNDERSTANDING EATING DISORDERS

Half of the people with one eating disorder will develop another eating disorder. Eating disorders have high rates of comorbidity with other psychological and medical problems.

A. Neurological Factors: Setting the Stage

It is difficult to tell if an eating disorder causes the neurological changes or if neurological changes cause the eating disorder.

1. Brain Systems

- People with anorexia have low activity in the frontal lobe (causing deficits in regulating behavior), portions of the temporal lobe (may increase feelings of fear), parietal lobes (distort body size), and anterior cingulated cortex (monitors competing responses and memory). These difficulties may lead to the inability to control dysfunctional behavior.
- When those with the restricting type of anorexia gain weight, activity in the parietal lobes increases (which represents spatial properties), while the basal ganglia and cerebellum activity (which controls repetitive behavior) decreases.

- Neuroimaging studies have revealed that anorexia has led to a loss of grey matter (neural cell bodies) and white matter (myelinated axons).
- These problems may decrease with recovery but may not disappear completely.

2. Neural Communication: Serotonin

- Serotonin activity is disrupted with these disorders but it is unclear whether this is a cause or effect of eating disorders.
- People with eating disorders exhibit an anxious temperament, which may be related to serotonin levels.
- People with anorexia have been found to be less responsive to serotonin.
- Eating less may reduce anxiety by lowering serotonin levels due to decreased tryptophan (a building block of serotonin) in the diet.
- The more severe the bulimia symptoms, the less responsive clients are to serotonin.
- More research is needed in this area.

3. Genetics

- People with eating disorders are more likely to have a family member with an eating disorder (though it may be a different type).
- Anorexia heritability rates range from 33% to 88%.
- Bulimia heritability rates range from 28% to 83%.
- Environment is also a factor in the development of eating disorders.

B. Psychological Factors: Thoughts of and Feelings About Food

Cognitions, conditioning, personality traits, eating patterns, and other psychological factors play a role in eating disorders.

1. Thinking About Weight, Appearance, and Food

Thoughts regarding weight and appearance and automatic distorted thoughts may play a role in eating disorders.

a. Excessive Concern with Weight and Appearance:

- People with eating disorders define their self-worth through their weight, body shape, and eating.
- Being dissatisfied with one's body is a consistent predictor of developing an eating disorder.

b. Abstinence Violation Effect:

- Automatic distorted thinking about food may play a role in eating disorders.
- Distorted thinking may lead to the *abstinence violation effect,* which is the condition that arises when the violation of a self-imposed rule about food restriction leads to feeling out of control with food, which then leads to overeating.

2. Operant Conditioning: Reinforcing Disordered Eating

- Symptoms may be reinforced through operant conditioning. For example, thinking about food can serve as a distraction from other life stressors (this is an example of negative reinforcement).
- Positive reinforcement may occur if the person feels a sense of power over one's appetite.

- Binge eating may be positively reinforcing if one eats foods one enjoys.
- Bingeing can also be negatively reinforcing if unpleasant thoughts or feelings are relieved during the binge.
- Purging can be negatively reinforcing as it relieves anxiety.
- Social isolation may occur during bingeing or purging episodes and may reduce anxiety (and thus is negatively reinforcing).

3. **Personality Traits as Risk Factors**

- *Perfectionism* is a persistent striving to attain perfection and excessive self-criticism about mistakes. Perfectionism is higher in people with eating disorders and is high even after people recover. Perfectionism causes a heightened awareness of one's imperfections (*aversive self-awareness*) and thus may lead to bingeing as a way to escape from one's thoughts. [See *Figure 10.2.*]
- People with eating disorders also exhibit *harm avoidance*, or the characteristic of trying to avoid potentially harmful situations or stimuli. For example, people high in this characteristic tend to be planners and watchful of their caloric intake.
- *Neuroticism*, which is characterized by a propensity toward anxiety and emotional reactivity, is also associated with eating disorders.
- Low self-esteem is also linked to eating disorders. People may control their food intake, thinking the results of these changes will improve their self-worth.

4. **Dieting, Restrained Eating, and Disinhibited Eating**

- *Restrained eating* occurs when one restricts the intake of specific foods, such as fats or carbohydrates, or overall caloric intake (as when dieting).
- *Disinhibited eating* is common among dieters and is where one binges on a restricted type of food or simply eats more of a nonrestricted type of food.
- The *last supper effect* is when disinhibited eating is triggered by an upcoming diet.
- Researchers compared the amount of food intake for those anticipating an upcoming diet as compared to those not anticipating an upcoming diet. Those anticipating the upcoming diet ate more than those without the upcoming diet. [See *Figure 10.3.*]
- Restrained eaters rely more heavily on external cues (such as portion size and time of meal) than on internal cues (such as hunger and fullness).

5. **Other Psychological Disorders as Risk Factors**

If a person develops a psychological disorder in early adolescence, he/she is at risk for developing disordered eating. [See *Figure 10.4.*]

LECTURE ENHANCEMENT 10.2: Pro MIA and Pro ANA Web Sites

Objective: To learn about additional psychological factors of eating disorders.

Time: 20 Minutes

Lecture Points:
I. What are Pro MIA and Pro ANA sites?
   A. Pro ANA refers to the promotion of anorexia, which is sometimes referred to as ANA.
   B. Pro MIA refers to the promotion of bulimia.
   C. Thinsporation refers to inspiration to lose weight through images.

II. Who visits these sites?
    A. People with eating disorders may visit these sites for support.
    B. Many people use these sites to learn new tricks to maintain their eating disorder and hide the symptoms from others.
III. Consequences
    A. These sites obviously fuel the symptoms of anorexia and bulimia.
    B. The images on these sites can trigger a person's symptoms.

Summary: Students will be shocked to learn about these pro anorexia and bulimia Web sites. Students will gain insight into the role that the Internet plays in the maintenance of eating disorders.

Resources: Warnings of Pro ANA and Pro MIA Web sites Listed in the National Eating Disorder Association's Educator's Toolkit (2008):
www.womensenews.org/article.cfm/dyn/aid/1529/context/archive
www.sirc.org/articles/totally_in_control.shtml
www.time.com/time/health/article/0,8599,169660,00.html
www.webmd.com/content/article/109/109381.htm
www.firstcoastnews.com/printfullstory.aspx?storyid=27567

Questions to Students and Discussion: Were you aware of these sites before? How do you think the Internet feeds eating disorders? What might be possible prevention strategies?

C. Social Factors: The Body in Context

Family, friends, culture, and the media are all factors that affect eating disorders.

1. The Role of Family and Peers

- Family members model eating behavior, body image concerns, and acceptance. (*Example:* A parent models body dissatisfaction and this behavior influences the child.)
- Family may respond to the child's body shape, weight, and food intake. (*Example:* parents question a child's food intake and lead the child to focus on his/her daily intake in an unhealthy way.)
- Teasing or criticism from friends may also impact one's perceptions of body image/satisfaction.
- Many women bond with one another through the preoccupation of food and weight.

2. The Role of Culture

- A meta-analysis revealed that there has only been a small increase in the number of eating disorders in the 20th century, but the concern about weight is relatively new.
- Rates of bulimia significantly increased from 1970 to 1990.
- Three cultural elements that increase eating disorders are cultural ideal of thinness, repeated exposure of the thin ideal, and individual assimilation of thinness.
- A comparison of *Playboy* centerfolds and the average U.S. woman's BMI shows an opposite trend. The centerfold BMI has decreased over the years while the average U.S. woman's BMI has increased. [See *Figure 10.5.*]
- Men are at a higher risk of developing an eating disorder if they are involved in modeling or wrestling or have a heightened awareness of appearance.

LEARNING ACTIVITY 10.3: Messages

Objective: To gain awareness of the messages we receive about our body image and food.

Time: 30 Minutes

Directions: Have students freewrite about the messages they have received about their body, food, eating habits, and exercise from their:
1. Family
2. Peers
3. Media

Summary: Students will learn about the overt and subtle messages they have received from numerous places about their body, food, eating habits, and exercise.

Questions to Students and Discussion: What messages did/do you receive from your family? What can you do about it? What messages did/do you receive from your peers? What can you do about it? What messages did/do you receive from the media? What can you do about it?

LEARNING ACTIVITY 10.4: What Is the Cultural Ideal?

Objective: To examine the cultural ideal in the media.

Time: 30 Minutes

Directions: Have students complete this activity on their own or in class. Students should bring in images from magazines, the Internet, or television of the cultural ideal of a man and a woman. Have students present the images to the class.

Summary: Students will see different and similar perspectives on the cultural ideal.

Questions to Students and Discussion: If you had to summarize the ideal man/woman, how would you describe the physical characteristics of this person? Does the image depend on culture? How do you think these "ideal" images have affected you?

3. **Eating Disorders Across Cultures**

   - Eating disorders are found mostly in Western and Westernized countries.

   - Eating disorders increase among those who immigrate to Western countries and among those who move into a higher economic status.

   - Rates vary by ethnicity, with Native Americans having the highest risk and African Americans the lowest. However, rates are increasing among African Americans and Latinas.

4. **The Power of the Media**

   - Three years after introducing television to Fiji in 1995, 75% of the population reported feeling "too big or fat."

   - Several studies have found a connection between media exposure and disordered eating.

   - One study found a positive correlation between the amount of television viewing among adolescent girls and disordered eating one year later.

5. **Objectification Theory: Explaining the Gender Difference**

   - *Objectification theory* posits that girls learn to consider their bodies as objects and commodities. [See *Figure 10.6.*]

- Objectification begins around puberty when females are increasingly viewed in sexual terms or as commodities.

- Research has shown that as women's power has increased (economically and politically), models have become thinner. Women then spend more time and money trying to reach this thin ideal, thus decreasing their economic and political power.

- Male ideals are becoming more unrealistic as male stars and action figures are becoming more muscular.

- Two-thirds of males in the United States report that they would like their bodies to be closer to the cultural ideal.

- Males are more likely to be diagnosed with EDNOS and express a focus on muscle building through excessive exercise or steroids. [See *Case 10.4.*]

   6. **FEEDBACK LOOPS IN ACTION: Eating Disorders**

   Neurological, psychological, and *social factors* influence the development and maintenance of eating disorders. [See *Figure 10.7.*]

IV. TREATING EATING DISORDERS

The goal of treatment of eating disorders is to help clients maintain a healthy weight by increasing eating and/or decreasing purging.

- Treatments vary in intensity and for in- or outpatient.

- Cognitive-behavior therapy is considered the best treatment.

- Clients will also meet with an internist or family doctor.

A. Targeting Neurological and Biological Factors: Nourishing the Body

Neurological treatments focus on healthy eating and reducing eating disorder–induced medical problems.

   1. **A Focus on Nutrition**

   - Healthy eating includes creating meal plans, identifying distorted thinking about food, and increasing nutrition and food variety.

   - *Refeeding syndrome* can occur in low-weight patients who increase food intake. This syndrome is caused by the rapidly shifting blood electrolyte levels and can cause heart failure, mental confusion, seizures, breathing difficulty, and possibly death. Thus, caloric intake should be increased at a moderate pace.

   - Gastrointestinal discomfort may result due to compression of the duodenum and limited amounts of bile (which are needed to digest fats but are decreased from the lack of eating).

MEDIA RECOMMENDATION 10.4: What Is Good Nutrition?

Objective: To learn what is considered proper nutrition.

Time: 30 Minutes

Media and Discussion: 40 Minutes

Discussion Only: 10 Minutes

Directions: Have students explore two Web sites related to nutrition. Students should write a summary of the various food groups needed for proper nutrition.

Explore Online: *Body Needs* at NOVA Online, http://www.pbs.org/wgbh/nova/thin/needs.html

Smart Nutrition 101, http://www.nutrition.gov/nal_display/index.php?info_center=11&tax_level=1&tax_subject=389

Summary: Students will learn the essential foods young adults need for healthy growth.

Questions to Students and Discussion: Are you eating enough of the right foods? What do you need more or less of? What are ways we can educate college students about proper nutrition?

2. **Medical Hospitalization**

- Medical hospitalization may be necessary if the client experiences heart problems, gastrointestinal bleeding, or significant dehydration.
- The goal of medical hospitalization is to stabilize the patient, not necessarily to "cure" the disordered behavior.

3. **Medication**

- Medications cannot help with weight gain; but once the patient has gained weight, SSRIs can reduce relapses in people with anorexia.
- SSRIs can reduce distorted eating, bingeing, vomiting, weight-gain concerns, and comorbid depression in those with bulimia.
- Benefits of medication decrease after discontinuation of the medication.

B. **Targeting Psychological Factors: Cognitive-Behavior Therapy (CBT)**

CBT focuses on changing eating-disorder thoughts, feelings, and behaviors.

1. **CBT for Anorexia**

- Cognitive restructuring can decrease irrational thoughts and increase realistic thoughts.
- CBT can help educate clients about the disorder and teach adaptive coping skills, self-monitoring skills, and relaxation training.
- Motivational enhancement therapy may be needed to motivate a client to change.

2. **CBT for Bulimia**

- CBT for bulimia focuses on thoughts and behaviors related to abnormal eating and the promotion of bingeing and purging; thoughts, feelings, and behaviors related to body image and appearance; perfectionism; low self-esteem and mood issues; and psychoeducation, cognitive-restructuring, self-monitoring, and relaxation.
- *Exposure with response prevention* is defined as when the client eats a moderate amount of a food he/she normally binges on. Afterward, the client is not allowed to purge (response prevention).
- CBT leads to normal eating; decreases dietary restrictions, which reduces risk of bingeing due to hunger or need for nutrients; and increases coping mechanisms.

3. **Using CBT Manuals to Treat Eating Disorders**

- Manual-based treatments offer a session-by-session guide.

- Sessions consist of three phases:
  - **i.** Phase 1 focuses on behavioral symptoms.
  - **ii.** Phase 2 examines thoughts underlying the symptoms.
  - **iii.** Phase 3 focuses on relapse prevention. [See *Table 10.5.*]

4. *Efficacy* **of CBT for Treating Eating Disorders**

- Most improvement can be seen within the first month; however, 50% of people still have symptoms after treatment ends.
- One study found that relapse risk factors include higher levels of food preoccupation and lower levels of motivation to change.
- Those with comorbid disorders respond less well to treatment.

C. Targeting Social Factors

Interpersonal and family therapy, inpatient groups, and prevention programs all target social factors.

1. Interpersonal Therapy

Interpersonal therapy (IPT) consists of 4 to 6 months of weekly sessions that focus on improving relationships and social interactions.

- IPT works by reducing interpersonal problems, which empowers people and increases their self-esteem.
- IPT affects people's disordered eating, reduces concern about appearance, increases social support and relationships, and reduces the interpersonal stressors that have previously triggered bingeing and purging.
- After one year, IPT and CBT have similar effectiveness, although CBT is slightly more effective.

2. Family Therapy

The Maudsley approach is the most widely used family treatment for anorexia. The *Maudsley approach* has a future-oriented focus that helps the parents to separate the patient from the illness and provides support for the parents as they figure out how to help their child.

- The parents are instructed to work together to feed their child.
- This approach requires constant monitoring of the child and thus may not work with all families, but it is the most effective treatment for adolescents and young adults with anorexia.

3. Psychiatric Hospitalization

Hospitalization is used when less intense treatments fail.

- Patients can attend groups that focus on body image, coping strategies, and relationships with food.
- Short-term goals include increasing the patient's weight to bring it into the normal range, establishing a normal eating pattern, reducing excessive exercise, and changing distorted thoughts.
- Symptoms seem to improve but do not endure as 30% to 50% of patients relapse once they have left the hospital. Possible explanations for the relapse rates include:
  - **i.** patients' lack of motivation to change

      ii. lack of outpatient follow-up care

      iii. reduced hospital stays due to insurance companies

   4. Prevention Programs

Prevention programs challenge distorted thinking and focus on decreasing overeating, fasting, and certain food avoidance.

- Programs may be a single or multiple sessions and come in the form of presentations and workshops that can be offered over the Internet.

- Prevention programs are associated with reduced disordered eating, yet other reviews have found these programs ineffective.

LEARNING ACTIVITY 10.5: Create a Prevention Program for Youth

Objective: To apply concepts of treatment in order to create a prevention program for youth.

Time: 20 Minutes

Directions: Have students work in small groups and create a prevention program for middle and high school students. Students should create one program for males and one for females. Have students incorporate ideas from the textbook. Then, have students outline the basic points on the board.

Summary: Students will synthesize and integrate material from this chapter by creating a prevention program.

Questions to Students and Discussion: How did your program differ for males and females? What differences in the program were related to gender? What factors did you seek to address in the program (neurological, psychological, and/or social)?

LECTURE ENHANCEMENT 10.3: Prevention: What Works

Objective: To learn key characteristics of prevention programs.

Time: 25 Minutes

Lecture Points:

I.   Youth intervention components should include:

   A. Nutrition education

      1. Emphasis on increasing physical activity

      2. Assessment of diet

      3. Parental involvement

      4. Modification of school meals

II. Systemic Prevention Programs—"Schools offer an excellent venue for reaching large numbers of adolescents. Within schools, formal activities may include:

   A. Staff training

   B. Classroom interventions

   C. Integration of relevant material into existing school curricula

   D. Small group or individual activities for high-risk youth

   E. A referral system for students suspected of having weight-related problems

   F. Opportunities for healthy eating at school

G. Modifications in physical education and sport activities

H. Outreach activities within the school and to the community

Resources:

Fleming M., & K. Towey, eds. (2003). *Educational forum on adolescent health: Adolescent obesity, nutrition, and physical activity.* Chicago: American Medical Association.

Neumark-Sztainer, D. (2007). Addressing the spectrum of adolescent weight-related problems: Engaging parents and communities. *The Prevention Researcher, 14*(3), 11–14.

Santrock, J. (2007). *Adolescence.* New York: McGraw-Hill.

Questions to Students and Discussion: Do you think the components listed here would have made a difference in disordered eating in your classmates? Why or why not? What parts of the prevention program had you not thought of? Would you make any additions?

5. FEEDBACK LOOPS IN TREATMENT: Eating Disorders

Neurological, psychological and social treatments influence one another. [See *Figure 10.8.*]

LECTURE ENHANCEMENT 10.4: Obesity

Objective: To learn about the obesity epidemic in the United States.

Time: 45 Minutes

Lecture Points:

I. What Is Obesity?

A. Obesity is an excess of body fat content and is determined by weight and energy level.

B. A BMI over 40 is considered morbidly obese.

C. For children and adolescents, a BMI equal to or higher than 30 is considered obese.

II. Rates of Obesity in the United States

A. The number of overweight Americans has increased since 1960 and now stands at 37%.

B. The percentage of those who are obese has doubled in the last 10 years.

C. 16% to 33% of teens are obese.

III. Causes

A. Significant differences exist between the various ethnic and racial groups. Data from the Centers for Disease Control and Prevention (CDC) and National Health and Nutrition Examination Survey (NHANES):

1. Boys and adolescents who are overweight or obese:
   - Mexican Americans 41.5%
   - Native Americans 39%
   - African Americans 37.5%
   - Caucasians 28%

2. Girls and adolescents who are overweight or obese:
   - Mexican Americans 40%
   - Native American 38%
   - African Americans 36%
   - Caucasians 27%

B. There is also a genetic component.

C. Education plays a role. While the prevalence of overweight and obese juveniles has increased across all educational levels, it is higher for adolescents with less education.

    D. Poor diet is also a factor (fast food, portion size, junk food in schools).

    E. Lack of exercise has an effect on weight, especially as young people spend more time in cars, playing video games, and watching television.

III. Consequences

    A. Type II diabetes leading to a failure of other functions (kidney, vision, heart)

    B. Increases in long-term health problems

Watch Online: *FAT: What No One Is Telling You,* http://www.pbs.org/wgbh/takeonestep/fat/index.html

This show examines the obesity epidemic, shows psychologists conducting studies on nutrition, and discusses food choices in cafeterias.

Summary: Students will be surprised to learn about the obesity epidemic and in particular how obesity rates differ by ethnicity.

Resources: Obesity in Children and Teens, http://www.aacap.org/cs/root/facts_for_families/obesity_in_children_and_teens

Koppel, T. (2005). *Nightline: Critical condition—America's obesity crisis* [Television program]. Princeton, NJ: Films for the Humanities & Sciences.

Questions to Students and Discussion: What explanations can you provide for the ethnic differences in obesity? Do you agree with the causes of the obesity epidemic? Do you think there are additional causes not mentioned? What can you do about this problem?

V. FOLLOW-UP ON MARYA HORNBACHER

Although the flagrant symptoms of eating disorders were mostly behind Marya Hornbacher by the time she finished her memoir *Wasted,* she later reported occasional periods of restricting or purging and other psychological struggles. She recounts that these periods of disordered eating were attempts to regulate her extreme moods, serving as an example of the frequent comorbidity among people with eating disorders.

ADDITIONAL READINGS

Alegria, M., Woo, M., Cao, Z., Torres, M., Meng, X., & Striegel-Moore, R. (2007). Prevalence and correlates of eating disorders in Latinos in the United States. *International Journal of Eating Disorders, 40,* S15–S21.

Gentile, K., Raghavan, C., Rajah, V., & Gates, K. (2007). It doesn't happen here: Eating disorders in an ethnically diverse sample of economically disadvantaged, urban college students. *Eating Disorders: The Journal of Treatment & Prevention, 15,* 405–425.

Keel, P. K., & Haedt, A. (2008). Evidence-based psychosocial treatments for eating problems and eating disorders. *Journal of Clinical Child and Adolescent Psychology, 37,* 39–61.

Nicdao, E. G., Hong, S., & Takeuchi, D. T. (2007). Prevalence and correlates of eating disorders among Asian Americans: Results from the National Latino and Asian American Study. *International Journal of Eating Disorders, 40,* S22–S26.

Ousley, L., Cordero, E. D., & White, S. (2008). Eating disorders and body image of undergraduate men. *Journal of American College Health, 56,* 617–621.

Olivardia, R. (2007). Muscle dysmorphia: Characteristics, assessment, and treatment. In J. K. Thompson, J. Kevin, and G. Cafri (Eds.), *The muscular ideal: Psychological, social, and medical perspectives* (pp. 123–139). Washington, DC: American Psychological Association.

Shaw, H., Stice, E., & Becker, C. B. (2009). Preventing eating disorders. *Child and Adolescent Psychiatric Clinics of North America, 18,* 199–207.

Wilson, G. T., Grilo, C. M., & Vitousek, K. M. (2007). Psychological treatment of eating disorders. *American Psychologist, 62*(3), 199–216.

Wonderlich, S. A., Joiner, T. E., Keel, P. K., Williamson, D. A., & Crosby, R. D. (2007). Eating disorder diagnoses: Empirical approaches to classification. *American Psychologist, 62*(3), 167–180.

Eating Disorder Books and Memoirs

Bowman, G. (2007). *Thin.* London: Penguin.
The memoir of a popular teenager who struggles with an eating disorder.

Covington, A. S. (2009). *Not all Black girls know how to eat: A story of bulimia.* Chicago: Lawrence Hill Books.
Covington discusses what it is like to be a Black female suffering from bulimia—a disorder largely thought of as a White woman's issue.

Hornbacher, M. (1998). *Wasted.* New York: Harper Collins.
This memoir, discussed throughout this chapter, provides a personal journey through the complexities of eating disorders.

Klein, M. (2008). *Moose: A memoir of fat camp.* New York: Harper Collins.
Klein discusses her time in the eighth grade when her parents sent her to a "fat camp."

Liu, A. (2007). *Gaining: The truth about life after eating disorders.* New York: Warner Books.
Through interviews with professionals and examples from her own experience, Liu describes the struggles one experiences after being treated for anorexia.

Saxon, R. (2007). *Good eater: The true story of one man's struggle with binge eating disorder.* Oakland: CA: New Harbinger Publications.
The memoir of a male model who becomes a binge eater.

ADDITIONAL MEDIA RECOMMENDATIONS

Blair, M. (Director). (2002). *Inside out: Stories of bulimia.* [Film]. New York: Fanlight Productions.
An amazing documentary that features men and women struggling with bulimia. The film participants represent diverse cultures and backgrounds. http://www.insideoutfilms.com/insideout/index.html

Cardoso, P. (Director). (2002). *Real women have curves.* [Film]. USA: HBO Independent productions.
A Latina who has recently graduated from high school tries to accept her curves as she resolves family tension. http://www.hbo.com/films/realwomen/

MCPhee, L. (2000). *Dying to be thin.* [Television broadcast]. WGBH Educational Foundation and Twin Cities Public Television, Inc. http://www.pbs.org/wgbh/nova/thin/program.html.
This powerful documentary features conversations with models and dancers as they discuss pressures to be thin and the long-term consequences of anorexia. http://www.pbs.org/wgbh/nova/thin/

Ling, L., Scherer, C., Arce, A., & Truong, C. (Authors). (2002). [Film]. *Body image for boys,* Monmouth Junction, NJ: Cambridge Educational.
An 18-minute film that explores body image issues among men and boys. http://ffh.films.com/id/4589/Body_Image_for_Boys.htm

Sargent, J. (Director). (1987). *The Karen Carpenter story.* [Film]. USA: Weintraub Entertainment Group.

This classic film documents the life and death of Karen Carpenter, a famous singer who suffered from anorexia.

Seidelman, A. A. (Director). (1986). *Kate's secret.* [Film]. USA: Andrea Baynes Productions.

Kate is a beautiful and successful woman secretly suffering from bulimia.

WEB SITES

National Eating Disorder Association: Provides information and resources for those with eating disorders. See: http://www.nationaleatingdisorders.org/

The National Eating Disorders Association Educator's Toolkit: This toolkit provides a number of resources and information for working with children and parents. See: http://www.nationaleatingdisorders.org/uploads/file/toolkits/NEDA-Toolkit-Educators_09-15-08.pdf

NIMH Eating Disorders: Describes the basics of anorexia, bulimia, and binge-eating disorders. See: http://www.nimh.nih.gov/health/publications/eating-disorders/what-are-eating-disorders.shtml

National Association for Males with Eating Disorders: Information for men with eating disorders and their families. See: http://www.namedinc.org/

National Association of Anorexia Nervosa and Associated Eating Disorders: Provides a list of support groups, resources, and school guidelines. See: http://www.anad.org/

Perfect Illusions: Eating Disorders and the Family: Listen to or read about men and women who struggle with eating disorders. See: http://www.pbs.org/perfectillusions/index.html and http://www.pbs.org/perfectillusions/aboutshow/watchvideo.html

The Academy for Eating Disorders: Provides academic information on eating disorders treatment and research. See: http://www.aedweb.org/

The F-Word: Food, Fat and Feminism: Examines the influence of social factors that affect our perceptions of food and fat. See: http://the-f-word.org/blog/index.php/about-the-site/

WORKSHEET 10.1

	Anorexia	Bulimia
Similarities		
Differences		
Physical Consequences		
Treatments		
Other		

Gender and Sexual Disorders

CHAPTER

11

CHAPTER OUTLINE

CHAPTER HEADINGS	INSTRUCTION IDEAS AND TEXTBOOK CORRELATIONS
GENDER IDENTITY DISORDER	
What Is Gender Identity Disorder?	**Learning Objective:** 11.1 **Learning Activity 11.1:** Variations of Biological Sex, Sexuality, and Gender **Media Recommendation 11.1:** *Boys Don't Cry* **Media Recommendation 11.2:** *Transparent* **Textbook Tools:** Tables 11.1, 11.2; Case 11.1
Criticisms of the DSM-IV-TR Definition	**Learning Objective:** 11.2 **Lecture Enhancement 11.1:** Transgendered Children
Understanding Gender Identity Disorder	**Learning Objectives:** 11.3, 11.4, 11.5 **Learning Concepts:** neurological factors; brain systems and neural communication; genetics; psychological factors: a correlation with play activities; social factors: responses from others **Textbook Tools:** Figure 11.1(a) and (b)
Treating Gender Identity Disorder	**Learning Objectives:** 11.6, 11.7 **Learning Concepts:** targeting neurological factors and other biological factors: altered appearance; targeting psychological factors: understanding the choices; targeting social factors: family support **Learning Activity 11.2:** Transgender Speaker
PARAPHILIAS	
What Are Paraphilias?	**Learning Objectives:** 11.8, 11.9, 11.10, 11.11, 11.12, 11.13, 11.14 **Learning Concepts:** paraphilias involving nonconsenting individuals; exhibitionism: physically exposing oneself; voyeurism: watching others; frotteurism: touching a stranger; pedophilia: sexually abusing children; sexual sadism and sexual masochism: pain and humiliation; sexual sadism: inflicting the pain; sexual masochism: receiving the pain; paraphilias involving nonhuman objects; fetishism: sexually arousing objects; transvestic fetishism: cross-dressing for sexual arousal

	Media Recommendation 11.3: Juvenile Sex Offenders **Media Recommendation 11.4:** Fetishes and Fantasies **Textbook Tools:** Tables 11.3, 11.4; Cases 11.2, 11.3, 11.4, 11.5, 11.6
Assessing Paraphilic Disorders	**Learning Objective:** 11.15 **Worth Video Tool Kit for Abnormal Psychology:** The Foot Fetish
Criticisms of the DSM-IV-TR Paraphilias	**Learning Objective:** 11.16
Understanding Paraphilias	**Learning Objective:** 11.17 **Learning Concepts:** neurological factors; psychological factors: conditioned arousal; social factors: more erotica?
Treating Paraphilias	**Learning Objective:** 11.18 **Learning Concepts:** targeting neurological and other biological factors: medication; targeting psychological factors: cognitive-behavior therapy; targeting social factors **Media Recommendation 11.5:** Treating Pedophilia
SEXUAL DYSFUNCTIONS	
An Overview of Sexual Functioning and Sexual Dysfunctions	**Learning Objectives:** 11.19, 11.20, 11.21, 11.22, 11.23, 11.24, 11.25 **Learning Concepts:** the normal sexual response cycle; sexual dysfunctions according to the DSM-IV-TR; sexual desire disorders; hypoactive sexual desire disorder; sexual aversion disorder; sexual arousal disorders; female sexual arousal disorder; male erectile disorder; orgasmic disorders; female orgasmic disorder; male orgasmic disorder; premature ejaculation; sexual pain disorders; dyspareunia; vaginismus; criticisms of the sexual dysfunctions in the DSM-IV-TR **Media Recommendation 11.6:** Female Sexual Health **Learning Activity 11.3:** Cultural Messages on Masturbation **Media Recommendation 11.7:** Premature Ejaculation and Treatments **Media Recommendation 11.8:** Sexual Pain Disorders **Textbook Tools:** Figures 11.2, 11.3; Tables 11.5, 11.6; Cases 11.7, 11.8, 11.9, 11.10, 11.11, 11.12, 11.13, 11.14
Understanding Sexual Dysfunctions	**Learning Objectives:** 11.26, 11.29 **Learning Concepts:** neurological and other biological factors; sexual side effects: disease, illness, surgery, and medication; aging; psychological factors: predisposing, precipitating, and maintaining sexual dysfunctions; social factors **Textbook Tools:** Figure 11.4; Table 11.7 **Worth Video Tool Kit for Abnormal Psychology:** Pathologizing of Women's Sexuality, Female Sexual Dysfunction
Assessing Sexual Dysfunctions	**Learning Objective:** 11.27 **Learning Concepts:** assessing neurological and other biological factors; assessing psychological factors; assessing social factors
Treating Sexual Dysfunctions	**Learning Objective:** 11.28, 11.29 **Learning Concepts:** targeting neurological and other biological factors: medications; targeting psychological factors: shifting thoughts, learning new sexual behaviors; targeting social factors: couples therapy **Media Recommendation 11.9:** Steps to Better Sex **Textbook Tools:** Figure 11.5; Table 11.8

LEARNING OBJECTIVES

After completing this chapter, students will be able to:

11.1 Describe the DSM-IV-TR criteria for gender identity disorder.

11.2 Name two criticisms of the DSM-IV-TR criteria for gender identity disorder.

11.3 Explain how brain systems, neural communication, and genetics play a role in gender identity disorder.

11.4 Describe the correlation among play activities and gender identity disorder.

11.5 Identify social factors that may play a role in gender identity disorder.

11.6 Name neurological and biological treatments for gender identity disorder.

11.7 Describe the psychological and social factors that affect gender identity disorder.

11.8 Define the sexual disorders called paraphilias.

11.9 List the DSM-IV-TR criteria for exhibitionism.

11.10 Describe the DSM-IV-TR criteria for voyeurism.

11.11 List the DSM-IV-TR criteria for frotteurism.

11.12 Describe the DSM-IV-TR criteria for pedophilia.

11.13 Compare and contrast sexual sadism and sexual masochism.

11.14 Name the characteristics of fetishism and transvestic fetishism.

11.15 Explain the different forms of assessing sexual disorders.

11.16 Articulate criticisms of the paraphilias.

11.17 Describe the neurological, psychological, and social factors that cause paraphilias.

11.18 Describe the neurological, psychological, and social treatments for paraphilias.

11.19 Define the four stages of the normal sexual response cycle.

11.20 Name the diagnostic criteria for sexual dysfunctions.

11.21 Name and describe the two sexual desire disorders.

11.22 Name and describe the two sexual arousal disorders.

11.23 Name and describe the three orgasmic disorders.

11.24 Name and describe the two sexual pain disorders.

11.25 Highlight the main criticisms of the DSM-IV-TR criteria for the sexual pain disorders.

11.26 Summarize the neurological, psychological, and social factors that cause sexual dysfunctions.

11.27 Summarize the neurological, psychological, and social assessments for sexual dysfunctions.

11.28 Summarize the neurological, psychological, and social treatments for sexual dysfunctions.

11.29 Describe how the neurological, psychological, and social factors and treatments influence one another.

KEY TERMS

Gender identity: The subjective sense of being male or female, as these categories are defined by the person's culture.

Gender role: The outward behaviors, attitudes, and traits that a culture deems masculine or feminine.

Gender identity disorder: A psychological disorder characterized by a cross-gender identification that leads the individual to be chronically uncomfortable with his or her biological sex.

Sex reassignment surgery: The procedure in which an individual's genitals (and breasts, for biological women) are surgically altered to appear like those of the other sex.

Paraphilia: A sexual disorder characterized by deviant fantasies, objects, or behaviors that play a role in sexual arousal.

Exhibitionism: A paraphilic disorder in which sexual fantasies, urges, or behaviors hinge on exposing one's genitals to a stranger, usually as a surprise.

Voyeurism: A paraphilia characterized by sexual fantasies, urges, or behaviors that involve observing someone who is in the process of undressing, is nude, or is engaged in sexual activity, when the person being observed has neither consented to nor is aware of being observed.

Frotteurism: A paraphilia characterized by recurrent, intense, sexually arousing fantasies, sexual urges, or behaviors that involve touching or rubbing against a nonconsenting person.

Pedophilia: A paraphilia characterized by recurrent sexually arousing fantasies, sexual urges, or behaviors involving a child who has not yet gone through puberty (typically aged 13 or younger).

Sexual sadism: A paraphilia characterized by recurrent sexually arousing fantasies, urges, and behaviors that inflict physical or psychological suffering on another person.

Sexual masochism: A paraphilia in which the individual repeatedly becomes sexually aroused by fantasies, urges, or behaviors related to being hurt—specifically, being humiliated or made to suffer in other ways—and this arousal pattern causes significant distress or impairs functioning.

Fetishism: A paraphilia in which the individual repeatedly uses nonliving objects to achieve or maintain sexual arousal and such an arousal pattern causes significant distress or impairs functioning.

Transvestic fetishism: A paraphilia in which a heterosexual man cross-dresses in women's clothes for sexual arousal and experiences distress or impaired functioning because of the cross-dressing; formerly called *transvestism.*

Sexual dysfunctions: Sexual disorders that are characterized by problems in the sexual response cycle.

Sexual response cycle: The four stages of sexual response—excitement, plateau, orgasm, and resolution—outlined by Masters and Johnson.

Hypoactive sexual desire disorder: A sexual dysfunction characterized by a persistent or recurrent lack of sexual fantasies or an absence of desire for sexual activity.

Sexual aversion disorder: A sexual dysfunction characterized by a persistent or recurrent extreme aversion to and avoidance of most genital sexual contact with a partner.

Female sexual arousal disorder: A sexual dysfunction marked by a woman's persistent or recurrent difficulty attaining or maintaining engorged genital blood vessels in response to adequate stimulation; formerly referred to as *frigidity.*

Male erectile disorder: A sexual dysfunction characterized by a man's persistent or recurrent inability to attain or maintain an adequate erection until the end of sexual activity; sometimes referred to as *impotence.*

Female orgasmic disorder: A sexual dysfunction characterized by a woman's persistent problem in progressing from normal sexual excitement to orgasm, such that orgasm is delayed or does not occur, despite a normal amount of appropriate stimulation.

Male orgasmic disorder: A sexual dysfunction characterized by a man's delay or absence of orgasm.

Premature ejaculation: A sexual dysfunction characterized by orgasm and ejaculation that occur earlier than the man expects, usually before, immediately during, or shortly after penetration.

Dyspareunia: A sexual dysfunction characterized by recurrent or persistent genital pain that is associated with sexual intercourse.

Vaginismus: A sexual dysfunction in females in which recurrent or persistent involuntary spasms of the musculature of the outer third of the vagina interfere with sexual intercourse.

Sensate focus exercises: A behavioral technique that is assigned as homework in sex therapy, in which an individual or couple seeks to increase awareness of pleasurable sensations that do not involve genital touching, intercourse, or orgasm.

CHAPTER GUIDE

Chapter Introduction

- Neuropsychosocial factors influence human sexuality.
- Sexuality is primarily a social activity because it involves relationships.
- Culture influences what is considered "normal" or "abnormal" sexual behavior, and thus behaviors are categorized accordingly in the DSM-IV-TR.
- Sexual disorders must cause distress or impairment to qualify for a diagnosis.

I. GENDER IDENTITY DISORDER

A. What Is Gender Identity Disorder?

- *Gender identity* is the subjective sense of being male or female, as these categories are defined by the person's culture. *Example:* A person may have male sexual anatomy but *feel* like a female.
- *Gender role* is defined by the outward behaviors, attitudes, and traits that a culture deems masculine or feminine. For example, gender roles for females allow a wider range of emotional expression than those for males.
- *Gender identity disorder* is a psychological disorder characterized by a cross-gender identification that leads the individual to be chronically uncomfortable with his or her biological sex.
- People with gender identity disorder identify with the other sex and deny their own sexual organs or sexual development, yet the disorder generally does not persist into adulthood.
  - **i.** Only 2% to 12 % of males had gender identity disorder in adulthood.
  - **ii.** As an adult, many people with gender identity disorder identify themselves as gay or lesbian.
  - **iii.** 40% to 80% of boys with gender identity disorder report being gay or bisexual in adulthood.
  - **iv.** There is not enough data on females with gender identity disorder to comment about the presence of the disorder in adulthood or adult sexual orientation. [See *Table 11.1.*]
- Symptoms include discomfort in living as one biological sex and preoccupation with the desire to be the other sex. The symptoms *cannot* arise due to being intersexed.
- Some may have medical and surgical treatments to change the appearance of their sex.
- The distress is often due to other people's responses to the client's cross-gender behavior. [See *Case 11.1.*]
- Most people with this disorder have heterosexual gender identifications. *Example:* A male who sees himself as female will tend to be attracted to men. [See *Table 11.2.*]

- Biological males experience this disorder at three times the rate as females. One cause of this difference may be due to society being more accepting of females who display a wide range of "masculine" behaviors than of males who exhibit some (or many) "feminine" behaviors.

LEARNING ACTIVITY 11.1: Variations of Biological Sex, Sexuality, and Gender

Objective: To increase student awareness of the complexity of sex, sexuality, and gender.

Time: 30–45 Minutes

Directions: Instructions to the students are on *Worksheet 11.1,* found at the end of the chapter.

Note to Instructor: Many people have a difficult time understanding the complex and multiple layers of sex, sexuality, and gender. This exercise divides each layer and shows how each layer can be expressed on a continuum. Each person is a complex array of sex, sexuality, and gender.

You may want to have students choose a celebrity and rate him or her on each of the layers of the continuum.

Source: This exercise is adapted from Augusta, B. (2007). Gay, lesbian, bisexual and transgender youth: Affectional identity development. GLBTQ Resource Teacher, Madison Metropolitan School District.

Summary: Students will be surprised to learn about the complexities of identity and sexuality. For example, an individual may be male, attracted to people of the same sex, identify himself as heterosexual, be treated as male, communicate in an androgynous style, and feel like his gender identity is in between.

Questions to Students and Discussion: What surprises you about these layers? Why? How might these different layers play a role in gender identity and sexual disorders?

MEDIA RECOMMENDATION 11.1: *Boys Don't Cry*

Objective: To learn about a real person who struggled with gender identity disorder.

Time: 118 Minutes

Film and Discussion: 148 Minutes

Discussion Only: 30 Minutes

Watch: Peirce, K. (Director). (1999). *Boys don't cry.* [Film]. USA: Twentieth Century Fox Home Entertainment. Official Web site: http://www.foxsearchlight.com/boysdontcry/
This site includes the trailer, facts, links, virtual gallery, and more.

Tells the true story of a Nebraska teen, Brandon Teena, who struggled with gender identity disorder in a small town.

Note to the Instructor: There are some extremely violent scenes in this film.

Summary: Students will become aware of how society often rejects someone with gender identity disorder. The film will reveal to students the personal and interpersonal struggles of someone with gender identity disorder and the negative consequences that can result from coming out.

Questions to Students and Discussion: What DSM-IV-TR criteria does Brandon Teena exhibit? How does her community accept her? How do you feel about Brandon's initial deception with Lana? What surprised you about the film?

MEDIA RECOMMENDATION 11.2: *Transparent*

Objective: To learn about parents who have struggled with gender identity disorder.

Time: 61 Minutes

Film and Discussion: 91 Minutes

Discussion Only: 30 Minutes

Watch: Rosskam, J. (Director). (2005). *Transparent.* [Film]. San Francisco: Framline Films. Official Web site: http://www.transparentthemovie.com/
This site includes a film synopsis, trailer, and more.

The film documents the experience of 19 female-to-male transsexuals in the United States who have given birth and are raising their biological children. The film explores the ways these individuals wrestle with "motherhood" while being male.

Summary: Students will gain awareness of the personal struggles of female-to-male transsexuals. For example, these men discuss the conflicts that arise from their children wanting to call them "mommy" while they are making the transition to becoming men.

Questions to Students and Discussion: Highlight the DSM-IV-TR criteria that some of these men meet. How does the community respond to them? How about their children? Partners? How do you feel about the struggle these men face? What surprised you about the film?

B. Criticisms of the DSM-IV-TR Definition

- Symptoms of distress seem to arise from other people's reactions, not the symptoms of the disorder itself.
- Some argue the DSM-IV-TR concepts of gender and gender "appropriate" behavior are too narrow.

LECTURE ENHANCEMENT 11.1: Transgendered Children

Objective: To explore the controversies of raising a child who is struggling with gender identity disorder.

Time: 13:38 Minutes (Video 1); 60 Minutes (Video 2)

Discussion and Media: 40 Minutes (Video 1); 90 Minutes (Video 2)

Discussion Only: 25 Minutes (Video 1); 30 Minutes (Video 2)

Watch Online: Search Google using the search terms "60 minutes my secret self," or http://www.sixtyminutes.ninemsn.com.au/stories/858237/my-secret-self
Learn about Jazz, the youngest documented case of gender identity disorder.

Search YouTube using the search terms "my secret self part 1 of 5," or http://www.youtube.com/watch?v=Utpam0IGYac&feature=related

This is part one of a five-part *20/20* episode featuring a number of children with gender identity disorder and their families.

Lecture Points:
I.   DSM-IV-TR Criteria Met by These Children
    A. Consistent desire to be the opposite sex
    B. Preference for cross-dressing
    C. Preference for cross-sex roles in make-believe play, games, and pastimes

        D. Preference for playmates of the other sex

II. The Struggle of Families

        A. Arguments against allowing cross-sex dressing, play, games, etc.

           1. This might be a phase.

           2. Other children will make fun of the child.

           3. How will the school handle the child? Which bathroom/dressing room should the child use?

        B. Arguments for allowing cross-sex dressing, play, games, etc.

           1. This might be a phase.

           2. If the child has gender identity disorder, early acceptance may be better.

           3. The child can feel free to express him/herself.

           4. The child will learn to accept him/herself because others accept him/her.

           5. If the root of gender identity is biological, the child cannot help his/her behavior.

Summary: Students will recognize the DSM-IV-TR criteria in these cases and will also gain insight into the struggles these families undergo; for example, should the families allow their children to receive hormone therapy?

Questions to Students and Discussion: Highlight the DSM-IV-TR criteria that some of these children meet. How do the families deal with their children's desire to be the opposite sex? How do you feel about the struggles expressed by these families and children?

C. Understanding Gender Identity Disorder

Neurological, psychological, and social factors are associated with gender identity disorder.

1. Neurological Factors

Researchers know little about the neurological factors contributing to gender identity disorder. However, they have:

- Begun to document differences in specific brain structures in people who both have and do not have the disorder
- Gathered evidence that hormones during fetal development play a role in producing this disorder
- Learned that genes are a big contributor to this disorder

a. Brain Systems and Neural Communication:

Research has found that the *bed nucleus of the stria terminalis* (an extension of the amygdala) in males with gender identity disorder has the same number of neurons as most females. Similarly, for women with gender identity disorder, the number of neurons in this structure is more similar to most males. This structural difference may be caused by the following:

- Prenatal exposure to hormones
- Maternal stress
  - i. A study found that maternal stress in rats can cause low levels of androgen and brain area changes in the fetus. After birth, the male pups showed more "female" behavior (female sexual posturing) versus male behavior (copulation and rough play).
  - ii. Another study found certain testosterone levels in human amniotic fluid were associated with later "male" behavior in 6- to 10-year-old girls, but less associated with behavior in 6- to 10-year-old boys.

b. Genetics:

Sixty-two percent of the variance in gender identity is due to genes, and the remaining percentage is due to the nonshared environment.

2. Psychological Factors: A Correlation with Play Activities

- Studies have shown that boys with gender identity disorder have lower levels of activity than other boys; girls with gender identity disorder engage in more rough-and-tumble play than other girls.

- Boys and girls with gender identity disorder are less likely to play with same-sex peers.

- However, these behaviors are just confirming the original criteria, which are problematic, and the disorder does not usually persist into adulthood.

3. Social Factors: Responses from Others

- One study argues that mothers who focused on their sons' physical attractiveness might have caused the mothers to interact with their sons as if the sons were girls, and this interaction may have influenced the development of gender identity disorder.

- See *Figure 11.1 (a)* and *(b),* which show how physical attractiveness is associated with gender identity disorder in males but in for females.

D. Treating Gender Identity Disorder

1. Targeting Neurological and Other Biological Factors: Altered Appearance

- Taking androgen, a male sex hormone, will lower a woman's voice, stop menstruation, and increase facial hair.

- Men may take estrogen and progesterone, female sex hormones, which enlarge breasts and redistribute fat to the hips and buttocks.

- *Sex reassignment surgery* is a procedure in which the genitals (and breasts, for biological women) are surgically altered to appear like those of the other sex.
  i. Sex reassignment surgery is easier for men than for women because it is difficult to create a satisfactory artificial penis.
  ii. Ten percent of people regret having this surgery, and thus most people are evaluated prior to the surgery.
  iii. Lack of family support, comorbid psychological disorders, and psychological instability lead to poorer post-surgery outcomes.

2. Targeting Psychological Factors: Understanding the Choices

- Mental health clinicians will help clients become aware of options and goals and provide education about medical and surgical options.

- Clinicians may also have clients examine how it feels to live part- or full-time as the other sex and discuss solutions to living as the other sex.

3. Targeting Social Factors: Family Support

- Family members may need education about the disorder and communication skills to more effectively discuss problems.

- Group therapy may provide additional support and information for the client.

LEARNING ACTIVITY 11.2: Transgender Speaker

Objective: To gain awareness of the experience of those with gender identity disorder.

Time: 60 Minutes

Directions:

1. Invite a person with gender identity disorder to speak in your class. Possible places to contact for speakers include:
   Transgender Forum Community Organization, http://www.transgender.org/
   National Transgender Advocacy, http://www.genderadvocates.org/links/national.html
   Transgender Tapestry, http://www.ifge.org/Web_Links-req-viewlink-cid-1.phtml
2. Have students prepare questions for the speaker based on the content in the textbook.

Note to Instructor: Guidelines for having a respectful discussion may need to be reviewed depending on the class dynamics.

Summary: Most students will be surprised to meet someone with gender identity disorder. Students should gain empathy for people with this disorder. Students should also be able to apply the information from the text to help understand the possible causes of gender identity disorder.

Questions to Students and Discussion: What surprised you about the guest speaker? What information was consistent or inconsistent with your textbook? What questions remain?

II. PARAPHILIAS

A. What Are Paraphilias?

Paraphilias (which means "beside/beyond fondness/love") focus on "deviant" fantasies, objects, or behaviors that play a role in sexual arousal.

- People with paraphilias have intense sexual fantasies or urges toward:
  i. Nonconsenting partners or children
  ii. Nonhuman objects
  iii. Suffering or humiliation of oneself or one's partner
- *Arousal pattern* is the predictable pattern of arousal, lasting at least 6 months, and must:
  i. Interfere with mutual and affectionate sexual activity
  ii. Impair functioning
  iii. Cause distress
  iv. Involve nonconsenting partners [see *Table 11.3*]
- The prevalence of this disorder is unknown.

1. Paraphilias Involving Nonconsenting Individuals

These types of paraphilic disorders include sexual fantasies, urges, or behaviors with nonconsenting partners. A diagnosis is given only if the person acts on the urges or if the urges cause him/her distress or interpersonal difficulties.

a. Exhibitionism: Physically Exposing Oneself:

Paraphilia *exhibitionism* is characterized by sexual fantasies, urges, or behaviors that hinge on a person's exposing his genitals to a stranger, usually as a surprise. [See *Table 11.3.*]

- Paraphilas must cause distress, relationship problems, or actual behavior of exposing oneself.
- Men with exhibitionism usually get an erection and may masturbate while exposing themselves.

- One man on average will flash 514 people over a lifetime; the median number of people is 34. [See *Case 11.2.*]

b. Voyeurism: Watching Others:

Voyeurism is a paraphilia characterized by sexual fantasies, urges, or behaviors that involve observing someone who is in the process of undressing, is nude, or is engaged in sexual activity.

- The person being observed neither has consented to nor is aware of being observed. [See *Table 11.3.*]
- Diagnostic criteria require that urges and fantasies must cause distress or one must have acted out urges upon someone who is unaware that the voyeurism is happening.

c. Frotteurism: Touching a Stranger:

Frotteurism is a paraphilia characterized by recurrent, intense, sexually arousing fantasies, sexual urges, or behaviors that involve touching or rubbing against a nonconsenting person. [See *Table 11.3.*]

- The diagnosis has two types: men who like to rub and men who like to touch.
- Diagnostic criteria require that urges and fantasies must cause distress or one must have acted on urges. [See *Case 11.3.*]

d. Pedophilia: Sexually Abusing Children:

Pedophilia is a paraphilia characterized by recurrent, sexually arousing fantasies, sexual urges, or behaviors involving a child who has not yet gone through puberty (typically aged 13 or younger). [See *Table 11.3.*]

- The individual must be at least 16 years of age and five years older than the child victim.
- A *child molester* is someone diagnosed with pedophilia who has had actual sexual activity with a child.
- Diagnostic criteria require that urges and fantasies must cause distress or one must have acted on urges.
- Sexual behaviors range from oral-genital contact to penetration; most often the victim is female.
- Twenty-five percent of victims are below age 6, 25% are between ages 6 to 10, and 50% are between ages 11 to 13.
- A person with this disorder believes that this form of contact is beneficial for the child and that the child played a role in the seduction, and thus he/she is not to blame for his/her behavior.
- The onset of pedophilia is in adolescence, is chronic, and has a higher relapse rate for those who molest boys versus those who molest girls.
- Not all sexual abuse occurs because of sexual arousal, but can also occur due to another psychological problem (such as substance abuse) or as an act of aggression.

MEDIA RECOMMEDATION 11.3: Juvenile Sex Offenders

Objective: To learn about the psychology behind juvenile sex offenders.

Time: 29 Minutes

Film and Discussion: 59 Minutes

Discussion Only: 30 Minutes

Watch: Stanton, W. R. (2005). *Givin' it up.* [Film]. Boston, MA: Frameline Films.
This powerful and disturbing documentary explores the sexual abuse history and psychology of several juveniles who are guilty of sex offenses. The film also highlights the difficulty in working with these youth as they are both survivors and perpetrators. See: http://www.fanlight.com/catalog/films/491_giu.php

Summary: Students will become aware of the limits of the DSM-IV-TR criteria of pedophilia. For example, these youth may not meet the age criteria, yet they meet all of the other criteria for pedophilia.

Questions to Students and Discussion: Why did these youth sexually abuse other youth? What did you learn about their history? What about their thought process? What difficulties do counselors face in treating these youth? What did you find surprising in this film?

2. **Sexual Sadism and Sexual Masochism: Pain and Humiliation**

   a. **Sexual Sadism: Inflicting the Pain:**

   Sexual sadism is a paraphilia characterized by recurrent, sexually arousing fantasies, urges, and behaviors that inflict physical or psychological suffering on another person. [See *Table 11.3.*]

   - Diagnostic criteria require that urges and fantasies must cause distress or one must have acted on urges toward a nonconsenting partner.
   - *Sadistic rapes* occur when the perpetrator is aroused by the violence and suffering of the victim.
   - Sadistic fantasies are present in childhood, but the behavior begins in early adulthood. [See *Case 11.4.*]

   b. **Sexual Masochism: Receiving the Pain:**

   Sexual masochism is a paraphilia in which the individual repeatedly becomes sexually aroused by fantasies, urges, or behaviors related to being hurt—specifically, being humiliated or made to suffer in other ways—and this arousal pattern causes significant distress or impairs functioning. [See *Table 11.3.*]

   - Diagnosed in both men and women, it is the only paraphilia that has measurable rates among women.
   - Twenty-five percent of women who engage in sexual masochism have a history of childhood sexual abuse.
   - Some inflict the pain and humiliation on themselves and others allow someone else to inflict the pain or humiliation.

3. **Paraphilias Involving Nonhuman Objects**

   These paraphilias include fetishism and transvestic fetishism.

   a. **Fetishism: Sexually Arousing Objects:**

   Fetishism is a paraphilia in which the individual repeatedly uses nonliving objects to achieve or maintain sexual arousal and such an arousal pattern causes significant distress or impairs functioning. [See *Table 11.3.*]

   - The *fetish* (or object) may be used to achieve sexual arousal or to maintain an erection with a partner or alone. *Example:* A man may become sexually aroused by seeing or smelling women's shoes.

- Severe fetishism is where the person is unable to have sexual relations without the object present.
- *Partialism* is where the object is a nonsexual body part (such as the foot).
- A study showed that men with fetishism are aroused by certain items of clothing (60%), rubber (25%), footwear (15%), partialism (15%), and stolen items of preferred fetish (37%). [See *Case 11.5.*]

MEDIA RECOMMENDATION 11.4: Fetishes and Fantasies

Objective: To learn about the different forms of sadism, masochism, and paraphilias.

Time: 2 Minutes

Media and Discussion: 10 Minutes

Discussion Only: 8 Minutes

Watch Online: Search Videojug.com using the search term "fetishes and fantasies," or http://www. videojug.com/interview/fetishes-and-fantasies-2

Eleanor McKenzie, a sex expert, describes the differences between sadism, masochism, and paraphilias.

Summary: Students will learn that sadists are ones who become aroused while humiliating or inflicting pain on their partners while masochists become aroused from receiving this treatment. Students will also learn about those with a paraphilia involving objects.

Question to Students and Discussion: Where is the line between sexual preferences and a sexual disorder? How might our culture influence the development of one of these disorders?

    b. Transvestic Fetishism: Cross-Dressing for Sexual Arousal:

    Transvestic fetishism is a paraphilia in which a heterosexual man cross-dresses in women's clothes for sexual arousal and experiences distress or impaired functioning because of the cross-dressing; formerly called *transvestism.* [See *Tables 11.3* and *11.4.*]

- Transvestic fetishism begins before age 10, and most adult males with this disorder are married with children. [See *Case 11.6.*]
- Nontransvestic fetish is where men may wear female clothes to achieve sexual arousal, but only if the clothes were previously worn by a woman.

B. Assessing Paraphilic Disorders

- A *penile plethysmograph* is an indirect measure of neurological events. It is placed on the penis to measure an erection. Men are then shown "normal" and "deviant" stimuli while their arousal is being recorded.
- Men with paraphilias show greater brain electrical activity in the left frontal lobe (indicating approach) when viewing "deviant" stimuli.
- Self-report surveys are also used to assess paraphilia.
- Reports from partners or the criminal justice system are additional methods to assess paraphilia.

C. Criticisms of the DSM-IV-TR Paraphilias

- "Normal" versus "deviant" depends on the current culture.
- Some sex crimes are included as a paraphilia but are not diagnosable (*Example:* rape).
- The wide range of paraphilias limits generalizability and discrimination.
- The DSM-IV-TR criteria do not consider the amount of control one has over the urges.
- Paraphilias should be considered a type of obsessive-compulsive disorder.

D. Understanding Paraphilias

Not enough is known about the neurological, psychological, and social factors in paraphilia. The text details the available knowledge, as given here.

1. Neurological Factors

- People with pedophilia have cognitive deficits in the basal ganglia and frontal lobes. These clients show impaired inhibiting responses and working memory.
- Research has shown dopamine and serotonin neurotransmitter dysfunction; SSRIs have been found to decrease sexual fantasies and behaviors.
- Paraphilias have a slight genetic cause.

2. Psychological Factors: Conditioned Arousal

- Research does not support a psychodynamic or cognitive-behavioral explanation.
- Some argue that classical conditioning may be a cause of paraphilia. If a boy sees a neutral object (for example, his mother's shoes) while unintentionally (accidentally) touching his penis, the neutral object then becomes associated with sexual arousal.
- The *Zeigarnik effect* may amplify these feelings because people are more likely to recall interrupted activities than ones that are completed. Thus, those people with paraphilia might have felt aroused as a child but were not allowed to complete the act.
- These explanations also argue that paraphilias occur more often in men because of the male anatomy and the ease at which this anatomy can be accidentally stimulated.

3. Social Factors: More Erotica?

- Nonindustrialized societies have lower prevalence of paraphilias than do Western societies.
- Western societies provide many erotic stimuli, such as magazines, movies, billboards, and television, and thus males, especially boys, are more likely to become interrupted, leading to a desire to complete the task (the *Zeigarnik effect*).

E. Treating Paraphilias

- *Sex offenders* are those people with paraphilic behaviors who have been brought into the criminal justice system.
- The goal of treatment is to reduce impulses by targeting neurological, psychological, and social factors.

1. Targeting Neurological and Other Biological Factors: Medication

Chemical castration is the use of medication (*medroxyprogesterone* [Depo-Provera] or *cyproterone* [Androcur]) to reduce testosterone, which lessens urges, fantasies, and behaviors.

- The medication does not decrease the deviant urges, so symptoms reappear when unmedicated.
- SSRIs decrease fantasies, urges, and behaviors with those who have an obsessive-compulsive element.

2. **Targeting Psychological Factors: Cognitive-Behavior Therapy**

CBT seeks to decrease cognitive distortions related to fantasies (*Example:* addressing distorted thinking of those who think their behavior is not harmful).

- Behavioral methods, such as extinction, decrease deviant sexual arousal and increase "normal" sexual arousal.
- Treatments may combine medication and CBT.
- *Relapse prevention training* helps to identify high-risk situations and avoidance techniques.

3. **Targeting Social Factors**

Increasing empathy toward victims is hoped to decrease future reoffending. However, many do not complete psychosocial treatments, and research has not shown these programs to be effective.

MEDIA RECOMMENDATION 11.5: Treating Pedophilia

Objective: To learn about various treatments of pedophilia.

Time: 6 minutes

Media and Discussion: 15 Minutes

Discussion Only: 9 Minutes

Watch Online: Search Investigation.discovery.com using the search term "pedophile," or http://investigation.discovery.com/videos/most-evil-pedophile-confessions.html
This short clip discusses the use of SSRIs, chemical castration, and other forms of treatment for pedophilia. People with pedophilia discuss their responses to these treatments.

Summary: Students will see how SSRIs reduce sexual desire and thus are used to treat pedophilia. Additionally, students will learn about the other forms of medication used to reduce testosterone levels.

Questions to Students and Discussion: How does this video complement or contradict your textbook? Do you believe these treatments are effective? Why or why not? Since pedophilia is difficult to treat, what might we do with those who are found guilty of such crimes?

III. SEXUAL DYSFUNCTIONS

A. An Overview of Sexual Functioning and Sexual Dysfunctions

- The human sexual response cycle is the normal progression of sexual pleasure.
- *Sexual dysfunctions* are disorders that are characterized by problems in the sexual response cycle.

1. **The Normal Sexual Response Cycle**

The *sexual response cycle* includes the four stages of sexual response (excitement, plateau, orgasm, and resolution) as outlined by Masters and Johnson. [See *Figure 11.2.*]

a. Excitement:

Sensory-motor, cognitive, and emotional stimulation causes muscle tension and engorged blood vessels. The penis swells in men, and in women the clitoris and external genital areas swell while the vagina becomes lubricated.

b. Plateau:

Body changes peak and then level out.

c. Orgasm:

The height of sexual pleasure marked by involuntary genital muscle contractions, and generally followed by ejaculation for men and vaginal contractions for women.

d. Resolution:

Relaxation and released tension, also called the *refractory period.* Men are unable to have an additional orgasm during this time, but with additional stimulation, women can return to the excitement stage.

Some researchers have suggested that *desire* should be the first stage, consisting of fantasies and thoughts about sexual activity.

2. Sexual Dysfunctions According to DSM-IV-TR

- Sexual dysfunctions are divided into four categories: sexual desire disorders, sexual arousal disorders, orgasmic disorders, and sexual pain disorders.
- People can have more than one kind of disorder, and the disorder can begin in early years or after a time of normal functioning.
- The disorder may occur in all situations *(generalized)* or in specific situations, with specific partners, or with certain types of stimulation *(situational).* [See *Table 11.5.*]
- Symptoms must cause distress or relationship problems.
- Many sexual disorders have a psychological cause and not a medical cause. [See *Case 11.7* and *Table 11.6.*]

3. Sexual Desire Disorders

- Sexual desire has at least three components: neurological and biological (hormones and brain activity), cognitive (inclination or desire to be sexual), and emotional and relational (willingness to engage in sex with a specific person).
- Any problems with these components can lead to hypoactive sexual desire disorder or sexual aversion disorder.

a. Hypoactive Sexual Desire Disorder:

Hypoactive sexual desire disorder is a sexual dysfunction characterized by a persistent or recurrent lack of sexual fantasies or an absence of desire for sexual activity. [See *Table 11.5.*]

- This disorder may be lifelong, and it may be generalized or situational.
- People with this disorder may lack sexual desire and be willing or unwilling to engage in a sexual relationship.
- Sexual desire disorder problems induced by a mood disorder do not qualify.
- Women have this disorder more often than men. [See *Case 11.8.*]
  - **i.** As women age, desire decreases possibly due to hormonal changes.
  - **ii.** Psychological and social factors also influence a woman's desire.

b. Sexual Aversion Disorder:

Sexual aversion disorder is a sexual dysfunction characterized by a persistent or recurrent, extreme aversion to and avoidance of most genital sexual contact with a partner. [See *Table 11.5.*]

- People with this disorder may have desire, interest, and fantasies and may masturbate.

- People will, however, become anxious when thinking of touching another person's genitals. [See *Case 11.9.*]

4. Sexual Arousal Disorders

Sexual arousal disorders occur when a person cannot become aroused or cannot maintain arousal during a sexual encounter.

- This disorder interrupts the excitement phase in one of three ways:
  - **i.** When *the pleasurable stimulation is interrupted* (*Example:* when one's child unexpectedly enters the room)
  - **ii.** When *other external stimuli interfere* (*Example:* a car alarm goes off)
  - **iii.** When *internal stimuli interfere* (*Example:* when a person becomes afraid, anxious, sad, or angry or has thoughts that intrude)
- Neurological, biological, cognitive, and/or emotional components can contribute to this problem. However, the DSM-IV-TR criteria focus on the biological aspects, such as blood flow impairment, that can cause problems with arousal.

a. Female Sexual Arousal Disorder:

Female sexual arousal disorder is a sexual dysfunction marked by a woman's persistent or recurrent difficulty attaining or maintaining engorged genital blood vessels in response to adequate stimulation; formerly referred to as *frigidity.* [See *Table 11.5.*]

- Less genital engorgement causes decreased lubrication.

- Menopause can cause vaginal dryness, and thus female sexual arousal disorder is more likely to occur in women who have been through menopause.

- When not part of menopause, female sexual arousal disorder co-occurs with desire and/or orgasm problems.

- The DSM-IV-TR criteria focus on the neurological and biological aspects of this disorder and not the subjective experience.

- The diagnostic criteria require that distress or relationship difficulties must be present and that the disorder is not caused by some other psychological or medical disorder.

MEDIA RECOMMENDATION 11.6: Female Sexual Health

Objective: To learn about the various factors that may influence female arousal.

Time: 10 Minutes

Media and Discussion: 30 Minutes

Discussion Only: 20 Minutes

Watch Online: Search Videojug.com using the search term "female sexual health," or http://www.videojug.com/interview/female-sexual-health-2
Dr. Jennifer Berman, a physician, discusses the changes in women's sexual health and factors that may influence a woman's sexual arousal.

Summary: Students may be surprised to learn that sexual interest tends to decrease with age. Students may also be surprised at the number of factors that can influence sexual arousal. For example, certain medications are known to decrease arousal.

Questions to Students and Discussion: What information complements or contradicts your textbook? What did you find surprising? What would you like to know more about? How might our gender role expectations influence these disorders?

b. Male Erectile Disorder:

Male erectile disorder is a sexual dysfunction characterized by a man's persistent or recurrent inability to attain an adequate erection or to maintain an adequate erection until the end of sexual activity; sometimes referred to as *impotence*. [See *Table 11.5* and *Case 11.10*.]

- Some men with this disorder are able to have erections under certain circumstances, whereas others have the problem during any type of sexual activity.
- Over half of men age 40 and over have some type of erectile problem, which may be a natural part of aging.

5. Orgasmic Disorders

An *orgasmic disorder* is diagnosed when a clinician determines that the individual has experienced normal excitement and adequate stimulation for orgasm in normal circumstances (based on the person's age and other factors), but fails to have an orgasm.

LEARNING ACTIVITY 11.3: Cultural Messages on Masturbation

Objective: To gain awareness of the cultural messages that American people have received about masturbation.

Time: 10 Minutes

Media and Discussion: 20 Minutes

Discussion Only: 10 Minutes

Directions:

Ask students to reflect on the following questions (this reflection can be a discussion or a silent reflection):
- What messages did you receive about masturbation growing up?
- Were these messages different for boys versus girls? How so?
- Do your religious or personal beliefs prohibit masturbation?

Watch Online: Search Sexsmartfilms.com using the search terms "joy spot what is healthy masturbation" or http://www.sexsmartfilms.com/free-videos/the-joy-spot-what-is-healthy-masturbation/
This clip provides an overview of male and female masturbation by a sex educator.

Summary: Students will be surprised to learn about the benefits of masturbation: for example, the health (better sleep) and sexual benefits (increase in sexual responsivity).

Questions to Students and Discussion: Do you agree with the sex educator that women perceive self-masturbation differently than men? Why or why not? Do you agree with the sex educator about the line she draws between adaptive masturbation versus maladaptive masturbation? What are some of the physical and sexual benefits of masturbation for men and women?

a. Female Orgasmic Disorder:

Female orgasmic disorder is a sexual dysfunction characterized by a woman's persistent problem in progressing from normal sexual excitement to orgasm, such that orgasm is delayed or does not occur, despite a normal amount of appropriate stimulation. [See *Table 11.5.*]

- The problem with achieving an orgasm must be persistent and not caused by lack of stimulation.
- The diagnosis requires that the lack of orgasm causes distress or relationship problems.
- The percentage of women who have female orgasmic disorder is 5% to 24%.
- There are two types
  - **i.** *Absolute* (woman does not have orgasm in all situations)
  - **ii.** *Situational* (the woman does not have an orgasm in specific situations) [see *Case 11.11*]

b. Male Orgasmic Disorder:

Male orgasmic disorder is a sexual dysfunction characterized by a man's delay or absence of orgasm. [See *Table 11.5.*]

- Male orgasmic disorder is different from female orgasmic disorder in the following ways:
  - **i.** It involves problems reaching an orgasm with a partner, whereas the person can achieve an orgasm through masturbation
  - **ii.** It involves problems only during vaginal intercourse
  - **iii.** It occurs in less than 10% of the male population
- Men do not usually seek treatment unless they want to have a baby (and thus will need to have an orgasm during vaginal sex). [See *Case 11.12.*]

c. Premature Ejaculation:

Premature ejaculation is a sexual dysfunction characterized by orgasm and ejaculation that occur earlier than the man expects, usually before, immediately during, or shortly after penetration. [See *Table 11.5.*]

- Premature ejaculation criteria include: ejaculation that occurs through "minimal sexual stimulation" (when the man ejaculates from briefer stimulation than normally needed for an orgasm), when the partner cannot control his ejaculation sufficiently enough for his partner 50% of the time, or when the man cannot voluntarily control the ejaculation reflex.
- This problem tends to be a couples problem, although some couples do not consider this a problem. [See *Case 11.13.*]

MEDIA RECOMMENDATION 11.7: Premature Ejaculation and Treatments

Objective: To learn about premature ejaculation and possible treatments.

Time: 11 Minutes

Media and Discussion: 20 Minutes

Discussion Only: 9 Minutes

Watch Online: Search Videojug.com using the search term "male sexual problems" or http://www.videojug.com/interview/common-male-sexual-problems
Dr. Phillip Werthman, a physician, discusses a number of male sexual disorders. The first disorder he talks about is premature ejaculation. Werthman also reviews various treatments for this disorder.

Summary: Students may be surprised that premature ejaculation can be treated with SSRIs or using a squeeze technique or a specific gel.

Questions to Students and Discussion: What information complements or contradicts your textbook? What did you find surprising? What would you like to know more about? How might our gender role expectations influence these disorders?

6. **Sexual Pain Disorders**

   Two disorders that are related to pain associated with sexual intercourse are dyspareunia and vaginisimus.

   a. **Dyspareunia:**

      Dyspareunia is a sexual dysfunction characterized by recurrent or persistent genital pain that is associated with sexual intercourse. [See *Table 11.5.*]

      • Males rarely have this condition, and it is usually caused by a medical condition.

      • In women, this condition may be caused by scar tissue, an infection, lack of lubrication, or a result of menopause; it occurs in 10% to 20% of women.

      • Persistent dyspareunia can lead to desire or excitement problems.

   b. **Vaginismus:**

      Vaginismus is a sexual dysfunction in females in which recurrent or persistent involuntary spasms of the musculature of the outer third of the vagina interfere with sexual intercourse. [See *Table 11.5.*]

      • Muscle spasms make it difficult to insert the penis, a tampon, finger, or *speculum* (device inserted vaginally and used during a pelvic exam).

      • This disorder is different than sexual aversion disorder, as the fear is a fear of penetration not of genital contact.

      • Most women with vaginismus also have dyspareunia, which can make the vaginismus worse.

      • Vaginismus typically does not lead to desire and excitement problems.

      • Women usually seek treatment when wanting to become pregnant. [See *Case 11.14.*]

MEDIA RECOMMENDATION 11.8: Sexual Pain Disorders

Objective: To learn more about the sexual pain disorders and their treatments.

Time: 7 Minutes

Media and Discussion: 15 Minutes

Discussion Only: 8 Minutes

Watch Online: Search Videojug.com using the terms "sexual pain disorders," or
http://www.videojug.com/interview/sexual-pain-disorders-2
Dr. Jennifer Berman, a physician, provides an overview of sexual pain disorders and treatment.

Summary: Students will learn about how vaginismus is a response to fear of pain and how the muscular response to this fear causes even more pain.

Questions to Students and Discussion: What are the different causes of sexual pain? What is the most common reason for sexual pain according to Dr. Berman? What is vaginismus? How is vaginismus treated?

7. **Criticisms of the Sexual Dysfunctions in DSM-IV-TR**

- The sexual response cycle may not apply as well to women. For women, arousal and desire may occur at the same time rather than desire always preceding arousal. [See *Figure 11.3.*]
- The criteria focus on body parts versus the subjective experience of the person or couple, which play a larger role in women.
- The criteria focus on the orgasm being the conclusion to the response cycle, although an orgasm is not always needed to feel satisfied.
- The definition of "normal" has been criticized as being based on an adolescent male, and as women and men age they are more likely to meet the criteria of dysfunction even when a dysfunction does not exist, except from growing older.
- The criteria do not include information about duration. For example, some symptoms are transient.
- The DSM-IV-TR definitions are not necessarily used by human sexuality specialists.
- Hypoactive sexual desire disorder has several criticisms:
    i.   An assessment of lack of sexual desire is subjective and may depend on the cultural and religious background of the clinician.
    ii. A diagnosis can be given when there is no disorder but instead only a difference in desire among partners.
    iii. Lack of desire may be a result of a poorly functioning relationship.
    iv. Different problems with desire—lifelong versus situational—may require different treatments.
- Dyspareunia is considered more of a pain disorder versus a sexual disorder by some.

B. **Understanding Sexual Dysfunctions**

Sexuality does not exist in a vacuum. Sexuality and any related problems develop through feedback loops among neurological, psychological, and social factors.

1. **Neurological and Other Biological Factors**

   Disease, illness, surgery, and medication can all, directly or indirectly, disrupt normal sexuality. The effects of normal aging can also produce sexual difficulties.

   a. **Sexual Side Effects: Disease, Illness, Surgery, and Medication:**
   - Disease or illness can cause sexual dysfunction *directly* (*Examples:* prostate or cervical cancer).
   - Surgery can also lead to sexual problems (*Example:* gynecologic cancer).
   - Disease or illness may also *indirectly* affect sexual functioning (*Example:* a heart attack may cause one to be afraid of having sex as it might bring on another attack).
   - Some medications interfere with sexual functioning (*Examples:* SSRIs, antipsychotics, beta-blockers, blood pressure medications, antiseizure medications, estrogen and progesterone medications, HIV medications, narcotics, and sedative hypnotics).
   - Alcohol can interfere with "normal" sexual functioning.

   b. **Aging:**
   - Normal aging can affect sexual functioning (*Example:* older women experience less lubrication, which can cause pain when having intercourse).
   - Men's testosterone levels decrease which increases the amount of stimulation needed for an erection.
   - Older men also experience decreased penis hardness and an increased refractory period.
   - Both sexes may develop illness or disease or take medications that affect sexual function.
   - Despite these limitations, older people report still enjoying sex.

2. **Psychological Factors: Predisposing, Precipitating, and Maintaining Sexual Dysfunctions**
   - Self-fulfilling prophecies can cause individuals to develop a sexual disorder. For example, a woman may believe she will lose her sexual desire as she ages (the belief then causes the decrease in interest), and men may think they should have sex twice a day (the belief causes a sense of inadequacy). [See *Table 11.7.*]
   - Childhood sexual abuse predisposes the development of a sexual disorder. Male survivors of childhood sexual disorders are three times more likely to have erectile dysfunction and twice as likely to have desire problems or premature ejaculation. Women survivors are more likely to have sexual problems.
   - Anxiety can trigger sexual dysfunctions (*Examples:* focusing on sex-related fears, feeling uncomfortable about one's body, or worrying about nonsexual matters).
   - A *maintaining factor* is when a person has a single failure in a sexual experience and then becomes afraid that the failure will occur again.

3. **Social Factors**

   Sexual relations are influenced by:
   - The expression and resolution of conflict
   - Communication of needs and desires

- How couples handle stress
- Level of attraction among partners

4. **FEEDBACK LOOPS IN ACTION: Sexual Dysfunctions**

See *Figure 11.4* to understand how the neurological, psychological, and social factors influence one another and contribute to sexual disorders. These factors also play a role in how sexual dysfunctions are caused and maintained.

C. Assessing Sexual Dysfunctions

Most patients see a physician first, who may refer them to a *sex therapist.*

- A *sex therapist* is usually a mental health clinician who is trained to assess and treat problems related to sexuality and sexual activity.
- An assessment is conducted to identify the specific neurological, psychological, and social factors contributing to the dysfunction.

1. **Assessing Neurological and Other Biological Factors**

To assess the health status and its affect on sexual disorders, the following are available:

- Lab tests to measure endocrine and hormone levels
- Ultrasound imaging
- Tests to assess sensory-nerve functioning
- Plethysmograph (to assess penile response)
- Vaginal probes (to measure vaginal lubrication, dilation, and relaxation)

2. **Assessing Psychological Factors**

To examine psychological factors that influence sexual disorders, clinicians may assess the client's:

- Personality (using an MMPI-2)
- Level of depression
- Thoughts, feelings, and expectations about sexual activity and masturbation
- Sexual history

3. **Assessing Social Factors**

An assessment will be made of how the relationship issues affect the sexual difficulties. The therapist will also examine how the couple decides on sexual activity timing, duration, and specific activities.

D. Treating Sexual Dysfunctions

1. **Targeting Neurological and Other Biological Factors: Medications**
   - *Table 11.8* highlights the medicalization of sex therapy.
   - Viagra (*sildenafil citrate;* a type of *phosphodiesterase type 5 inhibitor* or *PDE-5 inhibitor*) increases blood flow to the penis when a man is sexually excited.
   - Viagra and similar medications do not cure impotence but alleviate its symptoms.
   - Women may also use a PDE-5 inhibitor to increases blood flow to the clitoris.

- A drawback to this medication is that the PDE-5 inhibitor may actually lead to other dysfunctions. (*Example:* if a middle-aged man takes Viagra, his wife may find frequent sex painful if she lacks adequate lubrication.)

2. **Targeting Psychological Factors: Shifting Thoughts, Learning New Sexual Behaviors**

   - *Sex therapy* provides specific guidance and techniques to treat sexual problems.

   - Psychological therapies address feelings and thoughts that influence the sexual disorders.

   - Goals of therapy include human sexual response education and strategies to challenge negative thoughts, beliefs, or attitudes that interfere with sexual activity and to address self-image issues.

   - Masturbation can be used as a behavioral strategy to become more aware of sensations and fantasies.

   - ***Sensate focus exercises*** are behavioral techniques that are assigned as homework in sex therapy, in which an individual or couple seeks to increase awareness of pleasurable sensations that do not involve genital touching, intercourse, or orgasm.

   - The goals of behavioral therapy are to increase body awareness, orgasmic response, and control.

   - Treatment may also include making time for sexual activity or desensitization (for sexual aversion disorder).

   - Treatments for erectile dysfunction include psychoeducation and behavioral homework assignments.

   - Premature ejaculation is best treated using the *squeeze technique* where the man squeezes the base of the tip of the penis (just below the head) for 4 seconds, and when he feels in control he continues with the sexual activity.

   - Vaginismus is treated with systematic desensitization using a dilator.

   - Dyspareunia can be treated using biofeedback.

   - Orgasmic disorders are best treated by targeting psychological factors (for those who have never experienced an orgasm) and couples therapy or biological treatment (for those who have infrequent or situational orgasmic problems).

   - Many treatments need additional research.

3. **Targeting Social Factors: Couples Therapy**

   - Sex therapy may be conducted alone or with a partner.

   - Treatment may focus on the quality of the relationship and increasing communication, intimacy, and relationship skills or addressing power and control issues or may focus on assertiveness.

   - For gay or lesbian couples, treatment may include a focus on oppression or how to be intimate when HIV positive.

4. **FEEDBACK LOOPS IN TREATMENT: Sexual Dysfunctions**

   - *Figure 11.5* highlights how the neuropsychosocial treatments influence one another.

   - The effectiveness of treatments is difficult to measure because sexual disorders usually involve the client and his or her partner.

MEDIA RECOMMENDATION 11.9: Steps to Better Sex

Objective: To learn about treatments that target social factors that influence sexual disorders.

Time: 11 Minutes

Media and Discussion: 20 Minutes

Discussion Only: 9 Minutes

Watch Online: Search Oprah.com using the search terms "5 steps to better sex video," or http://www.oprah.com/media/20090116_sex-5steps
This video clip focuses on five steps to improve communication and in turn sexual relations in couples. The video also discusses how cultural messages can interfere with a healthy sex life.

Summary: Students will discover how cultural messages can inhibit healthy sexual responses. For example, if one receives negative messages about sexual activity, this may lead to difficulties into adulthood. Students will also learn about how to discuss their sexual needs more effectively and clearly with their partners.

Questions to Students and Discussion: What are the various factors that affect sexual activity? How do these factors complement or contradict the information in the text? Do you think scheduling a date night is a good or a bad idea for couples? Why or why not?

ADDITIONAL READINGS

Journal Articles

Beier, K., Ahlers, C., Goecker, D., et al. (2009). Can pedophiles be reached for primary prevention of child sexual abuse? First results of the Berlin Prevention Project Dunkelfeld (PPD). *Journal of Forensic Psychiatry & Psychology, 20*(6), 851–867.

Fee, E., Brown, T., & Laylor, J. (2003). One size does not fit all in the transgender community. *American Journal of Public Health, 93*(6), 899–900.

Kingsberg, S. (2009). Identifying HSDD in the family medicine setting. *Journal of Family Practice, 58,* S22–S25.

Lawrence, A. (2009). Erotic target location errors: An underappreciated paraphilic dimension. *Journal of Sex Research, 46*(2/3), 194–215.

Levine, S., & Solomon, A. (2009). Meanings and political implications of "psychopathology" in a gender identity clinic: A report of 10 cases. *Journal of Sex & Marital Therapy, 35*(1), 40–57.

Gender and Sexual Disorders Books and Memoirs

Ames. J. (2005). *Sexual metamorphosis: An anthology of transsexual memoirs.* New York: Vintage.
      This memoir questions traditional gender roles as several writers discuss the transformation from one sex to another.

Boylan, S. F. (2003). *She's not there: A life in two genders.* New York: Broadway Books.
      This autobiography of an English professor describes her male to female transformation.

Goldstein, A., Pukell, C., Goldstein, I., & Binik, Y. (2009). *Female sexual pain disorders: Evaluation and management.* New York: John Wiley & Sons.
      This book explores the research and treatments for dyspareunia. The book examines different causes of sexual pain and multidisciplinary forms of treatment.

Laws, R. D., & O'Donohue, W. T. (2008). *Sexual deviance: Theory, assessment, and treatment.* New York: Guilford Press.
   A comprehensive guide to different forms of sexual deviancy.

Salter, A. (2003). *Predators: Pedophiles, rapists, and other sex offenders.* New York: Basic Books.
   Anne Salter, a profiler, describes the techniques predators use on their victims.

ADDITIONAL MEDIA RECOMMENDATIONS

Clearway, A. (Director). (2007). *One in 2000.* [Film]. USA: Fanlight Productions.
   Powerful documentary that explores the life of intersexed individuals.

Field, T. (Director and Writer). (2006). *Little children.* [Film]. USA: New Line Cinema.
   This film explores different forms of sexual deviance from adultery to exhibitionism.

Kassell, N. (Director). (2004). *The woodsman.* [Film]. USA: Sony Pictures.
   A convicted pedophile is released and tries to live his life while he is tempted by his desires.

Mitchell, J. C. (Director). (2001). *Hedwig and the angry inch.* [Film]. USA: New Lines Production, Inc.
   A young man has a botched sex operation and spends his time singing with his band and pining after his love interest.

Palka, M. (Director and Writer). (2008). *Good dick.* [Film]. USA: Phase 4 Films.
   A woman has a difficult time with sexual intimacy after being sexually abused by her father.

Tucker, D. (Director and Writer). (2005). *Transamerica.* [Film]. USA: Weinstein Company.
   A male-to-female transgendered person discovers she has a son.

WEB SITES

American Association of Sexuality Educators, Counselors, and Therapists: Locate a professional, find books written by AASECT professionals, and learn about continuing education opportunities. See: http://www.aasect.org/

The Kinsey Institute for Research in Sex, Gender, and Reproduction: This Web site provides information about the institute, including current research and publications. See: http://www.kinseyinstitute.org/

Sex Smart Films: A resource for free films providing accurate sexual information. See: http://www.sexsmartfilms.com/

Transgender and Intersex Resources: This Web site provides information about "disorders of sex development," which includes intersex. The Web site contains a guide for parents and clinicians and additional resources. See: http://www.accordalliance.org/

Frameline: Provides a wealth of LGBT (lesbian, gay, bisexual, transgender) media. See: http://www.frameline.org/distribution/

WORKSHEET 11.1

SEX

Draw a continuum for biological sex (includes genitalia, hormonal makeup, chromosomes)

|——|

Male   Intersex   Female

SEXUALITY

Draw a continuum for sexual orientation (who we are attracted to)

|——|

Same sex   Bisexual   Opposite sex

Draw a continuum for sexual expression (our sexual behavior)

|——|

Same sex   Bisexual   Opposite sex

Draw a continuum for sexual identity (how we identify ourselves)

|——|

Gay/lesbian   Bisexual   Heterosexual

GENDER

Draw a continuum for gender roles (how society expects us to behave)

|——|

Male   Female

Draw a continuum for gender expression (gender communication style)

|——|

Masculine   Androgynous   Feminine

Draw a continuum for gender identity (our psychological sense of ourselves)

|——|

Man   Combination or third type   Woman

Schizophrenia and Other Psychotic Disorders

CHAPTER
12

CHAPTER OUTLINE

CHAPTER HEADINGS	INSTRUCTION IDEAS AND TEXTBOOK CORRELATIONS
WHAT ARE SCHIZOPHRENIA AND OTHER PSYCHOTIC DISORDERS?	
The Symptoms of Schizophrenia	**Learning Objectives:** 12.1, 12.2, 12.3, 12.4, 12.5, 12.6, 12.7, 12.8 **Learning Concepts:** positive symptoms; negative symptoms; cognitive deficits: the specifics; limitations of DSM-IV-TR criteria **Media Recommendation 12.1:** MINDSTORM: Sights and Sounds of Schizophrenia **Media Recommendation 12.2:** More on MINDSTORM: Sights and Sounds of Schizophrenia **Learning Activity 12.1:** Examples of Delusions **Media Recommendation 12.3:** The Case of Gerald **Media Recommendation 12.4:** Calalilly **Media Recommendation 12.5:** The Experience of Negative Symptoms of Schizophrenia **Learning Activity 12.2:** Role-Playing the Symptoms of Schizophrenia **Textbook Tools:** Figure 12.1; Table 12.1 **Worth Video Tool Kit for Abnormal Psychology:** Delusional Passenger on British Airways
Subtypes of Schizophrenia	**Learning Objectives:** 12.9 **Learning Concepts:** DSM-IV-TR subtypes; deficit/nondeficit subtypes **Media Recommendation 12.6:** Suffering from Paranoid Schizophrenia **Textbook Tool:** Case 12.1
Distinguishing Between Schizophrenia and Other Disorders	**Learning Objectives:** 12.10, 12.11, 12.12, 12.13, 12.14, 12.15, 12.16, 12.17 **Learning Concepts:** distinguishing between schizophrenia and other disorders; shared psychotic disorder; schizotypal personality disorder **Learning Activity 12.3:** Explore the Range of Psychotic Disorders **Textbook Tools:** Figure 12.2; Tables 12.2, 12.3

Schizophrenia Facts in Detail	**Textbook Tools:** Figure 12.3; Tables 12.4, 12.5, 12.6 **Learning Concepts:** schizophrenia facts in detail; prevalence; comorbidity; course; gender differences; prognosis
UNDERSTANDING SCHIZOPHRENIA	
Neurological Factors in Schizophrenia	**Learning Objectives:** 12.18, 12.19, 12.20, 12.21, 12.22 **Learning Concepts:** brain systems; a frontal lobe defect? impaired temporal lobe and thalamus? abnormal hippocampus? interactions among brain areas; possible causes of brain abnormalities; biological markers; neural communication; dopamine; serotonin and glutamate; stress and cortisol; effects of estrogen; genetics **Learning Activity 12.4:** Exploring the Biological Causes of Schizophrenia **Lecture Enhancement 12.1:** Childhood Onset Schizophrenia and Brain Wiring **Textbook Tools:** Figure 12.4; Table 12.7
Psychological Factors in Schizophrenia	**Learning Objectives:** 12.23, 12.24, 12.25, 12.26 **Learning Concepts:** mental processes and cognitive difficulties: attention, memory, and executive functions; beliefs and attributions; emotional expression **Textbook Tool:** Case 12.2
Social Factors in Schizophrenia	**Learning Objectives:** 12.27, 12.28 **Learning Concepts:** understanding the social world; stressful groups; immigration; economic factors; cultural factors: recovery in different countries; feedback loops in action: schizophrenia **Media Recommendation 12.7:** Theory of Mind **Textbook Tool:** Figure 12.5; Case 12.3
TREATING SCHIZOPHRENIA	
Targeting Neurological Factors in Treating Schizophrenia	**Learning Objectives:** 12.29, 12.30 **Learning Concepts:** medication; traditional antipsychotics; atypical antipsychotics: a new generation; discontinuing medication; preventive medication? brain stimulation: ECT and TMS **Media Recommendation 12.8:** Neurological Treatments for Schizophrenia
Targeting Psychological Factors in Treating Schizophrenia	**Learning Objective:** 12.31 **Learning Concepts:** cognitive-behavior therapy; cognitive rehabilitation; treating comorbid substance abuse: motivational enhancement
Targeting Social Factors in Treating Schizophrenia	**Learning Objectives:** 12.32, 12.33 **Learning Concepts:** family education and therapy; group therapy; social skills training; inpatient treatment; minimizing hospitalizations: community-based interventions; residential settings; vocational rehabilitation; feedback loops in treatment: schizophrenia **Lecture Enhancement 12.2:** Schizophrenia and Homelessness **Textbook Tool:** Figure 12.6

LEARNING OBJECTIVES

After reading this chapter, students will be able to:

12.1 Identify the positive and negative symptoms of schizophrenia.

12.2 Define hallucinations and provide an example of a hallucination.

12.3 Define delusions and provide an example of a delusion.

12.4 Describe the characteristics of disorganized speech.

12.5 Identify the symptoms of disorganized behavior.

12.6 Describe the characteristics of flat affect, alogia, and avolition.

12.7 Name and describe the cognitive deficits of schizophrenia.

12.8 Identify the limitations of the DSM-IV-TR criteria.

12.9 Identify and describe the five subtypes of schizophrenia.

12.10 Differentiate among mood disorders, substance-related disorders, and psychotic symptoms.

12.11 Describe the similarities and differences among schizophreniform, schizoaffective, delusional, shared psychotic, and schizotypal disorders.

12.12 Discuss the prevalence of schizophrenia worldwide.

12.13 Identify disorders that often occur with schizophrenia.

12.14 Describe the course of schizophrenia.

12.15 Articulate how gender and culture influence the development of schizophrenia.

12.16 Explain the rule of thirds regarding the prognosis of schizophrenia.

12.17 Describe the suicide and violence risk factors for those with schizophrenia.

12.18 Identify the various brain structures linked to schizophrenia.

12.19 Pinpoint three possible causes of brain abnormalities.

12.20 Define and describe biological markers of schizophrenia.

12.21 Describe the different neurotransmitters and hormones involved in schizophrenia.

12.22 Articulate the role of genetics in the development of schizophrenia.

12.23 Identify the mental processes and cognitive difficulties in schizophrenia.

12.24 Describe the beliefs and attributions of people with schizophrenia.

12.25 Explain the difficulties people with schizophrenia have with emotional expression and theory of mind.

12.26 Describe the role of expressed emotion in the development of schizophrenia.

12.27 Explain how immigration, economic, and cultural factors place people at risk for developing schizophrenia.

12.28 Describe how neurological, psychological, and social factors interact and cause schizophrenia.

12.29 Describe the advantages and disadvantages of traditional and atypical antipsychotics.

12.30 Discuss how brain stimulation can be used to treat schizophrenia.

12.31 Describe the various psychological treatments for schizophrenia.

12.32 Identify social factors that are helpful in treating schizophrenia.

12.33 Describe how neurological, psychological, and social factors influence one another when treating schizophrenia.

KEY TERMS

Schizophrenia: A psychological disorder characterized by psychotic symptoms that significantly affect emotions, behavior, and mental processes and mental contents.

Positive symptoms: Symptoms of schizophrenia that are marked by the *presence* of abnormal or distorted mental processes, mental contents, or behaviors.

Hallucinations: Sensations that are so vivid that the perceived objects or events seem real, even though they are not.

Delusions: Persistent false beliefs that are held despite evidence that the beliefs are incorrect or exaggerate reality.

Word salad: Disorganized speech consisting of a random stream of seemingly unconnected words.

Catatonia: A condition in which an individual remains in an odd posture or position, with rigid muscles, for hours.

Negative symptoms: Symptoms of schizophrenia that are marked by the *absence* or reduction of normal mental processes, mental contents, or behaviors.

Flat affect: A lack of, or considerably diminished, emotional expression, such as occurs when someone speaks robotically and shows little facial expression.

Alogia: A negative symptom of schizophrenia marked by speaking less than most other people and responding slowly or minimally to questions.

Avolition: A negative symptom of schizophrenia marked by difficulty in initiating or following through with activities.

Executive functions: Mental processes involved in planning, organizing, problem solving, abstract thinking, and exercising good judgment.

Paranoid schizophrenia: The subtype of schizophrenia characterized by the presence of delusions and auditory hallucinations that are limited to specific topics that have a coherent paranoid or grandiose theme.

Disorganized schizophrenia: The subtype of schizophrenia characterized by disorganized speech and behavior and inappropriate emotional expression.

Catatonic schizophrenia: The subtype of schizophrenia characterized by stiff or "frozen" postures or poses, bizarre jerky movements, or frozen facial expression.

Undifferentiated schizophrenia: The subtype of schizophrenia characterized by symptoms that do not completely match those specified for the paranoid, disorganized, or catatonic subtype.

Schizophreniform disorder: The psychotic disorder characterized by symptoms that meet all the criteria for schizophrenia *except* that the symptoms have been present for only 1 to 6 months and daily functioning may or may not have declined over that period of time.

Brief psychotic disorder: The psychotic disorder characterized by the sudden onset of positive or disorganized symptoms that last between a day and a month and are followed by a full recovery.

Schizoaffective disorder: The psychotic disorder characterized by the presence of both schizophrenia *and* a depressive, manic, or mixed mood episode.

Delusional disorder: The psychotic disorder characterized by the presence of nonbizarre but demonstrably incorrect beliefs that have persisted for more than 1 month.

Shared psychotic disorder: The psychotic disorder in which an individual develops delusions as a result of his or her close relationship with another person who has delusions as part of a psychotic disorder; also known as *folie à deux.*

Prodromal phase: The phase that precedes the onset of a psychological disorder (such as schizophrenia) when symptoms do not yet meet all the criteria for the disorder.

Active phase: The phase of a psychological disorder (such as schizophrenia) in which the individual exhibits symptoms that meet all the criteria for the disorder.

Biological marker: A neurological, bodily, or behavioral characteristic that distinguishes people with a psychological disorder (or a first-degree relative with the disorder) from those without the disorder.

Dopamine hypothesis: The view that schizophrenia arises from an overproduction of dopamine or an increase in the number or sensitivity of dopamine receptors.

Theory of mind: A theory about other people's mental states (their beliefs, desires, and feelings) that allows a person to predict how other people will react in a given situation.

High expressed emotion (high EE): A family interaction style characterized by hostility, unnecessary criticism, or emotional overinvolvement.

Social selection: The hypothesis that those who are mentally ill "drift" to a lower socioeconomic level because of their impairments.

Social causation: The hypothesis that the daily stressors of urban life, especially as experienced by people in a lower socioeconomic level, trigger mental illness in those who are vulnerable.

Tardive dyskinesia: An enduring side effect of traditional antipsychotic medications that produces involuntary lip smacking and odd facial contortions as well as other movement-related symptoms.

Atypical antipsychotics: A relatively new class of antipsychotic medications that affect dopamine and serotonin activity but create fewer movement-related side effects than do traditional antipsychotics; also referred to as *second-generation antipsychotics.*

Cognitive rehabilitation: A form of psychological treatment that is designed to strengthen cognitive abilities through extensive and focused practice; also called *neurocognitive remediation* or *cognitive mediation.*

Community care: Programs that allow mental health care providers to visit patients in their homes at any time of the day or night; also known as *assertive community treatment.*

CHAPTER GUIDE

Chapter Introduction

Four female quadruplets from one single fertilized egg were born in 1930. By age 20 all four had symptoms of or full-blown schizophrenia, which underscores the findings that 48% of identical twins will both develop schizophrenia and 16% of identical quads will all develop schizophrenia.

I.   WHAT ARE SCHIZOPHRENIA AND OTHER PSYCHOTIC DISORDERS?

Schizophrenia is a psychological disorder characterized by psychotic symptoms that significantly affect emotions, behavior, and mental processes and mental contents.

- Symptoms interfere with the person's ability to function in the world.
- Research suggests that schizophrenia is actually a set of related disorders, rather than one disorder, that have different symptoms, causes, courses, and treatment responses.

A. The Symptoms of Schizophrenia

There are two clusters of criteria for schizophrenia, positive and negative symptoms.

- Positive symptoms include delusions, hallucinations, and disorganized speech and behavior.
- Negative symptoms include the reduction of mental processing and contents, feelings, or behaviors (including speech, emotion, expression, and/or movement). [See *Table 12.1.*]

1. Positive Symptoms

- *Positive symptoms* of schizophrenia are marked by the *presence* of abnormal or distorted mental processes, mental contents, or behaviors.
- Positive symptoms include hallucinations, delusions, and disorganized speech and behavior and are intrusive, extensive, and powerful.

a. Hallucinations:

- *Hallucinations* are sensations that are so vivid that the perceived objects or events seem real, even though they are not.
- Hearing voices is the most common type of hallucination. Individuals with schizophrenia have difficulty differentiating whether the voice is internally or externally generated.
- People with schizophrenia are more likely to believe their internal conversations are coming from someone else.

MEDIA RECOMMENDATION 12.1: MINDSTORM: Sights and Sounds of Schizophrenia

Objective: To experience a simulation of hallucinations.

Time: 7 Minutes

Media and Discussion: 12 Minutes

Discussion Only: 5 Minutes

Watch Online: Search Google using the search terms "mindstorm schizophrenia," or http://www.janssen.com/janssen/mindstorm_video.html
This powerful video simulates both auditory and visual hallucinations.

Summary: Students will become aware of just how powerful and real auditory and visual hallucinations can be. They should gain more understanding and thus empathy for those who experience these positive symptoms of schizophrenia.

Questions to Students and Discussion: What do you think it is like to live every day with these types of hallucinations? What surprised you about this simulation? Why? What do you think would have happened if the patient did not have someone living with him or her (this refers to the person who comes in to help at the end)? What difficulties might arise when treating someone who has such delusions?

MEDIA RECOMMENDATION 12.2: More on MINDSTORM: Sights and Sounds of Schizophrenia

Objective: To gain an understanding of the hallucinations and delusions experienced by those with schizophrenia.

Time: 4 Minutes

Media and Discussion: 10 Minutes

Discussion Only: 6 Minutes

Watch Online: View the slideshow *Living with schizophrenia: A visit to the pharmacy* at NPR Online by visiting http://www.npr.org/programs/atc/features/2002/aug/schizophrenia/. Select the link "View a multimedia slideshow of highlights of one Janssen Pharmaceutical simulation of a schizophrenic episode."

This simulation highlights the hallucinatory symptoms of schizophrenia.

Summary: Students should become more aware of just how powerful and real auditory and visual hallucinations can be. They should gain more empathy for those who experience these positive symptoms of schizophrenia.

Questions to Students and Discussion: What do you think it is like to live every day with these types of hallucinations? What surprised you about this simulation? Why? What difficulties might arise when treating someone who has such delusions?

b. Delusions

- *Delusions* are persistent false beliefs that focus on a specific theme and are held despite evidence that the beliefs are incorrect or exaggerate reality.
- Types of delusions include:
  i. *Paranoid delusions:* Individuals believe they are being persecuted by others. (*Example:* believing that extraterrestrials are coming to take the person away)
  ii. *Delusions of control:* Individuals believe they are being controlled by other people who put thoughts into their heads, called *thought insertions.* (*Example:* believing that the pharmacist inserts thoughts into the person's head)
  iii. *Delusions of grandeur:* Individuals believe themselves to be more powerful, knowledgeable, or capable than in actuality. (*Example:* the person believing that he or she has created a new computer when this type of achievement is impossible for him or her)
  iv. *Delusions of reference:* Individuals believe that random, external events have special meaning for them. (*Example:* believing a song played in a movie was included specifically for the person)

LEARNING ACTIVITY 12.1: Examples of Delusions

Objective: To learn about the range of delusions that people with schizophrenia experience.

Time: 20 Minutes

Directions:
1. Search: http//www.psychexchange.co.uk using the search terms "examples of schizophrenic delusions," or visit http://www.psychexchange.co.uk/resource/1895/ for Leslie Ravenscroft's examples of delusions. Select several examples of delusions from the list and print them out.

2. Have students form small groups.
3. Hand out one example per group.
4. Ask students to identify the type of delusion in the example.
5. Then have students imagine what it must be like to live with that delusion.

This Web site provides a link to a downloadable worksheet that gives students a number of case studies from Haddock and Slade's (1996) *Cognitive-Behavioural Interventions with Psychotic Disorders.*

Summary: Students should be able to identify the type or types of delusions in each case. By imagining what it might be like to live with those delusions, students most likely will gain empathy for the clients.

Questions to Students and Discussion: Do you agree with your classmates' identifications of types of delusions? Why or why not? What is your opinion about what it must be like to live with that delusion? Is your opinion different from the opinions of your classmates? What do you think of your classmates' opinions?

c. Disorganized Speech
- Individuals with disorganized speech lack awareness that others cannot understand what they are trying to say.
- *Word salad* consists of disorganized speech characterized by a random stream of seemingly unconnected words. (*Example:* "Pots dog small is tabled")
- *Neologisms* are words that only have meaning to that individual. (*Example:* "wish-bell")

MEDIA RECOMMENDATION 12.3: The Case of Gerald

Objective: To observe the symptoms of disorganized speech.

Time: 8 Minutes

Media and Discussion: 14 Minutes

Discussion Only: 6 Minutes

Watch Online: Search YouTube using the search terms "Schizophrenia Gerald," or http://www.youtube.com/watch?v=gGnl8dqEoPQ
Gerald shows many different symptoms of schizophrenia, such as disorganized speech and neologisms.

Summary: Students will be able to identify examples of disorganized speech and other positive and negative symptoms of schizophrenia.

Questions to Students and Discussion: Provide examples of Gerald's organized speech. What other symptoms of schizophrenia does Gerald show? What do you think life is like for Gerald or his family members? How might you work with Gerald if he were your patient?

MEDIA RECOMMENDATION 12.4: Calalilly

Objective: To observe symptoms of childhood-onset schizophrenia.

Time: 1–3 Minutes

Media and Discussion: 10 Minutes

Discussion Only: 7 Minutes

Watch Online: Search Oprah.com using the search term "schizophrenia," or http://www.oprah.com/dated/oprahshow/oprahshow-20090828-schizophrenic
A number of these clips feature Jani Schoffield, a 7-year-old with schizophrenia who exhibits a number of positive symptoms.

Summary: Students should be able to identify Jani's word salad and neologisms.

Questions to Students and Discussion: What surprised you about Jani's symptoms? What do you think everyday life is like for Jani? How has this illness affected her family? Provide examples of Jani's symptoms using terms from the text or lecture.

d. Disorganized Behavior

- *Disorganized behavior* is unfocused, disconnected, or inappropriate behavior. The symptoms include inappropriate responses to a situation and/or the inability to perform daily tasks.

- Disorganized behavior also includes catatonia. *Catatonia* is a condition in which an individual remains in an odd posture or position, with rigid muscles, for hours.

2. Negative Symptoms

- *Negative symptoms* of schizophrenia are marked by the *absence* or reduction of normal mental processes, mental contents, or behaviors.

- Individuals must have a total of two of the three negative symptoms listed to meet the diagnostic criteria. [See *Table 12.1.*]

a. Flat Affect: Muted Expression

Flat affect is a lack of, or considerably diminished, emotional expression, such as occurs when someone speaks robotically and shows little facial expression. Even though individuals with schizophrenia do not express strong emotion, research has shown they do experience emotion similar to people without schizophrenia.

b. Alogia: Poverty of Speech

Alogia is a negative symptom of schizophrenia marked by speaking less than most other people and responding slowly or minimally to questions. It may take the individual more time to respond and choose his/her words.

c. Avolition: Difficulty Initiating or Following Through

Avolition is a negative symptom of schizophrenia marked by difficulty in initiating or following through with activities.

MEDIA RECOMMENDATION 12.5: The Experience of Negative Symptoms of Schizophrenia

Objective: To learn how people with schizophrenia live with and experience negative symptoms.

Time: 8 Minutes

Media and Discussion: 20 Minutes

Discussion Only: 12 Minutes

Watch Online: Search YouTube using the search terms "negative symptoms of schizophrenia," or http://www.youtube.com/watch?v=ujxcm524epo
A young woman discusses her experience of the negative symptoms of schizophrenia.

Summary: Students should be able to identify the negative symptoms that the woman discusses. Students should notice the woman's flat affect and avolition, yet absence of alogia.

Questions to Students and Discussion: Provide some examples of this woman's negative symptoms. How does she experience these symptoms? What surprised you about this video? Why? What would you like to know more about and why?

3. **Cognitive Deficits: The Specifics**

   Cognitive deficits or *neocognitive deficits* affect attention, memory, and executive functioning in people with schizophrenia.

   a. **Deficits in Attention**

   People with schizophrenia have difficulty sustaining and focusing attention.

   b. **Deficits in Working Memory**

   - *Working memory* consists of short-term memory and a set of executive processes that operate on information in short-term memory. Working memory encodes information for later use.

   - People with schizophrenia are unable to encode information for later use; however, information that is repeated numerous times can be encoded and remembered.

   - Memory problems can lead to difficulties with reasoning.

   c. **Deficits in Executive Functioning**

   Executive functions are mental processes involved in planning, organizing, problem solving, abstract thinking, and exercising good judgment. Deficits in executive functioning can cause impairments in tasks that require multiple steps and thus affect overall abilities.

   d. **Cognitive Deficits Endure over Time**

   Deficits can be seen in early childhood and may continue even after other symptoms improve.

LEARNING ACTIVITY 12.2: Role-Playing the Symptoms of Schizophrenia

Objective: To identify the symptoms of schizophrenia.

Time: 30 Minutes

Directions:
1. Have the class break up into small groups of 3–4 students.
2. Discuss the importance of not making fun of people with these symptoms, while emphasizing the importance of being able to identify the symptoms.
3. Give students 5 to 10 minutes to develop a skit where they show examples of positive, negative, and cognitive symptoms of schizophrenia.
4. Have each group perform their role-plays in front of the class while the rest of the class identify the symptoms with the assistance of their notes and textbook.

Summary: Students should be able to identify and apply the material they have learned about positive, negative, and cognitive symptoms of schizophrenia.

Questions to Students and Discussion: Do you think the role-plays accurately portrayed these symptoms? What specifics of any role-plays did you disagree with? What specifics of any role-plays did you heartily agree with? What do you think it would be like to live with these symptoms? Do you think the role-plays helped you learn to identify the symptoms? Why?

4. Limitations of DSM-IV-TR Criteria

Researchers point to drawbacks of the DSM-IV-TR criteria. They suggest that a more relevant set of symptoms would focus on the extent of cognitive deficits and the breadth and severity of symptoms. Limitations of the DSM-IV-TR include:

a. Absence of Focus on Cognitive and Social Functioning

- The criteria do not include the cognitive deficits, yet disorganized speech and behavior develop from cognitive deficits. For example, some people with schizophrenia have *loose associations,* where they skip from one topic to the next. Loose associations show how disorganized thinking can lead to disorganized speech.

- Cognitive deficits can lead to social difficulties. For example, people with schizophrenia may isolate themselves to avoid contact with others because they feel overwhelmed in social settings.

b. Categorical, Not Continual

- Currently, symptoms are listed as a category; that is, one does or does not have the symptom(s). However, researchers suggest that the symptoms should be located on a continuum so clinicians can note whether the symptoms are absent, mild, moderate, or severe.

- Symptoms could also be rated in three clusters: positive, disorganized, and negative. [See *Figure 12.1.*]

B. Subtypes of Schizophrenia

Types of schizophrenia are based on the presence or absence of certain symptoms, and the subtype can change over time depending on the shift in symptoms.

1. DSM-IV-TR Subtypes

There are five **DSM-IV-TR subtypes** of schizophrenia: paranoid, disorganized, catatonic, undifferentiated, and residual.

a. Paranoid Schizophrenia:

- *Paranoid schizophrenia* is a subtype of schizophrenia characterized by the presence of delusions and auditory hallucinations that are limited to specific topics that have a coherent paranoid or grandiose theme. (*Example:* A person believes the CIA is out to get him/her.)

- This subtype is commonly associated with aggressive behavior and also has the highest suicide rate of all of the schizophrenias (13%).

MEDIA RECOMMENDATION 12.6: Suffering from Paranoid Schizophrenia

Objective: To learn about cases of individuals with paranoid schizophrenia.

Time: 7 Minutes

Media and Discussion: 15 Minutes

Discussion Only: 8 Minutes

Listen Online: Search http://www.npr.org using the search terms "suffering from paranoid schizophrenia," or http://www.npr.org/templates/story/story.php?storyId=1025085
This audio clip discusses the difficulty in dealing with people who suffer from paranoid schizophrenia.

Summary: Students should be able to identify the client's delusions and highlight the difficulties families and professionals face when dealing with an individual with schizophrenia.

Questions to Students and Discussion: Describe the symptoms of paranoid schizophrenia discussed in the audio clip. What do you think about the difficulties the families and professionals face in treating schizophrenia? How do the laws both protect and hurt people with schizophrenia? What suggestions do you have to deal with these types of issues?

b. Disorganized Schizophrenia:

- *Disorganized schizophrenia* is a subtype of schizophrenia characterized by disorganized speech and behavior and inappropriate emotional expression. (*Example:* The person may giggle and dress inappropriately.)
- People with this type of schizophrenia have a poor prognosis because they require constant care. [See *Case 12.1.*]

c. Catatonic Schizophrenia:

- *Catatonic schizophrenia* is a subtype of schizophrenia characterized by stiff or "frozen" postures or poses, bizarre jerky movements, or frozen facial expression. (*Example:* The person may not speak or may repeat the words of others.)
- Individuals with catatonic schizophrenia need constant care.

d. Undifferentiated Schizophrenia:

Undifferentiated schizophrenia is a subtype of schizophrenia characterized by symptoms that do not completely match those specified for the paranoid, disorganized, or catatonic subtype.

e. Residual Schizophrenia:

- *Residual schizophrenia* is diagnosed when the positive and disorganized symptoms have subsided, but the individual still has negative symptoms (thus not meeting the full DSM-IV-TR criteria).
- This diagnosis may only apply for a short period of time or may last indefinitely.

2. Deficit/Nondeficit Subtypes

Deficit or nondeficit subtypes are alternative ways of looking at the DSM-IV-TR subtypes.

- An individual with a *deficit subtype* exhibits serious neurocognitive deficits in attention, memory, executive functioning and positive and negative symptoms. Those with the deficit subtype are more impaired than those with the nondeficit subtype and less likely to improve.
- The *nondeficit subtype* has mostly positive symptoms. Compared with the deficit subtype, this subtype is less impaired and has a better prognosis.

C. Distinguishing Between Schizophrenia and Other Disorders

Positive and negative symptoms can be present in nonschizophrenia disorders.

1. Psychotic Symptoms in Schizophrenia, Mood Disorders, and Substance-Related Disorders

- Hallucinations and delusions may be present in substance-related (during use or withdrawal) and mood disorders (during a mood episode). (*Example:* People with mania may have psychotic symptoms accompanying the mania symptoms; people with psychotic depression may experience delusions or hallucinations; or chronic use of stimulants may cause paranoid delusions.) [See *Table 12.2.*]

- These symptoms are distinguished from schizophrenia because they are caused by noncognitive deficits.
- People with schizophrenia can develop other comorbid disorders.

2. **Psychotic Disorders**

- *Psychotic disorders* require that psychotic symptoms are present.
- Psychotic disorders lie on a spectrum according to symptoms, duration, and severity.
- These disorders include schizophreniform disorder, brief psychotic disorder, schizoaffective disorder, delusional disorder, and shared psychotic disorder.

a. **Schizophreniform and Brief Psychotic Disorders:**

- Two disorders that do not meet the minimum 6-month duration criteria for schizophrenia are schizophreniform and brief psychotic disorders.
- *Schizophreniform disorder* is a psychotic disorder characterized by symptoms that meet all the criteria for schizophrenia *except* the symptoms have been present for only 1 to 6 months and daily functioning may or may not have declined over that period of time.
  - **i.** There may not be a decrease in daily functioning.
  - **ii.** If symptoms last 6 months, then a diagnosis of schizophrenia is given.
- *Brief psychotic disorder* is a psychotic disorder characterized by the sudden onset of positive or disorganized symptoms that last between a day and a month and are followed by a full recovery.
  - **i.** Negative symptoms are not present with this disorder.
  - **ii.** This disorder is marked by intense emotional episodes that make it difficult for the person to function and places the person at high risk for suicide.
  - **iii.** This disorder has a good prognosis for recovery.

b. **Schizoaffective Disorder:**

- *Schizoaffective disorder* is a psychotic disorder characterized by the presence of both schizophrenia *and* a depressive, manic, or mixed mood episode.
- Negative symptoms are less likely with this disorder.
- Since mood symptoms are a key feature of this disorder, there is a higher suicide risk.
- The prognosis for schizoaffective disorder is better than for schizophrenia.

c. **Delusional Disorder:**

- *Delusional disorder* is a psychotic disorder characterized by the presence of nonbizarre but demonstrably incorrect beliefs that have persisted for more than 1 month.
- The following are types of nonbizarre delusions:
  - **i.** *Erotomanic* is the belief that another person is in love with the client, the focus is on a romantic or spiritual connection, and the client may try to contact the person.
  - **ii.** *Grandiose* is the belief that one has a great talent or achievement (that has not been recognized).
  - **iii.** *Persecutory* is the belief that one is being spied on or harassed. People with this delusion may become violent toward the perceived threat.

iv. *Somatic* is the belief that the client is experiencing sensations or bodily malfunction. (*Example:* an odor coming from a part of the body)

v. *Jealous* is where the client believes his/her partner has been unfaithful when there is no evidence of it being true.

- People with delusional disorder may appear fully functioning when not discussing the delusion.

- The prognosis is mixed and tends to have a fluctuating impact on the client's life.

d. Shared Psychotic Disorder:

- *Shared psychotic disorder* is a psychotic disorder in which an individual develops delusions as a result of his or her close relationship with another person who has delusions as part of a psychotic disorder; also known as *folie à deux.*

- The "primary person" or original person with the disorder is usually diagnosed with schizophrenia or delusional disorder.

- The person with the shared psychotic disorder may still have the delusions even when the primary person no longer does.

e. Schizotypal Personality Disorder:

- **Schizotypal personality disorder** is marked by eccentric behaviors and relationship difficulties.

- Eccentric behaviors include unusual mannerisms, difficulty with eye contact, and difficulty with other social conventions. [See *Figure 12.2* and *Table 12.3.*]

LEARNING ACTIVITY 12.3: Exploring the Range of Psychotic Disorders

Objective: To find real-life examples of the range of psychotic disorders.

Time: 40 Minutes

Online Activity and Discussion: 60 Minutes

Discussion Only: 20 Minutes

Directions:
1. Have the class form small groups of 4 to 5 students.
2. Depending on the number of groups, assign each group 1 or 2 nonschizophrenia psychotic disorders (mood-related psychosis, substance-related psychosis, schizophrineform disorder, brief psychotic disorder, schizoaffective disorder, delusional disorder, shared psychotic disorder, or schizotypal personality disorder).
3. Ask students to find a real-life case of the disorder using the Internet (by searching Google or another search engine). Students should provide: real-life name(s), symptoms, and any additional important or interesting information.
4. Have student groups present the disorders they were assigned while the rest of the class fills in the chart in *Worksheet 12.1* located at the end of the chapter.

Summary: Students should begin to recognize the symptoms that help differentiate these disorders. Studying the real-life cases should help students improve their knowledge of each disorder.

Questions to Students and Discussion: What are some key differences among these disorders? What are some key similarities? Does the overlap among these disorders make them difficult to differentiate? Why or why not?

D. Schizophrenia Facts in Detail

This section discusses additional facts about schizophrenia:

- How common it is
- Disorders most frequently comorbid
- Related gender and cultural factors
- Prognosis for patients

1. Prevalence

- One percent of the population will develop schizophrenia at one point in their lives.
- In developed nations, schizophrenia is one of the top five causes of disability.
- In the United States, about 5% of people with schizophrenia are homeless and 6% are in jail or prison. [See *Figure 12.3.*]

2. Comorbidity

- Ninety percent of people with schizophrenia have at least one other disorder.
- The following are the most common comorbid disorders:

a. Mood Disorders and Anxiety Disorders:

- Eighty percent of people with schizophrenia also have a mood disorder, most commonly depression, and may meet the criteria for schizoaffective disorder.
- Some people also have anxiety problems and almost half of people have panic attacks.

b. Substance-Related Disorders:

- Sixty percent of people with schizophrenia have a non-tobacco-related substance-abuse problem.
- Ninety percent of people with schizophrenia smoke cigarettes and tend to inhale more deeply possibly, because the nicotine is self-medicating.
- Alcohol and other drugs may also help to relieve symptoms.
- A Swedish study on males found that those who smoked marijuana in adolescence were more likely to develop schizophrenia.
- A similar study on females with schizophrenia found that those who used marijuana by age 18 had more severe symptoms at age 26.
- Thus, research shows that frequent use of marijuana places someone at risk for schizophrenia or for more severe symptoms of schizophrenia; however, this research is only correlational.
- Another study found that marijuana use is associated with later psychosis and possibly predisposes one to developing schizophrenia.
- One study found that those with schizophrenia who used marijuana performed better on neuropsychological tests; thus marijuana has enhancing effects for some.
- fMRI studies show that marijuana use increases frontal lobe activity, which may compensate for the cognitive deficits found in those with schizophrenia.

3. Course

Schizophrenia develops in stages: It starts with the premorbid phase, leading to the prodromal phase, and finally to the active phase.

a. Premorbid Phase:

In the premorbid phase, individuals appear odd and eccentric and have difficulty interacting with others.

b. Prodromal Phase:

The *prodromal phase* may last from months to years; the individual exhibits suspiciousness, disorganized thinking, poor hygiene, anger, and social withdrawal. However, symptoms do not meet the level needed for a diagnosis of schizophrenia.

c. Active Phase:

The *active phase* (also called *episode of schizophrenia* or *psychotic episode*) features full-blown symptoms of schizophrenia. For up to 80% of people, symptoms go into remission with treatment. Although 60%–70% of people will have an additional episode, 30%–40% of people will never have a second episode.

d. Middle-to-Late Phase:

Cognitive functioning may decline during the first five years, which leads to disorganization and inability to care for oneself. Many begin to stabilize after 10 years, and after 30 years functioning may improve. [See *Table 12.4.*]

4. Gender Differences

- Men are at higher risk of developing schizophrenia than females, and the age of onset is earlier for males versus females (18–25 for males versus 26–45 for females).
- Women tend to have fewer negative but *more* mood symptoms.

5. Culture

- People in urban areas, of lower socioeconomic classes, and who are black are more likely to develop schizophrenia.
- People in non-Western countries have a better prognosis than those in Western countries. [See *Table 12.5.*]

6. Prognosis

- One-third improve, one-third stay the same, and one-third become disabled.
- Several factors are associated with a better prognosis in Western cultures. [See *Table 12.6.*]

a. Suicide:

- Ten percent to 15% of people with schizophrenia commit suicide, which places those with the disorder at a higher risk of death by suicide than other people.
- The paranoid subtype is the subtype with the highest rate of suicide.
- Risk factors for suicide include awareness of symptoms and effects, few negative symptoms, and pronounced positive symptoms.

b. Violence:

- Risk factors for violence include the male gender, comorbid substance abuse, medication noncompliance, and criminal or psychopathic history.
- Less than 10% of violent acts are caused by people with schizophrenia, mostly those who also abuse drugs and alcohol.
- Twenty percent of people with a psychotic disorder are more likely to be victims of violence.

II. UNDERSTANDING SCHIZOPHRENIA

Neuropsychological factors place people at risk for developing schizophrenia, while psychosocial factors contribute to the development of the disorder.

A. Neurological Factors in Schizophrenia

Neurological factors play a crucial role in schizophrenia, perhaps more so than for any other psychological disorder.

1. Brain Systems

- Autopsy studies have shown that people with schizophrenia have more atrophy and enlarged cerebrospinal ventricles.
- The enlarged ventricles cause a reduction in brain size. The smaller brain size can be seen prior to the development of the disorder.

a. A Frontal Lobe Defect?

- It appears that in people with schizophrenia, the brain excessively prunes connections in the frontal lobe.
- Some symptoms indicate abnormal activity in certain parts of the brain. (*Example:* Avolition is associated with too little activity in the left frontal lobe, and disorganized symptoms are associated with problems in the right frontal lobe.)

b. Impaired Temporal Lobe and Thalamus?

- Enlarged ventricles are associated with decreased size of the temporal lobes and thus affect the processing of auditory information, language, and visual recognition and may contribute to some of the positive symptoms (such as auditory hallucinations).
- The thalamus also appears to be smaller in people with schizophrenia and thus may affect a number of cognitive functions, such as attention, identification of relevant versus irrelevant stimuli, and memory.

c. Abnormal Hippocampus?

The hippocampi of people with schizophrenia (and their first-degree relatives) are smaller, and this may contribute to memory problems.

d. Interactions Among Brain Areas:

- Schizophrenia may be caused by disruptions in the frontal lobes, thalamus, and cerebellum. These disruptions cause the thalamus to be unable to fully screen out information, and thus this create confusion for the individual.
- Abnormal connections among the anterior cingulated cortex (involved in attention) and the hippocampus may contribute to the cognitive dysfunctions.

e. Possible Causes of Brain Abnormalities:

Several possible causes of the brain abnormalities listed here include maternal malnourishment or illness and oxygen deprivation.

(1) Maternal malnourishment:

Maternal malnourishment or poor diet during the first trimester may be a cause of brain abnormalities.

(2) Maternal illness and stress:

- *Maternal illness,* such as flu or a viral infection, during the sixth month of pregnancy may disrupt *cell migration* (when neurons establish their connections in the brain) and lead to abnormal connections.

- This problem rarely occurs among people who have no family history of schizophrenia.
- Maternal stress in the first trimester is also associated with schizophrenia.

(3) Oxygen deprivation:

Oxygen deprivation is inadequate oxygen before or during birth and is associated with smaller hippocampi in people with schizophrenia; however, not all babies who are oxygen deprived develop schizophrenia.

f. Biological Markers:

- A *biological marker* is a neurological, bodily, or behavioral characteristic that distinguishes people with a psychological disorder (or a first-degree relative with the disorder) from those without the disorder.
- *Smooth pursuit eye movement* is one distinct biological marker for schizophrenia. It is the inability to maintain smooth eye movement while tracking a light. This difficulty is due to neurological and irregular brain activities. [See *Figure 12.4*.]
- *Sensory gating,* or the ability to screen out information, is decreased in people with schizophrenia. When hearing two clicks, one right after the next, people with schizophrenia respond just as strongly to the second click as they do to the first click. Most people respond less to the second click.
- Another biological marker is involuntary movements—such as writhing or excessive movement of the tongue, lips, or arms—taking place from birth to age 2, and sometimes during adolescence.
  i. Some children also are more likely to cry when coming into contact with adults.
  ii. A Finnish study found that those with schizophrenia had poorer performance in sports and handicrafts (activities that require muscle coordination) but not other academic subjects.

2. Neural Communication

Neural communication involves a complex interplay of dopamine, serotonin, glutamate, cortisol, and possibly sex hormones.

a. Dopamine:

- Neuroimaging studies have found fewer **dopamine** receptors and an increase in dopamine production in the striatum.
- The *dopamine hypothesis* is the view that schizophrenia arises from an overproduction of dopamine or an increase in the number or sensitivity of dopamine receptors and triggers unrelated thoughts, feelings, and perceptions.
- Delusions are an attempt to organize these unrelated thoughts.
- Support for this hypothesis comes from research on dopamine-reducing medications, which decrease the positive symptoms, and from studies on people without schizophrenia who take LSD and report schizophrenic-like symptoms.
- Dopamine effects, and is affected by, other neurotransmitters.

b. Serotonin and Glutamate:

- **Serotonin** enhances the effects of glutamate (the most common, fast-acting excitatory transmitter), which may affect the glutamate receptor N-methyl-D-asparate (NMDA), which in turn affects learning and memory.
- High levels of **glutamate** in the frontal lobe have been found in people with schizophrenia, and this disrupts neural activity and impairs cognitive activities such as memory.

c. Stress and Cortisol:

- People with schizophrenia have a stronger reaction to **stress** and a higher **cortisol** baseline.
- A study found that during adolescence those with schizotypal disorder showed an increase in cortisol levels that may affect dopamine levels.

d. Effects of Estrogen:

- *Estrogen protection hypothesis* argues that **estrogen** positively affects the dopamine and serotonin levels in women and may explain why women have a later onset than men.
- Support for this hypothesis is that women with schizophrenia who have higher levels of estrogen have better cognitive functioning. Also, an estrogen skin patch reduced positive symptoms more so than did antipsychotic medications.

3. Genetics

- Genes play a role in schizophrenia. [See *Table 12.7.*]
- A family history of the disorder is the strongest predictor, but 85% of people with a parent or sibling with the disorder do not develop schizophrenia.
- Of co-twins, 46%–53% develop schizophrenia, indicating there must be other factors that lead to the development of this disorder even though both twins have the same *predisposition.*
- Children born to older fathers who are 45 years or older are three times more likely to develop schizophrenia than children born to fathers between the ages of 20 and 24. Researchers think a mutation in sperm produced by older men may be the culprit.
- Researchers are trying to identify the specific genes that cause schizophrenia. Thus far, researchers have found a mutated gene responsible for the symptoms of agitation.
- A Finnish study compared adopted children with a biological mother with schizophrenia and a control group. Of adopted children who had mothers with schizophrenia, those who were raised in a dysfunctional home were more likely to develop schizophrenia than those adopted into a nondysfunctional home. Thus, quality parenting seems to protect children from developing schizophrenia.

LEARNING ACTIVITY 12.4: Exploring the Biological Causes of Schizophrenia

Objective: To explore a number of biological causes of schizophrenia.

Time: 40 Minutes

Activity and Discussion: 1 Hour and 20 Minutes

Discussion Only: 40 Minutes

Directions:
1. Have students search the Genes to Cognition Web site to explore the multiple biological causes of schizophrenia, or http://www.g2conline.org/#Schizophrenia?aid=819&cid=520.
2. Direct students to read about three different biological causes of schizophrenia.
3. Then have students share their findings in class using the boldface headings in the book: Brain Systems, Neural Communication, and Genetics.

The Genes to Cognition Web site explores multiple factors that affect the development of schizophrenia. The Web site includes interviews with experts and more.

Summary: Students will gain awareness of the multiple biological explanations of schizophrenia.

Questions to Students and Discussion: Are you surprised by the number of biological causes? Why or why not? How do the biological causes impact the psychological and social factors? What surprised you about this exercise?

LECTURE ENHANCEMENT 12.1: Childhood Onset Schizophrenia and Brain Wiring

Objective: To learn about structural differences in the brains of those with childhood-onset schizophrenia.

Time: 20 Minutes

Lecture Points:
I. Background of study
   A. Twelve children with childhood-onset schizophrenia (COS) were compared to 12 children without schizophrenia over five years using magnetic resonance imaging.
   B. Tensor-based morphometry, developed by UCLA's Paul Thompson, superimposes the MRI scans onto another as the child develops.
II. Findings
   A. Those with COS had a 2.2% slower growth of white matter on the right side of the brain as compared to the controls.
   B. Those with COS who had a higher amount of white matter growth had better brain functioning and prognosis.
   C. The reduced white matter decreases the efficiency of nerve signals.

Note to Instructor: The following source also contains colorful images and video of these changes.

Source: Asher, J. (2008). *Brain's wiring stunted, lopsided in childhood onset schizophrenia: Front-to-back wave envelopes brain as child grows up.* National Institute of Mental Health, from http://www.nimh.nih.gov/science-news/2008/brains-wiring-stunted-lopsided-in-childhood-onset-schizophrenia.shtml.

Summary: Students will be surprised to learn about how white matter affects brain functioning and prognosis.

Questions to Students and Discussion: What role does white matter play in the function of the neuron? Why might the deterioration of white matter affect prognosis and functioning? What more would you like to know about the causes of childhood schizophrenia?

B. Psychological Factors in Schizophrenia

Schizophrenia arises from a combination of factors: For people with the disorder, neurocognitive deficits can also affect how the social world is perceived. Psychological underpinnings can influence the development of schizophrenia, despite the odds against this outcome.

1. Mental Processes and Cognitive Difficulties: Attention, Memory, and Executive Functions

- Cognitive difficulties arise prior to other symptoms appearing and remain after other symptoms are alleviated.
- Difficulties can occur with attention, making it difficult to discern between important and unimportant stimuli.

- Problems with memory lead to issues with problem-solving, planning, and judgment.
- People may also exhibit a *lack of insight* or awareness that they are having problems. [See *Case 12.2.*]

2. **Beliefs and Attributions**

- Children who exhibit these cognitive dysfunctions may experience peer rejection and may believe they are inferior and thus withdraw from others.
- The delusions can affect what the person pays attention to and believes is true. (*Example:* believing that a bad phone connection is due to FBI interference)
- Those with paranoid schizophrenia may tend to blame events on others, especially if it relates to the delusions. (*Example:* believing the FBI delayed a train from coming)
- People with schizophrenia do not tend to question the source of their auditory hallucinations and thus are more likely to believe what they hear.
- Those with negative symptoms tend to have lower expectations of themselves; cognitive therapy can effectively address this problem.

3. **Emotional Expression**

- People with schizophrenia have less intense facial expressions and are less accurate in correctly labeling the emotions of others.
- People with schizophrenia have problems reading nonverbal cues such as vocal tone, facial expression, and body language.
- These challenges can also be seen in the relatives of those with schizophrenia.

C. Social Factors in Schizophrenia

This section examines the difficulties in navigating the social world with schizophrenia and the influences of economic circumstances and cultural factors.

1. **Understanding the Social World**

- *Theory of mind* is a theory about other people's mental states (their beliefs, desires, and feelings) that allows a person to predict how other people will react in a given situation.
- People with schizophrenia have difficulty accurately understanding the theory of mind, and symptoms of paranoia and social withdrawal may be a natural result of this difficulty.

MEDIA RECOMMENDATION 12.7: Theory of Mind

Objective: To learn more about the interpersonal difficulties that people with schizophrenia have with the theory of mind.

Time: 2 Minutes

Media and Discussion: 10 Minutes

Discussion Only: 8 Minutes

Watch Online: Go to the Genes to Cognition Web site, http://www.g2conline.org, click on "schizophrenia," and then locate "Theory of Mind" on the network map, or http://www.g2conline.org/#Schizophrenia?aid=1119&cid=767

Dr. Sukhi Shergill discusses the difficulties that people with schizophrenia have when trying to understand what other people are thinking.

Summary: Students will learn about the theory of mind on a deeper level and connect the concepts from the text to the discussion by Dr. Shergill.

Questions to Students and Discussion: Why are theory of mind skills so useful? What do you think it would be like to have to live without those skills? How do you think the lack of these skills might contribute to some of the symptoms of schizophrenia?

2. **Stressful Groups**

   - Children who grow up in an orphanage are more likely to develop schizophrenia if they are genetically predisposed, even when compared to those who instead are adopted and have the genetic predisposition.
   - Families can create a stressful environment if they have high amount of expressed emotion.
     i. ***High expressed emotion (high EE)*** is a family interaction style characterized by hostility, unnecessary criticism, or emotional overinvolvement.
     ii. High expressed emotion does not cause schizophrenia and thus the research is only correlational.
     iii. There are ethnic differences in these findings; African American family members with schizophrenia actually have a better outcome with high expressed emotion.

3. **Immigration**

   - Being an immigrant places someone at a larger risk for developing schizophrenia.
   - Researchers are still looking for an explanation for this finding. [See *Case 12.3.*]

4. **Economic Factors**

   - Schizophrenia is more common among people living in urban areas and those from lower socioeconomic groups.
   - *Social selection* is the hypothesis that those who are mentally ill "drift" to a lower socioeconomic level because of their impairments.
   - *Social causation* is the hypothesis that the daily stressors of urban life, especially as experienced by people in a lower socioeconomic level, trigger mental illness in those who are vulnerable.
   - A study in Ireland found no difference in rates of schizophrenia among children in different social classes, but a study in Israel found higher rates among those in poorer groups.

5. **Cultural Factors: Recovery in Different Countries**

   - People from developing groups have higher rates of recovery as compared to people from industrialized countries, possibly because developing countries are more *collectivist* (emphasizing the group over the individual).
   - People in collectivist cultures might be more tolerant and supportive and have higher expectations for those with schizophrenia.

6. **FEEDBACK LOOPS IN ACTION: Schizophrenia**

   - Social factors, such as economics, may affect psychological and neurological factors.
   - Parent communication style affects children with a higher genetic risk for developing schizophrenia. [See *Figure 12.5.*]

- People with a genetic predisposition for schizophrenia *may* produce too much, or be too sensitive to, stress hormones. Social withdrawal might be a coping mechanism to deal with the stress, especially since people with schizophrenia have fewer cognitive resources to cope with stressors.

III. TREATING SCHIZOPHRENIA

There are four steps of treatment for schizophrenia, each targeting specific symptoms. The steps are:

STEP 1: Reduce the positive symptoms.
STEP 2: Reduce the negative symptoms.
STEP 3: Improve neurocognitive functioning.
STEP 4: Reduce problems with daily functioning.

A. Targeting Neurological Factors in Treating Schizophrenia

Currently most treatments focus on Steps 1 and 2 (reducing the positive and negative symptoms), although some treatments do focus on improving cognitive function.

1. Medication

- Thorazine was the first antipsychotic medication (also called a *neuroleptic*) and was developed in the 1950s.
- Various other antipsychotic medications have been developed, and each has its own side effects.

a. Traditional Antipsychotics:

- Dopamine antagonists, such as *Thorazine* (chlorpromazine) and other similar antipsychotics, block the action of dopamine.
- 75% to 80% of people with schizophrenia will have a decrease in positive symptoms.
- These traditional medications are the first response and lower the chance of relapse: Only 25% of those on traditional antipsychotics relapse versus a 65%–80% relapse rate for those not on medication.
- The medications cause sedation and are effective after 5 days to 6 weeks.
- *Tardive dyskinesia* is an unfortunate, enduring side effect of traditional antipsychotic medications that produces involuntary lip smacking and odd facial contortions as well as other movement-related symptoms. Tardive dyskinesia:
  i. Does not go away after stopping the medication, but can be reduced by other medications
  ii. In some cases, is part of the symptoms of schizophrenia and is not due to the medication
- Additional side effects of traditional antipsychotics include tremors, weight gain, and a sense of physical restlessness.

b. Atypical Antipsychotics: A New Generation:

- *Atypical antipsychotics* are a relatively new class of antipsychotic medications that affect dopamine and serotonin activity but create fewer movement-related side effects than do traditional antipsychotics; also referred to as *second-generation antipsychotics.*
- Atypical antipsychotics affect serotonin and dopamine but do not affect the motor areas of the brain as much as traditional antipsychotics.

- Atypical antipsychotics include *Risperdal* (risperidone), *Zyprexa* (olanzapine), and *Seroquel* (quetiapine).
- Long-term use will show a reduction in positive and negative symptoms. Research is mixed on the effects of these medications in reducing cognitive symptoms. The advantages and disadvantages of these medications follow.
- Advantages of atypical antipsychotics:
  - **i.** No tendency toward tardive dyskinesia
  - **ii.** Reduced comorbid anxiety and depression
  - **iii.** Improved daily functioning
- Similar advantage of both typical and atypical antipsychotics:
  - **i.** Decreased likelihood of relapse at least for one year
- Medical disadvantages of atypical antipsychotics:
  - **i.** Significant weight gain
  - **ii.** Increased risk of heart problems
  - **iii.** Side effects becoming so problematic that some people discontinue the medications
- The Clinical Antipsychotic Trials of Intervention Effectiveness (CATIE) research program was a large-scale study that included a wide range of patients over an 18-month period. Comparing traditional and atypical antipsychotics, the trials found that more than two-thirds of patients stopped taking their medications because either the medications didn't help or there were too many side effects.
- *Noncompliance* is when patients stop taking their medication without consulting their doctor.
- One study had healthy participants take a traditional antipsychotic (haloperidol), an atypical antipsychotic (risperidone), and a placebo. The side effects reflected the negative symptoms of schizophrenia, such as alogia due to drowsiness.
- Medications are needed that have fewer side effects and are more tolerable.

c. Discontinuing Medication:

- A study found that, of those who were noncompliant with their medication after 1 year of stability, 78% had symptoms return within 1 year after that time and 96% had symptoms return after 2 years' time.
- Those hospitalized and then discontinuing their medication were five times more likely to relapse.

d. Preventive Medication?

- Research has shown that those who receive medication after the first psychotic episode tend to have a better prognosis. Thus, some wonder if early and aggressive treatment might help reduce the overall long-term damage of schizophrenia to the brain.
- Risperidone was given to at-risk groups and decreased positive symptoms. However, some are hesitant to give children and adolescents such medication because it is unclear how it affects their developing brains.

2. Brain Stimulation: ECT and TMS

- When medication is not helpful, ECT may be administered. However, the effects are not long lasting.
- There is mixed support for the use of transcranial magnetic stimulation (TMS) to decrease hallucinations.

MEDIA RECOMMENDATION 12.8: Neurological Treatments for Schizophrenia

Objective: To learn about the various medical treatments of schizophrenia.

Time: 7:30 Minutes

Media and Discussion: 35 Minutes

Discussion Only: 25 Minutes

Watch Online: Go to the Genes to Cognition online Web site, click on "schizophrenia," and then click on the "Treatments for Schizophrenia" link on the network map, or http://www.g2conline.org/# Schizophrenia?aid=1185&cid=9. The following are just a few of the videos included on the Web site:
1. *Typical and Atypical Medications,* discussed by Professor Jeffrey Lieberman; Time: 2 Minutes.
2. Professor David Lewis discusses how it is easier to treat positive symptoms; Time: 2 Minutes.
3. Professor Jeffrey Lieberman discusses the importance of early intervention; Time: 2 Minutes.
4. Professor David Lewis discusses the response to antipsychotic medication; Time: 1:30 Minutes.

Note to Instructor: You may want to pick and choose from these resources.

Summary: Students will become aware of the number of treatments for schizophrenia. Students will also learn about the advantages and disadvantages of such treatments.

Questions to Students and Discussion: What are the advantages and disadvantages of the various treatments? Which treatment seems most appealing? Why? Which treatment seems least appealing? Why?

B. Targeting Psychological Factors in Treating Schizophrenia

There are four general treatments that target psychological factors:

- Cognitive-behavior therapy (CBT) to reduce psychotic symptoms
- CBT to reduce negative symptoms
- Cognitive rehabilitation to improve neurocognitive functioning
- Psychoeducation and motivational enhancement to improve quality of life and daily functioning

1. Cognitive-Behavior Therapy

- **Cognitive-behavior therapy (CBT)** helps clients manage symptoms by:
    - **i.** Distinguishing hallucinatory voices from real voices
    - **ii.** Emphasizing the importance of medication compliance
    - **iii.** Developing coping strategies
- CBT therapists do not challenge the delusions but address problems that arise from the delusions.
- CBT does improve overall functioning and decreases positive symptoms.

2. Cognitive Rehabilitation

- *Cognitive rehabilitation* is a form of psychological treatment that is designed to strengthen cognitive abilities through extensive and focused practice; also called *neurocognitive remediation* or *cognitive mediation.*
- Research has shown that cognitive rehabilitation improves attentional control (shifting and sustaining), reasoning ability, and mental flexibility.

3. Treating Comorbid Substance Abuse: Motivational Enhancement

Treatment that focuses on motivational enhancement helps clients develop and work toward their goals. (*Example:* One goal might be to take medication regularly.)

C. Targeting Social Factors in Treating Schizophrenia

Treatments that target social factors:

- Identify warning signs through family education and therapy, hospitalizing people who are unable to care for themselves
- Reduce some negative symptoms through social skills training
- Improve functioning and quality of life through community-based interventions

1. Family Education and Therapy

- Psychoeducation provides information to families about the illness, including recognizing consequences of the illness, signs of relapse, and side effects of medication, as well as how to manage crises. This knowledge can help to decrease the chance of relapse.
- Family-based treatments can also provide emotional support and more adaptive family interaction patterns.
- Family therapy can also reduce the high EE patterns, which lowers the relapse rate from 75% to 40%; but as discussed earlier families of certain cultures benefit from high EE.

2. Group Therapy: Social Skills Training

- **Social skills training** focuses on learning to "read" other people's behaviors, expected behaviors in certain situations, and adaptive responses to others.
- The training breaks down the complex behaviors, teaches specific components, and utilizes role-plays. (*Examples:* eye contact, taking turns speaking, adjusting voice loudness)
- Cognitive techniques focus on irrational beliefs, knowledge of social conventions, and underlying beliefs.
- Research shows that social skills training improves daily functioning; it has not been shown to prevent relapse or increase employment.

3. Inpatient Treatment

- Short- or long-term hospitalization may be necessary to stabilize the patient. Once the risk is reduced the patient will be discharged.
- Laws make it difficult to hospitalize people against their will; however, because of the nature of the disorder people may not realize they need help.

4. Minimizing Hospitalizations: Community-Based Interventions

- Many people with schizophrenia were institutionalized until the development of antipsychotic medication in the 1960s.
- As a result, *deinstitutionalization* became social policy, trying to help those with mental illness live in the community instead of a hospital; many were sent out without adequate resources and thus are now homeless.
- Some communities have developed programs to help those with serious disorders.

• *Community care* refers to programs that allow mental health care providers to visit patients in their homes at any time of the day or night; also known as *assertive community treatment*. Patients in these programs report greater satisfaction. However, treatments may not lead to better outcomes.

LECTURE ENHANCEMENT 12.2: Schizophrenia and Homelessness

Objective: To learn about how to help those with schizophrenia who are homeless.

Time: 20 Minutes

Lecture Points:
I.   The Homeless and the Mentally Ill
   A. Sixteen percent of homeless adults have a severe mental illness.
   B. In larger cities, the percentage can be as high as 35%.
   C. About 10 % of the homeless have schizophrenia.
II. Why Are Those with Mental Illness Homeless?
   A. It is difficult to find employment if one is mentally ill.
   B. Many homeless people with a mental illness have poor health.
   C. Many may be involved in the legal system.
III. Characteristics of Helpful Programs
   A. Respect for the individuals
   B. Help with finding adequate housing
   C. Help finding treatment
IV. Challenges to Effective Treatments
   A. A study found that homeless people have bad experiences with housing programs.
   B. Many feel they have been treated in a disrespectful manner and haven't been listened to.

Source: Price, M. (2009). More than shelter: Psychologists look at what it takes to get mentally ill homeless people into more stable environments. *Monitor on Psychology, 40*(11), 59–62.

Summary: Students will be surprised to learn about the number of homeless people who are mentally ill. Students should gain knowledge about more effective ways to address this issue.

Questions to Students and Discussion: Have you noticed the number of mentally ill people who are homeless in your own community? What have you observed? What does your community do to address this issue? What do you think *you* can do to address this issue? What role does the discovery of psychotropic medications play in this problem?

   a. Residential settings:
     • Highly supervised housing refers to a small number of people living with a staff member in a structured setting. (*Example:* Members take turns shopping, cooking, and doing chores and attend weekly scheduled meetings.)
     • Some settings include living in an apartment with other people with similar abilities and with a staff member who oversees.
     • Independent living refers to when a staff member has home visits in the patient's living quarters.
   b. Vocational rehabilitation:
     • *Sheltered employment* is designed to help people with emotional or intellectual problems find certain types of work (*Example:* in a hospital coffee shop or creating crafts).

- *Supported employment programs* place people with less severe symptoms in regular settings using a job coach to help them adjust. (*Example:* warehouse packaging or restocking)

5. **FEEDBACK LOOPS IN TREATMENT: Schizophrenia**

- Neurological, psychological, and social treatments are all necessary for those with schizophrenia.

- Changes in neurological and psychological factors can make social treatments more effective.

- Treatments that target psychological factors reduce symptoms and improve overall functioning.

- Social factors focus on improving family interactions, which may influence neurological functioning.

- Medication helps to alleviate some symptoms, but psychosocial treatments play an important role. [See *Figure 12.6.*]

ADDITIONAL READINGS

Journal Articles

Aghevli, M. A., Blanchard, J. J., & Horan, W. P. (2003). The expression and experience of emotion in schizophrenia: A study of social interactions. *Psychiatry Research, 119,* 261–270.

Andreasen, N. C., Arndt, S., Swayze, V., Cizadlo, T., Flaum, M., O'Leary, D., Ehrhardt, J. C., & Yuh, W. T. (1994). Thalamic abnormalities in schizophrenia visualized through magnetic resonance image averaging. *Science, 266,* 294–298.

Beck, A. T., & Rector, N. A. (2005). Cognitive approaches to schizophrenia: Theory and therapy. *Annual Review of Clinical Psychology, 1,* 577–606.

Brunelin, J., d'Amato, T., Brun, P., Bediou, B., Kallel, L., Senn, M., Poulet, E., & Saoud, M. (2007). Impaired verbal source monitoring in schizophrenia: An intermediate trait vulnerability marker? *Schizophrenia Research, 89,* 287–292.

Chattopadhyay, S. (2005). Do schizophrenics experience emotion but differ in expression? *Internet Journal of Mental Health, 2,* 1–6.

Freedman, R. (2008). Cannabis, inhibitory neurons, and the progressive course of schizophrenia. *American Journal of Psychiatry, 165*(4), 416–419.

Khashan, A. S., Abel, K. M., McNamee, R., Pedersen, M. G., Webb, R. T., Baker, P. N., Kenny, L. C., & Mortensen, P. B. (2008). Higher risk of offspring schizophrenia following antenatal maternal exposure to severe adverse life events. *Archives of General Psychiatry, 65,* 146–152.

Kurtz, M. M., & Mueser, K. T. (2008). A meta-analysis of controlled research on social skills training for schizophrenia. *Journal of Consulting and Clinical Psychology, 76,* 491–504.

Rosenfarb, I. S., Bellack, A. S., & Aziz, N. (2006). Family interactions and the course of schizophrenia in African American and white patients. *Journal of Abnormal Psychology, 115,* 112–120.

Tamminga, C. A. (2006). Practical treatment information for schizophrenia. *American Journal of Psychiatry, 163,* 563–565.

Books and Memoirs on Schizophrenia and Other Psychotic Disorders

Compton, K. A. (2007). *Discombobulated: An inspiring journey of hope through mental illness.* Victoria, BC: Trafford.
>A woman describes her journey from diagnosis to treatment of schizoaffective disorder.

McLean, R. (2005). *Recovered, not cured: A journey through schizophrenia.* Sydney: Allen & Unwin.
>An Australian man describes his experience with paranoia, and how he still managed to graduate from college and travel.

Saks, E. R. (2008). *The center cannot hold: My journey through madness.* New York: Hyperion.
>A law and psychiatry professor describes her experience living with paranoid schizophrenia.

Schiller, L., & Bennett, A. (1994). *The quiet room: A journey out of the torment of madness.* New York: Warner Books.
>A powerful book that explores the underlying social causes of schizophrenia.

Stafford, C. (2004). *The sublime detour: My experience with madness, the true story of Chad Stafford's hallucinations.* Baltimore, MD: Publish America.
>A man describes life with schizoaffective disorder.

ADDITIONAL MEDIA RECOMMENDATIONS

Howard, R. [Director]. (2001). *A beautiful mind.* [Film]. USA: Universal.
>Mathematician John Nash's experiences with visual hallucinations and powerful delusions.

Kelly, R. [Director & Writer]. (2001). *Donnie Darko.* [Film]. USA: 20th Century Fox Home Entertainment.
>A high school student suffers from intense visions of the future.

McGrath, P. [Writer]. (2002). *Spider.* [Film]. USA: Columbia TriStar Home Entertainment.
>This amazing film shows how realistic hallucinations and delusions can be, as experienced by a man who moves into a halfway house.

Murdock, D., Navasky, M., & O'Connor, K. [Producers]. (2002). *Frontline: A crime of insanity.* [Television series episode]. Boston: WGBH Educational Foundation, http://www.pbs.org/wgbh/pages/frontline/shows/crime/
>The true story of Ralph Tortorici, a man who, suffering from paranoid schizophrenia, committed a crime and became caught in conflicts among the legal and psychiatric systems.

Navasky, M., & O'Connor, K. (2005). *Frontline: The new asylums.* [Television series episode]. Boston: WGBH Educational Foundation, http://www.pbs.org/wgbh/pages/frontline/shows/asylums/
>This free film explores how the mentally ill are being housed in our nation's prison system.

Negroponte, M. [Director]. (1995). *Jupiter's wife.* [Film]. New York: New Video Group.
>This documentary explores the truth story of Maggie, a homeless woman living in Central Park.

Whol, I., & Cadigan, K. [Producers]. (2007). *People say I'm crazy.* [Film]. Princeton, NJ: Films for the Humanities & Sciences.
>A documentary made by an artist with schizophrenia. Official Web site: http://www.peoplesayimcrazy.org/

WEB SITES

Mental Health.Net Schizophrenia: Includes a list of videos, resources, and books. See: http://www.mentalhelp.net/poc/center_index.php?id=7

National Alliance for Research on Schizophrenia and Depression: Learn about prevention research for schizophrenia, bipolar disorder, and depression. See: http://www.narsad.org/index.php

Schizophrenia.com: Provides in-depth information, support and education related to schizophrenia, including videos and prevention materials. See: http://www.schizophrenia.com/

Schizophrenia Society of Canada: Contains educational materials, newsletters, resources, and links. See: http://www.schizophrenia.ca/heimEnglish1.htm

WORKSHEET 12.1

	Symptoms	Case example(s)
Mood-related		
Substance-related		
Schizophreniform		
Brief psychotic		
Schizo-affective		
Delusional		
Shared psychotic		
Schizotypal personality		

Personality Disorders

CHAPTER OUTLINE

CHAPTER HEADINGS	INSTRUCTION IDEAS AND TEXTBOOK CORRELATIONS
Chapter Introduction	**Learning Objective:** 13.1
DIAGNOSING PERSONALITY DISORDERS	
What Are Personality Disorders?	**Learning Objectives:** 13.2, 13.3, 13.4, 13.5, 13.6 **Learning Concepts:** why are personality disorders on Axis II instead of Axis I? assessing personality disorders, DSM-IV-TR personality clusters, criticisms of the DSM-IV-TR category of personality disorders **Media Recommendation 13.1:** Dancing Daniel **Media Recommendation 13.2:** Personality Disorders Mnemonics **Textbook Tools:** Figure 13.1; Tables 13.1, 13.2, 13.3; Case 13.1
Understanding Personality Disorders in General	**Learning Objectives:** 13.7, 13.8, 13.9, 13.10, 13.11 **Learning Concepts:** neurological factors in personality disorders: genes and temperament; psychological factors in personality disorders: temperament and the consequences of behavior; the role of temperament; the consequences of behavior; social factors in personality disorders: insecurely attached; feedback loops in action: understanding personality disorders **Learning Activity 13.1:** Dimensions of Temperament and Character **Textbook Tools:** Figures 13.2, 13.3
Treating Personality Disorders: General Issues	**Learning Objective:** 13.12 **Learning Concepts:** targeting neurological factors in personality disorders, targeting psychological factors in personality disorders, targeting social factors in personality disorders
ODD/ECCENTRIC PERSONALITY DISORDERS	
Paranoid Personality Disorder	**Learning Objective:** 13.13 **Media Recommendation 13.3:** Paranoid Personality Disorder Dramatization

	Media Recommendation 13.4: What Is Paranoid Personality Disorder? **Tools:** Tables 13.4, 13.5; Case 13.2
Schizoid Personality Disorder	**Learning Objective:** 13.14 **Media Recommendation 13.5:** What Is Schizoid Personality Disorder? **Textbook Tools:** Tables 13.6, 13.7; Case 13.3 **Worth Video Tool Kit for Abnormal Psychology:** Paranoid Personality Disorder
Schizotypal Personality Disorder	
What is Schizotypal Personality Disorder?	**Learning Objectives:** 13.15, 13.16 **Learning Concepts:** what is schizotypal personality disorder? distinguishing between schizotypal personality disorder and other disorders **Media Recommendation 13.6:** What Is Schizotypal Personality Disorder? **Textbook Tools:** Tables 13.8, 13.9; Case 13.4
Understanding Odd/Eccentric Personality Disorders	**Learning Objective:** 13.17 **Learning Concepts:** neurological factors in odd/eccentric personality disorders, psychological factors in odd/eccentric personality disorders, social factors in odd/eccentric personality disorders, feedback loops in action: understanding schizotypal personality disorder **Textbook Tools:** Figure 13.4; Table 13.10
Treating Odd/Eccentric Personality Disorders	**Learning Objective:** 13.17 **Learning Activity 13.2:** Compare and Contrast Cluster A Personality Disorders
DRAMATIC/ERRATIC PERSONALITY DISORDERS	
Antisocial Personality Disorder	**Learning Objectives:** 13.18, 13.19, 13.20, 13.21 **Learning Concepts:** the role of conduct disorder, psychopathy: is it different than antisocial personality disorder? understanding antisocial personality disorder, neurological factors in antisocial personality disorder and psychopathy, brain systems, neural communication, genetics, psychological factors in antisocial personality disorder and psychopathy, social factors in antisocial personality disorder and psychopathy, feedback loops in action: antisocial personality disorder and psychopathy, treating antisocial personality disorder and psychopathy **Media Recommendation 13.7:** What Is Antisocial Personality Disorder? **Learning Activity 13.3:** The Law and Mrs. Shelton **Textbook Tools:** Figures 13.5, 13.6, 13.7; Tables 13.11, 13.12, 13.13; Case 13.5
Borderline Personality Disorder	**Learning Objectives:** 13.22, 13.23, 13.24 **Learning Concepts:** distinguishing between borderline personality disorder and other disorders, understanding borderline personality disorder, neurological factors: born to be wild? brain systems, neural

	communication, genetics, psychological factors: emotions on a yo-yo, social factors: invalidation, feedback loops in action: understanding borderline personality disorder, treating borderline personality disorder: new treatments, targeting neurological factors: medication, targeting psychological factors: dialectical behavior therapy, targeting social factors: interpersonal therapy, feedback loops in treatment: borderline personality disorder **Media Recommendation 13.8:** What Is Borderline Personality Disorder? **Lecture Enhancement 13.1:** Self-Injury **Learning Activity 13.4:** Soothe-and-Share Kits **Lecture Enhancement 13.2:** Dialectical Behavior Therapy **Textbook Tools:** Figures 13.8, 13.9; Tables 13.14, 13.15; Case 13.6
Histrionic Personality Disorder	**Learning Objectives:** 13.25, 13.26 **Learning Concepts:** what is histrionic personality disorder? distinguishing between histrionic personality disorder and other disorders, understanding histrionic personality disorder, treating histrionic personality disorder **Media Recommendation 13.9:** What Is Histrionic Personality Disorder? **Textbook Tools:** Tables 13.16, 13.17; Case 13.7
Narcissistic Personality Disorder	**Learning Objectives:** 13.27, 13.28 **Learning Concepts:** understanding narcissistic personality disorder, treating narcissistic personality disorder **Media Recommendation 13.10:** What Is Narcissistic Personality Disorder? **Learning Activity 13.5:** Compare and Contrast Cluster B Personality Disorders **Textbook Tools:** Tables 13.18, 13.19, 13.20; Case 13.8 **Worth Video Tool Kit for Abnormal Psychology:** Histrionic Personality Disorder
FEARFUL/ANXIOUS PERSONALITY DISORDERS	
Avoidant Personality Disorder	**Learning Objectives:** 13.29, 13.30 **Learning Concepts:** what is avoidant personality disorder? distinguishing between avoidant personality disorder and other disorders **Media Recommendation 13.11:** What Is Avoidant Personality Disorder? **Textbook Tools:** Tables 13.21, 13.22; Case 13.9
Dependent Personality Disorder	**Learning Objectives:** 13.31, 13.32 **Learning Concepts:** what is dependent personality disorder? distinguishing between dependent personality disorder and other disorders **Media Recommendation 13.12:** What Is Dependent Personality Disorder? **Textbook Tools:** Tables 13.23, 13.24; Case 13.10

Obsessive-Compulsive Personality Disorder	**Learning Objectives:** 13.33, 13.34 **Learning Concepts:** what is obsessive-compulsive personality disorder? distinguishing between obsessive-compulsive personality disorder and other disorders **Media Recommendation 13.13:** What Is Obsessive-Compulsive Personality Disorder? **Textbook Tools:** Tables 13.25, 13.26; Case 13.11
Understanding Fearful/Anxious Personality Disorders	**Learning Objective:** 13.35 **Textbook Tool:** Table 13.27
Treating Fearful/Anxious Personality Disorders	**Learning Objective:** 13.35 **Learning Activity 13.6:** Compare and Contrast Cluster C Personality Disorders **Textbook Tool:** Table 13.28
FOLLOW-UP ON RACHEL REILAND	

LEARNING OBJECTIVES

After reading this chapter, students will be able to:

13.1 Define personality disorders.

13.2 Articulate the diagnostic criteria for personality disorders.

13.3 Describe the differences and similarities between Axis I and Axis II disorders.

13.4 Explain how psychologists assess personality disorders.

13.5 Describe the three clusters of personality disorders.

13.6 Articulate some of the major criticisms of the DSM-IV-TR category of personality disorders.

13.7 Describe the neurological role of genes and temperament in understanding personality disorders.

13.8 Identify the various dimensions of temperament.

13.9 Explain how consequences of behavior affect personality disorders.

13.10 Describe how the parent-child attachment affects personality disorders.

13.11 Explain how the interactions among neurological, psychological and social factors help us to understand personality disorders.

13.12 Describe the neurological, psychological and social treatments for personality disorders.

13.13 Identify the DSM-IV-TR criteria and additional facts for paranoid personality disorder.

13.14 Identify the DSM-IV-TR criteria and additional facts for schizoid personality disorder.

13.15 Identify the DSM-IV-TR criteria and additional facts for schizotypal personality disorder.

13.16 Compare and contrast schizotypal personality disorder with other disorders.

13.17 Describe how neurological, psychological, and social factors and their interactions can aid in the understanding and treatment of the odd/eccentric personality disorders.

13.18 Identify the DSM-IV-TR criteria and additional facts for antisocial personality disorder.

13.19 Describe the connection between antisocial personality disorder and conduct disorder.

13.20 Compare and contrast antisocial personality disorder with psychopathy.

13.21 Describe the neurological, psychological, and social factors and their interactions to help understand and treat antisocial personality disorder.

13.22 Identify the DSM-IV-TR criteria and additional facts for borderline personality disorder.

13.23 Compare and contrast borderline personality disorder with other disorders.

13.24 Explain how neurological, psychological, and social factors and their interactions help to understand and treat borderline personality disorder.

13.25 Identify the DSM-IV-TR criteria and additional facts for histrionic personality disorder.

13.26 Explain the factors that help to understand and treat histrionic personality disorder.

13.27 Identify the DSM-IV-TR criteria and additional facts for narcissistic personality disorder.

13.28 Explain the factors that help to understand and treat narcissistic personality disorder.

13.29 Identify the DSM-IV-TR criteria and additional facts for avoidant personality disorder.

13.30 Compare and contrast avoidant personality disorder with other disorders.

13.31 Identify the DSM-IV-TR criteria and additional facts for dependent personality disorder.

13.32 Compare and contrast dependent personality disorder with other disorders.

13.33 Identify the DSM-IV-TR criteria and additional facts for obsessive-compulsive personality disorder.

13.34 Compare and contrast obsessive-compulsive personality disorder with other disorders.

13.35 Describe the various factors that help to understand and treat the fearful/anxious personality disorders.

KEY TERMS

Personality disorders: A category of psychological disorders characterized by a pattern of inflexible and maladaptive thoughts, feelings, and behaviors that arise across a range of situations and lead to distress or dysfunction.

Personality: Enduring traits and characteristics that lead a person to behave in relatively predictable ways across a range of situations.

Cluster A personality disorders: Personality disorders characterized by odd or eccentric behaviors that have elements related to those of schizophrenia.

Cluster B personality disorders: Personality disorders characterized by emotional, dramatic, or erratic behaviors that involve problems with emotional regulation.

Cluster C personality disorders: Personality disorders characterized by anxious or fearful behaviors.

Paranoid personality disorder: A personality disorder characterized by persistent and pervasive mistrust and suspiciousness, accompanied by a bias to interpret other people's motives as hostile.

Schizoid personality disorder: A personality disorder characterized by a restricted range of emotions in social interactions and few, if any, close relationships.

Schizotypal personality disorder: A personality disorder characterized by eccentric thoughts, perceptions, and behaviors, in addition to having very few close relationships.

Antisocial personality disorder: A personality disorder characterized by a persistent disregard for the rights of others.

Conduct disorder: A psychological disorder that typically arises in childhood and is characterized by the violation of the basic rights of others or of societal norms that are appropriate to the individual's age.

Psychopathy: A set of emotional and interpersonal characteristics marked by a lack of empathy, an unmerited feeling of high self-worth, and a refusal to accept responsibility for one's actions.

Borderline personality disorder: A personality disorder characterized by volatile emotions, an unstable self-image, and impulsive behavior in relationships.

Histrionic personality disorder: A personality disorder characterized by attention-seeking behaviors and exaggerated and dramatic displays of emotion.

Narcissistic personality disorder: A personality disorder characterized by an inflated sense of importance, an excessive desire to be admired, and a lack of empathy.

Avoidant personality disorder: A personality disorder characterized by extreme social inhibition (i.e., extreme shyness) that usually stems from feeling inadequate and being overly sensitive to negative evaluation.

Dependent personality disorder: A personality disorder characterized by submissive and clingy behaviors, based on fear of separation.

Obsessive-compulsive personality disorder: A personality disorder characterized by preoccupations with perfectionism, orderliness, and self-control, as well as low levels of flexibility and efficiency.

CHAPTER GUIDE

Chapter Introduction

- Rachel Reiland, author of *Get Me Out of Here,* a memoir about living with a personality disorder, highlights the interpersonal problems that begin in childhood or adolescence and persist into adulthood.
- *Personality disorders* are a category of psychological disorders characterized by a pattern of inflexible and maladaptive thoughts, feelings, and behaviors that arise across a range of situations and lead to distress or dysfunction.

I. DIAGNOSING PERSONALITY DISORDERS

Reiland did not outgrow her difficulties. Instead, her difficulties continued into adulthood. Reiland's extreme behavior may be indicative of her personality or a personality disorder.

- *Personality* is defined as enduring traits and characteristics that lead a person to behave in relatively predictable ways across a range of situations.
- Personality traits occur on a continuum. For example, interpersonal warmth is on one end of the continuum while standoffishness is on the other end.

A. What Are Personality Disorders?

People with personality disorders have extreme and rigid traits that cause distress and dysfunction. [See *Table 13.1.*]

- Persistent patterns in affect, behavior, and cognition are seen in personality disorders and influence how the individual responds to a wide variety of situations:

    i. Affect refers to the range, intensity, and changeability of emotions, responsiveness, and emotion regulation.

    ii. Behavior refers to the ability to control impulses and interactions.

    iii. Cognition (mental processes and mental contents) refers to one's perceptions and interpretations. [See *Case 13.1.*]

Symptoms can improve with time, but these disorders are most resistant to treatment. [See *Figure 13.1.*]

- People with these disorders have less education; are more likely to never marry, to divorce, or to be separated; and are associated with suicide (about 30% of people who commit suicide and 40% of those who attempt suicide are believed to have a personality disorder).

MEDIA RECOMMENDATION 13.1: Dancing Daniel

Objective: To learn about the causes and treatments and the experience of living with a personality disorder.

Time: 40 Minutes

Film and Discussion: 60 Minutes

Discussion Only: 20 Minutes

Watch: BBC. (2008). *The Madness of Dancing Daniel.* [Film]. Films for the Humanities and Sciences. http://ffh.films.com/id/15736/The_Madness_of_Dancing_Daniel_A_Personality_Disorder_Case_Study.htm
Daniel is a young man who shows signs of several personality disorders. The film follows Dr. Peter Tyrer's work with Daniel.

Summary: After watching this film, students will be able to understand the complexities in diagnosing and treating personality disorders. Students will note how likeable Daniel is at times and how difficult he can be at other times.

Questions to Students and Discussion: What symptoms does Daniel have? How are these symptoms both Daniel's strengths and weaknesses? In what specific ways does Dr. Tyrer deal with Daniel's symptoms? How does Daniel's family cope with his illness? What surprised you about the film?

1. **Why Are Personality Disorders on Axis II Instead of Axis I?**

   - Mental retardation and personality disorders were placed on Axis II at the evolution of the DSM because they are disorders that start in childhood and were thought to be stable. However, there is little difference in childhood onset and stability between Axis I and Axis II disorders.

   - Personality disorders are difficult to diagnose because a person may be unaware of his/her own symptoms.

2. **Assessing Personality Disorders**

   - Diagnoses are usually made based on what the patient says or on patterns in what he or she says. [See *Case 13.1.*]

   - Clinicians may need additional visits with a patient before making a diagnosis.

- Personality inventories, questionnaires, and interviews with family members help in identifying interpersonal or chronic intrapersonal problems.
- Culture, ethnicity, and social background should be considered prior to the diagnosis. For example, immigrants may defer to family members or be unable to make decisions independently. This behavior should be interpreted within the cultural context.

3. DSM-IV-TR Personality Clusters

- There are 10 personality disorders in the DSM and they are divided into three clusters. [See *Table 13.2.*]
  - i. *Cluster A personality disorders* are personality disorders characterized by odd or eccentric behaviors that have elements related to those of schizophrenia.
  - ii. *Cluster B personality disorders* are personality disorders characterized by emotional, dramatic, or erratic behaviors that involve problems with emotional regulation.
  - iii. *Cluster C personality disorders* are personality disorders characterized by anxious or fearful behaviors. [See *Table 13.3.*]
- There is high comorbidity among the personality disorders in which half of the people with one personality disorder will have at least one other personality disorder.

MEDIA RECOMMENDATION 13.2: Personality Disorder Mnemonics

Objective: To develop a technique to remember the symptoms of each personality disorder.

Time: 20 Minutes

Media and Discussion: 30 Minutes

Discussion Only: 10 Minutes

Explore Online: Visit the following Web site for an acronym for each of the personality disorders: http://www.personalityresearch.org/pd.html

Summary: Students will find the acronyms helpful for remembering the symptoms of each of the disorders.

Questions to Students and Discussion: Do you find these acronyms helpful? Exactly why? What mnemonics can you make up to remember the disorders in each cluster—(1) P, S, S; (2) A, B, H, N; and (3) A, D, O.?

4. Criticisms of the DSM-IV-TR Category of Personality Disorders

- In the DSM-IV-TR, personality disorders are categorically different from normal personality. In contrast, researchers view personality disorders and normal personality on a continuum.
- There is an arbitrary cutoff for what distinguishes normal versus abnormal personality.
- The clusters have been organized by superficial commonalities that are not supported by research.
- The personality disorders are not distinct from one another. For example, schizoid and schizotypal share a pattern of poor social skills, social abilities, and social contacts.
- Some personality disorders are not distinct enough from Axis I disorders. For example, avoidant personality disorder and social phobia have a considerable amount of overlap.

- Research does not support the minimum number of symptoms designated for diagnosing a personality disorder.
- Number of symptoms and impairment level are different for the different disorders.
- The high comorbidity among the personality disorders suggests that disorders are not properly developed. For example, *personality disorder not otherwise specified* is the most common diagnosis among the personality disorders. *Not otherwise specified* is used when criteria are not met although the individual is experiencing distress or impairment.

B. Understanding Personality Disorders in General

There is evidence to support the theory that personalities run in families. For example, when examining her behavior, Rachel Reiland realized she had beaten her son just as her father had beaten her.

1. **Neurological Factors in Personality Disorders: Genes and Temperament**
   - Genes influence temperament (a person's affective state and emotional reactivity) through the effects of genes on brain structure and function.
   - Genes can predispose some people to develop a personality disorder if their temperament is extreme and rigid. *Example:* Reiland may have inherited aspects of her temperament from her father.

2. **Psychological Factors in Personality Disorders: Temperament and the Consequences of Behavior**
   - Temperament interacts with the environment to influence what life situations a person will face and his or her likely behavior in those situations.
   - Operant conditioning determines if the behavior will become repeatable.

   a. **The Role of Temperament:**
      - Cloninger proposed that temperaments and their contribution to personality disorders can be identified in the following two ways:
      (1) According to the strength of temperaments across each of four basic *temperament* dimensions:
          (a) Harm avoidance
          (b) Novelty seeking
          (c) Reward dependence
          (d) Persistence [see *Figure 13.2*]
      (2) According to the strength of temperaments across each of three *character* dimensions:
          (a) Cooperativeness
          (b) Self-directedness
          (c) Self-transcendence [see *Figure 13.2*]
      - Personality disorders are also sometimes categorized according to basic heritable characteristics using mathematical techniques. Such a process has yielded the following four dimensions:
      (1) Emotion dysregulation
      (2) Dissocial behavior or psychopathy
      (3) Inhibitedness or social withdrawal
      (4) Compulsivity

LEARNING ACTIVITY 13.1: Dimensions of Temperament and Character

Objective: To have students learn about the various dimensions of temperament.

Time: 30 Minutes

Directions: Explain to students that according to Cloninger there are four basic temperaments and three character dimensions that help to describe aspects of one's personality. (Use the information from *Figure 13.2* to help with this activity.) You are going to ask students to stand on a line on a continuum according to their temperament and character.

Temperament Dimensions:
1. *Harm avoidance:* Students who are high in risk-taking should stand close to the left side of the continuum, while students who are more careful should stand to the right side.
2. *Novelty seeking:* Students who are more compliant should stand close to the left side of the continuum, while students who are more rebellious should stand to the right side.
3. *Reward dependence:* Students who feel indifferent to rewards should stand close to the left side of the continuum, while students who are more indulgent with rewards should stand to the right side.
4. *Persistence:* Students who are high in apathy should stand close to the left side of the continuum, while students who are more fanatical should stand to the right side.

Character Dimensions:
1. *Cooperativeness:* Students who are antagonistic should stand close to the left side of the continuum, while students who are more agreeable should stand to the right side.
2. *Self-directedness:* Students who are careless should stand close to the left side of the continuum, while students who identify as responsible and goal-directed should stand to the right side.
3. *Self-transcendence:* Students who think they are more controlling or materialistic should stand close to the left side of the continuum, while students who are more imaginative and unconventional should stand to the right side.

Summary: Students should be surprised by the range of responses from their classmates. This activity also provides students with the opportunity to think about their own personalities and apply these concepts to their own lives.

Questions to Students and Discussion: How much did your classmates vary with regard to their temperament and character dimensions? Were you surprised with the wide (or narrow) range? How might temperament and character lead to a personality disorder?

b. The Consequences of Behavior:

Behavior is influenced by the environment. If **the consequences of behavior** are positive, the behavior will increase; if the consequences are negative, the behavior will decrease.

- These consequences can influence one's temperament and interpersonal expectations. *Example:* Misinterpretations may lead to a self-fulfilling cycle.
- People with personality disorders have pervasive and self-fulfilling dysfunctional beliefs that contain three elements:
  i. **Automatic thoughts** (*Example:* "No one should have to put up with me because I'm so bad.")
  ii. **Interpersonal strategies** (*Example:* "If I grovel or cry, maybe he'll forgive me.")
  iii. **Cognitive distortions** (*Example:* "He says he has to make a living—what he really means is that he thinks I'm not doing enough.")

3. **Social Factors in Personality Disorders: Insecurely Attached**

Child-parent *attachment style* in childhood affects the development of a personality disorder.

- People with personality disorders are likely to have an *insecure attachment,* in which they may view themselves negatively and/or assume that others will not meet their needs.
- Childhood abuse, neglect, or inconsistent discipline can lead to insecure attachments. (*Example:* Reiland's father was both physically and emotionally abusive.)

4. **FEEDBACK LOOPS IN ACTION: Understanding Personality Disorders**

- A social risk factor for developing a personality disorder is having a parent with an Axis I or II disorder.
- Temperament can influence psychological and social factors. [See *Figure 13.3.*]

C. Treating Personality Disorders: General Issues

- Reiland was suicidal and was encouraged to speak to her pastor.
- People with personality disorders don't see the problems as something that "happened" to them; instead, the problems are an integral part of the way they interact with the world.
- Thus people with personality disorders are unlikely to seek treatment unless they also have an Axis I disorder.
- People with personality disorders are more difficult to treat because of their ingrained patterns in thinking and behavior.

1. **Targeting Neurological Factors in Personality Disorders**

Neurological treatments include medication and are effective to treat comorbid Axis I disorder symptoms, not personality disorder symptoms per se. Medications *can,* however, provide some temporary relief.

2. **Targeting Psychological Factors in Personality Disorders**

- Psychodynamic therapy focuses on unconscious drives and motivations.
- Cognitive-behavioral therapy addresses maladaptive views and negative beliefs to increase confidence and modify beliefs in hopes of changing behaviors.
- Motivational enhancement strategies may be used to encourage change.
- The only psychological treatment studied in-depth is for borderline personality disorder.

3. **Targeting Social Factors in Personality Disorders**

- The relationship between the therapist and client is important and may become part of the therapy.
- Family education, family therapy, or couples therapy can help to educate families about the disorder and how to deal more effectively with it.
- Interpersonal or group therapy can provide clients with feedback about their interpersonal interactions.

II. ODD/ECCENTRIC PERSONALITY DISORDERS

People with Cluster A personality disorders exhibit odd or eccentric behaviors or thoughts, and oftentimes have an Axis I psychotic disorder. The three Cluster A personality disorders are paranoid, schizoid, and schizotypal.

A. Paranoid Personality Disorder

Paranoid personality disorder is a personality disorder characterized by persistent and pervasive mistrust and suspiciousness, accompanied by a bias to interpret other people's motives as hostile. [See *Table 13.4.*]

* A key feature of this disorder is distrust. (*Example:* A person might think his/her partner is having an affair despite the lack of evidence.)
* People with this disorder base their perceptions on reality and perceive threats from known individuals, and thus they have slightly different symptoms from those who have schizophrenia.
* A diagnosis of paranoid personality disorder is not given if the paranoia is substance induced or due to a psychotic episode of schizophrenia or a mood disorder. [See *Case 13.2.*]
* People with this disorder tend to be self-sufficient, critical, and blaming of others. When under stress their paranoia may reach the level of a delusion.
* The paranoia causes interpersonal difficulties. [See *Table 13.5.*]
* Racial and ethnic suspicions may reflect reality or misperceptions and thus make the etiology of the disorder difficult. (*Example:* If an immigrant has been harassed, he or she may have more guarded interactions.)

MEDIA RECOMMENDATION 13.3: Paranoid Personality Disorder Dramatization

Objective: To learn about the experience of someone with paranoid personality disorder through a dramatization.

Time: 5 Minutes

Media and Discussion: 11 Minutes

Discussion Only: 6 Minutes

Watch Online: Search YouTube using the search terms "paranoid LifeAtTheExtremes," or http://www.youtube.com/watch?v=YhoxarW69tY
This student dramatization reveals what it might be like to interact with someone with paranoid personality disorder.

Summary: Students will enjoy watching this student dramatization and applying the diagnostic criteria to this video. Students will be able to identify the following symptoms: perception of threats, delusions, and questioning the loyalty of one's partner.

Questions to Students and Discussion: How many DSM-IV-TR criteria were you able to identify in the main character? Which ones? What do you think it must be like living with this disorder? Please describe. What surprised you? Why?

MEDIA RECOMMENDATION 13.4: What Is Paranoid Personality Disorder?

Objective: To learn about paranoid personality disorder through an interview with an expert.

Time: 4 Minutes

Media and Discussion: 9 Minutes

Discussion Only: 5 Minutes

Watch Online: Search Videojug.com using the search terms "paranoid personality disorder," or http://www.videojug.com/interview/paranoid-personality-disorder/

Dr. Rhoda Hahn discusses the symptoms, causes of, and treatments for paranoid personality disorder.

Summary: Students will learn about the key symptoms and causes of paranoid personality disorder from a professional. Students will also learn about the genetic component of this disorder and its possible link to schizophrenia.

Questions to Students and Discussion: How many DSM-IV-TR criteria, as mentioned by Dr. Hahn, were you able to identify? Which ones? What do you think it must be like living with this disorder? What surprised you? Why? What issues might you face when trying to treat someone with this disorder?

B. Schizoid Personality Disorder

Schizoid personality disorder is a personality disorder characterized by a restricted range of emotions in social interactions and few, if any, close relationships. [See *Table 13.6.*]

- People with this disorder lack social skills and do not pick up on social cues. (*Example:* They may stare at someone who is smiling at them.)
- People also exhibit amotivation and passivity and seem expressionless, and thus they function best alone. [See *Table 13.7; Case 13.3.*]
- Behaviors should be evaluated with the client's culture of origin in mind. (*Example:* Some cultures value emotional detachment.)

MEDIA RECOMMENDATION 13.5: What Is Schizoid Personality Disorder?

Objective: To learn about schizoid personality disorder through an expert interview.

Media: 5 Minutes

Media and Discussion: 10 Minutes

Discussion Only: 5 Minutes

Watch Online: Search Videojug.com using the search terms "schizoid personality disorder," or http://www.videojug.com/interview/schizoid-personality-disorder
Dr. Rhoda Hahn discusses the symptoms and causes of and treatments for schizoid personality disorder.

Summary: Students will learn about key symptoms and causes of schizoid personality disorder from a professional. Students will also learn about the possible occupations for someone with this disorder and the possible link between this disorder and schizophrenia.

Questions to Students and Discussion: How many DSM-IV-TR criteria, as mentioned by Dr. Hahn, were you able to identify? Which ones? What do you think it must be like living with this disorder? What surprised you? Why? What issues might you face when trying to treat someone with this disorder?

C. Schizotypal Personality Disorder

Schizotypal personality disorder is the most researched Cluster A disorder and thus is the focus of this section.

1. What Is Schizotypal Personality Disorder?

Schizotypal personality disorder is a personality disorder characterized by eccentric thoughts, perceptions, and behaviors, in addition to very few close relationships. This personality disorder has 10 symptoms that are arranged in three categories. [See *Tables 13.8, 13.9; Case 13.4.*]

- **Cognitive-perceptual**
  i.   Magical thinking, where the person believes he/she has control over external events
  ii. Unusual perceptions, such as sensing the presence of a person not in the room
  iii. *Ideas of reference,* where the individual believes random events have meaning
  iv. Paranoid ideation or suspiciousness
- **Interpersonal**
  i.   Prefers being alone and lacks close friends
  ii. Shows only a narrow range of emotions
  iii. May exhibit social anxiety due to suspiciousness
  iv. May exhibit suspiciousness of others
- **Disorganized**
  i.   Odd, eccentric behavior, such as wearing unkempt clothing or odd social interactions
  ii. Odd speech

MEDIA RECOMMENDATION 13.6: What Is Schizotypal Personality Disorder?

Objective: To learn about schizotypal personality disorder through an expert interview.

Time: 5 Minutes

Media and Discussion: 10 Minutes

Discussion Only: 5 Minutes

Watch Online: Search Videojug.com using the search terms "schizotypal personality disorder," or http://www.videojug.com/interview/schizotypal-personality-disorder/
Dr. Rhoda Hahn discusses the symptoms and causes of and treatments for schizotypal personality disorder.

Summary: Students will learn about key symptoms and causes of schizotypal personality disorder from a professional. Students will also learn about the social anxiety experienced by someone with this disorder.

Questions to Students and Discussion: How many DSM-IV-TR criteria, as mentioned by Dr. Hahn, were you able to identify? Which ones? What do you think it must be like living with this disorder? What surprised you? Why? What issues might you face when trying to treat someone with this disorder?

2. **Distinguishing Between Schizotypal Personality Disorder and Other Disorders**

   Unlike schizoid personality disorder, schizotypal personality disorder includes cognitive-perceptual symptoms; however, there is overlap between these two disorders, and half of those persons with one of these disorders will be diagnosed with the other disorder.

   - Some propose that schizotypal is a milder form of schizophrenia.
   - Cultural and religious factors should be considered when looking at cognitive and perceptual distortions.

D. Understanding Odd/Eccentric Personality Disorders

1. Neurological Factors in Odd/Eccentric Personality Disorders

- Contributing factors toward the development of schizotypal personality disorder include:
    i. Genes and prenatal environment (maternal illness, malnourishment, and birth complications)
    ii. Abnormalities in brain structure (frontal and temporal lobes, thalamus, and hippocampus)
    iii. Abnormalities in neural function (dopamine, serotonin, and glutamate function)
- Genes also play a role in development: First-degree relatives of someone with a Cluster A personality disorder are more likely to have a schizophrenia-related disorder.

2. Psychological Factors in Odd/Eccentric Personality Disorders

- People with Cluster A disorders have cognitive deficits, such as problems with attention, memory, and executive functions.
- People with schizotypal personality disorder have mental-processing distortions.
- People with schizotypal personality disorder may have social problems due to the cognitive deficits. (*Example:* People with this disorder may have impaired *theory of mind,* defined as the ability to recognize emotions in others.)
- Most of the people with Cluster A disorders cope by isolating themselves. [See *Table 13.10.*]

3. Social Factors in Odd/Eccentric Personality Disorders

- Physical abuse, neglect, insecure parent-child attachment, discrimination, and other stressful events play a role in the onset of schizotypal disorder.
- Negative experiences can influence one's views of others as being harmful and untrustworthy.

4. FEEDBACK LOOPS IN ACTION: Understanding Schizotypal Personality Disorder

Early social stressors can affect the brain, which in turn will contribute to cognitive and emotional problems, which then affect the social interactions and increase stress, and so on. [See *Figure 13.4.*]

E. Treating Odd/Eccentric Personality Disorders

- Little research has been conducted on treatments for Cluster A disorders because many people with this disorder do not seek treatment or are reluctant to do so.
- Cognitive-behavioral therapy can improve social skills and other adaptive strategies.
- Relaxation techniques, exposure to avoided situations, and cognitive restructuring are also helpful.
- Medications and psychosocial treatments for schizophrenia can also be used for schizotypal personality disorder (such as cognitive-behavioral therapy, social skills training, and family therapy).
- Results suggest that social skills training can be effective.

LEARNING ACTIVITY 13.2: Compare and Contrast the Cluster A Personality Disorders

Objective: To identify the similarities and differences between the Cluster A personality disorders.

Time: 20 Minutes

Activity and Discussion: 45 Minutes

Discussion Only: 25 Minutes

Directions: Have students work in small groups to fill out *Worksheet 13.1* located in the back of this chapter. Assign each group to take a turn and present a portion of the chart to the class.

Summary: This activity will help students see the differences and similarities of these disorders more clearly. The chart will help them organize a large amount of material on these disorders.

Questions to Students and Discussion: What are key similarities among the disorders? What are key differences among the disorders? Based on your results, and using the textbook as a guide, what conclusions might you want to draw regarding overlap and differences of these disorders?

III. DRAMATIC/ERRATIC PERSONALITY DISORDERS

Reiland's impulsive, dramatic, and erratic reactions are typical of a person who has a Cluster B personality disorder.

- People with these disorders tend to have Axis I disorders, such as substance-related disorders, mood disorders, anxiety disorders, or eating disorders.
- Cluster B personality disorders include:
  i. Antisocial
  ii. Borderline
  iii. Histrionic
  iv. Narcissistic

A. Antisocial Personality Disorder

Antisocial personality disorder is a personality disorder characterized by a persistent disregard for the rights of others. [See *Table 13.11.*]

- People with this disorder violate rules or laws, act aggressively, hurt others, act impulsively, shirk responsibilities, and lack a moral conscience.
- The criteria for this disorder are behaviorally specific, thus making it the most reliably diagnosed personality disorder.
- A United Kingdom study found that clinicians were more likely to diagnose a white man with antisocial personality disorder than they were a black man.
- Signs of this disorder can be seen in childhood/adolescence and symptoms must be present by age 15.
- If one exhibits signs of this disorder prior to age 18 they are diagnosed with ***conduct disorder,*** a psychological disorder that typically arises in childhood and is characterized by the violation of the basic rights of others or of societal norms that are appropriate to the individual's age. [See *Table 13.12; Case 13.5.*]

1. The Role of Conduct Disorder

- Having conduct disorder prior to age 18 is not a criterion for having antisocial personality disorder. However, one must show symptoms of antisocial personality disorder prior to age 18.

- Conduct disorder is highly associated with later antisocial personality disorder, but most boys who have conduct disorder do not develop antisocial personality disorder. [See *Figure 13.5.*]

- Many women with antisocial personality disorder did not have *serious* conduct problems prior to age 18, yet girls who show a pattern of interpersonal and physical aggression develop antisocial personality disorder at higher rates than those girls who do not show these patterns.

- People from lower socioeconomic groups are at higher risk for developing antisocial personality disorder.

MEDIA RECOMMENDATION 13.7: What Is Antisocial Personality Disorder?

Objective: To learn about antisocial personality disorder through an expert interview.

Time: 6 Minutes

Media and Discussion: 10 Minutes

Discussion Only: 4 Minutes

Watch Online: Search Videojug.com using the search terms "antisocial personality disorder," or http://www.videojug.com/interview/antisocial-personality-disorder
Dr. Rhoda Hahn discusses the symptoms, causes of, and treatments for antisocial personality disorder.

Summary: Students will learn more about the key symptoms and causes of antisocial personality disorder from a professional. Students will also learn how individuals with this disorder must show symptoms before the age of 18.

Questions to Students and Discussion: How many DSM-IV-TR criteria, as mentioned by Dr. Hahn, were you able to identify? Which ones? What do you think it must be like living with this disorder? What surprised you? Why? What issues might you face when trying to treat someone with this disorder?

LEARNING ACTIVITY 13.3: The Law and Mrs. Shelton

Objective: To apply the DSM-IV-TR criteria for antisocial personality disorder to a real case.

Time: 25 Minutes

Discussion and Activity: 40 Minutes

Discussion Only: 15 Minutes

Explore Online: Leung, R. (2004). *48 Hours: The law and Mrs. Shelton.* CBS Worldwide Inc. http://www.cbsnews.com/stories/2004/06/22/48hours/main625447.shtml

Read about the strange circumstances surrounding Texas attorney Catherine Shelton and identify Shelton's symptoms of antisocial personality disorder and psychopathy.

Summary: Students will be surprised to learn about Mrs. Shelton's life and the number of symptoms she shows of antisocial personality disorder and psychopathy (such as disregard for others, involvement in crime, etc.).

Questions to Students and Discussion: Do you think Mrs. Shelton has antisocial personality disorder or shows signs of psychopathy? Why or why not? What are the dangers in diagnosing someone from a news article? What surprises you about this case? Why?

2. **Psychopathy: Is It Different Than Antisocial Personality Disorder?**

   - *Psychopathy* is a set of emotional and interpersonal characteristics marked by a lack of empathy, an unmerited feeling of high self-worth, and a refusal to accept responsibility for one's actions. [*See Figure 13.6.*]

   - *Psychopathy* (or *sociopathy*) focuses more on the emotional and interpersonal aspects versus breaking laws or stealing.

   - Research shows that the majority of those in prison meet the criteria for antisocial personality disorder (50%-80%) rather than for psychopathy (15% of male prisoners and 7.5% of female inmates).

   - Eighty-one percent of those with psychopathy also meet the criteria for antisocial personality disorder but only 38% of those with antisocial personality disorder meet the criteria for psychopathy—thus psychopathy is defined more narrowly.

3. **Understanding Antisocial Personality Disorder**

   - More research has been conducted on psychopathy than on antisocial personality disorder.

   - Research that has focused on antisocial personality disorder has been conducted on populations where it is difficult to isolate factors (*Example:* inmates).

   a. **Neurological Factors in Antisocial Personality Disorder and Psychopathy:**
   Abnormal brain structures, brain function, and genetic factors may contribute to the development of this disorder.

   (1) **Brain systems:**

      - People with antisocial personality disorder tend to have smaller frontal lobes and hippocampi and more white matter (coating on axons) in the corpus collosum.

      - Studies have shown that these individuals have less activation in the frontal and temporal lobes when a task involves classical conditioning and inhibiting responses.

   (2) **Neural communication:**

      - Genes that regulate dopamine and serotonin may play a role in antisocial personality disorder.

      - One study found that when medication is used to regulate these two systems in people with borderline personality disorder, there is a reduction of symptoms. However, this study has not been conducted on those with antisocial personality disorder.

      - Temperament may be influenced by abnormal brain functioning; some research has found that men who were later diagnosed with antisocial personality disorder were distractible, impulsive, and reckless as 3-year-olds.

  (3) Genetics:

    • Genes that influence dopamine and serotonin may influence specific aspects of temperament of those with antisocial personality disorder. Thus, people with antisocial personality disorder consistently exhibit the following temperament dimensions:

     i. High **reward dependence,** where an individual is motivated by a reward

     ii. Low **harm avoidance,** where the individual is not deterred by punishment

     iii. Low **persistence,** where a person has low frustration tolerance

    • Adoption studies have found that genetics raises one's risk of criminal behavior or antisocial behavior, especially if there are accompanying environmental factors associated with criminality. [See *Table 13.13.*]

 b. Psychological Factors in Antisocial Personality Disorder and Psychopathy:

  • Problems with classical and operant conditioning may also give rise to antisocial personality disorder.

  • Those criminals with psychopathic traits have difficulty learning to avoid painful stimuli unless given a medication to increase their sympathetic nervous system.

  • Low harm avoidance makes them less likely to be afraid of punishment.

  • They are also highly motivated by rewarding activities and thus are impulsive, have difficulty delaying gratification, and have poor judgment.

 c. Social Factors in Antisocial Personality Disorder and Psychopathy:

 When parents abuse or neglect their children or discipline them inconsistently, these children can develop insecure attachment and have a high risk of developing conduct and/or antisocial personality disorders.

 d. FEEDBACK LOOPS IN ACTION: Antisocial Personality Disorder and Psychopathy:

  • Neurological factors (such as predisposition or temperament) and social factors (such as the environment) may influence the development of antisocial personality disorder. [See *Figure 13.7.*]

  • Those children with conduct disorder who received punishment for their offenses were less likely to develop antisocial personality disorder (psychological factor).

  • Temperaments can influence normal classical and operant conditioning.

  • Social factors (such as abuse and neglect) may contribute to underarousal and may lead a person to seek out arousing activities.

 4. Treating Antisocial Personality Disorder and Psychopathy

  • Medication is only effective at treating comorbid disorders.

  • Treatments for psychopathy have a poor prognosis because the traits associated with the disorder interfere with treatment.

  • If the patient is violent, therapy will focus on *managing* the client versus *treating* the client.

  • People who are responsive to treatment have comorbid anxiety, and thus this may suggest that anxiety, rather than psychopathy, is the cause of the symptoms.

  • Treatments that focus on comorbid substance use and aggression have had some success.

- Effective treatments provide clear rules and consequences, and focus on behavior change and control using cognitive-behavioral therapy.

- Empathy training and social skills training are less effective.

- Social treatments improve family interactions.

- *Therapeutic communities* are 24-hour programs in prisons or jails that help to control an inmate's behavior and are effective for individuals with antisocial personality disorder and substance abuse disorder.

- Treatments are usually court ordered, and the outcome depends on one's motivation to change.

B. Borderline Personality Disorder

- *Borderline personality disorder* is a personality disorder characterized by volatile emotions, an unstable self-image, and impulsive behavior in relationships. [See *Table 13.14.*]

- "Borderline personality" was originally a psychodynamic term for those between neurosis and psychosis.

- A key symptom of the disorder is dysregulation, which is exhibited through emotional instability.

- Unstable relationship patterns is another key feature, one in which the person fluctuates between idealizing and devaluing a person.

- Reiland's thoughts, feelings, and behaviors meet the criteria for borderline personality disorder.

- Impulsive behaviors may result from strong responses to emotional stimuli (*Example:* feeling despair when someone is late).

- People with this disorder may also feel chronically empty, lonely, and isolated.

- Some individuals may use *parasuicidal* (or cutting) behavior to "feel something." This is most commonly done when a person dissociates after feeling rejected or abandoned.

- Ten percent of those with this disorder die by suicide. [See *Table 13.15.*]

- Women are more likely than men to be diagnosed with this disorder, but that may be due to a diagnostic bias.

- People with borderline personality disorder may have comorbid depression, which tends to increase suicidal thoughts, plans, or attempts. [See *Case 13.6.*]

MEDIA RECOMMENDATION 13.8: What Is Borderline Personality Disorder?

Objective: To learn about borderline personality disorder through an expert interview.

Media: 9 Minutes

Media and Discussion: 15 Minutes

Discussion Only: 6 Minutes

Watch Online: Search Videojug.com using the search terms "borderline personality disorder," or http://www.videojug.com/interview/borderline-personality-disorder/
Dr. Rhoda Hahn discusses the symptoms, causes of, and treatments for borderline personality disorder.

Summary: Students will learn more about key symptoms and causes of borderline personality disorder from a professional. Students will also learn about the key features of this disorder: instability and fear of abandonment.

Questions to Students and Discussion: How many DSM-IV-TR criteria, as mentioned by Dr. Hahn, were you able to identify? Which ones? What do you think it must be like living with this disorder? What surprised you? Why? What issues might you face when trying to treat someone with this disorder?

LECTURE ENHANCEMENT 13.1: Self-Injury

Objective: To learn more about the parasuicidal behavior of self-injury.

Time: 45 Minutes

Key Lecture Points:
I.   Why Do People Cut?
   A. As a way of coping or managing emotions
   B. To relieve "unbearable emotions"
   C. To end numbness
   D. As a form of self-soothing because self-soothing did not occur in childhood
   E. Usually *not* an attempt at suicide
II. History of Self-Mutilation
   A. Menninger was the first to make a category of self-injurious behavior.
   B. Graff and Mallin conducted a six-month study on "wrist-slashers" and found the following characteristics of cutters:
      1. Young
      2. Highly intelligent
      3. Substance abusers
      4. Interpersonal difficulties
      5. Cold mothers
      6. Critical fathers
III. Cause of Self-Injury Behavior
   A. Physical abuse
   B. Sexual abuse
   C. Neglect
   D. Dissociation (where one experiences extreme stress so he/she separates the mind from physical self)
   E. Unresolved feelings of pain, shame, and grief
IV. Treatments for Self-Injury
   A. Medications
      1. SSRIs
      2. Naltrexone (eliminates the high experienced from cutting—blocks release of opiates)
      3. Anticonvulsants (sometimes used to help with impulsivity)
   B. Therapy
      1. Learn self-soothing techniques
      2. Develop more honest connection between self and others
      3. Participate in SAFE (Self-Abuse Finally Ends)
      4. Attend Self-Mutilators Anonymous
      5. Seek out peer treatment

Summary: Students will find this discussion interesting since some youth who do not have border-line personality disorder use self-injury as a coping mechanism.

Sources: Selekman, M. D. (2009). *The adolescent and young adult self-harming treatment manual: A collaborative strengths-based brief therapy approach.* New York: Norton.

Strong, M. (1999). *A bright red scream.* New York: Viking.

Cambridge Educational Films. (2006). *Cutting: Addicted to self-injury.* [Film]. Films for the Humanities and Sciences. http://ffh.films.com/id/13082/Cutting_Addicted_to_Self-Injury.htm

Schneider, W., & Manson, S. (2007). *Cut: Teens and self-injury.* [Film]. Wendy Schneider. http://www.cutthemovie.com/

Questions to Students and Discussion: What have you heard about self-injurious behavior? Does this lecture complement or contradict what you know? What are other maladaptive forms of self-soothing? What surprises you about this topic? What interventions might be helpful to reduce the rates of self-injury?

1. **Distinguishing Between Borderline Personality Disorder and Other Disorders**

   Posttraumatic stress disorder, psychotic symptoms, mood fluctuations, impulsivity, interpersonal instability, and manipulation all overlap with symptoms of borderline personality disorder.

2. **Understanding Borderline Personality Disorder**

   The *biosocial theory* helps us to understand borderline personality disorder.

   a. **Neurological Factors: Born to Be Wild?**

      There has been much research on the neurological causes of borderline personality disorder.

      (1) **Brain systems:**
      - The frontal lobes, hippocampi, and amygdala are smaller and function abnormally in people with borderline personality disorder.
      - People with borderline personality disorder show no activation in the anterior cingulate, which helps in controlling affect. On the other hand, the amygdala (which aids in the production of strong emotion) is more active and is not regulated by the frontal lobes due to the decrease in activation.
      - People with this disorder have impaired memory and experience difficulty inhibiting their responses, focusing attention, organizing visual material, and making decisions.

      (2) **Neural communication:**
      - People with this disorder have less sensitive serotonin receptors. This characteristic is greater in women than in men.
      - The hypothalamic-pituitary-adrenal (HPA) axis is overly responsive, which leads to high levels of cortisol.
      - These findings are consistent with Marsha Linehan's theory that people with this disorder are neurologically vulnerable to emotion dysregulation and have a slow rate of returning to normal, baseline arousal.

(3) **Genetics:**

Studies support a genetic transmission of impulsivity, emotional volatility, and anxiety but do not support a genetic transmission of borderline personality disorder.

b. **Psychological Factors: Emotions on a Yo-Yo:**

- Dysregulation of emotion, sense of self, and behavior are key features of this disorder. (*Example:* People with this disorder can be in a rage one minute and break down in tears the next.)
- Self-destructive behaviors such as substance use or abuse, binge eating, and parasuicidal behaviors help to relieve feelings after interpersonal stressors and thus are negatively reinforcing.
- When experiencing heightened emotion, people with this disorder tend to have difficulty focusing their attention and are likely to misinterpret information.

c. **Social Factors: Invalidation:**

- Interpersonal dysregulation, especially with invalidation, is common for those with borderline personality disorder and may be the result of invalidation experienced in childhood.
- People with this disorder often become dependent on others to help them calm their emotions. However, this dependency then leads to a fear of abandonment.

d. **FEEDBACK LOOPS IN ACTION: Understanding Borderline Personality Disorder:**

- Neurological (brain systems), psychological (emotional reactions), and social (inability to soothe one's self) factors interact and help us understand borderline personality. [*See Figure 13.8.*]
- An invalidating parent-child relationship leads to later difficulties with trusting one's own experience, labeling emotions, and tolerating distress.

3. **Treating Borderline Personality Disorder: New Treatments**

- Parasuicidal and suicidal thoughts and behaviors make this disorder difficult to treat.
- The treatment of choice is *dialectical behavior therapy.*

a. **Targeting Neurological Factors: Medication:**

Medications target the symptoms of Axis I comorbid disorders such as mood, anxiety, impulsivity, and psychotic symptoms.

b. **Targeting Psychological Factors: Dialectical Behavior Therapy:**

- Linehan developed dialectical behavior therapy, a treatment for borderline personality disorder that uses aspects of cognitive-behavioral therapy, an emphasis on the quality of the therapist-client relationship, and the following additional elements:
  i. **An emphasis on validating the patient's experience:** Validating the person's thoughts, feelings, and behaviors in the context of the person's life experiences.
  ii. **A Zen Buddhist approach:** Being mindful and nonjudgmental about one's feelings and experiences.
  iii. **A dialectics component:** *Dialectics* is where one accepts the situation and the feelings while recognizing that something needs to change.
- This treatment, *dialectical behavior therapy,* includes individual and group therapy and seeks to reduce maladaptive behaviors. It lasts for one year.

- Research has shown lower dropout and hospitalization rates; the therapy has been used with Axis I disorders that have an impulsive component (*Example:* bulimia).
- Intensive psychodynamic and cognitive therapies are also effective.

LEARNING ACTIVITY 13.4: Soothe-and-Share Kits

Objective: To practice the dialectical behavior therapy (DBT) technique of self-soothing.

Time: 30 Minutes

Activity and Discussion: 60 Minutes

Discussion Only: 30 Minutes

Directions: Part of the difficulty people with borderline personality disorder face is the inability to control their emotions. One skill that DBT teaches is self-soothing skills. To learn about this skill, students will build their own "soothe-and-share" kits. Each kit should consist of a container filled with items that soothe the five senses (vision, smell, hearing, taste, touch). In addition to these items, students can write a list of soothing/distress-tolerance activities, which can include using positive or relaxing imagery, finding meaning in difficult situations, prayer, relaxation, learning to take one thing at a time, mini-vacations, or self-encouragements.

Write a brief description about your thoughts/feelings about doing this activity. How did you find this exercise?

Summary: Students will enjoy applying dialectical behavior techniques to their own lives. Students will identify multiple forms of self-soothing techniques.

Source: Linehan, M. (2009). *Dialectical behavior training course.* Cleveland, OH: Behavioral Tech, LLC. http://behavioraltech.org/index.cfm?CFID=26145730&CFTOKEN=11729169

Questions to Students and Discussion: Do you think a kit like this would help you when you are upset? Why or why not? Do you think this would help your future clients? Why or why not? How might this exercise be helpful to someone with borderline personality disorder?

LECTURE ENHANCEMENT 13.2: Dialectical Behavior Therapy

Objective: To learn additional information about dialectical behavior therapy.

Time: 40 Minutes

Key Lecture Points:
I.   Similarities to Cognitive-Behavioral Therapy
  A. Challenge maladaptive thinking
  B. New thought process should lead to change in behavior
II. Differences from Cognitive-Behavioral Therapy
  A. Acceptance of client by understanding the behavior within the moment and context. Therapist must accept client's behavior three times for every change request.
  B. Therapy focuses on behaviors that interfere with the therapeutic process and decrease therapeutic interfering behaviors.
  C. Relationship between client and therapist is the key to therapy.
III. Treatment Program
  A. There are four modules in the treatment program.
    1. Core mindfulness skills (acceptance)
      a. Observe the situation

       b. Describe the experience
       c. Become aware of reality as it is with no judgment
       d. Do one thing at a time—participate in the moment
    2. Distress tolerance and acceptance
       a. Crisis survival strategies for the short- and long-term
       b. Distress tolerance activities
         i. Create a Soothe-and-Share Kit
    3. Emotional regulation (change)
       a. Understand emotions
       b. Reduce vulnerability by living a balanced life (eat well, get enough sleep, etc.)
       c. Build positive emotions
       d. Increase positive experiences each day
       e. Decrease negative emotions through distraction and other skills
       f. Learn difference between unjustifiable and justifiable emotions
    4. Interpersonal effectiveness (change)
       a. Attending to relationships
         Examine factors that interfere with effectiveness
       b. Balance priorities and demands—learn when and how to say no
       c. Balance wants and shoulds
       d. Build mastery and self respect—learn conflict resolution skills
IV. Levels of Treatment
    A. Individual therapy and coaching phone calls
    B. Group therapy that is educational
    C. Multidisciplinary team for therapist

Summary: Students will find the detailed description of dialectical behavior therapy both interesting and personally helpful. In particular, students will benefit from learning specific distress-tolerance skills, ways to regulate emotion, and ways to improve interpersonal interactions.

Sources: *DBT Self Help: Life Skills for Emotional Health,* http://www.dbtselfhelp.com/html/dbt_skills_list.html

Linehan, M. (2009). *Dialectical behavior training course.* Cleveland, OH: Behavioral Tech, LLC. http://behavioraltech.org/index.cfm?CFID=26145730&CFTOKEN=11729169

Linehan, M. (1993). *Skills training manual for treating borderline personality disorder.* New York: Guilford Press.

Questions to Students and Discussion:
Why do you think this form of treatment is so helpful for those with borderline personality disorder? What aspects of the treatment did you find helpful?

    c. Targeting Social Factors: Interpersonal Therapy:

    Interpersonal therapy (IPT) seeks to increase interpersonal skills, balance extreme feelings about others, and lasts about 8 months.

    d. FEEDBACK LOOPS IN TREATMENT: Borderline Personality Disorder:

- Learning to regulate emotions (a psychological treatment) will affect the brain (a neurological factor), which may then improve interpersonal relationships (a social factor). [See *Figure 13.9.*]

- Feedback in the therapeutic environment will also change psychological and neurological factors.

C. Histrionic Personality Disorder

- *Histrionic personality disorder* is a personality disorder characterized by attention-seeking behaviors and exaggerated and dramatic displays of emotion.
- Reiland's behaviors show symptoms of histrionic personality disorder.

1. What Is Histrionic Personality Disorder?

- When people with this disorder feel bored, they seek excitement, have problems delaying gratification, and are frustrated with daily challenges. [See *Table 13.16.*]
- People with this disorder do not recognize their symptoms. [See *Table 13.17; Case 13.7.*]

2. Distinguishing Between Histrionic Personality Disorder and Other Disorders

- A desire for attention is what motivates someone with histrionic personality disorder, whereas power and gain motivate someone with antisocial personality disorder, and a need for nurturance motivates someone with bipolar disorder.
- Reiland might be diagnosed with histrionic personality disorder.

3. Understanding Histrionic Personality Disorder

- Little research has been done on this disorder, but it has been shown that people with this disorder believe they are special and that others admire them and are extra sensitive to being evaluated.
- Some of the behavior is motivated by entitlement and the inability to tolerate negative emotions.
- Receiving little attention in childhood may be one cause of this disorder.

4. Treating Histrionic Personality Disorder

- Treatment can include modifying maladaptive beliefs, increasing distress tolerance, learning about one's impact on others, and shifting focus from one's self to others.
- People with this disorder do not stay in treatment long.

MEDIA RECOMMENDATION 13.9: What Is Histrionic Personality Disorder?

Objective: To learn about histrionic personality disorder through an expert interview.

Time: 5 Minutes

Media and Discussion: 10 Minutes

Discussion Only: 5 Minutes

Watch Online: Search Videojug.com using the search terms "histrionic personality disorder," or http://www.videojug.com/interview/histrionic-personality-disorder/
Dr. Rhoda Hahn discusses the symptoms, causes of, and treatments for histrionic personality disorder.

Summary: Students will learn more about the key symptoms and causes of histrionic personality disorder from a professional. Students will also learn about the key feature of this disorder: a need to be the center of attention.

Questions to Students and Discussion: How many DSM-IV-TR criteria, as mentioned by Dr. Hahn, were you able to identify? Which ones? What do you think it must be like living with this disorder? What surprised you? Why? What issues might you face when trying to treat someone with this disorder?

D. Narcissistic Personality Disorder

- *Narcissistic personality disorder* is a personality disorder characterized by an inflated sense of importance, an excessive desire to be admired, and a lack of empathy.
- People with this disorder are overly focused on themselves and seek out praise from others. [See *Table 13.18, Table 13.19, Table 13.20; Case 13.8.*]
- People with narcissistic personality disorder can be grandiose.
- Reiland does not meet the criteria for narcissistic personality disorder.

1. Understanding Narcissistic Personality Disorder

- Little research has been done on this disorder.
- One theory argues that people with this disorder had overly attentive and permissive parents.

2. Treating Narcissistic Personality Disorder

Treatment focuses on changing maladaptive beliefs but many patients do not stay in treatment because they typically see other people as the problem.

MEDIA RECOMMENDATION 13.10: What Is Narcissistic Personality Disorder?

Objective: To learn about narcissistic personality disorder through an expert interview.

Time: 8 Minutes

Media and Discussion: 11 Minutes

Discussion Only: 3 Minutes

Watch Online: Search Videojug.com using the search terms "narcissistic personality disorder," or http://www.videojug.com/interview/narcissistic-personality-disorder

Dr. Rhoda Hahn discusses the symptoms, causes of, and treatments for narcissistic personality disorder.

Summary: Students will learn more about the key symptoms and causes of narcissistic personality disorder from a professional. Students will also learn about the key feature of this disorder: grandiosity.

Questions to Students and Discussion: How many DSM-IV-TR criteria, as mentioned by Dr. Hahn, were you able to identify? Which ones? What do you think it must be like living with this disorder? What surprised you? Why? What issues might you face when trying to treat someone with this disorder?

LEARNING ACTIVITY 13.5: Compare and Contrast the Cluster B Personality Disorders

Objective: To identify the similarities and differences between the Cluster B personality disorders.

Time: 30 Minutes

Activity and Discussion: 55 Minutes

Discussion Only: 25 Minutes

Directions: Have students work in small groups to fill out *Worksheet 13.2* located in the back of this chapter. Ask each group to take a turn and present a portion of the chart to the class.

Summary: This activity will help students clearly see the differences and similarities of these disorders. The chart will help them organize a large amount of material on these disorders.

Questions to Students and Discussion: What are key similarities among the disorders? What are key differences among the disorders?

IV.   FEARFUL/ANXIOUS PERSONALITY DISORDERS

Cluster C personality disorders are typified by anxiety and fear and include avoidant, dependent, and obsessive-compulsive personality disorders.

A. Avoidant Personality Disorder

Avoidant personality disorder is a personality disorder characterized by extreme social inhibition (*Example:* extreme shyness) that usually stems from feeling inadequate and being overly sensitive to negative evaluation.

1. **What Is Avoidant Personality Disorder?**

    - People with this disorder fear embarrassment and thus avoid social interactions. [See *Table 13.21.*]

    - People with this disorder report the lowest quality of life, as compared to the other personality disorders. [See *Table 13.22; Case 13.9.*]

2. **Distinguishing Between Avoidant Personality Disorder and Other Disorders**

    - Avoidant personality disorder shares some similar symptoms with social phobia, but the personality disorder symptoms are broader and more pervasive.

    - Cultural factors should be considered prior to diagnosis because language barriers and ethnic and religious norms may affect behavior.

MEDIA RECOMMENDATION 13.11: What Is Avoidant Personality Disorder?

Objective: To learn about avoidant personality disorder through an expert interview.

Time: 4 Minutes

Media and Discussion: 8 Minutes

Discussion Only: 4 Minutes

Watch Online: Search Videojug.com using the search terms "avoidant personality disorder," or http://www.videojug.com/interview/avoidant-personality-disorder

Dr. Rhoda Hahn discusses the symptoms, causes of, and treatments for avoidant personality disorder.

Summary: Students will learn more about the key symptoms and causes of avoidant personality disorder from a professional. Students will also learn about the key feature of this disorder: extreme fear of criticism.

Questions to Students and Discussion: How many DSM-IV-TR criteria, as mentioned by Dr. Hahn, were you able to identify? Which ones? What do you think it must be like living with this disorder? What surprised you? Why? What issues might you face when trying to treat someone with this disorder?

B. Dependent Personality Disorder

Dependent personality disorder is a personality disorder characterized by submissive and clingy behaviors, based on a fear of separation.

1. What Is Dependent Personality Disorder?

- People with this disorder have difficulty making even small decisions and prefer to have others make decisions for them. [See *Table 13.23.*]
- People with this disorder tend to choose dominant partners and may tolerate mental and physical abuse.
- Symptoms must cause significant impairment. [See *Table 13.24; Case 13.10.*]

2. Distinguishing Between Dependent Personality Disorder and Other Disorders

- People with avoidant personality disorder have social skills problems, while people with dependent personality disorder rely on others to take care of them.
- Cultures vary on their norms for men and women. (*Example:* Some cultures promote dependence on others.)

MEDIA RECOMMENDATION 13.12: What Is Dependent Personality Disorder?

Objective: To learn about dependent personality disorder through an expert interview.

Time: 5 Minutes

Media and Discussion: 9 Minutes

Discussion Only: 4 Minutes

Watch Online: Search Videojug.com using the search terms "dependent personality disorder," or http://www.videojug.com/interview/dependent-personality-disorder

Dr. Rhoda Hahn discusses the symptoms, causes of, and treatments for dependent personality disorder.

Summary: Students will learn more about the key symptoms and causes of dependent personality disorder from a professional. Students will also learn about the key feature of this disorder: extreme dependency.

Questions to Students and Discussion: How many DSM-IV-TR criteria, as mentioned by Dr. Hahn, were you able to identify? Which ones? What do you think it must be like living with this disorder? What surprised you? Why? What issues might you face when trying to treat someone with this disorder?

C. Obsessive-Compulsive Personality Disorder

- *Obsessive-compulsive personality disorder* is a personality disorder characterized by preoccupations with perfectionism, orderliness, and self-control as well as low levels of flexibility and efficiency.
- This personality disorder has the least disability and includes people with the highest levels of education.
- Reiland's father exhibited some symptoms of this disorder.

1. **What Is Obsessive-Compulsive Personality Disorder?**

   People with this disorder focus on details, appear rigid and inflexible, seek out perfection, adhere to rules, are formal, focus on logic and intellect, and have difficulty with others' perspectives. [See *Tables 13.25, 13.26; Case 13.11.*]

2. **Distinguishing Between Obsessive-Compulsive Personality Disorder and Other Disorders**

   - Obsessive-compulsive personality disorder does not include symptoms of obsessions and compulsions but, rather, a focus on details and inflexibility.

   - Research is still looking at the possible connection between these two disorders; people who have one of these disorders do not usually have the other.

MEDIA RECOMMENDATION 13.13: What Is Obsessive-Compulsive Personality Disorder?

Objective: To learn about obsessive-compulsive personality disorder through an expert interview.

Time: 5 Minutes

Media and Discussion: 9 Minutes

Discussion Only: 4 Minutes

Watch Online: Search Videojug.com using the search terms "obsessive-compulsive personality disorder," or http://www.videojug.com/interview/obsessive-compulsive-personality-disorder/

Dr. Rhoda Hahn discusses the symptoms, causes of, and treatments for obsessive-compulsive personality disorder.

Summary: Students will learn more about the key symptoms and causes of obsessive-compulsive personality disorder from a professional. Students will also learn about the key feature of this disorder: extreme rigidity.

Questions to Students and Discussion: How many DSM-IV-TR criteria, as mentioned by Dr. Hahn, were you able to identify? Which ones? What do you think it must be like living with this disorder? What surprised you? Why? What issues might you face when trying to treat someone with this disorder?

D. Understanding Fearful/Anxious Personality Disorders

- Little research has been done on these disorders.
- It is possible that the amygdala is involved, but this is just speculation.
- High harm avoidance (temperament) may also be a factor. [See *Table 13.27.*]
- Anxious or avoidant parent-child attachment style may also contribute to this disorder.

E. Treating Fearful/Anxious Personality Disorders

- CBT that includes exposure and cognitive restructuring can help with avoidant personality disorder.
- Family or couples therapy may also be used. [See *Table 13.28.*]

LEARNING ACTIVITY 13.6: Compare and Contrast the Cluster C Personality Disorders

Objective: To identify the similarities and differences between the Cluster C personality disorders.

Time: 20 Minutes

Activity and Discussion: 45 Minutes

Discussion Only: 25 Minutes

Directions: Have students work in small groups to fill out *Worksheet 13.3* located in the back of this chapter. Assign each group to take a turn and present a portion of the chart to the class.

Summary: This activity will help students clearly see the differences and similarities between these disorders. The chart will help them organize a large amount of material on these disorders.

Questions to Students and Discussion: What are key similarities between the disorders? What are key differences between the disorders?

V. FOLLOW-UP ON RACHEL REILAND

- Reiland clearly showed signs of borderline personality disorder, but also had some symptoms of histrionic and obsessive-compulsive personality disorder.
- Reiland was hospitalized a number of times and received psychotherapy and medication. Eight years after her treatment, she became more stable.

ADDITIONAL READINGS

Antisocial Personality Disorder

Cooke, D. J., Hart, S. D., & Michie, C. (2004). Cross-national differences in the assessment of psychopathy: Do they reflect variations in raters' perceptions of symptoms? *Psychological Assessment, 16,* 335–339.

Levy, T. M., & Orlans, M. (1999). Kids who kill: Attachment disorder, antisocial personality and violence. *The Forensic Examiner, 8,* 19–24.

Avoidant Personality Disorder

Chambless, D. L., Fydrich, T., & Rodebaugh, T. L. (2008). Generalized social phobia and avoidant personality disorder: Meaningful distinction or useless duplication? *Depression and Anxiety, 25,* 8–19.

Borderline Personality Disorder

Bandelow, B., Krause, J., Wedekind, D., Broocks, A., Hajak, G., & Rüther, E. (2005). Early traumatic life events, parental attitudes, family history, and birth risk factors in patients with borderline personality disorder and healthy controls. *Psychiatry Research, 134,* 169–179.

Becker, D., & Lamb, S. (1994). Sex bias in the diagnosis of borderline personality disorder and posttraumatic stress disorder. *Professional Psychology: Research and Practice, 25,* 55–61.

Schizotypal Personality Disorder

Berenbaum, H., Thompson, R. J., Milanek, M. E., Boden, M. T., & Bredemeier, K. (2008). Psychological trauma and schizotypal personality disorder. *Journal of Abnormal Psychology, 117,* 502–519.

BOOKS AND MEMOIRS

Antisocial Personality Disorder

Buttafuoco, M. J., & McCarron, J. (2009). *Getting it through my thick skull: Why I stayed, what I learned, and what millions of people involved with sociopaths need to know.* Deerfield Beach, FL: Health Communications.

Buttafuoco talks about her experiences with her husband who showed signs of being a sociopath long before his teenaged lover shot her.

Stout, M. (2005). *The sociopath next door.* New York: Broadway Books.

This book provides information about antisocial personality disorder and the sociopath and provides several case examples.

Borderline Personality Disorder

Reiland, R. (2004). *Get me out of here: My recovery from borderline personality disorder.* Center City, MN: Hazelden.

This book, which has been featured throughout this chapter, tells the story of one woman's struggle with borderline personality disorder.

Van Gelder, K. (2010). *Buddha & the borderline: My recovery from borderline personality disorder through dialectical behavior therapy, Buddhism, and online dating.* Oakland, CA: New Harbinger Publications.

This memoir features one woman's recovery from borderline personality disorder.

Narcissistic Personality Disorder

Brown, N. W. (2008). *Children of the self-absorbed: A grown-up's guide to getting over narcissistic parents.* Oakland, CA: New Harbinger Publications.

This book describes different types of narcissism and how to deal with one's parents, who have this disorder.

Campbell, L. C. (2009). *Daughter of narcissus: A family's struggle to survive their mother's narcissistic personality disorder.* Dynasty Press Limited.

An upper-class Jamaican family deals with their mother's narcissistic personality disorder.

ADDITIONAL MEDIA RECOMMENDATIONS

Brooks, J. L. (Director). (1997). *As good as it gets.* [Film]. USA: TriStar Pictures.

Melvin Udall has symptoms of both obsessive-compulsive disorder and obsessive-compulsive personality disorder.

Kubrick, S. (Director). (1971). *A clockwork orange.* [Film]. UK: Warner Brothers Pictures.

A group of young men, who show symptoms of antisocial personality disorder, terrorize community members.

Lynch, D. (Director). (1986). *Blue velvet.* [Film]. Wilmington, NC: De Laurentis Entertainment Group.

A woman with symptoms of dependent personality disorder is involved with an abusive man.

Lyne, A. (Director). (1987). *Fatal attraction.* [Film]. USA: Paramount Pictures.

A woman with symptoms of borderline personality disorder has an affair with a married man with terrifying consequences.

WEB SITES

Mental Health.Net: Provides an overview of each personality disorder and includes links for books and videos. See: http://www.mentalhelp.net/poc/center_index.php?id=8

Psychology Prof Online: Offers an overview of personality disorders, links, new research, and articles. See: http://www.psychologyprofonline.org/

Borderline Personality Disorder

BPDCentral: This Web site offers support groups, articles, books and more on borderline personality disorder. See: http://www.BPDCentral.com

Marsha Linehan's Faculty Web Page: Explore Linehan's clinic, PowerPoint presentations, books, and additional links. See: http://faculty.washington.edu/linehan/

WORKSHEET 13.1

Cluster A	Paranoid	Schizoid	Schizotypal
Symptoms			
Prevalence			
Gender differences			
Character from a film as example			
Treatment			
Other/misc.			

WORKSHEET 13.2

Cluster B	Antisocial	Borderline	Histrionic	Narcissistic
Symptoms				
Prevalence				
Gender differences				
Character from a film as example				
Treatment				
Other/misc.				

WORKSHEET 13.3

Cluster C	Avoidant	Dependent	Obsessive-Compulsive
Symptoms			
Prevalence			
Gender differences			
Character from a film as example			
Treatment			
Other/misc.			

Childhood Disorders

CHAPTER OUTLINE

CHAPTER HEADINGS	INSTRUCTION IDEAS AND TEXTBOOK CORRELATIONS
Chapter Introduction	**Learning Objective:** 14.1 **Learning Activity 14.1:** Class Discussion on Youth Mental Health and the Schools **Lecture Enhancement 14.1:** The State of Children's Mental Health
MENTAL RETARDATION	
What Is Mental Retardation?	**Learning Objectives:** 14.2, 14.3 **Learning Concept:** four levels of mental retardation **Textbook Tools:** Figure 14.1; Tables 14.1, 14.2; Case 14.1
Understanding Mental Retardation	**Learning Objectives:** 14.4, 14.5, 14.6 **Learning Concepts:** neurological factors: teratogens and genes; psychological factors: problem behaviors; social factors: understimulation **Textbook Tool:** Table 14.3
Treating Mental Retardation	**Learning Objectives:** 14.4, 14.7, 14.8 **Learning Concepts:** targeting neurological factors: prevention; targeting psychological and social factors: communication; targeting social factors: accommodation in the classroom—it's the law **Worth Video Tool Kit for Abnormal Psychology:** Mentally Disabled Couple Fights Michigan Law Keeping Them from Getting Married, "Best Buddies" Mental Retardation
PERVASIVE DEVELOPMENTAL DISORDERS	**Learning Objective:** 14.9
Autism Spectrum Disorders	**Learning Objectives:** 14.10, 14.11, 14.12, 14.13, 14.14 **Learning Concepts:** autism: what is autistic disorder? what is Asperger's disorder? distinguishing between Asperger's disorder and other disorders; understanding autism spectrum disorders; treating autism spectrum disorders

	Media Recommendation 14.1: Autistic Savant **Media Recommendation 14.2:** Red Flags for Autism Spectrum Disorder **Media Recommendation 14.3:** Mirror Neurons **Media Recommendation 14.4:** Applied Behavioral Analysis **Textbook Tools:** Tables 14.4, 14.5, 14.6, 14.7; Cases 14.2, 14.3 **Worth Video Tool Kit for Abnormal Psychology:** The Struggle with Autism
Other Pervasive Developmental Disorders	**Learning Objective:** 14.15 **Learning Concepts:** childhood disintegrative disorder; Rett's disorder
LEARNING DISORDERS: PROBLEMS WITH THE THREE Rs	
What Are Learning Disorders?	**Learning Objective:** 14.16 **Learning Concept:** three types of learning disorders **Media Recommendation 14.5:** What Is It Like to Have Dyslexia? **Textbook Tools:** Tables 14.8, 14.9; Case 14.4
Understanding Learning Disorders	**Learning Objective:** 14.17 **Learning Concepts:** neurological factors; psychological factors; social factors **Worth Video Tool Kit for Abnormal Psychology:** Discovering Carmen's Learning Disability Carmen's Strengths Help Her Overcome Her Learning Disability Dyslexia
Treating Learning Disorders	**Learning Objective:** 14.17 **Learning Concepts:** treating dyslexia; treating other learning disorders
DISORDERS OF DISRUPTIVE BEHAVIOR AND ATTENTION	
What Is Conduct Disorder?	**Learning Objectives:** 14.18, 14.19 **Learning Concepts:** adolescent-onset type; childhood-onset type **Textbook Tools:** Tables 14.10, 14.11; Case 14.5
What Is Oppositional Defiant Disorder?	**Learning Objectives:** 14.20, 14.21 **Textbook Tools:** Figure 14.2; Tables 14.12, 14.13; Case 14.6 **Worth Video Tool Kit for Abnormal Psychology:** Oppositional Defiant Disorder
What Is Attention-Deficit/Hyperactivity Disorder?	**Learning Objectives:** 14.22, 14.23, 14.24 **Learning Concepts:** distinguishing between attention-deficit/hyperactivity disorder and other disorders; criticisms of the DSM-IV-TR diagnostic criteria **Learning Activity 14.2:** Acting Out the Disruptive Disorders **Lecture Enhancement 14.2:** Bullying and Peer Victimization **Textbook Tools:** Figure 14.3; Tables 14.14, 14.15; Case 14.7 **Worth Video Tool Kit for Abnormal Psychology:** Adults Suffering from ADD, ADD Grows Up

Understanding Disorders of Disruptive Behavior and Attention	**Learning Objectives:** 14.25, 14.26, 14.27 **Learning Concepts:** neurological factors; psychological factors: recognizing facial expressions, keeping track of time; social factors: blame and credit; feedback loops in action: attention-deficit/hyperactivity disorder **Learning Activity 14.3:** Explore Genes to Cognition Online **Textbook Tool:** Figure 14.4
Treating Disorders of Disruptive Behavior and Attention	**Learning Objective:** 14.27 **Learning Concepts:** targeting neurological factors: medication; targeting psychological factors: treating disruptive behavior; targeting social factors: reinforcement in relationships; feedback loops in treatment: treating attention-deficit/hyperactivity disorder **Textbook Tool:** Figure 14.5
OTHER DISORDERS OF CHILDHOOD	
Separation Anxiety Disorder	**Learning Objectives:** 14.28, 14.29, 14.30 **Learning Concepts:** what is separation anxiety disorder? distinguishing between separation anxiety disorder and other disorders; understanding separation anxiety disorder; treating separation anxiety disorder **Media Recommendation 14.6:** Separation Anxiety Disorder in Children **Textbook Tools:** Tables 14.16, 14.17; Case 14.8
Other Types of Disorders of Childhood, in Brief	**Learning Objectives:** 14.31, 14.32 **Learning Concepts:** communication disorders; feeding and eating disorders; elimination disorders; tic disorders **Media Recommendation 14.7:** I Have Tourette's, but Tourette's Doesn't Have Me **Textbook Tool:** Figure 14.6

LEARNING OBJECTIVES

After completing this chapter, students will be able to:

14.1 Explain what is meant by "childhood disorders."

14.2 Identify the diagnostic criteria and additional facts for mental retardation.

14.3 Name the four levels of mental retardation and delineate the IQ criteria for each level.

14.4 Explain how neurological, psychological, and social factors and their interactions help to understand and treat mental retardation disorders.

14.5 Describe the genetic causes of the following abnormalities: Down syndrome, Rett's disorder, fragile X, Prader-Willi and Angelman syndromes, phenylketonuria, and congenital hypothyroidism [*Table 14.3*].

14.6 Identify the two types of problematic behaviors that are not mentioned in the DSM-IV-TR criteria.

14.7 Detail the benefits provided to children with disabilities under current government law.

14.8 Identify the goals of an individualized education program (IEP).

14.9 Define pervasive developmental disorders and name the four specific disorders that fall under this category of mental retardation.

14.10 Identify the diagnostic criteria and additional facts for autistic spectrum disorder.

14.11 Identify the diagnostic criteria and additional facts for Asperger's disorder.

14.12 Compare and contrast Asperger's disorder with other disorders.

14.13 Explain how neurological, psychological, and social factors and their interactions help to understand and treat autism spectrum disorders.

14.14 Define applied behavior analysis.

14.15 Identify the similarities and differences among childhood disintegrative disorder, Rett's disorder, and autism.

14.16 Identify the diagnostic criteria and additional facts for learning disorders.

14.17 Explain how neurological, psychological, and social factors and their interactions help to understand and treat learning disorders.

14.18 Identify the diagnostic criteria and additional facts for conduct disorders.

14.19 Describe the two types of conduct disorder.

14.20 Describe the diagnostic criteria and additional facts for oppositional defiant disorder.

14.21 Articulate the typical diagnostic paths that disruptive behavior disorders can take [*Table 14.2*].

14.22 Describe the diagnostic criteria and additional facts for attention-deficit/hyperactivity disorder (ADHD).

14.23 Compare and contrast attention-deficit/hyperactivity disorder with other disorders.

14.24 Articulate some of the major criticisms of the DSM-IV-TR category, ADHD.

14.25 Explain how neurological, psychological, and social factors and their interactions help to understand and treat disorders of disruptive behavior and attention.

14.26 Describe how the different factors related to ADHD create feedback loops.

14.27 Explain how neurological, psychological, and social factors and their interactions help to understand and treat disorders of disruptive behavior and attention.

14.28 Describe the diagnostic criteria and additional facts for separation anxiety disorder.

14.29 Compare and contrast separation anxiety disorder with other disorders.

14.30 Identify the factors and their interactions that help to understand and treat separation anxiety disorder.

14.31 Describe the symptoms and characteristics of communication disorders, feeding and eating disorders, the two types of elimination disorders, and tic disorders.

14.32 Define Tourette's disorder.

KEY TERMS

Mental retardation: Intelligence that is significantly below normal—an IQ approximately equal to or less than 70 (where the mean IQ is set at 100)—and that impairs daily functioning; also referred to as *intellectual disability.*

Teratogens: Substances or other stimuli that are harmful to a fetus.

Stereotyped behaviors: Repetitive behaviors—such as body rocking—that do not serve a function; also referred to as *stereotypes.*

Inclusion: The placement of students with disabilities in a regular classroom, with guidelines for any accommodations that the regular classroom teacher or special education teacher should make.

Pervasive developmental disorders: A set of developmental disorders that have in common severe deficits in communication and in social interaction skills and may also involve stereotyped behaviors and narrow interests.

Autistic disorder: A pervasive developmental disorder that arises in childhood and is characterized by delayed or impaired communication and social skills, along with restricted and repetitive behaviors and interests; also referred to as *autism.*

Asperger's disorder: A psychological disorder on the autism spectrum characterized by problems with social interaction and narrowed behaviors—similar to but less severe than autism—but in which language and cognitive development are in the normal range; also referred to as *Asperger's syndrome.*

Theory of mind: A theory about other people's mental states (their beliefs, desires, and feelings) that allows a person to predict how other people will react in a given situation.

Applied behavior analysis: A technique used to modify maladaptive behaviors by reinforcing new behaviors through shaping.

Childhood disintegrative disorder: A pervasive developmental disorder characterized by normal development until at least 2 years of age, followed by a profound loss of communication skills, normal types of play, and bowel control.

Rett's disorder: A pervasive developmental disorder that affects only females and is characterized by normal prenatal development and functioning after birth through at least 5 months of age, after which the growth of the child's head slows and she loses the ability to control normal muscle movements, interest in other people, and previously developed skills.

Learning disorder: A psychological disorder characterized by a significant disparity between an individual's academic performance and the expected level of performance based on his or her age, intelligence, and education level.

Dyslexia: A learning disorder characterized by difficulty with reading accuracy, speed, or comprehension that interferes with academic achievement or activities of daily functioning that involve reading.

Conduct disorder: A psychological disorder that typically arises in childhood and is characterized by the violation of the basic rights of others or of societal norms that are appropriate to the individual's age.

Oppositional defiant disorder: A psychological disorder that typically arises in childhood or adolescence and is characterized by overt disobedience, hostility, defiance, and negativity toward people in authority.

Attention-deficit/hyperactivity disorder (ADHD): A psychological disorder that typically arises in childhood and is characterized by inattention, hyperactivity, and/or impulsivity.

Contingency management: A procedure for modifying behavior by changing the conditions that led to, or are produced by, it.

Separation anxiety disorder: A psychological disorder that typically arises in childhood and is characterized by excessive anxiety about separation from home or from someone to whom the individual has become attached.

Communication disorders: A set of psychological disorders characterized by significant problems in understanding language or using language to express oneself.

Feeding and eating disorders: A set of psychological disorders characterized by problems with feeding or eating.

Elimination disorders: A set of psychological disorders characterized by inappropriate urination or defecation.

Encopresis: An elimination disorder characterized by a child's persistent defecation in improper locations—neither in a toilet nor in a diaper.

Enuresis: An elimination disorder characterized by a child's persistent urination in bed or in his or her clothes.

Tic disorders: A set of disorders characterized by persistent tics (motor or vocal) that occur many times a day on most days.

Tourette's disorder: A tic disorder characterized by recurrent motoric and vocal tics; also referred to as *Tourette syndrome.*

CHAPTER GUIDE

Chapter Introduction

- Lela and Carlos Enriquez have several children with social, academic, or developmental problems.
- This chapter covers disorders first diagnosed in infancy, childhood, or adolescence, some of which are lifetime disorders.
- Many of these disorders have not been well researched, so the interactions and feedback loops are not always known.

LEARNING ACTIVITY 14.1: Class Discussion on Youth Mental Health and the Schools

Objective: To understand the lack of mental health coverage in primary and secondary schools.

Time: 10 Minutes

Discussion and Reflection: 30 Minutes

Discussion Only: 20 Minutes

Directions: Ask students to reflect or free-write on the following question:

Think about your experiences in elementary, middle, and high school. What instruction did you receive about your physical, emotional, spiritual, and occupational development?

Summary: Students will note that both their emotional and spiritual development were either not addressed, or addressed very little, in primary and secondary classrooms.

Questions to Students and Discussion: Which areas were most emphasized and which were least emphasized? Why do you think certain areas were emphasized more than others? What are the consequences of the lack of coverage in these other areas?

LECTURE ENHANCEMENT 14.1: The State of Children's Mental Health

Objective: To learn about the current needs of U.S. youth.

Time: 20 Minutes

Lecture Points:
I.   Children's Mental Health Rates
   A. Twenty percent of children could qualify with a DSM-IV disorder, yet only a third receive services.
   B. Currently we only have enough services to meet the needs of 10% of children with mental health problems.
II. Consequences of Not Receiving Treatment
   A. Seventy-five percent of adults with disorders say they had symptoms in childhood.
   B. Children with emotional and behavioral disorders have the highest drop-out rates at 50.6%.
III. Addressing the Problem
   A. Policy changes
      1. Reform policies to ensure access
      2. Identify children at risk and provide preventative care
      3. Health and education centers need services to meet the mental health needs of children
      4. Create culturally sensitive care.
   B. Comprehensive health care for children
      1. Create accessible mental health services for children
      2. Include child mental health as a component in schools, regular office visits, and other settings
      3. Offer preventative care for high-risk children
      4. Create culturally sensitive care

Summary: Students will be surprised by the lack of services and treatment for children. Students will enjoy learning about policy changes and ways to create more comprehensive health care for youth.

Source: Tolan, P. H., & Dodge, K. A. (2005). Children's mental health as a primary care and concern. *American Psychologist, 60*(6), 601–614.

Questions to Students and Discussion: What did you find surprising about this lecture? How do you think the policy changes might affect the care people receive? How might a more comprehensive health care system change people's lives? What might you add to the policy and comprehensive care suggestions listed here?

I. MENTAL RETARDATION

A. What Is Mental Retardation?

- *Mental retardation* is defined as intelligence that is significantly below normal—an IQ approximately equal to or less than 70 (where the mean IQ is set at 100)—and that impairs daily functioning; also referred to as *intellectual disability*. [See *Table 14.1.*]
- There are four levels of mental retardation:
   i. **Mild mental retardation** is diagnosed with an IQ of 50–55 to 70; 85% of people with mental retardation fall into this group, and most in this group can function independently with occasional help.

ii. **Moderate mental retardation** is diagnosed with an IQ score of 35–40 to 50–55; 10% of people with mental retardation fall into this group, and people in this group cannot function independently but can perform unskilled work with supervision.

iii. **Severe mental retardation** is diagnosed with an IQ range between 20–25 to 35–40; 3%–4% of those with mental retardation fall into this category, and individuals can only perform simple tasks and must have close supervision.

iv. **Profound mental retardation** is diagnosed in those with IQ scores below 20 or 25; 1%–2% of those with mental retardation fall into this group, and this group needs constant supervision to perform simple tasks. [See *Figure 14.1.*]

- The most important criterion for determining the level of mental retardation is not necessarily IQ but an individual's ability to cope and function. [See *Case 14.1.*]

- People with mental retardation can have additional disorders and ranges of personality characteristics. [See *Table 14.2.*]

B. Understanding Mental Retardation

- Drugs, viruses, and other substances a fetus is exposed to are neurological causes of mental retardation.

- *Teratogens* are substances or other stimuli that are harmful to a fetus.

- Labor complications or exposure to high levels of lead prenatally or in early childhood can also cause mental retardation.

1. Neurological Factors: Teratogens and Genes

- Environmental toxins can enter the mother's bloodstream and expose the fetus through the placenta. (*Example:* Some harmful toxins are mercury, polychlorinated biphenyls [PCBs], and pesticides.)

- Exposure to these toxins in the first trimester can affect central nervous system development. [See *Table 14.3* for a detailed description of the genetic causes of mental retardation.]

- Abnormal brain structure causes abnormal processing, which leads to cognitive and behavioral deficits.

- Some studies have shown that those with mental retardation have larger heads and possibly larger brains. This size difference may be a result of enlarged ventricles in the brain or a higher number of glial cells.

- However, people with *fetal alcohol syndrome,* another form of mental retardation, have smaller heads.

- People with fetal alcohol syndrome have difficulties with coordination, smooth motor movement, and executive functions.

2. Psychological Factors: Problem Behaviors

- There are two problem behaviors that people with mental retardation show:
  i. *Stereotyped behaviors:* repetitive behaviors—such as body rocking—that do not serve a function; also referred to as *stereotypes*
  ii. **Self-injurious behaviors:** the patient doing harm to herself, such as hitting her head against something or hitting or biting herself

- Additional behaviors include preferring interactions with objects to people, inappropriate touching, and resisting contact and affection.

3. **Social Factors: Understimulation**

Mental retardation can result from understimulation or undernourishment; however, in 30%–40% of the cases there is no clear cause of this disorder.

C. Treating Mental Retardation

This disorder cannot be cured, but interventions help with daily functioning or reducing the causes of mental retardation.

1. **Targeting Neurological Factors: Prevention**

There are two successful prevention efforts:

- **Focus on phenylketonuria** (PKU) by testing newborns for difficulty metabolizing the enzyme phenylalanine hydroxylase. Those who test positive must avoid certain foods that will cause brain damage (which will prevent mental retardation).
- **Focus on lead exposure** by banning lead in paint (since 1978) and requiring people to inform potential buyers or tenants of any lead paint on a property. Lead has been removed from gasoline. These changes have lead to a decrease in lead-induced mental retardation.

2. **Targeting Psychological and Social Factors: Communication**

- Treatments depend on the symptoms of mental retardation and comorbid disorders.
- Treatment may target communication problems using the Picture Exchange Communication System (PECS), where children exchange the picture of what they want for the actual item. This system teaches recognition (a cognitive skill), giving the picture to a person (a social skill), and responding to "What do you want?" (social and communication skills).

3. **Targeting Social Factors: Accommodation in the Classroom—It's the Law**

- Children with disabilities between the ages of 3 and 21 are entitled to educational services at no cost to the parents due to the passage of the Americans with Disabilities Act (1990) and the Individuals with Disabilities Act (IDEA, 1997).
- These children are given an *individualized education program* (IEP), which articulates specific educational goals, services, and products.
- One goal may be *inclusion,* which is the placement of students with disabilities in a regular classroom with guidelines for any accommodations that the regular classroom teacher or special education teacher should make.
- *Mainstreaming* is where the child is placed in a regular classroom without adjustments.
- With inclusion, students meet with speech and language therapists and math and reading specialists.
- Those children with mental retardation who have disruptive behavioral problems will be transferred to a school for children with special needs.

II. PERVASIVE DEVELOPMENTAL DISORDERS

- Richie Enriquez shows signs of autism, a pervasive developmental disorder, as he avoids eye contact with others, spends hours playing with a ball, has no interest in playing with others, and becomes upset if the daily routine is altered.

- *Pervasive developmental disorders* are a set of developmental disorders that have in common severe deficits in communication and in social interaction skills and may also involve stereotyped behaviors and narrow interests.

- *Pervasive* means that the disorder affects all aspects of the person's life. Symptoms begin in infancy or early childhood for most of these disorders.

- There are four pervasive developmental disorders in the DSM-IV-TR:
  - **i.** *Autistic disorder*
  - **ii.** *Asperger's disorder*
  - **i.** *Childhood integrative disorder*
  - **ii.** *Rett's disorder*

- *Pervasive developmental disorder not otherwise specified* is the diagnosis given to children who do not meet the full criteria of these disorders.

- The term "spectrum" means that symptoms can occur on a continuum from mild to severe.

A. Autism Spectrum Disorders

1. Autism: What Is Autistic Disorder?

- *Autistic disorder* is a pervasive developmental disorder that arises in childhood and is characterized by delayed or impaired communication and social skills, along with restricted and repetitive behaviors and interests; also referred to as *autism*. [See *Table 14.4*.]

- People with autism tend to lack understanding of social cues and interactions.

- Some of the symptoms overlap with schizophrenia, but symptoms of autism are present before age 3, whereas symptoms of schizophrenia occur after age 3.

- Mental retardation is often diagnosed with the autism; but when clients are reevaluated using an intelligence test that does not rely on verbal instructions or responses, the intelligence level jumps to average or above average.

- Autism differs from mental retardation in that clients with autism are not impaired in all aspect and 20% show unique skills (referred to as *autistic savants*). [See *Case 14.2*.]

- [See *Table 14.5*].

MEDIA RECOMMENDATION 14.1: Autistic Savant

Objective: To observe someone who is considered an autistic savant.

Time: 5 Minutes

Media and Discussion: 11 Minutes

Discussion Only: 6 Minutes

Watch Online: Search YouTube using the search terms "Stephen Wiltshire: The Human Camera," or http://www.youtube.com/watch?v=a8YXZTlwTAU&feature=related
This clip shows Wiltshire's ability to re-create an accurate drawing of an entire city after only one visit.

Summary: Students will be amazed with the memory abilities of Wiltshire, who shows social impairments but has an amazing photographic memory.

Questions to Students and Discussion: What was most surprising about this video? Why do you think Wiltshire has impairments in so many other areas of his brain but not in his drawing abilities and his photographic memory?

MEDIA RECOMMENDATION 14.2: Red Flags for Autism Spectrum Disorder

Objective: To observe the "red flags" clinicians and physicians look for as early signs of the autism spectrum disorder.

Time: 2:20 Minutes (depending on video chosen)

Media and Discussion: 15 Minutes

Discussion Only: 13 Minutes

Watch Online: Go to the Autism Speaks Web site, http://www.autismspeaks.org/. Locate the video glossary and sign up for a free account. Click on "Social Interaction."
This video compares a typically developing child to a child with autism spectrum disorder.

Summary: Students will be able to see the different social interaction behaviors between a child with and a child without autism. Students will notice how the "typical" child interacts with adults, looking into the adults' eyes, while the child with autism fixates on an object and does not interact with the adults.

Questions to Students and Discussion: What symptoms of autism did you notice? What do you think it is like to be a parent of a child with autism? How might you work with this child to improve his social interactions?

2. **What Is Asperger's Disorder?**

   - *Asperger's disorder* is a psychological disorder on the autism spectrum characterized by problems with social interaction and narrowed behaviors—similar to but less severe than autism—but in which language and cognitive development are in the normal range; also referred to as *Asperger's syndrome.*
   - Subtle social cues and indirect meaning are difficult to understand for people with Asperger's disorder. [See *Table 14.6.*]
   - People with Asperger's avoid continued eye contact, lack the ability to show interest in others (are indifferent to others), and show impaired school function and self-care. [See *Table 14.7.*]
   - People with Asperger's may develop a narrow set of interests. [See *Case 14.3.*]
   - People with Asperger's tend to have two social patterns:
     i. Minimal contact with others, which results in social isolation
     ii. Limited social skills, which strain relationships

3. **Distinguishing Between Asperger's Disorder and Other Disorders**

   - The following are factors that are true for autism but not Asperger's:
     i. Problems with language
     ii. Extreme distress caused by change
     iii. Lack of interest in social interactions
   - Both schizoid personality disorder and Asperger's disorder have a lack of close friendships, but people with Asperger's have more desire for close friendships.
   - People with Asperger's are different from socially awkward people in that people with Asperger's have a narrow focus of interest that may interfere with eating and attending school.

4. **Understanding Autism Spectrum Disorders**

Autism has been researched more than Asperger's disorder; thus the outline here mostly addresses autism and the neuropsychosocial factors that cause it.

a. **Neurological Factors:**

Brain structure abnormalities, brain function, and genetics all play a role in the development of autism.

(1) **Brain systems:**

- Larger head circumference is associated with autism in children but not adults, which may indicate an increase in white and gray matter.

- In people with autism, certain areas of the brain have increased communication while the distant areas (the frontal lobes and other areas) have less communication.

- In autism, deficits in executive functioning may be due to decreased activity in the frontal lobe.

- The motor coordination problems seen in Asperger's may be due to problems with the central nervous system.

(2) **Genetics:**

- Eight percent (versus 0.2%) of people with a sibling with autism will be affected by the disorder.

- Monozygotic twins are nine times more likely to *both* have autism than are dizygotic twin pairs.

- Autism is thought to be developed by the interaction of a number of genes (possibly 15 genes).

- Fathers who are 40 years of age or older are six times more likely to have children with autism than fathers who are 30 years old or younger. Older mothers are also more likely to have children with an autism spectrum disorder.

- *Thimerisol,* an ingredient in vaccines, was thought to be a cause of autism, but this has not been supported by research; autism has increased despite the discontinuation of this substance in children's vaccines.

- In the United States, more children in the northwest have autism than in other parts of the country, which may be the result of too much time spent indoors leading to a increases in TV watching, vitamin D deficiency, or exposure to chemicals in household cleaning products.

- Relatives of those with Asperger's are more likely to have an autism spectrum disorder.

b. **Psychological Factors: Cognitive Deficits:**

- People with autism have cognitive deficits that make it difficult to switch from one activity to another.

- An EEG study of 3- and 4-year-olds found that children with autism respond the same to pictures of both neutral and fear faces.

- People with autism have difficulty taking the perspectives of others, also called *theory of mind.*

- ***Theory of mind*** is a theory about other people's mental states (their beliefs, desires, and feelings) that allows a person to predict how other people will react in a given situation.

- Children with autism fail the *false-belief test,* a test of theory of mind, 80% of the time. This test utilizes dolls to act out a scene and requires the viewer to take the perspective of one of the dolls.
- People with Asperger's show less severe theory of mind impairment.

MEDIA RECOMMENDATION 14.3: Mirror Neurons

Objective: To learn about the impact "broken" neurons might have on the development of autism.

Time: 14 Minutes

Media and Discussion: 24 Minutes

Discussion Only: 10 Minutes

Watch Online: Search Google using the terms "mirror neurons nova science now," or http://www.pbs.org/wgbh/nova/sciencenow/3204/01.html

This program highlights new research that may reveal how certain neurons help us imitate and understand the behaviors of others.

Summary: Students will find that new research suggests that broken mirror neurons inhibit those with autism from learning by watching others.

Questions to Students and Discussion: What surprised you about this short clip? How do mirror neurons help us with the theory of mind and empathy? What do you think it must be like if you lack fully functioning mirror neurons?

c. Social Factors: Communication Problems:

- People with autism focus on others' mouths, not eyes, and do not respond to their name or parents' voices. They lack "normal" communication skills and have an inability to recognize emotions, all of which makes interpersonal interactions challenging.
- Since autism is primarily caused by neurological factors, feedback loops were not included in this section.

5. Treating Autism Spectrum Disorders

- Time-intensive treatments (25 hours per week) are useful in treating the disorder, although there is no known cure.
- The American Academy of Pediatrics suggests that children be screened for autism before age 2.

a. Targeting Neurological Factors:

Medications (antipsychotics and SSRIs) are used to treat comorbid disorders with autism, but are less common for those with Asperger's disorder. Some research has shown that those with autism are more sensitive to the side effects of these medications.

b. Targeting Psychological Factors: Applied Behavior Analysis:

- *Applied behavioral analysis,* a technique used to modify maladaptive behaviors by reinforcing new behaviors through shaping, is the most common technique for changing problematic behaviors in children with autism.

- Complex behavior is broken down into smaller units of learning, where each unit can be taught and reinforced. *Example:* Glancing at a spoon or touching a spoon is reinforced when one is learning how to use a utensil when eating.

MEDIA RECOMMENDATION 14.4: Applied Behavioral Analysis

Objective: To observe and learn about applied behavioral analysis.

Time: 4 Minutes

Media and Discussion: 10 Minutes

Discussion Only: 6 Minutes

Watch Online: Search YouTube using the terms "applied behavioral analysis autism," or http://www.youtube.com/watch?v=iyCx-OLzgJw
This short video highlights the basics of behavioral analysis and shows several of the techniques.

Summary: Students will be surprised to learn that basic skills such as going to the grocery store need to be taught to children with autism. Students will enjoy learning how to use reinforcements to produce adaptive responses in children.

Questions to Students and Discussion: Highlight the key characteristics of applied behavioral analysis. What type of reinforcements did the instructor use to increase certain behaviors? What were some of the behaviors the children with autism needed to learn?

---

    c. Targeting Social Factors: Communication:

- Communication is facilitated through the use of a picture system (such as PECS).
- For those with high-functioning autism or Asperger's, communication skills are developed through the use of a social skills group, modeling, and role playing.
- Additional tools that develop communication skills include a computerized training program and social stories that teach specific social cues.

B. Other Pervasive Developmental Disorders

Childhood disintegrative disorder and Rett's disorder are also considered pervasive developmental disorders.

    1. Childhood Disintegrative Disorder

- *Childhood disintegrative disorder* is a pervasive developmental disorder characterized by normal development until at least 2 years of age, followed by a profound loss of communication skills, normal types of play, and bowel control.
- Unlike autism, these symptoms do not improve over time even with interventions.

    2. Rett's Disorder

- *Rett's disorder* is a pervasive developmental disorder that affects only females and is characterized by normal prenatal development and functioning after birth through at least 5 months of age, after which the growth of the child's head slows and she loses the ability to control normal muscle movements, and loses interest in other people and previously developed skills.
- Rett's disorder has three characteristics that differentiate it from autism:

       i. Delayed growth of head circumference
       ii. Problems with coordination
       iii. Loss of hand skills

- This is an X-linked genetic disorder and thus only affects females. Male fetuses who have this genetic mutation do not survive.

III. LEARNING DISORDERS: PROBLEMS WITH THE THREE Rs

A. What Are Learning Disorders?

- A *learning disorder* is a psychological disorder characterized by a significant disparity between an individual's academic performance and the expected level of performance based on his or her age, intelligence, and education level.
- According to the DSM-IV-TR, there are three types of learning disorders:
  i. *Reading*
  ii. *Mathematics*
  iii. *Written expression*
- *Dyslexia* is a learning disorder characterized by difficulty with reading accuracy, speed, or comprehension that interferes with academic achievement or activities of daily functioning that involve reading. [See *Table 14.8.*]
- The deficits for each type of learning are as follows:
  i. Reading disorder: difficulty with reading accuracy, speed, and comprehension, which causes achievement or functioning problems
  ii. Mathematics disorder: difficulty recognizing numbers, symbols, remembering mathematical steps, or translating word problems into mathematical symbols
  iii. Disorder of written expression: poor spelling *and* grammatical, punctuation, or organization problems [see *Case 14.4*]
- One consequence of learning disorders is that people with learning disorders are 50% more likely to drop out of school.
- Social factors, such as being an immigrant or frequent absences, can lead to a misdiagnosis of a learning disorder.

MEDIA RECOMMENDATION 14.5: What Is It Like to Have Dyslexia?

Objective: To observe through animation what it might be like to have dyslexia.

Time: 3 Minutes

Media and Discussion: 7 Minutes

Discussion Only: 4 Minutes

Watch Online: Search YouTube using the search terms "what is it like to have dyslexia animations and illustrations," or http://www.youtube.com/watch?v=gwZLFTW4OGY&feature=related
This video was created by Coventry University to show viewers the daily experience of having dyslexia.

Summary: Students will be surprised to see how difficult it is for dyslexics to read and the multiple forms that dyslexia can take.

Questions to Students and Discussion: After watching this video, what do you think it is like to have dyslexia? How might having dyslexia affect how one feels about himself or herself? How might you work with someone who has dyslexia?

B. Understanding Learning Disorders

Learning disorders are largely caused by neurological factors, but psychological and social factors do play a role.

1. Neurological Factors

Most neurological research has focused on dyslexia.

a. Brain Systems:

- Abnormal auditory processing in the brain is one cause of dyslexia. A study showed that children with dyslexia at 8 years of age had different brain wave patterns in infancy than those without dyslexia.

- Neuroimaging studies have shown reduced activity in rear areas in the left hemisphere: in particular the juncture of the parietal and temporal lobes and the junction of the occipital and parietal lobes in people with dyslexia.

- Part of the frontal lobe and the right occipital-temporal region have increased activity in children with dyslexia.

- People with dyslexia have reduced gray matter in the left temporal lobe while their frontal lobes are enlarged.

- Some people with dyslexia may have impaired visual abilities.

- The exact areas that affect dyslexia are influenced by culture. *Example:* In Chinese children with dyslexia, research has shown left frontal lobe impairment, since Chinese characters represent words that require memorization.

- The reversing of letters may be due to problems with visual stimuli processing.

b. Genetics:

- Four genes play a role in the development of dyslexia since it is a moderately to highly heritable disorder and affects how the neurons connect.

- Low quality schools or a disadvantaged family are environmental factors that may play a role in dyslexia.

2. Psychological Factors:

Motivation is influenced by successful experiences, determination, recognizing one's strengths, early identification, and coping mechanisms.

3. Social Factors:

Social factors like support and encouragement can affect the psychological factor of motivation.

C. Treating Learning Disorders

Accommodations and services are mandated by the Individuals with Disabilities Education Act (IDEA).

1. Treating Dyslexia

- Phonological practice includes dividing up words by sound and rhyming words.

- The *alphabetic principle,* where letters signal speech sounds, is another technique.

- These two techniques improve performance and brain function.

2. Treating Other Learning Disorders

- A trial-and-error process is used to find the best teaching techniques for the individual.

- Larger steps are broken down into smaller concepts and are followed with immediate feedback.

- Having a learning disability can affect a child's self-esteem, which may affect other aspects of the child's life, but not as much as other disorders might.

IV. DISORDERS OF DISRUPTIVE BEHAVIOR AND ATTENTION

- Clinicians must distinguish between "normal" and "pathological" behaviors.
- Three disruptive disorders are:
  - **i.** Conduct disorder
  - **ii.** Oppositional defiant disorder
  - **iii.** Attention-deficit/hyperactivity disorder

A. What Is Conduct Disorder?

- *Conduct disorder* is a psychological disorder that typically arises in childhood and is characterized by the violation of the basic rights of others or of societal norms that are appropriate to the individual's age. [See *Table 14.10.*]

- Conduct disorder is diagnosed in those under 18 years of age and who have three out of 15 criterion A behaviors (which are behaviors that violate the rights of others).

- People with conduct disorder show a lack of empathy and make negative attributions of others' behaviors.

- There are three intensity levels of symptoms:
  - **i. Mild:** the youth has only a few of the symptoms and causes minimal harm to others (*Example:* lying or staying out past one's curfew)
  - **ii. Moderate:** the youth shows a number of symptoms and has a mild to severe impact on others (*Example:* vandalism or stealing)
  - **iii. Severe:** the youth exhibits many of the symptoms and causes harm to others (*Example:* forced sex or using a weapon) [See *Case 14.5*]
- The age of onset helps to determine the course and prognosis:
  - **i. Adolescent-onset type:** no symptoms before age 10
  - **ii. Childhood-onset type:** symptoms appear before the age of 10

1. Adolescent-Onset Type

- Symptoms emerge after puberty and tend to be nonviolent symptoms such as theft, drunkenness, or property offenses.

- Symptoms tend to be temporary and do not affect peer relationships.

- As compared to females, males tend to develop the disorder at the ratio of 1.5 to 1.

2. Childhood-Onset Type

a. Childhood-Onset Type with Callous and Unemotional Traits:

- Youth with these traits are more aggressive, seek out exciting activities, seek out rewards, and react less to threatening or distressing stimuli.

- Individuals with this disorder are less sensitive to punishment and experience lower levels of fear. These qualities are what lead to callousness and aggressiveness in these children.
- Children with this disorder lack the skills to refrain from maladaptive behaviors and to understand social norms and empathy and are less likely to identify sadness in others.

b. Childhood-Onset Type Without Callous and Unemotional Traits:
- People with this disorder are unlikely to be aggressive unless they perceive a stimulus as a threat, since they have difficulty controlling their emotions.
- Individuals with this type of conduct disorder tend to react strongly to negative emotional stimuli and make inaccurate assumptions about social cues.
- A negative interaction with parents is likely. This type of interaction is cyclical and is where the individual responds to parental criticism with agitation, distress, and impulsivity.
- This type of conduct disorder is caused mostly by problemmatic parenting (versus genes) and these children usually have poor reasoning abilities. [See *Table 14.11.*]

B. What Is Oppositional Defiant Disorder?

- *Oppositional defiant disorder* is a psychological disorder that typically arises in childhood or adolescence and is characterized by overt disobedience, hostility, defiance, and negativity toward people in authority. [See *Table 14.12.*]
- Additional behaviors include refusing to negotiate, refusing to compromise, adhering to additional directions, and limit-testing.
- These behaviors need to be present for six months or longer.
- These behaviors are directed toward authority figures, are not usually violent, and are context-specific (such as with parents or well-known adults).
- Clinicians will need to obtain additional information from others since an individual with this disorder will not present these symptoms to the clinician. [See *Figure 14.2* for a visual depiction of the paths related to disruptive behavior disorders and *Table 14.13.*]
- The diagnosis of oppositional defiant disorder is not given if the behaviors do not affect functioning or if the behaviors are a result of a psychotic or mood disorder.
- [See *Case 14.6*].

C. What Is Attention-Deficit/Hyperactivity Disorder?

- *Attention-deficit/hyperactivity disorder (ADHD)* is a psychological disorder that typically arises in childhood and is characterized by inattention, hyperactivity, and/or impulsivity. [See *Table 14.14.*]
- The symptoms of ADHD must cause impairment in school and home. [See *Case 14.7.*]
- There are three types of ADHD:
  i. **Hyperactive/impulsive type:** disruptive, causes accidents, is rejected by peers
  ii. **Inattentive type:** academic problems due to executive function deficits
  iii. **Combined type:** symptoms of both of the other types
- These symptoms may change over time, and people can shift types. [See *Case 14.7.*]
- The following are ways to reduce symptoms:
  i. Reward appropriate behaviors

ii. Supervise the individual
iii. Work in a new context
iv. Provide interesting tasks
v. Help achieve focused attention [see *Figure 14.3*]

1. **Distinguishing Between Attention-Deficit/Hyperactivity Disorder and Other Disorders**

   - Those with hypomania, mania, or anxiety may exhibit impulsive symptoms seen in those with ADHD.

   - Inattention can also be seen in dissociative disorders as well as ADHD.

   - Substance-related disorders and some personality disorders show symptoms of inattention, hyperactivity, or impulsivity.

   - Childhood onset and high inattention and/or hyperactivity/impulsivity help to distinguish ADHD from the other disorders listed earlier.

   - There is high comorbidity between ADHD and oppositional defiant disorder and between ADHD and conduct disorder; however, those with ADHD are not intentionally cruel to others. Individuals can still exhibit symptoms of the two disorders at the same time. [See *Table 14.15.*]

LEARNING ACTIVITY 14.2: Acting Out the Disruptive Disorders

Objective: To help students differentiate among the disruptive disorders.

Time: 30 Minutes

Directions:
1. Form small groups of 2–3 students.
2. In your small group, come up with a scenario where one student acts out conduct disorder, oppositional defiant disorder, or ADHD.
3. After each performance, students in the class will determine if the behaviors represent conduct disorder, oppositional defiant disorder, or ADHD symptoms.

Summary: Students will find this task difficult, as there is much overlap among these disorders. Students will note that conduct disorder symptoms show more harmful behaviors to others and oppositional defiant disorder symptoms are mostly directed toward authority figures, while ADHD symptoms are unintentional.

Questions to Students and Discussion: What was most difficult about this exercise? Why? What are key symptoms that differentiate these disorders from one another? What symptoms overlap? How might the treatments for these disorders be similar? Different?

LECTURE ENHANCEMENT 14.2: Bullying and Peer Victimization

Objective: To discuss the social consequences of the disruptive disorders.

Time: 30 Minutes

Lecture Points:
I. Why Is It Important to Study Bullying and Peer Victimization?
    A. Three million bullying incidents occur each year—1700 per day
    B. Every 10 seconds a child is harassed, taunted, assaulted, or abused.

II. Characteristics of Bullied Children
   A. Smaller, weaker
   B. Lack of self-confidence
   C. Can be overly aggressive and disruptive
   D. Two types of bullied and victimized children:
      1. Aggressive:
         a. Are more often disliked by peers, but are unaware of how much they are disliked
         b. Receive reinforcement for aggressive behavior
         c. Usually have two or more friends
      2. Nonaggressive
         a. More aware of rejection
         b. More likely to experience extreme victimization
         c. Less social support
         d. Greater feelings of loneliness and dissatisfaction
         e. More self-blaming
III. Long-Term Consequences of Victimization and Bullying
   A. Poor adjustment in later life
   B. Dropping out of school
   C. Delinquent behavior
   D. Externalizing
   E. Helplessness, inadequacy, confusion, anxiety, tiredness, disorganization
   F. Males develop violent attitudes and behavior
   G. Females become depressed and suicidal
   H. Learned helplessness and external locus of control
   I. Loneliness because of unfulfilled relationships
      1. Lack of companionship
      2. Lack of acceptance, emotional support, and affection
      3. Lack of self-worth
   J. Later psychological disorders
      1. Schizophrenia
IV. Prevention and Intervention
   A. Systemic approaches
      1. Increase supervision in schools
      2. Establish antibullying policies
      3. Create a bully hotline
      4. Educate parents through programs
      5. Design school buildings to reduce the number of nonmonitored places
   B. Peer interventions
      1. Create seating assignments where popular and disliked children must interact
      2. Employ activities that reward cooperation
      3. Establish a "Safe Place" rule in the classroom where bullying and victimization are not allowed
      4. Model equal treatment of all students and interactions among students
   C. Parental interventions
      1. Keep a record of all incidents
      2. Talk to parents of bullies
   D. Child interventions
      1. Develop interpersonal and social skills
      2. Choose a play partner
      3. Teach them confidence
      4. Develop prosocial skills

Summary: Students will be surprised to learn that there are two types of victims of bullies: aggressive and nonaggressive. Students will also be able to understand some of the social consequences and how these consequences might lead to or result in symptoms of oppositional defiant disorder, conduct disorder, and/or ADHD (such as externalizing behavior, aggression, disruptiveness).

Sources: Asher, S. R., & Coie, J. D. (1990). *Peer rejection in childhood.* Cambridge University Press.

Beane, A. (1998). The trauma of peer victimization. In T. W. Miller (Ed.), *Children of trauma: stressful life events and their effects on children and adolescents.* Madison, CT: International Universities Press.

Questions to Students and Discussion: How can bullying or being a victim of bullying lead to disruptive behavior disorders? How can disruptive behavior disorders lead to bullying or being a victim of bullying? In what ways can we reduce the amount of bullying in school?

2. **Criticisms of the DSM-IV-TR Diagnostic Criteria**

   - The criteria do not fit adults who have ADHD since people can be impaired but not meet the minimum number of symptoms.

   - The diagnostic criteria require that symptoms must be present prior to age 7, yet research shows that people who showed symptoms after age 7 (but before age 12) were almost identical to those showing symptoms prior to age 7.

   - Females and males may express hyperactivity differently, as girls may show more talkativeness or emotional reactions than boys. This gender difference may lead to girls being underdiagnosed with ADHD and more likely to be treated for depression.

D. Understanding Disorders of Disruptive Behavior and Attention

ADHD is most understood and thus will be discussed in this section in more depth than conduct disorder or oppositional defiant disorder.

1. **Neurological Factors**

   Abnormal brain structure and function and the role neurotransmitters and genes play in the development of ADHD

   a. ADHD and Brain Systems:
   - People with ADHD have executive function impairment and thus have difficulty with time, planning, and achieving goals.

   - Smaller brain size, in particular the frontal and temporal lobes, corpus collosum, basal ganglia, and the cerebellum, have been found in children and adults with ADHD.

   - The smaller the cerebellum, the worse the symptoms of ADHD, since this structure is responsible for attention and timing.

   - Some differences do not last into adulthood and may be due to the fact that the brain adjusts for the impaired structures.

   - The combination of impairments is what contributes to ADHD versus impairment in a single area.

   - Neural structures in the frontal and parietal lobes (which aid in attention) are underactive in people with ADHD.

- These impairments in the brain can affect autonomic nervous system functioning and may cause reduced arousal to stimulation.

b. ADHD and Neural Communication:

- Multiple dysfunctions in the neurotransmitters (dopamine, serotonin, and norepinephrine) may cause coordination and organizational problems.
- Dopamine dysfunction includes the possibility of too few receptors or not enough removal of dopamine from the synapse.

c. ADHD and Genetics:

- This disorder runs in families; monozygotic twins have high concordance rates of ADHD, and ADHD is one of the most heritable disorders.
- Approximately a dozen genes affect the development of ADHD, and these genes may also contribute to conduct and oppositional defiant disorders.
- Genes interact with environmental risks (such as pregnant mothers who smoke).

d. Neurological Factors in Conduct Disorder and Oppositional Defiant Disorder:

- Those with oppositional defiant disorder or conduct disorder are more likely to have biological parents who are criminals or who are diagnosed with ADHD, oppositional defiant disorder, conduct disorder, antisocial personality disorder, substance use, or a mood disorder.
- The issues listed here all deal with externalizing behaviors (with the exception of mood disorders).
- Low harm avoidance temperament influences one's ability to recognize and follow social rules, and high reward temperament can lead to low persistence and frustration tolerance.

LEARNING ACTIVITY 14.3: Explore Genes to Cognition Online

Objective: To learn additional neurological factors that contribute to ADHD.

Time: 30 Minutes

Activity and Discussion: 45 Minutes

Discussion Only: 15 Minutes

Directions:
1. Form small groups with 3–4 students each.
2. Have each group select two videos on the ADHA section of the Genes to Cognition Web site, http://www.g2conline.org/#ADHD
3. Ask students to summarize the key findings of the videos and have each group present the highlights to class.

Questions to Students and Discussion: What findings are consistent with the text? Which findings are not? What information surprised you? What additional questions do you have about ADHD?

2. **Psychological Factors: Recognizing Facial Expressions, Keeping Track of Time**

- People with ADHD have difficulty recognizing the facial expressions of anger and sadness.

- One possible explanation for this difficulty is due to coping with bad experiences by tuning out people who express these emotions.
- One study has shown that boys with ADHD overestimate their abilities, become more frustrated when not succeeding, and are less likely to persist when challenged as compared to a control group.
- Another study revealed that children with ADHD are more likely to make negative internal attributions ("I am a failure") versus external/situational ones ("That was a challenging task"). This pattern of thinking is similar to those with low self-esteem.
- Students with ADHD report lower self-esteem and social skills than those without ADHD.
- Children with the other disruptive disorders have either low or overly inflated self-esteem.

3. Social Factors: Blame and Credit

- Parents of children with ADHD tend to attribute their children's behavior to random situations versus to the child.
- In one study, parents were given a personal digital assistant (PDA) that beeped at certain intervals. Participants were asked to record their activities and feelings when they heard the beep. Parents of children with ADHD recorded spending more time with their children "getting ready" (versus doing "other" things) and reported feeling more angry and stressed, less likely to report a good mood, and being more likely to argue with their children than those parents of children without ADHD. These feelings may be reflected in parent-child interactions, which may have an effect on children with ADHD.
- Psychological and social factors seem to play a larger role in the development of oppositional defiant and conduct disorders than ADHD, yet genes also play a role.
- Additional social factors include:
  i. Neglect
  ii. Observation by the ADHD child of antisocial behaviors in others
  iii. Inconsistent parenting
- Children may be more vulnerable to ADHD if they grow up in a house where there is lead paint.

4. FEEDBACK LOOPS IN ACTION: Attention-Deficit/Hyperactivity Disorder

- Those who are neurologically vulnerable to ADHD and are exposed to psychological and social factors will develop ADHD.
- Additional research has found that family conflict is higher in families that have a child with ADHD, yet the direction of this relationship is unclear. [See *Figure 14.4.*]

E. Treating Disorders of Disruptive Behavior and Attention

Treatments for ADHD tend to be comprehensive and treat all three factors.

1. Targeting Neurological Factors: Medication

- There are no specific medications for oppositional defiant and conduct disorders, but medication can treat comorbid disorders.
- Medication prevents the reuptake of dopamine, which produces more internal stimulation.

- Studies have found that those with ADHD perform better on memory and verbal tasks while listening to white noise as compared to controls.
- Stimulant medications (which may contain *methylphenidate* or amphetamines) and skin patches are also used to treat ADHD. These medications have the following side effects:
  - **i.** Headache
  - **ii.** Insomnia
  - **iii.** Decreased appetite
  - **iv.** Increased risk of heart problems
- Sixty-five to seventy-five percent of people improve on these medications, do not experience severe side effects, and show improvement in specific brain sites.
- *Atomoxetine* (Strattera), the treatment of choice, is a noradrenaline reuptake inhibitor and is not a stimulant. Side effects include those just mentioned.
- A reduction in ADHD behaviors and impulsivity can positively affect other aspects of the child's life.

2. **Targeting Psychological Factors: Treating Disruptive Behavior**

- Behavioral methods are used to reduce impulsivity and use rewards that are slowly replaced with verbal reinforcements.
- Behavioral methods can be used for all three disorders by delaying instant gratification and rewarding increases in restraint.
- Cognitive methods help with problem-solving and build skills through modeling and role playing.
- An IEP may be used to obtain accommodations for some children.

3. **Targeting Social Factors: Reinforcement in Relationships**

- Operant conditioning is used to shape children's behavior and is used by teachers and parents.
- Group therapy is used to improve social skills.

a. Contingency Management: Changing Parents' Behavior:

- *Contingency management* is a procedure for modifying behavior by changing the conditions that led to, or are produced by, the behavior.
- In this program, parents learn ways to consistently use praise, reinforcements, and punishments.
- The program begins with psychoeducation, where the parents learn about the symptoms and that the misbehavior is not intentional. The training then intends to:
  - **i.** Change parents' beliefs and help them develop realistic goals
  - **ii.** Help parents employ behavior modification techniques (showing attention for positive behaviors, providing clear and consistent directions, and creating a reward program)
  - **iii.** Teach parents how to respond to misbehavior
- Parent training is best for children with mild ADHD or preschoolers with ADHD.

b. Parent Management Training:

This training teaches contingency-management techniques, improves parent-child communication and warmth, and increases positive parent interest in the child.

c. Multisystemic Therapy:

- This treatment is based on family systems therapy and may include the following: family, couples, peers, the child, or the school.
- A small number of children with oppositional defiant and conduct disorders improve minimally or not at all, or treatment results may not generalize to other settings.

4. FEEDBACK LOOPS IN TREATMENT: Treating Attention-Deficit/Hyperactivity Disorder

- See *Figure 14.5* for the feedback loops in treatment for ADHD, which shows how medication leads to psychological and social changes.
- Other social treatments (such as multisystem therapy) can lead to psychological improvements.

V. OTHER DISORDERS OF CHILDHOOD

Children may exhibit the following behaviors that may or may not be pathological:

- Temporary anxiety when being separated by a loved one
- Delay in communication and language skills
- Unusual eating habits
- Accidents outside of the toilet
- Repetitive movements

A. Separation Anxiety Disorder

Separation anxiety disorder is a psychological disorder that typically arises in childhood and is characterized by excessive anxiety about separation from home or from someone to whom the individual has become attached.

1. What Is Separation Anxiety Disorder?

- Distress when separated occurs during normal stages of development. To qualify as a disorder, the anxiety, stress, or impairment must last over 4 weeks. [See *Table 14.16.*]
- Typical childhood activities are disrupted or impaired due to anxiety, the child needs constant reassurance about his parents' whereabouts, and/or the child experiences physical symptoms as a result of the anxiety (dizziness, stomachaches, nausea and vomiting, and feeling faint).
- If separation anxiety develops before age 6, it is noted as "early onset."
- Children may also fear and dream about getting permanently lost or being unable to leave the house, and may need to be next or close to the parent.
- Individuals with this disorder may have a constant fear of something harmful happening to themselves or their parents. [See *Case 14.8, Table 14.16,* and *Table 14.17.*]

2. Distinguishing Between Separation Anxiety Disorder and Other Disorders

- Symptoms can overlap with generalized anxiety disorder, but with separation anxiety disorder the worries are focused on separation from the parent.
- Symptoms also overlap with social phobia, but with separation anxiety the fear is focused on not wanting to leave the house versus fear of being criticized by others.

- Children may also have panic attacks but do not have panic disorder unless the fear of having additional attacks is debilitating.
- These children may also exhibit signs of depression.
- The children's behavior may also resemble oppositional defiant disorder when asked to do behaviors that lead to separation from the parents.
- Refusal to attend school could be caused by a number of other problems: mood disorder, social phobia, or oppositional defiant disorder, and thus a thorough evaluation must be done.

3. Understanding Separation Anxiety Disorder

- This disorder occurs more often in close families and is more common among those with close relatives, among those who have a mother with panic disorder, and in homes where fathers are absent.
- These factors can create feedback loops that reinforce the anxiety.

4. Treating Separation Anxiety Disorder

Cognitive-behavior therapy with exposure and cognitive restructuring and family therapy that examines any forms of inadvertent reinforcements are used to treat this disorder.

MEDIA RECOMMENDATION 14.6: Separation Anxiety Disorder in Children

Objective: To learn about symptoms and interventions for separation anxiety disorder.

Time: 5 Minutes

Media and Discussion: 10 Minutes

Discussion Only: 5 Minutes

Watch Online: Search YouTube using the search terms "child separation anxiety disorder," or http://www.youtube.com/watch?v=FzMExXi8hYo
Dr. Lynn Miller discusses the definition, symptoms, and interventions for separation anxiety disorder.

Summary: Students will learn about behavioral methods and the use of reinforcements to modify separation anxiety.

Questions to Students and Discussion: What are the key symptoms of separation anxiety disorder? Describe two interventions that are helpful in treating separation anxiety disorder. What questions do you still have about this disorder?

B. Other Types of Disorders of Childhood, in Brief

Communication disorders, feeding and eating disorders, elimination disorders, and tic disorders are all subcategories of childhood onset disorders and are extreme forms of behaviors.

1. Communication Disorders

- *Communication disorders* are a set of psychological disorders characterized by significant problems in understanding language or using language to express oneself.
- Clinicians are to evaluate the child for the following disorders that may be the cause of the communication difficulties: hearing problems, oppositional defiant disorder,

anxiety, schizophrenia, pervasive developmental disorder, mental retardation, or other disorder.

2. Feeding and Eating Disorders

- *Feeding and eating disorders* are a set of psychological disorders characterized by problems with feeding or eating.

- Behaviors include not eating enough, bizarre eating habits (*Example:* eating nonfood objects), and eating disorders.

- The diagnosis of this disorder is not given if the behavior is the result of a medical problem.

- Clinicians will also examine other psychological problems that may be causing the feeding and eating symptoms, such as depression, anxiety, oppositional defiant disorder, and others.

- Clinicians may treat the child and/or family.

3. Elimination Disorders

- *Elimination disorders* are a set of psychological disorders characterized by inappropriate urination or defecation.

- *Encopresis* is an elimination disorder characterized by a child's persistent defecation in improper locations—neither in a toilet nor in a diaper. This disorder may be caused by hard stool problems when the child delays defecating and then the looser stool leaks out. Changes in diet (more fluids and increase in fiber) can help alleviate this problem if it is caused by hard stool.

- *Enuresis* is an elimination disorder characterized by a child's persistent urination in bed or into his or her clothes.

- A tenth of children ages 5 to 16 wet their beds; it is caused by abnormal sleep patterns that prevent the children from realizing their bladders are full or in need of being relieved.

- A bed-wetting alarm [see *Figure 14.6*] is the most successful treatment. When the sensor detects wetness, the alarm signals the child to wake up and within 6 months or less the child learns to wake up on her own.

- Both of these disorders arise from biological factors, and thus it is important for caregivers to consult with a pediatrician.

- A mental health clinician is consulted if the behavior is the result of oppositional defiant disorder, anxiety, or sexual abuse.

4. Tic Disorders

- *Tic disorders* are a set of disorders characterized by persistent tics (motor or vocal) that occur many times a day on most days. Up to 12% of children between 6 to 15 years old will have a tic disorder at some point in their lives.

- *Tourette's disorder* is a tic disorder characterized by recurrent motoric and vocal tics; also referred to as *Tourette syndrome*. This disorder was named for the psychiatrist Gilles de la Tourette, who first connected and described the symptoms.

- The rare vocal tic (called *coprolalia*), where an individual screams out obscenities, occurs among only 10% of those with Tourette's.

- A neurologist examines a client for a tic disorder, though this can be difficult to differentiate from symptoms that arise from a pervasive developmental disorder.

However, in a pervasive developmental disorder, the repetitive behaviors are intentional and rhythmic, unlike those behaviors in Tourette's.

- Compulsive behaviors may seem similar to tics, but compulsive behaviors are often linked to an obsession and are not as unusual as the behaviors exhibited from a tic.

- Vocal tics are not the same as the disorganized speech seen in schizophrenia.

- People with this disorder experience a wide range of impairment or distress.

- Social rejection and/or interference with normal functioning may require medication or behavioral treatments.

MEDIA RECOMMENDATION 14.7: I Have Tourette's, but Tourette's Doesn't Have Me

Objective: To observe some real people with Tourette's disorder.

Time: 5 Minutes

Media and Discussion: 30 Minutes

Discussion Only: 25 Minutes

Watch Online: Search YouTube using the search terms "I Have Tourette's, but Tourette's Doesn't Have Me," or http://video.google.com/videoplay?docid=-5419952820725946842#
This powerful film shows young children who describe their symptoms of and experience with Tourette's disorder.

Summary: Students will be touched by the experiences of these youth. Additionally, students will be surprised to learn that boys have higher rates of this disorder than girls.

Questions to Students and Discussion: What symptoms did these children describe? What is it like for them to have Tourette's? Who is more at risk for Tourette's—males or females? What surprised you about these clips?

ADDITIONAL READINGS

Journal Articles

ADHD

Arnsten, A. F. (2006). Fundamentals of attention-deficit/hyperactivity disorder: Circuits and pathways. *Journal of Clinical Psychiatry, 67* (Suppl. 8), 7–12.

Clarke, A. R., Barry, R. J., McCarthy, R., Selikowitz, M., & Johnstone, S. J. (2007). Effects of stimulant medications on the EEG of girls with attention-deficit/hyperactivity disorder. *Clinical Neurophysiology, 118,* 2700–2708.

Autism and Asperger's

Bölte, S., & Poustka, F. (2003). The recognition of facial affect in autistic and schizophrenic subjects and their first-degree relatives. *Psychological Medicine, 33,* 907–915.

Cederlund, M., & Gillberg, C. (2004). One hundred males with Asperger syndrome: A clinical study of background and associated factors. *Developmental Medicine & Child Neurology, 46,* 652–660.

Conduct Disorder

Colman, I., Murray, J., Abbott, R., Maughan, B., Kuh, D., Croudace, T. J., & Jones, P. B. (2009). Outcomes of conduct problems in adolescence: 40 year follow-up of national cohort. *British Medical Journal, 338,* a2981.

Frick, P. J., & Morris, A. S. (2004). Temperament and developmental pathways to conduct problems. *Journal of Clinical Child and Adolescent Psychology, 33,* 54–68.

Dyslexia

Grigorenko, E. L. (2001). Developmental dyslexia: An update on genes, brains, and environments. *Journal of Child Psychology and Psychiatry, 42,* 91–125.

Shaywitz, B. A., Lyon, G. R., & Shaywitz, S. E. (2006). The role of functional magnetic resonance imaging in understanding reading and dyslexia. *Developmental Neuropsychology, 30,* 613–632.

Tic Disorders

Cook, C. R., & Blacher, J. (2007). Evidence-based psychosocial treatments for tic disorders. *Clinical Psychology: Science and Practice, 14,* 252–267.

Books and Memoirs

ADHD

Barkley, R. A. (2000). *Taking charge of ADHD: The complete authoritative guide for parents* (rev. ed.). New York: Guilford Press.
   Provides useful information to parents and teachers who work with ADHD children.

Hallowell, E. M., & Ratey, J. J. (1994). *Driven to distraction: Recognizing and coping with attention-deficit disorder from childhood through adulthood.* New York: Touchstone.
   Discusses some of the controversies surrounding ADHD as well as provides tips on how to live with this disorder.

Autism

Frith, U. (2003). *Autism: Explaining the enigma* (2nd ed.). Malden, MA: Blackwell Publishing.
   Provides a history of autism and current research.

Hermelin, B. (2001). *Bright splinters of the mind: A personal story of research with autistic savants.* London: Jessica Kingsley.
   Hermelin writes about her 20 years of research on savants.

Moore, C. (2006). *George & Sam: Two boys, one family, and autism.* New York: St. Martin's Press.
   Moore writes about her experiences raising two boys with autism.

Conduct Disorder

Kazdin, A. E. (1995). *Conduct disorders in childhood and adolescence* (2nd ed.). Thousand Oaks, CA: Sage Publications.
   Provides clinical research on conduct disorder.

Learning Disabilities

Lelewer, N. (1994). *Something's not right: One family's struggle with learning disabilities.* Acton, MA: VanderWyk & Burnham.
   One mother's struggle to get accommodations for her child.

ADDITIONAL MEDIA RECOMMENDATIONS

Autism and Asperger's

Johar, K. (Director). (2010). *My name is Khan.* [Film]. India: Dharma Productions.
   A Muslim man with Asperger's is mistaken as a terrorist post-9/11.

Levinson, B. (Director). (1998). *Rain man.* [Film]. USA: MGM Home Entertainment.
   A selfish young man discovers that he has a brother who is an autistic savant.

Mayer, M. (Director). (2009). *Adam.* [Film]. USA: Olympus Pictures.
   An intelligent young man with Asperger's has his first serious romantic relationship.

WEB SITES

Children and Adults with Hyperactivity Disorder: This Web site provides information, training, and support about ADHD. See: http://www.chadd.org/

Dr. Thomas Brown's Web Site: Provides articles, assessment tools, and additional resources. See: http://drthomasebrown.com/

Learning Disabilities

International Dyslexia Association: Provides information about events and conferences, new research findings, and downloadable material. See: http://www.interdys.org/

Tic Disorders

National Tourette's Syndrome Association: Provides news, events, videos, and more. See: http://www.tsa-usa.org/

Cognitive Disorders

CHAPTER
15

CHAPTER OUTLINE

CHAPTER HEADINGS	INSTRUCTION IDEAS AND TEXTBOOK CORRELATIONS
Chapter Introduction	**Lecture Enhancement 15.1:** Older Adults and Mental Health
NORMAL VERSUS ABNORMAL AGING AND COGNITIVE FUNCTIONING	
Cognitive Functioning in Normal Aging	**Learning Objectives:** 15.1, 15.2, 15.3 **Learning Concepts:** memory, processing speed, attention, working memory **Textbook Tool:** Figure 15.1
Psychological Disorders and Cognition	**Learning Objective:** 15.4 **Learning Concepts:** depression, anxiety disorders, schizophrenia **Media Recommendation 15.1:** Aging, Depression, and Suicide **Textbook Tools:** Table 15.1; Case 15.1
Medical Factors That Can Affect Cognition	**Learning Objective:** 15.5 **Learning Concepts:** diseases and illnesses, stroke, head injury, substance-induced changes in cognition **Media Recommendation 15.2:** Broca's Aphasia **Media Recommendation 15.3:** Wernicke's Aphasia **Media Recommendation 15.4:** Agnosia
DELIRIUM	
What Is Delirium?	**Learning Objective:** 15.6 **Textbook Tools:** Tables 15.2, 15.3; Case 15.2
Understanding Delirium: A Side Effect?	**Learning Objective:** 15.7 **Learning Concepts:** delirium that arises from substance use, delirium due to a general medical condition **Treating Delirium:** Rectify the Cause **Learning Objective:** 15.8

AMNESTIC DISORDER	
What Is Amnestic Disorder?	**Learning Objective:** 15.9 **Textbook Tools:** Tables 15.4, 15.5; Case 15.3
Understanding Amnestic Disorder	**Learning Objective:** 15.10 **Learning Concepts:** substance-induced persisting amnestic disorder; amnestic disorder due to a general medical condition **Textbook Tool:** Figure 15.2
Treating Amnestic Disorder	**Learning Objective:** 15.11 **Learning Concepts:** targeting psychological factors: developing and implementing new strategies; targeting social factors: organizing the environment **Textbook Tool:** Table 15.6 **Worth Video Tool Kit for Abnormal Psychology:** Living Without Memory
DEMENTIA	
What Is Dementia?	**Learning Objective:** 15.12 **Textbook Tools:** Tables 15.7, 15.8; Case 15.4
Distinguishing Between Dementia and Other Psychological Disorders	**Learning Objective:** 15.13 **Textbook Tool:** Table 15.9
Understanding Dementia	**Learning Objectives:** 15.14, 15.15 **Learning Concepts:** dementia of the Alzheimer's type; vascular dementia; dementia due to other general medical conditions **Lecture Enhancement 15.2:** Stages of Alzheimer's Disorder **Media Recommendation 15.5:** HBO Alzheimer's Project **Media Recommendation 15.6:** Amyloid Cascade Hypothesis **Textbook Tools:** Figure 15.3; Tables 15.10, 15.11, 15.12 **Worth Video Tool Kit for Abnormal Psychology:** Alzheimer's Disease
Treating Dementia	**Learning Objective:** 15.16 **Learning Concepts:** targeting neurological factors; targeting psychological factors; targeting social factors
DIAGNOSING MRS. B.'S PROBLEMS	

LEARNING OBJECTIVES

After completing this chapter, students will be able to:

15.1 Define the two types of intelligences.

15.2 Describe how memory can be affected by aging.

15.3 Discuss the effects of aging on processing speed, attention, and working memory.

15.4 Identify the common cognitive deficits and their characteristics experienced in late-life depression.

15.5 Name the four categories of medical problems that can affect cognition, and discuss the affects of each.

15.6 Identify the DSM-IV-TR criteria and additional facts for delirium.

15.7 Articulate the facts involved when delirium arises from substance use or from a general medical condition like an infection.

15.8 Articulate the facts involved and treatment approaches for delirium.

15.9 Identify the DSM-IV-TR criteria and additional facts for amnestic disorder.

15.10 Articulate the symptoms and facts involved when amnestic disorder arises from substance use or from a general medical condition.

15.11 Explain how psychological and social factors are used to help treat amnestic disorder.

15.12 Identify the DSM-IV-TR criteria and additional facts for dementia.

15.13 Compare and contrast dementia with other disorders.

15.14 Articulate the reasons, symptoms, and additional facts for the different types of dementia.

15.15 Describe the clinical characteristics of each of the five stages of dementia of the Alzheimer's type.

15.16 Explain how neurological, psychological, and social factors are used to treat dementia.

KEY TERMS

Cognitive disorders: A category of psychological disorders in which the primary symptom is significantly reduced mental abilities, relative to a prior level of functioning.

Crystallized intelligence: A type of intelligence that relies on using knowledge to reason; such knowledge has "crystallized" from previous experience.

Fluid intelligence: A type of intelligence that relies on the ability to create new strategies to solve new problems, without relying solely on information previously learned.

Stroke: The interruption of normal blood flow to or within the brain, which results in neuronal death.

Aphasia: A neurological condition characterized by problems in producing or comprehending language.

Broca's aphasia: A neurological condition characterized by problems producing speech.

Wernicke's aphasia: A neurological condition characterized by problems comprehending language and producing meaningful utterances.

Apraxia: A neurological condition characterized by problems in organizing and carrying out voluntary movements even though the muscles themselves are not impaired.

Delirium: A cognitive disorder characterized by a disturbance in consciousness and changes in cognitive functioning, particularly in attention.

Amnestic disorder: A cognitive disorder characterized by impaired memory while other mental processes remain relatively intact.

Confabulate: To create stories in order to fill in gaps in memory.

Errorless learning techniques: Techniques by which patients are explicitly guided in learning a new skill rather than being allowed to figure it out through trial and error.

Dementia: A set of cognitive disorders characterized by deficits in learning new information or recalling information already learned *plus* at least one other type of cognitive impairment.

Alzheimer's disease: A medical condition in which the afflicted individual initially has problems with both memory and executive function and which leads to progressive dementia.

Neurofibrillary tangles: The mass created by tau proteins that become twisted together and destroy the microtubules, leaving the neuron without a distribution system for nutrients.

Amyloid plaques: Fragments of protein that accumulate on the outside surfaces of neurons, particularly neurons in the hippocampus.

Vascular dementia: A type of dementia caused by reduced or blocked blood supply to the brain, which arises from plaque buildup or blood clots.

Dementia due to Lewy bodies: A type of progressive dementia caused by a type of protein (referred to as Lewy bodies) that builds up inside some types of neurons and can eventually cause them to die.

Huntington's disease: A progressive disease that kills neurons and affects cognition, emotion, and motor functions; it leads to dementia and eventually results in death.

CHAPTER GUIDE

Chapter Introduction

- A neuropsychologist evaluates Mrs. B. because she is having difficulty making it to the restroom on time, has impaired vision and hearing, and has fallen.
- A cognitive disorder might account for Mrs. B.'s behaviors.
- *Cognitive disorders* are a category of psychological disorders in which the primary symptom is significantly reduced mental abilities relative to a prior level of functioning.
- Cognitive symptoms are often present in the following disorders: depression, anxiety, psychosis, and substance use. However, these symptoms are secondary to the other symptoms.
- With the cognitive disorders, cognitive functioning and mental processes are the primary symptoms and are the result of a medical disease (such as Parkinson's, *stroke,* or substance withdrawal).
- Three types of cognitive disorders are discussed in this chapter: *delirium, amnestic disorder,* and *dementia.* These disorders mostly affect older adults.

LECTURE ENHANCEMENT 15.1: Older Adults and Mental Health

Objective: To learn about the current rates of mental disorders and other mental health issues among older adults.

Time: 20 Minutes

Lecture Points:
I. Overview (Surgeon General's Report)
  A. Twenty percent of those 55 years or older experience mental disorders.
  B. Suicide is highest among older white males.
  C. Cognitive capacity normally changes as we age, but the following are major changes in older adults:
    1. Slowness of processing
    2. Decrease in vocabulary past 70 years old
    3. Memory complaints
  D. The following are risk factors for mental health problems in older adulthood:
    1. Loss of social status and self-esteem

2. Loss of spouse
3. Less physical activity
4. Reduction in size and weight of brain/loss of neurons

Summary: Older adults experience a number of cognitive losses as part of typical aging; however, several risk factors increase one's risk of developing a mental health problem as an older adult.

Source: U.S. Department of Health and Human Services, *Chapter 5: Older adults and mental health.* In Mental Health: A Report of the Surgeon General—Executive Summary. Rockville, MD: U.S. Department of Health and Human Services, Substance Abuse and Mental Health Services Administration, Center for Mental Health Services, National Institutes of Health, National Institute of Mental Health, 1999. http://www.surgeongeneral.gov/library/mentalhealth/chapter5/sec1.html

Questions to Students and Discussion: How do the rates of mental illness in older adults compare to that of the general population? Highlight the major changes in older adults. What are neuropsychosocial factors that might help prevent or delay some of these changes?

I.   NORMAL VERSUS ABNORMAL AGING AND COGNITIVE FUNCTIONING

- The neuropsychologist uses a clinical interview to determine whether Mrs. B.'s behavior and symptoms are typical of someone her age.

- The clinician will compare current cognitive functioning with one's former abilities and with what is typical for the client's current age.

A. Cognitive Functioning in Normal Aging

- There are two types of intelligence:
  i. *Crystallized intelligence* relies on using knowledge to reason; such knowledge has "crystallized" from previous experiences and is assessed using verbal abilities tests.
  ii. *Fluid intelligence* relies on the ability to create new strategies to solve new problems without relying solely on information previously learned, relies on the *executive functions,* and is assessed using visual-motor skills, problem solving, and perceptual speed tests.

- Memory tests show that as adults age, their fluid intelligence declines, but these results do not apply when the test is untimed.

- The cognitive decline that occurs with aging affects those with a low IQ (85 or below) more than those with a high IQ.

- The memory, processing speed, attention, and executive functions are affected by typical aging.

1. **Memory**

   Two types of memory are implicit and explicit.

   - **Implicit memories** are made up of unconscious memories we gain through classical conditioning and our habits. These memories are not affected much by aging.

   - **Explicit memories** are voluntary and consist of words and images. Healthy people who are ages 65 and older have a more difficult time with these types of memories, more specifically with *recall* (which is the ability to "look up" information in our memory store).

2. **Processing Speed, Attention, and Working Memory**

- Older adults have a slower processing speed and thus require more time to learn new information.

- This reduction in processing speed may be the result of a deteriorating myelin sheath, which impairs communication among neurons.

- The ability to *multitask* also declines with age because single activities require more focused attention.

- The *Trail-Making Test* assesses both attention and processing speed. [See *Figure 15.1*.]

- This assessment examines working memory, which involves parts of the frontal lobes that keep information in mind while working on a problem.

B. Psychological Disorders and Cognition

- People who are older are less likely to have a psychological disorder; however, if one does have a psychological disorder when older, the symptoms are likely to impair one's cognitive abilities.

- Thus the clinician must determine whether the client's symptoms are the result of a psychological or cognitive disorder.

- Depression, anxiety disorders, and schizophrenia are psychological disorders that affect cognitive abilities.

1. **Depression**

- Those who are older and depressed are likely to exhibit more anxiety, agitation, and memory problems, as compared to younger people with depression.

- Depression will affect the following cognitive functions in older adults: memory, attention, concentration, and additional mental processes. [See *Table 15.1*.]

- However, a cognitive disorder can cause depression, and vice versa. [See *Case 15.1*.]

MEDIA RECOMMENDATION 15.1: Aging, Depression, and Suicide

Objective: To learn about depression in older adults.

Time: 4 Minutes

Media and Discussion: 10 Minutes

Discussion Only: 6 Minutes

Watch Online: Visit www.Mentalhelp.net, use the search box, and enter "Allan N. Schwartz aging depression suicide," or http://www.mentalhelp.net/poc/view_doc.php?type=doc&id=28741&w=5&cn=12

This video discusses mood disorders in older adults.

Summary: Students will enjoy hearing about the experience of mood disorders in older adults and will be surprised to learn about the suicidal and psychotic thoughts experienced by some of these adults.

Questions to Students and Discussion: What are the major symptoms reported by these older adults? What surprised you about this video? '

2. **Anxiety Disorders**

- Generalized anxiety disorder is the most common anxiety disorder among older adults as it affects 5% of people in this age range.
- The symptoms of generalized anxiety disorder can affect the cognitive skills of attention and concentration.

3. **Schizophrenia**

- Fifteen percent of people with schizophrenia experienced their first episode when they were over 44 years old.
- The positive and negative symptoms that arise with schizophrenia can also arise with cognitive disorders (such as delusions, hallucinations, alogia, and avolition).

C. Medical Factors That Can Affect Cognition

1. Diseases and Illnesses

- Encephalitis and brain tumors affect the brain and thus affect cognition.
- Chronic diseases and illnesses can create so much pain that they cause problems with concentration, attention, mental processes, and sleep.
- However, the client will need to be examined for hearing or vision problems because these may make the client *appear* to have a cognitive disorder when he/she does not.

2. Stroke

- A *stroke* is the interruption of normal blood flow to or within the brain, which results in neuronal death.
- Depending on what part of the brain is affected by the stroke, different problems occur and are described later.

a. Aphasia:

Aphasia is a neurological condition characterized by problems in producing or comprehending language. Two types of aphasia are:

- *Broca's aphasia* is a neurological condition characterized by problems in producing and comprehending speech. Symptoms include halting and telegraphic speech.

MEDIA RECOMMENDATION 15.2: Broca's Aphasia

Objective: To observe a client with Broca's aphasia.

Time: 2 Minutes

Media and Discussion: 9 Minutes

Discussion Only: 7 Minutes

Watch Online: Search YouTube using the search terms "Broca's aphasia," or http://www.youtube.com/watch?v=f2IiMEbMnPM
This video shows a patient with Broca's aphasia.

Summary: Students will be shocked at this patient's inability to produce basic speech and the length of time it takes for him to produce any speech.

Questions to Students and Discussion: What symptoms did the patient show? What do you think it would be like to experience these symptoms? What do you think it would be like to work with a patient like this?

- *Wernicke's aphasia* is a neurological condition characterized by problems comprehending language and producing meaningful utterances and caused by damage to the rear parts of the temporal lobe. Symptoms include mixing up word order and using nonsense words and can sometimes resemble those of schizophrenia; however, people with schizophrenia understand speech and can name objects better.

MEDIA RECOMMENDATION 15.3: Wernicke's Aphasia

Objective: To observe a client with Wernicke's aphasia.

Time: 4 Minutes

Media and Discussion: 9 Minutes

Discussion Only: 5 Minutes

Watch Online: Search YouTube using the search terms "Wernicke's aphasia," or http://www.youtube.com/watch?v=aVhYN7NTIKU
This video shows a patient with Wernicke's aphasia.

Summary: Students will be shocked at this patient's inability to produce basic speech.

Questions to Students and Discussion: What symptoms did the patient show? What do you think it would be like to experience these symptoms? What do you think it would be like to work with a patient like this?

b. Agnosia:
- Agnosia is where the client has difficulty understanding her perceptions.
- There are two types of agnosia: apperceptive agnosia and associative agnosia.
- (1) **Apperceptive agnosia:** The individual cannot organize visual input into objects and their spatial relations. *Example:* A person has a difficult time telling whether two objects are the same, and this can lead to disorientation.

- (2) **Associative agnosia:** The individual can visually organize shapes and can see objects but cannot associate the shape with meaning. *Example:* A stick figure would appear as lines and circles, not a human being.

MEDIA RECOMMENDATION 15.4: Agnosia

Objective: To observe a client with agnosia.

Time: 2 Minutes

Media and Discussion: 6 Minutes

Discussion Only: 4 Minutes

Watch Online: Search YouTube using the search term "agnosia," or http://www.youtube.com/watch?v=rwQpaHQ0hYw&feature=related
This video shows a patient with agnosia.

Summary: Students will be shocked at this patient's inability to identify common objects.

Questions to Students and Discussion: What symptoms did the patient show? What do you think it would be like to experience these symptoms? What do you think it would be like to work with a patient like this?

c. Apraxia:

Apraxia is a neurological condition characterized by problems in organizing and carrying out voluntary movements even though the muscles themselves are not impaired. This symptom can express itself through difficulty performing one muscle movement or a sequence of movements.

3. Head Injury

Head injuries and strokes can cause cognitive disorders.

4. Substance-Induced Changes in Cognition

- Substances can cause changes in attention, memory, judgment, or other cognitive functions.
- Older people are more sensitive to medication that may affect cognitive functioning.
- Clinicians will ask a series of questions to determine whether the decline in cognitive functioning is from psychological or medical disorders. These questions include interviewing and observing the patient, speaking with family and friends, a medical examination, lab tests, reviewing medications, examining daily functioning, and neurological testing.

II. DELIRIUM

Mrs. B. does not show the following signs of delirium: confusion, changes in consciousness, or lack of attention.

A. What Is Delirium?

- *Delirium* is a cognitive disorder characterized by a disturbance in consciousness and changes in cognitive functioning, particularly in attention.
- Symptoms can develop quickly, and the individual loses awareness of the environment and exhibits lack of focus and difficulty understanding.
- Interviews are difficult to conduct with these patients because of the attention problems. [See *Table 15.2.*]
- Individuals with delirium might not know where they are or the day or time. [See *Case 15.2.*]
- Additionally they may experience perceptual alterations such as:
  i. **Misinterpretations:** an incorrect interpretation of a sensory stimulus (*Example:* thinking the smell of smoke is a roaring fire)
  ii. **Illusions:** a misperception of an object (*Example:* seeing pants on the floor as a dog)
  iii. **Hallucinations:** seeing or hearing something not present
- The most common form of perceptual disturbance is visual, and these hallucinations seem real and may cause sleep disturbances and rapidly shifting emotions.
- Delirium is most common among elderly, terminally ill, and post-surgery patients. [See *Table 15.3.*]
- Symptoms similar to delirium include:
  i. **Psychotic symptoms:** These symptoms are unsystematic and thus not like psychotic symptoms found with schizophrenia and mood disorders.
  ii. **Mood, anxiety, or dissociative symptoms:** These tend to fluctuate with delirium unlike these symptoms with mood, anxiety, or dissociative disorder.
- The clinician should take into account a possible medical condition or cultural differences when conducting an assessment for delirium.

B. Understanding Delirium: A Side Effect?

Alcohol, medication, or a medical condition can also cause delirium.

1. Delirium That Arises from Substance Use

Delirium from taking or withdrawing from substances should only be diagnosed if the symptoms are so severe that the person requires attention and treatment; otherwise the person will be given the diagnosis of substance-related intoxication or withdrawal.

a. Delirium That Arises from Intoxication:

- Delirium as a result of intoxication takes only minutes to hours to manifest and can arise from prescribed medicines since 20% of older adults are prescribed the wrong medication.
- When the substance in the body decreases, the delirium ceases.

b. Delirium That Arises from Substance Withdrawal:

- Delirium tremens (DTs) lasts a few hours to 2–4 weeks after one withdraws from alcohol.
- Delirium is only diagnosed when the symptoms are more severe and require medical or mental health treatment.

2. Delirium Due to a General Medical Condition

- Various medical reasons can cause delirium such as an infection, dehydration, electrolyte imbalance, stroke, brain tumor, pneumonia, heart attack, head trauma, or surgery.
- A physical exam, lab tests, or review of the client's medical history can help understand the cause of the delirium.
- It may take up to several days to evaluate the client.
- Delirium may be caused by more than one factor.

C. Treating Delirium: Rectify the Cause

- Treatment for delirium targets neurological factors.
- Delirium can be alleviated after substance withdrawal has dissipated or through the treatment for a medical problem.
- Antipsychotic medications, such haloperidol or risperidone, can provide temporary relief or reduce delirium after an operation.
- The clinician can help the client initiate the following interventions that target psychological and social factors: using hearing aids and glasses to prevent sensory and perceptual problems; focusing on the present using clocks and calendars; creating a stimulating environment using enough light and minimizing noises; eating properly and staying warm; removing harmful objects; and becoming educated and educating family about delirium.

III. AMNESTIC DISORDER

Memory problems about recent events or the past may indicate that a person has amnestic disorder.

A. What Is Amnestic Disorder?

- *Amnestic disorder* is a cognitive disorder characterized by impaired memory while other mental processes remain relatively intact. It may be *transient* (lasting a few days to 1 month) or *chronic* (lasting more than 1 month), and the type of memory loss depends on the structure of the brain that is affected.

- Other cognitive disorders will not be present with amnestic disorder. [See *Table 15.4.*]

- This disorder is less likely to affect implicit memory but may affect one's memory for factual information.

- People with this disorder may **confabulate,** that is, create stories in order to fill in gaps in memory, friends and relatives may be needed to fill in missing information. [See *Case 15.3* and *Table 15.5.*]

- Amnestic disorder is different from dissociative disorder because the impairment in memory is not just for traumatic memories only, usually has a medical or substance use cause, and is more severe than the typical memory loss due to age.

B. Understanding Amnestic Disorder

- Amnestic disorder is caused by the neurological factors of substance use and/or medical condition.

- Memory loss is gradual when caused by substance abuse or toxin exposure.

- Memory loss is rapid when caused by a stroke or trauma.

1. Substance-Induced Persisting Amnestic Disorder

- A diagnosis of *substance-induced persistent amnestic disorder* is given when the memory impairment is due to substance use, toxins, or medication.

- *Alcohol-induced persistent amnestic disorder* is the diagnosis given to those with alcohol-induced memory loss.
    - **i.** Alcohol causes a *thiamine* deficiency that can lead to memory problems or *Korsakoff's syndrome,* which is an amnestic disorder.
    - **ii.** Symptoms show up after age 40 and are difficult to reverse.
    - **iii.** Alcohol-induced amnestic disorder has a worse prognosis than if induced by other substances.

- This disorder can also be caused by toxins in the environment (such as lead, mercury, and carbon monoxide).

- Medications (barbiturates or benzodiazepines) can also cause amnestic disorder.

2. Amnestic Disorder Due to a General Medical Condition

- Damage done to memory centers in the brain (such as the hippocampus, mamillary bodies, and the fornix) can cause memory problems and is called *amnestic disorder due to a medical condition.* [See *Figure 15.2.*]

- This diagnosis is given after a review of the patient's history, lab test, and/or physical.

C. Treating Amnestic Disorder

- There is no cure for amnestic disorder, but *rehabilitation* can help the patient learn to cope.

- Rehabilitation targets psychological and social factors by teaching coping strategies and making helpful changes in the environment.

1. Targeting Psychological Factors: Developing and Implementing New Strategies

- *Mnemonics* are memory strategies used to cope with the memory loss and include visualization.

- Additional strategies include notebooks, alarms, calendars, and a personal digital assistant. [See *Table 15.6.*]
- A clinician will:
  i. Explain how to use the strategies
  ii. Assign the clients to learn only one step at a time
  iii. Have the clients paraphrase the directions to ensure understanding
  iv. Link the new information to old information the clients already knows
  v. Have the clients rehearse and practice the strategy
  vi. Have the clients understand how to use the strategy in their own words
- Clinicians may also use *errorless learning techniques,* techniques by which patients are explicitly guided in learning a new skill rather than being allowed to figure it out through trial and error.
- The biggest challenge with these techniques is ensuring the clients will remember to use the strategies in their daily lives.

2. **Targeting Social Factors: Organizing the Environment**

Others can help clients by structuring the clients' environments and placing labels on all doors and rooms.

IV. DEMENTIA

Neuropsychological testing on Mrs. B. showed that she has difficulty with mental control, which is a symptom of *dementia.*

A. What Is Dementia?

- *Dementia* is a set of cognitive disorders characterized by deficits in learning new information or in recalling information already learned *plus* at least one other type of cognitive impairment.
- The types of cognitive impairment are:
  i. **Aphasia:** difficulty remembering the correct words for things
  ii. **Apraxia:** problem with carrying through motor tasks such as dressing or eating
  iii. **Agnosia:** problem recognizing family or friends
  iv. **Executive function problems:** difficulties in planning or organizing
- Dementia arises gradually and usually becomes worse, but must cause significant impairment to meet the diagnosis of dementia. [See *Table 15.7.*]
- There are two specifiers for dementia depending on the age of onset:
  i. **Late onset:** symptoms begin over age 65
  ii. **Early onset:** symptoms begin before age 65
- People with dementia may exhibit the following symptoms: inappropriate behavior, misperception of reality, or wandering away from home.
- These symptoms can lead to agitation or even violence.
- The most common cause of dementia is *Alzheimer's disease,* a medical condition in which the afflicted individual initially has problems with both memory and executive function and which then leads to progressive dementia. [See *Table 15.8* and *Case 15.4.*]

B. Distinguishing Between Dementia and Other Psychological Disorders

Disorders that have similar symptoms to dementia include:

- **Mental retardation:** Differentiated from dementia because it does not include symptoms of memory problems and is diagnosed in young people

- **Schizophrenia:** Includes symptoms of hallucinations and delusions, but is usually diagnosed in early adulthood
- **Depression:** Involves memory problems, poor concentration, and additional cognitive problems, but unlike dementia, individuals did not have these problems prior to the onset of depression and the symptoms usually come on rapidly
- **Delirium:** Difficult to differentiate from dementia, and the clinician may need to gather additional details from friends and family
- **Amnestic disorder:** Memory problems are involved in both this and dementia, but dementia also includes cognitive defects
- **Normal aging:** Will lead to some cognitive problems but not to the extent seen with dementia [see *Table 15.9*]

C. Understanding Dementia

The most common types of dementia are dementia of the Alzheimer's type, vascular dementia, and dementia due to other general medical conditions.

1. Dementia of the Alzheimer's Type

Three-fourths of those with dementia have Alzheimer's type dementias. This type is diagnosed by ruling out other causes.

a. The Progression of Alzheimer's Disease:

- The onset is gradual, but symptoms become worse.
- The early sign of the disease is difficulty with remembering recent events or new information.
- After a few years, clients may show signs of aphasia, apraxia, agnosia, decreased spatial skills, irritability, motor skills problems, and behavioral disturbances.
- Patients tend to die 8 to 10 years after the first symptoms begin. [See *Table 15.10.*]
- Those who show behavioral disturbances (such as wandering around) tend to have greater cognitive problems and need earlier institutional care. [See *Table 15.11.*]

LECTURE ENHANCEMENT 15.2: Stages of Alzheimer's Disorder

Objective: To learn about the progression of Alzheimer's.

Time: 30 Minutes

Lecture Points:
I. Overview
   A. Three stages
   B. Stages all total will last 8 to 10 years
II. Stage 1
   A. Features the following symptoms:
      1. Anterograde amnesia (loss of present and future memories)
      2. Amnesia especially for declarative/semantic memories
      3. Severe memory problems—forgetting names, dates, appointments, familiar routes of travel, or the need to turn off the kitchen stove
      4. Deficits in visuospatial skills—wandering
      5. Indifference, irritability, sadness
      6. Anomia—inability to name objects
      7. Depression often appears in the early phase of Alzheimer's

III. Stage 2

    A. Features the following symptoms:

        1. Increasing retrograde amnesia (loss of memories from the past)

        2. Flat or labile (changing) mood

        3. Restlessness and agitation

        4. Fluent aphasia—loss of ability to speak

        5. Acalculia—inability to perform math

        6. Ideomotor—involuntary movements

        7. Apraxia—inability to translate an idea into movement

IV. Stage 3

    A. Features the following symptoms:

        1. Severely deteriorated intellectual function

        2. Apathy

        3. Limb rigidity

        4. Urinary and fecal incontinence

Summary: Students will be surprised at the differences in severity of symptoms between Stages 1, 2, and 3.

Source: Alzhiemer's Association, Progression through the Brain, http://www.alz.org/brain/01.asp This Web site also provides excellent visuals of the brain, plaques, and stages of Alzheimer's.

Questions to Students and Discussion: What are the main changes you notice from Stage 1 to Stage 3? Have you observed anyone in these stages? How might families prepare for each stage?

MEDIA RECOMMENDATION 15.5: HBO Alzheimer's Project

Objective: To learn about real people dealing with Alzheimer's.

Time: 30 Minutes to 85 Minutes

Media and Discussion: 1 Hour, 10 Minutes to 4 Hours, 48 Minutes

Discussion Only: 40 Minutes

Watch Online: Search Google for "HBO Alzheimer's Project," or http://www.alz.org/news_and_events_16202.asp

This five-part series consists of the following films:
"Memory Loss Tape" (85 minutes): shows real people with symptoms of Alzheimer's

"Grandpa, Do You Know Who I Am? With Maria Shriver" (30 minutes): addresses grandchildren dealing with a grandparent suffering from Alzheimer's

"Momentum in Science," Part 1 (55 minutes) and Part 2 (70 minutes): explores the scientific side of Alzheimer's

"Caregivers" (48 minutes): discusses the experience of those caring for a loved one with Alzheimer's

Summary: Students will learn a lot about the personal side of Alzheimer's. Additionally students will learn about new research in this area.

Questions to Students and Discussion: What was most surprising in the videos you watched? What types of treatment or support would you want to provide for caregivers? What questions remain about the causes and treatments of Alzheimer's?

b. **Brain Abnormalities Associated with Alzheimer's Disease: Neurofibrillary Tangles and Amyloid Plaques:**

- *Neurofibrillary tangles* are masses created by tau proteins that become twisted together and destroy the microtubes, leaving the neuron without a distribution system for nutrients. [See *Figure 15.3.*]

- *Amyloid plaques* are fragments of protein that accumulate on the outside surfaces of neurons, particularly neurons on the hippocampus.

- Researchers do not know if the tangles and plaques cause Alzheimer's or the reverse, although both are found in autopsies and PET scans.

- Biomedical tests are also used to examine blood and cerebrospinal fluid to detect Alzheimer's and Parkinson's.

MEDIA RECOMMENDATION 15.6: Amyloid Cascade Hypothesis

Objective: To learn additional information about amyloid plaque and oligomers.

Time: 1 Minute

Media and Discussion: 5 Minutes

Discussion Only: 4 Minutes

Watch Online: Search the Genes to Cognition Web site, g2cogonline.org, using the search terms "amyloid plaque," and select the video featured Dr. Dennis Selkoe, or http://www.g2conline.org/#Alzheimers?aid=2134&cid=117
This video describes how the beta amyloid is formed when amyloid precursor protein is made but is snipped in the wrong place, creating beta amyloid 42—which is the cause of Alzheimer's.

Summary: Students will find this video fascinating as they will learn the intricate neurological underpinnings of Alzheimer's.

Questions to Students and Discussion: What are oligomers and plaques? What role do these substances play in Alzheimer's?

c. **Genetics:**
- A specific version of the *Apo E.* gene places people more at risk for Alzheimer's.
- Early-onset Alzheimer's is caused by a mutation in one of three other genes, and research has found that mutations in two of these genes lead to the development of Alzheimer's in 100% of cases.
- The third type of mutation is rare and is called *presenilin 2.* It does not always cause the disease, and thus other factors must play a role in the development of Alzheimer's.

2. **Vascular Dementia**

- *Vascular dementia* is a type of dementia caused by the reduction or blockage of blood supply to the brain, which arises from plaque buildup or blood clots.

- *Transient ischemic attacks,* or *ministrokes,* cause clots that prevent blood flow to the brain, which causes the cognitive impairments and has a gradual onset.

- A single large stroke may cause an abrupt onset of symptoms.

- A neurological exam includes blood work and examining abnormal reflexes and aids in the diagnosis.

- This form of dementia is more common in men.

- Symptoms worsen in a stepwise fashion with additional deficits appearing with reduced blood flow.

- Medication may help prevent additional strokes or blood clots.

3. **Dementia Due to Other General Medical Conditions**

Parkinson's, late-stage HIV infection, and Huntington's disease can also cause dementia.

a. **Dementia Due to Parkinson's Disease:**

- *Parkinson's disease* is where one slowly and progressively loses motor function.

- Symptoms include shaking hands, shuffling walk, and rigid muscles.

- Fifty percent of people with Parksinson's develop dementia, and these people are usually over age 65.

- Parkinson's damages the *substantia nigra* that contains dopamine-releasing neurons and plays a powerful role in motor and executive functions.

- Parkinson's is caused by genetic and neurological factors (such as toxin-caused brain damage).

b. **Dementia Due to Lewy Bodies:**

- *Dementia due to Lewy bodies* is a type of progressive dementia caused by a type of protein (referred to as Lewy bodies) that builds up inside some types of neurons and can eventually cause them to die.

- The neurons most affected are ones that play a role in memory and motor control.

- In the early stages of this form of dementia, people will experience hallucination, attention and consciousness problems, and stiff movements.

- About 20% of people with Alzheimer's have also been found to have Lewy bodies and can be differentiated from those with Alzheimer's using the following symptoms:
  i. Visual hallucinations
  ii. Retaining the ability to identify and name objects
  iii. Poor visuospatial ability
  iv. Impaired executive functions

- Patients usually deteriorate and die 8 to 10 years after the diagnosis.

c. **Dementia Due to HIV Disease:**

- HIV disease causes destruction of white matter and subcortical brain areas.

- Symptoms include:
  i. Impaired memory, concentration, and problem solving
  ii. Cognitive slowing
  iii. Apathy
  iv. Delirium
  v. Delusions
  vi. Hallucinations
  vii. Tremors
  viii. Repetitive movements
  ix. Balance problems

- Antiretroviral medications do slow the infection down, which can reverse the brain damage and thus improve cognitive functioning.

d. Dementia Due to Huntington's Disease:

- *Huntington's disease* is a progressive disease that kills neurons and affects cognition, emotion, and motor function; it leads to dementia and eventually results in death.

- Symptoms include mood swings, irritability, psychotic symptoms, restlessness, memory problems, executive dysfunction, and poor judgment.

- Five to seven people per 100,000 are affected, and men and women are equally affected by this disorder.

- Average age of diagnosis is between 30 and 40 years old, yet the age of onset can range from 4 to 85 years of age.

- This disorder is heritable and is attributed to one gene. Children have a 50% chance of getting the disorder if a parent has it.

e. Dementia Due to Head Trauma:

- Symptoms depend on the area damaged but usually include behavioral and memory problems and sensory motor and personality changes.

- This disorder is more common among males who engage in risk-taking behaviors, and the disorder will not get worse unless there are additional traumas.

f. Substance-Induced Persisting Dementia:

- *Substance-induced persisting dementia* is the diagnosis given when dementia is caused by a substance and lasts longer than the typical intoxication or withdrawal symptoms.

- Individuals with this disorder usually are substance dependent and older than 20 years old; the symptoms are irreversible.

- If someone has more than one of these disorders, both are diagnosed separately. [See *Table 15.12.*]

D. Treating Dementia

- There is no medication to reverse the cognitive problems, except the antiretroviral medication used in treat HIV infection.

- Since most people with dementia have Alzheimer's, this section will focus on treatments specific to this form of dementia.

1. Targeting Neurological Factors

- *Cholinesterase* (such as *galantamine* or *donepezil*) is used to treat mild or moderate cognitive symptoms by increasing the level of acetylcholine.

- *Memantine* is used to treat moderate to severe Alzheimer's dementia by affecting glutamate activity.

- Few studies have been conducted on these medications and long-term effects are unknown.

- These medications are also used with those who have dementia from Parkinson's.

- Antipsychotic medications are given to those who have psychotic symptoms, but the long-term effects are unknown.

- Those who have dementia due to Lewy bodies should not be given antipsychotic medication because the medication worsens the symptoms.

- High blood pressure increases the risk of vascular dementia and thus patients may also be given medication to address this as well.

2. Targeting Psychological Factors

- Maintaining a high quality of life is the first line of treatment for dementia.
- Friends and relatives need to develop strategies in the environment to cope with memory problems, structure daily activities so the schedule is predictable, and give patients a GPS tracking device in order to locate them if they get lost.
- Anxiety and depression are often experienced in the early stages and can be alleviated with *reality orientation therapy,* which helps patients focus on the present.
- *Reminiscence therapy* helps patients recall their early memories and life histories, which helps improve their mood.
- Agitation, aggression, and other behavioral problems can be addressed by identifying antecedents and consequences and learning how to modify these.

3. Targeting Social Factors

- *Elder day care* or other services target social factors and provide rest for caregivers.
- Full-time caretakers may be needed.
- Labeling the environment may also be useful.
- Caregivers may also need support, education, and treatment to learn how to deal with the stress.

V.   DIAGNOSING MRS. B.'S PROBLEMS

The neuropsychologist concluded that Mrs. B. had mild dementia, depression, and chronic pain.

ADDITIONAL READINGS

Journal Articles

Dementia

Atri, A., Shaughnessy, L. W., Locascio, J. J., & Growdon, J. H. (2008). Long-term course and effectiveness of combination therapy in Alzheimer disease. *Alzheimer Disease & Associated Disorders, 22,* 209–221.

Ayalon, L., Gum, A., Feliciano, L., & Areán, P. A. (2006). Effectiveness of nonpharmacological interventions for the management of neuropsychiatric symptoms in patients with dementia: A systematic review. *Archives of Internal Medicine, 166,* 2182–2188.

Delirium

Brown, T. M., & Boyle, M. F. (2002). The ABC of psychological medicine: Delirium. *BMJ: British Medical Journal, 325,* 644–647.

Books and Memoirs on Cognitive Disorders

Cooney, E. (2004). *Death in slow motion: A memoir of a daughter, her mother, and the beast called Alzheimer's.* New York: Perennial.
    Discusses her experience of taking care of a parent with Alzheimer's.

Farah, M. J. (2004). *Visual agnosia* (2nd ed.). Cambridge, MA: MIT Press/Bradford Books.
    A cognitive neuroscience perspective on visual disorders.

Folstein, S. E. (1989). *Huntington's disease: A disorder of families.* Baltimore: Johns Hopkins University Press.

    Part of a series on health.

Kessler, L. (2008). *Finding life in the land of Alzheimer's: One daughter's hopeful story.* New York: Penguin Group.

    A resident assistant at an Alzheimer's facility struggles to resolve her own issues surrounding her mother's death due to Alzheimer's.

ADDITIONAL MEDIA RECOMMENDATIONS

August, B. (Director). (2001). *A song for Martin.* [Film]. Australia: PAL Broadcast System.

    A composer and concertmaster falls in love and five years later discovers he is showing symptoms of Alzheimer's.

Jenkins, T. (Director). (2008). *Savages.* [Film]. USA: 20th Century Fox Home Entertainment.

    The Savage family must work together to take care of their father who has developed dementia.

Weis, J. (Director). (2007). *Away from her.* [Film]. USA: Lionsgate.

    A film about an Ontario couple who are married for 40 years before the wife develops Alzheimer's.

WEB SITES

Alzheimer's Association: Provides information, support, and the latest news, including *Alzheimer's disease facts and figures 2007.* See: http://www.alz.org/index.asp

American Association for Geriatric Psychiatry: Provides information for patients, caregivers, and media. See: http://www.aagpgpa.org/

American Geriatrics Society: Has information on health, research, and resources for patients, caregivers, and medical professionals. See: http://www.aagpgpa.org/

Mental Help Net: Includes an overview, latest news, and videos, as well as the report *An Introduction to Aging and Geriatrics.* See: http://www.mentalhealth.net

Ethical and Legal Issues

CHAPTER OUTLINE

CHAPTER HEADINGS	INSTRUCTION IDEAS AND TEXTBOOK CORRELATIONS
ETHICAL ISSUES	
An Ethical Principle: The Role of Confidentiality	**Learning Objectives:** 16.1, 16.2, 16.3, 16.4 **Learning Concepts:** ambiguities regarding confidentiality; limits of confidentiality: HIPAA in action; legal restrictions on confidentiality; privileged communication **Learning Activity 16.1:** APA Code of Ethics **Lecture Enhancement 16.1:** The Internet and Confidentiality **Textbook Tool:** Table 16.1
Informed Consent to Participate in Research on Mental Illness: Can Patients Truly Be Informed?	**Learning Objective:** 16.5
CRIMINAL ACTIONS AND INSANITY	**Media Recommendation 16.1:** A Crime of Insanity
While Committing the Crime: Sane or Insane?	**Learning Objective:** 16.6 **Learning Concepts:** the M'Naghten test; the irresistible impulse test; the Durham test, the American Legal Institute test; insanity defense reform acts **Learning Activity 16.2:** Comparison of the Insanity Tests **Textbook Tools:** Table 16.2; Case 16.1
The Insanity Defense: Current Issues	**Learning Objectives:** 16.7, 16.8, 16.9 **Learning Concepts:** assessing insanity for the insanity defense; states' rights: doing away with the insanity defense; with the insanity defense, do people really "get away with murder"? **Worth Video Tool Kit for Abnormal Psychology:** Clark Rockefeller Trial: A Delusional Disorder or a Defense Strategy?
After Committing the Crime: Competent to Stand Trial?	**Learning Objective:** 16.10 **Textbook Tool:** Case 16.2

DANGEROUSNESS: LEGAL CONSEQUENCES	**Learning Objective:** 16.11
Evaluating Dangerousness	**Learning Objectives:** 16.12, 16.13 **Textbook Tool:** Table 16.3
Actual Dangerousness	**Learning Objective:** 16.14 **Textbook Tool:** Figure 16.1
Confidentiality and the Dangerous Patient: Duty to Warn and Duty to Protect	**Learning Objective:** 16.15
Maintaining Safety: Confining the Dangerously Mentally Ill Patient	**Learning Objectives:** 16.16, 16.17, 16.18, 16.19 **Learning Concepts:** criminal commitment; civil commitment; sexual predator laws **Lecture Enhancement 16.2:** Mental Health Courts **Textbook Tools:** Cases 16.3, 16.4 **Worth Video Tool Kit for Abnormal Psychology:** Mental Health Courts
LEGAL ISSUES RELATED TO TREATMENT	
Right to Treatment	**Learning Objective:** 16.20
Right to Refuse Treatment	**Learning Objective:** 16.20
Competence to Refuse Treatment	**Learning Objective:** 16.20 **Learning Activity 16.3:** Debate on the Right to Refuse Treatment
Mental Health and Drug Courts	**Learning Objective:** 16.21 **Worth Video Tool Kit for Abnormal Psychology:** Crimes and Punishment: Drug Courts
THE WHEELS OF JUSTICE: FOLLOW-UP ON ANDREW GOLDSTEIN	

LEARNING OBJECTIVES

After completing this chapter, students will be able to:

16.1 Describe the role of and ambiguities regarding confidentiality in mental health ethics.

16.2 Articulate the changes in confidentiality that resulted from the Health Insurance Portability and Accountability Act (HIPAA) of 2002.

16.3 Detail the legal restrictions on confidentiality.

16.4 Expound on the definition of *privileged communication.*

16.5 Identify the general rule that defines informed consent to participate in research on mental illness.

16.6 Describe each of the five tests that have been used in the United States to determine whether a person is insane.

16.7 Identify the two unresolved issues regarding the federal requirements for the insanity defense.

16.8 Describe the factors to consider when assessing an insanity defense.

16.9 Identify two alternative options to pleading the insanity defense used in some states.

16.10 Detail the requirements for *competency to stand trial.*

16.11 Define *dangerousness* according to its four components regarding potential harm.

16.12 Articulate the research findings regarding the risk factors that could best identify which patients discharged from psychiatric facilities would subsequently act violently.

16.13 Identify under which two types of situations an incarcerated or hospitalized individual who is considered dangerous can continue to be incarcerated or hospitalized.

16.14 Identify the two circumstances related to mental illness that increase dangerousness.

16.15 Detail the options for mental health professionals who decide that a patient is about to harm a specific person.

16.16 Describe criminal commitment and civil commitment.

16.17 Describe the history and findings associated with both inpatient and outpatient commitment.

16.18 Expound on some of the problems encountered when trying to obtain appropriate treatment for people with chronic or severe mental illness.

16.19 Detail the history of sexual predator laws.

16.20 Describe each of the various court rulings regarding the rights of the mentally ill, including right to treatment, right to refuse treatment, and competence to refuse treatment.

16.21 Define the roles of drug courts and mental health courts.

KEY TERMS

Confidentiality: The ethical requirement not to disclose information about a patient (including whether someone even *is* a patient) to others unless legally compelled to do so.

Privileged communication: Confidential information that is protected from being disclosed during legal proceedings.

Criminally responsible: The determination that a defendant's crime was the product of both an *action* or attempted action (the alleged criminal behavior) and his or her *intention* to perform that action.

M'Naghten test (or rule): The legal test in which a person is considered insane if, because of a "defect of reason, from disease of the mind," he or she did not know what he or she was doing (at the time of committing the act) and did not know that it was wrong.

Irresistible impulse test: The legal test in which a person is considered insane if he or she knew that his or her criminal behavior was wrong but nonetheless performed it because of an irresistible impulse.

Durham test: The legal test in which a person is considered insane if an irresistible impulse to perform criminal behavior was due to a mental defect or disorder present at the time of the crime.

American Legal Institute test (ALI test): The legal test in which a person is considered insane if a defendant either lacks a substantial capacity to appreciate that his or her behavior was wrong or has a diminished ability to make his or her behavior conform to the law.

Competency to stand trial: The mental state during the time leading up to the trial that enables a defendant to participate in his or her own defense.

Dangerousness: The legal term that refers to someone's potential to harm self or others.

Tarasoff rule: A ruling by the Supreme Court of California (and later other courts) that psychologists have a duty to protect potential victims who are in imminent danger.

Criminal commitment: The involuntary commitment to a mental health facility of a person charged with a crime.

Civil commitment: The involuntary commitment to a mental health facility of a person deemed to be at significant risk of harming himself or herself or a specific other person.

CHAPTER GUIDE

Chapter Introduction

- Andrew Goldstein, who had a 10-year history of mental illness, pushed Kendra Webdale in front of a subway train in New York City in 1998, causing her immediate death. Although Goldstein was thought to have murdered Webdale, the case turned out not to be so simple.

- This chapter examines legal and ethical issues pertaining to mental health professionals and patients and also thoroughly examines criminal actions and their consequences when the actions are by those who are mentally ill.

I.   ETHICAL ISSUES

What are the clinician's ethical obligations when a patient threatens the safety of others?

A. An Ethical Principle: The Role of Confidentiality

Each mental health profession has its own code of ethics, with commonalities among all the codes. [See *Table 16.1.*]

- The most important commonality is the requirement to maintain *confidentiality*—not to disclose to others information about a patient at any time unless legally mandated to do so.
- Mental health records must remain confidential.
- Patients must be informed as to the limits of confidentiality.

LEARNING ACTIVITY 16.1: APA Code of Ethics

Objective: To expose students to the APA Code of Ethics.

Time: 40 Minutes

Discussion: 60 Minutes

Directions:
1. Print out a copy of the American Psychological Association's *Ethical Principles of Psychologists and Code of Conduct* (http://www.apa.org/ethics/code/index.aspx). The code of ethics covers the following areas:
   - Principles
   - Resolving ethical issues
   - Competence
   - Human relations

- Privacy and confidentiality
- Advertising and public statements
- Record keeping and fees
- Education and training
- Research and publication
- Assessment
- Therapy

2. Have the students break into small groups and divide the 11 topics mentioned here among the groups.
3. Have each group summarize the major points of each section for their classmates.

Summary: Students will be surprised to learn information about various ethical standards, such as having to wait two years before having relations with a former client and how long counselors are required to keep client records.

Questions to Students and Discussion: What surprised you about the Code of Conduct? What do you feel is missing from the Code? Describe what you learned about confidentiality. How does the information about confidentiality compare to what you learned about this topic in your text?

1. Ambiguities Regarding Confidentiality

- Issues surrounding confidentiality can be complex and difficult to resolve.
- Members of a counseling group (couples or group counseling) may choose to discuss what happens in therapy sessions with people who are not part of the group; group members are asked to maintain confidentiality about their sessions.
- A legal minor falls outside the bounds of confidentiality.
- The clinician will discuss, with a minor old enough to understand, the limits of confidentiality, pointing out possible circumstances that would require the clinician to share information with the parents.

2. Limits of Confidentiality: HIPAA in Action

- The Health Insurance Portability and Accountability Act (HIPAA) was passed in 2002 and widened the set of circumstances under which confidential information can be shared with other individuals and organizations that care for or monitor patients.
- A patient's information can be shared legally with other health providers without the patient's permission.
- A patient must give written consent to have psychotherapy notes shared with anyone. For other clinicians or organizations, only dates of treatment, diagnosis and prognosis, and medications prescribed can be shared.
- Patients have less control over their health records. Health care information can be shared without getting consent under the following circumstances:
  i. **Litigation:** The opposing lawyer in a lawsuit can request the health information of a patient from a provider and can also request medical records of witnesses.
  ii. **The person is a police suspect:** Police can request health information about a suspect without having a warrant or being under any judicial oversight.
  iii. **Marketing efforts by health providers and their business associates:** The patient's clinician or mental health center can notify the patient by mail of treatments, groups, etc., that may interest the patient.
  iv. **Research:** A patient's medical records may be used in a research study without the patient's permission.

- The law specifies that only minimal information be disclosed, unless the purpose of sharing information is to facilitate treatment.

3. Legal Restrictions on Confidentiality

States have laws of confidentiality, but there are exceptions. Typically, the exceptions include:

- When the patient gives the clinician permission to violate confidentiality (*Example:* giving explicit permission to a therapist to talk to the patient's spouse)
- When the clinician suspects abuse of children, the elderly, or the disabled (the clinician must then report the abuse to the authorities)
- When the clinician has reason to believe a patient is likely to harm himself/herself (the clinician must then take steps to protect the patient)
- When the clinician has reason to believe that a patient is likely to harm another, specific person (the clinician must then take steps to protect the other person)

LECTURE ENHANCEMENT 16.1: The Internet and Confidentiality

Objective: To learn about confidentiality and the Internet.

Time: 20 Minutes

Lecture Points:
I. Issues
    A. The California Healthcare Foundation examined the privacy documents for 21 Internet health sites.
    B. Most of these sites allow third-party advertisers to obtain information about clients.
    C. It was discovered that third-party ad networks received access to information that allowed them to build detailed, personally identified profiles of individual's health conditions and patterns of Internet use.
II. Suggestion to Clients
    A. Clients should be made aware that their personal information may be shared with a third party if they choose to use an Internet health site.
III. Suggestion to Companies
    A. Evaluate the privacy policy.
    B. Compare the policy to the actual information given to the third parties.
    C. Allow clients to have more privacy when they use the online resources.
    D. Develop a standard policy among Internet health care providers.

Source: Rabasca, L. (2000). Confidentiality not guaranteed by most health Web sites, report finds. *APA Monitor, 31*(4), 13.

Questions to Students and Discussion: What surprised you about this information? Why? Do you think it is ethical for health care companies to allow third-party access to client information? Why or why not? What suggestions would you add to the list?

---

4. Privileged Communication

- Although confidentiality is an ethical term, ***privileged communication*** is a legal term referring to confidential information that is protected from being disclosed during legal proceedings.

- Not all confidential information is privileged, and vice versa. When the law of privileged communication conflicts with the ethics of confidentiality, patients should be told of the limits of confidentiality as soon as possible.
- The patient usually, but not always, decides if information shared with a clinician can be revealed. Exceptions to privileged communication include:
  i. Mental health evaluations that are ordered by a judge (in some courts, depending on the jurisdiction)
  ii. Civil lawsuits that raise the issue of personal injury (with mental health consequences) in the suit (*Example:* a clinician's testimony if a patient or former patient sues his employer for anguish resulting from harassment at work)
- During lawsuits, judges decide on a case-by-case basis whether a therapist of a group therapy session must testify. Group members may be compelled to testify.

B. Informed Consent to Participate in Research on Mental Illness: Can Patients Truly Be Informed?

Potential participants in a psychological research study must be capable of understanding and reasoning about what they are consenting to, which may be more important to informed consent than whether the person is psychotic or otherwise impaired at the time of consent.

II. CRIMINAL ACTIONS AND INSANITY

- *Insanity,* a legal concept not found in DSM-IV-TR, is measured by determining if a person was **criminally responsible** (meaning a defendant's crime was the product of both an *action* or attempted action and his or her *intention* to perform that action) at the time of a crime.
- The legal system asks two sets of questions to determine if the defendant in a trial is suffering from a mental illness:
  i. What was the defendant's mental state at the time of the (alleged) criminal act? (Is the insanity defense appropriate?)
  ii. What was the defendant's mental state during the post-crime assessment, and what is his/her mental state now? (Can he/she assist in her own defense? Is he/she competent to stand trial?)

MEDIA RECOMMENDATION 16.1: A Crime of Insanity

Objective: To learn about a real case where the legal and mental health systems clashed.

Time: 66 Minutes

Media and Discussion: 111 Minutes

Discussion Only: 45 Minutes

Explore Online:

Murdock, D., Navasky, M. & O'Connor, K. *Frontline: A Crime of Insanity.* WGBH Educational Foundation. http://www.pbs.org/wgbh/pages/frontline/shows/crime/
Read about Ralph Tortorici, a paranoid schizophrenic charged with a violent crime, and the complex problems his lawyers faced in mounting an insanity defense.

Watch a short clip of Attorney Cheryl Coleman discussing the difficulty in finding a psychiatrist who is willing to testify that her client is sane at
http://www.pbs.org/wgbh/pages/frontline/shows/crime/etc/excerpt_hi.html

Summary: Students will learn the controversies and ethical issues surrounding an insanity defense. They will be surprised to learn that there are psychiatrists who are willing to testify for payment. Students will also learn about how the legal and mental health systems can clash with one another.

Questions to Students and Discussion: What standards did the lawyers use to determine Tortorici's sanity? Do you agree with the lawyers' actions? Why or why not? What interventions might have prevented this event from happening?

A. While Committing the Crime: Sane or Insane?

The following are the five tests that the United States legal system has used over time to determine insanity.

1. The M'Naghten Test

- A Scottish man in 1841 England, Daniel M'Naghten, attempted to kill British Prime Minister Sir Robert Peel, but killed his secretary instead, because M'Naghten believed that Peel was personally responsible for M'Naghten's woes.

- The *M'Naghten test (or rule)* asks at a trial whether the defendant, only at the time of committing the act, knew what he/she was doing and knew it was wrong.

2. The Irresistible Impulse Test

- In 1886, the *irresistible impulse test* focused on whether the defendant knew that the criminal behavior was wrong but nonetheless performed it because of an irresistible impulse.

- The test centered the legal definition of insanity on the extent to which the behavior was uncontrollable.

3. The Durham Test

- The *Durham test,* created after a 1954 Supreme Court ruling, broadened the test for the insanity defense again by seeking to determine whether the irresistible impulse was due to mental defect or a disorder present at the time of the alleged crime.

- The ruling shifted from considerations about morality (knowing right from wrong) to the realm of science (having a mental impairment), but left unclear the following:
  i.   What constituted a mental defect or disorder
  ii. Whether the criminal behavior was caused by the disorder or defect

- Only New Hampshire still uses this test.

4. The American Legal Institute Test

- The institute proposed two alternative criteria, known as the *American Legal Institute test (ALI test)* for insanity:
  i.   The person lacks a substantial capacity to appreciate that the behavior was wrong (versus no capacity).
  ii. The person has a diminished ability to make his or her behavior conform to the law (an irresistible impulse).

- The elements of the above American Legal Institute (ALI) test are referred to as *knowledge (cognition)* and *impulse (volition).*

- The test prevents people from using their antisocial personality disorder or illegal substance use as the basis for an insanity defense.
- This test continues to be used by many states.

5. **Insanity Defense Reform Acts**

- The insanity test changed again in 1984 after John Hinckley's 1981 assassination attempt on then-President Ronald Reagan. Hinckley was found not guilty by reason of insanity.
- Through the reform acts of 1984 and 1988, the legal system asks if an individual has a *severe* mental defect or disorder that causes a diminished capacity to understand right from wrong.
- The acts also eliminated the irresistible impulse element in federal courts.
- Having a disorder *in and of itself* does not constitute an insanity defense. [See *Table 16.2* and *Case 16.1.*]

LEARNING ACTIVITY 16.2: Comparison of the Insanity Tests

Objective: To compare and contrast the different tests used to determine whether someone is sane or insane.

Time: 30 Minutes

Directions: Ask students to fill out the chart on *Worksheet 16.1* to compare and contrast the different tests used to determine whether someone is insane.

Summary: The chart will help students easily compare and contrast these tests. Students will be able to see how the tests shifted from measuring one's impulsivity to examining one's mental capacity.

Questions to Students and Discussion: How has the test for sanity changed over time? What surprised you about these tests? What do you think is an appropriate measure of a person's sanity?

B. The Insanity Defense: Current Issues

The federal courts still need to resolve two ambiguous issues about how the insanity defense can be applied.

- Whether the person knew the act was wrong (moral issue) versus illegal (legal issue)
- Whether the person knew that the specific behavior was wrong in a particular circumstance versus whether he/she knew in the abstract that the act was wrong

1. **Assessing Insanity for the Insanity Defense**

- Juries, when determining whether a defendant was insane at the time a crime was perpetrated, rely on testimonies from friends, family members, witnesses, or mental health clinicians.
- Mental health clinicians, when determining whether a defendant was insane at the time a crime was perpetrated, may interview the defendant and administer and interpret psychological tests. These evaluations must take into account events that had happened after the crime and before the evaluation. *Examples:* experiences in jail, current medications, decision to plead Not Guilty By Reason of Insanity (NGBI),

reactions to the crime, coaching from a lawyer or other inmates, and responses to various assessment methods.

• Past psychiatric history does not necessarily indicate a person's mental state at the time he/she committed a crime.

2. States' Rights: Doing Away with the Insanity Defense

Some states have abolished the insanity defense, replacing it with a defense that a defendant did not have "free will" while committing a crime. Two alternative options are:

• **Diminished capacity:** A person, due to mental illness or defect, was less able to understand that the criminal act was wrong or to formulate a specific intention. The person receives a lesser sentence, is convicted of a lesser crime, or receives a modified form of punishment.

• **Guilty but mentally ill:** A convicted defendant is often sent to a psychiatric facility and may serve time in prison if his/her mental state improves over time, or the defendant may be sent to a prison immediately, where he/she may or may not receive psychiatric care.

3. With the Insanity Defense, Do People Really "Get Away with Murder"?

• A landmark study of 9,000 felony cases across eight states from 1976 to 1987 found that only 1% used the insanity defense, only one-fourth of that 1% were acquitted, and, of that one-fourth of 1%, only 7%, or two cases, were acquitted by a jury rather than a judge.

• The average time spent in jail by defendants who were found guilty (5 years) was comparable to the average time spent in a mental hospital by those where were found NGBI (4.7 years).

C. After Committing the Crime: Competent to Stand Trial?

• *Competency to stand trial* is based on an evaluation of mental state during the time leading up to the trial, resulting in a judgment as to whether a mental defect or disorder prevents the defendant from participating in his/her own defense. A person who is competent to stand trial will be able to:
  i. Understand the proceedings that will take place
  ii. Understand the facts in the case and the legal options available
  iii. Consult with his/her lawyer "with a reasonable degree of rational understanding"
  iv. Assist the lawyer in building the defense

• Until recently, the courts have viewed competency to stand trial as a black-and-white issue—a defendant either can or can't.

• Some scholars have proposed the alternative term, *adjudicative competence,* to address the mental competency of all defendants nearing legal proceedings. [See *Case 16.2.*]

• A MacArthur Foundation research project found that criminal defense attorneys viewed 15% of their clients as possibly having impaired competence. Those defendants were much less helpful to their attorneys than those who were clearly competent.

• A Supreme Court ruling states that mentally ill patients accused of nonviolent crimes cannot be forced to take medication in order to become competent to stand trial. However, if a person is not competent to stand trial and is released, he/she may be civilly committed to a psychiatric facility if deemed a danger to self or others.

III. DANGEROUSNESS: LEGAL CONSEQUENCES

Dangerousness is a legal term referring to someone's potential to harm self or others. The potential harm of someone who is determined dangerous is broken down into four components:

- **Probability:** Is the person likely to be dangerous?
- **Imminence:** How soon might the potential harm occur?
- **Frequency:** How often is the person likely to be dangerous?
- **Severity:** How much harm might the person inflict?

A. Evaluating Dangerousness

- Clinicians are asked to evaluate if a person is dangerous or not using severity, imminence, and likelihood of potential harm.
- Study findings regarding risk factors that can best identify which patients discharged from psychiatric facilities would subsequently act violently include:
    i. Within 5 months of discharge, 20% committed at least one violent act.
    ii. Men were only somewhat more likely than women to be violent; in general, family members were the victims of female patients who were violent.
    iii. A history of violence was a strong risk factor for later violence.
    iv. Persistent thoughts about harming others and higher scores on an anger scale predicted later violence.
    v. Childhood experiences of serious and frequent abuse and having a father who was a criminal or who engaged in substance abuse predicted future violent behavior.
    vi. Certain diagnoses (substance abuse and antisocial personality disorder) were better predictors of violence than other diagnoses (schizophrenia).
    vii. Delusions about suspicions of others and hallucinations that "commanded" a violent act also predicted later violence. [See *Table 16.3.*]
- A person is committed to incarceration or hospitalization only under two situations:
    i. When the person hasn't yet committed any violent crime, but is perceived to be at imminent risk to do so
    ii. When the person has already served a prison term or received mandated treatment in a psychiatric hospital and is about to be released but is perceived to be at imminent risk of behaving violently
- The definition of the word *imminent* remains unclear.

B. Actual Dangerousness

- Criminal behavior by the mentally ill is no more common than that by the general population.
- Two general situations increase dangerousness:
    i. When psychosis is involved and the person may be a danger to self and/or others
    ii. When serious mental illness is combined with substance abuse [see *Figure 16.1*]
- Most mentally ill people are not violent.

C. Confidentiality and the Dangerous Patient: Duty to Warn and Duty to Protect

- The Supreme Court of California ruled that psychologists have a duty to protect potential victims who are in imminent danger, a rule known as the *Tarasoff rule.*
- Clinicians who think their patients might harm a specific person can:
    i. Warn the intended victim or someone else who can warn the victim

ii. Notify law enforcement

iii. Take other reasonable steps, depending on the situation (*Example:* Have a patient committed to a psychiatric facility)

- The rule bounds clinicians with the duty to protect, not just warn.

- The rule does not cover danger to property.

D. Maintaining Safety: Confining the Dangerously Mentally Ill Patient

1. Criminal Commitment

- *Criminal commitment* happens when a person charged with a crime is involuntarily committed to a mental health facility. This can take place before or after a crime:

   i. Prior to the trial, the person will be evaluated on competence to stand trial and will be provided treatment to become competent to stand trial.

   ii. After the trial, a person acquitted due to insanity will be committed.

- Laws are unclear as to how long a person should remain committed.

2. Civil Commitment

- A person deemed dangerous who has not committed a crime can be judicially confined to a mental health facility, which is called *civil commitment*.

- There are two types of civil commitment:

   i. Inpatient commitment

   ii. Outpatient commitment with monitoring and/or treatment programs [see *Case 16.3*]

- Clinicians must base their judgments in part on known risk factors.

a. Inpatient Commitment:

- A study found that half of inpatients who thought they didn't need hospitalization later shifted their views.

- Patients did not feel coerced when family members used concern, persuasion, and inducements, whereas the use of force or threats or not being able to tell their "story" did feel like coercion.

b. Mandated Outpatient Commitment:

- This type of commitment was developed in the 1960s and 1970s as a less restrictive legally mandated alternative to inpatient care.

- It typically includes psychotherapy, medication, and periodic monitoring by a clinician.

- A study found that mandated outpatient commitment is more effective than inpatient treatment followed by freedom after discharge because it was more likely to:

   i. Keep the patient from being a danger to himself/herself or others

   ii. Result in less frequent hospitalizations

   iii. Result in patients taking their medicine or seeking other treatments

c. The Reality of Treatment for the Chronically Mentally Ill:

- State hospitals are pressured to move patients to less expensive programs, even if the patients are not ready.

- Space at psychiatric facilities is not always available for patients deemed mentally ill by the legal system.

- Deinstitutionalization options are not adequately funded, leaving all but the sickest to find other treatment options.

- Therefore, most people with severe mental illness lack adequate supervision, care, or housing.

- Not all people who are court mandated to receive treatment actually receive that treatment. [See *Case 16.4.*]

LECTURE ENHANCEMENT 16.2: Mental Health Courts

Objective: To learn about how mental health courts can treat defendants with more dignity and reduce recidivism.

Time: 30 Minutes

Lecture Points:
I. Issue
    A. There has been an increase in the number of mentally ill defendants in the United States.
    B. President Clinton passed the America's Law Enforcement and Mental Health Project Act (in 2000) to provide funds for those who wanted to establish mental health courts to deal with mentally ill defendants.
    C. Currently there are over 100 such courts in the United States.
    D. These courts seek to find the best treatment for the defendants.
II. Results
    A. Very little research has been conducted on these courts.
    B. However, Portland State researcher Heidi Herinckx found that the defendants were over four times less likely to reoffend, probation violations dropped 62%, and those with three or more arrests dropped from 26% to 3%.
III. Drawbacks
    A. These courts are short of funding and have few clients.
    B. Ensuring the judgments are carried out is difficult.

Summary: Students will enjoy hearing about a new method of treating those who are mentally ill and commit crimes. Students will also be surprised to learn about one researcher's amazing findings.

Source: A new justice system for the mentally ill, http://www.pbs.org/wgbh/pages/frontline/shows/asylums/special/courts.html

Questions to Students and Discussion: Do you believe such a program would be helpful in your community? Why or why not? What kind of issues does the use of an alternative court raise? What are your thoughts about other possible ways to work with those who have a mental illness and commit a crime?

3. **Sexual Predator Laws**

   - Repeat sexual offenders, or sexual predators, were treated as criminals before the 1930s and between 1980 and 1990, were viewed as mentally ill between the 1930s and 1980, and were sometimes incarcerated because of poor impulse control in the 1990s.

   - The government takes on the role of "parent" (*parens patriae*), protecting the public from threats and caring for those who cannot take care of themselves.

- After a 1997 Supreme Court ruling, sexual predators about to finish their prison sentence could be committed to a psychiatric hospital indefinitely if deemed likely to reoffend *and* if suffering from mental abnormalities or personality disorders.

- In 2002, the Court loosened the rules by requiring demonstration of people's difficulty in controlling their sexual behavior in order to commit them. The Court did not say how else to demonstrate this except through medical history.

IV. LEGAL ISSUES RELATED TO TREATMENT

Court decisions in the 1960s and 1970s addressed the right to treatment and right to refuse treatment.

A. Right to Treatment

- **1966:** Supreme Court ruled that people receiving treatment through civil commitment should be given the least restrictive alternative treatment available.

- **1967:** Supreme Court ruled that civil commitment must accompany appropriate treatment.

- **1970s:** Various courts outlined specific minimal criteria for treatment accompanying civil commitment:
  i.   Minimum staffing ratio
  ii. Minimum number of treatment hours per week
  iii. Individualized treatment plans for every person

- The Supreme Court also ruled that patients of civil commitment be released once they no longer meet the criteria for commitment and can survive on their own or with help from willing family members.

B. Right to Refuse Treatment

- A New Jersey federal district court ruled that civilly committed patients may refuse treatment. A hearing can take place that may or may not result in overriding this ruling.

- Factors to consider in a hearing to override a patient's right to refuse treatment include:
  i.   The patient is threatening to others.
  ii. The proposed treatment includes only a small risk of irreversible side effects.
  iii. No less restrictive treatment alternatives are available.
  iv. The patient cannot rationally decide about particular treatments.

C. Competence to Refuse Treatment

- About half of schizophrenia patients performed reasonably well on decision-making assessment tests.

- After two weeks of treatment, schizophrenia patients whose symptoms improved also improved in their decision-making abilities related to competence.

- About 75% of patients with the diagnosis of depression performed adequately on decision-making assessment tests.

- The law does not provide this same right to refuse treatment to those required to follow outpatient commitment treatment plans.

LEARNING ACTIVITY 16.3: Debate on the Right to Refuse Treatment

Objective: To learn about the different sides of the issue of the right to refuse treatment.

Time: 30 Minutes

Directions: Students should form two groups: One group defends the right to refuse treatment, while the other group defends the right to force people into treatment. Using their textbook, each group should develop support for its side in order to debate the issue in class.

Summary: Students will be surprised to learn about how complex the right to refuse treatment is: How do we respect individual rights while protecting others and the person in crisis?

Questions to Students and Discussion: How did your beliefs change from having this debate? If you were a clinician or attorney, how might you make the decision of whether or not to involuntarily commit someone? How difficult was it to switch sides of the argument?

D. Mental Health and Drug Courts

- Municipalities created two special courts to address more quickly legal cases related to the mentally ill: drug courts and mental health courts.
- As an alternative to jail, drug courts offer first-time drug abusers the opportunity to attend a drug treatment program; submit to random, frequent drug testing; and meet with the drug court judge regularly. These people are sent to jail immediately if they miss a court hearing.
- Participants in drug court programs are asked to:
    i.   Earn a GED
    ii. Hold a steady job
    iii. Have a mentor
    iv. Meet their financial obligations, such as child support
    v.   Become involved in community service
- Less than 10% of participants use drugs during these programs.
- Relapse rates are between 4% and 20% for those entering a program and less than 4% for those who complete a program.
- Some communities allow repeat offenders the opportunity to attend a drug court program.
- Mental health courts seek to treat, rather than incarcerate, mentally ill people charged with misdemeanors.
- Types of cases heard in mental health courts and features of these courts include:
    i.   The defendant's mental illness seems to contribute to the alleged criminal behavior.
    ii. The defendant seems likely to hurt herself or others.
    iii. Attendance to this court is voluntary—the defendant may choose to go through the usual court instead.
    iv. The court tries *not* to send the mentally ill to prison.
- Some courts accept violent defendants.
- According to studies, when mentally ill people receive treatment, they are subsequently less likely to become violent or to reoffend.

V. THE WHEELS OF JUSTICE: FOLLOW-UP ON ANDREW GOLDSTEIN

Goldstein had two trials. The jury found him guilty while acknowledging that he was mentally ill. Goldstein was sent to prison, where he was evaluated to determine whether he needed to be admitted to a psychiatric hospital, but only long enough to become stable and then to return to prison. After his conviction was overturned for a technical mishap, he pled guilty in a third trial, which sent him to jail for 23 years followed by 5 years of psychiatric oversight and supervision.

ADDITIONAL READINGS

Journal Articles

Egley, L. C. (1991). Defining the Tarasoff duty. *The Journal of Psychiatry and Law, 19,* 99–133.

Fazel, S., & Grann, M. (2006). The population impact of severe mental illness on violent crime. *American Journal of Psychiatry, 163,* 1397–1403.

Hiday, V. A., & Wales, H. W. (2003). Civil commitment and arrests. *Current Opinion in Psychiatry, 16,* 575–580.

McNiel, D. E., & Binder, R. L. (2007). Effectiveness of a mental health court in reducing criminal recidivism and violence. *American Journal of Psychiatry, 164,* 1395–1403.

Books and Memoirs on Ethical and Legal Issues

Bartol, C. R., & Bartol, A. M. (2004). *Psychology and law: Theory, research, and application.* Belmont, CA: Thomson/Wadsworth.
  A detailed overview of the ways psychology and the law interact.

Ewing, C. P., & McCann, J. T. (2006). *Minds on trial: Great cases in law and psychology.* New York: Oxford University Press.
  This book describes some famous cases and the role of psychologists in these cases.

La Fond, J. Q., & Durham, M. L. (1992). *Back to the asylum: The future of mental health law and policy in the United States.* New York: Oxford University Press.
  This book explores the mental health laws and policies in the United States, and the lack of emphasis on individual rights.

Wright, R. G. (2009). *Sex offender laws: Failed policies, new directions.* New York: Springer Publications.
  This book examines current laws on sex offenses and possible ways to prevent sex offender recidivism.

ADDITIONAL MEDIA RECOMMENDATIONS

Hoblit, G. (Director). (1996). *Primal fear.* [Film]. USA: Paramount Pictures.
  An attorney defends a boy who has witnessed a crime and the defendant claims he has multiple personality disorder.

Kasdan, L. (Director). (1999). *Mumford.* [Film]. USA: Touchstone Pictures.
  Shows a psychologist in a small town struggling with the ethical code.

Kassell, N. (Director). (2005). *The Woodsman.* [Film]. USA: Sony Pictures Home Entertainment.
  Shows some of the legal issues for sexual offenders.

WEB SITES

American Psychological Society, Division 41, American Psychology—Law Society: Includes latest news, career information, and research and publications. See: http://www.ap-ls.org/

Bazelon Center for Mental Health Law: Legal information about protecting the rights of people with mental illness. See: http://www.bazelon.org/

MacArthur Research Network on Mental Health and the Law: Information on mental health laws. See: http://www.macarthur.virginia.edu/mentalhome.html

WORKSHEET 16.1

	M'Naghten	Irresistible Impulse	Durham	American Legal Institute	Insanity Defense Reform Act
Year/Place					
Description					
Strengths					
Weaknesses					
Misc.					

APPENDIX

DSM-IV-TR Masters

Contents   **Description**

What's New in DSM-IV-TR?

The *DSM-IV Text Revision* (APA, 2000) has changed the diagnostic criteria for a number of disorders in DSM-IV.

Disorder	DSM-IV (APA, 1994)	DSM-IV Text Revision (APA, 2000)
Tourette's Disorder	Symptoms must cause marked distress or significant impairment in order to warrant diagnosis.	Diagnosis is warranted even if symptoms do not cause marked distress or significant impairment.
Chronic Motor or Vocal Tic Disorder	Symptoms must cause marked distress or significant impairment in order to warrant diagnosis.	Diagnosis is warranted even if symptoms do not cause marked distress or significant impairment.
Transient Tic Disorder	Symptoms must cause marked distress or significant impairment in order to warrant diagnosis.	Diagnosis is warranted even if symptoms do not cause marked distress or significant impairment.
Dementia Due to Other General Medical Conditions	Lists as Distinct Axis I disorders: *Dementia due to HIV disease Dementia due to head trauma Dementia due to Parkinson's disease Dementia due to Huntington's disease Dementia due to Pick's disease Dementia due to Creutzfeldt-Jakob disease*	These are no longer listed as distinct Axis I disorders. Instead, they are grouped together as *Dementia due to other general medical conditions*, with the particular medical condition coded on Axis III.
Personality Change Due to a General Medical Condition	Diagnosis is not warranted if the personality change occurs as part of dementia.	A diagnosis is warranted even in cases of dementia when the personality change is prominent.
Exhibitionism	Sexually arousing fantasies, sexual urges, or behaviors must cause significant distress or impairment in order to warrant diagnosis.	Diagnosis is warranted if person acts on sexual urges, even if such actions do not cause marked distress, impairment, or interpersonal difficulty. If person manifests only sexual urges or fantasies (not actions), these must cause marked distress or interpersonal difficulty to warrant diagnosis.
Frotteurism	Sexually arousing fantasies, sexual urges, or behaviors must cause significant distress or impairment in order to warrant diagnosis.	Diagnosis is warranted if person acts on sexual urges, even if such actions do not cause marked distress, impairment, or interpersonal difficulty. If person manifests only sexual urges or fantasies (not actions), these must cause marked distress or interpersonal difficulty to warrant diagnosis.

Source: APA, 2000, 1994

What's New in DSM-IV-TR? (Continued)

The *DSM-IV Text Revision* (APA, 2000) has changed the diagnostic criteria for a number of disorders in DSM-IV.

Disorder	DSM-IV (APA, 1994)	DSM-IV Text Revision (APA, 2000)
Pedophilia	Sexually arousing fantasies, sexual urges, or behaviors must cause significant distress or impairment in order to warrant diagnosis.	Diagnosis is warranted if person acts on sexual urges, even if such actions do not cause marked distress, impairment, or interpersonal difficulty. If person manifests only sexual urges or fantasies (not actions), these must cause marked distress or interpersonal difficulty to warrant diagnosis.
Sexual Sadism	Sexually arousing fantasies, sexual urges, or behaviors must cause significant distress or impairment in order to warrant diagnosis.	Diagnosis is warranted if person acts on sexual urges with a non-consenting person, even if such actions do not cause the patient marked distress, impairment, or interpersonal difficulty. If the individual manifests only sexual urges or fantasies (not actions), these must cause marked distress or interpersonal difficulty to warrant diagnosis.
Voyeurism	Sexually arousing fantasies, sexual urges, or behaviors must cause significant distress or impairment in order to warrant diagnosis.	Diagnosis is warranted if person acts on sexual urges, even if such actions do not cause marked distress, impairment, or interpersonal difficulty. If person manifests only sexual urges or fantasies (not actions), these must cause marked distress or interpersonal difficulty to warrant diagnosis.

Source: APA, 2000, 1994

Axis I Disorders in DSM-IV-TR

Disorders Usually First Diagnosed in Infancy, Childhood, and Adolescence
Disorders in this group tend to emerge and sometimes dissipate before adult life. They include pervasive developmental disorders (such as autism); learning disorders; attention-deficit hyperactivity disorder; conduct disorders; and separation anxiety disorder.

Delirium, Dementia, Amnestic, and Other Cognitive Disorders
These disorders are dominated by impairment in cognitive functioning. They include Alzheimer's disease and Huntington's disease.

Mental Disorders Due to a General Medical Condition
These are mental disorders that are caused primarily by a general medical disorder. They include mood disorder due to a general medical condition.

Substance-Related Disorders
These disorders are brought about by the use of substances that affect the central nervous system, such as alcohol use disorders, opioid use disorders, amphetamine use disorders, cocaine use disorders, and hallucinogen use disorders.

Schizophrenia and Other Psychotic Disorders
In this group of disorders, functioning deteriorates until the patient reaches a state of psychosis or loss of contact with reality.

Mood Disorders
Disorders in this group are marked by severe disturbances of mood that cause people to feel extremely and inappropriately sad or elated for extended periods of time. They include major depressive disorder and bipolar disorder.

Anxiety Disorders
Anxiety is the predominant disturbance in this group of disorders. They include generalized anxiety disorder, phobic disorders, panic disorder, obsessive-compulsive disorder, acute stress disorder, and posttraumatic stress disorder.

Somatoform Disorders
These disorders, marked by physical symptoms that apparently are caused primarily by psychological rather than physiological factors, include pain disorders, conversion disorders, somatization disorder, and hypochondriasis.

Factitious Disorders
People with these disorders intentionally produce or feign psychological or physical symptoms.

Source: APA, 2000, 1994

Axis I Disorders in DSM-IV-TR (Continued)

Dissociative Disorders

These disorders are characterized by a change in the usually integrated functions of memory and identity. They include dissociative amnesia; dissociative fugue, and dissociative identity disorder (multiple personality disorder).

Eating Disorders

People with these disorders display abnormal patterns of eating that significantly impair their functioning. The disorders include anorexia nervosa and bulimia nervosa.

Sexual Disorders and Gender Identity Disorders

These disorders in sexual functioning, behavior, or preferences include paraphilias, sexual dysfunctions, and gender identity disorder.

Sleep Disorders

People with these disorders display chronic sleep problems. The disorders include primary insomnia, primary hypersomnia, sleep terror disorder, and sleepwalking disorder.

Impulse-Control Disorders

People with these disorders are chronically unable to resist impulses, drives, or temptations to perform certain acts that are harmful to them or to others. The disorders include pathological gambling, kleptomania, pyromania, and intermittent explosive disorders.

Adjustment Disorder

The primary feature of these disorders is a maladaptive reaction to a clear stressor such as divorce or business difficulties that occur within three months after the onset of the stressor.

Other Conditions That May Be a Focus of Clinical Attention

This category consists of certain conditions or problems that are worth noting because they cause significant impairment, such as relational problems, problems related to abuse or neglect, medication-induced movement disorders, and psychophysiological disorders.

Source: APA, 2000, 1994

Global Assessment of Functioning (GAF) Scale

Consider psychological, social, and occupational functioning on a hypothetical continuum of mental health–illness. Do not include impairment in functioning due to physical (or environmental) limitations.

Code   [Note: Use intermediate codes when appropriate (e.g., 45, 68, 72).]

91–100   Superior functioning in a wide range of activities. Life's problems never seem to get out of hand, is sought out by others because of his or her many positive qualities. No symptoms.

81–90   Absent or minimal symptoms (e.g., mild anxiety before an exam), good functioning in all areas, interested and involved in a wide range of activities, socially effective, generally satisfied with life, no more than everyday problems or concerns (e.g., an occasional argument with family members).

71–80   If symptoms are present, they are transient and expectable reactions to psychosocial stressors (e.g., difficulty concentrating after family argument); no more than slight impairment in social, occupational, or school functioning (e.g., temporarily falling behind in schoolwork).

61–70   Some mild symptoms (e.g., depressed mood and mild insomnia) or some difficulty in social, occupational, or school functioning (e.g., occasional truancy, or theft within the household), but generally functioning pretty well; has some meaningful interpersonal relationships.

51–60   Moderate symptoms (e.g., flat affect and circumstantial speech, occasional panic attacks) or moderate difficulty in social, occupational, or school functioning (e.g., new friends, conflicts with peers or co-workers).

41–50   Serious symptoms (e.g., suicidal ideation, severe obsessional rituals, frequent shoplifting) or any serious impairment in social, occupational, or school functioning (e.g., no friends, unable to keep a job).

Source: APA, 2000, 1994
© 2011 by Worth Publishers

Global Assessment of Functioning (GAF) Scale (Continued)

31–40	Some impairment in reality testing or communication (e.g., speech is at times illogical, obscure, or irrelevant) or major impairment in several areas, such as work or school, family relations, judgment, thinking, or mood (e.g., depressed man avoids friends, neglects family, and is unable to work; child frequently beats up younger children, is defiant at home, and is failing at school).
21–30	Behavior is considerably influenced by delusions or hallucinations or serious impairment in communication or judgment (e.g., sometimes incoherent, acts grossly inappropriately, suicidal preoccupation) or inability to function in almost all areas (e.g., stays in bed all day; no job, home, or friends).
11–20	Some danger of hurting self or others (e.g., suicide attempts without clear expectation of death; frequently violent; manic excitement) or occasionally fails to maintain minimal personal hygiene (e.g., smears feces) or gross impairment in communication (e.g., largely incoherent or mute).
1–10	Persistent danger of severely hurting self or others (e.g., recurrent violence) or persistent inability to maintain minimal personal hygiene or serious suicidal act with clear expectation of death.
0	Inadequate information.

Source: APA, 2000, 1994

Diagnostic Criteria for Generalized Anxiety Disorder

A. Excessive anxiety and worry (apprehensive expectation), occurring more days than not for at least 6 months, about a number of events or activities (such as work or school performance).

B. The person finds it difficult to control the worry.

C. The anxiety and worry are associated with three (or more) of the following six symptoms (with at least some symptoms present for more days than not for the past 6 months). Note: Only one item is required in children.
   (1) restlessness or feeling keyed up or on edge
   (2) being easily fatigued
   (3) difficulty concentrating or mind going blank
   (4) irritability
   (5) muscle tension
   (6) sleep disturbance (difficulty falling or staying asleep, or restless unsatisfying sleep)

D. The focus of the anxiety and worry is not confined to features of an Axis 1 disorder, e.g., the anxiety or worry is not about having a Panic Attack (as in Panic Disorder), being embarrassed in public (as in Social Phobia), being contaminated (as in Obsessive-Compulsive Disorder), being away from home or close relatives (as in Separation Anxiety Disorder), gaining weight (as in Anorexia Nervosa), having multiple physical complaints (as in Hypochondriasis); and the anxiety and worry do not occur exclusively during Posttraumatic Stress Disorder.

E. The anxiety, worry, or physical symptoms cause clinically significant distress or impairment in social, occupational, or other important areas of functioning.

F. The disturbance is not due to the direct physiological effects of a substance (e.g., a drug of abuse, a medication) or a general medical condition (e.g., hyperthyroidism) and does not exclusively occur during a Mood Disorder, a Psychotic Disorder, or a Pervasive Developmental Disorder.

Source: APA, 2000, 1994

Diagnostic Criteria for Specific Phobia

A. Marked and persistent fear that is excessive or unreasonable, cued by the presence or anticipation of a specific object or situation (e.g., flying, heights, animals, receiving an injection, seeing blood).

B. Exposure to the phobic stimulus almost invariably provokes an immediate anxiety response, which may take the form of a situationally bound or situationally predisposed Panic Attack. Note: In children, the anxiety may be expressed by crying, tantrums, freezing, or clinging.

C. The person recognizes that the fear is excessive or unreasonable. Note: In children, this feature may be absent.

D. The phobic situation(s) is (are) avoided or else is endured with intense anxiety or distress.

E. The avoidance, anxious anticipation, or distress in the feared situation(s) interferes significantly with the person's normal routine, occupational (academic) functioning, or social activities or relationships, or there is a marked distress about having the phobia.

F. In individuals under 18 years, the duration is at least 6 months.

G. The anxiety, Panic Attacks, or phobic avoidance associated with the specific object or situation is not better accounted for by another mental disorder, such as Obsessive-Compulsive Disorder (e.g., fear of dirt in someone with an obsession about contamination), Posttraumatic Stress Disorder (e.g., avoidance of stimuli associated with a severe stressor), Separation Anxiety Disorder (e.g., avoidance of school), Social Phobia (e.g., avoidance of social situations because of fear of embarrassment), Panic Disorder With Agoraphobia, or Agoraphobia Without History of Panic Disorder.

Specify type:

Animal Type

Natural Environment Type (e.g., heights, storms, water)

Blood-Injection-Injury Type

Situational Type (e.g., airplanes, elevators, enclosed places)

Other Type (e.g., phobic avoidance of situations that may lead to choking, vomiting, or contracting an illness; in children, avoidance of loud sounds or costumed characters)

Source: APA, 2000, 1994

Diagnostic Criteria for Social Phobia

A. A marked and persistent fear of one or more social or performance situations in which the person is exposed to unfamiliar people or to possible scrutiny by others. The individual fears that he or she will act in a way (or show anxiety symptoms) that will be humiliating or embarrassing. Note: In children, there must be evidence of the capacity for age-appropriate social relationships with familiar people and the anxiety must occur in peer settings, not just in interactions with adults.

B. Exposure to the feared social situation almost invariably provokes anxiety which may take the form of a situationally bound or situationally predisposed Panic Attack. Note: In children, the anxiety may be expressed by crying, tantrums, freezing, or shrinking from social situations with unfamiliar people.

C. The person recognizes that the fear is excessive or unreasonable. Note: In children, this feature may be absent.

D. The feared social or performance situations are avoided or else are endured with intense anxiety or distress.

E. The avoidance, anxious anticipation, or distress in the feared social or performance situation(s) interferes significantly with the person's normal routine, occupational (academic) functioning, or social activities or relationships, or there is a marked distress about having the phobia.

F. In individuals under 18 years, the duration is at least 6 months.

G. The fear of avoidance is not due to the direct physiological effects of a substance (e.g., a drug of abuse, a medication) or a general medical condition and is not better accounted for by another mental disorder (e.g., Panic Disorder With or Without Agoraphobia, Separation Anxiety Disorder, Body Dysmorphic Disorder, a Pervasive Developmental Disorder, or Schizoid Personality Disorder).

H. If a general medical condition or another mental disorder is present, the fear in Criterion A is unrelated to it, e.g., the fear is not of Stuttering, trembling in Parkinson's disease, or exhibiting abnormal eating behavior in Anorexia or Bulimia Nervosa.

Source: APA, 2000, 1994

Criteria for Panic Attack

Note: A Panic Attack is not a codable disorder. Code the specific diagnosis in which the Panic Attack occurs (e.g., 300.21 Panic Attack with Agoraphobia).

A discrete period of intense fear or discomfort, in which four (or more) of the following symptoms developed abruptly and reached a peak within 10 minutes:

(1)   palpitations, pounding heart, or accelerated heart rate
(2)   sweating
(3)   trembling or shaking
(4)   sensations of shortness of breath or smothering
(5)   feeling of choking
(6)   chest pain or discomfort
(7)   nausea or abdominal distress
(8)   feeling dizzy, unsteady, lightheaded, or faint
(9)   derealization (feelings of unreality) or depersonalization (being detached from oneself)
(10) fear of losing control or going crazy
(11) fear of dying
(12) paresthesias (numbness or tingling sensations)
(13) chills or hot flushes

Source: APA, 2000, 1994
© 2011 by Worth Publishers

Criteria for Agoraphobia

Note: Agoraphobia is not a codable disorder. Code the specific disorder in which the Agoraphobia occurs (e.g., 300.21 Panic Attack with Agoraphobia or 300.22 Agoraphobia Without History of Panic Disorder).

A. Anxiety about being in places or situations from which escape might be difficult (or embarrassing) or in which help may not be available in the event of having an unexpected or situationally predisposed Panic Attack or panic-like symptoms. Agoraphobic fears typically involve characteristic clusters of situations that include being outside the home alone; being in a crowd or standing in a line; being on a bridge; and traveling in a bus, train, or automobile.

Note: Consider the diagnosis of Specific Phobia if the avoidance is limited to one or only a few specific situations, or Social Phobia if the avoidance is limited to social situations.

B. The situations are avoided (e.g., travel is restricted) or else are endured with marked distress or with anxiety about having a Panic Attack or panic-like symptoms, or require the presence of a companion.

C. The anxiety of phobic avoidance is not better accounted for by another mental disorder, such as Social Phobia (e.g., avoidance limited to social situations because of fear of embarrassment), Specific Phobia (e.g., avoidance limited to a single situation like elevators), Obsessive-Compulsive Disorder (e.g., avoidance of dirt in someone with an obsession about contamination), Posttraumatic Stress Disorder (e.g., avoidance of stimuli associated with a severe stressor), or Separation Anxiety Disorder (e.g., avoidance of leaving home or relatives).

Source: APA, 2000, 1994

Diagnostic Criteria for Panic Disorder Without Agoraphobia

A. Both (1) and (2):
   (1) recuurent unexpected Panic Attacks
   (2) at least one of the attacks has been followed by 1 month (or more) of one (or more) of the following:
       (a) persistent concern about having additional attacks
       (b) worry about the implications of the attack or its consequences (e.g., losing control, having a heart attack, "going crazy")
       (c) a significant change in behavior related to the attacks

B. Absence of Agoraphobia.

C. The Panic Attacks are not due to the direct physiological effects of a substance (e.g., a drug of abuse, a medication) or a general medication condition (e.g., hyperthyroidism).

D. The Panic Attacks are not better accounted for by another mental disorder, such as Social Phobia (e.g., on exposure to feared social situations), Specific Phobia (e.g., on exposure to a specific phobic situation), Obsessive-Compulsive Disorder (e.g., on exposure to dirt by someone with an obsession about contamination), Posttraumatic Stress Disorder (e.g., in response to stimuli associated with a severe stressor), or Separation Anxiety Disorder (e.g., in response to being away from home or close relatives).

Source: APA, 2000, 1994

Diagnostic Criteria for Obsessive-Compulsive Disorder

A. Either obsessions or compulsions:

Obsessions as defined by (1), (2), (3), and (4):
(1) recurrent and persistent thoughts, impulses, or images that are experienced, at some time during the disturbance, as intrusive and inappropriate and that cause marked anxiety or distress
(2) the thoughts, impulses, or images are not simply excessive worries about real-life problems
(3) the person attempts to ignore or suppress such thoughts, impulses, or images, or to neutralize them with some other thought or action
(4) the person recognizes that the obsessional thoughts, impulses, or images are a product of his or her own mind (not imposed from without as in thought insertion)

Compulsions are defined by (1) and (2):
(1) repetitive behaviors (e.g., hand washing, ordering, checking) or mental acts (e.g., praying, counting, repeating words silently) that the person feels driven to perform in response to an obsession, or according to rules that must be applied rigidly
(2) the behaviors or mental acts are aimed at preventing or reducing distress or preventing some dreaded event or situation; however, these behaviors or mental acts either are not connected in a realistic way with what they are designed to neutralize or prevent or are clearly excessive

B. At some point during the course of the disorder, the person has recognized that the obsessions or compulsions are excessive or unreasonable. Note: This does not apply to children.

C. The obsessions or compulsions cause marked distress, are time consuming (take more than 1 hour a day), or significantly interfere with the person's normal routine, occupational (or academic) functioning, or usual social activities or relationships.

D. If another Axis I disorder is present, the content of the obsessions or compulsions is not restricted to it (e.g., preoccupation with food in the presence of an Eating Disorder; hair pulling in the presence of Trichotillomania; concern with appearance in the presence of Body Dysmorphic Disorder; preoccupation with having a serious illness in the presence of Hypochondriasis; preoccupation with sexual urges or fantasies in the presence of a Paraphilia; or guilty ruminations in the presence of a Major Depressive Disorder).

E. The disturbance is not due to the direct physiological effects of a substance (e.g., a drug of abuse, a medication) or a general medical condition.

Source: APA, 2000, 1994

Diagnostic Criteria for Posttraumatic Stress Disorder

A. The person has been exposed to a traumatic event in which both of the following were present:
   (1) The person experienced, witnessed, or was confronted with an event or events that involved actual or threatened death or serious injury, or a threat to the physical integrity of self or others
   (2) The person's response involved intense fear, helplessness, or horror. Note: In children, this may be expressed instead by disorganized or agitated behavior.

B. The traumatic event is persistently reexperienced in one or more of the following ways:
   (1) recurrent and intrusive distressing recollections of the event, including images, thoughts, or perceptions. Note: In young children, repetitive play may occur in which themes or aspects of the trauma are expressed.
   (2) recurrent distressing dreams of the event. Note: In children, there may be frightening dreams without recognizable content.
   (3) acting or feeling as if the traumatic event were recurring (includes a sense of reliving the experience, illusions, hallucinations, and dissociative flashback episodes, including those that occur on awakening or when intoxicated). In young children, trauma-specific reenactment may occur.
   (4) intense psychological distress at exposure to internal or external cues that symbolize or resemble an aspect of the traumatic event
   (5) physiological reactivity on exposure to internal or external cues that symbolize or resemble an aspect of the traumatic event

C. Persistent avoidance of stimuli associated with the trauma and numbing of general responsiveness (not present before the trauma), as indicated by three (or more) of the following:
   (1) efforts to avoid thoughts, feelings, or conversations associated with the trauma
   (2) efforts to avoid activities, places, or people that arouse recollections of the trauma
   (3) inability to recall an important aspect of the trauma
   (4) markedly diminished interest or participation in significant activities
   (5) feeling of detachment or estrangement from others
   (6) restricted range of affect (e.g., unable to have loving feelings)
   (7) sense of a foreshortened future (e.g., does not expect to have a career, marriage, children, or a normal life span)

D. Persistent symptoms of increased arousal (not present before the trauma), as indicated by two (or more) of the following:
   (1) difficulty falling or staying asleep
   (2) irritability or outbursts of anger
   (3) difficulty concentrating
   (4) hypervigilance
   (5) exaggerated startle response

Source: APA, 2000, 1994

Diagnostic Criteria for Posttraumatic Stress Disorder
(Continued)

E.   Duration of the disturbance (symptoms in criteria B, C, D) is more than 1 month.

F.   The disturbance causes clinically significant distress or impairment in social, occupational, or other important areas of functioning.

Specify if:

   Acute: if duration of symptoms is less than 3 months

   Chronic: if duration of symptoms is 3 months or more

Specify if:

   With Delayed Onset: if onset of symptoms is at least 6 months after the stressor

Source: APA, 2000, 1994

Diagnostic Criteria for Acute Stress Disorder

A. The person has been exposed to a traumatic event in which both of the following were present:
    (1) the person experienced, witnessed, or was confronted with an event or events that involved actual or threatened death or serious injury, or a threat to the physical integrity of self or others.
    (2) the person's response involved intense fear, helplessness, or horror

B. Either while experiencing or after experiencing the distressing event, the individual has three (or more) of the following Dissociative symptoms:
    (1) a subjective sense of numbing, detachment, or absence of emotional responsiveness
    (2) a reduction in awareness of his or her surroundings
    (3) derealization
    (4) depersonalization
    (5) Dissociative amnesia

C. The traumatic event is persistently reexperienced in at least one of the following ways: recurrent images, thoughts, dreams, illusions, flashback episodes, or a sense of reliving the experience; or distress on exposure to reminders of the traumatic event.

D. Marked avoidance of stimuli that arouse recollections of the trauma (e.g., thoughts, feelings, conversations, activities, places, people).

E. Marked symptoms of anxiety or increased arousal (e.g., difficulty sleeping, irritability, poor concentration, hypervigilance, exaggerated startle response, motor restlessness).

F. The disturbance causes clinically significant distress or impairment in social, occupational, or other important areas of functioning or impairs the individual's ability to pursue some necessary task, such as obtaining necessary assistance or mobilizing personal resources by telling family members about the traumatic experience.

G. The disturbance lasts for a minimum of 2 days and a maximum of 4 weeks and occurs within 4 weeks of the traumatic event.

H. The disturbance is not due to the direct physiological effects of a substance or general medical condition, is not better accounted for by Brief Psychotic Disorder, and is not merely an exacerbation of a preexisting Axis I or Axis II disorder.

Source: APA, 2000, 1994

Diagnostic Criteria for Psychological Factors Affecting General Medical Condition

A.   A general medical condition (coded on Axis III) is present.

B.   Psychological factors adversely affect the general medical condition in one of the following ways:
   (1)   the factors have influenced the course of the general medical condition as shown by a close temporal association between the psychological factors and the development or exacerbation of, or delayed recovery from, the general medical condition
   (2)   the factors interfere with the treatment of the general medical condition
   (3)   the factors constitute additional health risks for the individual
   (4)   stress-related physiological responses precipitate or exacerbate symptoms of the general medical condition

Choose name based on the nature of the psychological factors (if more than one factor is present, indicate the most prominent):

Mental Disorder Affecting... *[Indicate the General Medical Condition]* (e.g., an Axis I disorder such as Major Depressive Disorders delaying recovery from a myocardial infarction)

Psychological Symptoms Affecting... *[Indicate the General Medical Condition]* (e.g., depressive symptoms delaying recovery from surgery; anxiety exacerbating asthma)

Personality Traits or Coping Style Affecting... *[Indicate the General Medical Condition]* (e.g., pathological denial of the need for surgery in a patient with cancer; hostile, pressured behavior contributing to cardiovascular disease)

Maladaptive Health Behaviors Affecting... *[Indicate the General Medical Condition]* (e.g., overeating; lack of exercise; unsafe sex)

Stress-Related Physiological Response Affecting... *[Indicate the General Medical Condition]* (e.g., stress-related exacerbations of ulcer, hypertension, arrhythmia, or tension headache)

Other of Unspecified Psychological Factors Affecting... *[Indicate the General Medical Condition]* (e.g., interpersonal, cultural, or religious factors)

Source: APA, 2000, 1994

Diagnostic Criteria for Somatization Disorder

A. A history of many physical complaints beginning before age 30 years that occur over a period of several years and result in treatment being sought or significant impairment in social, occupational, or other important areas of functioning.

B. Each of the following criteria must have been met, with individual symptoms occurring at any time during the course of the disturbance.
   (1) Four pain symptoms: a history of pain related to at least four different sites or functions (e.g., head, abdomen, back, joints, extremities, chest, rectum, during menstruation, during sexual intercourse, or during urination)
   (2) Two gastrointestinal symptoms: a history of at least two gastrointestional symptoms other than pain (e.g., nausea, bloating, vomiting other than during pregnancy, diarrhea, or intolerance of several different foods)
   (3) One sexual symptom: a history of at least one sexual or reproductive symptom other than pain (e.g., sexual indifference, erectile or ejaculatory dysfunction, irregular menses, excessive menstrual bleeding, vomiting throughout pregnancy)
   (4) One pseudoneurological symptom: a history of at least one symptom or deficit suggesting a neurological condition not limited to pain (conversion symptoms such as impaired coordination or balance, paralysis or localized weakness, difficulty swallowing or lump in throat, aphonia, urinary retention, hallucinations, loss of touch or pain, double vision, blindness, deafness, seizures; dissociative symptoms such as amnesia; or loss of consciousness other than fainting)

C. Either (1) or (2):
   (1) After appropriate investigation, each of the symptoms in Criterion B cannot be fully explained by a known general medical condition or the direct effects of a substance (e.g., a drug of abuse, a medication)
   (2) When there is a related general medical condition, the physical complaints or resulting social or occupational impairment are in excess of what would be expected from the history, physical examination, or laboratory findings

D. The symptoms are not intentionally produced or feigned (as in Factitious Disorder or Malingering).

Source: APA, 2000, 1994

Diagnostic Criteria for Conversion Disorder

A. One or more symptoms or deficits affecting voluntary motor or sensory function that suggest a neurological or other general medical condition.

B. Psychological factors are judged to be associated with the symptom or deficit because the initiation or exacerbation of the symptom or deficit is preceded by conflicts or other stressors.

C. The symptom or deficit is not intentionally produced or feigned (as in Factitious Disorder or Malingering).

D. The symptom or deficit cannot, after appropriate investigation, be fully explained by a general medical condition, or by the direct effects of a substance, or as a culturally sanctioned behavior or experience.

E. The symptom or deficit causes clinically significant distress or impairment in social, occupational, or other important areas of functioning or warrants medical evaluation.

F. The symptom or deficit is not limited to pain or sexual dysfunction, does not occur exclusively during the course of the Somatization Disorder, and is not better accounted for by another mental disorder.

Source: APA, 2000, 1994

Diagnostic Criteria for Pain Disorder

A.   Pain in one or more anatomical sites is the predominant focus of the clinical presentation and is of sufficient severity to warrant clinical attention.

B.   The pain causes clinically significant distress or impairment in social, occupational, or other important areas of functioning.

C.   Psychological factors are judged to have an important role in the onset, severity, exacerbation, or maintenance of the pain.

D.   The symptom or deficit is not intentionally produced or feigned (as in Factitious Disorder or Malingering).

E.   The pain is not better accounted for by a Mood, Anxiety, or Psychotic Disorder and does not meet criteria for Dyspareunia.

Diagnostic Criteria for Hypochondriasis

A.   Preoccupation with fears of having, or the idea that one has, a serious disease based on the person's misinterpretation of bodily symptoms.

B.   The preoccupation persists despite appropriate medical evaluation and reassurance.

C.   The belief in Criterion A is not of delusional intensity (as in Delusional Disorder, Somatic Type) and is not restricted to a circumscribed concern about appearance (as in Body Dysmorphic Disorder).

D.   The preoccupation causes clinically significant distress or impairment in social, occupational, or other important areas of functioning.

E.   The duration of the disturbance is at least 6 months.

F.   The preoccupation is not better accounted for by Generalized Anxiety Disorder, Obsessive-Compulsive Disorder, Panic Disorder, a Major Depressive Episode, Separation Anxiety, or another Somatoform Disorder.

Source: APA, 2000, 1994

Diagnostic Criteria for Body Dysmorphic Disorder

A. Preoccupation with an imagined defect in appearance. If a slight physical anomaly is present, the person's concern is markedly excessive.

B. The preoccupation causes clinically significant distress or impairment in social, occupational, or other important areas of functioning.

C. The preoccupation is not better accounted for by another mental disorder (e.g., dissatisfaction with body shape and size in Anorexia Nervosa).

Diagnostic Criteria for Factitious Disorder

A. Intentional production or feigning of physical or psychological signs or symptoms.

B. The motivation for the behavior is to assume a sick role.

C. External incentives for the behavior (such as economic gain, avoiding legal responsibility, or improving physical well-being, as in Malingering) are absent.

Code based on type:
  With Predominantly Psychological Signs and Symptoms
  With Predominantly Physical Signs and Symptoms
  With Combined Psychological and Physical Signs and Symptoms

Source: APA, 2000, 1994

Diagnostic Criteria for Dissociative Amnesia

A. The predominant disturbance is one or more episodes of inability to recall important personal information, usually of a traumatic or stressful nature, that is too extensive to be explained by ordinary forgetfulness.

B. The disturbance does not occur exclusively during the course of Dissociative Identity Disorder, Dissociative Fugue, Posttraumatic Stress Disorder, Acute Stress Disorder, or Somatization Disorder and is not due to the direct physiological effects of a substance (e.g., a drug of abuse, a medication) or a neurological or other general medical condition (e.g., Amnestic Disorder Due to Head Trauma).

C. The symptoms cause clinically significant distress or impairment in social, occupational, or other important areas of functioning.

Diagnostic Criteria for Dissociative Fugue

A. The predominant disturbance is sudden, unexpected travel away from home or one's customary place of work, with inability to recall one's past.

B. Confusion about personal identity or assumption of a new identity (partial or complete).

C. The disturbance does not occur exclusively during the course of Dissociative Identity Disorder and is not due to the direct physiological effects of a substance (e.g., a drug of abuse, a medication) or a general medical condition (e.g., temporal lobe epilepsy).

D. The symptoms cause clinically significant distress or impairment in social, occupational, or other important areas of functioning.

Source: APA, 2000, 1994

Diagnostic Criteria for Dissociative Identity Disorder

A. The presence of two or more distinct identities or personality states (each with its own relatively enduring pattern of perceiving, relating to, and thinking about the environment and self).

B. At least two of these identities or personality states recurrently take control of the person's behavior.

C. Inability to recall important personal information that is too extensive to be explained by ordinary forgetfulness.

D. The disturbance is not due to the direct physiological effects of a substance (e.g., blackouts or chaotic behavior during Alcohol Intoxication) or a general medical condition (e.g., complex partial seizures).

Diagnostic Criteria for Depersonalization Disorder

A. Persistent or recurrent experiences of feeling detached from, and as if one is an outside observer of, one's mental processes or body (e.g., feeling like one is in a dream).

B. During the depersonalization experience, reality testing remains intact.

C. The depersonalization causes clinically significant distress or impairment in social, occupational, or other important areas of functioning.

D. The depersonalization experience does not occur exclusively during the course of another mental disorder, such as Schizophrenia, Panic Disorder, Acute Stress Disorder, or another Dissociative Disorder, and is not due to the direct physiological effects of a substance (e.g., a drug of abuse, a medication) or a general medical condition (e.g., temporal lobe epilepsy).

Source: APA, 2000, 1994

Criteria for Major Depressive Episode

A. Five (or more) of the following symptoms have been present during the same 2-week period and represent a change from the previous functioning; at least one of the symptoms is either (1) depressed mood or (2) loss of interest or pleasure.

Note: Do not include symptoms that are clearly due to a general medical condition, or mood-incongruent delusions or hallucinations.

(1) depressed mood most of the day, nearly every day, as indicated by either subjective report (e.g., feels sad or empty) or observation made by others (e.g., appears tearful).

(2) markedly diminished interest or pleasure in all, or almost all, activities most of the day, nearly every day (as indicated by either subjective account or observations made by others)

(3) significant weight loss when not dieting or weight gain (e.g., a change of more than 5% of body weight in a month), a decrease or increase in appetite nearly every day. Note: In children, consider failure to make expected weight gains.

(4) insomnia or hypersomnia nearly every day

(5) psychomotor agitation or retardation nearly every day (observable by others)

(6) fatigue or loss of energy nearly every day

(7) feelings of worthlessness or excessive or inappropriate guilt (which may be delusional) nearly every day

(8) diminished ability to think or concentrate, or indecisiveness, nearly every day (either by subjective account or observed by others)

(9) recurrent thoughts of death (not just fear of dying), recurrent suicidal ideation without a specific plan, or a suicide attempt or a specific plan for committing suicide

B. The symptoms do not meet criteria for a Mixed Episode.

C. The symptoms cause clinically significant distress or impairment in social, occupational, or other important areas of functioning.

D. The symptoms are not due to the direct physiological effects of a substance (e.g., a drug of abuse, a medication) or a general medical condition (e.g., hypothyroidism).

E. The symptoms are not better accounted for by Bereavement, i.e., after the loss of a loved one, the symptoms persist for longer than 2 months or are characterized by marked functional impairment, morbid preoccupation with worthlessness, suicidal ideation, psychotic symptoms, or psychomotor retardation.

Source: APA, 2000, 1994

Criteria for Manic Episode

A. A distinct period of abnormally and persistently elevated, expansive, or irritable mood lasting at least 1 week (or any duration if hospitalization is necessary).

B. During the period of mood disturbance, three (or more) of the following symptoms have persisted (four if the mood is only irritable) and have been present to a significant degree:
    (1) inflated self-esteem or grandiosity
    (2) decreased need for sleep (e.g., feels rested after only 3 hours of sleep)
    (3) more talkative than usual or pressure to keep talking
    (4) flight of ideas or subjective experience that thoughts are racing
    (5) distractibility (i.e., attention too easily drawn to unimportant or irrelevant external stimuli)
    (6) increase in goal-directed activity (either socially, at work or school, or sexually) or psychomotor agitation
    (7) excessive involvement in pleasurable activities that have a high potential for painful consequences (e.g., engaging in unrestrained buying sprees, sexual indiscretions, or foolish business investments)

C. The symptoms do not meet the criteria for a Mixed Episode.

D. The mood disturbance is sufficiently severe to cause marked impairment in occupational functioning or in usual social activities or relationships with others, or to necessitate hospitalization to prevent harm to self or others, or there are psychotic features.

E. The symptoms are not due to the direct physiological effects of a substance (e.g., a drug of abuse, a medication, or other treatment) or a general medical condition (e.g., hyperthyroidism).

Criteria for Mixed Episode

A. The criteria are met both for a Manic Episode and for a Major Depressive Episode (except for duration) nearly every day during at least a 1-week period.

B. The mood disturbance is sufficiently severe to cause marked impairment in occupational functioning or in usual social activities or relationships with others, or to necessitate hospitalization to prevent harm to self or others, or there are psychotic features.

C. The symptoms are not due to the direct physiological effects of a substance (e.g., a drug of abuse, a medication, or other treatment) or a general medical condition (e.g., hyperthyroidism).

Source: APA, 2000, 1994

Criteria for Hypomanic Episode

A. A distinct period of persistently elevated, expansive, or irritable mood, lasting throughout at least 4 days, that is clearly different from the usual nondepressed mood.

B. During the period of mood disturbance, three (or more) of the following symptoms have persisted (four, if the mood is only irritable) and have been present to a significant degree:
    (1) inflated self-esteem or grandiosity
    (2) decreased need for sleep (e.g., feels rested after only 3 hours of sleep)
    (3) more talkative than usual or pressure to keep talking
    (4) flight of ideas or subjective experience that thoughts are racing
    (5) distractibility (i.e., attention too easily drawn to unimportant or irrelevant external stimuli)
    (6) increase in goal-directed activity (either socially, at work or school, or sexually) or psychomotor agitation
    (7) excessive involvement in pleasurable activities that have a high potential for painful consequences

C. The episode is associated with an unequivocal change in functioning that is uncharacteristic of the person when not symptomatic.

D. The disturbance in mood and the change in functioning are observable by others.

E. The episode is not severe enough to cause marked impairment in social or occupational functioning, or to necessitate hospitalization, and there are no psychotic features.

F. The symptoms are not due to the direct physiological effects of a substance (e.g., a drug of abuse, a medication, or other treatment) or a general medical condition (e.g., hypothyroidism).

Note: Hypomanic-like episodes that are clearly caused by somatic antidepressant treatment should not count toward a diagnosis of Bipolar II disorder.

Source: APA, 2000, 1994

Diagnostic Criteria for Major Depressive Disorder, Single Episode

A. Presence of a single Major Depressive Episode

B. The Major Depressive Episode is not better accounted for by Schizoaffective Disorder and is not superimposed on Schizophrenia, Schizophreniform Disorder, Delusional Disorder, or Psychotic Disorder Not Otherwise Specified.

C. There has never been a Manic Episode, a Mixed Episode, or a Hypomanic Episode. Note: This exclusion does not apply if all the manic-like, mixed-like, or hypomanic-like episodes are substance or treatment induced or are due to the direct physiological effects of a general medical condition.

Diagnostic Criteria for Major Depressive Disorder, Recurrent

A. A presence of two or more Major Depressive Episodes.

Note: To be considered separate episodes, there must be an interval of at least 2 consecutive months in which criteria are not met for a Major Depressive Episode.

B. The Major Depressive Episodes are not better accounted for by Schizoaffective Disorder and are not superimposed on Schizophrenia, Schizophreniform Disorder, Delusional Disorder, or Psychotic Disorder Not Otherwise Specified.

C. There has never been a Manic Episode, a Mixed Episode, or a Hypomanic Episode.

Note: This exclusion does not apply if all the manic-like, mixed-like, or hypomanic-like episodes are substance or treatment induced or are due to the direct physiological effects of a general medical condition.

Source: APA, 2000, 1994

Diagnostic Criteria for Dysthymic Disorder

A. Depressed mood for most of the day, for more days than not, as indicated either by subjective account or observation by others, for at least 2 years. Note: In children and adolescents, mood can be irritable and duration must be at least 1 year.

B. Presence, while depressed, of two (or more) of the following:
    (1) poor appetite or overeating
    (2) insomnia or hypersomnia
    (3) low energy or fatigue
    (4) low self-esteem
    (5) poor concentration or difficulty making decisions
    (6) feelings of hopelessness

C. During the 2-year period (1 year for children or adolescents) of the disturbance, the person has never been without the symptoms in Criteria A and B for more than 2 months at a time.

D. No Major Depressive Episode has been present during the first 2 years of the disturbance (1 year for children and adolescents); i.e., the disturbance is not better accounted for by chronic Major Depressive Disorder, or Major Depressive Disorder, In Partial Remission.

Note: There may have been a previous Major Depressive Episode provided there was a full remission (no significant signs or symptoms for 2 months) before development of the Dysthymic Disorder. In addition, after the initial 2 years (1 year in children or adolescents) of Dysthymic Disorder, there may be superimposed episodes of Major Depressive Disorder, in which case both diagnoses may be given when the criteria are met for a Major Depressive Episode.

E. There has never been a Manic Episode, a Mixed Episode, or a Hypomanic Episode, and criteria have never been met for Cyclothymic Disorder.

F. The disturbance does not occur exclusively during the course of a chronic Psychotic Disorder, such as Schizophrenia or Delusional Disorder.

G. The symptoms are not due to the direct physiological effects of a substance (e.g., a drug of abuse, a medication) or a general medical condition (e.g., hypothyroidism).

H. The symptoms cause clinically significant distress or impairment in social, occupational, or other important areas of functioning.

Specify if:

Early Onset: if onset is before age 21 years

Late Onset: if onset is age 21 or older

Source: APA, 2000, 1994
© 2011 by Worth Publishers

Diagnostic Criteria for Bipolar I Disorder, Single Manic Episode

A. Presence of only one Manic Episode and no past major Depressive Episodes.

    Note: Recurrence is defined as either a change in polarity from depression or an interval of at least 2 months without manic symptoms.

B. The Manic Episode is not better accounted for by Schizoaffective Disorder and is not superimposed on Schizophrenia, Schizophreniform Disorder, Delusional Disorder, or Psychotic Disorder Not Otherwise Specified.

Diagnostic Criteria for Bipolar II Disorder

A. Presence (or history) of one or more Major Depressive Episodes.

B. Presence (or history) of at least one Hypomanic Episode.

C. There has never been a Manic Episode or a Mixed Episode.

D. The mood symptoms in criteria A and B are not better accounted for by Schizoaffective Disorder and are not superimposed on Schizophrenia, Schizophreniform Disorder, Delusional Disorder, or Psychotic Disorder Not Otherwise Specified.

E. The symptoms cause clinically significant distress or impairment in social, occupational, or other important areas of functioning.

Source: APA, 2000, 1994

Diagnostic Criteria for Cyclothymic Disorder

A. For at least 2 years, the presence of numerous periods with hypomanic symptoms and numerous periods with depressive symptoms that do not meet criteria for a Major Depressive Episode. Note: In children and adolescents, the duration must be at least 1 year.

B. During the above 2-year period (1 year in children and adolescents), the person has not been without the symptoms in Criterion A for more than 2 months at a time.

C. No Major Depressive Episode, Manic Episode, or Mixed Episode has been present during the first 2 years of the disturbance.

D. The symptoms in Criterion A are not better accounted for by Schizoaffective Disorder and are not superimposed on Schizophrenia, Schizophreniform Disorder, or Psychotic Disorder Not Otherwise Specified.

E. The symptoms are not due to the direct physiological effects of a substance (e.g., a drug of abuse, a medication) or a general medical condition (e.g., hyperthyroidism).

F. The symptoms cause clinically significant distress or impairment in social, occupational, or other important areas of functioning.

Source: APA, 2000, 1994

Diagnostic Criteria for Anorexia Nervosa

A. Refusal to maintain body weight at or above a minimally normal weight for age and height (e.g., weight loss leading to maintenance of body weight less than 85% of that expected; or failure to make expected weight gain during period of growth, leading to body weight less than 85% of that expected).

B. Intense fear of gaining weight or becoming fat, even though underweight.

C. Disturbance in the way in which one's body weight or shape is experienced, undue influence of body weight or shape on self-evaluation, or denial of the seriousness of the current low body weight.

D. In postmenarcheal females, amenorrhea, i.e., the absence of at least three consecutive menstrual cycles. (A woman is considered to have amenorrhea if her periods occur only following hormone administration, e.g., estrogen.)

Specify type:

Restricting Type: during the current episode of Anorexia Nervosa, the person has not regularly engaged in binge-eating or purging behavior (i.e., self-induced vomiting or the misuse of laxatives, diuretics, or enemas)

Binge-Eating/Purging Type: during the current episode of Anorexia Nervosa, the person has regularly engaged in binge-eating or purging behavior (i.e., self-induced vomiting or the misuse of laxatives, diuretics, or enemas)

Source: APA, 2000, 1994

Diagnostic Criteria for Bulimia Nervosa

A. Recurrent episodes of binge-eating. An episode of binge eating is characterized by both of the following:
(1) Eating, in a discrete period of time (e.g., within any 2-hour period), an amount of food that is definitely larger than most people would eat during that similar period of time under similar circumstances
(2) A sense of lack of control over eating during the episode (e.g., a feeling that one cannot stop eating or control what or how much one is eating)

B. Recurrent inappropriate compensatory behavior in order to prevent weight gain, such as self-induced vomiting; misuse of laxatives, diuretics, enemas, or other medications; fasting; or excessive exercise.

C. The binge eating and inappropriate compensatory behavior both occur, on average, at least twice a week for 3 months.

D. Self-evaluation is unduly influenced by body shape and weight.

E. The disturbance does not occur exclusively during episodes of Anorexia Nervosa.

Specify type:

Purging Type: during the current episode of Bulimia Nervosa, the person has regularly engaged in self-induced vomiting or the misuse of laxatives, diuretics, or enemas.

Nonpurging Type: during the current episode of Bulimia Nervosa, the person has used other inappropriate compensatory behaviors, such as fasting or excessive exercise, but has not regularly engaged in self-induced vomiting or the misuse of laxatives, diuretics, or enemas.

Source: APA, 2000, 1994

Diagnostic Criteria for Substance Intoxication

A. The development of a reversible substance-specific syndrome due to recent ingestion of (or exposure to) a substance. Note: Different substances may produce similar or identical syndromes.

B. Clinically significant maladaptive behavioral or psychological changes that are due to the effect of the substance on the central nervous system (e.g., belligerence, mood lability, cognitive impairment, impaired judgment, impaired social or occupational functioning) and develop during or shortly after use of the substance.

C. The symptoms are not due to a general medical condition and are not better accounted for by another mental disorder.

Diagnostic Criteria for Substance Withdrawal

A. The development of a substance-specific syndrome due to the cessation of (or reduction in) substance use that has been heavy and prolonged.

B. The substance-specific syndrome causes clinically significant distress or impairment in social, occupational, or other important areas of functioning.

C. The symptoms are not due to a general medical condition and are not better accounted for by another mental disorder.

Source: APA, 2000, 1994
© 2011 by Worth Publishers

Criteria for Substance Abuse

A. A maladaptive pattern of substance use leading to clinically significant impairment or distress, as manifested by one (or more) of the following, occurring within a 12-month period:

(1) recurring substance use resulting in failure to fulfill major role obligations at work, school, or home (e.g., repeated absences or poor work performance related to substance use; substance-related absences, suspensions, or expulsions from school; neglect of children or household

(2) recurrent substance use in situations in which it is physically hazardous (e.g., driving an automobile or operating a machine when impaired by substance use)

(3) recurrent substance-related legal problems (e.g., arrests for substance-related disorderly conduct)

(4) continued substance use despite having persistent or recurrent social or interpersonal problems caused or exacerbated by the effects of the substance (e.g., arguments with spouse about consequences of intoxication, physical fights)

B. The symptoms have never met the criteria for Substance Dependence for this class of substance.

Source: APA, 2000, 1994

Criteria for Substance Dependence

A maladaptive pattern of substance use, leading to clinically significant impairment or distress, as manifested by three (or more) of the following, occurring at any time in the same 12-month period:

(1) tolerance as defined by either of the following:
- (a) a need for markedly increased amounts of the substance to achieve intoxication or desired effect
- (b) markedly diminished effect with continued use of the same amount of the substance

(2) withdrawal, as manifested by either of the following:
- (a) the characteristic withdrawal syndrome for the substance (refer to Criteria A and B of the criteria sets for Withdrawal from the specific substances)
- (b) the same (or a closely related) substance is taken to relieve or avoid withdrawal symptoms

(3) the substance is often taken in larger amounts or over a longer period than was intended

(4) there is a persistent desire or unsuccessful effort to cut down or control substance use

(5) a great deal of time is spent in activities necessary to obtain the substance (e.g., visiting multiple doctors or driving long distances), use the substance (e.g., chainsmoking), or recover from its effects

(6) important social, occupational, or recreational activities are given up or reduced because of substance use

(7) the substance use is continued despite knowledge of having a persistent or recurrent physical or psychological problem that is likely to be exacerbated by the substance (e.g., current cocaine use despite recognition of cocaine-induced depression, or continued drinking despite recognition that an ulcer was made worse by alcohol consumption)

Source: APA, 2000, 1994

Diagnostic Criteria for Hypoactive Sexual Desire Disorder

A. Persistently or recurrently deficient (or absent) sexual fantasies and desire for sexual activity. The judgment of deficiency or absence is made by the clinician, taking into account the factors that affect sexual functioning, such as age and the context of the person's life.

B. The disturbance causes marked distress or interpersonal difficulty.

C. The sexual dysfunction is not better accounted for by another Axis I disorder (except another Sexual Dysfunction) and is not due exclusively to the direct physiological effects of a substance (e.g., a drug of abuse, a medication) or a general medical condition.

Diagnostic Criteria for Sexual Aversion Disorder

A. Persistent or recurrent extreme aversion to, and avoidance of, all (or almost all) genital sexual contact with a sexual partner.

B. The disturbance causes marked distress or interpersonal difficulty.

C. The sexual dysfunction is not better accounted for by another Axis I disorder (except another Sexual Dysfunction).

Source: APA, 2000, 1994

Diagnostic Criteria for Female Sexual Arousal Disorder

A. Persistent or recurrent inability to attain, or to maintain until completion of the sexual activity, an adequate lubrication-swelling response to sexual excitement.

B. The disturbance causes marked distress or interpersonal difficulty.

C. The sexual dysfunction is not better accounted for by another Axis I disorder (except another Sexual Dysfunction) and is not due exclusively to the direct physiological effects of a substance (e.g., a drug of abuse, a medication) or a general medical condition.

Diagnostic Criteria for Male Erectile Disorder

A. Persistent or recurrent inability to attain, or to maintain until completion of the sexual activity, an adequate erection.

B. The disturbance causes marked distress or interpersonal difficulty.

C. The erectile dysfunction is not better accounted for by another Axis I disorder (other than a Sexual Dysfunction) and is not due exclusively to the direct physiological effects of a substance (e.g., a drug of abuse, a medication) or a general medical condition.

Source: APA, 2000, 1994

Diagnostic Criteria for Female Orgasmic Disorder

A. The persistent or recurrent delay in, or absence of, orgasm following a normal sexual excitement phase. Women exhibit wide variability in the type or intensity of stimulation that triggers orgasm. The diagnosis of Female Orgasmic Disorder should be based on the clinician's judgment that the woman's orgasmic capacity is less than would be reasonable for her age, sexual experience, and the adequacy of stimulation she receives.

B. The disturbance causes marked distress or interpersonal difficulty.

C. The orgasmic dysfunction is not better accounted for by another Axis I disorder (except another Sexual Dysfunction) and is not due exclusively to the direct physiological effects of a substance (e.g., a drug of abuse, a medication) or a general medical condition.

Diagnostic Criteria for Male Orgasmic Disorder

A. Persistent or recurrent delay in, or absence of, orgasm following a normal sexual excitement phase during sexual activity that the clinician, taking into account the person's age, judges to be adequate in focus, intensity, and duration.

B. The disturbance causes marked distress or interpersonal difficulty.

C. The orgasmic dysfunction is not better accounted for by another Axis I disorder (except another Sexual Dysfunction) and is not due exclusively to the direct physiological effects of a substance (e.g., a drug of abuse, a medication) or a general medical condition.

Source: APA, 2000, 1994

Diagnostic Criteria for Premature Ejaculation

A. Persistent or recurrent ejaculation with minimal sexual stimulation before, on, or shortly after penetration and before the person wishes it. The clinician must take into account factors that affect duration of the excitement phase, such as age, novelty of sexual partner or situation, and recent frequency of sexual activity.

B. The disturbance causes marked distress or interpersonal difficulty.

C. The premature ejaculation is not due exclusively to the direct effects of a substance (e.g., withdrawal from opioids).

Diagnostic Criteria for Dyspareunia

A. Recurrent or persistent genital pain associated with sexual intercourse in either a male or a female.

B. The disturbance causes marked distress or interpersonal difficulty.

C. The disturbance is not caused exclusively by Vaginismus or lack of lubrication, is not better accounted for by another Axis I disorder (except another Sexual Dysfunction), and is not due exclusively to the direct physiological effects of a substance (e.g., a drug of abuse, a medication) or a general medical condition.

Diagnostic Criteria for Vaginismus

A. Recurrent or persistent involuntary spasm of the musculature of the outer third of the vagina that interferes with sexual intercourse.

B. The disturbance causes marked distress or interpersonal difficulty.

C. The disturbance is not better accounted for by another Axis I disorder (e.g., Somatization Disorder) and is not due exclusively to the direct physiological effects of a general medical condition.

Source: APA, 2000, 1994
© 2011 by Worth Publishers

Diagnostic Criteria for Exhibitionism

A. Over a period of at least 6 months, recurrent, intense sexually arousing fantasies, sexual urges, or behaviors involving the exposure of one's genitals to an unsuspecting stranger.

B. The person has acted on these sexual urges, or the sexual urges or fantasies cause marked distress or interpersonal difficulty.

Diagnostic Criteria for Fetishism

A. Over a period of at least 6 months, recurrent, intense sexually arousing fantasies, sexual urges, or behaviors involving the use of nonliving objects (e.g., female undergarments).

B. The fantasies, sexual urges, or behaviors cause clinically significant distress or impairment in social, occupational, or other important areas of functioning.

C. The fetish objects are not limited to articles of female clothing used in cross-dressing (as in Transvestic Fetishism) or devices designed for the purpose of tactile genital stimulation (e.g., a vibrator).

Diagnostic Criteria for Frotteurism

A. Over a period of at least 6 months, recurrent, intense sexually arousing fantasies, sexual urges, or behaviors involving touching and rubbing against a nonconsenting person.

B. The person has acted on these sexual urges, or the sexual urges or fantasies cause marked distress or interpersonal difficulty.

Diagnostic Criteria for Pedophilia

A. Over a period of at least 6 months, recurrent, intense sexually arousing fantasies, sexual urges, or behaviors involving sexual activity with a prepubescent child or children (generally age 13 years or younger).

B. The person has acted on these sexual urges, or the sexual urges or fantasies cause marked distress or interpersonal difficulty.

C. The person is at least 16 years and at least 5 years older than the child or children in Criterion A.

Note: Do not include an individual in late adolescence involved in an ongoing sexual relationship with a 12- or 13-year-old.

Source: APA, 2000, 1994
© 2011 by Worth Publishers

Diagnostic Criteria for Sexual Masochism

A. Over a period of at least 6 months, recurrent, intense sexually arousing fantasies, sexual urges, or behaviors involving the act (real, not simulated) of being humiliated, beaten, bound, or otherwise made to suffer.

B. The fantasies, sexual urges, or behaviors cause clinically significant distress or impairment in social, occupational, or other important areas of functioning.

Diagnostic Criteria for Sexual Sadism

A. Over a period of at least 6 months, recurrent, intense sexually arousing fantasies, sexual urges, or behaviors involving acts (real, not simulated) in which the psychological or physical suffering (including humiliation) of the victim is sexually exciting to the person.

B. The person has acted on these sexual urges with a non-consenting person, or the sexual urges or fantasies cause marked distress or interpersonal difficulty.

Diagnostic Criteria for Transvestic Fetishism

A. Over a period of at least 6 months, in a heterosexual male, recurrent, intense sexually arousing fantasies, sexual urges, or behaviors involving cross-dressing.

B. The fantasies, sexual urges, or behaviors cause clinically significant distress or impairment in social, occupational, or other important areas of functioning.

Diagnostic Criteria for Voyeurism

A. Over a period of at least 6 months, recurrent, intense sexually arousing fantasies, sexual urges, or behaviors involving the act of observing an unsuspecting person who is naked, in the process of disrobing, or engaging in sexual activity.

B. The person has acted on these sexual urges, or the sexual urges or fantasies cause marked distress or interpersonal difficulty.

Diagnostic Criteria for Gender Identity Disorder

A. A strong and persistent cross-gender identification (not merely a desire for any perceived cultural advantages of being the other sex).

In children, the disturbance is manifested by four (or more) of the following:
   (1) repeatedly stated desire to be, or insistence that he or she is, the other sex
   (2) in boys, preference for cross-dressing or simulating female attire; in girls, insistence on wearing only stereotypical masculine clothing
   (3) strong and persistent preferences for cross-sex roles in make-believe play or persistent fantasies about being the other sex
   (4) intense desire to participate in the stereotypical games and pastimes of the other sex
   (5) strong preference for playmates of other sex

In adolescents and adults, the disturbance is manifested by symptoms such as a stated desire to be the other sex, frequent passing as the other sex, desire to live and be treated as the other sex, or the conviction that he or she has the typical feelings and reactions of the other sex.

B. Persistent discomfort with his or her sex or sense of inappropriateness in the gender role of that sex.

In children, the disturbance is manifested by any of the following: in boys, assertion that his penis or testes are disgusting or will disappear or assertion that it would be better not to have a penis, or aversion toward rough-and-tumble play and rejection of male stereotypical toys, games, and activities; in girls, rejection of urinating in a sitting position, assertion that she has or will grow a penis, or assertion that she does not want to grow breasts or menstruate, or marked aversion toward normative feminine clothing.

In adolescents and adults, the disturbance is manifested by symptoms such as preoccupation with getting rid of primary and secondary sex characteristics (e.g., request for hormones, surgery, or other procedures to physically alter sexual characteristics that simulate the other sex), or belief that he or she was born the wrong sex.

C. The disturbance is not concurrent with a physical intersex condition.

D. The disturbance causes clinically significant distress or impairment in social, occupational, or other important areas of functioning.

Source: APA, 2000, 1994

Diagnostic Criteria for Schizophrenia

A. Characteristic symptoms: Two (or more) of the following, each present for a significant portion of time during a 1-month period (or less if successfully treated):
   (1) delusions
   (2) hallucinations
   (3) disorganized speech (e.g., frequent derailment or incoherence)
   (4) grossly disorganized or catatonic behavior
   (5) negative symptoms, i.e., affective flattening, alogia, or avolition

   Note: Only one Criterion A symptom is required if delusions are bizarre or hallucinations consist of a voice keeping up a running commentary on the person's behavior or thoughts, or two or more voices conversing with each other.

B. Social/occupational dysfunction: For a significant portion of the time since the onset of the disturbance, one or more major areas of functioning such as work, interpersonal relations, or self-care are markedly below the level achieved prior to the onset (or when the onset is in childhood or adolescence, failure to achieve expected level of interpersonal, academic, or occupational achievement).

C. Duration: Continuous signs of the disturbance persist for at least 6 months. This 6-month period must include at least 1 month of symptoms (or less if successfully treated) that meet Criteria A (i.e., active-phase symptoms) and may include periods of prodromal or residual symptoms. During these prodromal or residual periods, the signs of the disturbance may be manifested by only negative symptoms or two or more symptoms listed in Criteria A present in an attenuated form (e.g., odd beliefs, unusual perceptual experiences).

D. Schizoaffective and Mood Disorder exclusion: Schizoaffective Disorder and Mood Disorder With Psychotic Features have been ruled out because either (1) no Major Depressive, Manic, or Mixed Episodes have occurred concurrently with active-phase symptoms; or (2) if mood episodes have occurred during active-phase symptoms, their total duration has been brief relative to the duration of the active and residual periods.

E. Substance/general medical condition exclusion: The disturbance is not due to the direct physiological effects of a substance (e.g., a drug of abuse, a medication) or a general medical condition.

F. Relationship to a Pervasive Developmental Disorder: If there is history of Autistic Disorder or another Pervasive Developmental Disorder, the additional diagnosis of Schizophrenia is made only if prominent delusions or hallucinations are also present for at least a month (or less if successfully treated).

Source: APA, 2000, 1994

Diagnostic Criteria for Paranoid Type

A type of Schizophrenia in which the following criteria are met:

A. Preoccupation with one or more delusions or frequent auditory hallucinations.

B. None of the following is prominent: disorganized speech, disorganized or catatonic behavior, or flat or inappropriate affect.

Diagnostic Criteria for Disorganized Type

A type of Schizophrenia in which the following criteria are met:

A. All of the following are prominent:
   (1) disorganized speech
   (2) disorganized behavior
   (3) flat or inappropriate affect

B. The criteria are not met for Catatonic Type.

Diagnostic Criteria for Catatonic Type

A type of Schizophrenia in which the following criteria are met:

   (1) motoric immobility as evidenced by catalepsy (including waxy flexibility) or stupor
   (2) excessive motor activity (that is apparently purposeless and not influenced by external stimuli)
   (3) extreme negativism (an apparently motiveless resistance to all instructions, or maintenance of a rigid posture against attempts to be moved) or mutism
   (4) peculiarities of voluntary movement as evidenced by posturing (voluntary assumption of inappropriate or bizarre postures), stereotyped movements, prominent mannerisms, or prominent grimacing
   (5) echolalia or echopraxia

Source: APA, 2000, 1994

Diagnostic Criteria for Undifferentiated Type

A type of Schizophrenia in which symptoms that meet Criterion A are present, but the criteria are not met for the Paranoid, Disorganized, or Catatonic Type.

Diagnostic Criteria for Residual Type

A type of Schizophrenia in which the following criteria are met:

A. Absence of prominent delusions, hallucinations, disorganized speech, and grossly disorganized or catatonic behavior.

B. There is continuing evidence of the disturbance, as indicated by the presence of negative symptoms or two or more symptoms listed in Criterion A for Schizophrenia, present in an attenuated form (e.g., odd beliefs, unusual perceptual experiences).

Source: APA, 2000, 1994

Diagnostic Criteria for Schizoaffective Disorder

A. An uninterrupted period of illness during which, at some time, there is either a Major Depressive Episode, a Manic Episode, or a Mixed Episode concurrent with symptoms that meet Criterion A for Schizophrenia.

Note: The Major Depressive Episode must include Criterion A1: depressed mood.

B. During the same period of illness, there have been delusions or hallucinations for at least two weeks in the absence of prominent mood symptoms.

C. Symptoms that meet criteria for a mood episode are present for a substantial portion of the total duration of the active and residual periods of the illness.

D. The disturbance is not due to the direct physiological effects of a substance (e.g., a drug of abuse, a medication) or a general medical condition.

Specify type:
Bipolar Type: if the disturbance includes Manic or a Mixed Episode (or a Manic or Mixed Episode and Major Depressive Episodes).

Depressive Type: if the disturbance only includes Major Depressive Episode.

Diagnostic Criteria for Schizophreniform Disorder

A. Criteria A, D, and E of Schizophrenia are met.

B. An episode of the disorder (including prodromal, active, and residual phases) lasts at least 1 month but less than 6 months. (When the diagnosis must be made without waiting for recovery, it should be qualified as "Provisional.")

Specify if:

Without Good Prognostic Features

With Good Prognostic Features: as evidenced by two (or more) of the following:
(1) onset of prominent psychotic symptoms within 4 weeks of the first noticeable change in usual behavior or functioning
(2) confusion or perplexity at the height of the psychotic episode
(3) good premorbid social and occupational functioning
(4) absence of blunted or flat affect

Source: APA, 2000, 1994

Diagnostic Criteria for Delusional Disorder

A. Nonbizarre delusions (i.e., involving situations that occur in real life, such as being followed, poisoned, infected, loved at a distance, or deceived by spouse or lover, or having a disease) of at least 1 month's duration.

B. Criterion A for Schizophrenia has never been met. Note: Tactile and olfactory hallucinations may be present in Delusional Disorder if they are related to the delusional theme.

C. Apart from the impact of the delusion(s) or its ramifications, functioning is not markedly impaired and behavior is not obviously odd or bizarre.

D. If mood episodes have occurred concurrently with delusions, their total duration has been brief relative to the duration of the delusional periods.

E. The disturbance is not due to the direct physiological effects of a substance (e.g., a drug of abuse, a medication) or a general medical condition.

Specify type (the following types are assigned based on the predominant delusional theme):

Erotomanic Type: delusions that another person, usually of higher status, is in love with the individual.

Grandiose Type: delusions of inflated worth, power, knowledge, identity, or special relationship to a deity or famous person.

Jealous Type: delusions that the individual's sexual partner is unfaithful

Persecutory Type: delusions that the person (or someone to whom the person is close) is being malevolently treated in some way.

Somatic Type: delusions that the person has some physical defect or general medical condition

Mixed Type: delusions characteristic of more than one of the above types but no one theme predominates

Unspecified Type

Source: APA, 2000, 1994

Diagnostic Criteria for Brief Psychotic Disorder

A. Presence of one (or more) of the following symptoms:
   (1) delusions
   (2) hallucinations
   (3) disorganized speech (e.g., frequent derailment or incoherence)
   (4) grossly disorganized or catatonic behavior

   Note: Do not include a symptom if it is a culturally sanctioned response pattern.

B. Duration of an episode of the disturbance is at least 1 day but less than 1 month, with eventual full return to premorbid level of functioning.

C. The disturbance is not better accounted for by a Mood Disorder with Psychotic Features, Schizoaffective Disorder, or Schizophrenia and is not due to the direct physiological effects of a substance (e.g., a drug of abuse, a medication) or a general medical condition.

Specify if:

With Marked Stressor(s) (brief reactive psychosis): if symptoms occur shortly after and apparently in response to events that, singly or together, would be markedly stressful to almost anyone in similar circumstances in the person's culture

Without Marked Stressor(s): if symptoms do *not* occur shortly after, or are not apparently in response to events that, singly or together, would be markedly stressful to almost anyone in similar circumstances in the person's culture

With Postpartum Onset: if onset is within 4 weeks postpartum

Source: APA, 2000, 1994
© 2011 by Worth Publishers

Diagnostic Criteria for Shared Psychotic Disorder
(Folie à Deux)

A. A delusion develops in an individual in the context of a close relationship with another person(s), who has an already established delusion.

B. The delusion is similar in content to that of the person who already has the established delusion.

C. The disturbance is not better accounted for by another Psychotic Disorder (e.g., Schizophrenia) or a Mood Disorder with Psychotic Features and is not due to the direct physiological effects of a substance (e.g., a drug of abuse, a medication) or a general medical condition.

Diagnostic Criteria for Psychotic Disorder due to
a General Medical Condition

A. Prominent hallucinations or delusions.

B. There is evidence from the history, physical examination, or laboratory findings that the disturbance is the direct physiological consequence of a general medical condition.

C. The disturbance is not better accounted for by another mental disorder.

D. The disturbance does not occur exclusively during the course of a delirium.

Source: APA, 2000, 1994

Diagnostic Criteria for Substance-Induced Psychotic Disorder

A.   Prominent hallucinations or delusions. Note: Do not include hallucinations if the person has insight that they are substance induced.

B.   There is evidence from the history, physical examination, or laboratory findings of either (1) or (2):

   (1)   the symptoms in Crierion A developed during, or within a month of, Substance Intoxication or Withdrawal

   (2)   medication use is etiologically related to the disturbance

C.   The disturbance is not better accounted for by a Psychotic Disorder that is not substance induced. Evidence that the symptoms are better accounted for by a Psychotic Disorder that is not substance induced might include the following: the symptoms precede the onset of the substance use (or medication use); the symptoms persist for a substantial period of time (e.g., about a month) after the cessation of acute withdrawal or severe intoxication, or are substantially in excess of what would be expected given the type or amount of the substance used or the duration of use; or there is other evidence that suggests the existence of an independent non-substance-induced Psychotic Disorder (e.g., a history of recurrent non-substance-related episodes).

D.   The disturbance does not occur exclusively during the course of a delirium.

   Note: This diagnosis should be made instead of a diagnosis of Substance Intoxication or Substance Withdrawal only when symptoms are in excess of those usually associated with the intoxication or withdrawal syndrome and when the symptoms are sufficiently severe to warrant independent clinical attention.

Specify if:

   With Onset During Intoxication: if criteria are met for Intoxication with the substance and the symptoms develop during the intoxication syndrome

   With Onset During Withdrawal: if criteria are met for Withdrawal from the substance and the symptoms develop during, or shortly after, a withdrawal syndrome

Source: APA, 2000, 1994

General Diagnostic Criteria for a Personality Disorder

A. An enduring pattern of inner experience and behavior that deviates markedly from the expectations of the individual's culture. This pattern is manifested in two (or more) of the following areas:

   (1) cognition (i.e., ways of perceiving and interpreting self, other people, and events)
   (2) affectivity (i.e., the range, intensity, ability, and appropriateness of emotional response)
   (3) interpersonal functioning
   (4) impulse control

B. The enduring pattern is inflexible and pervasive across a broad range of personal and social situations.

C. The enduring pattern leads to clinically significant distress or impairment in social, occupational, or other important areas of functioning.

D. The pattern is stable and of long duration and its onset can be traced back at least to adolescence or early childhood.

E. The enduring pattern is not better accounted for as a manifestation or consequence of another mental disorder.

F. The enduring pattern is not due to the direct physiological effects of a substance (e.g., a drug of abuse, a medication) or a general medical condition (e.g., head trauma).

Source: APA, 2000, 1994

Diagnostic Criteria for Paranoid Personality Disorder

A. A pervasive distrust and suspiciousness of others such that their motives are interpreted as malevolent, beginning by early adulthood and present in a variety of contexts, as indicated by four (or more) of the following:
   (1) suspects, without sufficient basis, that others are exploiting, harming, or deceiving him or her
   (2) is preoccupied with unjustified doubts about the loyalty or trustworthiness of friends or associates
   (3) is reluctant to confide in others because of unwarranted fear that the information will be used maliciously against him or her
   (4) reads hidden, demeaning, or threatening meanings into benign remarks or events
   (5) persistently bears grudges, i.e., is unforgiving of insults, injuries, or slights
   (6) perceives attacks on his or her character or reputation that are not apparent to others and is quick to react angrily or to counterattack
   (7) has recurrent suspicions, without justification, regarding fidelity of spouse or sexual partner

B. Does not occur exclusively during the course of Schizophrenia, a Mood Disorder With Psychotic Features, or another Psychotic Disorder and is not due to the direct physiological effects of a general medical condition.

Diagnostic Criteria for Schizoid Personality Disorder

A. A pervasive pattern of detachment from social relationships and a restricted range of expression of emotions in interpersonal settings, beginning in early adulthood and present in a variety of contexts, as indicated by four (or more) of the following:
   (1) neither desires nor enjoys close relationships, including being part of a family
   (2) almost always chooses solitary activities
   (3) has little, if any, interest in having sexual experiences with another person
   (4) takes pleasure in few, if any, activities
   (5) lacks close friends or confidants other than first-degree relatives
   (6) appears indifferent to the praise or criticism of others
   (7) shows emotional coldness, detachment, or flattened affectivity

B. Does not occur exclusively during the course of Schizophrenia, a Mood Disorder With Psychotic Features, another Psychotic Disorder, or a Pervasive Developmental Disorder and is not due to the direct physiological effects of a general medical condition.

Source: APA, 2000, 1994
© 2011 by Worth Publishers

Diagnostic Criteria for Schizotypal Personality Disorder

A. A pervasive pattern of social and interpersonal deficits marked by acute discomfort with, and reduced capacity for, close relationships as well as by cognitive or perceptual distortions and eccentricities of behavior, beginning by early adulthood and present in a variety of contexts, as indicated by five (or more) of the following:

(1) ideas of reference (excluding delusions of reference)

(2) odd beliefs or magical thinking that influences behavior and is inconsistent with subcultural norms (e.g., superstitiousness, belief in clairvoyance, telepathy, or "sixth sense"; in children and adolescents, bizarre fantasies or preoccupations)

(3) unusual perceptual experiences, including bodily illusions

(4) odd thinking and speech (e.g., vague, circumstantial, metaphorical, overelaborate, or stereotyped)

(5) suspiciousness or paranoid ideation

(6) inappropriate or constricted affect

(7) behavior or appearance that is odd, eccentric, or peculiar

(8) lack of close friends or confidants other than first-degree relatives

(9) excessive social anxiety that does not diminish with familiarity and tends to be associated with paranoid fears rather than negative judgments about self

B. Does not occur exclusively during the course of Schizophrenia, a Mood Disorder With Psychotic Features, another Psychotic Disorder, or a Pervasive Developmental Disorder.

Source: APA, 2000, 1994

Diagnostic Criteria for Antisocial Personality Disorder

A. There is a pervasive pattern of disregard for and violation of the rights of others occurring since age 15 years, as indicated by three (or more) of the following:
   (1) failure to conform to social norms with respect to lawful behaviors as indicated by repeatedly performing acts that are grounds for arrest
   (2) deceitfulness, as indicated by repeated lying, use of aliases, or conning others for personal profit or pleasure
   (3) impulsivity or failure to plan ahead
   (4) irritability and aggressiveness, as indicated by repeated physical fights or assaults
   (5) reckless disregard for safety of self or others
   (6) consistent irresponsibility, as indicated by repeated failure to sustain consistent work behavior or honor financial obligations
   (7) lack of remorse, as indicated by being indifferent to or rationalizing having hurt, mistreated, or stolen from another

B. The individual is at least age 18 years.

C. There is evidence of Conduct Disorder with onset before age 15 years.

D. The occurrence of antisocial behavior is not exclusively during the course of Schizophrenia or a Manic Episode.

Diagnostic Criteria for Borderline Personality Disorder

A pervasive pattern of instability of interpersonal relationships, self-image, and affects, and marked impulsivity beginning by early adulthood and present in a variety of contexts, as indicated by five (or more) of the following:

(1) frantic efforts to avoid real or imagined abandonment. Note: Do not include suicidal or self-mutilating behavior covered in Criterion 5.
(2) a pattern of unstable and intense interpersonal relationships characterized by alternating between extremes of idealization and devaluation
(3) identity disturbance: markedly and persistently unstable self-image or sense of self
(4) impulsivity in at least two areas that are potentially self-damaging (e.g., spending, sex, substance abuse, reckless driving, binge eating). Note: Do not include suicidal or self-mutilating behavior covered in Criterion 5.
(5) recurrent suicidal behavior, gestures, or threats, or self-mutilating behavior
(6) affective instability due to a marked reactivity of mood (e.g., intense episodic dysphoria, irritability, or anxiety usually lasting a few hours and only rarely more than a few days)
(7) chronic feelings of emptiness
(8) inappropriate, intense anger or difficulty controlling anger (e.g., frequent displays of temper, constant anger, recurrent physical fights)
(9) transient, stress-related paranoid ideation or severe dissociative symptoms

Source: APA, 2000, 1994
© 2011 by Worth Publishers

Diagnostic Criteria for Histrionic Personality Disorder

A pervasive pattern of excessive emotionality and attention seeking, beginning by early adulthood and present in a variety of contexts, as indicated by five (or more) of the following:

(1) is uncomfortable in situations in which he or she is not the center of attention
(2) interaction with others often characterized by inappropriate sexually seductive or provocative behavior
(3) displays rapidly shifting and shallow expression of emotions
(4) consistently uses physical appearance to draw attention to self
(5) has a style of speech that is excessively impressionistic and lacking in detail
(6) shows self-dramatization, theatricality, and exaggerated expression of emotion
(7) is suggestible, i.e., easily influenced by others or circumstances
(8) considers relationships to be more intimate than they actually are

Diagnostic Criteria for Narcissistic Personality Disorder

A pervasive pattern of grandiosity (in fantasy or behavior), need for admiration, and lack of empathy, beginning by early adulthood and present in a variety of contexts, as indicated by five (or more) of the following:

(1) has a grandiose sense of self-importance (e.g., exaggerates achievements and talents, expects to be recognized as superior without commensurate achievements)
(2) is preoccupied with fantasies of unlimited success, power, brilliance, beauty, or ideal love
(3) believes that he or she is "special" and unique and can only be understood by, or should associate with, other special or high-status people (or institutions)
(4) requires excessive admiration
(5) has a sense of entitlement, i.e., unreasonable expectations of especially favorable treatment or automatic compliance with his or her expectations
(6) is interpersonally exploitative, i.e., takes advantage of others to achieve his or her own ends
(7) lacks empathy: is unwilling to recognize or identify with the feelings and needs of others
(8) is often envious of others or believes that others are envious of him or her
(9) shows arrogant, haughty behaviors or attitudes

Source: APA, 2000, 1994
© 2011 by Worth Publishers

Diagnostic Criteria for Avoidant Personality Disorder

A pervasive pattern of social inhibition, feelings of inadequacy, and hypersensitivity to negative evaluation, beginning by early adulthood and present in a variety of contexts, as indicated by four (or more) of the following:

(1) avoids occupational activities that involve significant interpersonal contact, because of fears of criticism, disapproval, or rejection

(2) is unwilling to get involved with people unless certain of being liked

(3) shows restraint within intimate relationships because of the fear of being shamed or ridiculed

(4) is preoccupied with being criticized or rejected in social situations

(5) is inhibited in new interpersonal situations because of feelings of inadequacy

(6) views self as socially inept, personally unappealing, or inferior to others

(7) is unusually reluctant to take personal risks or to engage in any new activities because they may prove embarrassing

Diagnostic Criteria for Dependent Personality Disorder

A pervasive and excessive need to be taken care of that leads to submissive and clinging behavior and fears of separation, beginning by early adulthood and present in a variety of contexts, as indicated by five (or more) of the following:

(1) has difficulty making everyday decisions without an excessive amount of advice and reassurance from others

(2) needs others to assume responsibility for most major areas of his or her life

(3) has difficulty expressing disagreement with others because of fear of loss of support or approval. Note: Do not include realistic fears of retribution.

(4) has difficulty initiating projects or doing things on his or her own (because of lack of self-confidence in judgment or abilities rather than a lack of motivation or energy)

(5) goes to excessive lengths to obtain nurturance and support from others, to the point of volunteering to do things that are unpleasant

(6) feels uncomfortable or helpless when alone because of exaggerated fears of being unable to care for himself or herself

(7) urgently seeks another relationship as a source of care and support when a close relationship ends

(8) is unrealistically preoccupied with fears of being left to take care of himself or herself

Source: APA, 2000, 1994
© 2011 by Worth Publishers

Diagnostic Criteria for Obsessive-Compulsive Personality Disorder

A pervasive pattern of preoccupation with orderliness, perfectionism, and mental and interpersonal control, at the expense of flexibility, openness, and efficiency, beginning by early adulthood and present in a variety of contexts, as indicated by four (or more) of the following:

(1) is preoccupied with details, rules, lists, order, organization, or schedules to the extent that the major point of the activity is lost

(2) shows perfectionism that interferes with task completion (e.g., is unable to complete a project because his or her own overly strict standards are not met)

(3) is excessively devoted to work and productivity to the exclusion of leisure activities and friendships (not accounted for by obvious economic necessity)

(4) is overly conscientious, scrupulous, and inflexible about matters of morality, ethics, or values (not accounted for by cultural or religious identification)

(5) is unable to discard worn-out or worthless objects even when they have no sentimental value

(6) is reluctant to delegate tasks or to work with others unless they submit to exactly his or her way of doing things

(7) adopts a miserly spending style toward both self and others; money is viewed as something to be hoarded for future catastrophes

(8) shows rigidity and stubbornness

Source: APA, 2000, 1994

Diagnostic Criteria for Separation Anxiety Disorder

A. Developmentally inappropriate and excessive anxiety concerning separation from home or from those to whom the individual is attached, as evidenced by three (or more) of the following:

   (1) recurrent excessive distress when separation from home or major attachment figures occurs or is anticipated

   (2) persistent and excessive worry about losing, or about possible harm befalling, major attachment figures

   (3) persistent and excessive worry that an untoward event will lead to separation from a major attachment figure (e.g., getting lost or being kidnapped)

   (4) persistent reluctance or refusal to go to school or elsewhere because of fear of separation

   (5) persistently and excessively fearful or reluctant to be alone or without major attachment figures at home or without significant adults in other settings

   (6) persistent reluctance or refusal to go to sleep without being near a major attachment figure or to sleep away from home

   (7) repeated nightmares involving the theme of separation

   (8) repeated complaints of physical symptoms (such as headaches, stomachaches, nausea, or vomiting) when separation from major attachment figures occurs or is anticipated

B. The duration of the disturbance is at least 4 weeks.

C. The onset is before age 18 years.

D. The disturbance causes clinically significant distress or impairment in social, academic (occupational), or other important areas of functioning.

E. The disturbance does not occur exclusively during the courses of a Pervasive Developmental Disorder, Schizophrenia, or other Psychotic Disorder and, in adolescents and adults, is not better accounted for by Panic Disorder With Agoraphobia.

Early Onset: if onset occurs before age 6 years

Source: APA, 2000, 1994
© 2011 by Worth Publishers

Diagnostic Criteria for Oppositional Defiant Disorder

A. A pattern of negativistic, hostile, and defiant behavior lasting at least 6 months, during which four (or more) of the following are present:

(1) often loses temper
(2) often argues with adults
(3) often actively defies or refuses to comply with adults' requests or rules
(4) often deliberately annoys people
(5) often blames others for his or her mistakes or misbehavior
(6) is often touchy or easily annoyed by others
(7) is often angry or resentful
(8) is often spiteful or vindictive

Note: Consider a criterion met only if the behavior occurs more frequently than is typically observed in individuals of comparable age and developmental level.

B. The disturbance in behavior causes clinically significant impairment in social, academic, or occupational functioning.

C. The behaviors do not occur exclusively during the course of a Psychotic or Mood Disorder.

D. Criteria are not met for Conduct Disorder, and, if the individual is age 18 years or older, criteria are not met for Antisocial Personality Disorder.

Source: APA, 2000, 1994

Diagnostic Criteria for Conduct Disorder

A. A repetitive and persistent pattern of behavior in which the basic rights of others or major age-appropriate societal norms or rules are violated, as manifested by the presence of three (or more) of the following criteria in the past 12 months, with at least one criterion present in the past 6 months:

Aggression to people and animals
(1) often bullies, threatens, or intimidates others
(2) often initiates physical fights
(3) has used a weapon that can cause serious physical harm to others (e.g., a bat, brick, broken bottle, knife, gun)
(4) has been physically cruel to people
(5) has been physically cruel to animals
(6) has stolen while confronting a victim (e.g., mugging, purse snatching, extortion, armed robbery)
(7) has forced someone into sexual activity

Destruction of property
(8) has deliberately engaged in fire setting with the intention of causing serious damage
(9) has deliberately destroyed others' property (other than by fire setting)

Deceitfulness or theft
(10) has broken into someone else's house, building, or car
(11) often lies to obtain goods or favors or to avoid obligations (i.e., "cons" others)
(12) has stolen items of nontrivial value without confronting a victim (e.g., shoplifting, but without breaking and entering; forgery)

Serious violations of rules
(13) often stays out at night despite parental prohibitions, beginning before age 13 years
(14) has run away from home overnight at least twice while living in parental or parental surrogate home (or once without returning for a lengthy period)
(15) is often truant from school, beginning before age 13 years

B. The disturbance in behavior causes clinically significant impairment in social, academic, or occupational functioning.

C. If the individual is age 18 years or older, criteria are not met for Antisocial Personality Disorder.

Source: APA, 2000, 1994

Diagnostic Criteria for Conduct Disorder (Continued)

Specify type based on age at onset:

Childhood-Onset Type: onset of at least one criterion characteristic of Conduct Disorder prior to age 10 years

Adolescent-Onset Type: absence of any criteria characteristic of Conduct Disorder prior to age 10 years

Specify severity:

Mild: few if any conduct problems in excess of those required to make the diagnosis and conduct problems cause only minor harm to others

Moderate: number of conduct problems and effect on others intermediate between "mild" and "severe"

Severe: many conduct problems in excess of those required to make the diagnosis or conduct problems cause considerable harm to others

Source: APA, 2000, 1994

Diagnostic Criteria for Attention-Deficit/ Hyperactivity Disorder

A. Either (1) or (2):

(1) six (or more) of the following symptoms of inattention have persisted for at least 6 months to a degree that is maladaptive and inconsistent with developmental level:

Inattention

(a) often fails to give close attention to details or makes careless mistakes in schoolwork, work, or other activities

(b) often has difficulty sustaining attention in tasks or play

(c) often does not seem to listen when spoken to directly

(d) often does not follow through on instructions and fails to finish schoolwork, chores, or duties in the workplace (not due to oppositional behavior or failure to understand instructions)

(e) often has difficulty organizing tasks and activities

(f) often avoids, dislikes, or is reluctant to engage in tasks that require sustained mental effort (such as schoolwork or homework)

(g) often loses things necessary for tasks or activities (e.g., toys, school assignments, pencils, books, or tools)

(h) is often easily distracted by extraneous stimuli

(i) is often forgetful in daily activities

(2) six (or more) of the following symptoms of hyperactivity-impulsivity have persisted for at least 6 months to a degree that is maladaptive and inconsistent with developmental level:

Hyperactivity

(a) often fidgets with hands or feet or squirms in seat

(b) often leaves seat in classroom or in other situations in which remaining seated is expected

(c) often runs about or climbs excessively in situations in which it is inappropriate (in adolescents or adults, may be limited to subjective feelings of restlessness)

(d) often has difficulty playing or engaging in leisure activities quietly

(e) is often "on the go" or often acts as if "driven by a motor"

(f) often talks excessively

Impulsivity

(g) often blurts out answers before questions have been completed

(h) often has difficulty awaiting turn

(i) often interrupts or intrudes on others (e.g., butts into conversations or games)

B. Some hyperactive-impulsivity or inattentive symptoms that caused impairment were present before age 7 years.

Source: APA, 2000, 1994

Diagnostic Criteria for Attention-Deficit/ Hyperactivity Disorder (Continued)

C. Some impairment from the symptoms is present in two or more settings (e.g., at school [or work] and at home).

D. There must be clear evidence of clinically significant impairment in social, academic, or occupational functioning.

E. The symptoms do not occur exclusively during the course of a Pervasive Developmental Disorder, Schizophrenia, or other Psychotic Disorder and are not better accounted for by another mental disorder (e.g., Mood Disorder, Anxiety Disorder, Dissociative Disorder, or a Personality Disorder).

Attention-Deficit/Hyperactivity Disorder, Combined Type: if both Criteria A1 and A2 are met for the past 6 months

Attention-Deficit/Hyperactivity Disorder, Predominantly Inattentive Type: if Criterion A1 is met but Criterion A2 is not met for the past 6 months

Attention-Deficit/Hyperactivity Disorder, Predominantly Hyperactive-Impulsive Type: if Criterion A2 is met but Criterion A1 is not met for the past 6 months

Source: APA, 2000, 1994

Diagnostic Criteria for Enuresis

A. Repeated voiding of urine into bed or clothes (whether involuntary or intentional).

B. The behavior is clinically significant as manifested by either a frequency of twice a week for at least 3 consecutive months or the presence of clinically significant distress or impairment in social, academic (occupational), or other important areas of functioning.

C. Chronological age is at least 5 years (or equivalent developmental level).

D. The behavior is not due exclusively to the direct physiological effect of a substance (e.g., a diuretic) or a general medical condition (e.g., diabetes, spina bifida, a seizure disorder).

Diagnostic Criteria for Encopresis

A. Repeated passage of feces into inappropriate places (e.g., clothing or floor) whether involuntary or intentional.

B. At least one such event per month for at least 3 months.

C. Chronological age is at least 4 years (or equivalent developmental level).

D. The behavior is not due exclusively to the direct physiological effects of a substance (e.g., laxatives) or a general medical condition except through a mechanism involving constipation.

Source: APA, 2000, 1994
© 2011 by Worth Publishers

Diagnostic Criteria for Autistic Disorder

A. A total of six (or more) items from (1), (2), and (3), with at least two from (1), and one each from (2) and (3):

 (1) qualitative impairment in social interaction, as manifested by at least two of the following:

   (a) marked impairment in the use of multiple nonverbal behaviors such as eye-to-eye gaze, facial expression, body postures, and gestures to regulate social interaction

   (b) failure to develop peer relationships appropriate to developmental level

   (c) a lack of spontaneous seeking to share enjoyment, interests, or achievements with other people (e.g., by a lack of showing, bringing, or pointing out objects of interest)

   (d) lack of social or emotional reciprocity

 (2) qualitative impairments in communication, as manifested by at least one of the following:

   (a) delay in, or total lack of, the development of spoken language (not accompanied by an attempt to compensate through alternative modes of communication such as gesture or mime)

   (b) in individuals with adequate speech, marked impairment in the ability to initiate or sustain a conversation with others

   (c) stereotyped or repetitive use of language or idiosyncratic language

   (d) lack of varied, spontaneous make-believe play or social imitative play appropriate to developmental level

 (3) restricted repetitive and stereotyped patterns of behavior, interests, and activities, as manifested by at least one of the following:

   (a) encompassing preoccupation with one or more stereotyped and restricted patterns of interest that is abnormal either in intensity or focus

   (b) apparently inflexible adherence to specific, nonfunctional routines or rituals

   (c) stereotyped and repetitive motor mannerisms (e.g., hand or finger flapping or twisting, or complex whole-body movements)

   (d) persistent preoccupation with parts of objects

B. Delays or abnormal functioning in at least one of the following areas, with onset prior to age 3 years: (1) social interaction, (2) language as used in social communication, or (3) symbolic or imaginative play.

C. The disturbance is not better accounted for by Rett's Disorder or Childhood Disintegrative Disorder.

Source: APA, 2000, 1994

Diagnostic Criteria for Asperger's Disorder

A. Qualitative impairment in social interaction, as manifested by at least two of the following:
    (1) marked impairment in the use of multiple nonverbal behaviors such as eye-to-eye gaze, facial expression, body postures, and gestures to regulate social interaction
    (2) failure to develop peer relationships appropriate to developmental level
    (3) a lack of spontaneous seeking to share enjoyment, interests, or achievements with other people (e.g., by a lack of showing, bringing, or pointing out objects of interest to other people)
    (4) lack of social or emotional reciprocity

B. Restricted repetitive and stereotyped patterns of behavior, interests, and activities, as manifested by at least one of the following.
    (1) encompassing preoccupation with one or more stereotyped and restricted patterns of interest that is abnormal either in intensity or focus
    (2) apparently inflexible adherence to specific, nonfunctional routines or rituals
    (3) stereotyped and repetitive motor mannerisms (e.g., hand or finger flapping or twisting, or complex whole-body movements)
    (4) persistent preoccupation with parts of objects

C. The disturbance causes clinically significant impairment in social, occupational, or other important areas of functioning.

D. There is no clinically significant general delay in language (e.g., single words used by age 2 years, communicative phrases used by age 3 years).

Source: APA, 2000, 1994

Diagnostic Criteria for Mental Retardation

A.   Significantly subaverage intellectual functioning: an IQ of approximately 70 or below on an individually administered IQ test (for infants, a clinical judgment of significantly subaverage intellectual functioning).

B.   Concurrent deficits or impairments in present adaptive functioning (i.e., the person's effectiveness in meeting the standards expected for his or her age by his or her cultural group) in at least two of the following areas: communication, self-care, home living, social/interpersonal skills, use of community resources, self-direction, functional academic skills, work, leisure, health, and safety.

C.   The onset is before age 18 years.

Code based on degree of severity reflecting level of intellectual impairment:

Mild Mental Retardation:	IQ level 50–55 to approximately 70
Moderate Mental Retardation:	IQ level 35–40 to 50–55
Severe Mental Retardation:	IQ level 20–25 to 35–40
Profound Mental Retardation:	IQ level below 20 or 25

Source: APA, 2000, 1994

Diagnostic Criteria for Mathematics Disorder

A. Mathematical ability, as measured by individually administered standardized tests, is substantially below that expected given the person's chronological age, measured intelligence, and age-appropriate education.

B. The disturbance in Criterion A significantly interferes with academic achievement or activities of daily living that require mathematical ability.

C. If a sensory deficit is present, the difficulties in mathematical ability are in excess of those usually associated with it.

Diagnostic Criteria for Disorder of Written Expression

A. Writing skills, as measured by individually administered standardized tests (or functional assessments of writing skills), are substantially below those expected given the person's chronological age, measured intelligence, and age-appropriate education.

B. The disturbance in Criterion A significantly interferes with academic achievement or activities of daily living that require the composition of written texts (e.g., writing grammatically correct sentences and organized paragraphs).

C. If a sensory deficit is present, the difficulties with writing skills are in excess of those usually associated with it.

Diagnostic Criteria for Reading Disorder

A. Reading achievement, as measured by individually administered standardized tests of reading accuracy or comprehension, is substantially below that expected given the person's chronological age, measured intelligence, and age-appropriate education.

B. The disturbance in Criterion A significantly interferes with academic achievement or activities of daily living that require reading skills.

C. If a sensory deficit is present, the reading difficulties are in excess of those usually associated with it.

Source: APA, 2000, 1994

Diagnostic Criteria for Phonological Disorder

A. Failure to use developmentally expected speech sounds that are appropriate for age and dialect (e.g., errors in sound production, use, representation, or organization, such as, but not limited to, substitutions of one sound for another [use of /t/ for target /k/ sound] or omissions of sounds such as final consonants).

B. The difficulties in speech sound production interfere with academic or occupational achievement or with social communication.

C. If Mental Retardation, a speech-motor or sensory deficit, or environmental deprivation is present, the speech difficulties are in excess of those usually associated with these problems.

Diagnostic Criteria for Expressive Language Disorder

A. The scores obtained from standardized individually administered measures of expressive language development are substantially below those obtained from standardized measures of both nonverbal intellectual capacity and receptive language development. The disturbance may be manifest clinically by symptoms that include having a markedly limited vocabulary, making errors in tense, or having difficulty in recalling words or producing sentences with developmentally appropriate length or complexity.

B. The difficulties with expressive language interfere with academic or occupational achievement or with social communication.

C. Criteria are not met for Mixed-Receptive-Expressive Language Disorder or a Pervasive Developmental Disorder.

D. If Mental Retardation, a speech-motor or sensory deficit, or environmental deprivation is present, the language difficulties are in excess of those usually associated with these problems.

Coding note: If a speech-motor or sensory deficit or a neurological condition is present, code the condition on Axis III.

Diagnostic Criteria for Mixed Receptive/Expressive Language Disorder

A. The scores obtained from a battery of standardized individually administered measures of both receptive and expressive language development are substantially below those obtained from standardized measures of nonverbal intellectual capacity. Symptoms include those for Expressive Language Disorder as well as difficulty understanding words, sentences, or specific types of words, such as spatial terms.

B. The difficulties with receptive and expressive language significantly interfere with academic or occupational achievement or with social communication.

C. Criteria are not met for a Pervasive Developmental Disorder.

D. If Mental Retardation, a speech-motor or sensory deficit, or environmental deprivation is present, the language difficulties are in excess of those usually associated with these problems.

Coding note: If a speech-motor or sensory deficit or a neurological condition is present, code the condition on Axis III.

Source: APA, 2000, 1994

Diagnostic Criteria for Stuttering

A. Disturbance in the normal fluency and time patterning of speech (inappropriate for the individual's age), characterized by frequent occurrences of one or more of the following:

   (1) sound and syllable repetitions
   (2) sound prolongations
   (3) interjections
   (4) broken words (e.g., pauses within a word)
   (5) audible or silent blocking (filled or unfilled pauses in speech)
   (6) circumlocutions (word substitutions to avoid problematic words)
   (7) words produced with an excess of physical tension
   (8) monosyllabic whole-word repetitions (e.g., "I-I-I-I see him")

B. The disturbance in fluency interferes with academic or occupational achievement or with social communication.

C. If a speech-motor or sensory deficit is present, the speech difficulties are in excess of those usually associated with these problems.

Coding note: If a speech-motor or sensory deficit or a neurological condition is present, code the condition on Axis III.

Source: APA, 2000, 1994
© 2011 by Worth Publishers

Diagnostic Criteria for Developmental Coordination Disorder

A. Performance in daily activities that require motor coordination is substantially below that expected given the person's chronological age and measured intelligence. This may be manifested by marked delays in achieving motor milestones (e.g., walking, crawling, sitting), dropping things, "clumsiness," poor performances in sports, or poor handwriting.

B. The disturbance in Criterion A significantly interferes with academic achievement or activities of daily living.

C. The disturbance is not due to a general medical condition (e.g., cerebral palsy, hemiplegia, or muscular dystrophy) and does not meet criteria for a Pervasive Developmental Disorder.

D. If Mental Retardation is present, the motor difficulties are in excess of those usually associated with it.

Coding note: If general medical condition or sensory deficit is present, code the condition on Axis III.

Source: APA, 2000, 1994
© 2011 by Worth Publishers

Diagnostic Criteria for Dementia of the Alzheimer's Type

A. The development of multiple cognitive deficits manifested by both
 (1) Memory impairment (impaired ability to learn new information or to recall previously learned information)
 (2) one (or more) of the following cognitive disturbances:
   (a) aphasia (language disturbance)
   (b) apraxia (impaired ability to carry out motor activities despite intact motor function)
   (c) agnosia (failure to recognize or identify objects despite intact sensory function)
   (d) disturbance in executive functioning (i.e., planning, organizing, sequencing, abstracting)

B. The cognitive deficits in Criteria A1 and A2 each cause significant impairment in social or occupational functioning and represent a significant decline from a previous level of functioning.

C. The course is characterized by gradual onset and continuing cognitive decline.

D. The cognitive deficits in Criteria A1 and A2 are not due to any of the following:
 (1) Other central nervous system conditions that cause progressive deficits in memory and cognition (e.g., cerebrovascular disease, Parkinson's disease, Huntington's disease, subdural hematoma, normal-pressure hydrocephalus, brain tumor)
 (2) systemic conditions that are known to cause dementia (e.g., hypothyroidism, vitamin B12 or folic acid deficiency, niacin deficiency, hypercalcemia, neurosyphilis, HIV infection)
 (3) Substance-induced conditions

E. The deficits do not occur exclusively during the course of a delirium.

F. The disturbance is not better accounted for by another Axis I disorder (e.g., Major Depressive Disorder, Schizophrenia).

Code based on presence or absence of a clinically significant behavioral disturbance:

 Without Behavioral Disturbance: if the cognitive disturbance is not accompanied by any clinically significant behavioral disturbance.

 With Behavioral Disturbance: if the cognitive disturbance is accompanied by a clinically significant behavioral disturbance (e.g., wandering, agitation).

Specify subtype:

 With Early Onset: if onset is age 65 years or below

 With Late Onset: if onset is after age 65 years

Source: APA, 2000, 1994

Diagnostic Criteria for Dementia Due to Other General Medical Conditions

A. The development of multiple cognitive deficits manifested by both
   (1) memory impairment (impaired ability to learn new information or to recall previously learned information)
   (2) one (or more) of the following cognitive disturbances:
      (a) aphasia (language disturbance)
      (b) apraxia (impaired ability to carry out motor activities despite intact motor function)
      (c) agnosia (failure to recognize or identify objects despite intact sensory function)
      (d) disturbance in executive functioning (i.e., planning, organizing, sequencing, abstracting)

B. The cognitive deficits in Criteria A1 and A2 each cause significant impairment in social or occupational functioning and represent a significant decline from a previous level of functioning.

C. There is evidence from the history, physical examination, or laboratory findings that the disturbance is the direct physiological consequence of one of the general medical conditions listed below.

D. The deficits do not occur exclusively during the course of a delirium.

Code based on presence or absence of a clinically significant behavioral disturbance:

Without Behavioral Disturbance: if the cognitive disturbance is not accompanied by any clinically significant behavioral disturbance.

With Behavioral Disturbance: if the cognitive disturbance is accompanied by a clinically significant behavioral disturbance (e.g., wandering, agitation).

Also code the general medical condition on Axis III (e.g., HIV infection, head injury, Parkinson's disease, Huntington's disease, Pick's disease, Creutzfeldt-Jakob disease)

DSM-IV-TR Classification

From the American Psychiatric Association: Diagnostic and Statistical Manual of Mental Disorders, Fourth Edition, Washington, DC, American Psychiatric Association, 1994, Revised, 2000. Reprinted by permission.

(All categories are on Axis I except those indicated otherwise.)

Disorders Usually First Diagnosed in Infancy, Childhood, or Adolescence

Mental Retardation

Note: These are coded on Axis II.
Mild mental retardation
Moderate mental retardation
Severe mental retardation
Profound mental retardation
Mental retardation, severity unspecified

Learning Disorders

Reading disorder
Mathematics disorder
Disorder of written expression
Learning disorder NOS*

Motor Skills Disorder

Developmental coordination disorder

Communication Disorders

Expressive language disorder
Mixed receptive-expressive language
    disorder
Phonological disorder
Stuttering
Communication disorder NOS*

Pervasive Developmental Disorders

Autistic disorder
Rett's disorder
Childhood disintegrative disorder
Asperger's disorder
Pervasive development disorder NOS*

Attention-Deficit and Disruptive Behavior Disorders

Attention-deficit/hyperactivity disorder
    Combined type
    Predominantly inattentive type
    Predominantly hyperactive-impulsive
        type
Attention-deficit/hyperactivity disorder
    NOS*
Conduct disorder
Oppositional defiant disorder
Disruptive behavior disorder NOS*

Feeding and Eating Disorders of Infancy or Early Childhood

Pica
Rumination disorder
Feeding disorder of infancy or early
    childhood

Tic Disorders

Tourette's disorder
Chronic motor or vocal tic disorder
Transient tic disorder
Tic disorder NOS*

Elimination Disorders

Encopresis
    With constipation and overflow
        incontinence
    Without constipation and overflow
        incontinence
Enuresis (not due to a general medical
    condition)

Other Disorders of Infancy, Childhood, or Adolescence

Separation anxiety disorder
Selective mutism
Reactive attachment disorder of infancy or
    early childhood
Stereotypic movement disorder
Disorder of infancy, childhood, or
    adolescence NOS*

*NOS = Not otherwise specified
© 2011 by Worth Publishers

DSM-IV-TR Classification (Continued)

From the American Psychiatric Association: Diagnostic and Statistical Manual of Mental Disorders, Fourth Edition, Washington, DC, American Psychiatric Association, 1994, Revised, 2000. Reprinted by permission.

(All categories are on Axis I except those indicated otherwise.)

Delirium, Dementia, and Amnestic and Other Cognitive Disorders

Delirium

Delirium due to . . . *(indicate the general medical condition)*
Substance intoxication delirium
Substance withdrawal delirium
Delirium due to multiple etiologies
Delirium NOS*

Dementia

Dementia of the Alzheimer's type, with early onset
Dementia of the Alzheimer's type, with late onset
Vascular dementia

Dementia Due to Other General Medical Conditions

Dementia due to HIV disease
Dementia due to head trauma

Dementia due to Parkinson's disease
Dementia due to Huntington's disease
Dementia due to Pick's disease
Dementia due to Creutzfeldt-Jakob disease
Dementia due to . . . *(indicate the general medical condition not listed above)*
Substance-induced persisting dementia
Dementia due to multiple etiologies
Dementia NOS*

Amnestic Disorders

Amnestic disorders due to . . . *(indicate the general medical condition)*
Substance-induced persisting amnestic disorder
Amnestic disorder NOS*

Other Cognitive Disorders

Cognitive disorder NOS*

Mental Disorders Due to a General Medical Condition Not Elsewhere Classified

Catatonic disorder due to . . . *(indicate the general medical condition)*
Personality change due to . . . *(indicate the general medical condition)*

Mental disorder NOS* due to . . . *(indicate the general medical condition)*

DSM-IV-TR Classification (Continued)

From the American Psychiatric Association: Diagnostic and Statistical Manual of Mental Disorders, Fourth Edition, Washington, DC, American Psychiatric Association, 1994, Revised, 2000. Reprinted by permission.

(All categories are on Axis I except those indicated otherwise.)

Substance-Related Disorders

[Specific substance categories: Alcohol; Amphetamine; Caffeine; Cannabis; Cocaine; Hallucinogen; Inhalant; Nicotine; Opioid; Phencyclidine; Sedative, Hypnotic, or Anxiolytic; Polysubstance; Other or unknown]

Substance Use Disorders

Substance dependence
Substance abuse

Substance-Induced Disorders

Substance intoxication
Substance withdrawal

Substance intoxication delirium
Substance withdrawal delirium
Substance-induced persisting dementia
Substance-induced persisting amnestic
   disorder
Substance-induced psychotic disorder
Substance-induced mood disorder
Substance-induced anxiety disorder
Substance-induced sexual dysfunction
Substance-induced sleep disorder
Substance-related disorder NOS*

Schizophrenia and Other Psychotic Disorders

Schizophrenia
   Paranoid type
   Disorganized type
   Catatonic type
   Undifferentiated type
   Residual type
Schizophreniform disorder
Schizoaffective disorder

Delusional disorder
Brief psychotic disorder
Shared psychotic disorder
Psychotic disorder due to . . . *(indicate the general medical condition)*
Substance-induced psychotic disorder
Psychotic disorder NOS*

Mood Disorders

Depressive Disorders

Major depressive disorder
Dysthymic disorder
Depressive disorder NOS*

Bipolar Disorders

Bipolar I disorder

Bipolar II disorder
Cyclothymic disorder
Bipolar disorder NOS*
Mood disorder due to . . . *(indicate the general medical condition)*
Substance-induced mood disorder
Mood disorder NOS*

DSM-IV-TR Classification (Continued)

From the American Psychiatric Association: Diagnostic and Statistical Manual of Mental Disorders, Fourth Edition, Washington, DC, American Psychiatric Association, 1994, Revised, 2000. Reprinted by permission.

(All categories are on Axis I except those indicated otherwise.)

Anxiety Disorders

Panic disorder without agoraphobia
Panic disorder with agoraphobia
Agoraphobia without history of panic
  disorder
Specific phobia
Social phobia
Obsessive-compulsive disorder

Posttraumatic stress disorder
Acute stress disorder
Generalized anxiety disorder
Anxiety disorder due to . . . (indicate the
  general medical condition)
Substance-induced anxiety disorder
Anxiety disorder NOS*

Somatoform Disorders

Somatization disorder
Undifferentiated somatoform disorder
Conversion disorder
Pain disorder
Associated with psychological factors
Associated with both psychological factors

  and a general medical condition
Hypochondriasis
Body dysmorphic disorder
Somatoform disorder NOS*

Factitious Disorders

Factitious disorder
With predominantly psychological signs and
  symptoms
With predominantly physical signs and
  symptoms

With combined psychological and physical
  signs and symptoms
Factitious disorder NOS*

Dissociative Disorders

Dissociative amnesia
Dissociative fugue
Dissociative identity disorder

Depersonalization disorder
Dissociative disorder NOS*

DSM-IV-TR Classification (Continued)

From the American Psychiatric Association: Diagnostic and Statistical Manual of Mental Disorders, Fourth Edition, Washington, DC, American Psychiatric Association, 1994, Revised, 2000. Reprinted by permission.

(All categories are on Axis I except those indicated otherwise.)

Sexual and Gender Identity Disorders

Sexual Dysfunctions

Sexual Desire Disorders

Hypoactive sexual desire disorder

Sexual aversion disorder

Sexual Arousal Disorders

Female sexual arousal disorder

Male erectile disorder

Orgasmic Disorders

Female orgasmic disorder

Male orgasmic disorder

Premature ejaculation

Sexual Pain Disorders

Dyspareunia (not due to a general medical condition)

Vaginismus (not due to a general medical condition)

Sexual Dysfunction Due to a General Medical Condition

Substance-induced Sexual Dysfunction

Sexual Dysfunction NOS*

Paraphilias

Exhibitionism

Fetishism

Frotteurism

Pedophilia

Sexual Masochism

Sexual Sadism

Transvestic Fetishism

Voyeurism

Paraphilia NOS*

Gender Identity Disorders

Gender identity disorder

  In children

  In adolescents or adults

Gender identity disorder NOS*

Sexual disorder NOS*

Eating Disorders

Anorexia nervosa

Bulimia nervosa

Eating disorder NOS*

Sleep Disorders

Primary Sleep Disorders

Dyssomnias

Primary insomnia

Primary hypersomnia

Narcolepsy

Breathing-related sleep disorder

Circadian rhythm sleep disorder

Dyssomnia NOS*

Parasomnias

Nightmare disorder

Sleep terror disorder

Sleepwalking disorder

Parasomnia NOS*

Sleep Disorders Related to Another Mental Disorder

Other Sleep Disorders

Sleep disorder due to . . . (indicate the general medical condition)

Substance-induced sleep disorder

DSM-IV-TR Classification (Continued)

From the American Psychiatric Association: Diagnostic and Statistical Manual of Mental Disorders, Fourth Edition, Washington, DC, American Psychiatric Association, 1994, Revised, 2000. Reprinted by permission.

(All categories are on Axis I except those indicated otherwise.)

Impulse-Control Disorders Not Elsewhere Classified

Intermittent explosive disorder
Kleptomania
Pyromania

Pathological gambling
Trichotillomania
Impulse-control disorder NOS*

Adjustment Disorders

Adjustment disorder
   With depressed mood
   With anxiety
   With mixed anxiety and depressed mood

With disturbance of conduct
With mixed disturbance of emotions and
   conduct
Unspecified

Personality Disorders

Note: These are coded on Axis II.
Paranoid personality disorder
Schizoid personality disorder
Schizotypal personality disorder
Antisocial personality disorder
Borderline personality disorder

Histrionic personality disorder
Narcissistic personality disorder
Avoidant personality disorder
Dependent personality disorder
Obsessive-compulsive personality disorder
Personality disorder NOS*

DSM-IV-TR Classification (Continued)

From the American Psychiatric Association: Diagnostic and Statistical Manual of Mental Disorders, Fourth Edition, Washington, DC, American Psychiatric Association, 1994, Revised, 2000. Reprinted by permission.

(All categories are on Axis I except those indicated otherwise.)

Other Conditions That May Be a Focus of Clinical Attention

Psychological Factors Affecting Medical Condition

Mental disorder affecting medical condition

Psychological symptoms affecting medical condition

Personality traits or coping style affecting medical condition

Maladaptive health behaviors affecting medical condition

Stress-related physiological response affecting medical condition

Other or unspecified psychological factors affecting medical condition

Medication-Induced Movement Disorders

Neuroleptic-induced Parkinsonism

Neuroleptic malignant syndrome

Neuroleptic-induced acute dystonia

Neuroleptic-induced acute akathisia

Neuroleptic-induced tardive dyskinesia

Medication-induced postural tremor

Medication-induced movement disorder NOS*

Other Medication-Induced Disorder

Adverse effects of medication NOS*

Relational Problems

Relational problem related to a mental disorder or general medical condition

Parent-child relational problem

Partner relational problem

Sibling relational problem

Relational problem NOS*

Problems Related to Abuse or Neglect

Physical abuse of child

Sexual abuse of child

Neglect of child

Physical abuse of adult

Sexual abuse of adult

Additional Conditions That May Be a Focus of Clinical Attention

Noncompliance with treatment

Malingering

Adult antisocial behavior

Child or adolescent antisocial behavior

Borderline intellectual functioning

Age-related cognitive decline

Bereavement

Academic problem

Occupational problem

Identity problem

Religious or spiritual problem

Acculturation problem

Phase of life problem

Source: APA, 2000, 1994